*The Handbook of
Child and Adolescent
Systems of Care*

The Handbook of
Child and Adolescent
Systems of Care

The New Community Psychiatry

Andres J. Pumariega
Nancy C. Winters
Editors

Foreword by Clarice L. Kestenbaum

A Publication of the Work Group on
Community-Based Systems of Care of the American
Academy of Child and Adolescent Psychiatry

JOSSEY-BASS
A Wiley Imprint
www.josseybass.com

Published by Jossey-Bass
A Wiley Imprint
989 Market Street, San Francisco, CA 94103-1741   www.josseybass.com

Jossey-Bass books and products are available through most bookstores. To contact Jossey-Bass directly call our Customer Care Department within the U.S. at 800-956-7739, outside the U.S. at 317-572-3986 or fax 317-572-4002.

Jossey-Bass also publishes its books in a variety of electronic formats. Some content that appears in print may not be available in electronic books.

Library of Congress Cataloging-in-Publication Data

The handbook of child and adolescent systems of care : the new community psychiatry / edited by Andres J. Pumariega, Nancy C. Winters.
p. cm.
Includes bibliographical references and index.
ISBN 0-7879-6239-2
1. Child mental health services—Handbooks, manuals, etc.
2. Community mental health services—Handbooks, manuals, etc.
I. Pumariega, Andres J. II. Winters, Nancy C., 1952-
RJ499.3 .H362 2002
362.2'083—dc21
                                                    2002007180

Printed in the United States of America
FIRST EDITION
HB Printing 10 9 8 7 6 5 4 3 2 1

CONTENTS

PART FOUR: ADMINISTRATION AND EVALUATION OF SYSTEMS OF CARE

TABLES AND FIGURES

FOREWORD

The year 1999 was a banner year for public awareness of the mental health needs of children and adolescents, and their families. In June, the first White House Conference on Mental Health was chaired by Tipper Gore, who described the conference as "a first step in ending the stigma and discrimination that for so long have prevented people from seeking the treatment that can help them live healthy, positive lives." In December of the same year, David Satcher, the surgeon general, presented his landmark *Report on Mental Health*, which brought widespread media attention to the number of Americans with a mental disorder (one in five) and documented the effectiveness of a range of treatments. This report, which took over two years to prepare, gave a mandate to strengthen the public health approach and left little room for policymakers to deny or limit treatment for emotional disorders, concluding that "the journey ahead must finally establish mental health as a cornerstone of health." The accomplishments of 1999 set out an ambitious agenda for addressing the mental health needs and disparities facing children with emotional disturbances and their families.

The *Handbook of Child and Adolescent Systems of Care* is an important contribution toward that agenda. It is a product of a dedicated group of child and adolescent psychiatrists, the Work Group on Community-Based Systems of Care, cochaired by Andres J. Pumariega and Nancy C. Winters. Building on its advocacy efforts since 1994 for children with mental health needs and their families, the work group has held a series of full-day symposia in cities throughout the

United States to describe and support the systems of care approach for children's mental health. This book represents the efforts of the work group to address issues of national concern in children's mental health in the context of administrative, legal, and funding challenges.

This book integrates a variety of clinical modalities and perspectives, from psychopharmacology to psychosocial interventions, always keeping in mind a developmental paradigm within a framework of diverse cultures and populations. This book provides a firm base for mental health workers of every discipline: psychiatrists, psychologists, social workers, counselors, pediatricians, nurses, educators, lawyers and judges, politicians, child advocates, and, of course, parents and families. Despite increasingly effective medications, treatment algorithms, manualized therapies, and diagnostic criteria, many children continue to fall through the cracks in our communities. No child can be evaluated today without consideration of the complex contexts of our communities and health care systems.

Andres Pumariega and Nancy Winters have provided an approach that should serve as a model for programs dealing with the mental health needs of children in this new millennium. The American Academy of Child and Adolescent Psychiatry is proud to support their efforts and this work.

Clarice J. Kestenbaum
American Academy of Child
and Adolescent Psychiatry
President (1999–2001)

PREFACE

In J. D. Salinger's *The Catcher in the Rye* (1945), the narrator, Holden Caulfield, pictures himself at the edge of a cliff. Thousands of children are playing in a field of rye, in danger of falling off the cliff. He has to catch the children if they start to fall over the cliff. This poignant image exemplifies the emotions and motivations of those of us who work with children with serious emotional disorders and their families. Jane Knitzer expressed much the same sense of urgency and duty in her groundbreaking work, *Unclaimed Children* (1982), which sparked the movement toward community-based systems of care. Children were falling through the cracks and being lost to their communities. Someone had to step in and catch them.

The early development of system of care philosophy was in many ways a reaction to the medical model that was developing in child mental health in the early 1980s. This model focused on diagnosis, treatment, and the use of medical facilities and residential programs in preference to community-based programs. Although it emphasized high-quality interventions for clinical conditions, it did not address the context within which our most vulnerable children found themselves. Their lack of family and community supports and disengagement from their cultural and social roots and strengths truly left them at the edge of the abyss. Children often were treated far away from their homes over months and years. While they demonstrated symptomatic improvement at these placements, their problems recurred on their return to the same challenging environments.

Their families had no connection with those treating their children and ultimately, and most important, lost their connection to their children.

The system of care philosophy was indeed beneficial in addressing many of the needs of children with serious emotional disturbance and their families. It emphasized much-needed coordination of care, natural support services, partnerships with families, an ecological and contextual approach to care, and least restrictive treatment in the most developmentally normative environment possible. However, in some respects, the baby was thrown out with the bath water by inadvertently excluding physicians, especially child and adolescent psychiatrists, from the array of professionals engaged with these systems in the early system of care programs. The exclusion of the clinical psychiatric perspectives from systems of care also impoverished the intervention resources available to these children with serious disturbances and their families who were most in need of these perspectives. The contributions of child and adolescent psychiatrists as diagnosticians, consultants, treatment coordinators and implementers, and systems change agents were diminished. Also, this ignored a tradition from the early history of child and adolescent psychiatry of commitment to working within community settings and to an interdisciplinary collaboration with our child-serving colleagues.

The formation of the Work Group on Community-Based Systems of Care of the American Academy of Child and Adolescent Psychiatry (AACAP) was a response by our specialty to these trends in the system of care field. Its mission was both to the integration of child and adolescent psychiatrists (and their expertise and skills) into systems of care philosophy and programs. The work group was also to promote system of care philosophy among our child and adolescent psychiatric colleagues in order to broaden the scope of their clinical and professional roles and perspectives.

Movement toward the formation of the work group began at the 1994 Georgetown TA Center Biennial Institute with a meeting of child and adolescent psychiatrists who were engaged in systems of care, led by Mary Jane England, president of the Washington Business Group on Health and president of the American Psychiatric Association. A monograph by the Washington Business Group on Health (1994) summarized the proceedings of this meeting and described the value of the involvement in systems of care of child and adolescent psychiatrists. England then approached the leadership of the AACAP to support the formation of a task force to address system of care issues within child and adolescent psychiatry, especially with the emerging influence and possible threats of managed care to systems of care. The task force (and later work group) first met and constituted in October 1994 and quickly proceeded to pursue its mission.

The work group has become a tightly knit, highly committed group of child and adolescent psychiatrists who serve dual roles as experts and advocates for community-based systems of care. They are driven by their commitment to children with serious emotional disturbances and their families and to the goals of access and quality of care. The group's dedication and productivity has become widely recognized within and outside the AACAP and has been regularly recognized by the AACAP leadership in its organizational reports. Its numerous activities and accomplishments have been highly effective in addressing the relationship between child and adolescent psychiatry and the system of care movement:

- Our first product, *Best Principles for Managed Care Medicaid RFP's* (American Academy of Child & Adolescent Psychiatry, 1996a; Pumariega et al., 1997), addressed the impact of public managed care on children's systems of care. It also outlined guidelines for managed Medicaid contracts between states and private contractors that incorporate system of care principles. Furthermore, it served to operationalize the application of system of care philosophy in larger state systems. These guidelines have had a significant influence on Medicaid policies in numerous states and counties across the nation.
- A companion document, *Best Principles for Measuring Outcomes in Managed Care Medicaid Programs* (American Academy of Child and Adolescent Psychiatry, 1998), addressed approaches to evaluating emerging state-level systems of care in multiple stakeholder-relevant domains beyond the financial focus of these systems.
- *Guidelines for Training Towards Community-Based Systems of Care for Children with Serious Emotional Disturbances* (American Academy of Child and Adolescent Psychiatry, 1996b) addressed the conceptual basis, areas of knowledge and skill, and clinical and didactic curricula needed to train child and adolescent psychiatrists (and other mental health professionals) for these emerging systems of care. It has had a national influence on child and adolescent training programs across the nation and has been featured in two panel presentations by the work group at the annual meeting of the American Association of Directors of Psychiatric Residency Training.
- *Best Principles for Early Childhood Systems of Care* (American Academy of Child and Adolescent Psychiatry, in press-a) outlines the conceptual basis for systems of care for infants, toddlers, and preschool-aged children, as well as operationalizes the critical components of such systems of care.
- The *Child and Adolescent Level of Care Utilization System* (CALOCUS; American Academy of Child and Adolescent Psychiatry and American Association of Community Psychiatry, 1999) and its *User's Manual* (Klaehn, O'Malley, Vaughan, & Kroeger, 1999) is a level-of-care determination tool designed for use with children ages six to seventeen and brings a developmental perspective to system of care philosophy. It was based on the successful Level of Care Utilization System (American Association of Community Psychiatry, 2000; Sowers, 1998) and developed in collaboration with the American Association of Community Psychiatry. The work group also undertook a national multisite evaluation of the CALOCUS,

funded by the Center for Mental Health Services (CMHS), which has demonstrated good reliability and validity for this instrument (Fallon et al., 2001). The CALO-CUS has already achieved a high level of acceptability as a well-designed and useful instrument based on peer reviews and has achieved initial use in state and local systems of care (Lyons & Abraham, 2001). The work group is currently working on the development of the *Toddler and Infant LOCUS,* a tool for level-of-care determination for early childhood systems of care.

• A study of collaboration between juvenile justice and mental health in the CMHS-funded system of care sites, also funded by CMHS, examined the critical components that led to successful integration of mental health and juvenile justice services and positive outcomes for youth at risk of entering the juvenile justice system. The methodology used both objective data and site visits to the programs and interviews with the critical stakeholders. The results will be published shortly (Fallon et al., in press).

• *Best Principles for Confidentiality and Information Sharing in Community-Based Systems of Care* (American Academy of Child & Adolescent Psychiatry, in press-b) is a conceptual discussion and a set of guidelines that address information sharing and privacy protection within systems of care, balancing these with the values of interagency and interprofessional collaboration and respect for families and children.

• The work group began to sponsor local and regional conferences across the nation in conjunction with its quarterly meetings. These have focused on increasing child and adolescent psychiatrists' interest in, understanding of, and involvement in systems of care; the building of alliances among child and adolescent psychiatrists, family members, and other child mental health professionals in systems of care; and addressing specific challenges facing local and regional systems of care. The success of these conferences prompted CMHS to award a grant to the work group to pursue additional conferences oriented to current and prospective CMHS-funded SOC grant communities.

Salinger's *The Catcher in the Rye* (1945) became highly meaningful to our work group in 2001, when we received the Catchers in the Rye Award from the AACAP, awarded by its Assembly of Regional Organizations, for the development of the CALOCUS. As an advocacy award and as suggested by its title, it captures the essence and motivation behind the system of care movement. In addition to feeling honored by the recognition awarded by our peers, this award was further encouragement for us to stay on this track.

This book is undoubtedly one of the work group's major projects and a culmination of a three-year process of development. Our aim in it is to conceptually integrate system of care philosophy practice with the clinical, conceptual, and policy perspectives of modern child and adolescent psychiatry. It is produced in collaboration with many nonpsychiatric professional and family colleagues from system of care programs across the nation. In presenting this work, we wish to facilitate the arrival of child and adolescent psychiatry to its natural home in systems of care and reassert its commitment to serve children and families not only with system of care principles, but using the best clinical approaches at our disposal.

Andres J. Pumariega
Nancy C. Winters

References

American Academy of Child and Adolescent Psychiatry (1996a). *Best principles for managed care Medicaid RFP's: How decision makers can select and monitor high quality programs.* Washington, DC: Author.

American Academy of Child and Adolescent Psychiatry. (1996b). *Guidelines for training towards community-based systems of care for children with serious emotional disturbances.* Washington, DC: Author.

American Academy of Child and Adolescent Psychiatry. (1998). *Best principles for measuring outcomes in managed care Medicaid programs.* Washington, DC: Author.

American Academy of Child and Adolescent Psychiatry and American Association of Community Psychiatry. (1999). *Child and Adolescent Level of Care Utilization System, Version 1.1.* Washington, DC: Author.

American Academy of Child and Adolescent Psychiatry (in press-a). *Best principles for early childhood systems of care.* Washington, DC: Author.

American Academy of Child and Adolescent Psychiatry (in press-b). *Best principles for confidentiality and information sharing in community-based systems of care.* Washington, DC: Author.

American Association of Community Psychiatry. (2000). *Level of Care Utilization System, Version 2.0.* Author.

Fallon, T., Pumariega, A. J., Winters, N., Chenven, M., Grimes, K., Heffron, W., Marx, L., O'Malley, K., Vaughan, T., & Zachik, A. (in press). *Juvenile justice/mental health collaborations in the service of adolescents with serious emotional and behavioral disturbances.* Washington, DC: Center for Mental Health Services, Substance Abuse and Mental Health Administration.

Fallon, T., Winters, N., Pumariega, A. J., Huffine, C., O'Malley, K., Zachik, A., Grimes, K., & Dominguez, E. (2001). CALOCUS: Comparative and face validity. In *Scientific Proceedings of the Annual Meeting of the American Academy of Child and Adolescent Psychiatry.* Washington, DC: American Academy of Child & Adolescent Psychiatry. [Research abstract.]

Klaehn, R., O'Malley, K., Vaughan, T., & Kroeger, K. (1999). *User's manual for the Child and Adolescent Level of Care Utilization System, Version 1.1.* Washington, DC: American Academy of Child and Adolescent Psychiatry.

Knitzer, J. (1982). *Unclaimed children.* Washington, DC: Children's Defense Fund.

Lyons, J., & Abraham, M. E. (2001). Designing level of care criteria. In L. Kiser, P. Lefkovitz, & L. Kennedy (Eds.), *The integrated behavioral health continuum: Theory and practice.* Washington, DC: American Psychiatric Association Press.

Pumariega, A. J., Nace, D., England, M. J., Diamond, J., Mattson, A., Fallon, T., Hanson, G., Lourie, I., Marx, L., Thurber, D., Winters, N., Graham, M., & Wiegand, D. (1997). Community-based systems approach to children's managed mental health services. *Journal of Child and Family Studies, 6,* 149–164.

Salinger, J. D. (1945). *The catcher in the rye.* New York: Bantam Books.

Sowers, W. (1998). Level of care determinations in psychiatry. *Harvard Review of Psychiatry, 5,* 286–290.

Washington Business Group on Health. (1994). *The roles of child and adolescent psychiatrists in community-based systems of care.* Washington, DC: Author.

ACKNOWLEDGMENTS

We wish to acknowledge the contributions of numerous colleagues and supporters in the completion of this book, as well as the mission and work of the Work Group on Community-Based Systems of Care of the American Academy of Child and Adolescent Psychiatry (AACAP).

First, we thank our chapter authors, without whom this book would not have been possible. They not only labored long hours and contributed their considerable knowledge and wisdom, but also suffered the frequent missives of the coeditors. We also acknowledge the individual members of the work group, each of whom has devoted extraordinary time and energy on behalf of children and their families. The current members (besides Nancy Winters) are Mark Chenven (current co-chair), Debbie Carter, Theodore Fallon, William Heffron, Robert Klaehn, Larry Marx, Kaye McGinty, Kieran O'Malley, Thomas Vaughan, and Al Zachik. We also wish to acknowledge the contributions of past work group members: Alan Axelson, John Diamond, Emilio Dominguez, Mary Jane England, Katherine Grimes, Ira Lourie, David Nace, Albert Solnit, and Deborah Thurber. Our work group consultants have also included Robert F. Cole, Charles Huffine, and Wesley Sowers. Their dedication to the needs of children with serious emotional disturbances and their families and their professionalism and productivity have always been inspiring and energizing.

We readily acknowledge the strong support the work group (and we personally) has received in pursuing our mission and goals. In addition to Kristen Kroeger, we acknowledge the outstanding contributions of Virginia Anthony, executive director of the AACAP (and "Mother" of the academy) and Mary Crosby, associate executive director of the AACAP. They make it happen for all of us in the AACAP with their dedication, hard work, and grace. We also thank the past and current presidents of the AACAP who provided us their wise counsel and unfailing support, including William Stone, Larry Stone (our solid foundation was built on two Stones), David Pruitt, Clarice Kestenbaum, and Marilyn Benoit.

We acknowledge the heroes of the systems of care movement for their conceptual, programmatic, and advocacy contributions. Mary Jane England first comes to mind, since she was the founder and "Godmother" of the work group; it was through her advocacy within and outside the AACAP that we came into being. Jane Knitzer, Beth Stroul, Robert Friedman, Barbara Friesen, and Barbara Burns provided us the conceptual, philosophical, and evidence base for community-based systems of care on which we strive to build. Ira Lourie was the first child and adolescent psychiatrist who stood as a voice and advocate (often a lone one) for systems of care and continues to stand there for us. The Center for Mental Health Services, particularly Bernard Arons (director), Gary DeCarolis, Rolando Santiago (of the Child and Family Branch), and Gayle Porter and David Osher (of the Technical Assistance Center at the American Research Institutes) have been critical supporters of systems of care and of our work. The Federation of Families for Children's Mental Health, particularly Trina Osher, Carolyn Nava, and Vera Pena, have been great supporters and sources of inspiration and challenge to help us strive for a greater understanding of and collaboration with families. Charles Huffine deserves added mention for his intense and passionate advocacy for the voice of youth within systems of care.

The staff at Jossey-Bass Publishers has been a delight to work with, and we thank them for their enthusiasm and collegiality. We particularly thank Alan Rinzler for giving us this unique opportunity to address a wider audience through this book and for his enthusiasm for the project, even including attending a work group meeting at the AACAP annual meeting. We also sincerely thank Amy Scott and Susan Geraghty for their responsiveness, professionalism, focused editorial feedback, flexibility, and (above all) patience.

Last but not least is a special acknowledgment to those children and families and colleagues who live and work in community-based systems of care. They have taught us invaluable and unforgettable lessons about collaboration, partnership, and perseverance.

The Handbook of
Child and Adolescent
Systems of Care

*We wish to dedicate this book to
those closest and most supportive of us:*

*Andres Pumariega:
To my dear wife, JoAnne (Buttacavoli),
whose love, dedication, and support make possible and inspire all
that I do in my work and career. To my dear daughters, Christina and
Nicole, who both support and challenge me to be a good parent as
well as a more understanding child and adolescent psychiatrist.*

*Nancy Winters:
To my husband, Scott Murray,
my "system of care," whose love, abiding support, and humor
(and late-night cups of tea) have enriched my life beyond measure.
In memory of my mother, Barbara Edwards Winters, whose warmth
and dedication to her children shall never be forgotten.*

*We both wish to dedicate this book to
Kristin Kroeger Ptakowski,
director of clinical affairs of the American Academy of Child and
Adolescent Psychiatry. Without her dedication, focus, and professionalism, this book and the many other accomplishments of the Work Group
on Community-Based Systems of Care would not have been possible.*

*During the preparation of this book,
Dr. Albert Solnit,
Sterling Professor of Child Psychiatry at Yale University and a founder
of our work group, died an untimely death. This was a serious loss to
all of us who had the privilege of knowing him, all of us who work in
the field of children's mental health, and the children and families
whom we serve. We also wish to dedicate this book to him and to his
monumental legacy of scholarship, service, mentorship, and caring.*

PART ONE

CONCEPTUAL FOUNDATIONS OF SYSTEMS OF CARE

CHAPTER ONE

A History of
Community Child
Mental Health

Ira S. Lourie

It is difficult to conceive of the history of community child mental health as separate from the history of child mental health itself. A large segment of the field of child mental health has always focused on the delivery of service in the community for the population of children in need regardless of their social status or standing. In fact, the earliest child mental health services were aimed at a population of homeless and wayward youth, following from an advocacy movement that grew out of the industrial revolution at the end of the nineteenth century and the spate of immigration at the beginning of the twentieth century in the United States. The child guidance movement grew out of these early beginnings and focused on serving the entire population. As a result, by the time the formal community mental health movement began in the United States in the early 1960s, the concepts of treating the mental health needs of children and adolescents in the context of their communities were already being practiced by child guidance centers and had become the accepted practice of the field.

Over the more recent history of the child mental health movement, several underserved populations have emerged around which the need for specialized community mental health services has been recognized: the alienated adolescents of 1960s and 1970s and children and adolescents with severe emotional disturbances as recognized in the 1980s. This chapter traces the four major community mental health movements for children that have occurred over the past hundred years: child guidance, the community mental health center program, the alternative youth

1

services movement, and now the system of care concept for children and adolescents with serious emotional disturbances and their families.

CHILD GUIDANCE

The history of child mental health began as a progressive movement toward social welfare in the late nineteenth century described as the "child savers" (Jones, 1999). This group of advocates aimed at rescuing wayward children from the destructive forces of poverty. This movement then expanded to ameliorating the effects of those same forces, along with mental retardation, as the causes of juvenile delinquency. Beginning in the 1880s, problematic behavior in children, most often manifesting as delinquency, was seen as the product of moral and mental defects, compounded by the lack of appropriate resources. While one might find these concepts simplistic and antiquated by today's standards, we should be reminded that poverty and racism remain overwhelming social problems that leave their mark on the development and mental health of children growing up in their shadows.

Jones (1999) describes the forces that moved child mental health to a more professional child guidance during the first thirty years of the twentieth century. The first child mental health services began as child guidance clinics that functioned much like court clinics today. The first child mental health service agency, which was in Chicago, still bears its original name, the Institute for Juvenile Research, and another of the still existing early such programs, the Judge Baker Child Guidance Center, was named for the judge who was instrumental in its inception.

Child guidance was aimed at guiding youth in the right direction. Jones (1999) describes a Judge Baker Foundation document from 1915, *Strengthening the Twig*, which presents the concept of taking a young organism and helping it grow in the proper straight direction. A general professional acceptance of this premise is reflected in the fact that the primary professional organization for child mental health professionals from 1930 through the 1970s was the American Orthopsychiatric Association, in which the term *orthopsychiatric* is derived from the Greek root of the word *ortho,* meaning to straighten.

The first major advancement in our understanding and treatment of children and adolescents with problematic behavior that grew from child guidance was the shift from punishment to correction: we should fix troubled children, not further harm them. This community-focused concept was built on the premise that if children and adolescents misbehaved, it was not necessarily their own fault. Rather, society was to blame because it deprived youth of the resources necessary to meeting their needs. The accepted position that most delinquents came from the lower economic sectors of society was used as support for this supposition. At the same time, early thoughts on individual and family development were emerging, building on the earlier understanding that development was affected by economics and organicity (primarily retardation).

In the 1920s and 1930s, child guidance expanded from a primarily delinquency-based movement to one aimed more at the middle and upper classes. Jones (1999) calls this the "popularization of child guidance," which was driven by both the desire for mental health professionals to have their gospel more generally accepted and a youth movement of the 1920s unlike any before it. A broad audience for child guidance followed from a growing understanding that problematic youth behavior was found in all classes. Jones's theory is that the public became fascinated by the Leopold and Loeb trial of two upper-class youth convicted of a senseless murder, which led not only to a focus on upper-class problems but also served as a lesson in the relationship between developmental issues and youth behavior. What followed was a conceptualization of delinquency prevention, which led to a better understanding of how the deviations from the normal developmental course could lead to poor behavior. A movement followed from this to teach parents how to avoid these problems by using better methods in rearing their children.

Most of the early growth in the field of child mental health that Jones described consisted of a new understanding of children and their development and was exemplified by the focus on individual development, the role of the family in that development, and the effects of societal forces that children and families had to deal with. Unfortunately, it was during this era late in the first half of the twentieth century that child guidance accepted an increasing role as a private practice–like setting for middle- and upper-class populations. Although most child guidance clinics continued to provide publicly supported and charitable services to those who could not afford them, the field of child mental health as a whole slipped from being a primarily community mental health service to a private practice model.

COMMUNITY MENTAL HEALTH CENTER PROGRAM

A major shift in mental health policy in the United States occurred in the early 1960s with the advent of the Federal Community Mental Health Center program. In adult psychiatry, the public system had no community mental health alternative equal to the child guidance centers, and most communities did not have access to those centers. Public psychiatry consisted for the most part as state hospitals serving mainly a population with chronic psychotic disorders. For children, there were child guidance centers and some residential treatment, funded primarily as child welfare and juvenile justice institutions. The advent of phenothiazine treatment of psychotic symptoms in the 1950s had begun to create a population of adults with serious and persistent mental health problems who had been deinstituionalized and were living in communities.

Federal Community Mental Health Center Act

The U.S. Congress responded by the passage of the Mental Retardation Facilities and Community Mental Health Center Construction Act of 1963 (P.L. 88–164) to begin to meet the needs of this population. The purpose of the mental health portion of that legislation was to create a nationwide network of community-based mental health clinics that could serve this deinstitutionalized population, among others. The program was aimed at the development of community mental health centers (CMHCs) in every community in the country (the plan was to have one center for each catchment area of about 135,000 people). These centers were to provide five essential services: inpatient (short term), outpatient therapy, emergency services, crisis stabilization, and consultation and education.

Although children and adolescents were not excluded from the use of these services, their needs were not specifically addressed. Under the earliest iterations of the CMHC program, there was no requirement that services specifically aimed at children and adolescents be offered by the centers. As a result, the plight of children was left up to each center; unfortunately, only about half of the centers had any children's services at all (Ad Hoc Committee, 1971). Two major forces tended to inhibit the development of community mental health services for children and adolescents. The first of these was the predominance of adult focus within the field of mental health itself. This tendency, which still exists, causes the community mental health leadership not even to think about specialized services for children and adolescents. Some of this is related to their unfamiliarity with the differences in the needs of the populations. In addition, the needs of the adult population are so great that they alone could easily use up all the existing funds available and still require more.

The second factor is the high cost of children's services. CMHCs were most often created with money from the federal CMHC program, which offered start-up staffing grants and which decreased over the period of eight years (there were also some funds available specifically for the building of new centers). As the federal funds decreased, they were made up with state funds and other public and private reimbursement sources. For adults, this process worked fairly well. As the federal monies dried up, the state was able to replace them with state mental health funds (which had been primarily aimed at this population of serious and persistently mental ill adults in the first place) and with newly developed federal funding streams such as supplemental security income, Medicaid, and Medicare, all of which the adult mentally ill population had easy access to. Children and adolescents had less access to these sources of funding.

Children's services require a greater degree of indirect services that are not reimbursable by most public or private insurance programs: informal case management tasks, consultation with schools and other programs for children and adolescents, and internal teaming time by the group of professionals at the mental health program who work with one family. During the time that a CMHC was receiving federal funding, many of these nonreimbursable child-oriented services were covered under the rubric of consultation and education services. But as soon as the federal monies were gone, state resources rarely were used to fill in, and the services dried up. When this happened, the cost of children's services became too high for the CMHCs to afford. Centers that had started children's services under the federal CMHC program dropped them when the federal monies went away, and other centers never even started them.

Compounding these problems was the fact that the state departments of mental health, which had the responsibility for continuing the CMHC program after the federal government's eight-year commitment was over, often did not have a child mental health capacity or expertise to support children's services. In 1982, Knitzer found that twenty-one states did not have a full-time person assigned to children's mental health services at the state level or a specific children's mental health allocation in their state mental health budgets. With such a lack of interest and support for children's services, it is no wonder that not many such services grew within the early days of the CMHC movement.

Part F of the Community Mental Health Center Act

The failure of adequate child and adolescent community mental health services to develop led child advocates to push for the development of a special child and adolescent program under the CMHC Act. In 1972, Congress passed an amendment to that act that provided for a special children's program, Part F. Part F was one of the most exciting advances in children's mental health services since the emergence of the child guidance centers some sixty years earlier. Under this program, around four hundred CMHCs developed and supported children's services, about a third of the total number of CMHCs (Lourie, 1992). Many of these children's programs were exciting and innovative and led the way to defining the delivery of mental health services to children, adolescents, and their families during that era. This program was deemed a success, and in 1974, the CMHC program was changed so as to require children's services in every federally funded CMHC. Unfortunately, the same CMHC act amendment of that year also added six other required services, raising the number from five to twelve but without increased funds to provide for these new services. As a result, each of the seven new services was insufficiently funded to be properly implemented, and status quo was the general rule. In addition, there were no longer special monies available to start new children's services as there had been under Part F. However, CMHCs that had received Part F grants did continue to receive these special children's funds for the full eight years of their original Part F grant.

Joint Commission on the Mental Health of Children

Around the same time that the Community Mental Health Center Program was started, there was another major step in community child mental health: the Joint Commission on the Mental Health of Children. Congress established this national study of the needs of children and adolescents with emotional problems in 1965. In *Crisis in Child Mental Health* (1970), the Joint Commission laid the framework for a child advocacy approach to children's services. This child advocacy reflected the full range of children's needs—welfare, corrections, education, health, and mental health—and was to be based on the principles of child guidance. This advocacy was felt to be needed at the national, state, local, and individual levels. Congress made two attempts to enact legislation implementing the recommendations of the Joint Commission, but both failed. This major setback for the field of child mental health reflected the waning of the federal government's commitment to child mental health from its earliest support of child guidance.

The 1970s saw few advances in community child mental health, and there was minimal impact from the Joint Commission in spite of the major advances in providing mental health services in general during that period through the national CMHC program, which was flourishing at its height nationwide, covering over half of the communities in the country with community mental health centers supported by federal monies. Unfortunately, this movement had little impact on child mental health because most of these community mental health centers offered few services for children and adolescents.

ALTERNATIVE YOUTH SERVICES MOVEMENT

One area in which there *was* a great deal of growth and change in the 1970s was the field of youth services. Like the founding child savers of the child guidance movement, a group of individuals became concerned about the spirit of alienation of the late 1960s and early 1970s between the youth culture and the adult culture (not unlike the forces of the 1920s that helped drive child guidance). Adolescents in the 1970s were less likely than prior generations to participate in the traditional child guidance approach. Not only were these youth rebelling against their parents as had generations before; they also rebelled against adult authority in general, including the professional authority embedded in child mental health. Child mental health as a field responded to these alienated youth with the popularization of family therapy, which sought to treat the problems of youth as the result of a family system gone wrong rather than focusing on the alienation itself. Family therapists viewed the problems of youth as being the result of dysfunctional dynamics that developed among various family members, including the youth.

Another response to this population was embodied by a totally new set of services that grew out of the youth work movement, which over the previous forty years had primarily focused on gangs and had little, if any, relationship to child mental health. From this service sector came what was to be called the alternative services: untraditional programs that viewed the alienation of youth from their families as a societal change rather than as a form of psychopathology. This new perspective dictated a different set of goals for mental health interventions. Mental health workers first needed to connect with the youth by helping them with the problems they perceived as important and only later, when the youth was ready to participate, offer counseling. Even later (and only if it made sense) did mental health workers try to reconnect these youth with their families. Drop-in centers, runaway houses, and multiservice walk-in services, as well as traditional street work, became the tools of the alternative service movement, while the formal principles of child guidance and community mental health were looked on as being irrelevant to the needs of youth. As we will see, these alternative services created the service milieu model in which many of the more innovative current child mental health services are provided.

THE SYSTEM OF CARE CONCEPT

Community child mental health is currently embodied by the system of care for children with severe emotional disturbances and their families. The conceptualization of the system of care derived originally from the underlying principles of child guidance and the findings of the Joint Commission on the Mental Health of Children. These principles were modified to fit the perceived service needs of the last two decades of the twentieth century and reflect the lessons of the alternative service movement of the 1970s.

The National Plan for Mental Health

The convening of the President's Commission on Mental Health in 1978 led to a major shift in mental health policy. The recommendations from this commission (President's Commission on Mental Health, 1978), which followed from first lady Rosalynn Carter's interest in mental health, were enacted through the development of a National Plan for the Chronically Mentally Ill, through which the National Institute of Mental Health set the course for the current era in spite of the fact that the children's chapter of the National Plan was relegated to the status of an appendix (Lourie et al., 1980). The President's Commission and the National Plan highlighted two underserved mental health populations: adults with chronic mental illness (today referred to as serious and persistent mental illness) and children and adolescents with serious emotional disturbances. The blame for this underservice was laid on the failure of community mental health centers to address these populations and meet these public needs adequately. The governmental response to the national plan was rapid for adults, and the Community Support Program, a very successful program to develop state and local social and rehabilitation resources for the population of those individuals with serious and persistent mental illness, which had been developed the year before, was expanded.

The Most-in-Need Program. The programmatic response for children was similar to that of the children's chapter of the National Plan: an appendix (Lourie et al., 1980). All that followed was a tiny program of services for those children who were most in need. This program, called the Most-in-Need Program, commonly known as MIN, had a strong community mental health focus and was conceptualized in a way to allow communities to apply the principles of the Joint Commission to those children in their locality with the most unique needs, no matter what those needs were and regardless of the degree of mental health focus reflected. Unfortunately, this program was never embraced by Congress or the National Institute of Mental Health in which it was developed. In fact, it was funded only by the Indian Health Service in the form of short-term grants in only twelve reservation and urban Native American communities.

The Mental Health System Act. The final result of the President's Commission on Mental Health was the 1980 passage of the Mental Health System Act (P.L. 96–398). Under this legislation, a federal grant program was to be developed that created community-based systems for approaching the needs of the underserved populations identified by the commission: chronically mentally ill adults (now recognized as adults with serious and persistent mental illness) and severely emotionally and mentally disturbed children and adolescents. Unlike the Community Mental Health Center Program, which created federal-local partnerships to develop these centers, the Mental Health System Act aimed at including state government as a more important and active partner in this local community mental health capacity start-up program. Including the state in the partnership process was aimed at encouraging the development of state mental health funding streams that would support those nonreimbursable services that the community mental health centers had tended to drop when the federal monies disappeared, under the Community Mental Health Center Program.

The Block Grant Program. The Mental Health System Act was never implemented. After a year of National Institute of Mental Health planning and developing both adult and child programs to create local mental health systems, the act, along with the entire Community Mental Health Center Program, was repealed and replaced by the Alcohol, Drug Abuse and Mental Health Block Grant Program (part of the Omnibus Budget Reconciliation Act of 1981, P.L. 97–35). The block grant concept was a governmental shift toward state control over the federal monies. The states were to receive all of the funds they had received previously under the Community Mental Health Center Program and prospectively under the Mental Health System Act to spend as they saw fit in their community mental health programs. There were some guidelines, but the result of the block grant legislation rapidly shifted the emphasis of using federal dollars from the development of new centers and systems to the ongoing support of existing centers; there were no provisions specifically allocating funds for children's services in the original act. So few new children's services or service systems were being developed under the block grant program that Congress instructed at various times that at least 10 to 25 percent of all monies to a state under the block grant be allocated to the development of new children's services (Lourie et al., 1996). This provision was never well monitored, and the block grant program has never proved effective in expanding children's community mental health services or creating service systems for the most severely affected children and adolescents.

Unclaimed Children

The full children's response to the President's Commission and the National Plan had to wait for six more years. In 1982, Jane Knitzer reported on her Children's Defense Fund–supported study of services for severely emotionally disturbed children and adolescents. The report, *Unclaimed Children,* documented the sorry state of services for children with the most severe mental health problems and the failure of federal, state, and local governments to respond to that crisis. This report has become a classic and served as the battle cry for a new wave of child advocacy based on the findings of the Joint Commission fifteen years earlier. Finally, in 1984, the federal government funded a program to meet the needs of this population better: the Child and Adolescent Service System Program, better known as CASSP.

The Child and Adolescent Service System Program

CASSP came on the scene at a time when the more serious the emotional problem or mental illness that a child or adolescent had, the more likely that that child would not be able to obtain the full range of appropriate and needed services. A comprehensive service system for children and adolescents had failed to be created. The roots that had grown into child guidance—child welfare, juvenile justice, special education, health, and mental health—had developed several major branches, each of which represented a branch of government that had taken some child mental health responsibility but which was no longer interconnected.

Mental Health. Child guidance and community mental health centers were not playing a major role in providing child mental health services and had little public funding. These programs had come to act like private practices, primarily meeting the needs of middle-class children with mild to moderate problems. Ironically, youth with the most severe mental health problems were unable to find adequate services within mental health. They often found themselves in out-of-home services funded by welfare, justice, and education agencies. To obtain these services, a youth had to qualify for services from one of these agencies.

Education. The education system was a major route for a child to obtain mental health services. In 1974, the federal government passed special education legislation, known today as the Individuals with Disabilities Education Act. This law, originally known as the Education for All Handicapped Children Act (P.L. 94–142), was the result of a civil rights action brought on behalf of students who were being denied education on the basis of their disabilities. Its purpose was to entitle every child a free and appropriate education regardless of the restrictions created by a disability; this included emotional and behavioral problems. Children and adolescents whose education was being hampered by their emotional disabilities were required to receive those services, including, but not limited to, mental health and educational, that were necessary in order for them to learn. Regardless of the many exemplary education-based programs created across the country to serve the needs of children with emotional problems better, the system has never become complete or comprehensive in all jurisdictions, and many, if not most, school districts underidentify youth with emotional and behavioral disabilities or fail to develop the services many of them need (Knitzer, Steinberg, & Fleisch, 1990).

Juvenile Justice. The juvenile justice system was another avenue to obtaining mental health services that reflects its child guidance roots. But as Jones (1999) pointed out, the current movement in juvenile justice is away from guidance toward punishment; juvenile justice now has an increasingly adult penal orientation. As with education, many jurisdictions continue to provide excellent mental health services for their juvenile justice populations, and many court clinics still exist, but in general, appropriate services are hard to find nationally for the population of children and youth with serious emotional disturbances—ironically, just the population that the entire juvenile justice system was concerned with at the advent of child guidance.

Child Welfare. Child welfare agencies have become the most prominent among the child-serving agencies that support mental health services for the most seriously disturbed children and adolescents. Like juvenile justice, child welfare was closely connected to child guidance at its birth. This grew from the preponderance of troubled children coming from families struggling with poverty and other troubles and the propensity for these youth to be abandoned or become victims of domestic violence, and thus wards of the state. Many such children bounce from foster home to foster home, psychiatric hospitalization to psychiatric hospitalization, and finally to residential treatment, often out of state and far from their homes and families. Because child welfare may be the only agency with the resources for the purchase of high-intensity mental health services, many parents are obliged, sometimes forced, to give up custody of their child with emotional disturbance to the welfare agency. To do this, the parents must either declare themselves inadequate to the task of rearing their child or, more destructively, as being abusive.

An Interagency Approach. CASSP was developed as a federal program aimed at ensuring that children and adolescents with the most serious emotional problems would get their needs met without having to qualify for child welfare, juvenile justice, or special education services. A further goal was for mental health to work with these other systems in helping families obtain the full range of services that their children might need. CASSP was based on the original principles of child guidance and the understanding that children and adolescents with emotional problems and their families have multiple needs that must be met before the problems can be alleviated. Similarly, it was based on the principles of the Joint Commission and the concepts of child advocacy at the federal, state, local, and individual family levels. The embodiment of advocacy within CASSP is the concept of the system of care, which is a multiagency approach to the delivery of services that need to be community based, child centered, and family focused, as described by Stroul and Friedman (1986) in their classic monograph, *A System of Care for Children and Youth with Severe Emotional Disturbances.*

The first goal of CASSP was to encourage states and communities to create interagency systems of care for the purpose of ensuring that the multiagency needs of this population of children, adolescents, and their families would be met (Lourie, Katz-Leavy, DeCarolis, & Quinlan, 1996). Initially, individual states responded to this federal initiative by developing an interagency process at the state level that brought the mental health, child welfare, juvenile justice, and special education agencies together for joint planning of how they could work better among themselves. Ultimately, these state-level interagency processes were applied at the community level to create systems of care, the mission of which was to provide individual children, adolescents, and their families in those communities the most appropriate and better coordinated services.

CASSP's second major goal was to develop a better response for child mental health agencies within systems of care and to enhance their role within them. Many states and communities have a paucity of mental health resources available to participate in such systems of care. Knitzer had pointed out that fewer than half of the states had an individual at the state level who was responsible for child mental health services. And fewer than half of the states had a specific budget for child mental health services. These facts, along with the failure of community mental health to address the mental health needs of children adequately, left the population in need with few mental health resources and no governmental agency with responsibility for ensuring their availability. CASSP acted to create a specific child mental health presence in the governments of all states, increase state child mental budgets, and develop mechanisms for passing this increased state-level focus on child mental services down to the community level.

Enhancing the role of the family was another major goal of CASSP (Friesen & Huff, 1996). Early in its development, CASSP recognized the destructive nature of parent blaming that had first emerged in the early days of child guidance and was reified through the dysfunctional family concepts of family systems theory, and moved toward its abolition. The family was seen as the child's most important resource, even when the situation was such that the family was not able to care for that child directly for a period of time. If the system of care was to function properly, family members must help define it and run it, as well as benefit from its services. The parent movement that grew out of CASSP, embodied in the Federation of Families for Child Mental Health and the National Alliance for the Mentally Ill—Child and Adolescent Network and the numerous local chapters of these organizations, has had a major impact on improving the systems of care that have developed nationally and have gone a long way in proving that parents need to be supported in the care of their children in need rather than being blamed for those needs.

Cultural competence was the other major goal of CASSP. Public systems of care have a higher representation of individuals and families from cultural and ethnic minority groups than does the general population. Yet child guidance had grown in a manner that was essentially color blind. While this had the advantage of trying to be fair and racially neutral, it had the disadvantages of applying the predominant cultural standards to all people, even when it was inappropriate to do so. This has been recognized most prominently in the case of standardized psychological testing, which has proven to be culturally biased against many minority groups. CASSP recognized the need for members of culturally diverse groups to have input into how the system of care is created and how the interventions they and their children receive approach their unique cultural values. At the highest level of cultural competence, child mental health and its systems of care practices need to celebrate cultural differences and use them in the interventions offered to children and families (Cross, Bazron, Dennis, & Isaacs, 1989).

Wraparound Services. CASSP was not only based on the traditions of child guidance and the Joint Commission; it also borrowed heavily from the alternative youth service philosophies of the 1970s. From these, CASSP encompassed the concepts of wraparound services, which were adopted as the CASSP-oriented intervention. Wraparound is the application of alternative youth service philosophies and practices to children and adolescents with serious emotional disturbance and their families (Katz-Leavy, Lourie, & Dendy, 1992). With wraparound, a team of individuals, including the family, who know a youth well, like him or her, and can see his or her strengths comes together with the youth to plan interventions. This team makes an unconditional commitment to stick with that youth until help is no longer needed. The implication is that the group will work to modify the intervention approach until a successful combination of services is discovered. In order to make this happen, the team explores the youth's strengths and develops interventions that build on them, while at the same time creating interventions aimed at protecting the youth and others from problematic behaviors. The family takes a major role in wraparound planning and caring for the child, and the family's strengths are used as part of the plan. What follows is a truly individualized and flexible planning process and intervention. Thus, wraparound encompasses the alternative service–derived principles of unconditional care, strength-based approaches, individually developed, culturally relevant, and flexible services, along with the CASSP system of care principles of community-based and family-centered services delivered in the context of multiagency systems of care, and gives professionals and families a way to maximize the resources available to them.

Heritage of CASSP. CASSP has had a positive effect on overcoming the forces that have limited the effectiveness of community child mental health and child guidance principles. It has encouraged the multidisciplinary approach, going even further to describe a multiagency approach. It has worked to bring juvenile justice and mental health closer together again in meeting the needs of children and youth with emotional problems and fighting delinquency; it has gone even further by also bringing other agencies, child welfare, and special education together as part of the multiagency system of care. It has helped to create a parent movement that has taken major steps in undermining the concepts of parent blaming; it has gone even further by recognizing the major role that family members must play in the development and running of systems of care, as well as acting as the major resource for their children. It has institutionalized the concepts of cultural competence. It has created a governmental response that has encouraged expansion of the principles of child guidance and the system of care necessary for its application to the most seriously disturbed youngsters; by 1995, it had been noted that all of the states had at least one full-time child mental health specialist at the state level (Davis, Yelton, Katz-Leavy, & Lourie, 1995). In addition, it added the wraparound service philosophy and practice as a new force to move the field ahead.

The concepts of systems of care for children and adolescents with serious emotional disturbance and their families that emerged from CASSP were first applied to local service delivery on a large scale in 1989 through the Mental Health Services Program for Youth (MHSPY) of the Robert Wood Johnson Foundation. This program initially funded eight five-year grants for state-local collaborations to provide services based on CASSP principles in a particular community to children and adolescents with serious emotional disturbances and their families (in one instance, the grant affected an entire state). Major contributions of MHSPY include the practical definition of the population in need of an interagency service system, the development of models for organizing and running those systems, and the definition of the role of child psychiatry in the system of care concept.

Other local system of care development projects were started by states themselves without the Robert Wood Johnson support, and by 1992 I was able to identify enough such sites to perform a study of the principles of local system development (Lourie, 1992). The major finding of this study was that the development of a productive local system of care relied most on the cooperation and leadership of several local public children's agencies, such as child welfare, mental health, juvenile justice, and special education. The type of collaborative processes that developed relied on those leaders' accepting a joint mission that followed not just from the CASSP principles but also from the beginning concepts of child guidance (Cole & Poe, 1993).

The CASSP concepts became codified in law in 1992 when Congress, impressed by the success of MHSPY, passed an act that created the Comprehensive Community Mental Health Services for Children and Their Families Program (Children's Services Program) (P.L. 102–321), which has supported the development of systems of care based on the CASSP principles and MHSPY service delivery models across the country. The Children's Services Program, administered by the Center for Mental Health Services, had funded service component development in more than forty-five additional communities by 1999, which are developing system of care approaches (U.S. Department of Health and Human Services, 1999).

The public support of local system of care development concept has not been without some controversy. Although CASSP and its principles have received wide acceptance and acclaim, several researchers have found that some system of care demonstrations have not proven to be more effective than the more traditional services systems (Bickman, Guthrie, & Foster, 1995). Others have argued that the systems so studied were not fully developed systems of care and that the CASSP principles and system of care philosophy are so ingrained in service systems that it is impossible to find a community that has not incorporated some system of care practices and can act as a true control for the purpose of rigorous research design (Friedman & Burns, 1996). Regardless of the controversy, the U.S. Congress continues to support the Child Mental Health Services Initiative at a rate of nearly $80 million a year, the second largest federal mental health program behind the community mental health center block grant program.

Community mental health as applied to children, adolescents, and their families has endured from its beginnings with the first child guidance concepts and centers. It flourished under Part F of the Community Mental Health Center Program. Today it is alive and well within the system of care concepts and practice that emerged from CASSP and incorporated the alternative youth service principles embodied in wraparound service interventions and other similar concepts and practices. The particulars of the system of care for children and adolescents are the subjects of the chapters that follow.

References

Ad Hoc Committee on Child Mental Health. (1971). *Ad Hoc Committee on Child Mental Health: Report to the director, National Institutes of Mental Health.* Rockville, MD: National Institute of Mental Health.

Bickman, L., Guthrie, P. R., & Foster, E. M. (1995). *Evaluating managed mental health care: The Fort Bragg experiment.* New York: Plenum.

Cole, R. F., & Poe, S. (1993). *Partnerships for care: Systems of care for children with serious emotional disturbances and their families.* Washington, DC: Washington Business Group on Health.

Cross, T., Bazron, B., Dennis, K., & Isaacs, M. (1989). *Towards a culturally competent system of care: A monograph on effective services for minority children who are severely emotionally disturbed.* Washington, DC: Georgetown University Child Development Center, National Technical Assistance Center for Child Mental Health.

Davis, M., Yelton, S., Katz-Leavy, J., & Lourie, I. (1995). Unclaimed children revisited. *Journal of Mental Health Administration, 22,* 142–166.

Friedman, R. A., & Burns, B. (1996). The evaluation of the Fort Bragg demonstration project: an alternative interpretation of the findings. *Journal of Mental Health Administration, 23,* 128–136.

Friesen, B. J., & Huff, B. (1996). Family perspectives on systems of care. In B. A. Stroul (Ed.), *Children's mental health: Creating systems of care in a changing society.* Baltimore, MD: Brooks Publishing.

Joint Commission on the Mental Health of Children. (1970). *Crisis in child mental health: Challenge for the 1970s.* New York: Harper & Row, 1970.

Jones, K. (1999). *Taming the troublesome child: American families, child guidance, and the limits of psychiatric authority.* Cambridge, MA: Harvard University Press.

Katz-Leavy, J., Lourie, I. S., & Dendy, C. (1992). *Individualized services in a system of care.* Washington, DC: Georgetown University Child Development Center, National Technical Assistance Center for Child Mental Health.

Knitzer, J. (1982). *Unclaimed children.* Washington, DC: Children's Defense Fund.

Knitzer, J., Steinberg, Z., & Fleisch, B. (1990). *At the schoolhouse door.* New York: Bank Street College of Education.

Lourie, I. S. (1992). *Principles of local system development.* Chicago: Kaleidoscope.

Lourie, I. S., Katz-Leavy, J., DeCarolis, G., & Quinlan W. (1996). The role of the federal government. In B. A. Stroul (Ed.), *Children's mental health: Creating systems of care in a changing society.* Baltimore, MD: Brooks Publishing.

Lourie, I. S., with Fishman, M., Hersh, S., Platt, L., Schulterbrandt, L. S., & Smith, E. (1980). *Chronically mentally ill children and adolescents: A special report for the National Plan for the Chronically Mentally Ill.* Rockville, MD: National Institutes of Mental Health.

President's Commission on Mental Health. (1978). *Report to the president from the President's Commission on Mental Health,* Washington, DC: U.S. Government Printing Office.

Stroul, B. A., & Friedman, R. A. (1986). *A system of care for children and youth with severe emotional disturbances* (Rev. ed.). Washington, DC: Georgetown University Child Development Center, National Technical Assistance Center for Child Mental Health.

U.S. Department of Health and Human Services. *Mental health: A report of the surgeon general.* Rockville, MD: U.S. Department of Health and Human Services, National Institutes of Health, 1999.

CHAPTER TWO

Systems of Care

A Framework for Children's Mental Health Care

Beth A. Stroul

The system of care concept and philosophy have provided a framework for system reform in the children's mental health arena since the mid-1980s by offering a new paradigm for comprehensive, community-based, individualized, and culturally competent services for children and adolescents with emotional disorders and their families. After nearly two decades of experience in implementing this concept and philosophy, it is essential to revisit and clarify the basic premises of the framework, incorporate perspectives from accumulating experience, and consider its continued relevance.

WHY IS SYSTEM REFORM NEEDED FOR CHILDREN'S MENTAL HEALTH CARE?

Calls for reform in children's mental health date back to the 1960s, with numerous task forces and reports citing shortcomings in services for children with emotional disorders and their families and recommending changes (Joint Commission on the Mental Health of Children, 1969; President's Commission on Mental Health, 1978; U.S. Congress Office of Technology Assessment, 1986; Knitzer, 1982). Nearly all of the reports and documents advocating system reform had these major themes:

- Most children in need were not getting mental health services.
- Those served were often in excessively restrictive settings.
- Services typically were limited to outpatient, inpatient, and residential treatment; few, if any intermediate, community-based options were available.
- The various child-serving systems sharing responsibility for children with mental health problems rarely worked together.
- Families typically were blamed and were not involved as partners in their child's care.
- Agencies and systems rarely considered or addressed cultural differences in the populations they served.

The proposed solution to these systemic problems was comprehensive, coordinated, community-based systems of services and supports.

In 1984, the federal Child and Adolescent Service System Program (CASSP) was initiated by the National Institute of Mental Health (and later administered by the Center for Mental Health Services within the Substance Abuse and Mental Health Services Administration) to help states and communities plan for and implement system reform in children's mental health. This program and its successors have been promoting system reform that focuses on creating these community-based service systems, which eventually became known as systems of care.

Since the mid-1980s, there has been tremendous progress across the nation in developing systems of care for children with emotional disorders and their families. Perhaps most notable is the $92 million federal program (the Comprehensive Community Mental Health Services for Children and Their Families Program) to support the development of systems of care in communities across the nation. Sixty-seven have been funded thus far, with more to come in the future. In addition, there has likely been even greater investment of state and local resources to create services consistent with the system of care philosophy. Although much progress has been made, many communities still lack well-developed systems of care, many challenges have frustrated system of care development, and there is much work yet to be done.

WHAT IS THE MEANING OF THE SYSTEM OF CARE CONCEPT?

Since the introduction of the concept, many meanings have been attributed to the term *system of care*. It has been called a model; many have tried to replicate the model, to operationalize it, measure it, evaluate it, and compare it to traditional services. Despite these interpretations, systems of care are neither unitary nor easy to define.

Stroul and Friedman (1986) were the first to define *system of care*: "A comprehensive spectrum of mental health and other necessary services which are organized into a coordinated network to meet the multiple and changing needs of children and adolescents with serious emotional disturbances and their families" (p. 3). Although this definition refers to a spectrum of services, the concept of a system of care represents more than a network of individual service components. The system of care concept represents a philosophy about the way in which services should be delivered to children and their families. Although the actual components and organizational configuration of systems of care may differ from state to state and community to community, inherent in the concept is a set of basic values and operational philosophies that guide the character and quality of service delivery (Stroul & Friedman, 1986, 1996). Three core values have been identified for systems of care:

1. *Systems of care should be child centered and family focused.* The first core value specifies that the needs of the child and his or her family should drive the system and dictate the types and mix of services provided. This child-centered and family-focused approach is seen as a commitment to adapt services to the child and family rather than expecting them to adapt to the constraints of agencies and programs. It is also seen as a commitment to providing services in an environment and a manner that enhances the personal dignity of children and families, respects their wishes and individual goals, and maximizes opportunities for involvement and self-determination in the planning and delivery of services. Implicit in this value is a commitment to serving the child in the context of the family. In most cases, parents are the primary caregivers for children with serious emotional disorders, and systems of care should support and assist parents in this role, as well as involve families in all decisions regarding service delivery.

2. *Systems of care should be community based.* The historic overuse of restrictive institutional facilities in serving children with serious emotional disorders has been well documented (Knitzer, 1982). The system of care philosophy is built on the notion of a community-based network of services for youth with emotional disturbances and their families, offering less restrictive, more normative treatment environments within or close to the child's home community. The notion of a community-based system of care extends beyond the actual services and includes the control and management of the system. Decisions about the mix of services to be offered, service coordination mechanisms, and the use of resources should be made at the community level in cooperation with state government. Such flexibility and decision-making authority encourage communities to accept responsibility for serving their youngsters.

3. *Systems of care should be culturally competent.* The third core value asserts that agencies, programs, and services in systems of care must be responsive to the cultural, racial, and ethnic differences of the populations they serve (Isaacs & Benjamin, 1991). The need to create culturally competent systems of care assumes greater urgency in view of the changing demographics of the American population, with whites continuing to decline as a proportion of the population and ethnic minorities growing. Furthermore, a number of external stressors have been found to place ethnic minority children at increased risk for emotional disorders. Thus, children of color are likely to comprise an increasing proportion of the country's population of youth and an even larger proportion of youngsters receiving mental health and other services from child-serving agencies. Cultural competence is inherent in the concept of a system that emphasizes child-centered, family-focused, and community-based care: values that dictate that children and families be served within their own unique and specific contexts.

Culture and ethnicity comprise a significant part of the context for children of color and their families. Isaacs and Benjamin (1991) emphasize that ethnicity shapes beliefs about what constitutes mental health and mental illness, manifestations of symptoms and patterns of coping, help-seeking patterns, and use and response to treatment. Thus, the critical importance of culture and ethnicity necessitates the development of culturally competent systems of care (Cross, Bazron, Dennis, & Isaacs, 1989; U.S. Department of Health and Human Services, 2001).

In addition to these three fundamental values for systems of care, ten principles have been identified that enunciate other basic guidelines about the way services should be delivered within systems of care (see Figure 2.1):

1. *Comprehensiveness.* Children should have access to a broad array of mental health services, going well beyond the limited inpatient, outpatient, and residential treatment that has typically been available to them. Even with a broad array of mental health services, children with serious and complex behavioral health disorders are likely to require additional services and supports to meet their multidimensional needs and those of their families. Mental health treatment services can be effective only within the context of a larger network of services and supports that are directed at meeting the child's health, educational, recreational, family support, and vocational needs. Thus, the scope and array of services provided in systems of care must be sufficiently broad to account for the diverse treatment and support needs of children and their families.

2. *Individualization.* Individualizing services means that the types, mix, and intensity of services must be designed to fit the child's needs. The assessment process offers the opportunity to consider the child and family's strengths and problems, level of functioning, age and developmental stage, and any special needs

---

Core Values

---

1. The system of care should be child centered and family focused, with the needs of the child and family dictating the types and mix of services provided.
2. The system of care should be community based, with the locus of services as well as management and decision-making responsibility resting at the community level.
3. The system of care should be culturally competent, with agencies, programs, and services that are responsive to the cultural, racial, and ethnic differences of the populations they serve.

Guiding Principles

---

1. Children with emotional disturbances should have access to a comprehensive array of services that address their physical, emotional, social, and educational needs.
2. Children with emotional disturbances should receive individualized services in accordance with the unique needs and potentials of each child and guided by an individualized service plan.
3. Children with emotional disturbances should receive services within the least restrictive, most normative environment that is clinically appropriate.
4. The families and surrogate families of children with emotional disturbances should be full participants in all aspects of the planning and delivery of services.
5. Children with emotional disturbances should receive services that are integrated, with linkages between child-serving agencies and programs and mechanisms for planning, developing, and coordinating services.
6. Children with emotional disturbances should be provided with case management or similar mechanisms to ensure that multiple services are delivered in a coordinated and therapeutic manner and that they can move through the system of services in accordance with their changing needs.
7. Early identification and intervention for children with emotional disturbances should be promoted by the system of care in order to enhance the likelihood of positive outcomes.
8. Children with emotional disturbances should be ensured smooth transitions to the adult service system as they reach maturity.
9. The rights of children with emotional disturbances should be protected, and effective advocacy efforts for children and adolescents with emotional disturbances should be promoted.
10. Children with emotional disturbances should receive services without regard to race, religion, national origin, sex, physical disability, or other characteristics, and services should be sensitive and responsive to cultural differences and special needs.

FIGURE 2.1. System of Care Values and Principles.

Source: Stroul and Friedman (1986).

that bear on service delivery. The culmination of the assessment process should be an individualized service plan that identifies strengths and needs across all life domains, establishes goals, and specifies appropriate interventions. Many communities now use multiagency teams convened by a case manager, and with the full participation of the child, family, providers, and significant others, to develop a comprehensive, individualized service plan.

The concept of individualized services has been given new meaning with the advent and increasing use of the wraparound approach to services delivery (Katz-Leavy, Lourie, Stroul, & Zeigler-Dendy, 1992; Kendziora, Bruns, Osher, Pacchiano, & Mejia, 2001). The approach involves constructing a service plan for a child and family and using flexible funds to develop a package of services and supports that are specifically tailored to address each child and family's unique needs. This may involve enlisting existing treatment and support resources in the community, as well as purchasing or designing services and supports for a particular child and family. In addition to more familiar treatment services, an individualized wraparound approach may enlist services and supports such as hiring behavioral aides, professional roommates, or mentors for the home or classroom; providing special recreational or vocational services; and purchasing reinforcers. These individually tailored service packages, designed to surround the child and family with a full network of resources based on their needs and wishes, are increasingly being used for youngsters with the most serious disorders.

3. *Least restrictive setting.* Children and adolescents should be served in as normal an environment as possible. An implicit goal of systems of care is to maintain as many children as possible in their own homes by providing a full range of family-focused and community-based services and supports. Although out-of-home or protective placements may be indicated at times, frequently they are used because less restrictive, community-based alternatives are not available (Behar, 1985, 1986; Friedman & Street, 1985; Stroul, 1988, 1993; Rosenblatt, Attkisson, & Mills, 1992). Often the concepts of treatment *setting,* treatment *intensity,* and treatment *restrictiveness* are confused. The setting of a particular service does not necessarily determine how intensive the treatment is. For example, the services provided by day treatment programs and home-based service programs are highly treatment intensive, working with children and families for many hours each day and providing a whole range of therapeutic interventions. Thus, highly intensive treatment services do not necessarily require restrictive settings.

Even within the residential arena, there is a range of more normative options that attempt to approximate the child's natural environment. For example, therapeutic foster homes and family-style group homes create a family-type atmosphere and allow children to attend public schools and remain involved in community activities. These services may have more potential for helping youngsters realize the goal of returning to their own family and school than do residential services that cut youngsters off from normal family and educational environments (Friedman, 1983; Stroul, 1989).

4. *Family orientation.* This principle emphasizes that families or surrogate families should be active participants in all aspects of the planning and delivery of services. In a word, parents should be partners in systems of care. In order to be established as partners, parents should be involved in all phases of service delivery for their children: assessment, development of the individualized service plan, service provision, service coordination, and evaluation of progress. In addition, an array of services and supports should be offered to families to strengthen their coping skills and their ability to care for their children effectively, such as parent support, parent education, counseling, respite services, and home aid services. There is increasing evidence that when adequate family support is available, many families are able to maintain children with serious emotional disturbances at home and avoid their placement in residential or institutional settings. Even when children are in out-of-home placements, the participation and involvement of parents should be encouraged. Involving and providing supports to families maximize the opportunities for successful return of the child to the family. Furthermore, families should not be forced to relinquish legal custody in order to obtain expensive, but needed, residential treatment for their children (Bazelon Center for Mental Health Law and Federation of Families for Children's Mental Health, 1999).

The principle of family involvement applies not only to participation in planning and delivering services for their own children but to participation at the system level as well. Families should be involved as full partners in policymaking, planning, priority setting, and evaluating the overall system of care for children with emotional disturbances in their communities. Only when parents are active participants in decision making for both their own youngsters and the overall service system will they be full partners in systems of care.

5. *Service integration.* This principle refers to systematizing systems of care: there should be structures and processes in place to ensure that the various child-serving agencies and programs work together to develop and oversee systems of care. Most youngsters served in systems of care have multiple problems and are involved with multiple agencies and systems. Coordination at the service delivery level is essential to coordinate their care. Coordination is also needed at the system level to ensure that the services provided by mental health, education, child welfare, health, substance abuse, juvenile justice, and other agencies are interwoven into a coherent and effective system. Many states and communities have created interagency entities comprising the representatives of the major child-serving systems to fulfill these system-level coordination functions. Another critical system-level coordination function is the capacity to review difficult cases that cannot be resolved through other mechanisms within systems of care. This

interagency case review and problem-solving function often is handled by inter-agency structures created in communities for this specific purpose.

6. *Case management.* Case management is critical for the effective operation of systems of care, because it is the function that ensures care coordination at the level of the child and family (Friesen & Poertner, 1995). Case management or care coordination is intended to ensure that children and families receive the services they need, the services are coordinated, and the services are appropriate to their changing needs over time. The role of the case manager includes a number of essential functions: coordinating the comprehensive interagency assessment of the child's needs; planning for services to address the needs of the child and family; arranging for needed services; linking the various parts of the child's system, including family, agencies, school, and significant others; monitoring the adequacy and appropriateness of services; ensuring continuity of service; advocating for the child and family; and establishing linkages with the adult service system to facilitate transition (Stroul, 1995).

7. *Early identification.* Systems of care must strike a balance between services designed for early intervention in children identified as at risk for serious emotional problems and those designed for youngsters already identified as seriously disturbed. Evidence indicates that early identification and intervention can have a significant effect on the course of emotional disorders in children (Friedman, 1984; Cowen et al., 1975). Systems of care have also become increasingly focused on creating appropriate behavioral health services for young children (infants, toddlers, and preschoolers) and their families assessed to be at high risk for emotional problems or already exhibiting symptoms (Kaufmann & Dodge, 1997; Cohen & Kaufmann, 2000).

8. *Smooth transition.* The transition from systems of care for children and youth with emotional disturbances to the adult service system is fraught with problems. Children who age out of systems of care become young adults who often are in need of long-term mental health care, vocational services, and a range of other support services. A number of factors complicate this transition: difficulties in accessing the mental health and other needed services from the adult service system, lack of independent living and vocational skills, and philosophical differences with adult service systems that are based on disability and rehabilitation concepts. In addition, adult agencies that have specialized in serving persons with severe and persistent mental illnesses often are ill prepared to serve many of the youth who have been served by systems of care for children, and the programs they offer often are inappropriate to the needs and characteristics of this youth-in-transition population. Systems of care should develop specific services for youth in transition to adulthood and establish functional linkages with relevant adult agencies to ensure continuity of services for individual youth and families, as well as to work with the adult system to become more responsive to the needs of these youth (Clark & Davis, 2000).

9. *Rights protection and advocacy.* Systems of care should include mechanisms to protect the rights of children, particularly with respect to actions involving removal from families, placement in restrictive settings, or denial of services in managed care systems. Such mechanisms may include statutes, statements of the rights of children, grievance procedures, case review committees, and protection and advocacy systems. In addition to rights protection, systems of care should promote advocacy activities on behalf of children and adolescents with emotional disorders. Case advocacy is defined as efforts on behalf of an individual child to ensure that the child and family receive appropriate services, benefits, or protections; class advocacy involves efforts to seek improvements in services, benefits, or rights on behalf of all children and youth with emotional disturbances (Knitzer, 1989). Both types of advocacy are vital to the success of systems of care.

10. *Nondiscrimination.* The final principle states that systems of care should uphold a policy of nondiscrimination in the delivery of services and that all children with emotional disorders and their families should have access to quality services. This principle means that services should be accessible to children and family members with physical disabilities, that interpreters should be available to those with hearing impairments, translation services should be provided for those with language barriers, and systems of care should be sufficiently flexible to remove any barriers to service delivery for children and families with special needs or from diverse ethnic groups. Without such efforts, systems of care could not truly be child centered.

The actual system of care model is organized in a framework consisting of eight major dimensions of service, as shown in Figure 2.2. Each dimension represents an area of need for children and families and a set of functions that must be fulfilled in order to provide comprehensive services to meet these needs. The framework does not specify which type of agency should fulfill any of the particular functions; this is determined by each individual community. The mental health dimension, of critical importance for this population, consists of a range of nonresidential and residential services:

Nonresidential Services	*Residential Services*
Prevention	Therapeutic foster care
Early identification and intervention	Therapeutic group care
Assessment	Therapeutic camp services
Outpatient treatment	Independent living services
Home-based services	Residential treatment services
Day treatment	Crisis residential services
Crisis services	Inpatient hospitalization

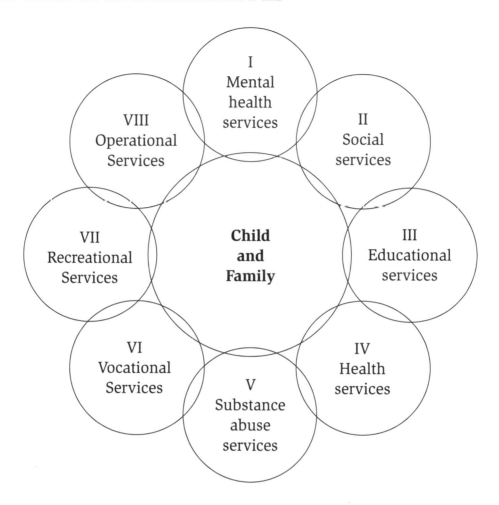

FIGURE 2.2. System of Care Framework

Additional services from other dimensions such as respite care, school-based mental health services, and case management have also been shown to be essential.

All of these components are interrelated, and the effectiveness of any one component is related to the availability and effectiveness of all other components. For example, the same day treatment program is likely to be more effective in a community that also has strong outpatient services, crisis services, and respite services than in a community lacking these other services and supports. Because all of the components of systems of care are interdependent, it is not advisable to devote a lot of resources to developing one or two of the services without paying sufficient attention to the entire system. In addition, an appropriate balance between the components of systems is essential, particularly between the more restrictive and the less restrictive services. If a system is not in balance, youngsters will be placed in restrictive service settings without having an opportunity to receive other types of intensive services like day treatment or home-based services or therapeutic foster care.

This system of care framework can be used as a guide for planning and policymaking, as well as for assessing existing services and planning improvements; it has been described as a blueprint for a service system that establishes directions and goals. It was designed as a starting point for states and communities as they seek to build their systems, a baseline from which changes can be made as additional research, experience, and innovation dictate. States and communities are encouraged to adapt the framework to conform with their needs, environments, and service systems.

WHAT CLARIFICATIONS OF THE SYSTEM OF CARE CONCEPT ARE NEEDED?

After nearly two decades of experience, a number of myths and misconceptions have surfaced with respect to the system of care concept—for example:

- Systems of care focus not on clinical interventions but primarily on system infrastructure.
- The system of care philosophy is primarily focused on family involvement and cultural competence.
- Systems of care are different from or do not involve evidence-based interventions.
- No traditional services are included in systems of care.
- Systems of care place greater value on nonprofessional service providers and natural supports than on other clinicians, providers, and treatment modalities.

Debunking the myths is important in order to ensure that progress in improving service systems for children with emotional disorders and their families is not impeded. A review of the system of care values, principles, and framework makes it clear that service coordination and interagency collaboration are elements of the system of care philosophy, as are family involvement and cultural competence. The development of the necessary infrastructure for a system of care is important. However, none of these is the sole focus of system of care development. First and foremost, *systems of care are a range of treatment services and supports guided by a philosophy.*

Systems of care not only include clinical services; they are the very core. Accordingly, they must involve evidence-based interventions. A goal of systems of care is to provide state-of-the-art, effective clinical services and supports. It is important to note, however, that most interventions have not been tested on the population typically served by systems of care. In clinical research, the emphasis has been on the application of a well-defined treatment delivered to a set of children with well-demarcated problems. In contrast, systems of care serve a highly diverse population of children with multiple needs and problems and who receive multiple services and supports. Little is actually known about whether these treatments are effective within operating systems of care (Friedman & Hernandez, 2001).

Thus, systems of care involve clinical interventions, and they involve traditional services such as outpatient, inpatient, and residential treatment, as well as newer, more nontraditional service modalities such as home-based services, therapeutic foster care, and mentoring, many of which do have an emerging evidence base from research in community settings (Burns & Hoagwood, 2002). In addition, systems of care involve highly trained clinicians of all disciplines, as well as paraprofessionals, families as providers, and other creative staffing strategies to meet different needs.

Systems of care involve all of these things. It is essential to recognize that the development of a system of care is a multifaceted, multilevel intervention that encompasses the following components:

- Changing state and local policies, financing mechanisms, and other structures and processes to support systems of care

- Making changes at the local system level needed to plan, implement, manage, and evaluate systems of care

- Making changes at the service delivery level to provide a broad array of effective, state-of-the-art treatment services and supports to children and their families

Developing a system of care is a difficult and complex intervention with many challenges at each of these levels. Furthermore, the system of care concept is a framework and a guide, not a prescription. Different communities implement systems of care in different ways, with different service arrays and different organizational arrangements designed for each unique environment (Hernandez & Hodges, 2002). It is the philosophy that is the constant. Flexibility and creativity in implementing systems of care are inherent in the concept and are encouraged to adapt to local needs.

WHY SHOULD WE CONTINUE TO ADVOCATE
AND DEVELOP SYSTEMS OF CARE?

Most people would say that the field should continue to advocate and develop systems of care only if they are proven to be effective. To that end, researchers have been attempting to assess the effectiveness of systems of care. In reviewing the literature, the recent surgeon general's report states that research has shown positive outcomes at the system level, but that the relationship between the system level and practice level remains unclear and that questions remain about cost (U.S. Department of Health and Human Services, 1999).

An important concern in asking whether systems of care are effective is that the most basic characteristics of systems of care often are not considered:

- They are multifaceted, multilevel interventions and thus difficult to measure. After nearly two decades of experience, it is clear that systems of care are more complex, more difficult to implement, and take more time to implement than had ever been realized.

- The services in systems of care are difficult to measure because children are likely to be receiving multiple services—a package of flexible, individualized services and supports—rather than a single treatment that can be isolated.

- Systems of care do not comprise a unitary approach; they are substantially different in every community. It is therefore difficult, if not impossible, to group them and measure them all in the same way.

- They are not static interventions but rather are constantly changing and evolving.

- Most communities have some elements of the philosophy and services associated with systems of care, so it is complicated to try to compare those with and those without.

Given these complexities and variations, it is a significant challenge to evaluate systems of care, and there is no one objective truth or simplistic answer about their effectiveness. The central issue in considering the effectiveness of systems of care is to ask, "Effective for what?" There are goals and desired outcomes at each level of the intervention, all of which are important and all of which should be considered and measured appropriately. It is important for policymakers and researchers to be clear about what is being measured at which level of the intervention and make sure that appropriate indicators and methods are used. For example, it is inappropriate to examine system-level changes and measure them by looking at clinical and functional outcomes. Clinical and functional outcomes must be linked to what occurs at the service delivery or practice level. And one would not expect improved clinical and functional outcomes if the intervention involves only system-level changes, such as building an infrastructure or coordinating. A major challenge as the field moves forward is to understand better the relationship between variables at the system level and variables at the practice level, the challenge stated in the surgeon general's report (U.S. Department of Health and Human Services, 1999). In the interim, care must be taken to ensure that the outcomes measured are reasonably linked and related to the level and the aspect of the intervention that is being assessed.

Research and evaluation activities will yield some of the answers about why the system of care concept and philosophy should continue to guide system change in children's mental health. As the concept and philosophy are reviewed and clarified after nearly two decades of experience, another reason for continuing to apply them as a guide for system reform in children's mental health becomes obvious: it is the right thing to do. The systems of care philosophy has the following critical elements:

- Providing a broad array of individualized services and supports
- Serving children in the most normative and least restrictive environments possible
- Serving children in community-based programs and not institutionalizing them unless absolutely necessary
- Supporting and involving families in caring for their children, since in most cases, families are the most important and lifelong resource for their children
- Agencies and programs working together and not at cross-purposes when serving children with multiple needs
- Recognizing and addressing cultural differences

These and the other elements of the system of care philosophy now represent a widely accepted value base for services to children and their families, not only in mental health systems but across child-serving systems in this country.

There has been extraordinary progress toward the development of community-based systems of care. Accomplishments are evident at the national, state, and local levels and span areas including the elucidation of the system of care concept and philosophy, the development of new services, the formation of an advocacy movement, the improvement of interagency collaboration, and the stimulation of research. Although gains have been substantial, great challenges lie ahead in the endeavor to develop systems of care. Some of these represent areas in which the field has not focused attention; others result from changes in the environment in which systems of care are evolving. Contemplation of the reasons that it has been difficult to implement systems of care raises a number of questions:

- Is the system of care concept still not sufficiently known, understood, or accepted?
- Are the incentives to implement systems of care inadequate?
- Is there insufficient funding by mental health and other child-serving systems to accomplish system development and develop needed service capacity?
- Are managed care reforms and other cost-containment and financial retrenchment measures across states diverting attention and investment away from system of care development?
- Is system development impeded by the lack of a pool of staff who are prepared with the philosophy and skills needed to work within a system of care context?
- Has insufficient attention been focused on working with front-line staff in order to work toward changing attitudes and practices at the service delivery level?

These and other factors pose formidable and continuing challenges to developing and improving systems of care. Despite these implementation challenges, however, the system of care concept and philosophy continues to offer a value base and blueprint to guide the development and improvement of services for children and adolescents with serious emotional disorders and their families.

References

Bazelon Center for Mental Health Law and Federation of Families for Children's Mental Health. (1999). *Staying together: Preventing custody relinquishment for children's access to mental health services. A guide for family advocates.* Washington, DC: Author.

Behar, L. B. (1985). Changing patterns of state responsibility: A case study of North Carolina. *Journal of Clinical Child Psychology, 14,* 188–195.

Behar, L. B. (1986). A model for child mental health services: The North Carolina experience. *Children Today, 15,* 16–21.

Burns, B. J. & Hoagwood, K. (2002). *Community treatment for youth: Evidence-based interventions for severe emotional and behavioral disorders.* New York: Oxford University Press.

Clark, S., & Davis, M. (2000). *Transition to adulthood: A resource for assisting young people with emotional or behavioral difficulties.* Baltimore, MD: Brookes Publishing.

Cohen, E., & Kaufmann, R. (2000). *Early childhood mental health consultation.* Washington, DC: U.S. Department of Health and Human Services, Substance Abuse and Mental Health Services Administration, Center for Mental Health Services.

Cowen, E. L., Trost, M. A., Lorion, R. P., Dorr, D., Izzo, L. D., & Isaacson, R. V. (1975). *New ways in school mental health: Early detection and prevention of school maladaptation.* New York: Human Science Press.

Cross, T., Bazron, B., Dennis, K., & Isaacs, M. (1989). *Towards a culturally competent system of care: Vol. 1. A monograph on effective services for minority children who are severely emotionally disturbed.* Washington, DC: Georgetown University Child Development Center, National Technical Assistance Center for Children's Mental Health.

Friedman, R. (1983). *Children's mental health services and policy in Florida.* Unpublished manuscript. Tampa: University of South Florida, Louis de la Parte Florida Mental Health Institute.

Friedman, R. (1984). *Seriously emotionally disturbed children: An underserved and ineffectively served population.* Unpublished manuscript. Tampa: University of South Florida, Louis de la Parte Florida Mental Health Institute.

Friedman, R., & Hernandez, M. (2001). The national evaluation of the comprehensive community mental health services for children and their families program: A commentary. *Children's Services: Social Policy, Research, and Practice, 5,* 67–74.

Friedman, R., & Street, S. (1985). Admission and discharge criteria for children's mental health services: A review of the issue and options. *Journal of Clinical Child Psychology, 14,* 229–235.

Friesen, B. J., & Poertner, J. (Eds.). (1995). *From case management to service coordination for children with emotional, behavioral or mental disorders.* Baltimore, MD: Brookes Publishing.

Hernandez, M., & Hodges, S. (2002). *Building upon the theory of change for systems of care.* Manuscript submitted for publication.

Isaacs, M., & Benjamin, M. (1991). *Towards a culturally competent system of care: Vol. 2. Programs which use culturally competent services.* Washington, DC: Georgetown University Child Development Center, National Technical Assistance Center for Children's Mental Health.

Joint Commission on the Mental Health of Children. (1969). *Crisis in child mental health.* New York: HarperCollins.

Katz-Leavy, J., Lourie, I., Stroul, B., & Zeigler-Dendy, C. (1992). *Individualized services in a system of care.* Washington, DC: Georgetown University Child Development Center, National Technical Assistance Center for Children's Mental Health.

Kaufmann, R., & Dodge, J. (1997). *Prevention and early interventions for young children at risk for mental health and substance abuse problems and their families: A background paper.* Washington, DC: Georgetown University Child Development Center, National Technical Assistance Center for Children's Mental Health.

Kendziora, K., Bruns, E., Osher, D., Pacchiano, D., & Mejia, B. (2001). *Wraparound: Stories from the field.* Washington, DC: Center for Effective Collaboration and Practice, American Institutes for Research.

Knitzer, J. (1982). *Unclaimed children.* Washington, DC: Children's Defense Fund.

Knitzer, J. (1989). Children's mental health: The advocacy challenge. In R. Friedman, A. Duchnowski, & E. Henderson (Eds.), *Advocacy on behalf of children with serious emotional problems* (pp. 15–27). Springfield, IL: Charles C. Thomas.

President's Commission on Mental Health. (1978). *Report of the sub-task panel on infants, children, and adolescents.* Washington, DC: Author.

Rosenblatt, A., Attkisson, C., & Mills, N. (1992). *The California AB377 evaluation, three year summary report.* San Francisco: University of California.

Stroul, B. (1988). *Home-based services.* Washington, DC: Georgetown University Child Development Center, National Technical Assistance Center for Children's Mental Health.

Stroul, B. (1989). *Therapeutic foster care.* Washington, DC: Georgetown University Child Development Center, National Technical Assistance Center for Children's Mental Health.

Stroul, B. (1993). *Systems of care for children and adolescents with severe emotional disturbances: What are the results?* Washington, DC: Georgetown University Child Development Center, National Technical Assistance Center for Children's Mental Health.

Stroul, B. (1995). Case management in a system of care. In B. Friesen & J. Poertner (Eds.), *From case management to service coordination for children with emotional, behavioral, or mental disorders: Building on family strengths* (pp. 3–25). Baltimore, MD: Brookes Publishing.

Stroul, B., & Friedman, R. (1986). *A system of care for children and youth with severe emotional disturbances* (Rev. ed.). Washington, DC: Georgetown University Child Development Center, National Technical Assistance Center for Children's Mental Health.

Stroul, B., & Friedman, R. (1996). The system of care concept and philosophy. In B. Stroul (Ed.), *Children's mental health: Creating systems of care in a changing society* (pp. 1–22). Baltimore, MD: Brookes Publishing.

U.S. Congress. Office of Technology Assessment. (1986). *Children's mental health: Problems and services: A background paper.* Washington, DC: Author.

U.S. Department of Health and Human Services. (1999). *Mental health: A report of the surgeon general.* Rockville, MD: U.S. Department of Health and Human Services,

Substance Abuse and Mental Health Services Administration, Center for Mental Health Services, National Institutes of Health, National Institute of Mental Health.

U.S. Department of Health and Human Services. (2000). *Report of the Surgeon General's Conference on Children's Mental Health: A national action agenda.* Washington, DC: Author.

U.S. Department of Health and Human Services. (2001). *Mental health: Culture, race, and ethnicity: A supplement to mental health: A report of the surgeon general.* Rockville, MD: U.S. Department of Health and Human Services, Public Health Service, Office of the Surgeon General.

CHAPTER THREE

Family Advocacy Development in Systems of Care

Charles Huffine
Deborah Anderson

Families are the core of any civilization's social structure. Supporting families to raise their children, participate meaningfully in the community, and care for their sick and aged is a central goal for any society. Tragically, in our society, as in so many others around the world, some families do not experience that support. In the United States, families of color, immigrant families, and families living in poverty have often suffered prejudice by the larger society and oppression by government and social agencies. Our recent history is rife with examples of such families demanding full inclusion in their communities. Their struggle is not unlike that of families who suffer the tragedy of an adult family member with a mental illness or a child with serious emotional disturbance. Children with mental disorders often express their distress behaviorally, thus providing their families, schools, and communities with many challenges.

It is essential to have family-centered care as a central organizing concept in system of care reform. In all aspects of the emerging system are families caught in the ambivalent response of their communities to their having a child who presents such challenges. Families with emotionally and behaviorally disturbed children and adolescents are often treated as pariahs in their communities, suffering similar prejudice and discrimination as have other misunderstood and oppressed minorities.

This painful fact has led to a growing movement of families acting as advocates for child and adolescent mental health. Prejudice and discrimination within the system of care meant to serve emotionally disturbed youth have long been recognized by those involved in the creation of the Child and Adolescent Service System Program (CASSP; Stroul & Friedman, 1994). They supported the concept that families need to be involved actively in all aspects of the system of care to ensure it is family centered and focused on the needs of the children it purports to serve. It was recognized that families need to be involved in all aspects of the system of care, from partnership with professionals who serve their children to full participation on the policy committees that govern the programs serving such youth.

The ideal of family-centered care applies to all elements of a child-serving system, from mental health and substance abuse treatment to social services, juvenile justice, and the schools. The ideal envisions that families be involved in planning and governing programs for children and adolescents at a policy level and in monitoring the operation of programs, evaluating programs through quality management techniques and research. Family-centered care presumes that a child or adolescent will be served in the least restrictive setting, preferably the family home, based on a highly individualized care plan that promotes the most normative possible inclusion of the child and family in the life of the community. Models of care embracing these ideals are termed a wraparound process (VanDenBerg & Grealish, 1996; Yoe, Santarcangelo, Atkins, & Burchard, 1996). Such programs are emerging all around the United States with the support of the Center for Mental Health Services (CMHS), a division of the federal Substance Abuse and Mental Health Services Administration (SAMHSA), which sponsors a massive grant program, the Children's Mental Health Initiative. This grant program aims to reform the system of care for children and youth in all communities in the United States. Current thinking defines a leadership role for parents and consumer youth in such national efforts. In local programs using a wraparound process, families and youth are defined as centrally important to a method of care that promotes the original CASSP values of family-centered, child-focused, culturally competent, and coordinated care. Thus, system of care reform stands for placing families in the leadership role of determining the course of the care their family member receives. This leadership is delivered through the vehicle of a child and family team.

FAMILIES AS ESSENTIAL PARTNERS IN A REFORMED SYSTEM OF CARE

Various approaches have been used to engage families as partners in systems of care.

Model of Child and Family Teams

Central to the concept of family-centered care and the wraparound process is the concept of the child and family team. Such teams, in well-constructed care programs for youth, are the driving force of planning, purchasing, and evaluating professional services and all other community-based activities that support a child's strengths and serve his or her needs. It is crucial that the parents or the youth for whom the team is formed be empowered to have the ability to be the driving force. In many cases, with younger children or very challenged youth, parents are in effect the team leaders. In other cases, with youth who have no family or whose family is unable to be involved, the young person who receives the services is empowered to be the team leader.

Essential to this empowering process is enabling the family (parents and youth) to gather about them people who are central to their lives and from their community. This may include close relatives, neighbors, close friends, or coworkers. It may include those who have shown some caring for the family but may have not previously been close, such as a shopkeeper or hair dresser. Clergy, coaches, community leaders, or family advocates from the family's community may be asked to be part of the team. It is critical for older youth to be able to include peers on their team should they so choose.

Ideally, in the pure model, those who offer professional services are not included as part of the team, but in reality many families identify some who have provided services as among those closest to the family and want such individuals on the team. A rough guide is that a team should never be more than 50 percent professional and may have only one professional: a care manager who serves as an adviser and bridge to the professional world. The team may ask professionals to attend from time to time as advisers or consultants. A psychiatrist who is not involved as a service provider for the child or youth in need of care may serve a critically useful role as a consultant for reviewing a current treatment plan or evaluating the efficacy of a recommended treatment. Team membership may vary from three or four to ten to twelve. Larger teams may get cumbersome, but often can provide access to a network of supports for the family and the child, such as respite or activities for the child (examples are summer employment or sports activities).

In a more evolved system, where coordination is the rule between systems, service providers may form treatment or service teams to discuss the care of patient-clients. A child and family team can relate to such a process through establishing a clear relationship to that group of professionals. A parent, youth, or advocate may be invited to attend all meetings of the treatment or care team or be included in all communications of such a professional team. In some systems where funds for the care of troubled children and youth are blended, the child and family team may serve as a purchaser of services. This is the case with the King County Blended Funding Project (KCBFP) in Washington State. As purchasers of services, such teams collectively can ask for and fund the development of missing services and thus shape the nature of service provision in a community. Even when not formally in control of the funds that feed services, families who are empowered can have a great influence on the ways that professional teams relate to families. They can and do insist on respect for the consumer family perspective.

Ideally, child and family teams will empower parents to be able to keep their challenging children in their home and in the community through the development of a wraparound process and a care plan. The care plan should evolve to relying less on professional services and more on natural community activities, such as schools, youth activity programs, sports, youth employment, and informal networking of peers. A crisis plan is a crucial element of a team's activity, as is recognizing, and finding resources to meet, specific needs of a youth, such as for psychiatric services, individual psychotherapy, medical care, or tutoring. Families that are networking to get advice, identifying family-friendly resources, and providing strategic approaches to those elements of the system that may not be family friendly gives power to distressed families. Families tend to become isolated and dispirited when struggling alone with the constant demand generated by a very difficult child. More experienced parents serving as advocates for the consumer family and as a team member can be a critical element in empowering families. Family advocates may go with a frightened mother or youth to court hearings. They may intercede when those offering professional services to a child or youth may not be communicating well with parents, or they may support a parent in asserting her perspective on a treatment plan proposed by a therapist.

The Role of Family Advocates

The role of family advocates is crucial in the development of child and family teams. Families who emerge as advocates have been through the trials of dealing with a very challenging child. They have experienced the frustrations of dealing with the usually fragmented system of care for children with problems and have experienced the alternative of a strength-based approach to caring for difficult children and youth. They are likely to be perceived by overwhelmed and distressed consumer families as relevant helpers. As members of the team, they have a unique opportunity to support families having difficulties in negotiating a very confusing system of care. Advocates often provide the type of practical advice that can only be imagined by one who has been in the situation. Their perspectives allow for deep caring, hugs, and humor. These attributes are rare in service providers due to the confines of professional boundaries. Many family advocates who are members of formal advocacy organizations are in a position to provide training for child and family teams.

The advocacy organizations in children's mental health have access to national resources for training materials, advice on best practices, and technical assistance. Some of these are the national Federation of Families for Children's Mental Health (FFCMH), the National Mental Health Association (NMHA), the

Children and Adults with Attention Deficit Disorder (CHADD), and the Child and Adolescent Bipolar Foundation (CABF). The National Alliance for the Mentally Ill (NAMI) is focusing on the problems of youth with serious emotional disorders. CMHS and its system of technical assistance contractors offer a wealth of information regarding the important roles of families and family advocates in the formation of teams around troubled children and youth within a wraparound process. While all families raising emotionally and behaviorally challenged children have common needs and share common experiences it is not a given that they will be comfortable affiliating. Class, race, and culture can divide families engaged in caring for such children just as in the larger society. Some advocacy groups include parents passionate regarding a single diagnostic entity, such as CHADD or the CABF. Others, such as NAMI, have only recently explored the nature of mental illness in children. NAMI has built a powerful organization focused primarily on mental illness and adults. Many in NAMI have in the past doubted that behavioral problems are indicative of true mental illnesses and warrant their concern.

Family Involvement in the System of Care

An optimally functioning family movement, whether embodied in one organization or several culturally diversified, regional, or specialty organizations, is essential if families are to be fully included in all aspects of the system of care. Families who seek to do advocacy must develop some sophistication regarding the fiscal context and unique culture of policy-setting bodies and the administration of service-providing agencies. This sophistication will enable them to approach professionals in ways that do not threaten and that promote collaboration. Such knowledge and skills will help families be regarded as partners with professionals and empowered as decision makers regarding the care of their own children and youth. Family advocates must demand that family representatives be fully involved in policy development, program management, and quality assurance activities. They must also develop the skills and understand the nature of caregiving sufficiently to be effective players at that level.

Families sitting on committees with professionals must be provided with adequate orientation, given all necessary information on an issue being discussed, and given support to come to a full understanding of the information being provided. In professional meetings, those who have jobs in the system of care are being paid to participate. It is an issue of basic justice and common sense that to promote families' full participation; adequate remuneration, transportation, and child care must be made available to the families willing to be involved in policy development or administration.

Family representatives on the boards of organizations and the policy councils of government agencies are representing a consumer constituency and are able to represent grievances of consumers to these bodies. A functional family advocacy program will have a structure in place to ensure all families are adequately represented by their advocate. Advocates should be reporting back and gaining advice from the many families who do not sit on the committees and boards.

Family Involvement in Systems of Care Evaluation

Families have a critical role in designing quality assurance programs and program evaluations. They should be expected to ally with scientists who have technical expertise in evaluation design but lack the practical experience of knowing what to measure or what is functionally significant. This is an area of expertise of families who have experienced being served by the system of care. Measuring the outcomes of system of care ideals, including the impact of full family participation in a culturally competent, community-based system of care for children with emotional and behavioral problems, is easier to articulate than to create. Many communities where the principles of family-centered care are held in highest regard have struggled to make the ideal a fact. The advantages of family empowerment in system of care reform in realizing substantial changes in outcomes have been especially difficult to measure. Two early studies of pioneering efforts to practice family-centered care yielded disappointing results when outcome was defined as measurable improvements in a child's functioning (Bickman, Summerfelt, & Noser, 1997). However, aggregate data from the Children's Mental Health Initiative grants have indicated that the situation is a bit more complicated than what was presumed in the Bickman studies. Results to date show that families of children with serious emotional disturbances demonstrate higher levels of satisfaction and inclusion in system of care programs (Holden, Friedman, & Santiago, 2001; Osher, Van Kammen, & Zaro, 2001).

One interesting result comes from a program evaluation of a system of care project in King County associated with the CMHI grant. A program evaluation of the KCBFP was codesigned by a psychiatric epidemiologist and a group of parent advocates (Vander Stoep, Williams, Jones, Green, & Trupin, 1999). The parents were initially disappointed that conventional measures of a child's functional improvement seemed not relevant to their children and others they knew who had serious emotional and behavioral disorders. They were introduced to a number of functional assessment scales, including the Child and Adolescent Functional Assessment Scale (CAFAS; Hodges & Wong, 1996). These families engaged in a research design meeting with the scientist and contributed the vital ingredients to a more relevant program evaluation.

The key contribution of the parents on the evaluation design team was to formulate a theory of change as a direct result of their practical experience raising very challenging children. They also built into the evaluation plan a mechanism for regular feedback to the child and family teams. The evaluation was designed to be an aid to the team on the progress of their efforts to provide a context for supporting healthy development and meeting the unique needs of the consumer child. It was the families' theory of change that empowered families could better ally with professionals, and this alliance would lead to a better-defined sense of the needs of the children. Meeting these needs would lead to a greater ability and a clearer commitment to integrating these children into their communities. They postulated that measures of family empowerment (Koren, DeChillo, & Friesen, 1992) and of needs met and community connections (Vander Stoep et al., 1999; Vander Stoep, Green, Jones, & Huffine, 2001) would allow them to measure this change process. They contended that these measures were valid results by themselves because meeting needs and fostering community integration were defined goals of the program for their children. The parents insisted that measuring clinical improvement alone was misleading and that more realistic goals for the very disturbed children in the KCBFP needed to be defined. Although CAFAS scores were included in the project evaluation, it seemed to the families not to capture the youth they knew in the program. They sensed that this tool was not a fine enough measure of functional improvement. Indeed, the KCBFP first- and second-year evaluations showed little change in CAFAS scores. However, they demonstrated that improved family empowerment was correlated with improvements in meeting needs and in children being better connected in their communities in several domains of their life. Family empowerment was facilitated by integrating family advocates on child and family teams (Vander Stoep et al., 1999, 2001). Prior to the third-year evaluation, problems that developed between the key family advocacy organization and consumer families led to disruption in parent support services. Although the results of that evaluation are not yet available, it appears that they will show less favorable results in the key elements of the process of change (A. Vander Stoep, personal communication, 2002).

The KCBFP includes some children who have no family at all and have spent years in residential treatment. As they are enrolled in the program and discharged to a treatment-oriented foster home, they often do not have the benefit of a child and family team grounded in their birth family and community. Many of these foster parents relate more naturally with professionals and often ask that only professionals be on their teams. They are more likely to view professionals in agencies as more primary to the process of change than do birth families or foster families, who have a more natural and long-lasting connection to the child. Needs for more normative experiences in their communities by consumer children in professional foster homes often go unmet as a result. To date, there are no measures of outcomes between the "true-to-the-model" teams and more professional teams.

YOUTH PERSPECTIVE AND
THE DEVELOPMENT OF YOUTH VOICE

Many older teenagers served by the system have little voice in their care or the rules that govern their care in foster care or from probation departments. The perspective of youth and parents often deviates, particularly as it relates to issues of safety versus freedom to experiment in the service of personal growth. Although youth and their parents have many common goals and values, differences in perspective must be reflected in any comprehensive view of family voice. In many parts of the country, with the support of CMHS Children's Mental Health Initiative (CMHI) grants, youth groups have been formed, often nurtured by family advocacy organizations, for the purpose of developing youth leadership to articulate youth voice in policy. In limited ways, youth advocates who have had experience in the system of care are beginning to offer their support to peers in child and family teams.

The national leadership in CMHS, which administers the CMHI grants, and their technical assistance partners have acknowledged the need for a unique youth voice in policy. The leadership of the Federation of Families has been very sympathetic and supportive of including the distinctive perspective of youth as part of their concept of a family voice. This leadership realizes that any youth movement nationally will take considerable resources and organizational efforts. Youth are not in a position to obtain the resources to be successful in such an organizational building task. Local youth advocacy movements also take extra resources if a viable organization is to emerge. To date, the resources have not been deployed as integral parts of the grants. Youth voice is not required as a condition of the grants, and no resources are allocated to the development of youth organizations.

Around the country, small organizations have emerged, often in grant communities, that enable young people who have been in the system of care to organize and develop leadership. Social service meetings seek articulate youth in foster care to speak on panels about their experiences. Youth consumers in mental health systems informally meet as part of a NAMI affiliate or other advocacy group. Grantee meetings regularly have had youth in breakout panels and as plenary speakers at their meetings. Youth who tell their story, simply and with great honesty, tend to gain rapt attention from adults, both parents and professionals, in the system of care. But so often the youth who gain the ear of adults are regarded as special and charming, examples of the system working well. Youth are the ultimate tokens when included in a work group with adults. Parents may promote their son or daughter as a youth leader due to their justifiable pride in their successes in overcoming emotional or behavioral problems, but these youth do not represent a larger constituency of youth. Organizing meaningful youth involvement in system of care reform is a daunting process.

Those who have worked with youth on the streets of Seattle—who have served them in homeless shelters and specialized schools for homeless youth and have housed them in foster homes and small group homes—know that consumer youth have a story to tell that may be very different from the stories told by parents. In Seattle, 48 percent of the youth on the streets are refugees from a marginally functional foster care system. Many have unmet mental health and substance abuse service needs. Some surveys say that 70 percent are "throwaway kids," forced to leave their homes due to abuse or neglect or due to the fact that their parents were unable and unprepared to meet the challenges of their difficult adolescence (Trupin, Low, Forsyth-Stephens, Tarico, & Cox, 1988, cited in testimony by youth advocates before the Washington State legislature in 1999). Youth touched by the system need to have a voice in how the system works, just as do their parents.

King County developed plans for meaningful family inclusion as we anticipated receiving our CMHS grant, Children and Families in Common. The psychiatrist associated with the grant, who is experienced as a mental health provider to adolescents and has been active as an advocate for youth in his community, led the grant management to committing some resources for the development of a youth advocacy group. There was essentially no shared experience in grant communities on how to make this happen. There was great appreciation of our efforts by the CMHS and its technical assistance contractors. They acknowledged the need for a youth voice. But there was no substantial technical assistance and no resources other than the part-time support of a series of three excellent staff from the technical assistance partnership who were assigned be youth coordinators.

With the blessings of CMHS and determination by the CFIC grant staff, King County set out to build an organization that would offer youth voice in policy throughout the system of care. Several attempts were made to communicate to youth in the community. Youth consumers of services, such as youth with juvenile court experience or those in foster care, were sought out. Fliers were distributed in communities with a high incidence of youth at risk. Essentially, no youth came to planned meetings despite promises of food, fun, and good works. What we did encounter were preexisting groups of youth affiliated with other aspects of the human services system who were supportive but wondered if we were duplicating their efforts. None of these groups seemed committed to the idea of creating an organization for the expressed purpose of providing youth voice in policy for the entire system of care.

A group of homeless youth had organized as Peace on the Streets by Kids from the Streets (PSKS) with the support of a committed foster parent. A strong youth leader had emerged in this organization who as a late teen had already had experience speaking to groups of professionals. She had found ways to be effective in meetings and had helped write grants. She was clear that she was not able or willing to form a new group but nevertheless was supportive and allied with our efforts. Within our county's Department of Community and Human Services, there had been a grant-supported youth group, Youth 'N' Action, that had mobilized young people to provide youth voice on a full range of topics, from social issues to issues of environmental degradation. These young people had engaged in projects in the community and had spoken to a number of service and governmental groups. In Youth 'N' Action, leaders had emerged who were willing to do some organizational work.

Many youth in this organization had wanted to explore issues of health, including mental health, as this related to teens. Their youth adviser embraced our activities, and a subcommittee, Health 'N' Action (HnA), was formed. The psychiatrist and the project director for the grant committed to meeting monthly with this group and overseeing its formation into an organization with structure, a mission, and some definable projects. A core of eight to ten youth came to HnA meetings regularly and defined two goals. First, they agreed to deploy their members to grant-organizing committees and to mobilize youth to attend other councils and meetings relating to the broad issues of youth health and development. This embraced all the agencies and activities of the system of care reform efforts of our grant. Second, they committed to organizing a teen health summit. They envisioned having a youth-run and youth-friendly health fair with entertainment, celebrity involvement, breakout sessions on topics of concern to youth, and booths for providers.

The enthusiasm and energy of the group was enormous as young people who had already come to know each other shared their ideals and good intentions. It was clear, however, that the job of nurturing and supporting true youth leadership properly fell on the adult sponsors. Without time and organizational support from the adults, the good intentions of the youth would not be realized. The youth would become discouraged and the efforts would die. Four months into the formation of HnA, the group was blessed by having an older, experienced university student volunteer to be the youth coordinator. She was working toward an M.S.W. degree and was able to include the HnA experience as a two-year internship with the grant. She had her own history in the system of care as a consumer of mental health services. She also had high energy, strong commitment, and inherent skills as a youth leader. The grant was able to provide her a student stipend for her work and create a formal relationship for her with the King County mental health authority and the CFIC grant.

The youth leader began the laborious process of helping youth turn good ideas into concrete action for the teen health summit. Slowly the groundwork for this community event was laid. Youth came into the offices of King County's mental health authority, made calls, and used the computer. They accompanied the youth coordinator to seek corporate sponsorship and donations. They participated and assumed leadership in specific tasks, but always with the close oversight of the youth leader. The psychiatrist and grant director also played an active role in their meetings, giving of time and energy, and occasionally personal resources, to make sure the youth had all they needed to fulfill their goals. The grant provided cash payments for all youth involvement. The professionals, including the student volunteer, received money for their work with HnA. The same principle was applied as had been applied for parent advocates who volunteered their time. They would receive twenty dollars for a two-hour meeting and fifty dollars for any all-day activity (one lasting four to six hours). The initial leadership, who appreciated the cash incentives, were crucial in recruiting more consumer youth later in the development of HnA. We began to gather some members who were in desperate circumstances: living with relatives in tenuous arrangements, suffering extreme poverty, being homeless, and having a multitude of extreme needs. These youth became the passion of the youth coordinator, who spent ever more time doing basic social work with needy youth, helping them get basic needs met, while mobilizing them to participate in the projects of HnA.

In May 2001, HnA carried out its plan for a youth summit. The Teen Health Summit drew about two hundred young people and had youth buzzing about booths, learning from providers about their services, talking with medical students who brought human body organs diseased by poor health practices, enjoying a topical musical review organized by an HnA leader with talent, and hearing a pep talk by their youth-friendly county executive. They participated in focus groups and breakout sessions. There was tension at the "doughnut dialogue" between youth and county sheriff representatives over racial profiling and perceived oppression of youth by police. This event marked the culmination of efforts for some youth, who then became less involved. It also cemented others' commitment and drew in even more youth to the organization. Many of the original leaders have moved on, leaving the group to reform and make new decisions regarding its goals and activities.

Shortly after the launching of HnA, the surgeon general asked the CMHS grant sites to send ten youth to a conference in Washington, D.C., to discuss the findings of the surgeon general's report on children's mental health. The CFIC accepted the invitation to send three youth to this meeting: the PSKS leader and two HnA leaders, all nineteen or twenty years old and sophisticated in dealing with adults in policy settings. The psychiatrist and the youth leader accompanied them to the meeting. The expenses were met by the surgeon general's office and did not require spending resources from the grant.

The King County group joined seven other youth of varying levels of sophistication. They attended the plenary sessions and were deployed as token youth representatives, along with token parent representatives, in breakout sessions with national leaders in research and service provision who had been invited to this meeting. Most of the ten youth felt overwhelmed and ignored in the break-out sessions. Clearly, the adults in attendance had a high level of intensity in their wish to be meaningful participants at this meeting. The youth sensed that the leaders assembled had agendas that did not include hearing the concerns of youth participants. With the strong support of the King County and the other youth advisers and some strong family advocates from the Federation of Families, the youth boycotted the next breakout sessions and formed their own discussion group. They drafted a statement and demanded time to read it to the entire meeting in the closing session. The adult attendees were puzzled by the assertive action of the youth. They learned that the youth were not pleased with their disregard for youth and family voice in the meeting. The youth's statement was read at the closing plenary session. The professional leaders, including the surgeon general, were silenced and awed by the reading of the youth's statement. It was read by a fifteen-year-old Alaska Native girl, CeCelia Nation, who had walked out of a prior breakout session in anger. The statement (see Figure 3.1) was thoughtful and well balanced between an appreciation for research and a demand for relevant "real-world practice as it affects the life experiences of young people receiving services." For the King County youth, bonding with the other youth and youth leaders from around the country and the drama of this experience proved pivotal in developing leadership for HnA.

We are young but need to be treated as human beings and not as a problem or a disorder. We are prototypes, not to be treated as stereotypes.

School officials and health care providers must be trained to recognize and understand mental illness and its effects on us. The ignorance of the people who don't understand hurts us. For example, sometimes teachers who don't understand that mental illness is not just a behavior problem say that we "choose" to act that way. Some professionals only take or only have a few minutes to deliver a diagnosis and "figure the whole thing out."

People who are supposed to be helping end up hurting us because they are not prepared and their training and our lives have not been made a priority. They contribute to the stigma of mental illness which is perhaps one of the biggest barriers to our service. It hurts even more when a doctor or teacher rejects you than when a peer does.

Now, I'm sure many of you are thinking that you would never do this to us, or that you are not ignorant in this way, so it's not your concern. We tell you from our own

---

FIGURE 3.1. Youth Statement from the Surgeon General's
Conference on Children's Mental Health.

Source: Transcript from the Surgeon General's Conference on Children's Mental Health.

FIGURE 3.1. *continued*

experience of the professionals out there that are ignorant in this way that it is your concern—because it's not going to change unless the system changes. And at least we hope that systems change is why you are all here.

Too often, once we get services (after fighting for them, or hitting a breaking point, or waiting on a waiting list for months), our services are hurried and disrespectful, and they don't respond to who we are as people, who we are in the context of our families and communities, and who we will one day become. Let's not forget that a lot of this is about who we will become and whether or not we will be able to dream and achieve our dreams.

I want to tell a story that one of us shared.

I had two friends—doing something that took them before a judge. One was sentenced to a detention center and one to a rehabilitation center (don't know why there was this difference). Six months later they both came back and it was amazing to see the differences. The one who went to the detention center got worse, more surly, more troublesome. The other one came back transformed and really made a change in his path. Why are we so comfortable devoting resources to locking youth up, and so reluctant to put money toward treatment? Treatment is cost effective and beneficial for all of us. If you lock someone up at a young age with others who are like them (or more hardened) without people to really help them, they will get worse.

Young people will live up to or down to the expectations of adults, teachers and professionals in their environment. Providers and systems must highly value and expect the best from us.

We need early prevention, better training for our parent, teachers and professionals, more awareness about mental health so that youth with mental health issues are not stigmatized and thrown away.

We need systems that can and do work together. Families, schools, and health care providers must collaborate in a collective effort to mobilize and train our communities to work together.

We need accountability with checks and balances.

Services goals should be developed by youth and families—before services are delivered.

Services must be evaluated according to how these goals are achieved.

- For example—has the provider established a connection with us that we can trust?
- Are we being treated like an ordinary person rather than a disability?

You can do all the research you want, but if you forget who we are and what we need as people, and if you don't respond to our needs in the system and in our individual treatment, you will fail, the system will fail, and we will bear the burden as we do now. You must include youth, bring us to the table and when we show up, you must listen. LISTEN.

Most of the grant communities with youth committees were able to send the same youth as had attended the surgeon general's meeting to subsequent grantee meetings. King County's HnA was one of the only youth programs that had a significant number of young people involved. They were faced with a need for a policy on who would attend meetings involving travel. Opportunity for national travel became a benefit of participation because selection was to be based on length of participation in HnA and the amount of time devoted to projects. King County's decision to send different youth to each meeting has affected HnA's ability to join in the emerging group of young people seeking to provide national leadership in articulating youth voice.

The grant specified no money specifically for youth participation in national meetings. It specified only that at least one family member must attend. Given the constraints of the county, no money could be allocated, even from grant resources, for youth travel. CMHS and its technical assistance contractors worked hard to help King County finance sending youth and youth leaders to grantee meetings. The barriers for this type of national-level youth participation are daunting. The county, ever more in financial difficulty, banned all travel not required by contracts such the grant. Federal resources for supporting youth involvement at more recent grant meetings have not been forthcoming. The technical assistance organization leading the national effort on youth participation had only one-third of a full-time equivalent devoted to this effort. Nevertheless, HnA youth had been active participants in grant meetings in Atlanta and San Juan, Puerto Rico, and to a youth meeting organized by the state of Missouri. They have also participated actively in local meetings and in various grant-related committees.

Despite the lack of resources, youth leaders, including the designated part-time youth program director from the Technical Assistance Partnership, have facilitated the development of youth leadership through programs at national meetings. To compensate for HnA youth not having had prior opportunities to participate and forge close peer relationships with other youth at national meetings, the youth advisers from both King County and the Technical Assistance Partnership have made special efforts to prepare HnA youth and integrate them quickly into the leadership training. An e-mail list has helped this effort to some degree. However, there remain questions regarding the creation of an advocacy elite versus a more grassroots representation of youth voice who may have very diverse stories to share at national meetings.

King County youth who have participated in such meetings have told their stories of personal difficulties and their struggles to overcome adverse circumstances. These have had great impact at grant meetings, particularly as several King County youth were chosen with full recognition that they were still dealing with their issues. The youth leaders at King County hoped that an opportunity to exercise some leadership skills would bolster their strength and resilience. So far, this strategy has been successful in developing our HnA program. Our youth have been involved in many local meetings and are regular attendees at the state Children, Youth and Family Mental Health Advisory Board. They were instrumental in having this board include the word *youth* in its title as a demand for respect for older youth who feel insulted by being termed children. Other youth have served on grant oversight committees and other committees of the mental health authority. Youth were involved with juvenile justice leaders in a grant application, and others will be involved with the King County drug and alcohol service system in their new federal Safe Futures grant.

The prime lesson from King County's efforts to sponsor an organization representing youth voice in policy is that ensuring youth voice demands strong adult leadership. This leadership, however, must respect and facilitate the inherent leadership potential of young people. It is clear that leadership development is an essential ingredient in any such organization. In dealing with youth participation, it is essential to show respect for youth needs for cash support, transportation, times to meet that are youth friendly, and needs for even the most committed young leaders to move on. It has become ever clearer that youth who participate may have enormous problems, including mental health issues, that have never before been tended to. One cannot provide leadership to a group of young people without attending to the reality of the system's problems, such as access to services, prejudice toward youth with problems, and occasional outrageously bad practice by system providers. Personal experience with such problems will be embodied in the lives of those who participate in a program that seeks to promote youth voice in policy. In fact, it is this reality that makes youth voice so relevant to those of us who might want to rest on our laurels for having put together good programs for children and adolescents.

The fact of stigma and discrimination is the overriding principle that ensures that the movement for ensuring youth voice is in reality part of the complex of family voice. Families and those who support and care for families struggling with adolescent issues can lose sight of this fact when coping with the sometimes outrageous behavior displayed by their disturbed adolescent children. Society tends to magnify such situations and presumes that adolescent rebellion is the rule. Researchers for thirty years have documented that over two-thirds of adolescents do not display rebellious behavior and are mostly decent, though at times stressed, family members (Offer & Offer, 1975). According to the surgeon general's report (U.S. Department of Health and Human Services, 1999), 20 percent of teens have a diagnosable mental disorder, and only a quarter of these are the disorders characterized by severe behavioral symptoms. Those who work well with teens in such trouble know that despite periods of estrangement, young people long for reconciliation and an alliance with their parents. The presence of a youth voice in system of care reform would be a healing force for those youth and families suffering a breach of trust and family upheaval. In such situations, the whole of the family, despite internal dissention and turmoil, needs to be considered a source of strength that, when mobilized, makes possible the positive changes in a family-centered system of care. Youth voice, along with that of adult family members, is an essential ingredient for positive change (Coutinho & Denny, 1996).

THE EVOLUTION OF FAMILY MOVEMENTS

The challenge for those who value building diverse communities is to transcend the suspicion and divisiveness that so often accompanies differences. The commonality of experience in raising challenging children must be the force that draws families together. This is a basic human experience that can transcend issues of culture, socioeconomic status, and individual style. Nationally, the FFCMH has achieved a high degree of success in providing an umbrella for many family advocacy groups from around the United States. The FFCMH has pioneered having youth as members of their board. However, many communities struggle with finding the best model for supporting the growing strength of family voice in programs for children and youth. Advocacy groups are subject to the forces at play in all social systems. As one group gets some recognition and power, another group feels slighted. As another group is recognized by the human services bureaucracies through contracts for services, some parents see that group as part of the establishment. These dynamics are inevitable and must be understood lest advocates and their professional allies become disillusioned. The experience of two communities illustrates some of these dynamics.

Two Communities in the Context of the National Experience

Since 1992, concerned citizens of Kentucky have been focusing intensely on creating opportunities for families of children with emotional and behavioral disabilities to participate at all levels of the system of care. Initiatives have included empowering consumer families to participate as service coordinators or advocates for their own child through the development of a wraparound process including child and family teams. The state has enabled family advocates to become major players in system evaluation, policy development, and program direction.

In 1992, the Kentucky Department for Mental Health and Mental Retardation Services created a program within the Division of Mental Health to support families of children with emotional disabilities and to develop a network of families across the state. A parent of a child with emotional disabilities was hired to lead the newly formed state office, Opportunities for Family Leadership, and began to expand the family movement in Kentucky. Many regional interagency councils (RIACs) hired family advocates to represent family voice. Although the concept seemed relatively simple, issues nevertheless arose between family leaders and consumer families and between families and professionals. Problems caused system of care leaders in Kentucky to reevaluate the meaning of family participation.

The evolution of family participation in King County, Washington, has been much the same as in Kentucky. A succession of initiatives since 1986 has led to a strong commitment on the part of families and professionals to realize the concept of family participation. Since 1986, King County's system of care reform efforts have championed the development of child and family teams using a wraparound process. The KCBFP and other grant programs have encouraged the involvement of family advocates on these teams and in representing family voice in policy settings. Initial enthusiasm for a new family advocacy movement has been followed by disillusionment with its leadership and reevaluation of how to structure family involvement in the system of care. King County has seen the evolution of family participation grow, falter, and evolve much as it has in Kentucky

Both communities based their initiatives on groundbreaking research conducted in 1982 by Jane Knitzer. At that time, Knitzer concluded that parents received little assistance in finding services for their children. They were ignored or coerced by public agencies, and few advocacy efforts were aimed at relieving the problems for families. Knitzer called for revolutionary changes in the way the system dealt with families. Her *Unclaimed Children* was applauded by Congress and prompted Congress's creating CASSP. The CASSP Values and Principles, articulated by Stroul and Friedman in their concept paper for this program (1994), have guided not only the original CASSP grants, but successions of grant programs from NIMH and SAMHSA, as well as private foundations. Over the past two decades, recognition of and response to the plight of families has become increasingly widespread. These principles are now defining a new best practice for the delivery of services to children in all aspects of the system of care.

Kentucky and Washington State were early participants in the CASSP program. Each embraced CASSP values and principles enthusiastically, including that of family inclusion, at a time where there was essentially no practice of family participation. The common experience of families involved in the system of care was one of being excluded, denigrated as the likely cause of a child's problems, and seen as subjects for family therapy, not coequal partnership. King County's interagency staffing teams (ISTs) were developed in 1988 primarily to facilitate system coordination. Family participation in ISTs was the first experimentation with realizing this value. The KCBFP was established in 1998, and the initiation of the Child and Families in Common (CFIC) grant a year later. Both were grounded on the principle of family-centered care.

Lessons from the Two Communities

In comparing the problems experienced in Kentucky and King County, we by no means imply that the principles common to both experiences represent a developmental scheme that is universal or inevitable. To the contrary, there is a great diversity of experience in the development of family voice (Briggs, 1996). Many communities have been blessed with a smooth developmental process, and many professionals and administrators have nurtured the growth and partnered well with family organizations. Not all problems will be comparable to those we describe in Kentucky and King County, yet it is important to offer some analysis of these experiences and articulate some general principles in order to initiate some methods of looking at problematic developmental issues in the evolution of the family movement. Examining these experiences may contribute to an orderly way of organizing our thoughts about problems for future research. It is also important to hypothesize some theoretical basis for problems as they are described.

Difficulties must be placed in context if they are to be properly understood. Central to understanding problems in the movement to empower and include families in the system of care is the fact of prejudice and stigma against mental illness, particularly in children. It must be recognized that the family inclusion and disability rights movements are siblings of the civil rights movement, and so developmental problems can be noted in these movements that may have some common themes (Solomon, 1976). In each, stigmatizing stereotypes, prejudices, and discrimination have an impact on the ability of oppressed people. Sometimes the development of these movements is impaired by such social attitudes from outside their group or by prejudicial laws or policies. Because all members of these movements are part of their society and are affected by negative stereotypes, these attitudes can be found, sometimes disguised, within the group or even within the self-concept of an individual within the group. Negative stereotypes and stigma can be insidious. Thus, reform movements must cope with forces—sometimes socially empowered groups and other times hurting and embittered individuals—that embrace such negative attitudes toward those deemed different and dangerous. Yet despite such social forces, some communities are amazingly resilient and can avoid any negative impact on movements for social reform. But the impact of such negative forces is often hidden. Unless they are recognized and understood, they may lead to the fragmentation of these movements (Kieffer, 1981).

Parents of children with emotional disabilities face an uncommon amount of prejudice in their daily lives. Children who have serious emotional difficulties often exhibit behaviors that are not well tolerated by communities. Others may view this behavior as the fault of the parent, who is therefore blamed as being the cause of the child's illness. The stigma of being the "bad" parent because of passing down bad genes, or being too strict or not strict enough, or being neglectful or abusive in some other way, can be overwhelming. In addition, mental illness is often viewed by Americans as nothing more than a weakness or a willful act. Families with children suffering serious emotional disabilities are members of a society that places blind value on self-reliance and the Horatio Alger myth of pulling oneself out of difficulties. Often these social biases cause family members to fail to understand the functional limits that come with a mental illness. This failure can be stigmatizing to the child with the problems and self-stigmatizing to their parent. The level of the stigma and blame tends to be highest toward biological parents, but it is also significant with adoptive parents, grand-parents, other relative caregivers, and even foster parents. A sense of helplessness and a negative view of oneself and one's family is often the result. Regrettably, the mental health system, in place to assist the child, often simultaneously op-presses the parent. Frequently subtle, but even blatant, measures are used to block even the most superficial involvement of the parent in treatment, policymaking, or evaluation. The result is to unjustly keep a parent's role separate and diminished. These results occur even when the values of family-centered care are present in all of the system statements and documents (Curtis & Singh, 1996; Scheel & Rieck-mann, 1998).

With the growth that has occurred in family inclusion in Kentucky and King County and the problems that developed, certain stages were recognized as common to both communities. These stages clearly reflect the dynamics of stigma and prejudice as they have affected both parents and professionals. They affect entire systems, including professional and family agencies, boards, and support groups. Let us look at the family movement in each of these communi-ties, examine the successes of each as well as their problems, and explore lessons learned and opportunities for further growth.

Developmental Stage One: No Involvement. The first stage is perhaps the eas-iest to identify and understand in each of the community's movement for fami-lies of children with emotional disabilities. It is likely universal. In this stage, families are shut out from participation in the care of their child in any form other than in the most minimal ways. Even then, the involvement must be at the direction of the professional. In Kentucky, this stage was noted to have two ele-ments. The first was a clear apathy on the part of professionals for family par-ticipation in a system of care. System leaders had peripheral knowledge of the family movement but had not bought into the value of the movement. Rather than focus on change and inclusion, they found it easier to ignore the issues. The second element to this stage was that of blatant prejudice against families and a concerted effort to prevent family involvement at all levels. This effort to exclude families was partially disguised as professional leaders politely claimed they just did not have enough money, staff, or time to develop a family network or other methods to include families in their daily operations. Other times, how-ever, they made clear prejudicial statements about families. The message was clear that they believed families were too uneducated, lazy, or crazy to be of any use to the professional community.

The prejudices and oppression described against Kentucky families that were raising severely emotionally and behaviorally disturbed youth paralleled the ex-periences in King County. Families who now are the vanguard of the family advocate movement tell of gross insults and insensitivity in all aspects of the system as they attempted to get services for their children. They describe a

Kafkaesque experience of being told only bits and pieces of information regarding their child and were given the clear implication that they were at fault for the problems of their child, but they were never told how, why, or what to do to improve the situation. Meetings with caregivers were terrifying and left parents with a sense of failure and despair. Yet parents were expected to attend every meeting regarding their child in each of several systems: school special education meetings, meetings with parole officers and court appearances, and family therapy sessions. Each system was oblivious of the burden on the parent from all the other elements of the system of care. Little regard was made for a parent's work requirements. When they could not attend meetings, their adequacy as parents was further impugned

Stage Two: Tokenism. The second stage of development noted in the two communities is tokenism: the policy of making a perfunctory effort or a symbolic gesture toward the accomplishment of a goal. It is likely that other communities have experienced that phenomenon as well. Families served by the system of care are pleased to see some acknowledgment of the importance of family voice but are disillusioned by an ineffectual implementation of the principle. In this stage, the state of Kentucky or local King County agencies invite parents to meetings. But the parents were not provided orientation on the purpose of the meeting, were not told the rules or the agenda, and were left off the distribution list for documents to be discussed. Parents dealing with being tokens are often kept in the dark about the overall mission of a project. Staff are very proud that they have a parent at the table and often boast of their accomplishment, especially in annual reports or grant applications. Tokenism can also occur when parents are invited into the governing councils of a mental health agency.

In Kentucky at this stage, the state mental health authority took the unusual step of hiring a family member to represent consumer families throughout the state. Within a few years, several regional agencies had also hired family members as advocates. The parent was invited to volunteer and eventually was hired by state officials to meet state and federal mandates on consumer and family involvement. The state agency pronounced it was now obviously family sensitive because a parent was serving as a family liaison. Those in the agency believed themselves to be no longer prejudiced toward families. Yet the agency tied the family participant's hands by not providing that person with the education, access, or resources needed to function in the new role. This, for a while, blocked the increase in family involvement beyond the liaison. Hiring the parent to develop and run a program without providing funding or even basic supplies reduces the parent and the position to tokenism. A peculiar phenomenon of this stage was the vehemence with which the agency personnel defended the notion that having hired a family liaison, they were now family sensitive. Of course, hiring one person did not make an entire agency suddenly family sensitive to the concerns of all families. What actually occurred is that they become sensitive to the issues of the one family member they had hired.

Another example of tokenism in relation to the family movement in Kentucky concerns parents appointed to RIACs. Parents are appointed to represent other parents within the region whose children are being served by RIAC programs. Once appointed, however, the parent representative may be blocked from contacting the families he or she represents. Prohibited from receiving basic information and isolated from other parents, the parent representatives are still expected to consider themselves an equal with all of the agency staff on the council.

In King County, tokenism involved the inclusion of families in the interagency staffing teams. In reality, these teams were professionals from all agencies who came together to solve problems stemming from the poorly coordinated system of care. A permanent team of leaders from the system's agencies heard the dilemmas regarding a particular case presented by a professional who had sought collaboration from all the service providers involved with the case. The leaders of these teams were steeped in CASSP literature and held the value of family inclusion, yet no permanent family representative sat on the team. Consumer families were encouraged to attend the team meeting as they discussed the fate of their child. The team members felt that they had included the family member as a full participant. In reality, this was an intimidating, unsettling experience for most such families. They were often ignored as the subtle maneuvering between agencies occurred as a subtext to the meeting discourse, thus confusing families and making them feel unwelcome. Instead of insults, the families experienced some indulgence but no real role.

Stage Three: Pedestal. At some point, the message of the importance of family involvement and equal partnerships becomes fashionable. Once someone in authority catches on to the shift, the system begins to change. In both Kentucky and King County, parents who had been denigrated as troublemakers for their "outsider" advocacy became indulged. The token family advocates within the system were placed on a pedestal. The family advocacy movement was suddenly thrust into a position of power.

During this stage, professionals became fearful of saying anything that could be considered offensive or challenging. Some feared offending parents and being accused of "parent bashing." Any such change is a striking power shift. In previous stages, all of the power rested with the professional; now the parents had a share of real power.

In cases where parents or other family members have been given power, they often experience the sudden transition from ineffectual token or outside agitator to being a pedestaled "star" parent as confusing. It is entirely human for them to enjoy the power this new phase brings. This was likely the first time that they have been told that what they have to offer as a parent is valuable and that they, as parents, have worth. As would any other parents thrust into such a position, family leaders in each community who had been disempowered most of their adult lives had little experience using the advantages of being on a pedestal to create a more solid family movement.

Unfortunately during this phase, growth in the family movement slows. The stars fear being removed from the pedestal as they were overwhelmed with expectations to offer leadership they were not prepared to deliver. They avoid sharing the spotlight with others. Sometimes leaders on the pedestal go to great lengths to keep other families from becoming involved except at very superficial levels. They may start to criticize and bash other parents. Consumer parents who are in the throes of crisis with their difficult children find the expectations from parent leaders as oppressive as those sometimes offered by professionals. When consumer parents fail to feel supported by parent leaders, they became disillusioned and began to criticize. Professionals may adopt politically correct attitudes with respect to family inclusion with conversing with pedestaled parent advocates. They learned quickly the correct words to say, whether they believed in the philosophy or not. This pedestal stage is inherently superficial and transitory and sets up the family participants for great turmoil.

In Kentucky, as family voice became trendy among progressive agency leaders, the cadre of family members appointed as both regional representatives and family liaisons were given some real authority and responsibilities. They were expected to contact and support consumer families in their region. Some dutifully called on their constituents, feeling that a call on a regular basis was what their job required. But they were not trained on how they could be helpful in such contacts and often took pride in the fact of a contact rather than in their being effective in helping consumer families in such contacts. Many were set up by being placed on a pedestal.

In the early 1990s in King County, the ISTs worked hard to get families together and form a family organization. No family leader emerged in these efforts, and the families remained heavily dependent on their professional sponsors. In 1996, the planning for a blended funding project (combining multiple funding sources without categorical restrictions on spending) was initiated through a Robert Wood Johnson replication grant. As part of this planning process, a leader emerged who had been a strong advocate for her own foster children. She had been much reviled by professionals she had attacked in many agencies throughout the system. She turned all her energy to forming a chapter of the Federation of Families and participating as part of the planning group. She built a family organization with considerable energy and intelligence. Several families participated in these pioneering efforts and emerged as a cadre of strong family advocates in all planning efforts. Families worked as codesigners with an innovative social scientist to put together an evaluation system for blended funding that would reflect families' concerns and interests. The local Federation of Families chapter exerted leadership to bring other family groups together in a parent council and planned to deploy council members to all major policy forums in the system. The federation chapter was given an award for outstanding advocacy by the county mental health authority.

By this point, leaders in the county and state had become enamored with this nascent family movement and gave the new leader of the King County Federation of Families ever more responsibilities, including contracts that made them part of the vendor system. As the federation rose to be the premier family advocacy organization, provider agencies in the system of care began to show signs of resentment and resisted the efforts of advocates to participate with consumer families in the care of their children.

Stage Four: Storming. Disillusionment with the pedestal stage led the family movement in Kentucky and King County toward the developmental stage of storming. The pedestaled parents became defensive and discouraged some newer families from becoming involved, particularly if they came with some criticism of the advocate's role and with new ideas. Other families in the community, not having been a part of the earliest struggles, perceived the "star" parent as too close to the policymakers and service agencies and began to attack, or "storm," this leader, as well as policymakers and agency heads.

The family movement will always tend to have insiders and newcomers. Inside leaders are quick to be defensive, and newcomers have no history and are quick to criticize. This dynamic is inherent in any movement. The advantage of the insider-newcomer tension is that it can balance the stability of the advocacy movement with freshening innovations. When it is a malignant process, the two factions begin to turn on themselves and fight one another for power and control. If the malignant aspect of storming is not contained and resolved, the infighting will likely affect the professional communities' regard for family advocates. The glow in the hearts of professionals for having a family liaison hired will begin to fade. Professional staff may become frustrated when they are not able to provide beneficial advice or assistance to a family for fear that it will be construed as putting the family down or not being sensitive to the families' needs. Parent bashing within the agency may increase dramatically as the romance with family advocacy seems over.

In some areas of Kentucky, there was a period when leaders of the family movement faced serious problems. Many of the original leaders came under attack from their constituents. Divisiveness and anger seemed to arise from all areas, often erupting into hostile arguments at public meetings. Executive directors of the family organizations and family liaisons had their jobs threatened, agency staff were bombarded with calls from legislators, and many quit out of frustration. Similarly, parent support groups and family organizations imploded, divided into two or more totally separate groups, or they failed altogether.

In King County, the burdens and responsibilities on the Federation of Families chapter grew beyond their ability to handle them, and the director worked harder to fill the breach. She became more impatient and offended some key families, who began to attack her. Complaints about the methods that the federation used grew, and the leadership fractured; some became entrenched, and others left the organization. The professionals in the system of care, including new agencies that had arisen to address the needs identified by families and their advocates, complained that they could not work with the federation. The professional teams serving the Child and Families in Common grant rejected the federation and complained loudly about their functioning in the system. For a while, the staff at King County Mental Health took different sides in the disputes between the leadership of the family advocacy movement and the dissatisfied parents.

Stage Five: Apathy. Following storming, a stage of great strife and turmoil in both Kentucky and King County, exhaustion, and apathy set in. There was a wish to avoid dealing with a depressing issue, and many family advocates drifted away from the movement. Sympathetic administrators, on the edge of conflict over how to address the problems, decided to put the issues on the back burner. No one wanted to address what had happened. Many acknowledged the need for change but were confused about what changes to make. Professionals and administrators neither helped to increase family involvement, nor openly tried to stop it. New family support groups and family organizations acknowledged one another and refrained from negativity but also failed to work together.

In Kentucky, parents working as family liaisons who had fallen from the pedestal and had experienced the disillusionment of their constituents began to assimilate into their agencies. The role of the liaison became expanded to meet other agency needs, such as clerical worker, receptionist, and training coordinator. Some family liaisons requested these changes. They realized they would have to look for other ways to regain their status within the agency. The family liaison began to see this role primarily as a staff person to an agency rather than as an internal advocate for other families. Parent representatives on RIACs began to question if Kentucky had experienced model drift from the core CASSP principles that served as the basis of the system of care reforms.

Confusion, exhaustion, and despair followed the demise of the King County's Federation of Families as a viable leader of a family advocacy movement. The Children and Families in Common grant struggled to keep family involvement in their main planning meetings. They worried that they would be in violation of their grant mandate to build a viable and sustainable family involvement in our system of care. The leaders of the blended funding project sought new leaders and worked hard to encourage families who had been hurt by the recent conflicts. Provider agencies resumed old methods of working outside family collaboration, although a value of family participation had been seeded and did not disappear.

Stage Six: Advanced Tokenism. Following the period of apathy, family involvement appeared to revitalize in Kentucky and King County. Families and professionals were likely to be lulled into thinking that equal partnership was occurring. New advocates found jobs working within the system that has institutionalized family involvement. No longer is the movement considered a fad or a whim but rather a piece of the system, just as is outpatient therapy. Slow growth within the movements was occurring with the support of some professionals. New support groups were developed. Paid family liaisons or parent representatives found their way back to policy committees and boards. Professionals feel certain that they have achieved the ultimate goals of family involvement and tout their initiatives in glowing terms. Parent-professional partnerships are the byword of this stage. Initially, this stage was in reality a less pedestaled version of an earlier stage and could be followed by a second storming and more apathy. But with a more diversified advocacy movement, seasoned by earlier painful growth experiences, family inclusion may deepen and mature. If it does, a true bridging of professional and family perspective may occur.

This could be by far the most difficult of the stages to this point. The emotions involved around the issues can become very personal. The inclination from both sides is to hide any painful issues. Change comes only from soul searching and listening objectively to the person who has felt the sting of subtle prejudice. When the lessons of the earlier stages have been learned and the leadership becomes more secure, true family inclusion may emerge. New consumer families will be respected and given real support from parent-to-parent efforts. System glitches may be enthusiastically addressed by the hired family liaison, and policy decisions may be affected by more viable parent-professional partnerships.

In Kentucky, the family liaisons became completely assimilated into their agencies. Liaisons were no longer viewed as parent advocates but rather as professional administrators hired to oversee the parent program. Some family organizations changed their role to become providers of mental health services rather than providing resource and educational information to families. In many ways, the family organizations duplicated the professional system they found fault with at the beginning of the movement. Financial stability and program and system development began to take priority over the needs of the "outside" families. Family liaisons became an elitist group, and the system became one of the haves (the insiders) and the have-nots (the outsiders).

Prejudice and oppression were clearly evident in this stage in Kentucky. Prejudice from professional staff was still present. However, at this stage, discussing that prejudice was met with heated reactions. Just as people will clearly state they are not prejudiced against other races, professional staff just as vehemently denied being insensitive to family needs or inclusion. Attempts to address family sensitivity issues incited the same response one could expect when someone is accused of being a racist. Currently, some family advocates are beginning to reexamine the viability of the family liaison system and contemplating alternative ways for promoting family inclusion.

In King County, new family advocacy leadership began to emerge with the active encouragement of the CFIC grant staff who were very discouraged with the gross disruption in the family advocacy movement. The grant staff facilitated new and more experienced families meeting at informal picnics. Younger professional staff steeped in system of care principles for their work on grant sponsored wraparound programs were also invited to the picnics and became part of the community of concern that emerged to revitalize the family movement in King County. New leadership is now emerging. The Federation of Families has stabilized, and although some families remain angry and hurt from their encounters with this organization, other families are finding support there. A diversity of groups, formal and informal, is emerging. Several alternative family organizations are in the early stages of development. Once again, families are regularly included in planning and policy meetings for the grant programs. The Blended Funding Project has hired a family advocate to work with the care managers who serve child and family teams. A scaled-down Federation of Families has retained its role in the blended funding project evaluation. Through strong support from the system of care reform leadership in King County, a more diversified family movement is emerging that is less ambitious in its role in the system and has absorbed the lessons of the painful conflicts of a few months earlier.

Stage Seven: Integrated Family Inclusion. Neither Kentucky nor King County has achieved the final stage of integrated family inclusion. Other communities may be much closer. The nature of an evolutionary process is that the ultimate goal stays just out of grasp and yet guides communities to approximate the ideal. Problems born of changing personalities, new twists on old problems, and the nature of human communities assure us that the work of building a system of care that has truly integrated family inclusion will never be complete. What will stabilize policy that embraces the values of family inclusion will be administrative structures that ensure effective family participation at all levels.

Whether institutionalized with hired staff or contracted from advocacy groups for tasks such as program evaluation or parent-to-parent support, family advocacy functions must be subject to quality assurance mechanisms just as is the rule with clinical services. Furthermore, the concepts of quality assurance and quality improvement must embrace the best practice concepts of family inclusion as they are designed for service providers. While these ideas are being included in many system of care sophisticated mental health services, social services, juvenile justice, education, and all other elements of the system of care must embrace the principles as well. When the stage of true integration of family inclusion has been achieved, all elements of the system of care will have in place a family advocacy function that permeates the organization: policy bodies, boards, legislative liaison groups, ombuds functions and other consumer relations mechanisms, program evaluation and research, clinical and other service consultations, training and orientation of new staff (administrative and service), and parent-to-parent service providers integrated into service teams. Family advocates will include not only experienced parents but youth who have experienced difficulties and have been in the system. All family advocates, older and young, will receive adequate orientation as they begin their responsibilities and will be paid for what they do in ways that are commensurate with those responsibilities. There is no integrated family involvement unless some means is found to pay those involved in such a way that allows commitment to the task on the part of family representatives. This is a key element of a fully evolved system (Simpson, Koroloff, Friesen, & Gac, 1999).

The omnipresence of family advocates will ensure that child and family teams will function true to model, and this will integrate care for troubled children and youth in communities. Networks of informal community resources will emerge that are ultimately community based and based in a consumer family's culture. Youth with difficulties will have increasing opportunities for a more normative community-based life with all the supports they may need to achieve such a life. Family involvement will ensure community mobilization and, eventually, changes in social attitudes that marginalize and stigmatize families who struggle with emotionally and behaviorally disturbed children. In a fully integrated system of care, professionals will experience the advantages of working with parents and communities outside the formal service providers. Those who have positive experiences will teach others new ways of regarding families in the SOC, and a new care culture will emerge.

As we build for a future that approximates the final goals of Stage Seven, it is time to take stock of what we have learned along the way. Clearly the principles that emerge from the experiences in both communities have relevance to many who share the same struggles.

LESSONS LEARNED AND STRATEGIC QUESTIONS FOR GROWTH

The difficulties and successes with including families in the system of care reforms in Kentucky and King County, Washington, typify stories from around the country, especially in communities working to improve their system within the CMHS Children's Mental Health Initiative grants. Although the principles remain deceptively simple, the practice is complicated with a full array of human issues: fears, misperceptions, differing points of view, turf protection issues, and politics. It is important not to be discouraged by these factors that are common to all human endeavors. Some family advocates have compared participation in a family inclusion program as analogous to Mr. Toad's Wild Ride. Despite the disappointments and travails, there have been many heartening stories of families better served and positive relationships formed with professionals.

Have Kentucky and King County found the keys to effective family inclusion? Not yet. Have these communities and others with similar experiences reached equal partnership in their family inclusion movements? It is doubtful that many have. Will there ever be a community that is completely placed in Stage Seven? Probably not. However, as communities approximate the vision, practice and policy will begin to change, leading to real change in the culture of care. Has traveling through the various stages been worthwhile, and has it made a difference in those communities willing to endure the struggles? Absolutely.

Following are some of the practical implications of the lessons learned from looking at the evolution of family inclusion in these two communities:

- Family voice is a complex phenomenon. There is no one voice; rather, there are as many voices as there are families being served or who have taken their past experiences into a role as advocates. The process for including family voice must ensure that diverse perspectives have a hearing. This may involve families forming a variety of support and advocacy groups. It may involve a constant evolution of the structures of family advocacy as new parents with new concerns mobilize and assume leadership. National technical assistance systems must provide models and supports for ensuring diverse representation of families in communities building a reformed system of care.

- Youth voice is a unique and fragile element of family voice, and it is essential if system of care reform is to be complete. Resources must be identified to build and give expression to the youth perspective at all levels in the system. Such efforts must respect the developmental fact that adult support for youth leadership development will be essential. Turnover of youth leadership will be more rapid, requiring programmatic structure and support. Each community should have an adult youth leader identified, and the national technical assistance system should deploy adequate resources to develop a system of youth advocacy.

- At the level of service provision, the concept of child and family teams is the best vehicle for ensuring family voice in care plans. Family-to-family involvement, properly managed, is an essential aspect of this element of the wraparound process.

- Psychiatric and other professional consultation to child and family teams by professionals who understand the vision of family inclusion may be a vehicle for addressing service questions and internal difficulties in teams and in advocacy groups and may help families develop a more sophisticated knowledge of the culture of care they are trying to modify.

- Accessing consumer family perspective is often very difficult, but if it is ignored, the value of implementing family involvement can be quickly undercut. Reaching out to consumers must be innovative and respectful of consumers' strengths and limitations. Such outreach must be relentless.

- There are as many professional perspectives as there are service providers. Line clinicians will see family involvement case by case, and their supervisors and program administrators will view family inclusion from a very different perspective. All perspectives must be acknowledged and valued.

- Parent and professional leadership must appreciate that various family constituencies, agencies, and professional groups may have different needs that may conflict. Great skill must be exercised by both family and professional leaders to understand the other's needs and perspective and that disputes must be resolved within a consensus on the common vision for system of care reform.

- Structures for receiving, digesting, and resolving conflicting perspectives on family inclusion must be developed. These must be defined in the administrative structures of each element of the system of care with a strong commitment from both government administrative and political leadership.

- Social forces are at play in dealing with seriously emotionally disturbed children and youth. Prejudice and stigma against families raising such children is pervasive and similar to other oppressed and marginalized groups. It is sometimes subtle, sometimes overt, but always hurtful to the child or youth consumer and family. Occasionally, laws protecting the rights of those with disabilities and educational handicaps must be invoked, and these laws must be protected and strengthened.

- It must be accepted that the process of giving voice to diverse elements of the system of care—families, youth, consumers, line staff, and administrators—can be intense and threatening to many, involve hurt and anger, and be very messy. But it is essential. It will take courage and a willingness to rise above personal concerns to understand the perspective of others.

Articulating a vision for system of care reform is essential. Methods for achieving the vision must be articulated, such as in defining child and family team functions or a more evolved system that achieves full advantage of the wraparound process as described in Stage Seven. The inevitable difficulties are all part of building the foundations on which a better system of care can rest. If change is to occur, growth pains, failure, despair, and renewal all must occur. At certain points, we can take stock and look at our gains and see where we have come.

Through the early efforts of the CASSP program, through the demonstration projects of the Robert Wood Johnson grants, to the grant programs of CMHS, we have seen amazing progress in redefining appropriate care for children and youth with severe emotional problems. Many professionals have changed their concepts regarding family involvement as a result of exposure to new forms of family inclusion in the system of care. There is great hope among those who have been involved in the process of redefining family involvement that the value regarding family-centered care, first articulated by Stroul and Friedman, is permeating the thinking of all involved in this movement. Yet it is possible to get lost in the nuts and bolts of implementation of the principles and values. The implementation difficulties examined here are both understandable and inevitable. They can be endured and worked through on the way to meaningful family inclusion in system of care reform.

References

Bickman, L., Summerfelt, W., & Noser, K. (1997). Comparative outcomes of emotion ally disturbed children and adolescents in a system of services and usual care. *Psychiatric Services, 84,* 1543–1548.

Briggs, H. E. (1996). Creating independent voices: The emergence of statewide family networks. *Journal of Mental Health Administration, 23,* 447–457.

Coutinho, M. J., & Denny, R. K. (1996). National leadership for children and youth with seriously emotional disturbance: Progress and prospects. *Journal of Child and Family Studies, 5,* 207–227.

Curtis, W. J., & Singh, N. N. (1996). Family involvement and empowerment in mental health service provision for children with emotional and behavioral disorders. *Journal of Child and Family Studies, 5,* 503–517.

Hodges, K., & Wong, M. (1996). Psychiatric characteristics of a multidimensional measure to assess impairment: The Child and Adolescent Functional Adolescent Scale. *Journal of Child and Family Studies, 5,* 445–467.

Holden, W., Friedman, R., & Santiago, R. (2001). Overview of the national evaluation of the Comprehensive Community Mental Health Services for Children and Their Families Program. *Journal of Emotional and Behavioral Disorders, 9,* 4–12.

Kieffer, C. H. (1981). *The emergence of empowerment: The development of participatory competence among individuals in citizen organizations.* Unpublished doctoral dissertation, University of Michigan, Ann Arbor.

Knitzer, J. (1982). *Unclaimed children.* Washington, DC: Children's Defense Fund.

Koren, P. E., DeChillo, N., & Friesen, B. J. (1992). Measuring empowerment in families whose children have emotional disabilities: A brief questionnaire. *Rehabilitation Psychology, 37,* 305–321.

Offer, D., & Offer, J. (1975). *From teenage to young manhood: A psychological study.* New York: Basic Books.

Osher, T., Van Kammen, W., & Zaro, S. (2001). Family participation in evaluating systems of care: Family, research, and service systems perspectives. *Journal of Emotional and Behavioral Disorders, 9,* 63–70.

Rappaport, J. (1987). Terms of empowerment/exemplars of prevention: Toward a theory for community psychology. *American Journal of Community Psychology, 15,* 121–145.

Scheel, M. J., & Rieckmann, T. (1998). An empirically derived description of self-efficacy and empowerment for parents of children identified as psychologically disordered. *American Journal of Family Therapy, 26,* 15–27.

Simpson, J. S., Koroloff, N., Friesen, B. F., & Gac, J. (1999). *Promising practices in family-provider collaboration.* Washington, DC: Center for Effective Collaboration and Practice, American Institutes for Research.

Solomon, B. B. (1976). *Black empowerment: Social work in oppressed communities.* New York: Columbia University.

Stroul, B. A., & Friedman, R. M. (1994). *A system of care for children and youth with severe emotional disturbances* (Rev. ed.). Washington, DC: Georgetown University Child Development Center, Child and Adolescent Service System Program Technical Assistance Center.

Stroul, B. A., Lourie, I, Goldman, S., & Katz-Leavy, J. (1992). *Profiles of local systems of care for children and adolescents with severe emotional disturbances* (Rev. ed.). Washington, DC: Georgetown University, Child and Adolescent Service System Program Technical Assistance Center.

Trupin, E., Low, B., Forsyth-Stephens, A., Tarico, V., & Cox, G. R. (1988). *Washington State children's mental health system analysis: Final report.* Seattle: Division of Community Psychiatry, University of Washington.

U.S. Department of Health and Human Services. (1999). *Mental health: A report of the surgeon general.* Rockville, MD: Department of Health and Human Services, Substance Abuse and Mental health Administrative Center for Mental Health Services.

VanDenBerg, J. E., & Grealish, E. M. (1996). Individualized services and supports through the wraparound process: Philosophy and procedures. *Journal of Child and Family Studies, 5,* 7- 21.

Vander Stoep, A., Green, L., Jones, R., & Huffine, C.(2001). A family empowerment model of change. In M. Hernandez & S. Hodges (Eds.), *Developing outcome strategies in children's mental health.* Baltimore, MD: Brooks Publishing Co.

Vander Stoep, A., Williams, M., Jones, R., Green, L., & Trupin, E (1999). Families as full research partners: What's in it for us? *Journal of Behavioral Health Services and Research, 26*(3), 329–344.

Yoe, J. T., Santarcangelo, S., Atkins, M., & Burchard, J. D. (1996). Wraparound care in Vermont: Program development, implementation, and evaluation of a statewide system of individualized services. *Journal of Child and Family Studies, 5,* 23–39.

CHAPTER FOUR

Collaboration Across Disciplines and Among Agencies Within Systems of Care

Mark Chenven
Barbara Brady

Interest in collaboration within systems of care derives from a maturing awareness by all participants in service delivery systems that no discipline, no single approach, and no solitary action or intervention can reliably provide the comprehensive and overarching support for recovery that seriously emotionally ill youth and their families need. Whether at the individual case level or as a systemic initiative at an agency level, success in achieving positive outcomes requires coordination of resources and the joining of efforts by numerous persons and entities. Simply put, helping troubled youth not only takes a village, but it takes an exceptional village, one that works together focused on the goal of helping its children and families achieve their optimal potential. Such a village makes fullest use of all of its members and resources to provide services in the most normative and least restrictive levels of care. Collaborative processes are fundamental in achieving these goals.

In prior decades, traditional community mental health systems sought to establish a comprehensive continuum of care with services ranging from prevention efforts on to restrictive residential and hospital care. These efforts resulted in significant enhancement of services in many communities, yet they fairly routinely failed to integrate the mental health system fully with other child-serving agencies. The potential for patients to get lost in the cracks was substantial, as mechanisms for coordination across program and agency boundaries were often poorly developed (Knitzer, 1982).

Henry, a depressed youth residing at a receiving facility for abused children operated under the auspices of a child protective agency, did not have access to appropriate mental health service absent his escalation to a high level of suicidal threat. Coordinated multidisciplinary mental health treatment was simply not available at the facility, and he received appropriate assessment and treatment only after his condition had exacerbated so that he needed inpatient intervention. Once stabilized, he was returned to the receiving home, where the limitations in service capacity ultimately resulted in his needing re-referral for hospitalization. A victim of a crisis-oriented revolving door service system, Henry did not have the benefit of an integrated system of care to address his multiple emotional and social needs.

THE SYSTEMS OF CARE APPROACH

The system of care movement has sought to improve on the base of traditional community mental health systems by focusing resources on wraparound services centered on youth and family needs, within a strength-based paradigm. Services are offered by teams of multidisciplinary providers and are organized with the full coordination of involved agencies. Such systems, in more advanced communities, have evolved to the point that capacity now exists to serve even the most severely challenged at-risk youth.

Timothy, a multiply handicapped and traumatized sixteen year old, had been "raised by the system" since the age of four, with innumerable placements in foster, group, residential, and hospital facilities. He had received multiple treatment efforts including psychotherapies, behavior modification, and medications, but without sustained success. Because of the severity of his behavioral, emotional, and educational disabilities, he had spent the past four years in a state hospital facility more than a hundred miles from his home community. He continued to have explosive and self-destructive behaviors. Probably destined to a life of restrictive institutional care, he was the first of nearly twenty youth enrolled in a community reentry project coordinated by the local mental health program along with the local department of social services, the community school district and local advocacy groups.

Tim was progressively moved from the out-of-county facility to a local inpatient unit, where community integration strategies were implemented. His mother, who had a history of recurrent alcoholism and homelessness, was located, provided support, and gradually reinvolved in visitation with Tim. An intensive mentoring program was instituted that allowed Tim to go on supervised outings in the community. He was reengaged with his mother's church, providing him with his first experiences of normative community attachment. After several months of these efforts, in conjunction with the multidisciplinary supports of the hospital, Tim was able to make the transition to an intensive residential program, where the process of assertive case management, family linkage, and community engagement continued.

His mother's recovery was supported by various adult service providers, and though she continued with significant limitations, her increased stability allowed for ongoing contacts with Tim. By the age of eighteen, Tim, who previously had not known how to manage cash or shop in a local store, was able to negotiate within the community, had moved on to a small group residential program, and was working part time as a janitorial assistant at his church.

Other youth from this community, who like Tim had been sent off to the distant state hospital in prior decades, were successfully reintegrated in their home community. Funds previously spent to support the state hospital placements are now expended exclusively in local programs.

In the compartmentalized bureaucratic systems that provide psychosocial services for children and families in need, effective collaboration is essential. Collaborative practice provides the foundation for successful system of care programs as described by Child and Adolescent Service System Program (CASSP) principles (Stroul & Friedman, 1986). Along with other core CASSP fundamentals, such as full engagement and empowerment of families, ready access to an array of comprehensive services, support for cultural and clinical competencies, appropriate and flexible funding, and continuity of services throughout a youth's development, collaborative practice is the sine qua non without which none of these other components can be expected to achieve optimum outcomes.

Multidisciplinary Coordination

Traditional community mental health systems also pioneered multidisciplinary practice patterns, now standard in most progressive public and private sector programs. In both outpatient child guidance centers and inpatient hospital programs, mental health professionals developed service models that enable the collaborative work of psychiatrists, psychologists, nurses, social workers, and occupational and recreational therapists, along with other specialists. While the pressures of managed care and constrained resources have reduced the use of comprehensive multidisciplinary treatment teams in assessment and treatment activities, there remains within the mental health professions a strong tradition and inclination to work collaboratively across professional areas of expertise.

Rosa Ana is a delightful but shy and sensitive fourth grader who is struggling with her schoolwork. At school she is well behaved and quiet, but at home she has begun to exhibit emotional outbursts and increasing distress with the challenges of homework assignments. Her mother brings her to the community health clinic for assessment. At intake, the clinical social worker finds clues in Rosa Ana's drawings that are suggestive of mild organicity. A psychological assessment documents specific learning disabilities, mild attentional problems, and some depressive trends. These findings are shared with the family and with school personnel. A student study team, attended by the parents, school personnel, and the clinic social worker, develops a coordinated service plan that includes adaptive educational services and continued supportive psychotherapy to assist Rosa Ana in her self-esteem and problem management skills. A psychiatric consultation is arranged to explore whether medication should be considered. The cooperative work of this multidisciplinary team identifies and intervenes in a comprehensive manner to meet this girl's needs.

Interagency Cooperation

The system of care movement has expanded and enriched the concept of collaboration in mental health services. The evolving standard of care now requires collaboration between professional and paraprofessional personnel and does so with a mandate for comprehensive interagency cooperation. Increasingly, it has become standard practice to colocate multidisciplinary mental health treatment services within other service system programs, such as schools, receiving homes, juvenile detention facilities, and other community settings. In the best of these model programs, there is a comprehensive coordination and virtual integration of staffing and program responsibilities across agency boundaries. Blended and braided staffing and funding patterns are now realities in many community programs and represent one of the major advances achieved through the application of collaborative strategies to meet the needs of youth.

Michael, diagnosed with paranoid schizophrenia, typically receives services through a community mental health clinic in his neighborhood, but his compliance with medication treatment is inconsistent. At times of psychotic decompensation, he is prone to minor acts of antisocial behaviors, for which he is detained at Juvenile Hall. The recently expanded mental health treatment clinic in that facility has access to his mental health records and is able to reinstitute medication treatment to speed his reconstitution. Court-mandated referral to an outreach case management program is instituted to break Michael's cycle of treatment noncompliance in the future.

Shirley, age fourteen, has a long history of foster placement with episodic emotional outbursts that result in brief respite stays at a crisis residential facility during times of stress. Her community therapist and the facility-based therapist have an established relationship that allows for open and consistent communication about Shirley's egressions, and over time her need for separations from her foster home have decreased in frequency and duration.

Collaborative Practice Within the National Context

The vision of truly collaborative service systems for youth is a realizable opportunity in many communities. The recently published *Report of the Surgeon General's Conference on Children's Mental Health: A National Action Agenda* (U.S. Department of Health and Human Services, 2000), itself a collaboration among three major federal departments (Health and Human Services, Education, and Justice), supports system of care models that prioritize collaboration and cooperation across service systems, between providers, and with families. The report states that "children's mental health care is dispersed across multiple systems: schools, primary care, the juvenile justice system, child welfare and substance abuse treatment" and calls for "integrating family, child and youth-centered mental health services into all systems that serve children and youth" (p. 3). The report also calls for the enhancement of "the infrastructure for children's mental health services, including support for . . . interventions across professions" and for increased "access to and coordination of quality mental health services" (p. 4).

The report identifies a host of issues where stronger collaborations would have positive impacts. It notes that the number of children needing treatment is large and that many, perhaps most, are neither identified nor served; that the morbidity associated with inadequate treatment is lifelong and costly; that there are vast disparities in access to care based on socioeconomic and ethnic variables; and that even with a significant and expanding scientific base of knowledge about childhood disorders and efficacious treatment methods, implementation of these technologies lags. The need for substantial investment in collaborative endeavors across child-serving systems, between universities and public agencies, with minority and ethnic social service and religious organizations, with parent advocacy organizations, and with the media is evident. Expanded collaborations across these domains could reduce the prevalence and morbidity of mental illness for children at risk.

Numerous efforts are underway to expand awareness of system of care opportunities and the importance of collaborative institutional structures to improve the care for youth and families. Nationally, the systems of care initiative grants sponsored by the Center for Mental Health Services have been the key driving force in these efforts (U.S. Department of Health and Human Services, 1999). This grant program has moved state and local systems to explore, endorse, and establish collaborative services within their local programs. Support has also come from numerous nonprofit organizations dedicated to improving the lives of children. Their support for systemic intervention in model programs has been critical in the growing commitment to improve service methods and systems. Family organizations, mental health advocacy groups, and, more recently, professional organizations have also played important roles in raising consciousness and investment in system of care efforts.

Collaborative Practice as a Support to Children and Families

Implicit in system of care concepts is the understanding that all youth, whether emotionally ill or in optimal health, require family and community supports in multiple arenas to achieve their full potential. Ideally, all children should have access to developmentally informed caretaking at home, mental health screening in physical health settings, psychosocial services in the schools, and multimodal supports in a broad array of community settings. In our complex and demanding world, obtaining appropriate services in all of these domains of care and caring is a challenge.

Well-functioning families obtain services to meet the needs of their children by engaging community resources. An empowered and supported parent is, among many other things, an effective case manager: coordinating care and accessing multiple services from the arenas of health care, schools, religious organizations, and other social resources. Minor and even modestly complicated mental health and psychosocial problems are routinely handled in this fashion. Parents access health care providers, work with school personnel, and engage other public and private resources to obtain services for their children.

Ali is an active but moody teenager who is often the center of his peer group's attention. Following the death of two relatives in a brief period of time, his mother begins to notice signs of withdrawal that persist beyond the normal period of mourning that other family members have experienced. She contacts the school counselor and one of Ali's favorite teachers, and they confirm that he has been out of sorts in recent weeks with decreased classroom involvement and activity. Initially resistant, Ali is encouraged by his mother and eventually agrees to see a psychotherapist. In short order, he returns to his premorbid level of functioning. A follow-up parent-teacher conference confirms that Ali is back on track, engaged in his typical teenage antics.

For children and families with more substantial behavioral health and related social difficulties, the challenges can be substantial. These children (and their families) often have an exceptional need for external agencies to provide specialized services and supports. These needs may occur in all spheres of the youth's life: intrapsychically, within the family, with peers, in school, and in myriad other settings. Other chapters in this book address the multiplicity of specialized arenas (child welfare, dual disorders, education, juvenile justice) where supplemental mental health services can be brought to bear to provide more comprehensive care for these individuals. Successful practice across this broad array of service sectors is dependent on effective interdisciplinary and cross-agency collaboration.

Bruce and Barbara are two siblings recently taken into court custody by the local child protective agency because of parental dysfunction (substance abuse and domestic violence). They are jointly placed in a specialized residential treatment facility that provides protective care and multimodal treatment services, including health, special education, recreational, and mental health services. The parents, self-motivated but also under court mandate, pursue relevant treatment services for themselves and engage in parent training programs to prepare themselves for eventual reunification and responsible caretaking of their children. Active collaboration by the residential treatment team, the local social service agency and court, and the various service providers supporting the parents' recovery allows for progressive identification and intervention for a variety of problems and needs of the children and their parents. At discharge, a comprehensive service plan to sustain the parents' recovery and to support the children in their reengagement with their parents and community is instituted.

To be effective, all involved staff need skills in both their respective fields of expertise and their collaborative interchange with each other and the children's parents. Working as a functional team, these multiple professionals and agency staff can prepare troubled families for reunification and independent functioning.

When children and youth have serious emotional disturbances, their needs and the needs of their families are multiple. The resolution or mitigation of problems requires the integrated and coordinated application of resources from multiple arenas. In many communities, the systems that provide these elements of care are limited in their capability, flexibility, and resources to do the job on their own. Many do admirable work, but even in the best of systems, there are constraints and barriers to optimal services and supports for youth with mental health and associated biopsychosocial problems. Building an effective village for every child and family invariably requires collaborative efforts across multiple systems.

Collaboration as a Systemic Value and Process

Collaboration in systems of care needs to occur at all levels: at the case level, within agency practice, and on the administrative plane. At the case level, family members, clinicians, caseworkers, educators, and other community members need to engage as partners. As team players, they need to develop and implement multidimensional interventions within each youth and family's individualized treatment plan. Seamless collaboration by agency staff from different service systems is essential. At the level of agency involvement, in both middle management and upper management, collaboration is needed to ensure that programs working with the same clients have policies and protocols that support complementary clinical, case management, and service efforts, including flexible resource allocation when needed. Ultimately, involvement and engagement of the community's political leadership in enhancing system of care initiatives is essential to ensure adequate funding and provide incentives for policy and planning efforts. Finally, the efforts of advocates, parents, and providers are also needed to ensure sustained attention to the larger vision and goals.

Five-year-old Jeff lives under the guardianship of his widowed working grandmother, who is struggling to maintain a steady income, coordinate Jeff's school and after-school placements, and negotiate and coordinate the court-sanctioned contacts between Jeff and his mother, who struggles with her own social-emotional problems. An intensive outreach mental health program operating in coordination with the local elementary school district provides thorough diagnostic assessment, initiates supportive psychotherapies in school and at home, refines medication management, offers counsel and "buffering" with the mother, consults with the local social service agency, and provides crisis management services (locating a temporary after-school program when the youth is expelled for misbehavior). After four months of intensive service delivery, a period of maintenance support is provided. After eight months of services, medication management responsibility is returned to the pediatrician, and normative community resources of the school and local child care agencies provide the needed daytime supervision and support.

Prerequisites for this program's success include engagement with all family members; cooperation within the mental health team; coordination across mental health, school, and after-school providers; and administrative support of the involved agencies. The end result of this multitiered collaborative service program is that Jeff's life is normalized, and the long-term risk and cost of his potential dislocation from family and community are averted.

Clinical Dimensions of Collaboration Among Staff

Clinicians have long recognized the need for collaboration with patients in the concept of the therapeutic alliance and in recognition of the impact of both transference and countertransference as factors in treatment relationships. In publicly funded human services agencies, clinical mental health providers have the added challenge of negotiating these intensely interpersonal phenomena within the context of layers of complex institutional and bureaucratic rules and regulations. They must work in close contact and interdependence with peers and coworkers not necessarily of their choosing and must develop collaborative partnerships with other service providers and agency staff from multiple organizations, each of whom brings unique personnel, professional, conceptual, and institutional perspectives to their activities. Working through areas of conflict, maximizing the potential for positive contributions, and compensating for limited resources are major challenges in the collaborative process.

After nearly two years of intensive school and community outreach work with seven-year-old Joan and her twenty-nine-year-old mother, who are mired in an enmeshed multigenerational pattern of domestic victimization, Joan's therapist notes that the girl has begun to show increasing autonomy from her troubled relationship with her mother and is performing at more age-appropriate levels in school and after-school activities. Initially presenting as very deviant and with psychotic-like ideation, Joan has progressed considerably. Although her mother has made significant gains and demonstrates intellectual insight into the nature of her problematic parenting style, her basic pattern of child rearing remains negative and damaging to Joan's self-esteem and developmental progress. In therapy, Joan has begun to demonstrate awareness of the distortions in her interactions with her mother and has expressed a desire to live away from home in "a normal place." Concurrently, her mother reports that Joan herself has begun to verbalize threats toward her younger siblings.

Efforts to obtain an emergency respite foster placement through the local child protective agency are initially met with resistance. An extended process of telephone and written communications begins between the clinic staff and the social service agency, bouncing up to the supervisory level because of mutual frustration experienced by the line staff. An interagency meeting is held to work through the conflicts experienced by the staff of the two agencies, and a thorough discussion of each agency's capacities and responsibilities allows for development of a service plan to meet the family's needs. The boundaries of each agency's responsibilities are clarified, and a temporary placement is secured.

In supervision, Joan's therapist reports that she felt blamed and victimized during her contacts with the social service agency and reports feeling hostility toward her cross-agency peer. The parallel between her frustration and rage in seeking help from a seemingly unresponsive agency mirrors the psychological condition of her patient, Joan, in her struggles with her mother and in her own behaviors toward her siblings. Though very demanding of time and emotionally draining, this complex case collaboration was successfully resolved and has led to stronger interagency understanding and cooperation.

Partnership with Parents as Collaborative Practice

Any discussion of the personal nature of collaboration needs to address the opportunities for partnering with patients and parents within the paradigm of cooperative strength-based interactions. True collaborative practice entails including youth and family as active participants and team members in intervention planning and system design. The challenges and possibilities of staff-family collaborations are both substantial and compelling. Just as the strength-based approach to treatment planning efforts has been recognized as the gold standard for intervention efforts, a similar strength-based approach has enormous applicability to the process of collaboration in interdisciplinary, interagency, and provider-client activities.

Alfredo is a thirteen year old on his way to a "career" in the juvenile justice system. Although his non-English-speaking parents managed to obtain adequate supports for him during his latency years and he had managed to make it through elementary school in spite of significant learning disabilities and moderate behavioral problems, with the onset of adolescence, he has become involved in petty delinquencies, and his functioning in school and with peers has deteriorated substantially. After several incidents, he was placed in a court-authorized, probation-supervised day school program capable of containing his behavior while meeting many of his basic educational needs and providing a variety of mental health treatment interventions.

After this program, Alfredo needs extensive community-based supports. His parents are faced with the need to negotiate for the multiple services to support their son. He is referred to a linguistically and culturally sensitive intensive case management program that engages with the parents to coordinate an appropriate school placement, obtain psychiatric consultation for medication management, and develop after-school linkages for social peer involvements. Home visits, guidance with paperwork, and participation with the parents during initial contacts with the new providers help build bridges for the youth and family. The bilingual, bicultural paraprofessional case manager provides the glue to create a successful alliance between the family and these community service systems. The family-centered continuity of care provided in this collaboration between mental health services, the school, probation, and the family provides Alfredo a second chance to obtain the multimodal and multi-agency services he will need to proceed successfully through adolescence.

For parents, the experience of working with a collaborative and accepting service team is a critical component in their progression from a position of frustration and vulnerability to one of empowerment and positive self and family management. This dynamic is true for all families, mainstream and minority; however, effective collaboration with minority clients also requires explicit efforts to bridge cultural and linguistic barriers that may impede communication and collaborative accomplishment.

Organizational Collaboration

At organizational and administrative levels, collaborative activities invariably are complex. The work required varies depending on the size of the organization and level of the manager (middle manager or upper-level administrator), yet in this arena, agency rules and regulations, legislative mandates, budgetary concerns and constraints, and local politics all enter as variables that can either enhance or undercut efforts to optimize service delivery. In the ideal situation, the managers and administrators of multiple systems are able to come together in material ways to set standards for collaborative practice and remove barriers to implementation of coordinated care across agency boundaries.

Various strategies can be employed to strengthen collaborative practice within organizations, including efforts that support positive cross-agency interactions by line staff, as well as those that move or build organizational capacity to support fuller integration of services. In the realm of staff support, building in consultation time as a component of a line staff's job, offering cross-training opportunities to inform staff of others areas of expertise, scheduling multidisciplinary case conferencing, organizing didactic conferences, and colocating staff from different agencies are activities that can create the team knowledge and team connections needed to make collaborative work more feasible. When effective, these efforts result in the development of meaningful personal relationships between individual staff members as well as the creation of institutional connections that support workers in collaborative practice.

A program manager obtained administrative support in negotiating with a child and adolescent psychiatrist interested in working for a public sector program. The psychiatrist made clear her desire to have adequate "indirect" time for interdisciplinary collaboration in team meetings, clinical supervision, and case consultation prior to accepting the job offer. In addition, a workload standard was established that allowed for reasonable time slots to be dedicated to direct service contacts (assessments and medication checks). Her job satisfaction and her performance in serving clients were enhanced by the program manager's accommodation of these needs for adequate collaborative work time. Staff at the clinic displayed improved morale consequent to the increased consultative services available to them.

Working at the level of bureaucracy, strategies such as the creation of focused task groups, pursuit of grant initiatives, establishing comanagement teams, developing integrated or interdependent budgets, and even reorganizing administrative reporting channels can be productive if they are well planned.

A group of program managers responsible for the care and placement of high-end seriously challenged youth for their community had often found themselves in crisis or conflict over who would or could take primary responsibility for placement and service delivery for a child. A meeting of representatives from mental health, social services, probation, and developmental services was convened monthly to review cases where roadblocks in case management were preventing appropriate disposition and service provision. Informally known as the "Hot Potatoes Group," this multidisciplinary forum allowed for creative case management strategies to meet client needs and reduce interagency conflicts. One teenage girl who had been bounced back and forth between mental health, social service, and developmental disability agencies in several states was ultimately placed in a skilled nursing facility, where her underlying neurological and medical disabilities were better able to be served, ending years of being bounced around in inappropriate placements.

Ultimately, a system's capacity for effective collaboration depends very much on the existence of positive and personalized professional relationships among key participants. Although public systems often receive criticism because of their bureaucratic rigidities, effective public servants with years of expertise, strong personal ties to peers, and a growth-promoting institutional environment can mobilize enormous resource in support of effective collaborations.

A group of managers of various state, county, and private nonprofit human service entities initiated a reading group focused on the literature on best practices in the arena of early childhood services. Participants from mental health, social services, early education, pediatrics, developmental services, and other sectors met regularly, with much of the study conducted at home as part of their personal professional development activities. In addition to developing strong and positive relationships with each other that aided in their existing responsibilities, this group was able to use the knowledge of best practice literature in responding to various grants and program development activities that arose within the community in ensuing years.

At higher levels within systems, the impact of an exceptional key leader with clout can move bureaucracies and garner resources quickly and effectively.

The recently appointed presiding juvenile court judge in one community quickly realized that court orders for sobriety were without backbone in both dependency cases (with substance-abusing parents) and delinquency cases involving teenagers in trouble with the law. Having learned the first lesson in parenthood—"Don't make a rule you cannot enforce"—he obtained foundation grant support and corralled agency leadership. Effective programs for routine drug testing and treatment referral of these populations were developed. With the dependency cases, the period of court involvement decreased, and the time spent awaiting permanency planning decreased, with children returned home or removed from parental custody and control in a more timely and developmentally appropriate manner. For the adolescents, referrals to appropriate levels of drug treatment were made, and increased rates of abstinence were achieved.

PROBLEMS AND CHALLENGES IN COLLABORATIVE PROCESSES

With all of its potential promise, however, requests for collaboration are often seen ambivalently and engender outright resistance. As often as not, the roadblocks and barriers are covert, with individual and institutional resistances coming into play. Turf issues, self-esteem, and professional narcissism can be barriers to collaborative efforts. Even when the results are productive, collaboration is rarely a simple matter or an easy experience. There are invariably challenges and frustrations, and no collaboration is guaranteed to be successful, so the risk of failure needs to be recognized as a potential outcome.

Collaborative efforts are most difficult in the earliest stages before trust, cooperation, boundaries, responsibilities, and overall protocols are clearly established. Not infrequently, participants from different agencies do not have a clear appreciation of each other's responsibilities and resource bases, leading to conflicts that disrupt collaborative processes. The training, mandate, and mind-set of social workers, judges, educators, mental health professionals, and others are distinct from the other. Conflicts invariably arise when the child welfare worker's concerns about protection of the child conflict with the therapist's interest in bonding relationships with the parent and the attorney is concerned about the parents' due process rights.

These differing perspectives can be accommodated in successful collaborative efforts, but even with success, there is an ongoing need to support and nurture mutual understanding and cooperative relationships in ongoing collaborative activities. As with all other dynamic interpersonal processes, cooperative spirit and mutual support need to be sustained, particularly as the conditions of the participants and the background situation evolve and change.

The adage, "If you need a job done, do it yourself," has considerable relevance for a front-line clinician or agency worker who may well prefer to go it alone rather than become dependent on another person or agency to assist in implementing a treatment plan or intervention. This may be particularly true when time constraints or fiscal implications may limit the priority given by the second party to the proposed task. Unless a reliable and trusting relationship exists, requests for collaborative support may be fruitless and more frustrating than going it alone.

Additional threats to successful collaboration can develop when the going gets tough and the potential for splitting, blaming, and defensive reactivity can get out of hand and create more problems than the potential benefit that is being sought. This can occur between peers at the same level within organizations or vertically between subordinate and superordinate layers of the organization. As in most other interactions, a negotiated compromise that addresses each party's needs and is sensitive to each party's level of resource should be the desired goal in collaborative ventures.

Responding to an invitation to get to know the community resources, a newly appointed inpatient unit director agreed to visit the local social service receiving home to understand that facility better. He was received with enthusiasm, and his general consultative comments about the exceptional mental health needs of the population were well received. Encouraged to return again later in the month, he was presented with three cases with explicit expectations that all would be transferred to the inpatient service because of their high acuity. Delicate negotiations ensued regarding the mutual capacities and needs of the two facilities, and over time a mutual and balanced collaboration was established whereby acutely ill youth from the receiving home were preferentially considered for hospital admission, while protocols for support and treatment were developed within the receiving home, enabling the hospital program to discharge no-longer-acute inpatients to that facility for after-care placement.

At the case (or clinical) level, proposed partnerships can flounder when communications between prospective partners are unclear, all stakeholders to a collaboration are not included, the strengths and the limitations of the participants are not appreciated, the purported goals are not defined and mutually agreed on, and the external constraints (such as agency policy among many others) confound otherwise rational or even obvious solutions to the problems being addressed.

Clinicians working in inpatient settings or in group or marital therapy modalities are well aware of the critical need for clarity of focus and unanimity of purpose in any therapeutic effort. The role of treatment teams, milieu development, and open communications across the organization and between staff and clients is well recognized. These same principles apply to work across agencies where differences in training and work priorities need to be understood and openly addressed.

A school-based outreach program working with educationally disabled young delinquents with psychiatric illnesses determined that it was critical for the psychiatrist to have dedicated time in order to participate in team meetings and provide in-service training to staff. All initial encounters of patients with the psychiatrist were structured to include the therapist or case manager to obtain full cooperation in evaluation and treatment interventions. Not only did the clinical team work together more smoothly, but the youth were reassured that all staff working with them were on the same track. Similar principles were applied to contacts with the family members as part of the engagement and partnering process. This team-oriented work style resulted in significantly better outcomes with fewer glitches than when the clinicians operated in greater isolation from each other.

Most services provided for youth with serious emotional disturbance are organized as components within much larger bureaucracies. For this reason, the challenges and opportunities for meaningful collaborative intervention must address both individual stakeholder issues and institutional and organizational considerations. Collaborative efforts arising as initiatives from middle management typically require support from peers in parallel posts in other service agencies and from nonclinical branches of the organization (such as budgetary and human resources). They must also address both upstream and downstream resistance. Upstream, the middle manager must elicit the support (or hope for the forgiveness) of supervisors who themselves may have different agendas or organizational values. Downstream, he or she will need to mobilize subordinates to change established practice patterns and provide the support and training needed to make change possible.

Efforts to coordinate databases, colocate staff from different agencies in adjoining office quarters, and integrate staff development divisions are all vehicles that can lead to the types of relationship and connectivity so necessary for effective collaborative work between parallel service agencies. Developing integrated funding pools for projects and other joint venture activities can also advance coordination of services.

A middle management task force, convened at the direction of a leading politician in the community, was brought together to improve collaboration between children's serving agencies; however, there was little clarity as to which problems, if any, might need to be addressed. All participants at the table had established relationships with each other and generally managed to operate their system's interactions with mutuality and respect. After months of meetings, creation of inventories of "collaborativeness," and a variety of other make-work activities, the participants were feeling worn down while their superiors were pressing hard for some substantive project or product that seemed beyond the capacity of this management group to deliver. Lofty goals of coordinated case management and other systemic enhancements were considered but were wisely recognized as being beyond the group's organizational capacity and beyond the overall system's capacity to implement at that stage. Ultimately, a more limited interagency challenge (ensuring quality and coordination of outpatient mental health services for dependent children of the court by private contract providers) was addressed.

At higher levels of administration, the risqué definition of collaboration as "an unpleasurable activity performed by nonconsenting adults in public" highlights the tensions and risks intrinsic to collaborative activities. The risks of public disclosure of organizational problems, the dangers of unrealistic expectations, and the intrusion of disaffected advocates during collaborative discussions can be a source of concern and vulnerability. Media exposure can create added challenges for upper-level administrators. Political influences, legislative demands and constraints, public and community relations issues, and budgetary concerns may all bear down on organizational leaders to inhibit or restrict their freedom to work collaboratively and creatively in effecting system changes. The balancing act of addressing external community pressures while sustaining and supporting the efforts of subordinate organizational components and staff requires commitment and dedication.

In various communities, the issues of where and how the governance and budget of children's mental health should be managed has been an important issue. In most locales, they are consolidated with the adult mental health system, where the special interests and needs of the children's system often become peripheral to the challenges and efforts of the larger system. Many children's advocates and providers see more natural linkages with other agencies also serving children, and some have made efforts to build firewalls to protect children's fair share of budgets and integrate administrative structures in closer alliance with other child serving agencies. Efforts of this nature can result in stronger collaboration and greater mutuality across agency barriers. But these efforts have also been criticized as exacerbating divisions within the mental health community, creating barriers in the transition of older youth to adult service programs, and creating additional administrative support costs. While the results of these various organizational approaches to enhancing collaboration and outcomes for clients served by children's mental health programs are still uncertain, the underlying need to support system of care principles in administrative efforts remains a priority. For clients and consumers, the underlying organizational chart is far less relevant than that system services are accessible, available, and appropriate.

Collaboration is ultimately about people solving real problems and achieving meaningful outcomes through cooperative work. At its core, collaboration facilitates the solving of a problem situation in a new way that actively recognizes and accommodates to both the strengths and the needs of all involved in the work process. When collaboration is effective, the result should be actions that make a difference on the ground, providing all participants with a win.

Within the framework of the expanding new community systems of care effort, collaboration ultimately entails breaking down barriers between disciplines and across agency and institutional barriers, between providers and clients, between professionals and paraprofessionals, and at management and administrative levels. Close and respectful personal relationships are an essential component; institutional and organizational commitments and structures (often reaching far beyond the nexus of the involved participants) are critical to the maintenance and sustenance of such activities.

In the best of all worlds, efforts from the grassroots level of clients, ideas from service staff (professional and paraprofessional), guidelines from agency managers, policy directives from administrators, and the vision of politicians all will be in synergy. Under these conditions, the work of collaboration can proceed, though it will remain a challenge given the numbers of persons and interests involved. A stable focus and a clear commitment of resource, whether at the level of the youth, the family, line workers, middle management, administration, or political governance or in financing, regulatory, or legislative mandates helps the process along.

As with so many other things, talking the talk is different from walking the walk. The goal of system of care efforts and all who participate in them is ultimately to meet the needs of individual clients not able to respond to cookie-cutter cures. The challenge is to adapt and develop programs within larger systems that flexibly and efficiently meet the needs of all involved. Collaborative practice is one of the most important tools in this effort.

References

Knitzer, J. (1982). *Unclaimed children.* Washington, DC: Children's Defense Fund.

Stroul, B. A., & Freidman, R. M. (1986). *A system of care for children and youth with severe emotional disturbances* (Rev. ed.). Washington, DC: Child and Adolescent Service System Program Technical Assistance Center, Georgetown University Child Development Center.

U.S. Department of Health and Human Services. (1999). *Mental health: A report of the surgeon general.* Rockville, MD: U.S. Department of Health and Human Services, National Institutes for Health.

U.S. Department of Health and Human Services. (2000). *Report of the Surgeon General's Conference on Children's Mental Health: A national action agenda.* Rockville, MD: U.S. Department of Health and Human Services, National Institutes for Health, 2000.

CHAPTER FIVE

Cultural Competence
in Systems of Care
for Children's Mental Health

Andres J. Pumariega

Child and adolescent mental health has always recognized that culture is a critical component of development, mental health, and disorder in children and adolescents. Child psychiatry in particular has had a history of interest in the impact of cross-cultural issues on children and families from its inception. This was exemplified by the work of early pioneers on child development (Erikson, 1968), family therapy (Minuchin, 1974), community mental health (Berlin, 1978, 1983), and issues of racial identity and discrimination (Spurlock, 1985; Wilkinson & Spurlock, 1986). However, the focus on serving culturally diverse children and families has traditionally been narrowly defined toward narrow segments of the population, such as children living in inner cities or Indian reservations.

Recent demographic changes in the United States have served to underscore the significance of these issues and place them in the forefront of service delivery and policy in child mental health. In the past twenty years, there has been a remarkable growth in culturally diverse populations, at a much faster rate than the mainstream European-background population in America. In many areas, including most large cities and many states in the Southwest, there are no longer minority populations but a plurality of different ethnic, racial, and cultural groups. This will be the case for the United States as a whole before the year 2050 and among the under-eighteen-year-old population by the year 2030. These changes are happening most rapidly in areas not typically associated with multiple racial and ethnic groups, such as the South and Midwest. Most of this growth in culturally diverse populations has resulted from higher birthrates and increased immigration by people of color. Youth of color already constitute 30 percent of the population under the age of eighteen and close to 40 percent by 2020 (U.S. Bureau of the Census, 1998).

It would be a mistake to assume that these growing culturally diverse populations are in any way monolithic or homogeneous. They comprise a wide array of national origins, ethnicities, and races, many of them overlapping. For example, there are numerous nationalities of Hispanics and Latinos in the United States, with Mexican Americans comprising the majority, but also including Puerto Ricans, Dominicans, Cubans, different Central American nationalities, and different South American nationalities. Hispanic and Latinos have a varied racial and cultural heritage, including a strong American Indian background in mainland Latinos, but also including a strong African heritage among Caribbean Latinos and strong European backgrounds among South Americans. Similarly, Asian–Pacific Islanders include a wide range in nationality and racial origin: Chinese, Japanese, Southeast Asians (such as Vietnamese, Filipino, and Cambodian), Indian, Pakistani, Afghans, Polynesians, and other Pacific Islanders. They have come to the United States for a number of reasons: economic immigration, political exile and refuge, and relocation by multinational corporations. Many groups have been in the United States for decades, some even before the landing of the *Mayflower* (such as American Indians and northern New Mexico Hispanics). Immigrants range linguistically from being monolingual in their native tongue, being monolingual in English, being bilingual, to speaking many different dialects. Although these populations are rapidly becoming the numerical majority in the United States, they still suffer from inequities in socioeconomic status, education, and access to health and human services. This is reflected in significantly lower mean household income and levels of education, higher mortality rates (including infant mortality), higher unemployment, and higher rates of physical health problems and morbidities.

Culturally diverse groups, and particularly those in the four underserved and underrepresented ethnic and racial groups (African Americans, Latinos and Hispanics, Asian Americans, and American Indians), are still discriminated against by the U.S. mental health system. A number of barriers to access to mental health care exist for these populations: a lack of minority practitioners, lack of culturally appropriate services, and lack of knowledge and skill among majority practitioners around cross-cultural issues. In addition, the persistent lack of public child and adolescent mental health services disproportionately affects these underserved groups. As a result, culturally diverse children are underrepresented in mental health settings, shunted to other service systems (child welfare and juvenile justice), or placed in overly restrictive levels of care such as in residential facilities or incarceration or juvenile detention (Pumariega, Glover, Holzer, & Nguyen, 1998; Pumariega, Johnson, Sheridan, & Cuffe, 1995; Cuffe, Waller, Cuccaro, Pumariega, & Garrison, 1995; Pumariega et al., 1999). The morbidity and mortality resulting from such neglect are already resulting in high social and financial costs for society at large, as well as high personal costs for minority children and their families. Such problems as high homicide and suicide rates, substance abuse, homelessness, teenage pregnancy, and school dropout and illiteracy are at least partially results of these barriers and the policies that created them.

CONCEPTS OF CULTURE AND IMPACT ON HEALTH AND BEHAVIOR

A conceptual framework of the role of culture in health and human behavior is necessary to understand the health needs of culturally diverse individuals and populations.

Cultural Influences on Health

Spiegel (1971) and Kluckhorn (1953) saw culture as part of a transactional field, ranging from the somatic, individual, familial, societal, and cultural levels to the level of the universe. Culture, at the interface between society and the greater universe, is where the guidelines for the maintenance of social system, linguistic systems, systems of beliefs and values, and behavioral norms are found. Basic cultural values attempt to define human relationships to four basic domains: nature, time, activity, and relationships. Different cultures define these domains in ways that are adaptive to the group's environmental contexts. Value orientations can be influenced by socioeconomic status and personality and cannot be stereotyped across individuals, though some commonalities can be found within cultures. For example, non-Western cultures adopt harmonious or fatalistic attitudes toward nature, focus on the present or on past traditions and customs, emphasize familial and tribal membership for their identity, and value kinship or hierarchical relations. Western culture adopts a dominant attitude toward nature, is future oriented, focuses on activity or occupational roles to define identity, and values individualism.

Value orientation greatly influences health beliefs and practices. For example, nature, time, and activity orientations influence health maintenance or preventive practices, as well as health risk behaviors. Value orientations influence the health locus of control, or the degree the individual believes health is under personal control or under external influences. The role of the family as arbiter of health practices and provider of caregiving support is influenced by relational value orientations. While some cultures expect the healer to assume an authority role, others prefer a more egalitarian role (Good, 1994).

Attributional beliefs about physical and mental illness are largely culturally determined. Illness can be viewed through a Western biopsychosocial perspective, or through the perspective of religion (God's will), spirituality (spirit possession), or interpersonal and supernatural beliefs (caused by hexes or spells). Culture also defines the sick role, with individuals expected to behave in a fragile or invalid manner, carry on responsibilities in spite of their illness, or have a special spiritual role for the society. Finally, cultural values and beliefs influence patterns of help-seeking behavior. People of different cultures seek different types of assistance: neighborhood wise ladies or *co-madres,* traditional healers (such as *curanderos, santeros, espiritas,* root doctors, or medicine men and women), clergy (ministers, priests, rabbis, mullahs), physicians, and mental health professionals. The orientation of healers and healing approaches are governed by attributional beliefs, and their practices may differ greatly from those of the professional establishment (ceremonies and rituals, incantations, prayers, herbal remedies, sweat lodges, spiritual counseling, psychopharmacology; Rogler & Cortes, 1993).

Cultural Influences on Human Development

Human psychological development is a key process through which culture has significant impact on behavior and adaptation. The definition of behavioral and emotional normality is largely culturally determined. Cultural values help define developmental norms and expectations and child rearing patterns. Normative expectations for such landmarks as toilet training, when to leave a child unsupervised, readiness for expression of sexuality and intimacy, and readiness to leave the parental home are all governed by culture. Expected role functioning in different contexts is also largely culturally governed, including gender (female versus male characteristics), familial, and occupational roles. Patterns of interpersonal communication are also largely culturally governed. For example, even within Hispanic and Latino groups, there are differences in affective expressiveness, with some groups more reserved and others expressive and voluble. Norms around behaviors or behavioral patterns and adaptive psychological strategies differ widely among cultures. For example, hyperactivity in male children is not seen as abnormal by different groups, including Latinos and African Americans; for others, such as Caucasians and Asian Americans, it may be seen as highly deviant. Some cultures value coping mechanisms such as sublimation of emotions into productivity, while others may value humor, abreaction, and the use of rituals or artistic forms.

Children respond to cultural expectations in their environment for role functioning, interpersonal relationships and communication patterns, and behavioral norms. For most culturally diverse children, this may involve being conversant with at least two cultural systems. A number of authors, including deAnda (1984), have already proposed that an optimal adaptation for minority children, and particularly adolescents, is the development of the capacity to be bicultural or even multicultural. Such adaptation implies the development of knowledge and skills in at least two cultural traditions, with the youth retaining his or her original cultural heritage while becoming adept at meeting the expectations of a different culture. It also implies the development of flexibility to operate in different cultural contexts, the development of a stable self-image and values based on selective adoption of the best values and beliefs of different cultures, and openness to different cultural viewpoints and perspectives. An inability to develop these adaptational characteristics results in a number of patterns with adverse psychological consequences: marginalization, reification or mummification of the culture of origin, overacculturation to the mainstream culture and resultant identity diffusion or negative identity formation as defined by Erikson (1968), and cultural conflict that is either internalized or externalized between generations in the family (Szapocznik & Kurtines, 1980).

It is important to view the lack of development of these cross-cultural skills in culturally diverse youngsters not as a disorder but as developmental tasks that they can achieve given the proper environmental support and opportunities, which are often lacking in the difficult socioeconomic and social circumstances in which they grow up. Remarkably, many do develop them in spite of very adverse circumstances, including poverty and discrimination. In fact, with an increasingly pluralistic society, these may also be critical (and equally difficult) tasks for children from the mainstream culture. Sue (1981) describes the process of racial identity formation and provides a developmental framework for understanding these mental health issues. Sue's work suggests that the identity formation process can be assessed and that therapeutic interventions can be designed to facilitate the development of a healthy bicultural adjustment. However, behaviors that may be offensive to the larger society are likely to be exhibited during identity development, causing many helpers to see a healthy but painful process as pathological. Inappropriate responses may inhibit healthy outcomes and contribute to role confusion and identity diffusion.

Cultural Influences on Mental Health

Culture has a major influence on how we experience, understand, express, and address emotional, behavioral, and mental distress and dysfunction. It greatly influences the symptoms used to express distress and may characterize different disorders. Somatization, for example, is a symptom frequently associated with depression and anxiety disorders in minority groups (Roberts, 1992; Glover, Pumariega, Holzer, & Rodriguez, 1999). Differences in language and idiomatic expressions can determine how different symptoms are identified. For example, the term *feeling blue* may have clinical significance to a psychiatrist, but to an African American it reflects a state resulting from chronic oppression, and to a Hispanic it does not make sense when interpreted literally (as a color). Cultural values may also dictate who are reliable reporters and observers, as well as where it is appropriate to discuss different symptoms and problems. For example, recent research demonstrated that Asian Americans report somatic symptoms to physicians but identify emotional responses and symptoms to close friends and family. Different clustering of symptoms may also vary among different groups. For example, many fewer Africans than Britons identified as depressed meet diagnostic criteria for major depression (Draguns, 1984). In addition, there are many culture-bound syndromes that are expressions of distress or psychopathology (such as *susto* or *ataques de nervios* in Hispanics) and do not fit any standard diagnostic criteria (Mezzich & Berganza, 1984).

Various risk factors for psychopathology are influenced by cultural background and immigration status. Risks for certain forms of psychopathology or morbidity that are commonly seen in mainstream populations, such as substance abuse, eating disorders, and suicidality, increase with increased exposure to Western cultural values and practices (Swanson, Linskey, Quintero-Salinas, Pumariega, & Holzer, 1992; Pumariega, 1996; Miller & Pumariega, 2001). This increase in risk may be a result of the loss of previously protective cultural values and beliefs (such as different attitudes about the use of substances, suicide, and body image and family support) and exposure to risk-enhancing factors such as media exposure and peer pressure with lesser family support (Pumariega, Swanson, Holzer, Linskey, & Quintero-Salinas, 1992; Pate, Pumariega, Hester, & Garner, 1992).

Added stressors from the process of immigration and acculturation can lead to increased risk for emotional disturbance. These include previous traumatic exposure in their homelands (war, terrorism, famine), loss of extended family, difficult and traumatic journeys to the United States (crossing rivers, capsizing in rafts, witnessing deaths), the process of acculturation, slavery, discrimination, and poverty. For example, Arroyo and Eth (1985) and Rothe, Castillo-Moros, Brinson, and Lewis (2000) found high rates of posttraumatic stress disorder in Central American and Cuban refugee children as a result of traumas prior to and during immigration. Szapocznik et al. (1978) found that among Cuban Americans, youth had an increased risk for conduct disturbance and substance abuse, which was correlated to the degree of generational difference in acculturation from their parents and resulting conflict. Other authors have also pointed to increased risk for depression (Roberts, Roberts, & Chen, 1997) and anxiety disorders (Glover et al., 1999) among immigrant youth. Many of these effects can have an impact over multiple generations, such as the residual trauma of the African American diaspora (Wilkinson & Spurlock, 1986).

THE CULTURAL COMPETENCE MODEL

Cultural competence became one of the core principles of the system of care movement. Cross, Bazron, Dennis, and Isaacs (1989) defined the prerequisites for culturally appropriate or competent services for minority children and their families. They defined the cultural competence model as a set of congruent behaviors, attitudes, and policies that are found in a system, agency, or a group of professionals that enables them to work effectively in a context of cultural difference. They identified a spectrum of cultural competence that has been demonstrated by society at large and institutions in particular that ranges across cultural destructiveness (genocide, lynching, ethnic cleansing), cultural incapacity (segregation, discrimination, immigration quotas, services which break up families), cultural blindness ("equal" treatment for all but not making distinctions in services offered on differences in values or beliefs), cultural precompetency (realization of differences but insufficient provision of services), cultural competence, and cultural proficiency (provision of innovative services and research).

Cross and colleagues (1989) went on to define the particular qualities that culturally competent practitioners and agencies must embody and achieve. For the individual practitioner, they include qualities such as being aware and accepting of cultural differences, being aware of their own culture and the biases it may create, understanding the dynamics of working across cultures, acquiring cultural knowledge, and acquiring and adapting practice skills to fit the cultural context of the client. They also drew on the work of Wilson (1982), who summarized a number of the qualities to be developed under areas of attitudes, knowledge, and skill. Many of these attributes do not differ from qualities found in good clinicians or mental health professionals, but others are specifically oriented to the needs of culturally diverse children and families.

Cross et al. (1989) also define five main qualities that culturally competent agencies or institutions should demonstrate: valuing and adapting to cultural diversity; ongoing organizational self-assessment; understanding and managing the dynamics of cultural difference; the institutionalization of cultural knowledge and skills through training, experience, and literature; and instituting service adaptations to serve culturally diverse clients and their families better. They go on to specify that such adaptations include addressing barriers to care (cultural, linguistic, geographic, or economic), levels of staffing that reflect the composition of the community being served, needs assessment and outreach, training in communication or interviewing skills, and modifications in actual assessment and treatment procedures and modalities.

CULTURAL COMPETENCE PRINCIPLES IN CLINICAL CARE

The concept of cultural competence has direct applications in the clinical setting, at the interface between the child and adolescent psychiatrist and the child and family.

Even before the child and the family present for a clinical visit, clinicians must be aware of how cultural differences can determine access to the care desired. The clinic or facility may have inadvertently developed barriers such as how the telephone referral is handled (for example, too formal or impersonal or not sufficiently respectful), the geographical location of the clinic (away from accessible transportation or the neighborhoods), and the appointment hours available (which may not match the work and activity hours of the family). The clinic setting and decor may not reflect the cultural values of the populations being served, such as having sufficient room for extended family or kin. In fact, some clinics may discourage attendance by such related individuals during initial visits, even though they may have critical information for the diagnostic process. Registration and financial procedures may contribute to an atmosphere of impersonality and mistrust.

Engagement and Therapeutic Alliance

The establishment of a therapeutic alliance may be the most critical factor in treatment success with culturally diverse youth and families (Bernal, Bonilla, Padilla-Cotto, & Perez-Prado, 1998). Once the child and family present for their initial appointments, the clinician must be attentive to how his or her nonverbal and verbal cues and those of the family are perceived within their cultural context and relate to the establishment of a therapeutic alliance. Even the manner in which a handshake is approached can have vastly different meanings in different cultures. Among many tribes, a soft handshake is the appropriate sign of respect and trust with Native Americans of either gender. Hispanic males expect a firm handshake and females a softer one. Avoidance of eye contact, which may be misperceived as a sign of dishonesty or even psychopathology by majority clinicians, is a sign of respect among Asian and Hispanic youth and a self-protective adaptational stance among African Americans. It may be important to establish quickly who is the main spokesperson for the family and to direct inquiries through that individual, at least initially. Gender-based differences in different cultures in interpersonal communication, communication of intimate information, and boundaries need to be recognized and addressed (Bracero, 1998).

A number of factors may impinge on the minority family's motivation for clinical assistance. It is important to establish whether the motivation is primarily their own or enforced by some outside agent or agency (such as a school or welfare department), which may lead to resentment and disinterest. If the referral resulted from the failure of a cultural practitioner to address the problem, the family may be dealing with demoralization and frustration. Whether such care is sanctioned by the family elders or other decision makers, such as grandparents, is very important, and they should be involved as soon as possible. The clinician should ascertain the degree of stigma associated with mental illness and seeking psychiatric help in the culture and how this could have an impact on the family's comfort with the consultation. The expectations and outcomes hoped for out of the evaluation should be readily established so they may be dealt with openly in order to prevent misconceptions or disappointment (Cross et al., 1989).

Other important factors that can have an adverse impact on the establishment of a therapeutic alliance with culturally diverse youth and families is that of pre-existing biases and stereotypes by clinicians. Some studies have established how such biases can have an adverse impact on the perception of minority clients from the outset of the clinical interaction (Abreu, 1999). Clinicians need to become aware of their own perceptions of diverse cultural and racial groups and prevent these from entering into their interaction with diverse clients.

Clinical Assessment

The principles of cultural competence can be applied to the assessment of the psychosocial functioning of the individual child within his or her sociocultural context. The earlier points about cultural factors involved in the expression, reporting, and assessment of symptoms need to be accounted for in clinical evaluations. Such differences in the interpretation of emotional experiences, the labeling and interpretation of symptomatology, and degree of self-disclosure affect the cross-cultural and cross-ethnic validity of most of the diagnostic instruments used in clinical assessment, since the large majority of these were normed with primarily Anglo American populations. Results from any such instruments require interpretation within the youngster's sociocultural context and support by careful clinical observation (Canino et al., 1987; Knight, Virdin, Ocampo, & Roosa, 1994).

The cultural and family context of symptomatology must also be considered in the assessment of a minority child. Symptomatology may be occurring in the context of a culturally normative period of transition, such as a grief or mourning period or a maturational stage. Clinicians must assess whether cross-cultural dynamics may play a role in the symptomatology, such as intergenerational conflicts around acculturation, discrimination, and marginalization from the majority culture or the youth's own culture. The impact of experiences such as poverty and deprivation or traumatic immigration experiences should also be considered (Koss-Chioino & Vargas, 1999).

The expected norms of behavior and psychosocial development of minority children may differ considerably by cultural group, with different psychological and cognitive skills being reinforced according to different cultural values. Minority children are also exposed to different family structures, role expectations, and communication patterns than majority children are. When minority children are evaluated against the norms for the majority European American culture, they may be erroneously found to be deficient or abnormal. For example, African American children are frequently overrepresented in the disruptive behavior diagnoses, but the greater emphasis on motoric development in Afrocentric cultures is not taken into account in coming to such diagnostic conclusions (Fabrega, Ulrich, & Mezzich, 1993; Kilgus, Pumariega, & Cuffe, 1995). Another misconception, that African American children have lower levels of self-esteem than whites, was proven erroneous by a number of studies that found that they actually had higher levels of self-esteem and used each other as models for comparison. Native American children are often assessed as quiet or lacking in social skills due to being socialized to use longer pauses between turns at conversation. When the Native American child pauses for a polite silence of up to thirty seconds after the previous speaker, children or adults of other cultures usually break the silence, leaving the Native child out of the conversation. In the diagnostic interview, this behavior is often misinterpreted. In fact, a particular source of stress for culturally diverse children are the conflicting developmental expectations from within and outside their families and communities, with the risk of being labeled as dysfunctional by either (Powell, Yamamoto, Romero, & Morales, 1983; Gibbs & Huang, 1989; Philips, 1983).

Ethnography and Language

Clinicians must become knowledgeable about the behavioral and developmental norms and parenting and child-rearing patterns of the populations that they serve. Although there are excellent resource materials for reference, the best source of such information is the family itself. Modifications to the traditional diagnostic interview are needed for this purpose. The techniques used, often termed *ethnographic interviewing* (Green & Leigh, 1989; Spradley 1979), involve having the family member serve as the cultural guide for the clinician by making open-ended inquiries about different cultural aspects of family life. The clinician needs to mark a transition from the typical clinical interview and enlist the cooperation of the family member in this task. The clinician might also incorporate some of these techniques in the interview with the child to evaluate his or her understanding of cultural expectations. In addition, consultants from the cultural group or community to which the family belongs can provide much contextual information about normal development, behavioral norms, and role functioning expectations. In interviewing the child, the clinician should as much as possible include in the interview or the interview area symbols significant to the child's culture so as to facilitate expression of conflicts in culturally syntonic ways. This might include having dolls and figures of the appropriate racial group or reading materials that could elicit cultural themes.

It is not uncommon in clinical settings to serve children from families who do not speak English. Unfortunately, the importance of language and communication in obtaining accurate clinical information is totally overlooked in many mental health settings. Translation and interpretation are relegated as a menial or informal task rather than one that is central to the clinical process. This is reflected in the use of disembodied telephonic translating services or untrained translators, such as housekeeping or lower-level care staff, and the use of family members without regard to the impact on family relations, particularly the use of siblings or the child. This latter practice should be absolutely prohibited except in emergencies due to the adverse impact it can have on family relations. Interpreters should have proper training in both their skill and the content area of interpretation—in this case, child mental health. They should understand the culture of the child and family and be ready to address verbal, nonverbal, and implicit communications (Altarriba & Santiago Rivera, 1994).

Care Planning and Selection of Interventions

The treatment planning and interpretive process are critical in the effective treatment of minority children. The minority family may well feel a strong power differential between themselves and the professional, which is often the case when dealing with agents of the majority culture. They often choose to acquiesce passively and later not follow recommendations. It is important to address this perception and empower the family in making treatment decisions for their child. Clinicians must ensure that a true consensus is developed with the family around the understanding of the child's problems and possible illness. This may involve using terminology and concepts acceptable in their cultural belief system. It is also important to present treatment options in a demystifying manner understandable to the family yet in a manner that is not condescending to them. Such options should include cultural or folk practitioners and consultants whenever indicated, as well as the option not to pursue treatment at all.

One of the most obvious care planning decisions in the mental health treatment of culturally diverse children and their families is around clinician assignment. The assignment of a culturally diverse therapist or clinician from the same or similar cultural, ethnic, or racial background would seem to be the most culturally competent approach to treatment. In fact, some studies suggest that such matching leads to better engagement in treatment and better outcomes (O'Sullivan & Lasso, 1992). However, there are some realities that mitigate against this choice. First, the availability of a matched clinician is likely to be low, especially in geographical areas where the child belongs to a marked numerical minority. Overall, minority mental health clinicians are far outnumbered by culturally diverse children and families seeking services. Moreover, minority clinicians are not necessarily culturally competent in terms of their clinical skills, and the acculturation process inherent in professional training may reduce their degree of cross-cultural effectiveness. Also, there are times when minority families deliberately do not want to see a clinician from their own community out of concern for confidentiality and potential stigma.

Explanatory models of illness or psychological distress play a role in the family's acceptance of the care plan and therapeutic approaches being recommended (Callan & Littlewood, 1998). It is important that in selecting target behaviors for intervention or role function expectations for improvement goals, cultural norms for these be taken into account. In addition, for behavioral interventions, the selection of family intervenors needs to be consonant with the normative family roles for the culture. For example, if grandparents have a greater role in discipline than parents, grandparents need to be highly involved in developing and implementing any protocols for behavioral interventions for disruptive behaviors.

Pharmacotherapy

A common assumption about psychopharmacotherapy is that since this is an area of intervention that is biologically based, cultural competence principles are not important in its implementation. However, emerging research challenges this assumption and makes cultural competence a critical principle in psychopharmacotherapy, as well as in other areas of mental health treatment and services. The interpretation, expression, measure, and threshold of behavioral and emotional symptoms can also vary across cultures, making the establishment of baselines and outcomes more challenging. Significant cultural bias found in clinical psychiatric diagnostic assessment of children and adolescents (Kilgus et al., 1995; Fabrega et al., 1993) can readily lead to the inappropriate use or withholding of psychopharmacotherapy for culturally diverse children. For example, Zito, Safer, dosReis, Magder, and Riddle (1997) found that African American children were less likely to receive stimulant medications than Caucasian children in treatment settings. The perception by ethnic and racial minorities of psychopharmacological agents as a means for social control adversely influences the acceptability of these agents among such populations. Cultural and ethnic norms around family medical decision making and consent need to be considered in presenting the recommendations to use such agents and soliciting informed consent, where elders assume a greater role than in traditional white middle-class families. It is important to educate and obtain true informed consent from the true family decision makers or elders in order to obtain optimal treatment compliance. This also involves demystifying the use of medications and addressing misperceptions based on both traditional cultural beliefs and the perceived power differential with the clinician (for example, that the medication will "control his thinking"). Discussion of biological and genetic factors can also serve to alleviate feelings of guilt on the part of the family, who may often feel responsible for the child's illness or problems as a result of their socioeconomic limitations.

Cross-racial and cultural biological considerations need to be attended to in psychopharmacological treatment. A new science of ethnopsychopharmacology is developing its own body of literature pointing to genetic and nutritional factors that can contribute to differential pharmacological response across ethnic and racial groups (Lin, Poland, & Nakasaki, 1993). A case in point relates to the metabolism of most pharmacological agents, especially the serotonin reuptake inhibitor (SSRI) antidepressants. These agents are metabolized by a series of liver enzymes called cytochrome P450 enzymes, with various of these enzymes responsible for the metabolism of different agents. Genetic polymorphisms have been described for many drug-metabolizing enzymes in Caucasian, Asian, and African-origin populations (Smith & Mendoza, 1996). In addition, nutritional factors such as citrus and corn content in the diet, which vary by ethnic group, inhibit the action of some of these enzymes. The level of action of the cytochrome P450 enzymes can determine the dosage needed to achieve therapeutic action, as well as the emergence of side effects (Rudorfer & Potter, 1999).

Psychosocial Therapies

In individual psychotherapy, the clinician must address the dynamics of cultural difference and power differential with the child as clearly as with the family. The presence of identity or role confusion as a result of acculturation conflicts should also be addressed empathetically, but also empowering the child to make flexible choices around cultural values and identification. It is also important to address specific areas of cultural conflict, such as role pressures on the child to serve as a cultural broker with the family, pressures not to "betray" their culture, and negative identification against their culture of origin. A value-neutral approach, where the clinician models openness to the diverse cultural influences the child is exposed to, is quite effective in achieving these goals. Therapists can also use judicious self-disclosure with the child when they have experienced any of these conflicts in their own experience. Confidentiality in psychotherapy must be addressed so the clinician is not perceived as driving a wedge between the patient and family or used by the patient to resist dealing with family issues (Gibbs & Huang, 1989; Baker, 1999).

Culturally diverse children and families have been shown to be more accepting and responsive to psychotherapeutic approaches that have a practical problem-focused, here-and-now focus. Cognitive-behavioral approaches, which are oriented toward these principles, are most frequently used; results from studies and case reports suggest good response by culturally diverse clients (Elligan, 1997; Williams, Chambless, & Steketee, 1998; Longshore, Grills, & Annon, 1999). Interpersonal approaches, which focus on an important attributional issue in emotional and behavioral problems for non-Western cultures, show promise in their use with diverse populations (Mufson, Weissman, Moreau, & Garfinkel, 1999; Rosello & Bernal, 1999; Brown, Schulberg, Sacco, Perel, & Houck, 1999). Psychoanalytically insight-oriented interventions are not contraindicated but have tended to include inherent cultural biases (such as encouraging separation-individuation and challenge of traditional parental authority and roles), which can be counterproductive in engaging more culturally traditional families (Cabaniss, Oquendo, & Singer, 1994). When cultural values and beliefs are effectively addressed, culturally diverse clients also benefit from these approaches (Aslami, 1997). Some therapists have developed interventions that are specific for particular ethnic and racial groups, which have been evaluated for efficacy (Malgady, Rogler, & Costantino, 1990; Costantino, Malgady, & Rogler, 1994; De Rios, 1997). Group psychotherapy, particularly group approaches that integrate cultural and ethnic identity themes as well as a psychoeducational approach addressing culturally consonant coping approaches, have also been reported as both well accepted and successful (Guanipa, Talley, & Rapagna, 1997; Yancey, 1998; Salvendy, 1999).

Contextual Orientation and Interventions

All treatment of minority children must have a contextual orientation in order to address cultural issues effectively. This means that therapists must evaluate the familial, neighborhood, community, and cultural contexts of the child's dysfunctional behaviors; address the environmental factors that contribute to the problem behaviors; and draw on the strengths that the child and family bring to the problem solving (Koss-Chioino & Vargas, 1999). Therapists should help parents develop effective behavioral management skills that are consonant with their values and beliefs. They must respect culturally established means of communication and family role functioning, but at the same time foster flexibility on the part of the family to accommodate differing points of view that might be espoused by their more bicultural offspring. This involves addressing intergenerational acculturation conflicts, which may stem from parental fears of abandonment by their acculturating child, while also facilitating the family in its role of transmission of traditional cultural values and beliefs in a nonconflictual fashion. The family can accept greater acculturation by the child if the members are empowered in dealing with the majority culture more effectively (Montalvo & Gutierrez, 1983; Szapocznik & Kurtines, 1989; Koss-Chioino & Vargas, 1999).

In a contextual approach, therapists should engage the family in using community resources that can facilitate both the enhancement of their traditional strengths as well as the introduction into new cultural viewpoints. This includes the use of school settings, churches, community organizations, and informal kinship networks, which the family is often cut off or marginalized from (Spurlock, 1985; Gutierrez-Mayka & Contreras-Neira, 1998; Garrison, Roy, & Azar, 1999; Koss-Chioino & Vargas, 1999). The use of a cultural consultant in therapy, with the family's consent, can be useful in dealing with issues around the interpretation of traditional beliefs and values, as well as potential distortion of these for dysfunctional purposes.

APPLYING CULTURAL COMPETENCE PRINCIPLES TO SYSTEMS OF CARE

Culturally competent practice can occur only within a system of care that has internalized and integrated cultural competence principles into every aspect of its organization and functioning (Cross et al., 1989). This requires an operationalization of how cultural competence is to be applied within these systems.

Further impetus for this operational definition of cultural competence has been provided by managed care. Managed behavioral health has a particular impact on culturally diverse populations, particularly children and their families. Many are covered under Medicaid, while states increasingly pursue managed behavioral health approaches for these programs. Public managed behavioral health, combined with the privatization of many of these services, has adopted approaches oriented toward middle-income populations. These do not deal with the multiple stressors faced by culturally diverse children and families and use different types of services, particularly fewer social support services. Managed care implementation has also relocated many mental health services away from traditional ethnic community and neighborhood settings and toward unfamiliar and uncomfortable suburban settings. The exclusive provider panels developed for such plans tend to select against culturally diverse practitioners due to their having fewer formal credentials as well as their serving higher-risk, higher-using (and thus higher-cost) clients.

The response to these challenges has been to develop standards for cultural competence at both the provider and the systems levels, for use by practitioners, provider organizations, health plans, and organized systems of care. Examples of such standards are the Guidelines for Culturally Competent Managed Mental Health Services by the National Latino Behavioral Workgroup, sponsored by the Western Interstate Commission on Higher Education (Pumariega et al., 1997), the Standards for Cultural Competence in Managed Care Mental Health by the Center for Mental Health Services (Four Racial/Ethnic Panels, 1999), and the California Cultural Competence Plan for Mental Health (California Department of Mental Health, 1997).

Governance

Cultural competence needs to be at the top of the priorities for any system of care and considered in all its policies and procedures. Where this is often best reflected is in its inclusion in the organizational mission and vision and statements of such systems. The leadership of systems of care should be reflective of the populations served, in either racial and ethnic composition or extensive expertise with such populations.

Systems of care require that the populations that they serve participate in decision making. Organized ways in which this can occur include community representatives on governing boards and advisory boards, though the latter often serve more as window dressing than empowering underserved populations. Organized planning around the cultural needs of the population is essential, including access to epidemiological data about the population served, as well as conducting community-based needs assessments. Consumer satisfaction and input should be obtained through surveys conducted by community entities independent of the service agencies and have credibility within the diverse populations served, also conducted using language and methods acceptable to the population.

Benefits Design

Benefits and services delivered by the system of care should be consonant with the cultural values of the populations served and responsive to their needs. These should include not only clinical and psychosocial support services but also traditional cultural healing services where applicable. Overall, there should be comparability of benefits for underserved populations as for mainstream middle-class populations leading to comparable clinical and functional outcomes.

Quality Assurance and Improvement

Quality assurance and improvement assessments and studies should always undertake analysis of outcomes by race, ethnicity, and socioeconomic status of critical quality indicators. Quality plans should also include special studies on issues and indicators that are critical for underserved minority populations. These include access to services, quality of linguistic support, addressing cultural support issues in service and treatment plans, and negative outcomes, such as institutionalization, homicide, suicide, and school dropout. Such plans should be informed by cultural consultants and specialists within the system of care.

Information Systems

Information systems need to capture data on race, ethnicity, socioeconomic status, geographical distribution, linguistic proficiency, and functioning (for example, employment and school attendance), in addition to data on clinical outcomes on the population it served. These data need to be analyzed cross-culturally for the development of new services and enhancement of existing services. Epidemiological data as well as data from multiple serving agencies (such as schools, child welfare, and juvenile justice agencies) need to be used, along with the mental health database in examining processes of care and outcomes for culturally diverse populations.

Staff Training and Support

Systems of care need to have active training plans designed to develop cultural competence in all staff members, from the top leaders to the lowest levels of the organization. Such training needs to address areas of cultural knowledge and skills relating to the populations served at all these different levels. It also needs to address issues of attitude that are often thorny and can produce conflict, such as attitudes about the existence of discrimination, affirmative action, limited English proficiency (LEP), and bilingual education. For clinicians, such training needs to address clinical issues relating to specific populations served in depth.

Systems of care need to develop in-house cultural expertise on the population it served. They need to include programs to recruit, retain, and promote individuals of color within their ranks, including providing educational and advancement opportunities. The development of cultural mental health specialists is also recommended within the Center for Mental Health Services (CMHS) standards; these are clinicians with high levels of expertise in specific cultural groups who can consult at various levels, such as screening and triage protocols, case planning, clinical consultation and supervision, placement at higher levels of care, and quality assurance and improvement plans.

Case Management

Trained individuals who are intimately familiar with the culture of the client family (preferably from the same culture) and the resources of their community should provide case management. Case management should be respectful of the culturally specific decision-making process of the family and as much as possible have the family drive case management decisions. Case managers should optimize the use of natural resources from the ethnic community and the deployment of strengths based on the cultural origin of the family.

Linguistic Support

Systems of care need to provide accessible and high-quality translation services for children, and especially families with LEP to avoid having the janitor or even the child serve in this capacity. Standards for such services should be at the level of court translators, who have an understanding of the cultural group and proficiency not only in the language but also in the idioms and nonverbal communications. Furthermore, systems of care need to train providers on communication issues that are relevant to the diverse populations they serve, such as nonverbal cues, mannerisms, and colloquialisms.

This is a critical issue for equalizing access to care for immigrant and culturally diverse populations. Access to services for individuals with LEP has been termed a civil rights issue under the 1964 Civil Rights Act. However, many service providers, governmental agencies, and even professional organizations resist the implementation of requirements for translation services because of concerns over the cost of such services. The approach recommended by the CMHS standards is to designate a threshold of population numbers for such services to be readily available. The California cultural competence standards (California Department of Mental Health, 1997) defined the threshold at three thousand covered individuals or 5 percent of the population, whichever is less, within a county behavioral health entity. For example, Los Angeles has twelve threshold languages for which it must provide professional translation services or bilingual providers, while San Jose has seven.

TOWARD CULTURAL PROFICIENCY

Work in the field of cultural competence continues to evolve and develop as the fields of business, health care, and human services become aware of its importance to our multicultural society. The surgeon general's supplement on mental health, culture, race, and ethnicity (U.S. Department of Health and Human Services, 2001) has outlined significant issues in ethnic and racial mental health disparities and the need for expanding research in this important area. This report has complemented the federal initiative on health disparities, which involves the identification inequalities not only in mental health status but also in physical health. (U.S. Office of Minority Health, 2000). Research in epidemiology and services research examining mental health disparities for minority and underserved youth is also pointing the way toward the system of care reforms needed to improve the cultural competence of child mental health services (Glover & Pumariega, 1998; U.S. Department of Health and Human Services, 2001).

However, as Cross and colleagues (1989) clearly asserted, the advancement of knowledge and skills needs to be matched with similar progress in attitudes in order for progress toward a true culturally pluralistic and proficient system of care. It will be up to front-line practitioners in systems of care to use the new knowledge about the influence of culture, race, and ethnicity in mental health and also to face the ugly specters of prejudice and discrimination that persist.

References

Abreu, J. (1999). Conscious and nonconscious African-American stereotypes: Impact on first impression and diagnostic ratings by therapists. *Journal of Consulting and Clinical Psychology, 67,* 387–393.

Altarriba, J., & Santiago Rivera, A. (1994). Current perspectives on using linguistic and cultural factors in counseling the Hispanic client. *Professional Psychology: Research and Practice, 25,* 388–397.

Arroyo, W., & Eth, S. (1985). Children traumatized by Central American warfare. In S. Eth & R. Pynoos (Eds.), *Post-traumatic stress disorder in children* (pp. 103–120). Washington, DC: American Psychiatric Press.

Aslami, B. (1997). Interracial psychotherapy: A report of the treatment of an inner-city adolescent. *Journal of the American Academy of Psychoanalysis, 25,* 347–356.

Baker, A. (1999). Acculturation and reacculturation influence: Multilayer contexts in therapy. *Clinical Psychology Review, 19,* 951–967.

Berlin, I. N. (1978). Anglo adoptions of Native Americans: Repercussions in adolescence. *Journal of the American Academy of Child and Adolescent Psychiatry, 17,* 387–388.

Berlin, I. N. (1983). Prevention of emotional problems among Native American children: Overview of developmental issues. In S. Chess & A. Thomas (Eds.), *Annual progress in child psychiatry and development* (pp. 320–333). New York: Brunner Mazel.

Bernal, G., Bonilla, J., Padilla-Cotto, L., & Perez-Prado, E. (1998). Factors associated to outcome in psychotherapy: An effectiveness study in Puerto Rico. *Journal of Clinical Psychology, 54,* 329–342.

Bracero, W. (1998). Intimidades: Confianza, gender, and hierarchy in the construction of Latino-Latina therapeutic relationships. *Cultural Diversity and Mental Health, 4,* 264–277.

Brown, C., Schulberg, H., Sacco, D., Perel, J., & Houck, P. (1999). Effectiveness of treatments for major depression in primary care practice: A post-hoc analysis of outcomes for African-American and white patients. *Journal of Affective Disorders, 53,* 185–192.

Cabaniss, D., Oquendo, M., & Singer, M. (1994). The impact of psychoanalytic values on transference and countertransference: A study in transcultural psychotherapy. *Journal of the American Academy of Psychoanalysis, 22,* 609–621.

California Department of Mental Health. (1997). *Plan for culturally competent specialty mental health services. Consolidation of specialty mental health services (phase II).* Sacramento: Department of Mental Health, State of California.

Callan, A., & Littlewood, R. (1998). Patient satisfaction: Ethnic origin or explanatory model? *International Journal of Social Psychiatry, 44,* 1–11.

Canino, G., Bird, H., Rubio-Stipec, M., Woodbury, M., Ribera, J., Huertas, S., & Seeman, M. (1987). Reliability of child diagnosis in a Hispanic sample. *Journal of the American Academy of Child and Adolescent Psychiatry, 26,* 560–565.

Costantino, G., Malgady, R. G., & Rogler, L. H. (1994). Storytelling through pictures: Culturally sensitive psychotherapy for Hispanic children and adolescents. *Journal of Clinical Child Psychology, 23,* 13–20.

Cross, T. L., Bazron, B. J., Dennis, K. W., & Isaacs, M. R. (1989). *Towards a culturally competent system of care.* Washington, DC: Child and Adolescent Service System Program Technical Assistance Center, Georgetown University Child Development Center.

Cuffe, S., Waller, J., Cuccaro, M., Pumariega, A. J., & Garrison, C. Z. (1995). Race and gender differences in the treatment of psychiatric disorders in young adolescents. *Journal of the American Academy of Child and Adolescent Psychiatry, 34,* 1536–1543.

deAnda, D. (1984). Bicultural socialization: Factors affecting the minority experience. *Social Work, 29,* 101–107.

De Rios, M. (1997). Magical realism: A cultural intervention for traumatized Hispanic children. *Cultural Diversity and Mental Health, 3,* 159–170.

Draguns, J. G. (1984). Assessing mental health and disorder across cultures. In P. B. Petersen, N. Sartorius, & A. J. Marsella (Eds.), *The cross-cultural context* (pp. 31–58). Thousand Oaks, CA: Sage.

Elligan, D. (1997). Culturally sensitive integration of supportive and cognitive-behavioral therapy in the treatment of a bicultural dysthymic patient. *Cultural Diversity and Mental Health, 3,* 207–213.

Erikson, E. H. (1968). *Identity, youth, and crisis.* New York: Norton.

Fabrega, H., Ulrich, R., & Mezzich, J. (1993). Do Caucasian and black adolescents differ at psychiatric intake? *Journal of the Academy of Child and Adolescent Psychiatry, 32,* 407–413.

Four Racial/Ethnic Panels. (1999). *Cultural competence standards for managed care mental health for four racial/ethnic underserved/underrepresented populations.* Rockville, MD: Center for Mental Health Services, Substance Abuse and Mental Health Administration, U.S. Department of Health and Human Services.

Garrison, E., Roy, I., & Azar, V. (1999). Responding to the mental health needs of Latino children and families through school-based services. *Clinical Psychology Review, 19,* 199–219.

Gibbs, J. T., & Huang, L. N. (1989). A conceptual framework for assessing and treating minority youth. In J. T. Gibbs & L. N. Huang (Eds.), *Children of color: Psychological interventions with minority youth* (pp. 1–29). San Francisco: Jossey-Bass.

Glover, S., & Pumariega, A. J. (1998). The importance of children's mental health epidemiological research with culturally diverse populations. In M. Hernandez & M. Isaacs (Eds.), *Promoting cultural competence in children's mental health services.* Baltimore: Brookes Publishing.

Glover, S., Pumariega, A. J., Holzer, C. E., & Rodriguez, M. (1999). Anxiety symptomatology in Mexican-American adolescents. *Journal of Child and Family Studies, 8,* 47–57.

Good, B. (1994). *Medicine, rationality, and experience: An anthropological perspective.* Cambridge: Cambridge University Press.

Green, J. W., & Leigh, J. W. (1989). Teaching ethnographic methods to social service workers. *Practicing Anthropology, 11,* 8–10.

Guanipa, C., Talley, W., & Rapagna, S. (1997). Enhancing Latin American women's self-concept: A group intervention. *International Journal of Group Psychotherapy, 47,* 355–372.

Gutierrez-Mayka, M., & Contreras-Neira, R. (1998). A culturally receptive approach to community participation in system reform. In M. Hernandez & M. Isaacs (Eds.), *Promoting cultural competence in children's mental health services.* Baltimore, MD: Brookes Publishing.

Kilgus, M., Pumariega, A. J., & Cuffe, S. (1995). Race and diagnosis in adolescent psychiatric inpatients. *Journal of the American Academy of Child and Adolescent Psychiatry, 34,* 67–72.

Kluckhorn, F. R. (1953). Dominant and variant value orientations. In C. Kluckhorn & H. A. Murray (Eds.), *Personality in nature, society, and culture.* New York:

Knopf.

Knight, G. P., Virdin, L. M., Ocampo, K. A., & Roosa, M. (1994). An examination of the cross-ethnic equivalence of measures of negative life events and mental health among Hispanic and Anglo-American children. *American Journal of Community Psychology, 22,* 767–783.

Koss-Chioino, J., & Vargas, L. (1999). *Working with Latino youth: Culture, development, and context.* San Francisco: Jossey-Bass.

Lin, K., Poland, R., & Nakasaki, G. (1993) *Psychopharmacology and psychobiology of ethnicity.* Washington, DC: American Psychiatric Press.

Longshore, D., Grills, C., & Annon, K. (1999). Effects of a culturally congruent intervention on cognitive factors related to drug-use recovery. *Substance Use and Misuse, 34,* 1223–1241.

Malgady, R. G., Rogler, L. H., & Costantino, G. (1990). Hero/heroine modeling for Puerto Rican adolescents: A preventive MH intervention. *Journal of Consulting and Clinical Psychology, 58,* 469–474.

Mezzich, J., & Berganza, C. (Eds.). (1984). *Culture and psychopathology.* New York: Columbia University Press.

Miller, M., & Pumariega, A. J. (2001). Culture and eating disorders: A historical and cross cultural review. *Psychiatry: Interpersonal and Biological Processes, 64,* 93–110.

Minuchin, S. (1974). *Families and family therapy.* Cambridge, MA: Harvard University Press.

Montalvo, B., & Gutierrez, M. (1983). A perspective for the use of the cultural dimension in family therapy. In C. J. Fallicov (Ed.), *Cultural perspectives in family therapy.* Gaithersburg, MD: Aspen.

Mufson, L., Weissman, M., Moreau, D., & Garfinkel, R. (1999). Efficacy of interpersonal psychotherapy for depressed adolescents. *Archives of General Psychiatry, 56,* 573–579.

O'Sullivan, M., & Lasso, B. (1992). Community mental health services for Hispanics: A test of the culture compatibility hypothesis. *Hispanic Journal of Behavioral Sciences, 14,* 455–468.

Pate, J., Pumariega, A., Hester, C., & Garner, D. (1992). Cross-cultural patterns in eating disorders. *Journal of the American Academy of Child and Adolescent Psychiatry, 31,* 802–809.

Philips, S. U. (1983). *The invisible culture.* New York: Longman.

Powell, G. J., Yamamoto, J., Romero, A., & Morales, A. (Eds.). (1983). *The psychosocial development of minority group children.* New York: Brunner/Mazel.

Pumariega, A. J. (1996). Culturally competent program evaluation in systems of care for children's mental health. *Journal of Child and Family Studies, 5,* 389–397.

Pumariega, A. J., Atkins, D. L., Rogers, K., Montgomery, L., Nybro, C., Caesar, R., & Millus, D. (1999). Mental health and incarcerated youth. II: Service utilization in incarcerated youth. *Journal of Child and Family Studies, 8,* 205–215.

Pumariega, A. J., Balderrama, H., Garduno, R., Hernandez, M., Hernandez, P., Martinez, F., Romero, J., Saenz, J., Torres, J., Sanchez, M., & Keller, A. (1997). *Cultural competence guidelines in managed care mental health services for Latino populations.* Boulder, CO: Western Interstate Commission for Higher Education, 1997.

Pumariega, A. J., Glover, S., Holzer, C. E., & Nguyen, N. (1998). Utilization of mental health services in a tri-ethnic sample of adolescents. *Community Mental Health Journal, 34,* 145–156.

Pumariega, A. J., Johnson, P., Sheridan, D., & Cuffe, S. (1995). Race, gender, age, depressive symptomatology, and substance abuse in high-risk adolescents. *Cultural Diversity and Mental Health, 2,* 115–123.

Pumariega, A. J., Swanson, J., Holzer, C. E., Linskey, A., & Quintero-Salinas, R. (1992). Cultural context and substance abuse in Hispanic adolescents. *Journal of Child and Family Studies, 1,* 75–92.

Roberts, R. (1992). Manifestation of depressive symptoms among adolescents: A comparison of Mexican-Americans with the majority and other minority populations. *Journal of Nervous and Mental Disease, 180,* 627–633.

Roberts, R., Roberts, C., & Chen, Y. (1997). Ethnocultural differences in prevalence of adolescent depression. *American Journal of Community Psychology, 25,* 95–110.

Rogler, L. H., & Cortes, D. E. (1993). Help-seeking pathways: A unifying concept in mental health care. *American Journal of Psychiatry, 150,* 554–561.

Rosello, J., & Bernal, G. (1999). The efficacy of cognitive-behavioral and interpersonal treatments for depression in Puerto Rican adolescents. *Journal of Consulting and Clinical Psychology, 67,* 734–745.

Rothe, E., Castillo-Moros, H., Brinson, K., & Lewis, J. (2000). La odisea de los balseros cubanos: Sintomas post-traumaticos y caracteristicas de viaje en niños y adolescentes. *Medico Interamericano, 19,* 578–581.

Rudorfer, M., & Potter, W. (1999). Metabolism of tricyclic antidepressants. *Cell and Molecular Biology, 19,* 373–409.

Salvendy, J. (1999). Ethnocultural considerations in group psychotherapy. *International Journal of Group Psychotherapy, 49,* 429–464.

Smith, M., & Mendoza, R. (1996). Ethnicity and pharmacogenetics. *Mount Sinai Journal of Medicine, 63,* 285–290.

Spiegel, J. (1971). *Transactions: The interplay between individual, family, and society* (J. Papajohn, Ed.). New York: Science House.

Spradley, J. (1979). *The ethnographic interview.* New York: Holt, Rinehart.

Spurlock, J. (1985). Assessment and therapeutic interventions of black children. *Journal of the American Academy of Child and Adolescent Psychiatry, 24,* 168–174.

Sue, D. W. (1981). *Counseling the culturally different.* New York: Wiley.

Swanson, J., Linskey, A., Quintero-Salinas, R., Pumariega, A. J., & Holzer, C. E. (1992).

Depressive symptoms, drug use and suicidal ideation among youth in the Rio Grande Valley: A bi-national school survey. *Journal of the American Academy of Child and Adolescent Psychiatry, 31,* 669–678.

Szapocznik, J., & Kurtines, W. (1980). Acculturation, biculturation, and adjustment among Cuban-Americans. In A. M. Padilla (Ed.), *Acculturation: Theory, models, and some new findings* (pp. 139–159). Boulder, CO: Westview Press.

Szapocznik, J., & Kurtines, W. (1989). *Breakthroughs in family therapy with drug abusing and problem youth.* New York: Springer.

Szapocznik, J., Scopetta, M. A., Aranalde, M. A., & Kurtines, W. M. (1978). Cuban value structure: Clinical implications. *Journal of Consulting and Clinical Psychology, 46,* (5), 961–970.

U.S. Bureau of the Census. (1998). *Resident population of the United States: Estimates by sex, race, and Hispanic origin.* Washington, DC: U.S. Department of Commerce.

U.S. Department of Health and Human Services. (2001). *Mental health: Culture, race, and ethnicity. A supplement to mental health: A report of the surgeon general.* Rockville, MD: U.S. Department of Health and Human Services, Substance Abuse and Mental Health Services Administration, Center for Mental Health Services, National Institutes of Health, National Institute of Mental Health.

U.S. Office of Minority Health (2000). *Assuring cultural competence in health care: Recommendations for national standards and an outcomes-focused agenda.* Washington, DC: U.S. Department of Health and Human Services, Public Health Service.

Wilkinson, C., & Spurlock, J. (1986). *The mental health of black Americans: Psychiatric diagnosis and treatment.* New York: Plenum Press.

Williams, K., Chambless, D., & Steketee, G. (1998). Behavioral treatment of obsessive-compulsive disorder in African-Americans: Clinical issues. *Journal of Behavioral Therapy and Experimental Psychiatry, 29,* 163–170.

Wilson, L. (1982). *The skills of ethnic competence.* Unpublished manuscript; Seattle: University of Washington,

Yancey, A. (1998). Building positive self-image in adolescents in foster care: The use of role models in an interactive group approach. *Adolescence, 33,* 253–267.

Zito, J., Safer, D., dosReis, S., Magder, L., & Riddle, M. (1997). Methylphenidate patterns among Medicaid youths. *Psychopharmacological Bulletin, 33,* 143–147.

PART TWO

INTEGRATING CLINICAL MODALITIES INTO SYSTEMS OF CARE

CHAPTER SIX

Strengthening
the Clinical Perspective

Theodore Fallon Jr.

In the care of children and adolescents with serious emotional disturbances, coordination of resources, including fiscal and organizational resources, has been critical to the provision of effective services. Strong efforts have been made to adjust national, state, and local legislation, funding mechanisms, organizational structure, collaborative relationships, and service design in an attempt to improve the care of this population. Now that there is considerable experience in adjusting this infrastructure, it is useful to ask what gains have been made in the face-to-face clinical care of these children, adolescents, and their families and what challenges remain.

HISTORICAL PERSPECTIVE

The federally funded Child and Adolescent Service System Program (CASSP), which began in 1984, was the culmination of an increasing awareness of and concern for the needs of children and adolescents and a desire to coordinate an ever growing number of previously uncoordinated public services, such as public health, mental health, school, welfare, child protection, and juvenile justice, to name a few. Within a few years of this initiative, it became clear that the children and adolescents most in need of these coordinated services were the ones who had disturbances in multiple domains of their lives: school, home, community, and within themselves.

These children and adolescents were defined as having serious emotional disturbances. One of the key challenges in working clinically with this population was that their lives were characteristically filled with cataclysms and abrupt changes that created discontinuities in their development. These discontinuities made it difficult, if not impossible, for providers to establish a coordinated program of care. These children and adolescents and their families were in need of services in multiple domains of their lives; without a coordinated system of care, services and treatment were next to impossible.

Experience with CASSP led the Robert Wood Johnson Foundation to fund the Mental Health Service Program for Youth (RWJ-MHSPY), which allowed seven sites from around the country to develop into what might arguably be called the first fully functional implementation of child-focused coordinated systems of care. As demonstration projects, these RWJ-MHSPY sites provided rich experiences in addressing the needs of children and youth with serious emotional disturbances and their families.

Personnel from diverse disciplines and backgrounds came together to design and work side by side in complex coordinated constellations of services. The RWJ-MHSPY project realized many of the promises made by CASSP in the coordination of resources. State and local legislation along with public and private service administrators organized resources for children and adolescents in need and their families.

The resounding organizational success of the demonstration projects led to the federal funding of the Center for Mental Health Services Comprehensive Community Mental Health Services for Children and Their Families (CMHS-CCMHSC) grant program, which is now working to propagate this approach to the rest of the country. Despite the organizational success, the question remained as to whether the clinical care of this population had improved. To answer this question, a sampling was done of the actual clinical care provided by the RWJ-MHSPY sites (Solnit, Adnopoz, Saxe, Gardner, & Fallon, 1997). This sampling revealed important observations about the successes of this work, as well as the challenges that remain.

A CLINICAL EXAMPLE

An example from one RWJ-MHSPY site is illustrative (Solnit et al., 1997).

Lonny was a physically imposing fifteen year old, outsizing even the largest staff by at least fifty pounds and a few inches in height. Up to this point in life, he had over a dozen arrests for auto theft, petty theft, robbery, drug charges, and resisting arrest. He had made suicidal gestures and was reported to be stubborn and inarticulate. Previous residential placement at age ten for a year had yielded little gain. Previous involvement with child protective services as well as mental health (both individual and family therapy), law enforcement, and juvenile justice had been unsuccessful.

At age fourteen, he was enrolled in a system of care with a residential setting, staff to work with his mother, and juvenile justice involvement, which included a fifteen-year veteran probation officer. Because Lonny was intimidating toward residential staff, the probation officer used a detention center as a temporary time-out for a few days several times to get Lonny back under control. This informal use of juvenile hall, although not in accord with standard policy, allowed Lonny to begin to improve his functioning. This cooperative work in the best interest of the child provided enhanced efficacy over what had been attempted previously by juvenile justice and mental health alone.

By seven months into his residential placement, Lonny held a leadership position in the therapeutic community, was getting A's and B's in school, and was feeling good about his work. His participation in group therapy also went well, although individual and family therapy did not proceed as smoothly. In a presentation of this case, it was clear that the probation officer had developed a significant influential alliance with Lonny to the point that time-outs in the detention center were no longer necessary.

Nine months after enrollment, because of funding issues, Lonny was discharged from the residential treatment center, and although he was doing well, it was apparent to mental health staff that he had not consolidated his gains. It was expected that returning to the environment from which he came would likely lead to a recurrence of at least some of his previous illegal activities, especially since few gains had been made within his family system.

Months after discharge, with repeated probation violations and school attendance waning, his probation officer felt betrayed by Lonny. The probation officer began to falter in his ability to maintain his previously excellent rapport with Lonny. This officer previously had gone to bat for Lonny, going against policy to do what was right for Lonny. And even at this time, he was able to come up with strategies that would continue to support the healthy part of Lonny (for example, to see Lonny every day and get him off to school every morning); however, the probation officer was unable to bring himself to go to bat for Lonny yet again and carry through on his own recommendations. He eventually resigned from the case. The subsequent probation officer made preparations to send Lonny to the state prison system, a most discouraging outcome for a potentially hopeful case.

The initial successes and the final difficulties in this case highlight the benefits and challenges that this coordinated system of care had on Lonny's clinical care. Because of the system of care, a number of elements were coordinated: the residential care setting and staff, expert mental health clinicians, and juvenile justice personnel. His RWJ-MHSPY team developed an intuitive understanding of Lonny's needs and attempted to advocate for appropriate and sorely needed resources, including a structured environment outside the family and recruitment of the mother in the advocating process.

In the initial successes, it was the probation officer in particular who was able to engage and develop a significant influential alliance with Lonny. The probation officer used techniques he had learned from his own experience. But it was only together that the team was able to accomplish what individual providers, including mental health and juvenile justice personnel, had not been able to do on their own previously.

The success of this case highlights the important contributions from both the creative adaptation that grew out of necessity and experience (as with the probation officer) and the understanding derived from the collective knowledge and experience developed in the fields of mental health. In fact, the RWJ-MHSPY experiment repeatedly highlighted the tremendous importance and usefulness of collaboration of various personnel and disciplines. The cooperative tension created by the broad knowledge base, diverse background experiences, and viewpoints allowed a new picture to fall into view for these cases individually and for the field as a whole.

This approach highlights two important viewpoints. First is the child as an individual in the context of his development. What are the specific child's capacities (psychological and physical), and where is he in relation to his potential? For example, what was Lonny's ability to relate to others? At the beginning of his residential treatment, Lonny was unable to relate to the staff other than as threatening impediments to what he felt he wanted. Later, he was much more appropriate developmentally; he was able to work out with staff (and even peers in group therapy) a relationship that was much more satisfying to both him and others. This viewpoint incorporates the knowledge and technologies brought by psychology, psychiatry, and medicine where the individual is considered as an independent functioning unit. These fields ask, "How is this individual functioning?" and "What interventions to the individual will assist him to function better?"

The second viewpoint is the child in the context of his environment: family, school, and community. What unique role can this child identify for himself and be accepted by his community? Lonny's role was initially as a delinquent, bully, and violator of others' rights. In the context of the residential treatment setting, he became a student and a community leader who could excel. The difficulty came when his environment was unable to continue to support this role for him. This viewpoint, which incorporates the understanding that no individual, especially a child or adolescent, functions as an independent entity, is the foundation for family therapy and public services such as child welfare, child protective services, and juvenile justice.

Together, these two viewpoints allow the melding of the medical model, the rehabilitation model, the family systems model, and an ecological model into one that takes into account the biological, psychological, family, social, and greater community. This model has been called the biopsychosocial model (Engel, 1980).

Lonny's case also demonstrates that although the organizational collaborations are necessary and important components of an effective system of care, they are not sufficient. After discharge from the residential placement, it was anticipated that Lonny's functioning might deteriorate. With this challenge, the probation officer's rapport and intuitive understanding of Lonny would have been invaluable to Lonny in his continued development. The probation officer himself, however, lost sight of what was healthy within Lonny. With the loss of this influential alliance, Lonny's healthy development was not likely to continue despite the continued organizational collaborations that the RWJ-MHSPY team offered.

A CLINICAL PERSPECTIVE IN SYSTEMS OF CARE

The design and implementation of a coordinated system of care is a mammoth task that involves political, governmental, funding, academic, informational, advocacy, and public and private agencies. Although the goal is to provide the highest-quality care to children, adolescents, and their families, it is not surprising that with such a large task involving so many people, many of them not trained in the psychological development and functioning of children and their families, there have been times that the goal has been lost sight of. If we are to pursue improved care in this area, it is advantageous to revisit this goal, assess how we are doing, and consider what other components are necessary to strengthen the clinical care of children and adolescents with serious emotional disturbances.

Direct face-to-face clinical work with children and adolescents and their families has as its ultimate goal assisting the individual in understanding how to operate as a content, productive individual within the bounds of society. An important intermediary goal for a disturbed child or adolescent is to get him or her back on track in psychological development and return to a level of functioning that approaches that of healthy peers (Freud, 1962).

The Holding Environment

In order to accomplish this goal, children must feel comfortable and motivated to grow. This requires meeting their physical needs of food, clothing, and shelter. Just as important, it also requires that children feel adequately safe (protected), loved (valued), and cared for (nurtured). In addition, the environment provides stimulation that is not overwhelming and challenges that they are able to meet. These challenges and stimulations promote growth and development of good self-esteem. When all goes well, the needs of children can be met by the environment, including parents, relatives, neighborhood, school, and community.

For the exceptional children, such as those with serious emotional disturbances, however, environmental resources are often not adequate. In addition, when those in the children's environment cannot determine what is either overstimulated or understimulated, when these children fail in the challenges that they encounter and continue to be frustrated, psychological development goes awry.

This is not to say that the environment is responsible for the psychiatric disorders seen in children. Rather, it is the fit between the child and the environment; the demands from the child for developmental support at times cannot be met by the environment. In these cases, specialized help is often needed in addition to parental care. This formulation of fit between the child and environment leads to a response suggesting that clinical therapeutic efforts can be directed toward both the environment and the child.

Clinical work usually begins by assisting those in the child's environment, such as parents and teachers, to create such an adequate environment. This holding environment keeps the child safe and provides appropriate physical and psychological supplies. For Lonny, a great deal of attention, creativity, and resources were necessary to create a setting to minimize the risk of harm for Lonny and the staff.

For this population of adolescents, systems of care have excelled in thinking about and creating such holding environments. It is the personnel such as Lonny's probation officer, who often have minimal formal training in child development, who have been the experts in designing creative holding environments. These personnel include law enforcement officers, probation officers, juvenile court judges, and even school bus drivers, to name just a few. Many of these dedicated front-line staff who have learned from their own experiences have devised techniques to work and build rapport with these difficult youth in a way that has eluded professionally trained mental health staff.

The Psychotherapeutic Process

This holding environment is necessary; however, it is many times not sufficient for a disturbed child to mature psychologically (Meyer, 1993). These children many times need assistance to negotiate the impediments that stand in the way of normal development. This individual therapeutic work with children has been overlooked many times and has led to some programs to substitute wraparound and ecological supports for individual work.

This oversight may have occurred because with environmental and psychotherapeutic support, many times the overt manifestations of the developmental difficulties will abate. However, if the child does not receive help in understanding his own inner state and in promoting his own inner growth, there will not be a progression toward healthy adulthood. When environmental supports are withdrawn, the difficulties may return if the child has not resumed normative development.

The residential treatment setting was able to support Lonny, but the underlying developmental difficulties had not resolved. For Lonny, as for most other adolescents, the goal of his development was to find his place in the world, to learn how to interact effectively with others, and to face his own physical and psychological strengths and limitations (Erikson, 1956). These conditions allow children to develop good self-esteem as well as build the capacity to manage frustration psychologically. On discharge from the residential treatment center, Lonny was working toward this goal but was not there yet. His community environment was not able to support this goal, but there was the possibility that in a continued therapeutic alliance, his probation officer might be able to assist him in this area.

This individual therapeutic work can be carried out in a variety of settings by various personnel using a number of approaches. A considerable body of knowledge regarding this process has been amassed in the fields of psychology, psychiatry, psychoanalysis, and social work. It contains considerable information regarding both normal and aberrant human psychological development and illuminates both strengths and weaknesses of a child.

The implementation of a therapeutic process requires not only knowledge but skill—a working knowledge of child development and effective techniques derived from experience. Although there are many workers who can be effective in initiating a therapeutic process, to sustain this process usually requires extensive training, supervision, and experience. Unfortunately, there is no one commonly accepted certification or licensing of this skill.

CLINICAL WORK IN SYSTEMS OF CARE

With this perspective in mind, it is useful to consider how to do clinical work in the context of a system of care. The knowledge base of clinical work comes from the fields of psychology, psychiatry, education, child development, medicine, psychoanalysis, criminology, social work, and public health. The knowledge base provides information as well as an organizing structure for compiling and processing information about the child and his environment. This structure includes assessment, formulation and intervention planning, monitoring of responses to interventions, and repeated assessment, revised formulation, and revision of planned interventions.

The Clinical Process

First and foremost, clinical care requires assessment, which lies at the foundation of all use of this knowledge base. This assessment occurs at initial contact and is ongoing throughout the clinical work with a child and family. The assessment has several facets:

• Collecting information such as developmental milestones, medical events, and interventions throughout the child and family's life, social history (including past and present friendships and acquaintances), school history (including grades, promotions, and failures), family history, behavior, and interpersonal relations, moves, losses, and other traumatic events.

• Direct evaluation of the child, including a general mental status exam and any detailed examinations that are deemed relevant after this general exam, including cognitive testing (IQ, aptitude, achievement), adaptive functioning, competence, psychiatric, and medical diagnostic testing.

• An evaluation of the environment, including stressors and supports that it provides. This would include an evaluation of the parents' ability to parent, other supports, threats, and stressors (including the physical living environment, cohabitants, neighbors, relatives, school setting, neighborhood, and availability of community services).

The formulation then calls for organizing this history and data and synthesizing it all into a coherent picture that is consistent with what is known about children, families, and the world in general. This clinical picture will offer hypotheses about contributors to the child's difficulties and environmental stressors, as well as the child's strengths and environmental supports. These strengths and weaknesses will suggest possible interventions, which will then be shaped into a plan, depending on available resources.

The initial formulation is only an approximation of who the child is and what his environment is like. Careful observation of the child's and environment's response to interventions made, as well as further data gathering, will lead to revisions of the formulation and a closer approximation to the actual child and environment.

This process goes on at a number of levels and requires personnel from different fields with different expertise. Which experts are involved and what their role in the treatment team are depends on the particular child and family. One example of an evaluation might require a pediatrician to assess for and treat possible medical problems such as endocrine abnormalities, sexually transmitted diseases, abnormal physical growth, occult brain diseases, or skin problems. A child psychiatrist might need to evaluate for disruptive behaviors such as are seen in oppositional defiant disorder and conduct disorder, anxieties such as are seen in separation anxiety, panic and agoraphobia disorders, mood disturbances as seen in depression, dysthymia, and bipolar disorder, and even psychotic disorders such as schizophrenia, and ultimately consider treatment options such as psychotherapy and the use of psychotropic medication. A psychologist, along with educational personnel, may need to perform formal testing to assess cognitive ability and personality functioning and address learning disorders. Juvenile court personnel may need to design a probation plan including drug testing. There may be others who assess the parents' ability to parent, triage siblings, and the like.

Roles in the Clinical Process

Each of these roles requires particular expertise. Although some personnel may be qualified to assess and address a number of issues, personnel are not interchangeable. For example, while many child psychiatrists are trained to assess the individual as well as the family, they are not qualified to do psychological or educational testing. Many times an understanding of particular areas of the child's life may require the cooperative work of multiple personnel; for example, the assessment of a child's neighborhood and cultural context may require a family advocate and a child psychiatrist together.

Translation of Clinical Knowledge

Use of this knowledge base requires translation, which must occur in two ways. The first is taking clinical observations of the individual child and his setting and organizing them and interpreting them into a meaningful picture that fits with what we know about the development and functioning of children and adolescents. The second is using the clinical picture that was developed to formulate interventions that will be effective with the particular child in his particular setting.

These translations to and from the child (and family) are particularly important and sensitive aspects of the therapeutic process in systems of care and require careful attention. There are two major synergistic reasons for the need for such careful attention. First, children and families in these settings are usually far from the mainstream, which sometimes means having different cultural, ethnic, or familial beliefs; sometimes it means having exceptional origins, background, or development. These differences make misunderstandings and misinterpretations of expressions and actions quite likely. That is, a clinician can easily misinterpret observations because of his or her lack of familiarity with particular ethnic, cultural or familial settings.

Second, these adolescents and families usually feel quite disenfranchised, which leads, among other things, to a feeling of powerlessness. Because of this feeling of powerlessness, the children and families are much less likely to advocate on their own behalf and less able or willing to correct misunderstandings and misinterpretations. This is why empowerment has become such an important concept in the system of care literature.

In fact, the CASSP principles of being child centered, family focused, and culturally sensitive (Stroul & Friedman, 1996) are built around these vulnerabilities. In systems of care, effective therapeutic process means using our knowledge and understanding of psychological development and at the same time keeping in perspective the individual, family, and cultural environments with all of their supports as well as risks, demands, and pressures.

Psychotherapeutic Work

The setting for clinicians in a system of care has other similarities as well as differences when compared with a traditional setting of an office or clinic. The most striking difference between the two settings is that in a system of care, much more care, attention, time, and resources are directed toward the design and implementation of a holding environment for the child when compared with a traditional setting.

The individual therapeutic work in systems of care also has similarities as well as differences when compared with traditional settings. In working with an individual child in a system of care, as in any other clinical situation, there is not a clear understanding of that child at the beginning of the clinical work. Data are gathered in an initial assessment, a formulation and treatment plan is derived, and then more data are gathered as the child is observed in response to the treatment. A new treatment plan is devised, and the cycle begins again. Each cycle yields an improved clinical picture.

The focus in both settings is on understanding where the child is in his development in terms of managing anxieties, frustrations, and interpersonal relationships and offering an interpersonal environment that is safe, caring, and at the same time developmentally and appropriately challenging and stimulating.

In the initial assessment phase of the therapeutic process, traditional settings are more appropriate for patients with a more normative background who, by virtue of their coming to the office, demonstrate their ability to advocate for themselves and their families. But children with serious emotional disturbances and their families in systems of care come to the therapeutic process very much more unknown, since a mainstream, normative history, background, development, and values cannot be assumed. System of care clinicians must more actively assess this background and, when information is unavailable, consider the possibility that significant information is missing.

To offset this disadvantage, clinicians working in a coordinated system of care have ready access to multiple treatment team members who can gather data from outside sources, provide background information (cultural, ethnic, neighborhood, familial), and offer different interpretations and points of view regarding the child and family. For example, family advocates many times have insights into cultural differences that others on the treatment team do not.

This team approach has the potential to create a full and complex clinical picture quickly. Although these multiple sources of data and multiple formulations can be cumbersome, the persistent effort at collecting and integrating the data and formulations can lead to a powerful process. Formally, this work of integrating can be done in a clinical case conference or team meeting. Such meetings can be scheduled as appropriate—usually two or three times a year per child. The clinical case conference offers a forum for the treatment team members to share the information they have gathered and observations they have made of the child or adolescent and to coordinate the work with the child among the various personnel present. Records about the child and family—for example from the school, welfare, child protective services, hospitals, and clinics—can be brought to these meetings and shared (Solnit et al., 1997).

Although this presentation of the data can be time-consuming, sometimes taking two hours or longer, it pieces together an important picture that many times has never been clear to the child or adolescent, family, or providers. With time for discussion and an experienced clinician to guide the questions, discussion, and interpretations, a clinical picture of the child and his environment develops in a way that becomes a shared understanding among the team members.

This shared clinical picture is key to a coherent, coordinated collaboration among the team members because it drives the treatment, which further supports data gathering and new formulations. In this way, the assessment and formulation becomes a group process. This group process depends on more than just collaboration and cooperation. It is dependent on good interpersonal relationships among team members.

With the completion of the initial assessment and formulation, a key part of the therapeutic process, treatment moves to center stage. Techniques of treatment vary considerably, even within settings (office based versus systems of care).

Treatment usually follows from the clinical picture view and must be planned with an understanding of the cultural, ethnic, familial, and personal background in mind. Treatment, which might be labeled psychotherapy in a traditional setting, might consist of a patient who presents himself because he is troubled by feelings, thoughts, or even actions. The treatment is then an exploration to understand these feelings, thoughts, or actions in a developmental context. This exploration might lead to connections with other thoughts, feelings, and memories; an understanding of painful feelings; realizations of maladaptive patterns of behavior; and trials of new types of behavior first in thought and then in action.

This particular version of individual psychotherapy might incorporate a psychodynamic approach. There are, of course, many other approaches as well, including cognitive and behavioral ones. Each has many variations in terms of styles, techniques, frequencies, and intensities. In the context of individual therapies, psychopharmacology also needs to be mentioned.

In a system of care setting, the focus tends to be more external to the child and family, and although the child or adolescent might be in considerable psychological pain, the presenting disturbances tend to involve others in system of care settings. That is, rather than the presenting problems lying just within the child, there are others who are motivated to have the child treated: people within the child's school, family, and community. With this presentation, traditional psychotherapeutic techniques are many times not useful initially, although there may be opportunities to use them as the child or adolescent becomes better able to locate the difficulties within the self.

To assist in this process, other forms of therapy that are not for the individual child may be used more commonly in systems of care than in an office-based practice. These forms of therapy include family, group, and milieu therapy and use the disturbances surrounding the child to understand and modify the presenting difficulties.

One classic set of techniques that can be successfully used in a system of care setting was first developed by Aichhorn (1935). This work, although based on psychoanalytic principles, focuses on the interpersonal relationship and the rapport that develops between clinician and child or adolescent. The clinician provides developmentally appropriate stimulation and challenges that promote the progression of healthy psychological maturation of the child or adolescent and, eventually, improved self-esteem. This type of treatment can be provided within the milieu of detention, hospital, group home, or somewhere else.

Systems of care also offer an entire team to contribute to the treatment process. The multiple personnel who work with the child or adolescent present multiple opportunities to track changes in the client's environment. These data can be critical in monitoring the child's or adolescent's development and response to therapeutic interventions.

There are opportunities to have others on the treatment team offer interventions. In some cases, the patient may choose as primary contact a member of the treatment team not formally trained in psychotherapeutic work. If the team supports this choice, then it is incumbent on the clinician to provide the necessary supervision and support.

For Lonny, the probation officer had a central therapeutic role. At the outset, he functioned quite well, stimulating and challenging Lonny at an appropriate level. The failure in this case occurred when the necessary support and supervision were not there for the probation officer in an expected time of difficulty. It is particularly at difficult times, when the therapeutic process has gone on for some time, that more clinical expertise is necessary to carry a case through.

Because systems of care have had to focus so heavily on organizational aspects and the components of a holding environment, clinical expertise has not necessarily been emphasized in the past. The array of child care personnel from diverse disciplines and backgrounds filling so many roles within systems of care has also created confusion as to the strengths and utility of each of the team members.

The purpose of a team is to involve all personnel involved with the child in the decision-making process. Included in this process must be child care workers, personnel from the juvenile justice system (when involved), representatives from the educational system, representatives from the family, as well as expert-level clinicians trained and experienced in child development, child assessment, and child psychotherapy.

Systems of care have provided necessary and vital components in the care of children and adolescents. These systems of care are complicated and require many personnel with many roles and responsibilities attached to these personnel. However, without clinical expertise and technologies, the organizational components are not sufficient for effective care. Experience from systems of care demonstrations projects such as the RWJ-MHSPY and CMHC-CCMHS has taught us much, but there is clearly much more to learn in the care of children with serious emotional disturbances.

References

Aichhorn, A. (1935). *Wayward youth.* New York: Viking Press.

Engel, G. L. (1980). The clinical application of the biopsychosocial model. *American Journal of Psychiatry, 137,* 535–544.

Erikson, E. (1956). The problem of ego identity. *Journal of the American Psychoanalytic Association, 4,* 56–121.

Freud, A. (1962). Assessment of childhood disturbances. *Psychoanalytic Study of the Child, 17,* 149–158.

Meyer, W. S. (1993). In defense of long-term treatment: On the vanishing holding environment. *Social Work, 38,* 571–578.

Solnit, A. J., Adnopoz, J., Saxe, L., Gardner, J., & Fallon, T. (1997). Evaluating systems of care for children. *American Journal of Orthopsychiatry, 67,* 554–567.

Stroul, B., & Friedman, R. (1996). *A system of care for children and youth with severe emotional disturbances.* Washington, DC: Georgetown University Child Development Center, Child and Adolescent Service System Program Technical Assistance Center.

CHAPTER SEVEN

Pharmacotherapy in Systems of Care for Children's Mental Health

Andres J. Pumariega
Theodore Fallon

Systems of care for children's mental health have the promise of making child mental health services accessible and effective for the majority of children in the United States. The effectiveness of these systems is not only a result of the coordination of agencies and the integration of interventions in the child's natural environment, but also due to the advances in treatment itself. One important treatment to consider is psychopharmacology, the use of psychoactive medications (Jensen, Hoagwood, & Petti, 1996).

The use of psychoactive medication in general child psychiatric practice has always been surrounded by some controversy since its inception over fifty years ago, with the first reported use of stimulants for hyperactivity (Bradley, 1937). Some have expressed concern about the excessive and unnecessary use of psychotropic medication with children to compensate for inadequate resources for psychosocial interventions or inadequate time and skills available to teachers or parents in dealing with disruptive behaviors (Barkley, 1988). Some have voiced a fear of "medicalizing" and "pathologizing" childhood behavior, thus either stigmatizing the child or disempowering parents, teachers, and children themselves. Due to the technical nature of medical decision making, parents and children may be excluded from the decision-making process (Gadow, 1997). Heightening these concerns are the sociopolitical and religious agendas often played out around the use of pharmacotherapy, with alarmist overtones that complicate the legitimate concerns of families and child-serving professionals.

In spite of these concerns and vagaries, however, psychotropic medication use in children has increased over the past two decades.

In terms of the effect of the medications themselves, there have been concerns about short-term side effects, the lack of data on the long-term impact of the developing child, and potential for addiction (Jensen et al., 1999). Research on the benefits and risks of psychopharmacological treatment for children is still in its early stages. In recent years, however, an increasing number of well-designed clinical trials of psychotropic agents with children and adolescents have led to a clearer understanding of these agents. Weisz and Jensen (1999) report more than eighty psychopharmacological trials with children and adolescents for disorders not involving attention deficit hyperactivity disorder (ADHD) and over two hundred trials for ADHD itself. This compares to over four hundred published child psychotherapy clinical trials. They found significant limitations of these studies. In general, the studies are small, have little or no long-term follow-up, give insufficient attention to age, gender, and ethnic differences, and lack standardized, verifiable outcomes. Only a few studies, mostly in the treatment of ADHD, compare the relative benefits of medication with other available treatments. Jensen and Payne (1998), in their review of fifteen well-controlled studies comparing medication and psychotherapeutic approaches in the treatment of ADHD, found that medication treatment alone was consistently superior to behavioral treatments alone in treating ADHD symptoms. However, medication treatment was found to be equivalent to behavioral treatments in addressing non-ADHD types of behavior.

The field is moving toward the state of multisite trials examining comparative efficacy and effectiveness. The Multimodal Treatment Study of ADHD (MTA Cooperative Group, 1999a, 1999b) has been the largest (579 participants) and longest (fourteen months) comparative study of pharmacological and behavioral treatment for children so far. This study randomized participants to medication alone, behavioral therapy alone, combination treatment, and usual community treatment. Medication and combination treatment were found to be more effective than behavioral therapy alone or the usual community treatment, a surprising finding given that over two-thirds of community treatment involved medication at some point. Experimental medication treatment may have been more effective since it adhered to a strict protocol of careful monitoring of adherence, thrice-daily dosing, regular coordination with teachers, and sufficient time during appointments for close communication and education with the child and family as well as careful adjustment. Although combination therapy was slightly better than medication alone, this difference was significant in focused areas, such as parent-child relations, academic achievement, and reducing coexisting symptoms of anxiety. A similar study under way is evaluating the comparative effectiveness of pharmacotherapy and cognitive-behavioral therapy for the treatment of depression in adolescents (March, 1999).

These two studies support the idea that combined treatments (medication and behavioral therapies) may allow clinical benefits to be achieved at lower medication dosages. Ultimately, studies may point to an understanding that pharmacotherapy and psychotherapy address different symptoms and provide different benefits. This conclusion supports the importance of individualization of treatment interventions, which makes inherent sense in the treatment of children with serious emotional or mental disorders and is consistent with systems of care principles.

PSYCHOPHARMACOLOGICAL INTERVENTIONS

For the purposes of this brief review, psychotropic medications are grouped in the following categories: tricyclic antidepressants, monoamine oxidase inhibitors, newer antidepressants, mood stabilizers, stimulants, neuroleptics and antipsychotics, antihypertensive agents, anxiolytic agents, and miscellaneous agents.

Tricyclic Antidepressants

The tricyclic antidepressants (TCAs) include amitriptyline (Elavil), clomipramine (Anafranil), desipramine (Norpramin), imipramine (Tofranil), and nortriptyline (Pamelor). Prior to the development of newer antidepressants, the TCAs were the most widely used drugs for the treatment of depression. Because of their lower cost, they are still widely used in spite of their relative lack of scientific evidence for efficacy (especially in depression) and significant side effects. They have also been used in a variety of childhood clinical syndromes, including enuresis, pavor nocturnes (night terrors), separation anxiety and school phobia, and disruptive behavior disorders that fail to respond to stimulants (Geller, Reising, Leonard, Riddle, & Walsh, 1999). Although they were effective with adults, double-blind, placebo-controlled trials with TCAs have failed to demonstrate efficacy in the treatment of depression with children and adolescents, except for one study of intravenous clomipramine (Sallee, Vrindavanam, Deas-Nesmith, Carson, & Sethuraman, 1997). Tricyclic antidepressants are well known to produce a high incidence of adverse effects, especially with children. These include dry mouth, blurred vision, constipation, drowsiness, ataxia, anxiety, insomnia, nightmares, confusion, decreased cognition, and seizures. In addition, TCAs can precipitate delusions and worsen psychosis in patients with schizophrenia. TCAs are potentially life threatening in the case of an overdose, resulting in seizures, coma, respiratory depression, hypotension, cardiac arrhythmia, acute renal failure, and death. Children are more vulnerable than adults to the toxic effects of TCAs because they produce a greater proportion of cardiotoxic or nephrotoxic metabolites (Pumariega, Muller, & Rivers-Buckeley, 1982; Geller et al., 1999). The TCAs are now primarily used for children who do not respond to other medications.

Their use in children should be accompanied with careful monitoring of vital signs, electrocardiogram, and blood levels.

Monoamine Oxidase Inhibitors

The monoamine oxidase inhibitors (MAOIs) are another class of antidepressants that has been primarily reserved for treatment-resistant depression with adults; MAOIs have potentially toxic side effects due to their interaction with foods high in the amino acid tyramine (which include many wines, cheeses, and nuts). These side effects make the risk associated with their use in children and adolescents far outweigh any potential benefits. Newer forms of these agents, which do not have the same degree of side effects, are showing efficacy in treating depressed adults (Elmslie, Walkup, Plizka, & Ernst, 1999).

Newer Antidepressants

This category includes all nontricyclic, non-MAOI antidepressants. The main class of these newer agents is the selective serotonin reuptake inhibitors (SSRIs), whose relatively high therapeutic index has led to their widespread use. This group includes fluoxetine hydrochloride (Prozac), paroxetine (Paxil), sertraline (Zoloft), fluvoxamine (Luvox), citalopram (Celexa), and trazodone (Desyrel). These agents are currently in the process of undergoing Food and Drug Administration (FDA) trials for children and adolescents.

Double-blind, placebo-controlled trials studies of SSRIs in the treatment of children with depression have shown efficacy greater than placebo (Simeon, Dinicola, Ferguson, & Copping, 1990; DeVane & Salle, 1996; Elmslie et al., 1997; Keller et al., 2001). The SSRIs are being increasingly used to treat children with anxiety disorders. Both fluvoxamine and sertraline are FDA approved for the treatment of obsessive-compulsive disorder in children, with large multisite placebo-controlled trials supporting efficacy as well as other placebo-controlled studies (Elmslie et al., 1999). A small placebo-controlled study supports the use of fluoxetine in selective mutism, which is often associated with social anxiety disorder in young children (Black, Udhe, & Tancer, 1992). Noncontrolled studies have suggested effectiveness in the cognitive aspects of these disorders, such as worrying, rumination, decreased concentration, and repetitive or intrusive thinking or behaviors (Murdoch & McTarish, 1992; Bernstein, Borchardt, & Perwien, 1996). The SSRIs have also been demonstrated to diminish obsessive-compulsive and stereotypical behaviors and to improve social reciprocity and learning in children and adults with autism and other developmental disorders in uncontrolled and a few controlled studies (McDougle, 1998; Elmslie et al., 1999). Trazodone, with its longer-acting profile, may be used as a sleep aid in children who have problems with both initial and intermittent insomnia.

The SSRIs have a relatively lower side-effect profile and easy once-a-day administration due to longer serum half-life. The most frequent adverse effects are nausea, headache, diarrhea or loose stools, insomnia, dry mouth, and, predominantly in males, sexual dysfunction. Adverse effects appear to decrease in frequency and severity with chronic dosing. The SSRIs also appear to be safer than TCAs in acute overdose, with some reports showing no adverse sequelae and others showing more serious effects, such as tachycardia, hypertension, hallucinations, and coma.

Newer agents, such as buproprion (Wellbutrin), venlafaxine (Effexor), nefazodone (Scrzone), and mirtazapine (Remeron), have dual adrenergic and serotonergic action, with the balance of these often related to dose level. They are being increasingly used in treatment-resistant depression as alternatives to the MAOIs and the TCAs. These have side effect profiles that are even more favorable than those of the SSRIs. The results of small trials with children and adolescents so far are mixed, but larger-scale studies are underway (Elmslie et al., 1999). Buproprion has demonstrated efficacy in the treatment of ADHD in double-blind, controlled studies, though its effect is somewhat less robust than that of stimulants. It is being rapidly considered as a second-line agent in the treatment of ADHD (Casat, Pleasants, Schroeder, & Parler, 1989; Elmslie et al., 1999).

There is conflicting evidence of the benefits for anorexia nervosa from antidepressants, though there is some indication of reduced frequency of bingeing and purging resulting from treatment with the TCAs, the SSRIs, and the MAOIs (Jacobi, Dahme, & Rustenbach, 1997). Buproprion is contraindicated in the treatment of bulimia due to the risk of seizures (Steiner & Lock, 1998).

Mood Stabilizers

Lithium has been considered the treatment of choice for bipolar illness (Geller et al., 1999; Ryan, Bhatara, & Perel, 1999). It has also been used for impulse control symptoms (such as aggressive and violent behaviors) and as an adjunctive treatment in major psychiatric disorders, such as treatment-resistant depression and schizophrenia (Strober, Freeman, Rigali, Schmidt, & Diamond, 1992). Lithium has multiple potential side effects, including gastrointestinal, neurological, renal, endocrine, and cardiovascular effects, as well as a high overdose lethality (Ryan et al., 1999).

Anticonvulsants (antiseizure medications) are used in a variety of psychiatric syndromes, including impulse control symptoms, severe anxiety disorders (especially posttraumatic stress disorder, PTSD), and bipolar disorders (Ryan et al., 1999). Medications in this category typically include carbamazepine (Tegretol), phenytoin (Dilantin), and valproic acid (Depakote), with newer agents such as gabapentin (Neurontin), lamotrigine (Lamictal), oxcarbamazepine (Trileptal), and topiramate (Topomax) coming into increasing use among children and adolescents. Although it was impossible to tell if these medications were used to treat seizures or impulse disorders or to stabilize moods, or some combination thereof, children taking these medications are reported to demonstrate improvement in such behavioral and emotional symptoms. However, there are no controlled studies on the psychiatric use of anticonvulsants in children and limited safety data. There are some promising uncontrolled studies of valproate as a mood stabilizer (Ryan et al., 1999). Valproate and carbamazepine have the added beneficial feature that blood levels can be measured, with established norms for therapeutic ranges and toxic levels. Severe skin rashes, tremor, confusion, and weight gain are among the many side effects known for these agents. There are reports associating the use of valproate with a metabolic syndrome characterized by obesity, hyperinsulinemia, lipid abnormalities, polycystic ovaries, and hyperandrogenism, particularly in younger women being treated for seizures (Isovarji, Laatikainen, Pakarinen, Juntunen, & Myllyla, 1993), though its generalizability to psychiatric populations is still unknown.

Stimulants

Stimulants have been the first-choice treatment for attentional problems and hyperactivity. Methylphenidate (Ritalin) and dextroamphetamine (Dexedrine) are the main stimulant agents used in the treatment of ADHD in children, both of which are shorter-acting agents. Pemoline (Cylert) and Adderall (a combination of various amphetamines), which are longer-acting stimulant preparations, are useful alternatives for nonresponders or children who require more extensive symptom coverage. Longer-acting preparations of methylphenidate (Ritalin SR, Metadate, and Concerta) and Adderall (Adderall XR), which use sustained release delivery systems, are also available.

Stimulant medication continues to be the most effective treatment available for ADHD. In more than 170 controlled short-term studies involving over five thousand school-age children with ADHD, 70 percent of participants responded to a single stimulant medication (Schachar & Tannock, 1993). Short-term studies support response to the most salient symptoms of ADHD. However, few show across-the-board symptom resolution and long-term benefits in academic achievement and social skills. Stimulant medication is superior to placebo, other drug classes, and nonpharmacological treatments. Four large prospective long-term studies also support the long-term effectiveness of stimulant medications, including the recent National Institute of Mental Health's Collaborative Multi-Site Multi-Modal Treatment Study of Children with ADHD (Greenhill et al., 1996; Greenhill, Halperin, & Abikoff, 1999; National Institutes of Health, 1999; MTA Cooperative Group, 1999a). There is considerable concern about possible overprescription of stimulants for the treatment of ADHD; however, available data suggest a mixed picture of both over- and underdiagnosis and treatment (Greenhill et al., 1999).

Common side effects from the stimulants include decreased appetite, dizziness, drowsiness, lack of sleep, stomachache, headache, tics and other nervous movements, anxiety, disinterest in others, euphoria, nightmares, sadness, and staring into space. Most of these side effects are dosage related and subject to individual differences. Side effects, however, appear to be mild, short-lived (except possibly tics), and responsive to dosage adjustments, making the stimulants among the safest pharmacological agents with children. Side effects can be reduced by giving the child small dosages at the beginning of therapy and working up slowly to the smallest dosage that achieves meaningful results. Earlier reports of growth retardation with the stimulants have not been proven in controlled studies, with any effect on growth being related to its effect on appetite. Studies have not supported a greater risk of abuse or dependence by children using stimulants, although these can be diverted for abuse by peers (Greenhill et al., 1999).

Narcolepsy, a rare sleep disorder that involves continual involuntary transition into sleep at all hours of the day, is another condition for which stimulants are efficacious agents (Dahl, Holttum, & Trubnick, 1994).

Neuroleptics and Antipsychotics

These medications are used for children with major psychiatric disorders that are characterized by mania (such as bipolar disorder), schizophrenia, and psychosis associated with other psychiatric disorders. Their use has been reported for children with severe impulse control or disruptive disorders, children with serious self-injurious behaviors, and children with severe anxiety disorders (such as posttraumatic disorders and obsessive-compulsive disorders (Gadow, 1997).

The older antipsychotics such as chlorpromazine (Thorazine), thioridazine (Mellaril), haloperidol (Haldol), trifluoperazine (Stelazine), perphenazine (Trilafon), thiothixene (Navane), loxapine (Loxitane), and fluphenazine (Prolixin) have been proven efficacious in the treatment of the psychotic symptoms associated with schizophrenia in a number of controlled studies with children. However, these agents have significant short-term side effects, such as oversedation, Parkinsonian-like extrapyramidal symptoms, anticholinergic-like side effects (such as dry mouth, blurred vision, difficulty with urination, and effects on cardiac conduction), and neuroleptic malignant syndrome (the acute onset of muscle rigidity, fever, severe extrapyramidal symptoms, tachycardia, tachypnea, diaphoresis, altered consciousness, and altered blood chemistries, which is potentially fatal). They are also not particularly efficacious in addressing negative symptoms in schizophrenia, such as amotivation and cognitive blunting. Tardive dyskinesia, an involuntary movement disorder that can become irreversible, is associated with chronic use or high dosage of these agents. Children and adolescents may be at higher risk for tardive dyskinesia as a result of their possible use over a longer life span. As a result of these adverse effects, these medications are less frequently prescribed for ongoing use. They continue to have a role in the management of acute psychosis, especially in their injectable form, and as second-line agents (Campbell, Rapaport, & Simpson, 1999).

The newer atypical antipsychotics, such as risperidone (Risperidal), olanzapine (Zyprexa), quetiapine (Seroquel), ziprazidone (Geodon), and clozapine (Clozaril), may prove more useful in the treatment of schizophrenia and psychotic symptoms in general given both their relatively lower side effects and better efficacy in treating negative symptoms (Campbell et al., 1999). Clozapine has already been demonstrated superior to haloperidol in one controlled study of children across all measures of psychosis, although agranulocytosis, neutropenia, and seizures were significant problems for one-third of participants (Kumra et al., 1996). Reports of new-onset diabetes, obesity, and elevated lipids with these medications in adults indicate that significant caution should be exercised with children, especially with a higher dosage or long-term use. In open studies, risperidone is also showing similar promise but is associated with high rates of extrapyramidal symptoms and weight gain (Armenteros, Whitaker, Welikson, Stedge, & Gorman, 1997).

Antipsychotics are the most frequently used agents for the reduction of target symptoms such as stereotypies, aggression, self-injurious behavior, and hyperactivity in children with autism and developmental disorders. Haloperidol has demonstrated efficacy in addressing these symptoms in a number of controlled studies, and thiothixine, pimozide, and risperidone have demonstrated promise in uncontrolled trials (Perry, Pataki, Munoz-Silva, Armenteros, & Silva, 1997). Antipsychotic agents have been used to manage severe aggressiveness, with haloperidol, molindone, and thioridazine demonstrating efficacy in controlled studies and many increasingly using the atypical antipsychotics in low dosages. Some antipsychotic medications have demonstrated efficacy in controlled studies of the treatment of tic disorders, including antipsychotics, such as haloperidol and pimozide (Campbell et al., 1999).

Antihypertensive Agents

These agents were originally developed to control hypertension, but now have many psychiatric applications. Beta blockers (propranolol) and alpha-adrenergic agonists have been suggested for use in controlling anxiety symptoms. No systematic studies of a beta blocker or alpha agonists have been completed with children and adolescents with anxiety disorders, though uncontrolled studies are promising in the treatment of PTSD and hyperventilation syndrome associated with panic disorder. These medications have associated risks of hypotension, bradycardia and other significant cardiac side effects, sedation, bronchoconstriction, hypoglycemia, and others, so they need to be carefully titrated (Riddle et al., 1999).

Clonidine (Catapres), one of the alpha-adrenergic antagonists, has been used as an adjunctive medication along with stimulants for children with ADHD, with significant difficulties with impulsivity and aggression, and with sleep disturbances (Riddle et al., 1999). Two small single-use controlled studies with children suggest efficacy over placebo but not superior to stimulants (Hunt, Minderas, & Cohn, 1985; Gunning, 1992). Its use in combination with stimulants for the control of aggression and impulsivity, though widespread, lacks supporting evidence from controlled studies, with only two uncontrolled studies supporting its use as an adjunct (Hunt, 1987; Comings, Comings, Tacket, & Li, 1990). It has also been suggested for the adjunctive management of Tourette's disorder (Riddle et al., 1999). There are four reported cases of sudden death with the combined use of clonidine and methylphenidate and about twenty emergency room reports of significant cardiac side effects, all thought to be related to a rare adverse interaction between these agents (Swanson et al., 1995). Guanefacine (Tenex), another alpha agonist, has been shown to have potential benefits in ADHD in uncontrolled trials, with potential advantages over clonidine in terms of longer half-life and greater selectiveness of action on attention (Riddle et al., 1999).

Anxiolytic Agents

This category of psychotropic drugs includes the benzodiazepines, the antihistamines, and buspirone. The few studies of benzodiazepines, such as alprazolam (Xanax) and clonazepam (Klonopin), in children and adolescents with anxiety disorders show mixed results. Uncontrolled studies are supportive of efficacy, but placebo-controlled studies show marginally better efficacy than placebo in sustained anxiety disorders, while they show efficacy with acute anxiety precipitated by medical procedures. Problems such as risks for abuse and dependence, sedation, withdrawal symptoms, and disinhibition of impulsive or aggressive behaviors and psychotic symptoms have been reported. Their short-term use may be considered in acute situational anxiety such as posttrauma or surgery, or in the short-term management of anxiety disorders prior to the onset of action of other agents (Riddle et al., 1999).

Antihistamines, such as diphenhydramine (Benadryl) and hydroxyzine (Atarax or Vistaril), are commonly used in treating anxiety and sleep disorder in children, though their effects are mostly those of general sedation. They are typically safe to administer, with oversedation and behavioral disinhibition being the most common side effects (Popper & Zimnitzky, 1995).

Buspirone, a serotonergic receptor agonist, has also been used for the treatment of anxiety disorders in adults and has some support from noncontrolled studies with children, but no controlled studies with children or adolescents have been reported (Riddle et al., 1999). Buspirone has anxiolytic but not sedative properties.

Other Miscellaneous Agents

Naltrexone, an opiate antagonist, was at first thought to be promising as a treatment for autism in noncontrolled studies, but in subsequent controlled studies, it was not found effective in autistic symptoms other than hyperactivity, with no effect on self-injurious behavior. However, its use has been reported in open trials for self-injurious behavior associated with other disorders, with some success (Sandman, 1991; Riddle et al., 1999).

Cyproheptadine (Periactin), a drug with antihistaminic and antiserotonergic properties, is an effective adjunct in the treatment of patients with the restricting type of anorexia nervosa, either as an appetite stimulant or through reduction of gastrointestinal malaise (Steiner & Lock, 1998).

Desmopressin acetate (DDAVP), an antidiuretic administered intranasally, has been shown to be effective in reducing enuresis. Electrolyte levels should be checked early in treatment (Thompson & Rey, 1995).

STUDIES ON THE USE OF PHARMACOTHERAPY IN SYSTEMS OF CARE

Systems of care present a unique context for medication use and therefore require separate consideration compared with other settings. For the most part, children and adolescents seen in the contexts of systems of care are those with the most serious emotional disturbances. For this population, psychotropic medication use is usually high (Cullinan, Gadow, & Epstein, 1987; Kaplan, Simms, & Busner, 1994; Wilk, Greenbaum, & Kline, 1995). For example, Landrum, Singh, Nemil, Ellis, and Best (1995), studying children at risk of residential placement, found that 40 percent were using medication. Holden and Santiago (2001) in a sampling of twenty-two of the federally funded Comprehensive Community Mental Health Services for Children (CCMHSC) and their families system of care sites found that over 47 percent of youth had taken medication for the six months preceding enrollment in a system of care. Hallfors, Fallon, and Watson (1998) in a sampling of the two Robert Wood Johnson funded—Mental Health Service Program for Youth (RWJ-MHSPY) sites, found that 40 percent of Children enrolled in this project were on medication.

Even within the population of serious emotional disturbed children and adolescents, however, medication use varied considerably. For example, Landrum et al. (1995) found that 56 percent of children identified by school personnel as having serious emotional disturbances (SED) were on medication, compared with the overall use rate of 40 percent. Holden and Santiago (2001) found that 62 percent of males versus 38 percent of females used medication, while Hallfors et al. (1998) found girls more than twice as likely to receive medication when compared with boys. In comparing use of medication in urban versus rural sites, Hallfors et al. (1998) found a rate of 37 percent and 45 percent respectively, although this difference may have been due to different demographics of the population. When this was examined in detail, they found that being in special education (2.79), female (1.82), in a restrictive placement (1.79), Caucasian (1.60), and younger (1.12) all had a higher prevalence of taking medication (odds ratios in parenthesis).

Medication use appears most strongly associated with type of disorder. Hallfors et al. (1998) found that children with a diagnosis of psychosis, ADHD, or mood disorder were over six times as likely to receive medication when compared with the rest of the SED population. In contrast, only 25 percent of those with conduct disorder received medication (odds ratio 0.64). Holden and Santiago (2001) found medication use of 86 percent in those diagnosed with psychotic disorders, 83 percent in autism and other pervasive developmental disorders, and 78 percent in children with ADHD. The diagnoses least associated with medication use at these CMHS-CCHMSC sites were adjustment disorders (19 percent), substance abuse disorders (28 percent), and anxiety disorders (30 percent). Children and adolescents who took medication at these sites had higher levels of symptoms on the Child Behavior Checklist (Achenbach, 1991), a higher level of impairment on the Child and Adolescent Functional Assessment Scale (Hodges & Wong, 1996) except in the area of substance abuse, and lower levels of strengths as measured by the Behavioral and Emotional Rating Scale (Epstein & Sharma, 1998).

Holden and Santiago (2001) also found that children who had participated in particular treatment modalities (outpatient services, school-based services, day treatment, and residential treatment) received medications significantly more than those who had not, while there was no greater medication use in children who had used substance abuse services over those who had not. Prior history of physical abuse, sexual abuse, running away, and attempted suicide were all associated with higher rates of medication use, but prior substance abuse was not.

Hallfors et al. (1998) found that the most commonly prescribed medications were stimulants, followed by tricyclic medication, neuroleptic medications, and anticonvulsant medications. Anxiolytics and lithium were the drug types least frequently used. A single group of medications dominated any single diagnosis category in a few instances. For example, stimulants clearly dominated the ADHD diagnoses, although tricyclics were also used for these types of disorders. Neuroleptics were the most commonly used drug type within the psychotic disorders. Anticonvulsants were also heavily represented among the psychotic disorders and in children with ADHD plus other disorders.

The types of medications prescribed were quite different in rural versus urban sites in the Hallfors et al. study (1998). TCAs were most widely prescribed in the rural site (over half the children receiving medications were prescribed tricyclics), while less than one-fifth of medicated children in the urban site received TCAs. Newer antidepressants were used twice as often in the urban site than in the rural site. In the city, 35 percent of the children were prescribed antipsychotics, while only 13 percent of the children in the rural site received these agents. Lithium (12 percent versus 10 percent), stimulants (37 percent), anticonvulsants (24 percent), and antihypertensive agents (19 percent versus 16 percent) were prescribed relatively equally to children in the urban site and the rural site. Drugs categorized as anxiolytics were administered to 5 percent of urban children and 13 percent of rural children. A somewhat greater proportion of urban children (51 percent) had records of medication that fell into two or more drug types as compared with rural children (41 percent).

The most discouraging finding in the area of medication use among youth with SED was that although a large proportion are prescribed these medications, only a small proportion are seen for follow-up monitoring visits (Kelleher, Hohmann, & Larson, 1989; Wolraich et al., 1990; Hallfors et al., 1998). In addition, students with SED often receive medications in school settings despite the absence of school personnel who are well versed in the basics of psychopharmacology (Singh, Epstein, Luebke, & Singh, 1990).

In summary, although the literature on pharmacotherapy in the context of systems of care programs is still in its infancy, a number of trends are evident:

- Medication use in children served by these programs is widespread.

- Medication use in these programs is far from consistent, with wide variations in practice across diagnoses, regions and settings, gender, and race. For any given condition, a variety of medications is used. The only consistency is that children with a greater level of disturbance or symptomatology were more likely to receive medications.

- Psychiatrists and other prescribing physicians were not an integral part of care. Rather, they were treated as a separate service. This separation interferes with communication between physicians and the rest of the system of care and contributes to inadequate follow-up care and monitoring.

THE PRACTICE OF PHARMACOTHERAPY WITHIN SYSTEMS OF CARE

A number of important issues need to be addressed within system of care programs or settings in order to ensure the success and effectiveness of pharmacological interventions. Addressing these issues ensures that pharmacotherapy can be successfully integrated within other therapeutic modalities within this approach.

Value versus Limitations of Diagnosis

Psychiatric diagnostic nomenclature since the publication of the third edition of the *Diagnostic and Statistical Manual of Mental Disorders* (American Psychiatric Association, 1980), which is more descriptive and nontheoretical, has facilitated more specific testing of the efficacy of treatment modalities on different clinical populations, including medications, and has led to further advances in the development of such treatments (Gittleman-Klein, Spitzer, & Cantwell, 1978). However, these diagnostic systems are far from flawless. They are in constant evolution depending on advances in epidemiological, biological, and psychological research. The application of psychiatric diagnoses to children and adolescents also has limitations. The process of emotional and cognitive development is superimposed on the process of a disease or disorder, often leading to incomplete symptom expression or symptoms being expressed in different ways at different times in the child's life. The epidemiological study of childhood and adolescent disorders has also been limited in scope, particularly the longitudinal relationship between childhood-onset disorders and adult disorders. Some studies suggest clarity and continuity in childhood disorders into adulthood (Rao et al., 1995), while others support a lack of clarity and validity in clinical child diagnosis, especially in relation to the child's prognosis. In addition, children with SED served by agencies within systems of care are more likely to suffer from multiple comorbid diagnoses, especially comorbidities involving disruptive behavior disorders, substance abuse, and developmental disorders (Caron & Rutter, 1991; Pumariega, Johnson, & Sheridan, 1995; Atkins et al., 1999).

As a result of this lack of clarity, the severity of a child's condition may not be necessarily related to diagnosis, but may be more clearly expressed in his or her functional ability to successfully negotiate roles within the family, with peers, in school, and in other community settings. In fact, the difficulty in demonstrating the efficacy of certain pharmacological agents for certain disorders may be due to the difficulty with the diagnostic assessment of the population of children or adolescents studied, as with antidepressant treatment of adolescents (Geller et al., 1999). In addition, the efficacy of a pharmacological agent may not be predictive of diagnostic certainty for a given child. For example, the stimulants have nonspecific effects on attention and activity level (Rapoport et al., 1980). Therefore, response to these agents does not predict the diagnosis of ADHD, and many children who do not have this disorder may respond nonspecifically to these agents and others, complicating the diagnostic picture.

There are also problems with the reliability and validity of clinician-administered diagnoses, which often do not adhere to the criteria set by the diagnostic nosology. These limitations are overcome in research settings using structured diagnostic interviews such as the Diagnostic Interview Schedule for Children (Shaffer et al., 1996), the Diagnostic Interview for Children and Adolescents (Reich, Welner, & Herjanic, 1994), and the child version of the Schedule of Affective Disorders and Schizophrenia (Chambers et al., 1985), which systematically cover the DSM criteria and have established reliability and validity. These instruments are typically burdensome to use and costly for clinical settings, but a new generation of structured diagnostic interviews using computer algorithms that are self-administered can reduce this burden. The results of such interviews should always be matched with those of clinical assessment for clinical relevance and child-specific validity.

The benefits of diagnostic assessment can outweigh its limitations for children and adolescents who more clearly meet diagnostic criteria for one of multiple disorders, since these can guide clinicians on the pharmacological interventions that should be considered. Ultimately, the combination of diagnostic assessment and the determination of target symptoms can be most useful. A lack of diagnostic clarity should not serve as an absolute contraindication to pharmacological treatment, especially when behavioral, psychotherapeutic, and environmental interventions have been given adequate trials without sufficient results.

Value of Symptomatic and Functional Assessment

Symptomatically based assessment can overcome some of the limitations presented by the lack of clear diagnostic assessments. The careful selection and measurement of target symptoms is already the basis for measuring efficacy in pharmacological trials. Even when diagnostic assessments are the basis for treatment selection or study inclusion, establishing baseline and posttreatment measures of certain target symptoms (using symptom rating scales) is essential in order to establish treatment efficacy. However, there is a small but growing body of research that evaluates the use of psychopharmacological agents independent of diagnostic criteria, focusing on problem behaviors, such as aggression or self-injurious behaviors, and using target behaviors as the main criteria for both treatment selection and the determination of efficacy. This approach is similar to that used in the application of behavioral interventions (Pelham & Murphy, 1986). It may be useful in the treatment of children with SED, who do not easily fit diagnostic criteria outlined in the fourth edition of the *Diagnostic and Statistical Manual of Mental Disorders* (DSM-IV; American Psychiatric Association, 1994) but have clear target behaviors that interfere in daily functioning.

The use of target symptoms to evaluate the effectiveness of a pharmacological agent for a particular child or adolescent should parallel the assessment of the effectiveness of other treatment modalities. These should be integrated into the child's individualized treatment plan, with adequate assessment of baseline symptom and behavioral levels to allow for effective assessment of treatment response. The model that is most useful in this process is that of a single case design commonly used to evaluate behavioral interventions. Ideally, different interventions should be introduced sequentially, allowing for multiple baselines to be measured as interventions are added, though the exigencies of real-life needs and urgencies may preclude this approach at times.

Assessment in child mental health requires information from multiple observers in the evaluation of symptomatology, given the unreliable nature of the report of any single observer (parents, teachers, friends, or the child). The report of any single observer of a child's behavior usually has very limited reliability, but the composite picture from multiple reports is often highly reliable. A number of instruments have been designed to collect and score multi-informant data in an integrative manner for diagnostic assessment and treatment outcome monitoring. Empirically derived instruments, which measure behavioral symptomatology and social functioning, have been developed as a means of identifying children with significant emotional or behavioral disturbances and assessing them across different settings and environments. They offer a complementary alternative to diagnostically driven identification. In addition, they serve as an efficient means of screening populations of children, since many are directly self-administered by key informants, such as the child, parent, and teacher, without needing significant interviewer assistance. The Child Behavior Checklist/Teacher Report Form/Youth Self Report (Achenbach, 1991) is the prime example of this type of instrument. Instruments that evaluate a child's global level of functioning or across different life domains also have been found to be invaluable in assessing the effectiveness of treatment modalities.

Multi-informant information is also needed to evaluate specific types of behaviors or symptoms and their response to pharmacological intervention across different settings and environments. The Conners' Scales (for ADHD: Conners, 1969; Conners & Wells, 1997), the Children's Depression Rating Scale (Poznanski, Freeman, & Mokros, 1985), the Child Depression Inventory (Kovacs, 1981), the State-Trait Anxiety Scale (Spielberger, 1973), the Multidimensional Anxiety Scale for Children (March, Parker, Sullivan, Stallings, & Conners, 1997), and the Yale-Brown Obsessive Compulsive Scale for Children (Goodman & Price, 1992) are examples of instruments that measure specific areas of symptomatology. To determine efficacy and adjust dosages, these rating scales should be obtained from parents, teachers, other child service professionals, and youth. This information benefits the clinician, child services professionals, and parents by organizing information about drug responsiveness in ways that are most directly usable. The multiple informants available for a child involved in multiple child-serving systems can be important assets in such assessments, each providing an important perspective about the child's symptoms and level of functioning across different settings. Continuities or disparities in the child's behavior across different settings or contexts are invaluable in determining the use of different therapeutic modalities, such as whether the dosing of a medication should be changed temporally or whether a behavioral intervention should be implemented instead of adding a medication.

There are also additional limitations around the use of diagnosis and even symptomatology to evaluate the effectiveness of psychopharmacotherapy. Interventions may at times improve clinical symptoms but not address the child's level function in the significant areas of his or her life. This may be explained by the focus on negative behaviors or symptoms (such as aggression, hyperactivity, or sadness) in symptomatic and diagnostic assessment. The child's development of positive adaptive capacities or skills (such as social skills and delay of gratification) receives secondary or incidental attention, though they are equally important for true improvement and recovery. In children with SED, level of function is often more severely impaired than symptomatology would indicate. Therefore, the use of functional assessment measures to evaluate the child's baseline and progress is also critical. The Child and Adolescent Functional Assessment Schedule (Hodges & Wong, 1996) and the Children's Global Assessment of Function (Shaffer et al., 1983) are examples of such functional instruments, while the Behaviorial and Emotional Rating Scale (Epstein & Sharma, 1998) exemplifies functional measures that use a strength-based perspective.

Monitoring Psychopharmacological Treatment

When antidepressant or mood-stabilizing agents are used, the need for an adequate period to allow for buildup of serum levels should be considered. It often takes two to three weeks or even longer before adequate response can be seen. This is in contrast to shorter-acting agents such as the stimulants and short-acting benzodiazepines, with effects often seen in hours or days. Therefore, adequate treatment periods should be considered before discontinuing a medication. Another complicating factor is the differential time course and dosage in different agents to affect different symptoms. For example, in ADHD, a complicating phenomenon in evaluating medication-dose efficacy is the reported findings of a curvilinear relationship between dose and attentional improvement, resulting in a therapeutic window effect, as compared to a more linear relationship between dose and efficacy in reducing hyperactivity and impulsivity (Rosenberg, Holttum, & Gershon, 1994). This latter finding may complicate the validity and reliability of different observers. For example, teachers may be torn between identifying the effect on attention and learning versus the effects of disruptive behavior and classroom disruptions. Dosage levels and schedules need to be carefully assessed and adjusted to fit the child's educational needs and function and activity levels (for example, timing for peak action, reduction of side effects, and improvement of sleep hygiene).

The use of pharmacological agents also requires the baseline and reassessment monitoring of common or most serious medication side effects, as well as biochemical or physiological measures of various bodily functions to prevent adverse events, such as cardiac monitoring through electrocardiograms and the monitoring of liver enzymes or blood counts for hematological effects. Physiological factors that may contribute to dose adjustment and drug interactions need to be considered and reassessed periodically, such as interactions with other medications or medical conditions, the child's physical size and weight, nutritional patterns, and other maturational and hormonal factors (which clearly change over time).

The use of pharmacological agents with children requires closer monitoring than is common with adults, so this requires some adjustment in the expectations and practices of mental health services within systems of care. This needs to be considered within case management plans within systems of care as well as in the plans for resource availability for such systems.

Integration with Other Modalities

Pharmacotherapy is never a sole modality in treating children and adolescents with serious emotional disorders or mental illnesses. It has a number of inherent limitations, such as its limited targets of intervention, side effects, lack of efficacy in addressing complex behavioral and psychosocial needs, and potential for overreliance when other interventions (or resources for their implementation) are in short supply. For children with serious emotional disturbance, their propensity to have multiple comorbidities and serious functional impairments often dictates the need for multiple interventions to address multiple complex needs.

A multimodal treatment approach guided by a multidisciplinary team is the most effective approach. Pharmacotherapy is being increasingly used for rapid symptom relief and return to functioning, while cognitive, behavioral, and psychosocial therapies are being seen as most effective in relapse prevention and the development of long-term adaptive skills (Cantwell, 1996; Weisz & Jensen, 1999). The MTA study results (MTA Cooperative Group, 1999a, 1999b) suggest the added value of combined interventions (pharmacological and behavioral) to address comorbid conditions.

The use of multiple interventions in a well-integrated, multimodal treatment approach requires the education of and close communication among different clinicians, child service professionals, and parents. Joint definition of intervention and treatment goals, tracking of target symptoms, evaluation of level of function, close monitoring of medication side effects, and fidelity and adherence to treatment modality techniques and dosage need to be achieved for such an approach to be successful. Ideally, such an integrated treatment plan should be coordinated across agencies or settings in which the child or adolescent is involved. Another level of integration that can be achieved is to have a single mental health professional, particularly child and adolescent psychiatrists, deliver both pharmacological and psychotherapeutic interventions for youngsters who are most seriously impaired. There is some evidence from the adult literature that such integration is more cost-effective than having two separate professionals delivering the same treatment (Dewan, 1999).

Unfortunately, such integration may not be encouraged as agencies worry about incurring significant portions of the total costs of treatment, including medical treatment. This is most often seen in the lack of coordination across school, other community, and home settings around behavioral and pharmacological management, or the lack of coordination and continuity of care plans when a child is transferred across different care settings or levels of care. Interagency systems of care with clear interagency agreements can set the stage for such treatment integration (Pumariega et al., 1997).

Parental and Child Education, Consent, and Alliance

True informed consent is the cornerstone of decision making about pharmacological interventions. The parents and the child, where appropriate, need to be fully informed of the risks and benefits of any medication in an interactive discussion using appropriate language that is understandable and allows for questions and responses. Side effects of medications and what the parents and child can do in the event side effects occur should be carefully discussed. Parents should also understand the importance of regular follow-ups to monitor response to medication and side effects. Collaboration with parents is essential in making dosage adjustments and ensuring adherence with medication treatment. This involves helping parents feel empowered to make the ultimate decisions around medication and feeling an equalization of the power differential associated with dealing with medical professionals (Werry & Aman, 1993).

It is also extremely important to educate parents as well as child services professionals (such as teachers, counselors, case workers, and probation officers) about emotional and psychiatric disorders and the use of pharmacological agents as a means of empowerment and of demystifying psychopharmacology, with a resultant increase in comfort with such treatment. In the age of consumerism, there is ready information access on the World Wide Web and through advocacy groups, lay-oriented books, and educational materials. Parents and child service professionals should be suspicious of clinicians who hide behind technical language and incomprehensible terminology.

An issue that often arises in pharmacological treatment is the reluctance on the part of parents to allow school personnel or other human services professionals to know whether a child is on a psychotropic medication. Parents in such situations often fear discrimination and stigma from the resultant labeling of their child if this information is disclosed publicly. However, lack of information by such professionals can result in serious problems if the child experiences adverse effects without their knowledge or inappropriate expectations if the child's condition is poorly understood. The achievement of a stigma-free environment in schools needs to be a high priority among child services and mental health professionals. This should involve educating child service professionals and children, as well as the development of appropriate procedures for medication administration or side effect management that do not single out children in public settings such as educational or recreational settings.

The importance of addressing medication treatment directly with the child cannot be overlooked. Clinicians should evaluate and address the child's self-concept, self-esteem, and perceived stigma as a result of taking medications. They should also address the child's fears of side effects as well as the realities. Children and teens with serious emotional disturbances can externalize the responsibility and locus of control for their control of symptoms or problems, which is counter to their expected progress developmentally. Their active involvement and control in medication selection, administration, and monitoring need to be encouraged. Clinicians need to enlist treatment adherence by the child, including honest reporting of beneficial and adverse effects and developmentally appropriate responsibility for taking and keeping track of medications (Werry & Aman, 1993).

Cultural Competence in Psychopharmacotherapy

A common assumption about psychopharmacotherapy is that since this is an area of intervention that is biologically based, racial and cultural differences are not important factors in its implementation. However, emerging research challenges this assumption and makes cultural competence critical in psychopharmacology, as well as in other areas of mental health treatment and services. The interpretation, expression, measure, and threshold of behavioral and emotional symptoms can vary across cultures, making the establishment of baselines and outcomes more challenging. Significant cultural bias found in clinical psychiatric diagnostic assessment of children and adolescents (Kilgus, Pumariega, & Cuffe, 1995; Fabrega, Ulrich, & Mezzich, 1993) can readily lead to the inappropriate use or withholding of psychopharmacotherapy for culturally diverse children. For example, Landrum and colleagues (1995) and Zito, Safer, dosReis, Magder, and Riddle (1997) found in different studies that African American children were less likely to receive medications than Caucasian children in treatment settings. Hallfors et al. (1998), in their study of the MHSPY systems of care sites, found that race was not a significant variable until site, referral source, custody, and Medicaid were removed from their logistical regression model for analysis. However, race was highly correlated with site, referral source (nonwhites tend to be referred through the schools, whereas whites tend to be referred through child welfare), and custody status (whites were more likely to be in state custody). When these variables were dropped from the model, their combined influence allowed race to become a significant, albeit weak, predictor. Such findings may indicate that white youth are more likely to have access to a physician, resulting in a greater likelihood of receiving medication.

The perception by ethnic and racial minorities of psychopharmacological agents as means for social control adversely influences the acceptability of these agents among such populations. Cultural and ethnic norms around family medical decision making and consent need to be considered in presenting the recommendations to use such agents and soliciting informed consent, where elders assume a greater role than in traditional white middle-class families.

Cross-racial and cultural biological considerations also need to be attended to in psychopharmacological treatment. A new science of ethnopsychopharmacology is developing its own body of literature pointing to genetic and nutritional factors that can contribute to differential pharmacological response across ethnic and racial groups (Lin, Poland, & Nakasaki, 1993). A case in point relates to the metabolism of most pharmacological agents, especially the SSRIs. These agents are metabolized by a series of cytochrome P450 liver enzymes, with several of these enzymes responsible for the metabolism of different agents. Genetic polymorphisms have been described for many drug-metabolizing enzymes in Caucasian, Asian, and African-origin populations (Smith & Mendoza, 1996; Masimirembwa & Hasler, 1997). These can lead to the slow metabolism of many agents, including potentially toxic ones such as the TCAs. In addition, nutritional factors such as citrus and corn content in the diet, which vary by ethnic group, inhibit the action of some of these enzymes. The level of action of the cytochrome P450 enzymes can determine the dosage needed to achieve therapeutic action as well as the emergence of side effects (Smith & Mendoza, 1996; Sramek & Pi, 1996; Rudorfer & Potter, 1999).

Role of Professionals in Pharmacotherapy

The close and effective collaboration among different professionals of different disciplines can ensure the success of pharmacotherapy within the context of school-based mental health services, as well as that of the overall treatment program for children. Communication among these professionals needs to be structured and facilitated and should include such issues as functional and symptomatic change, side effects, attitudes about medications, logistical limitations and factors in medication administration, and coordination across modalities. Systems of care programs should provide the necessary support for such communication, including the time for this most critical task. The practice of interdisciplinary treatment conferences and teams where information is shared is critical for effective pharmacological and psychosocial treatment. Information technology such as e-mail, telecommunication, and unified electronic records can also assist members of the child and family's care team in communicating critical information.

Case Managers and Therapists. Case managers have critical roles to play in the implementation of pharmacotherapy. They can provide objective assessment (and reassessment) of the child's baseline symptoms and behaviors and side effects, at times also using many of the rating instruments already described. They can also facilitate the communication of observations and concerns from the child and family relating to the use of medications. The maintenance of adherence with medication regimens should become a major focus of their work by supporting the child and family in this endeavor and providing valuable feedback to the psychiatrist or other medical professional about the practicality of the regimen prescribed. Therapists who are not case managers can provide important information and feedback about the effectiveness of pharmacotherapy through their evaluation of the child, both clinically and through the use of systematic measures, supporting the child and family in pursuing pharmacotherapy, and ensuring their active participation in treatment, bringing up questions and concerns and accessing information about medications.

Psychiatrists. Child and adolescent psychiatrists or general psychiatrists in areas with a shortage of these professionals have critical roles in the treatment of children with serious emotional disturbances. They provide effective diagnostic evaluation for children suspected of serious disorders and can serve as clinical consultants to other professionals in interdisciplinary treatment teams in the construction, implementation, and reevaluation of treatment plans. They initiate pharmacotherapeutic treatment and, when the child's condition is stabilized, and guide the transition of care to other medical professionals, or continue pharmacotherapy (and even psychotherapy) for children with more serious disturbances and needs. They consult with other mental health professionals on the implementation of a wide range of therapeutic modalities, including psychotherapeutic, behavioral, group, and family interventions. Child and adolescent psychiatrists are involved in program consultation, community education around emotional and psychiatric disorders, and systems consultation. Child and adolescent psychiatrists, with their combined medical and mental health training, can serve as effective liaisons between medical and nonmedical professionals. They can also help design protocols as well as policy and procedures for pharmacological treatment within school settings (Pumariega et al., 1997).

Other Medical Professionals. Pediatricians are actively involved in monitoring the physical and cognitive development of children. They provide screening assessment and first-line treatment for children with less complicated emotional and behavioral disorders, as well as assume care for children with more serious disorders in consultation with child psychiatrists. They can also care for concomitant physical illnesses in children with behavioral and emotional disturbances. Family physicians serve some of the roles defined above, but their more limited training in childhood development and psychopathology limits their involvement in assessment. They can work closely with families on the child's overall physical and emotional health.

Nurse practitioners and school nurses play important roles in providing screening, evaluation, and monitoring of the efficacy of pharmacotherapy in consultation with child psychiatrists, and in outreach to the home and the community around education about emotional disorders and mental illness.

Teachers and Other Educational Professionals. Educational professionals serve important roles in effective pharmacotherapy. They can readily provide objective observations on a child's behavior naturalistically or with the aid of rating tools. This is due to their ready access to other children in the classroom environment for comparative assessment, which can be invaluable in diagnosis and in monitoring medication efficacy and outcomes. They can help destigmatize emotional and psychiatric disorders and their treatment with pharmacotherapy among other students and their families through their attitudes and education. They are in excellent positions to observe and report side effects, especially those affecting learning or cognition. Educational professionals can also reassure children and parents as they face the decisions about initiating pharmacotherapy and adhering to it. School psychologists serve important roles through their performance of psychoeducational testing, which can help to refine the selection of target symptoms and evaluation of the efficacy of treatment on educational function. They develop behavioral interventions to complement pharmacological treatment and improve the child's overall functioning.

FUTURE DIRECTIONS

Psychopharmacological treatments are progressively becoming more important treatment modalities within systems of care for children's mental health. The efforts of clinicians and researchers should be to formalize and fully integrate their use within the array of interventions available to children, so that treatment can be truly individualized to meet the needs of individual children. Research should move beyond simple efficacy studies and increasingly toward studies of the effectiveness of these treatments within community-based, interagency treatment settings, including the evaluation of multimodal treatments and their impact on the child's functioning and the family's burden of care (Weisz & Jensen, 1999). Clinicians in interagency systems of care need to attend to the evidence base in pharmacotherapy given the rapidly changing knowledge base about these agents. The knowledge base incorporated into systems of care should include not only the indications, contraindications, side effects, and dosing of these agents, but also the state of the art in assessment and reassessment tools and instruments that improve decision making about treatment modalities. Knowledge and skills in the effective implementation of evidence-based psychosocial and behavioral interventions by clinicians also need to be stressed within such systems. The lack of these alternatives within systems of care leads to premature implementation of pharmacotherapy.

Systems of care for children's mental health must also institute structural changes to incorporate the effective use of pharmacotherapy. Practice guidelines for the treatment of various disorders and disturbances need to be institution-alized within systems of care that provide direction about the initiation of med-ication treatment. Increasingly, professional organizations and federal agencies are developing and promoting such practice guidelines, which are regularly up-dated to account for new research findings (American Psychiatric Association, 1997). These guidelines can direct appropriate referral practices to either pedi-atricians or child and adolescent psychiatrists for evaluation for pharmacother-apy when other less invasive interventions, such as cognitive and behavioral therapies and parent training, have failed or have proven insufficient. Such prac-tice guidelines are best implemented within systems that are adequately staffed with well-trained clinicians working within interdisciplinary teams where fam-ilies are integral members and collaborators on behalf of the child. The goal for children's mental health should be to achieve this level of access and quality of care for all children.

References

Achenbach, T. (1991). *Integrative guide for the CBCL 4–18, YSR, and TRF Profiles.* Burlington: University of Vermont Department of Psychiatry.

American Psychiatric Association. (1980). *Diagnostic and statistical manual for mental disorders* (3rd ed.). Washington, DC: American Psychiatric Press.

American Psychiatric Association. (1994). *Diagnostic and statistical manual for mental disorders* (4th ed.). Washington, DC: American Psychiatric Press.

American Psychiatric Association. (1997). *Supplement to the Journal of the American Academy of Child and Adolescent Psychiatry: Practice Parameters, 36*(10), 1s–202s.

Armenteros, J., Whitaker, A., Welikson, M., Stedge, D., & Gorman, J. (1997). Risperi-done in adolescents with schizophrenia: An open pilot study. *Journal of the Amer-ican Academy of Child and Adolescent Psychiatry, 36,* 694–700.

Atkins, D. L., Pumariega, A. J., Montgomery, L., Rogers, K., Nybro, C., Jeffers, G., & Sease, F. (1999). Mental health and incarcerated youth. I: Prevalence and nature of psychopathology. *Journal of Child and Family Studies, 8,* 193–204.

Barkley, R. (1988). The effects of methylphenidate on the interactions of preschool ADHD children with their mothers. *Journal of the American Academy of Child and Adolescent Psychiatry, 27,* 336–341.

Bernstein, G., Borchardt, C., & Perwien, A. (1996). Anxiety disorders: A review of the past 10 years. *Journal of the American Academy of Child and Adolescent Psychia-try, 35,* 1110–1119.

Black, B., Udhe, T., & Tancer, M. (1992). Fluoxetine for the treatment of social phobia. *Journal of the American Academy of Child and Adolescent Psychiatry, 34,* 36–44.

Bradley, C. (1937). The behavior of children receiving benzedrine. *American Journal of Psychiatry, 94,* 577–585.

Campbell, M., Rapaport, J., & Simpson, G. (1999). Antipsychotics in children. *Journal of the American Academy of Child and Adolescent Psychiatry, 38,* 537–545.

Cantwell, D. (1996). Attention deficit disorder: A review of the past 10 years. *Journal of the American Academy of Child and Adolescent Psychiatry, 35,* 978–987.

Caron C., & Rutter, M. (1991). Co-morbidity in child psychopathology: Concept, issues, and research strategies. *Journal of Child Psychology and Psychiatry, 32,* 1063–1080.

Casat, C., Pleasants, D., Schroeder, D., & Parler, D. (1989). Buprorion in children with attention deficit disorder. *Psychopharmacological Bulletin, 25,* 198–201.

Chambers, W., Puig-Antich, J., Hirsch, M., Paez, P., Ambrosini, P., Tabrizi, M., & Davies, M. (1985). The assessment of affective disorders in children and adolescents by semistructured interview: Test-retest reliability of the schedule for affective disorders and schizophrenia for school-age children, present episode. *Archives of General Psychiatry, 42,* 696–702.

Comings, D., Comings, B., Tacket, T., & Li, S. (1990). The clonidine patch and behavior problems. *Journal of the American Academy of Child and Adolescent Psychiatry, 29,* 667–668.

Conners, C. (1969). A teacher rating scale for use in drug studies with children. *American Journal of Psychiatry, 126,* 884–888.

Conners, C., & Wells, K. (1997). *Conners-Wells Self-Report Scale.* North Tonawanda, NY: Multi-Health Systems.

Cullinan, D., Gadow, K. D., & Epstein, M. H. (1987). Psychotropic drug treatment among learning-disabled, educable mentally retarded, and seriously emotionally disturbed students. *Journal of Abnormal Psychology, 15,* 469–477.

Dahl, R. E., Holttum, J., & Trubnick, L. (1994). A clinical picture of child and adolescent narcolepsy. *Journal of the American Academy of Child and Adolescent Psychiatry, 33,* 834–841.

DeVane, C., & Salle, F. (1996). Serotonin selective reuptake inhibitor in child and adolescent psychopharmacology: A review of published experience. *Journal of Clinical Psychiatry, 57,* 56–66.

Dewan, M. (1999). Are psychiatrists cost-effective? An analysis of integrated versus split treatment. *American Journal of Psychiatry, 156,* 324–326.

Elmslie, G., Rush, J., Weinberg, W., Kowatch, R., Hughes, C., Carmody, T., & Rintelmann, J. (1997). Double-blind, placebo-controlled trial of fluoxetine in depressed children and adolescents. *Archives of General Psychiatry, 54,* 1031–1037.

Elmslie, G., Walkup, J., Plizka, S., & Ernst, M. (1999). Nontricyclic antidepressants: Current trends in children and adolescents. *Journal of the American Academy of Child and Adolescent Psychiatry, 38,* 517–528.

Epstein, M. H., Cullinan, D., Quinn, K., & Cumblad, C. (1995). Personal, family and service use characteristics of young people served by an interagency community-based system of care. *Journal of Emotional and Behavioral Disorders, 3,* 55–62.

Epstein, M., & Sharma, J. (1998). *Behavioral and Emotional Rating Scale (BERS): A strength based approach to assessment. Examiner's manual.* Austin, TX: PRO-ED Publishers.

Fabrega, H., Ulrich, R., & Mezzich, J. (1993). Do Caucasian and black adolescents differ at psychiatric intake? *Journal of the Academy of Child and Adolescent Psychiatry, 32,* 407–413.

Gadow, K. (1997). An overview of three decades of research in pediatric psychopharmacology. *Journal of Child and Adolescent Psychopharmacology, 7,* 219–236.

Geller, B., Reising, D., Leonard, H., Riddle, M., & Walsh, T. (1999). Critical review of tricyclic antidepressant use in children and adolescents. *Journal of the American Academy of Child and Adolescent Psychiatry, 38,* 513–516.

Gittleman-Klein, R., Spitzer, R., & Cantwell, D. (1978). Diagnostic classification and psychopharmacologic indications. In J. Werry (Ed.), *Pediatric psychopharmacology: The use of behavior modifying drugs in children.* New York: Brunner/Mazel.

Goodman, W., & Price, L. (1992). Assessment of severity and change in obsessive-compulsive disorder. *Psychiatric Clinics of North America, 15,* 861–869.

Greenhill, L., Abikoff, H., Arnold, L., Cantwell, D., Conners, C., Elliott, G., Hechtman, L., Hinsaw, S., Hoza, B., Jensen, P., March, J., Newcorn, J., Pelham, W., Severe, J., Swanson, J., Vitiello, B., & Wells, K. (1996). Medication treatment strategies in the MTA: Relevance to clinicians and researchers. *Journal of the American Academy of Child and Adolescent Psychiatry, 35,* 1304–1313.

Greenhill, L., Halperin, J., & Abikoff, H. (1999). Stimulant medications. *Journal of the American Academy of Child and Adolescent Psychiatry, 38,* 503–512.

Gunning, B. (1992). *A controlled trial of conidine in hyperactive children.* Unpublished doctoral dissertation, Academic Hospital, Rotterdam, the Netherlands.

Hallfors, D., Fallon, T., & Watson, K. (1998). An examination of psychotropic drug treatment for children with serious emotional disturbance. *Journal of Emotional and Behavioral Disorders, 6,* 56–63.

Hodges, K., & Wong, M. (1996). Psychometric characteristics of a multidimensional measure to assess impairment: The Child and Adolescent Functional Assessment Scale. *Journal of Child and Family Studies, 5,* 445–467.

Holden, E. W., & Santiago, R. (2001). Medication use for children entering systems of care. *System of Care Evaluation Briefs, 2*(8), 1–3.

Hunt, R. (1987). Treatment effects of oral and transdermal clonidine in relation to methylphedinate: An open pilot study in ADD-H. *Psychopharmacological Bulletin, 23,* 111–114.

Hunt, R., Minderas, R., & Cohn, D. (1985). Clonidine benefits children with attention deficit disorder and hyperactivity: Report of a double blind, placebo-crossover therapeutic trial. *Journal of the American Academy of Child and Adolescent Psychiatry, 24,* 617–629.

Isovarji, J., Laatikainen, T., Pakarinen, A., Juntunen, K., & Myllyla, V. (1993). Polycystic ovaries and hyperandrogenism in women taking valproate for epilepsy. *New England Journal of Medicine, 329,* 1383–1388.

Jacobi, C., Dahme, B., & Rustenbach, S. (1997). Comparison of controlled psycho-and pharmacotherapy studies in bulimia and anorexia nervosa. *Psychotherapy and Psychosomatic Medical Psychology, 47,* 346–364.

Jensen, P., Bhatara, V., Vietello, B., Hoagwood, K., Feil, M., & Burke, L. (1999). Psychoactive medication prescribing practices for U.S. children: Gaps between research and clinical practice. *Journal of the American Academy of Child and Adolescent Psychiatry, 38,* 557–565.

Jensen, P., Hoagwood, K., & Petti, T. (1996). Outcomes of mental health care for children and adolescents: II. Literature review and application of a comprehensive model. *Journal of the American Academy of Child and Adolescent Psychiatry, 35,* 1055–1063.

Jensen, P., & Payne, J. (1998). Behavioral and medical treatments for attention deficit hyperactivity disorder: Comparisons and combinations. In *NIMH Consensus Development Conference: Diagnosis and treatment of attention deficit hyperactivity disorder* (pp. 143–155). Bethesda, MD: National Institutes of Health, Office of the Director.

Kaplan, S. L., Simms, R. M., & Busner, J. (1994). Prescribing practices of outpatient child psychiatrists. *Journal of the American Academy of Child and Adolescent Psychiatry, 33,* 35–44.

Kelleher, K. J., Hohmann, A. A., & Larson, D. B. (1989). Prescription of psychotropics to children in office-based practice. *American Journal of Diseases of Children, 143,* 810–813.

Keller, M., Ryan, D., Strober, M., Klein, R. G., Kutcher, S., Birmaher, B., Hagno, O., Koplewicz, H., Carlson, G., Clarke, G., Elmslie, G., Feinberg, D., Geller, B., Kusumakar, V., Papatheodorov, G., Sack, W., Sweeney, M., Wagner, K., Weller, E., Winters, W., Oakes, R., & McCafferty, J. (2001). Efficacy of paroxetine in the treatment of adolescent major depression: A randomized controlled trial. *Journal of the American Academy of Child and Adolescent Psychiatry, 40,* 762–772.

Kilgus, M., Pumariega, A., & Cuffe, S. (1995). Influence of race on diagnosis in adolescent psychiatric inpatients. *Journal of American Academy of Child and Adolescent Psychiatry, 35,* 167–172.

Kovacs, M. (1981). Rating scales to assess depression in school-aged children. *Acta Paedopsychiatrica, 46,* 305–315.

Kumra, S., Frazier, J., Jacobsen, L., McKenna, K, Gordon, C., Lenane, M., Hamburger, S., Smith, A., Albus, K., Alghband-Rad, J., & Rapaport J. (1996). Childhood onset schizophrenia: A double blind clozapine-haloperidol comparison. *Archives of General Psychiatry, 53,* 1090–1097.

Landrum, T. J., Singh, N. N., Nemil, M. S., Ellis, C. R., & Best, A. M. (1995). Characteristics of children and adolescents with serious emotional disturbance in systems of care. Part II: Community-based services. *Journal of Emotional and Behavioral Disorders, 3,* 141–149.

Lin, K., Poland, R., & Nasaki, G. (1993). *Psychopharmacology and psychobiology of ethnicity.* Washington, DC: American Psychiatric Press.

March, J. (1999, June 1). *Multi-site trial in adolescent depression: Purpose, design, and methods.* Paper presented at the Thirty-Ninth Annual New Clinical Drug Evaluation Unit Meeting, Boca Raton, FL.

March, J., Parker, J., Sullivan, K., Stallings, P., & Conners, C. (1997). The Multidimensional Anxiety Scale for Children (MASC): Factor structure, reliability, and validity. *Journal of the American Academy of Child and Adolescent Psychiatry, 36,* 554–565.

Masimirembwa, C., & Hasler, J. (1997). Genetic polymorphism of drug metabolizing enzymes in African populations: Implications for the use of neuroleptics and antidepressants. *Brain Research Bulletin, 44,* 561–571.

McDougle, C. (1998). Psychopharmacology. In D. Cohen & F. Volkmar (Eds.), *Handbook of autism and pervasive developmental disorders* (pp. 707–729). New York: Wiley.

Multisite Treatment of ADHD Cooperative Group. (1999a). A fourteen-month randomized clinical trial of treatment strategies for attention-deficit/hyperactivity disorder. *Archives of General Psychiatry, 56,* 1073–1086.

Multisite Treatment of ADHD Cooperative Group. (1999b). Moderators and mediators of treatment response for children with attention deficit hyperactivity disorder. *Archives of General Psychiatry, 56,* 1088–1096.

Murdoch, D., & McTarish, D. (1992). Sertraline: A review of its psychodynamic and pharmacokinetics properties, and therapeutic potential in depression and obsessive-compulsive disorders. *Drugs, 44,* 604–624.

National Institutes of Health. (1999). Diagnosis and treatment of attention deficit hyperactivity disorder. *NIH Consensus Statements 1998,* Nov. 16–18, 1–37.

Pelham, W., & Murphy, H. (1986). Attention deficit and conduct disorders. In M. Hersen (Ed.), *Pharmacological and behavioral treatment: An integrated approach* (pp. 108–148). New York: Wiley.

Perry, R., Pataki, C., Munoz-Silva, D., Armenteros, J., & Silva, R. (1997). Risperidone in children and adolescents with pervasive developmental disorder: Pilot trial and follow-up. *Journal of Child and Adolescent Psychopharmacology, 7,* 167–179.

Popper, C., & Zimnitzky, B. (1995). Child and adolescent psychopharmacology update: January, 1994-December, 1994. *Journal of Child and Adolescent Psychopharmacology, 5,* 1–40.

Poznanski, E., Freeman, L., & Mokros, H. (1985). Children's depression rating scale—revised. *Psychopharmacology Bulletin, 21,* 979–989.

Pumariega, A. J., Johnson, N. P., & Sheridan, D. (1995). Emotional disturbance and substance abuse in adolescents in residential group homes. *Journal of Mental Health Administration, 22,* 426–431.

Pumariega, A., Muller, B., & Rivers-Buckeley, N. (1982). Acute renal failure secondary to amoxapine overdose. *Journal of the American Medical Association, 282,* 3141–3142.

Pumariega, A., Nace, D., England, M., Diamond, J., Mattson, A., Fallon, T., Hansen, G., Lourie, I., Marx, L., Thurber, D., Winters, N., Graham, M., & Weigand, D. (1997). Community-based systems approach to children's managed mental health services. *Journal of Child and Family Studies, 6,* 149–164.

Rao, U., Ryan, N., Birmaher, B., Dahl, R., Williamson, D., Kaufman, J., Rao, R., & Nelson, B. (1995). Unipolar depression in adolescents: Clinical outcome in adulthood. *Journal of the American Academy of Child and Adolescent Psychiatry, 34,* 566–578.

Rapoport, J., Buchsbaum, M., Weingartner, H., Zahn, P., Ludlow, C., & Mikkelsen, F. (1980). Dextroamphetamine: Cognitive and behavioral effects in normal and hyperactive boys and normal men. *Archives of General Psychiatry, 37,* 933–943.

Reich, W., Welner, Z., & Herjanic, B. (1994). *Diagnostic Interview for Children and Adolescents, Revised (for DSM-IV) Computer Program: Child/ Adolescent Version and Parent Version.* North Tonawanda, NY: Multi-Health Systems.

Riddle, M., Bernstein, G., Cook, E., Leonard, H., March, J., & Swanson, J. (1999). Anxiolytics, adrenergic agents, and naltrexone. *Journal of the American Academy of Child and Adolescent Psychiatry, 38,* 546–556.

Rosenberg, D., Holttum, S., & Gershon, S. (1994). *Psychostimulant textbook of pharmacotherapy for child and adolescent psychiatric disorders* (pp. 19–50). New York: Brunner/Mazel.

Rudorfer, M., & Potter, W. (1999). Metabolism of tricyclic antidepressants. *Cell and Molecular Biology, 19,* 373–409.

Ryan, N., Bhatara, V., & Perel, J. (1999). Mood stabilizers in children and adolescents. *Journal of the American Academy of Child and Adolescent Psychiatry, 38,* 529–536.

Sallee, F., Vrindavanam, N., Deas-Nesmith, D., Carson, S., & Sethuraman, G. (1997). Pulse intravenous clomipramine for depressed adolescents: Double blind, controlled trial. *American Journal of Psychiatry, 154,* 668–673.

Sandman, C. (1991). The opiate hypothesis in autism and self injury. *Journal of Child and Adolescent Psychopharmacology, 1,* 237–248.

Schachar, R., & Tannock, R. (1993). Childhood hyperactivity and psychostimulants: A review of extended treatment studies. *Journal of Child and Adolescent Psychopharmacology, 3,* 81–97.

Shaffer, D., Fisher, P., Dulcan, M., Davies, M., Piacentini, J., Schwab-Stone, M., Lahey, B., Bourdon, K., Jensen, P., Bird, H., Canino, G., & Regier, D. (1996). The NIMH Diagnostic Interview Schedule for Children Version 2.3 (DISC 2.3): Description, acceptability, prevalence rates, and performance in the MECA study. *Journal of the American Academy of Child and Adolescent Psychiatry, 35,* 865–877.

Shaffer, D., Gould, M., Brasic, J., Ambrosini, P., Fisher, P., Bird, H., & Aluwahlia, S. (1983). A Children's Global Assessment Scale (CGAS). *Archives of General Psychiatry, 40,* 1228–1231.

Simeon, J., Dinicola, V., Ferguson, H., & Copping, W. (1990). Adolescent depression: A placebo controlled fluoxetine study and follow-up. *Progress in Neuropharmacology and Biological Psychiatry, 14,* 791–795.

Singh, N. N., Epstein, M. H., Luebke, J., & Singh, Y. N. (1990). Psychopharmacological intervention. I: Teacher perceptions of psychotropic medication for students with serious emotional disturbance. *Journal of Special Education, 24,* 283–295.

Smith, M. & Mendoza, R. (1996). Ethnicity and pharmacogenetics. *Mount Sinai Journal of Medicine, 63,* 285–290.

Spielberger, C. (1973). *Preliminary Test Manual for the State-Trait Anxiety Inventory for Children.* Palo Alto, CA: Consulting Psychologists Press.

Sramek, J., & Pi, E. (1996). Ethnicity and antidepressant response. *Mount Sinai Journal of Medicine, 63,* 320–325.

Steiner, H., & Lock, J. (1998). Anorexia nervosa and bulimia nervosa in children and adolescents: A review of the past 10 years. *Journal of the American Academy of Child and Adolescent Psychiatry, 37,* 352–359.

Strober, M., Freeman, R., Rigali, J., Schmidt, S., & Diamond, R. (1992). The pharmacotherapy of depressive illness in adolescence. II. Effects of lithium augmentation in non-responders to imipramine. *Journal of the American Academy of Child and Adolescent Psychiatry, 31,* 16–20.

Swanson, J., Flockhart, D., Udea, D., Cantwell, D., Connor, D., & Williams, L. (1995). Clonidine in the treatment of ADHD: Questions about safety and efficacy. *Journal of Child and Adolescent Psychopharmacology, 5,* 301–304.

Thompson, S., & Rey, J. (1995). Functional enuresis: Is desmopressin the answer? *Journal of the American Academy of Child and Adolescent Psychiatry, 34,* 266–271.

Weisz, J., & Jensen, P. (1999). Efficacy and effectiveness of child and adolescent psychotherapy and pharmacotherapy. *Mental Health Services Research, 1,* 125–157.

Werry, J., & Aman, M. (1993). *Practitioner's guide to psychoactive drugs for children and adolescents.* New York: Plenum, 1993.

Wilk, R. J., Greenbaum, P., & Kline, C. J. (1995, Mar.). *Predictors of psychotropic medication usage in children and adolescents.* Paper presented at the Eighth Annual Research Conference of the Center for Children's Mental Health, University of South Florida, Tampa.

Wolraich, M. L., Lindgren, S., Stromquist, A., Milich, R., Davis, C., & Watson, D. (1990). Stimulant medication use by primary care physicians in the treatment of attention deficit hyperactivity disorder. *Pediatrics, 86,* 95–101.

Zito, J., Safer, D., dosReis, S., Magder, L., & Riddle, M. (1997). Methylphenidate patterns among Medicaid youths. *Psychopharmacological Bulletin, 33,* 143–147.

CHAPTER EIGHT

Evidence-Based Community-Based Interventions

Kenneth Rogers

Beginning with the Community Mental Health Centers Act of 1964, there has been an increased emphasis on community-based mental health services. Although services were initially focused on treating adults, there was increased recognition that children and adolescents suffer from mental illnesses that are responsive to clinical intervention. Many interventions have been widely used, but it has been only within the past ten years that empirical evidence that supporting their efficacy has been available.

In 1986, Stroul and Friedman pointed out the lack of community-based services for youth with serious emotional disturbances. Despite the twenty-two years that had passed since President Kennedy had signed his historic legislation, few organized approaches had been implemented to care for these youth. Most agencies that served children and adolescents functioned in an atmosphere that did not foster collaboration even though most of these agencies were responsible for serving the various needs of these youth.

Estimates are that 4.5 to 6.3 million children have serious emotional disturbance. These mental health problems have a significant impact on the future development of these youth and have been linked to increased morbidity, mortality, and disability. Appropriate treatment can prevent the sequelae of untreated emotional disturbance, which include substance abuse, juvenile delinquency, and increased behavioral problems.

GENERAL PHILOSOPHY OF
COMMUNITY-BASED INTERVENTIONS

The general philosophy of interventions with children and adolescents is to provide appropriate services in the least restrictive setting. Although treatment in restrictive placements such as residential treatment centers and group homes are beneficial in treating the behavioral aspects of emotional disturbance, these gains are often short-lived. Community-based interventions involve family and community members and focus on changing the youth's environment or allowing them to function more effectively in their natural environment. These interventions should be (and often are) more effective in providing stable long-term gains.

The goal of clinicians who are treating children and adolescents who need mental health services is to provide appropriate treatment that will return them to their optimal level of functioning while decreasing their degree of distress. The ultimate goal of community-based interventions is to enable youth to function optimally in their environment while reducing emotional and behavioral symptoms as much as possible. In choosing the best treatment for a child or adolescent, clinicians have generally relied on what they learned during training or during the course of clinical practice. In either case, their exposure to different treatment modalities is limited. Many of the treatments they use have never been adequately studied or, in some cases, have been studied and found to be ineffective. Although there are myriad reasons why clinicians continue to use these treatments, some reasons are very common: they feel effective using their current treatment strategies; they are unaware of treatments that have been demonstrated to be more effective than their current treatment modalities; they feel ill equipped to use newer modalities of treatment; and they feel that the evidence for the proposed treatments is too weak to warrant change from their standard clinical practice. Finally, many changes in treatment modalities require system changes that may be beyond the scope of individual clinicians or groups of clinicians to effect.

WHEN IS A TREATMENT MODALITY EVIDENCE BASED?

The discussion of the term *evidence based* requires that we define the term in a manner that is commonly accepted. Hoagwood, Burns, Kiser, Ringeisen, and Schoenwald (2001) refer to evidence-based practice as "a body of scientific knowledge about service practice or about the impact of clinical treatments or services on the mental health problems of children and adolescents" (p. 1179). In the area of child mental health services research, the term *evidence based* implies that some degree of scientific study has been applied to those treatments labeled as evidence based versus those that have not been subjected to scientific study.

There are several approaches to defining criteria for determining whether a treatment is evidence based. Several authors have used meta-analyses of previously existing bodies of work to demonstrate the effectiveness of psychosocial treatments. This approach lacks the level of scientific rigor of other approaches but does suggest treatments that may be promising.

The American Psychological Association convened a task force to develop a comprehensive approach to evaluating the evidence base for treatments. The task force developed two sets of criteria to be used for determining the evidence base of proposed treatments and placed the treatments into two categories: well-established psychosocial interventions and probably efficacious psychosocial interventions (Lonigan, Elbert, & Johnson, 1998). These proposed criteria stated that treatments should be supported by group design or single-subject experiments. A treatment is considered to be well established if two or more studies find it superior to medication, placebo, or alternative treatment or if treatment is equivalent to an already established treatment. Treatments were considered as probably efficacious if two or more studies showed it to be superior to wait-list control conditions or one experiment must meet criteria for a well-established treatment or three single case studies must be conducted.

An alternative set of criteria for defining evidenced-based treatment has been proposed by the Interdisciplinary Committee on Evidence Based Youth Mental Health Care, with formal input from the American Academy of Child and Adolescent Psychiatry, the American Academy of Pediatrics, and the American Psychological Association. The definitions were broadened to include both psychosocial and pharmacological therapies that have been scientifically evaluated (Weisz & Jensen, 1999). Treatment is considered evidence based if there are at least two studies with between-group comparisons from the same age group and receiving the same treatment for the same problem or if there are at least two studies within a group or single case design with the same parameters. The majority of studies should demonstrate a positive result.

Once there is substantial evidence to determine that a treatment intervention is effective at addressing a clinical disorder, the next problem faced is its dissemination into widespread use. The issue of identifying scientifically proven prevention and treatment services and disseminating those findings is a national priority (U.S. Department of Health and Human Services, 1999).

Many interventions are developed and tested in practice settings where the environment is well controlled and may differ substantially from the community-based practices where the interventions are most likely to be used. In the past, the attributes of the practice context have largely been ignored and considered to be nuisance variables (Schoenwald & Hoagwood, 2001). The differences in the sites where many of these treatments were developed and the locations where they are used must be addressed before the issue of transportability is addressed. In child and adolescent mental health treatment, these conditions may vary more drastically than in other areas of mental health or physical health care because of all of the variables and service sector differences that must be addressed. For example, the philosophy of a local school district or other child-serving agency could have a dramatic impact on the ability of a program that is very efficacious from being as successful in another location.

In addition, barriers that may not have been present in the original location may be prominent in a second location. Minor changes such as the location and accessibility of the program or cultural differences that may differ between communities may have a dramatic impact on the success of the program. Without adequate research of the transportability of an intervention, it is unclear if "evidence-based treatment" in location A is "evidence-based treatment" in location B. Therefore, one must examine dimensions and variables from the intervention to compare research and practice settings. Schoenwald and Hoagwood (2001) have identified six characteristics to make such comparisons: intervention, practitioner, client, service delivery, organizational, and service system characteristics.

REVIEW OF COMMUNITY-BASED TREATMENTS

This section reviews community-based treatments, describes their evidence base, and describes how they work.

Wraparound Services

Wraparound services are a method of delivering services to children and families with multiple problems and often being served by multiple agencies. These services are individually designed to address problems specific to an individual youth and may include treatment services as well as support services that allow the youth to stay in a home environment and in the community. Wraparound services require interagency collaboration to provide appropriate services: crisis intervention, educational advocacy, individual and family therapy, psychological evaluation, medication evaluation and management, and social service interventions, among others. Services may be provided in various locations, including the client's home, school, or community. The goal of the intervention is to provide appropriate interventions while preventing the youth from progressing into more restrictive levels of care.

Wraparound services are more than just a set of services; they are "a philosophy that includes a definable planning process involving the child and family that result in a unique set of community services and natural supports individualized for that child and that family to achieve a positive set of outcomes"

(Goldman, 1999, p. 10). Because of the tendency to view wraparound services as simply a group of services brought together to address various problems experienced by the client, it became essential to define these services clearly.

In 1998, a group of leaders in wraparound, including developers, trainers, providers, family members, administrators, and researchers, met to address the issues of defining the core elements of these services. They agreed on ten key elements that constitute the essence of wraparound services (Goldman, 1999, pp. 12–13):

1. Wraparound must be based in the community.

2. Services and supports must be individualized, built on strengths, and meet the needs of children and families across the life domains in order to promote success, safety, and permanency in home, school, and the community.

3. The process must be culturally competent.

4. Families must be full and active partners in every level of the wraparound process.

5. The wraparound approach must be a team-driven process involving the family, child, natural supports, agencies, and community services working together to develop, implement, and evaluate the individualized service plan.

6. Wraparound teams must have flexible approaches with adequate and flexible funding.

7. Wraparound plans must include a balance of formal services and informal community and family resources.

8. The community agencies and teams must make an unconditional commitment to serve their children and families.

9. A service support plan should be developed and implemented based on an interagency, community-neighborhood collaborative process.

10. Outcomes must be determined and measured for each goal established with the child and family, as well as for those goals established at the program and system levels.

Wraparound services are widely disseminated, with 88 percent of states reporting their use. Most wraparound programs are based in mental health systems, although many other service systems actively participate in these programs.

Burns and Goldman (1998) examined the evidence base for wraparound services and reviewed fourteen studies representing programs in nine states: Alaska, Florida, Illinois, Indiana, Kentucky, Maryland, New York, Vermont, and Wisconsin. The populations targeted for these programs were always youth for risk of out-of-home placements and youth returning from residential placements. The studies were most often pre-post studies comparing baseline and follow-up without a control group (ten studies) followed by randomized clinical trials (two studies), and case study design (two studies). The studies generally showed that the programs were moderately successful at producing behavioral adjustment, family adjustment, and school adjustments. Some programs appeared very successful, while others appeared only minimally successful.

Two areas identified as needing additional research pertain to the integrity of the intervention and the effectiveness of the intervention: Do the outcomes associated with the wraparound process differ from those associated with other types of interventions? The authors expressed concern that as more evidence is found for the efficacy of wraparound services, more and more services are identified as wraparound even though they do not adhere to the values, requirements, and philosophy of wraparound services.

Case Management

Case management is often viewed as the central service that drives many other services. The main purpose of the case manager is to coordinate services received by children and families who may require multiple services, often from multiple agencies. Although the model of functioning may differ from one system to another, the case manager may serve as a broker of services or a coordinator of services, or may provide some of the services. Case managers may be classified into two groups: traditional case managers (those who primarily coordinate and broker services) and clinician case managers (those who serve as part of the treatment team by providing services in addition to coordinating the overall treatment plan). Some programs offer intensive case management in which the case manager has fewer cases and may have more flexibility to purchase additional services. Some case managers function as part of a team in providing an array of services; others function individually and do not work as members of an interdisciplinary team.

The evidence for the effectiveness of case management services derives from two sets of studies of two types of programs: those using traditional case managers and those using a clinician case manager. Three controlled studies that have examined programs using a traditional case manager show that case management increased the amount of individual services received and services were more coordinated and comprehensive (Koren et al., 1997). Furthermore, intensive case management using traditional case management has been found to allow youth to spend more days in the community between episodes of more restrictive services such as hospitalization and when hospitalized youth are hospitalized for fewer days (Evans, Banks, Huz, & McNulty, 1994).

Several studies examine case management services where the case manager serves as part of the interdisciplinary team. A randomized trial in North Carolina (Burns, Farmer, Angelo, Costello, & Behar, 1996) found that youth served by an interdisciplinary team headed by a case manager were more likely to receive community-based services, spend fewer days in psychiatric hospitals, and receive more comprehensive services than youth served by treatment teams headed by their primary clinician. Youth receiving team-based services were also found to have fewer behavioral symptoms and significantly better overall functioning than youth receiving multiple services without the benefit of a case manager (Evans, Huz, McNulty, & Banks, 1996). Using the case manager approach with youth in foster care placements has been found to keep youth in placements longer, increase social skills, decrease absenteeism from school, and decrease delinquency compared to youth in traditional foster care without a case manager (Clark et al., 1998).

Overall, case management appears to be an effective approach to treating youth with emotional and behavioral problems. Although studies report positive outcomes in multiple areas of functioning and the ability to access and remain in services, further outcomes are difficult to assess and compare because of the wide variation in programs using case management services.

Partial Hospitalization and Day Treatment

Day treatment programs are interventions designed to be more intensive than traditional outpatient services such as individual, group, or family therapy, but they are less restrictive than inpatient care. The programs may be located in schools, hospitals, clinics, or community settings. Most programs offer a range of services, including individual, family, and group therapy, and educational interventions. Youth spend up to eight hours in the program during the day and return home in the evening to be with their families. Day treatment programs are sometimes used as an alternative to hospitalization for those who are having a crisis that may require significant intervention but can be managed outside the hospital. For other youth, day treatment programs may serve as a transition from the hospital by providing services that may help with their transition back to a community setting and community-based treatments.

Most of the research done on day treatment programs shows positive results; however, most of these studies are uncontrolled. These studies show an improvement in family functioning and improvement in the youth behavioral symptoms (Kutash & Rivera, 1995). Most studies found improvement in the youth's academic functioning, though some found no improvement. Day treatment services were also found to reduce the use of more costly and restrictive services such as hospitalization and residential treatment. Controlled studies examining day treatment services demonstrated decreased behavioral problems and improved family functioning (Grizenko, Papineau, & Sayegh, 1993; Grizenko, 1997).

Multisystemic Therapy

Multisystemic therapy (MST), perhaps the best-studied family and community-based treatment model, is an intensive short-term home-based treatment for youth with serious emotional disturbances. Its central focus is to determine the factors that are contributing to or maintaining identified youth problems across the youth's and family's social ecology (Schoenwald, Brown, & Henggeler, 2000). The MST clinician does a comprehensive and individualized evaluation to determine the individual, family, peer, neighborhood, and school factors that are contributing to the youth's problems. The goal is to use the MST model to produce positive change in the youth and family by increasing the competency of the family to parent the youth, developing a support system in the community to help the youth make and maintain positive change, and helping the youth develop the skills needed to make positive change. It is hoped that the changes obtained during this intensive intervention lasting three to five months will endure.

The objective of MST is to deliver services in the youth's natural environment (home, school, and community) using a home-based model of service delivery. MST seeks to eliminate barriers to service access so the youth who are at imminent risk for out-of-home placement receive services that allow them to remain in their homes. MST therapists are high-level, highly trained therapists with at least a master's degree. Each therapist has a caseload of three to five families and is available at all times to respond to crises. The MST therapist has daily contact with families, and appointments are scheduled at times that are convenient for families, including evenings and weekends.

The efficacy of MST has been demonstrated in three randomized controlled trials for youth in the juvenile justice system. MST programs were compared to usual community treatment interventions in Memphis, Tennessee, and Simpsonville, South Carolina. These studies found that MST was superior to usual community treatment in decreasing adolescent behavioral problems and improving family relations (Henggeler et al., 1986); the number of arrests and self-reported delinquent behaviors were lower in youth treated in MST programs versus usual community treatment (Henggeler, Pickrel, Brondino, & Crouch, 1996). In Columbia, Missouri, MST was found to be superior to individual therapy in ameliorating adjustment problems in individual family members and preventing future criminal behavior (Borduin et al., 1995). More recently, MST has been used with success in psychiatrically impaired youth without a history of juvenile justice involvement (Rowland et al., 2000) and in youth with substance abuse and dependence (Henggeler, Pickrel, Brondino, & Crouch, 1996). Although the efficacy of MST has been demonstrated in multiple settings, including juvenile justice, substance abuse, child welfare, and mental health, the findings have been demonstrated by only one group and need to be replicated by others.

Therapeutic Foster Care

Therapeutic foster care differs from regular foster care in that the foster parents are trained to deal with youth with severe emotional and behavioral problems. Care is delivered in a home setting using a family-based model to provide youth with a nurturing home environment. Although therapeutic foster care can differ substantially from one locale to another, there are common features present in each program:

- Therapeutic foster parents receive extensive training in dealing with special needs youth.
- Therapeutic foster homes have a very low census—usually only one youth.
- Case managers overseeing these homes also have low caseloads, allowing them provide more oversight, training, and care coordination to therapeutic foster parents. These services may include in-home interventions or crisis interventions.

Four randomized controlled studies of therapeutic foster care programs demonstrated that therapeutic foster care improved behavior, decreased the use of institutional care, and lowered costs compared to other settings for previously hospitalized youth (Chamberlain & Reid, 1991). Emotional and behavioral adjustment were greater for youth in therapeutic foster care than in regular foster care (Clark et al., 1994). Reincarceration and residential care decreased for youth receiving therapeutic foster care who had a history of delinquency compared to delinquent youth in residential placements (Chamberlain & Moore, 1998).

Kutash and Rivera (1995), in a review of eighteen reports of uncontrolled trials, found that 60 to 90 percent of youth treated in therapeutic foster home were discharged to less restrictive settings. Most were able to remain in these less restrictive settings for substantial periods of time.

EVIDENCE-BASED PSYCHOLOGICAL INTERVENTIONS

There has been an increased interest in using evidence-based psychological interventions to treat specific psychiatric disorders. Many of the psychosocial interventions used in the treatment of emotional and behavioral disorders have little evidence to demonstrate their efficacy. Among those treatments that have demonstrated efficacy, many of these studies were conducted in adults and their results extrapolated to youth with little evidence that they are efficacious in the younger population. Many childhood and adolescent disorders (including autism, bipolar disorder, posttraumatic stress disorder, obsessive-compulsive disorder, panic disorder, substance abuse, and eating disorders) do not have any well-established or probably efficacious psychosocial treatments. Well-established treatments have been identified for attention deficit hyperactivity disorder (ADHD) and phobias. Probably efficacious treatments have been identified for ADHD, conduct disorder, and phobias. We will briefly outline treatments that have proven efficacious for treating specific child and adolescent disorders.

Major Depressive Disorder

The primary psychosocial treatments for major depressive disorders have been various forms of psychotherapy, including play therapy, cognitive behavior therapy (CBT), interpersonal therapies, and family therapy. Most of these therapies were initially developed for use with adults and later tailored for use with children and adolescents. Using the American Psychological Association criteria outlined earlier in this chapter, there are no well-established treatments for major depressive disorder in children and adolescents.

In a comprehensive review article, Kaslow and Thompson (1998) found only one form of CBT to be probably effective. This intervention was based on the Coping with Depression course developed for adults by Lewinsohn, Clarke, and Hoberman (1989) and adapted by Clarke and colleagues (1992) to treat adolescent depression. Youth receiving this treatment reported lower rates of depression, less self-reported depression, improved cognition, and increased activity levels compared to wait-list controls (Lewinsohn et al., 1996). These twelve-session group interventions based on self-control therapy or behavior-solving therapy were found to be superior to a wait-list control group in reducing the symptoms of depression and anxiety (Stark, Reynolds, & Kaslow, 1987). The self-control therapy, which was found to be superior to behavior-solving therapy, was compared to traditional counseling. Self-control therapy consisting of social skills training, assertiveness training, relaxation training, and imagery and cognitive restructuring reduced the number of depressive symptoms (Stark, Rouse, & Livingston, 1991). CBT has also been used as a prevention intervention; it has recently been demonstrated to have a substantial positive effect on adolescents at risk for developing depressive disorders (Beardslee, Versage, Wright, & Salt, 1997; Clarke et al., 2001).

Attention Deficit Hyperactivity Disorder

ADHD is among the most controversial disorders in mental health and perhaps in the entire medical field. For that reason, it may also be among the best studied of the childhood disorders.

ADHD is characterized by two sets of symptoms: inattention and hyperactivity-impulsivity. Inattention symptoms include careless mistakes in schoolwork, not appearing to listen when spoken to, difficulty sustaining attention, inability to follow through on instructions, difficulty with organization, losing things easily, and being forgetful and easily distracted. Hyperactive-impulsive symptoms include fidgetiness, difficulty playing quietly, excessive talkativeness, being constantly on the go, running or climbing excessively, blurting out answers, interrupting others, and difficulty awaiting turn. Although many youth are diagnosed with ADHD prior to school age, most are identified when the child is presented with a school environment where there are clear expectations and challenges that were not present prior to that age. For example, this may be the first time that a child is expected to sit still for an extended period of time or have schoolwork to complete. By definition, the symptoms must be present by age seven.

Many children with ADHD adjust and function well in adolescence and adulthood. Hyperactivity symptoms are more likely to remit, while inattention symptoms are more likely to persist into adulthood. Many youth have prominent difficulty with socialization and may have poor relationships with peers, a negative prognostic sign for future behavior because many of these youth are more likely to drop out of school or have substance abuse or legal difficulties. Often they develop other disruptive behavior disorders, including oppositional defiant disorder and conduct disorder.

Although pharmacological treatment with stimulants or a combination of stimulants and psychosocial treatments has been demonstrated to be superior to psychosocial treatments alone, there is significant evidence for the efficacy of behavioral approaches over usual or no treatment. Behavioral training is the most widely used psychosocial modality used to treat ADHD. These therapies have included behavior training for children, teachers, and youth. Although there is evidence that each of these is efficacious under certain conditions, only behavior training for teachers is a well-established treatment for ADHD.

Parent training is one of the most commonly used outpatient interventions. Most often it is used in a clinic setting in conjunction with other treatments, including medication and behavior training interventions for children. The interventions are often done in a group setting and cover issues of discipline, behavior-shaping strategies to use at home, and training on child development. The evidence for the efficacy of parent training is mixed. Parent training has been compared to the use of stimulants (Firestone, Crowe, Goodman, & McGrath, 1986; Horn, Ialongo, Popovich, & Peradotto, 1987; Horn et al., 1990, 1991; Pelham, Wheeler, & Chronis, 1998). Although there was some improvement in behavioral symptoms, core inattention hyperactive, and impulsive symptoms are not substantially affected. Parent training is often beneficial only when the youth are with parents; there are usually no substantial changes in other settings such as school and other social settings. In comparisons of parent training to wait-list controls or other behavioral strategies, parent training has been found to improve ADHD symptoms, reduce behavioral problems, and increase grades in school-age children (Sonuga et al., 2001; Stein, 1999). However, other studies have demonstrated no impact on behavior problems in youth, although there was an increased sense of competency among parents (Weinberg, 1999).

Multimodal treatment has long been the method of treatment for ADHD. However, the National Institute of Mental Health Multimodal Treatment Study of ADHD (MTA Study) was the first to examine this treatment paradigm. The MTA Study compared three treatment conditions: medication management alone, behavioral treatment alone, or a combination of behavioral and medication treatments. At fourteen months, medication was found to be superior to behavioral treatment alone; however, the combined treatment was most effective in improving social skills, parent-child relations, internalizing symptoms, reading achievement, aggressive behaviors, and parent satisfaction (Jensen et al., 2001). The study concluded that medication alone or combined with behavior treatment was beneficial for reducing the core symptoms of ADHD over a fourteen-month period. The addition of behavior therapy provided no improvement in core ADHD symptoms but did provide improvement in associated behavioral problems (Jensen et al., 2001).

Conduct Disorder

Many clinicians view conduct disorder as untreatable. The disorder is characterized by a repetitive and persistent pattern of behavior in which the basic rights of others are violated (American Psychiatric Association, 1994). The behaviors fall into four main categories: aggressive conduct that causes or threatens harm to other people or animals, nonaggressive conduct that causes property loss or damage, deceitfulness or theft, and serious violation of rules. These youth often fight, bully, intimidate, assault, sexually coerce, or are cruel to others. They present a problem in community treatment settings because they constantly challenge the system and engage in behaviors that make them difficult to manage. In many cases, these youth are treated in restrictive settings such as group homes and residential treatment facilities for extended periods of time but usually make the transition back to community-based programs once their restrictive treatments are completed.

The etiology of conduct disorder is not fully known, but it appears to have environmental and genetic components (Hendren, 1999). Environmental risk factors include maternal rejection, separation from parents, family neglect, physical and sexual abuse, exposure to violence, parental psychiatric illness, and poverty. Genetic and biological risks include low birthweight complications, learning impairments, and neurological complications during birth and pregnancy. Because many of these risk factors are present very early in development and tend to become more problematic with time, it is important to intervene as early as possible to prevent the development of more serious sequelae.

Despite popular notions of hopelessness about treating youth with conduct disorder, there are several well-established and probably efficacious treatments for intervening with youth with conduct disorder. Brestan and Eyberg (1998) conducted a review of psychosocial interventions for child and adolescent conduct problems, including oppositional defiant disorder and conduct disorder. Of the eighty-two studies they reviewed, they identified two treatments as well established and several others as probably efficacious. The well-established treatments, which include a series of videotapes modeling parent training (Spaccarelli, Cotler, & Penman, 1992) and a parent training manual (Bernal, Klinnert, & Schultz, 1980), follow Patterson and Gullion's *Living with Children* (1971), which is based on operant conditioning and teaches parents to reward desirable behaviors and punish deviant behaviors. The videotapes cover parent training lessons followed by a therapist-led discussion about the videotaped lesson.

Other treatments that are probably efficacious include some that focus on intervening early with youth and include parent training and MST. The treatments that are successful seem to show that identifying and intervening early in the process of development and using interventions that cover multiple domains, including home, school, and the community, are most successful. Although a number of treatments are successful for youth with conduct disorder, relatively little information is available for special populations, including ethnic minorities and females. There is a relative paucity of programs aimed at these populations, and where programs exist, there are relatively few studies examining their effectiveness.

Anxiety Disorders

The group of disorders comprising the category of anxiety disorders is prevalent and wide ranging among children and adolescents. The category is composed of separation anxiety disorder, generalized anxiety disorder, social phobia, obsessive-compulsive disorder (OCD), and posttraumatic stress disorder (PTSD). The commonality of these disorders is that the individual becomes nervous or anxious as a result of real or perceived threats. In separation anxiety disorder, the symptoms may arise as a result of separation from a parent, while fear of being embarrassed in a social situation is the trigger in social anxiety disorder. PTSD symptoms arise as a result of traumatic event experienced by the child. In OCD and generalized anxiety disorder, the trigger is not always identifiable or may be very diffuse. Many anxiety symptoms are appropriate for younger children to display but are developmentally inappropriate for the older child or adolescent. For example, a three-year-old child may become extremely anxious when separated from his mother for a brief period. This response is appropriate at age three; a similar response at age fifteen would be less appropriate and may be indicative of a psychiatric illness.

The standard of treatment for most anxiety disorders is a combination of pharmacotherapy and psychobehavioral interventions. The psychosocial treatments are commonly used despite a paucity of information on their efficaciousness. Phobic disorders are the only anxiety disorders for which a well-established treatment exists. Contingency management, which attempts to alter behavior by manipulating consequences through shaping and positive reinforcement, is deemed well established in the treatment of phobic disorders. Other commonly used interventions considered probably efficacious are systematic desensitization, which includes exposure and response prevention, and modeling. CBT has shown promise as a treatment for both phobic disorders and OCD.

There is evidence from laboratory settings that CBT is probably efficacious in the treatment of phobic disorders by reducing symptoms of anxiety and helping individuals cope with anxiety symptoms that persist (Kendell, 1994). However, these findings have not been replicated in real-world settings. CBT is sometimes effective in the treatment of OCD, but the results are inconclusive.

PHARMACOLOGICAL VERSUS PSYCHOLOGICAL INTERVENTIONS

Many parents, because of cultural, religious, or other beliefs, prefer to use psychological rather than pharmacological interventions to treat youth with emotional disturbances. In a review of the evidence supporting the use of psychotherapy in children and adolescents from more than five hundred studies, Weisz and Jensen (1999) reported that the evidence for the effectiveness of psychotherapy in everyday practice suggests little benefit. However, the evidence supporting more structured treatments is more positive and shows substantial evidence of their effectiveness. As Weisz and Jensen suggest, psychotherapies have more of a translational barrier moving from research to clinical practice than pharmacological interventions do. Ease of use, access to knowledge about the intervention, and more widely disseminated knowledge about the intervention aid clinicians in using pharmacological interventions, whereas similar barriers may slow the translation of psychological interventions into clinical practice.

PREVENTIVE INTERVENTIONS

The risk factors for the development of emotional and behavioral disturbances are well researched. These include biological influences such as parental and familial mental disorders, poor nutrition, toxin exposure, pre- and perinatal trauma, and childhood illness (U.S. Department of Health and Human Services, 2000). They also include psychosocial factors such as family discord, large family size and overcrowding, poverty, physical and sexual abuse, and stressful life events (U.S. Department of Health and Human Services, 2000). The goal of prevention programs is to address the risk factors that can be modified and to enable children to cope as effectively as possible with those that are cannot be modified.

Because childhood is so short and problems can develop very early without intervention, it is important to intervene in the lives of children as early as possible and across as many facets of the child's life as possible so that no child is left behind. This type of intervention requires a coordinated effort among agencies serving youth, including education, mental health, physical health, law enforcement, social service agencies, and community-based agencies. We outline four interventions that have been successful at primary prevention for emotional and behavioral problems.

Project Head Start

Project Head Start, conceived as a primary prevention program for poor and disadvantaged preschool youth, has become one of the largest and best-known prevention programs since it began in 1965. The goal of the program is to increase social competence and learning ability by intervening in a comprehensive manner with children and families through social, health, and education services. Repeated evaluations of Project Head Start have shown that early intervention can increase IQ and test scores compared to youth not in Head Start programs, but these findings are transient, and scores are comparable for Head Start and non–Head Start youth in early elementary school (Lee, Brooks-Gunn, Schnur, & Liaw, 1990). Other changes appear to be more sustained: lower enrollment in special education classes, higher rates of promotion to next grade level, and higher high school graduation rates (Barnett, 1995). Social competence and decreased antisocial behavior are higher in adolescents who received Head Start services as children (Webster-Stratton, 1998; Weikart, 1998). The positive findings of the studies demonstrating the benefits of Head Start have often been called into question and viewed with skepticism because of the lack of randomized controlled trials and the high degree of variability among programs.

The Carolina Abecedarian Project

The Carolina Abecedarian Project, unlike Project Head Start, was a carefully controlled study that began in infancy rather than during childhood. The project involved fifty-seven infants from low-income families who were randomly assigned to receive early intervention in a high-quality child care setting and fifty-four infants in a nontreated control group. Treated children received a full-time, individualized educational intervention from infancy through age five. These interventions addressed social, emotional, and cognitive development, with particular attention to language.

Children receiving the intervention had significantly higher scores on cognitive tests, and these differences remained through adolescence. A follow-up study of young adults found that individuals who had received the intervention as infants and children had higher mental test scores, better language skills, higher reading and math achievement scores; were more likely to remain in school and attend college; and had higher employment rates. The study demonstrated that very early childhood education significantly improves the education achievements of poor children (Campbell & Ramey, 1994).

Elmira Prenatal/Early Infancy Project

The Elmira Prenatal/Early Infancy Project, which began in the early 1980s, is a preventive intervention targeting economically disadvantaged first-time mothers. The intervention targeted an at-risk population to prevent the onset of health, social, and mental health problems in children and their parents. The study is a randomized control trial involving four hundred first-time mothers who were less than thirty weeks gestation. The mothers were assigned one of four groups: home visitation intervention only during pregnancy, home visitation until the child was two years of age, control group with transportation to usual prenatal care appointments and well-child visits, and control group with no services except for developmental screenings at age one and two years. The intervention group received home visits by nurses trained in parent education, methods of involving family and friends in assisting and supporting the mother, and linking the family to other services. The goal was to provide long-term follow-up to observe the impact of the intervention into adolescence.

The study found significant short- and long-term advantages for both the mothers and children in the intervention groups. Mothers reported decreased cigarette use, better nutrition, and better attendance at childbirth classes, and there were fewer reports of child abuse and neglect (Olds, Henderson, Tatelbaum, & Chamberlain, 1986). Children had fewer visits to hospital emergency rooms and received more appropriate play materials from their parents.

Primary Mental Health Project

The Primary Mental Health Project (PMHP) is an early detection and prevention program that addresses emotional and behavioral problems that interfere with effective learning. The program, which focuses on children in grades K through 3, systematically uses a screening instrument to identify children with early adjustment problems. Once problems are identified, students receive assistance through an individualized program consisting of play therapy and relationship skill building to help resolve home and school difficulties. Students are seen individually or in small groups once or twice a week for thirty- to sixty-minute sessions.

School-based mental health professionals, parents, the classroom teacher, and other pertinent school professionals, such as the school guidance counselor, provide the coordinated services for the child. The program also uses child associates who are carefully selected and trained nonprofessionals (such as college students and aides), working under close professional supervision. They act as extenders who increase the number of children who can be helped. PMHP represents a successful intervention that does not require highly trained mental health professionals to complete.

The intervention has been used in multiple setting with children from various ethnic backgrounds. Over thirty program evaluations have been completed in programs in two thousand schools in seven hundred school districts. The program is effective in improving school grades, achievement test scores, and adjustment ratings by teachers.

Other Interventions

There are other promising interventions that have not met criteria for effective or probably efficacious interventions, but show tremendous promise for preventing psychiatric sequelae among children who are abused or neglected. Zeanah and colleagues (2001) developed the most rigorously studied of these programs. The intervention focuses on providing assessments for emotional and behavioral problems for maltreated infants and toddlers who were placed in the foster care system and designing treatments for issues identified during the course of these assessments. Children receiving the intervention were less likely to return for another episode of abuse and were more likely to be freed for adoption.

CLINICIAN USE OF INTERVENTIONS AND RESULTS

The interventions outlined in this chapter range from those that can be implemented in the individual clinician's practice to those that require systemwide or multisystem change to implement. These interventions represent those that have been well studied and perhaps offer the best opportunity for improving emotional and behavioral disorders that affect youth.

The goal of every clinician who treats children and adolescents is to effect positive change in the lives of these individuals. In fact, most clinicians use the principle of using evidence-based treatments. For example, when a patient comes into the treatment setting, the clinician chooses treatments that he or she has found to be effective with similar patients in the past. The problem is that most of the techniques that clinicians use are the ones they learned in their training or have had direct exposure to in the course of their professional lives. For most clinicians, this represents a small fraction of the treatments that are available and effective.

RECOMMENDATIONS FOR FUTURE RESEARCH

Many of the studies explored in this chapter have been evaluated in optimal settings, which may not reflect real-world situations. The fact that a treatment may have been very successful when used in a research setting with a great deal of support from multiple sources does not mean that it will be successful in a public mental health center where the support may be less substantial. In these settings, the nuisance variables described by Schoenwald and Hoagwood (2001), may make the intervention less effective or require significant modification. Research on the transportability of effective treatments is important so that the most effective treatments reach the greatest number of children and adolescents.

A second issue is the notion of cultural competence and culturally related issues. As the United States moves more toward becoming a nation without a majority population, the issue of cultural competence will become increasingly important. The success of interventions may be heavily dependent on ethnic or other socioeconomic characteristics. These characteristics can differ substantially from one setting to another, and the intervention may require modifications to be successful or may not be successful in a different setting. Studying interventions in varied settings is important in being able to match interventions with settings in which they may be successful rather than employing a one-size-fits-all philosophy.

References

American Psychiatric Association. (1994). *Diagnostic and statistical manual of mental disorders* (4th ed.). Washington, DC: American Psychiatric Association.

Barnett, W. W. (1995). Long term effects of early childhood programs on cognitive and school outcomes. *Future of Children, 5*(3), 25–50.

Beardslee, W. R., Versage, E. M., Wright, E. J., & Salt, P. (1997). Examination of preventive interventions for families with depression: Evidence of change. *Development and Psychopathology, 9,* 109–137.

Bernal, M. E., Klinnert, M. D., & Schultz, L. A. (1980). Outcome evaluation of behavioral parent training and client-centered parent counseling for children with conduct problems. *Journal of Applied Behavior Analysis, 13,* 677–691.

Borduin, C. M., Mann, B. J., Cone, L. T., Henggeler, S. W., & Fucci, B. R., Blaske, D. M., & Williams, R. A. (1995). Multisystemic treatment of serious juvenile offenders: Long-term prevention of criminality and violence. *Journal of Consulting and Clinical-Psychology, 63,* 569–578.

Brestan, E. V., & Eyberg, S. M. (1998). Effective psychosocial treatments of conduct-disordered children and adolescents: 29 years, 82 studies, and 5,272 kids. *Journal of Clinical Child Psychology, 27,* 180–189.

Burns, B., Farmer, E., Angelo, A., Costello, E., & Behar, L. (1996). A randomized trial of case management for youth with serious emotional disturbance. *Journal of Clinical Child Psychology, 25,* 476–486.

Burns, B. J., & Goldman, S. K. (1998). *Promising practices in wraparound for children with severe emotional disturbance and their families.* In Center for Mental Health Services, *Systems of care: Promising practices in children's mental health.* Rockville, MD: Center for Mental Health Services, Substance Abuse and Mental Health Administration, U.S. Department of Health and Human Services.

Campbell, F., & Ramey, C. (1994). Effects of early intervention on intellectual and academic achievement: A follow-up study of children from low income families. *Child Development, 65,* 684–698.

Chamberlain, P., & Moore, K. (1998). A clinical model for parenting juvenile offenders: A comparison of group care versus family care. *Clinical Child Psychology and Psychiatry, 3,* 375–386.

Chamberlain, P., & Reid, J. B. (1991). Using a specialized foster care community treatment model for children and adolescents leaving the state mental hospital. *Journal of Community Psychology, 19,* 266–276.

Clark, H. B., Prange, M. E., Lee, B., Boyd, L. A., McDonald, B. A., & Stewart, E. S. (1994). Improving adjustment outcomes for foster children with emotional and behavioral disorders: Early findings from a controlled study on individualized services. *Journal of Emotional and Behavioral Disorders, 2,* 207–218.

Clark, H. B., Prange, M. E., Lee, B., Stewart, E. S., McDonald, B. B., & Boyd, L. A. (1998). An individualized wraparound process for children in foster care with emotional/behavioral disturbances: Follow-up findings and implications from a controlled study. In M. H. Epstein, K. Kutash, & A. J. Duchnowski (Eds.), *Outcomes for children and youth with emotional and behavioral disorders and their families: Programs and evaluation best practices* (pp. 686–707). Austin, TX: Pro-Ed.

Clarke, G., Hops, H., Lewinsohn, P. M., Andrews, J., Seeley, J. R., & Williams, J. (1992). Cognitive-behavioral group treatment of adolescent depression: Prediction of outcome. *Behavior Therapy, 23,* 341–354.

Clarke, G., Hornsbrook, M., Lynch, F., Polen, M., Gale, J., Beardslee, W., O'Connor, E., & Seeley, J. (2001). A randomized trial of a group cognitive intervention for preventing depression in adolescent offspring of depressed patients. *Archives of General Psychiatry, 58,* 1127–1134.

Evans, M. E., Banks, S. M., Huz, S., & McNulty, T. L. (1994). Initial hospitalization and community tenure outcomes of intensive case management for children and youth with serious emotional disturbance. *Journal of Child and Family Studies, 3,* 225–234.

Evans, M., Huz, S., McNulty, T., & Banks, S. (1996). Child, family, and systems outcomes of intensive case management in New York State. *Psychiatric Quarterly, 67,* 273–287.

Firestone, P., Crowe, D., Goodman, J. T., & McGrath, P. (1986). Vicissitudes of follow-up studies: Differential effects of parent training and stimulant medication with hyperactives. *American Journal of Orthopsychiatry, 56,* 184–194.

Goldman, S. K. (1999). The conceptual framework for wraparound: Definition, values, essential elements, and requirements for practice. In B. J. Burns & S. K. Goldman (Eds.), *Promising practices in wraparound for children with severe emotional disturbance and their families* (1998 series, Vol. 4). Washington, DC: Center for Effective Collaboration and Practice, American Institute for Research.

Grizenko, N. (1997). Outcome of multimodal day treatment for children with severe behavior problems: A five-year follow-up. *Journal of the American Academy of Child and Adolescent Psychiatry, 36,* 989–997.

Grizenko, N., Papineau, D., Sayegh, L. (1993). Effectiveness of a multimodal day treatment program for children with disruptive behavior problems. *Journal of the American Academy of Child and Adolescent Psychiatry, 32*, 127–134.

Hendren, R. L. (1999). *Disruptive behavior disorders in children and adolescents.* Washington, DC: American Psychiatric Press.

Henggeler, S. W., Pickrel, S. G., Brondino, M. J., & Crouch, J. L. (1996). Eliminating (almost) treatment dropout of substance abusing or dependent delinquents through home-based multisystemic therapy. *American Journal of Psychiatry, 153*, 427–428.

Henggeler, S. W., Rodrick, J. D., Borduin, C. M., Hanson, C. F., Watson, S. M., & Vrey, J. R. (1986). Multisystemic treatment of juvenile offenders: Effects on adolescent behavior and family interaction. *Developmental Psychology, 22*, 132–141.

Henggeler, S. W., Schoenwald, S. K., Borduin, C. M., Rowland, M. D., & Cunningham, P. B. (1998). *Multisystemic treatment of antisocial behavior in children and adolescents.* New York: Guilford Press.

Hoagwood, K., Burns, B., Kiser, L., Ringeisen, H., & Schoenwald, S. (2001). Evidence-based practice in child and adolescent mental health services. *Psychiatric Services, 52*(9), 1179–1189.

Horn, W. F., Ialongo, N., Greenberg, G., Packard, T., & Smith-Winberry, C. (1990). Additive effects of behavioral parent training and self-control therapy with attention deficit hyperactivity disordered children. *Journal of Clinical Child Psychology, 19*, 98–110.

Horn, W. F., Ialongo, N. S., Pascoe, J. M., Greenberg, G., Packard, T., Lopez, M., Wagner, A., & Putler, L. (1991). Additive effects of psychostimulants, parent training, and self-control therapy with ADHD children. *Journal of the American Academy of Child and Adolescent Psychiatry, 30*, 233–240.

Horn, W. F., Ialongo, N., Popovich, S., & Peradotto, D. (1987). Behavioral parent training and cognitive-behavioral self-control therapy with ADD-H children: Comparative and combined effects. *Journal of Clinical Child Psychology, 16*, 57–68.

Jensen, P. S., Hinshaw, S. P., Swanson, J. M., Greenhill, L. L., Conners, C. K., Arnold, L. E., Abikoff, H. B., Elliott, G., Hechtman, L., Hoza, B., March, J. S., Newcorn, J. H., Severe, J. B., Vitiello, B., Wells, K., & Wigal, T. (2001). Findings from the NIMH Multimodal Treatment Study of ADHD (MTA): Implications and applications for primary care providers. *Journal of Developmental and Behavioral Pediatrics, 22*, 60–73.

Kaslow, N. J., & Thompson, M. P. (1998). Applying the criteria for empirically supported treatments to studies of psychosocial interventions for child and adolescent depression. *Journal of Clinical Child Psychology, 27*, 146–155.

Kendell, P. C. (1994). Treating anxiety disorders in children: Results of a randomized clinical trial. *Journal of Consulting and Clinical Psychology, 62*, 100–110.

Koren, P. E., Paulson, R., Kinny, R., Yatchmenoff, D., Gordon, L., & DeChillo, N. (1997). Service coordination in children's mental health: An empirical study from the caregiver's perspective. *Journal of Emotional and Behavioral Disorders, 5*, 162–172.

Kutash, K., & Rivera, V. R. (1995). Effectiveness of children's mental health services: A review of the literature. *Education and Treatment of Children, 18,* 443–477.

Lee, V. E., Brooks-Gunn, J., Schnur, E., & Liaw, F. R. (1990). Are Head Start effects sustained? A longitudinal follow up comparison of disadvantaged children attending Head Start, no preschool, and other preschool programs. *Child Development, 61,* 495–507.

Lewinsohn, P. M., Clarke, G. N., & Hoberman, H. M. (1989). The Coping with Depression Course: Review and future directions. *Canadian Journal of Behavioural Science, 21,* 470–493.

Lewinsohn, P. M., Clarke, G. N., Rohde, P., Hops, H., & Seely, J. (1996). A course in coping: A cognitive-behavioral approach to the treatment of adolescent depression. In D. Hobbs & P. S. Jensen (Eds.). *Psychosocial treatments for child and adolescent disorders: Empirically based strategies for clinical practice* (pp. 109–135). Washington, DC: American Psychological Association.

Lonigan, C. J., Elbert, J. C., & Johnson, S. B. (1998). Empirically supported psychosocial interventions for children: An overview. *Journal of Clinical Psychology, 27,* 138–145.

Olds, D. L., Henderson, C., Tatelbaum, R., & Chamberlain, R. (1986). Improving the delivery of prenatal care and outcomes of pregnancy: A randomized trial of nurse home visitation. *Pediatrics, 77,* 16–28.

Patterson, G. R., & Brodsky, G. (1966). A behavior modification program for a child with multiple behavior problems. *Journal of Child Psychology and Psychiatry, 7,* 277–295.

Patterson, G., & Gullion, E. (1971). *Living with children.* Champaign, IL: Research Press.

Pelham, W.E.J., Wheeler, T., & Chronis, A. (1998). Empirically supported psychosocial treatments for attention deficit hyperactivity disorder. *Journal of Clinical Child Psychology, 27,* 190–205.

Pickrel, S. G., & Henggeler, S. W. (1996). Multisystemic therapy for adolescent substance abuse and dependence. *Child and Adolescent Psychiatric Clinics of North America, 5,* 201–211.

Rowland, M. D., Henggeler, S. W., Gordon, A. M., Pickrel, S. G., Cunningham, P. B., & Edwards, J. E. (2000). Adapting multisystemic therapy to serve youth presenting psychiatric emergencies: Two case studies. *Child Psychology and Psychiatry Review, 5,* 30–43.

Schoenwald, S. K., Brown, T. L., & Henggeler, S. W. (2000). Inside multisystemic therapy: Therapist, supervisory, and program practices. *Journal of Emotional and Behavioral Disorders, 8,* 113–127.

Schoenwald, S., & Hoagwood, K. (2001). Effectiveness, transportability, and dissemination of interventions: What matters when? *Psychiatric Services, 52,* 1190–1197.

Sonuga, B., Edmund, J. S., Daley, D., Thompson, M., Laver Bradbury, C., & Weeks, A. (2001). Parent-based therapies for preschool attention-deficit/hyperactivity disorder: A randomized, controlled trial with a community sample. *Journal of the American Academy of Child and Adolescent Psychiatry, 40,* 402–408.

Spaccarelli, S., Cotler, S., & Penman, D. (1992). Problem-solving skills training as a supplement to behavioral parent training. *Cognitive Therapy and Research, 16,* 1–17.

Stark, K. D., Reynolds, W. M., & Kaslow, N. J. (1987). A comparison of the relative efficacy of self-control therapy and a behavioral problem-solving therapy for depression in children. *Journal of Abnormal Child Psychology, 15,* 91–113.

Stark, K. D., Rouse, L. W., & Livingston, R. (1991). Treatment of depression during childhood and adolescence: Cognitive-behavioral procedures for the individual and family. In P. Kendall (Ed.), *Child and adolescent therapy: Cognitive behavioral procedure.* New York: Guilford Press.

Stein, D. B. (1999). A medication-free parent management program for children diagnosed as ADHD. *Ethical Human Sciences and Services, 1,* 61–79.

Stroul, B. A., & Friedman, R. M. (1986). *A system of care for severely emotionally disturbed children and youth.* Washington, DC: Child and Adolescent Service System Program Technical Assistance Center, Georgetown University Child Development Center.

U.S. Department of Health and Human Services. (1999). *Mental health: A report of the surgeon general.* Rockville, MD: U.S. Department of Health and Human Services, Substance Abuse and Mental Health Services Administration, Center for Mental Health Services, National Institutes of Health, National Institute of Mental Health.

U.S. Department of Health and Human Services. (2000). *Mental health: A report of the surgeon general.* Washington, DC: U.S. Government Printing Office.

Webster-Stratton, C. (1998). Preventing conduct problems in Head Start children: Strengthening parenting competencies. *Journal of Consulting and Clinical Psychology, 66,* 715–730.

Weikart, D. P. (1998). Changing early childhood development through educational intervention. *Preventive Medicine, 27,* 233–237.

Weinberg, H. A. (1999). Parent training for attention-deficit hyperactivity disorder: Parental and child outcome. *Journal of Clinical Psychology, 55,* 907–913.

Weisz, J., & Jensen, P. (1999). Efficacy and effectiveness of child and adolescent psychotherapy and pharmacotherapy. *Mental Health Services Research, 1,* 125–157.

Zeanah, C. H., Larrieu, J. A., Heller, S. S., Valliere, J., Hinshaw Fuselier, S., Aoki, Y., & Drilling, M. (2001). Evaluation of a preventive intervention for maltreated infants and toddlers in foster care. *Journal of the American Academy of Child and Adolescent Psychiatry, 40,* 214–221.

CHAPTER NINE

Case Management

The Linchpin of Community-Based Systems of Care

Nancy C. Winters
Elizabeth Terrell

C ase management is widely viewed as an essential, if not *the* essential, component of systems of care for children and adolescents. It has been described as the "glue that holds the system together" (Stroul & Friedman, 1986, p. 109) and the "linchpin for an effective interagency system" (England & Cole, 1992, p. 632). Although the advent of case management for children and adolescents with serious emotional disturbance (SED) is more recent than its use for adults with severe and persistent mental illness (SPMI), its prominence for children with SED parallels the growing emphasis on case management for adults with severe mental disorders (Rosen & Teesson, 2001). Case management for adults has been described as a cornerstone of community care (Kanter, 1989) and "the most significant innovation in the organization of mental health services since the asylum in the early 1800s" (Holloway & Carson, 2001, p. 21).

Despite the widespread use of case management and the increasing belief in its centrality in systems of care for children and adults, case management is not a single concept but a range of functions about which there is no agreed-on terminology or definition. The research literature on case management suffers from a myriad of different terms, which are often used interchangeably, creating confusion as to what interventions are actually being compared. In fact, there are probably more terms for case management approaches in the adult and child literature than there are distinct case management functions. Such terms include *case management, care management, care coordination, service coordination, intensive case management, clinical case management, broker case management, family-centered case management, strengths case management, rehabilitation case management, assertive community treatment, therapeutic case advocacy; as well as the primary therapist model, interdisciplinary team model, family as case manager,* and *paraprofessional* or *volunteer case manager model.*

The variations in terminology do have significance, however, and they imply functional differences along broad dimensions. For example, Friesen and Poertner (1995) make the distinction that *case management* is an intervention at the client (that is, child and family) level, whereas *care coordination* implies working at the system level, emphasizing coordination and linking of services, activities that are particularly relevant for the multi-agency-involved children served in systems of care. The terms *care coordination* and *service coordination* are also seen as more supportive of family members' wish to avoid the stigmatizing connotation of "case" and the implication of being "managed" (Illback & Neill, 1995). This terminology is consistent with the goal of family empowerment that would promote the natural role of parents as case managers for their children. Although arguments in favor of these other terms have merit, *case management* continues to be the most inclusive term in the child and adult mental health literature, and for that reason we use it in this chapter.

DEFINITIONAL ISSUES AND CASE MANAGEMENT FUNCTIONS

Despite the many forms and functions embedded in the concept of case management, certain core elements generally hold true. Case management includes a set of functions intended to mobilize, coordinate, and maintain an array of services (Stroul & Friedman, 1996); to overcome fragmentation of services and offer a continuum of care; and to provide continuity of care. Case management ensures that services are suited to the individual child and family, are clinically and culturally appropriate, and lead to desired outcomes.

Stroul and Friedman (1996) articulated basic elements of case management in systems of care: (1) assessment; (2) service planning; (3) service implementation, including linking, brokering (procuring), resource development, and troubleshooting obstacles; (4) service coordination (ensuring multiple services are directed at the same goal); (5) monitoring and evaluation; and (6) advocacy, including empowering families and overcoming barriers. This model is similar to the adult broker model described by Intagliata (1982), whose functions are assessment, planning, linking to services, monitoring, and advocacy.

Case Management Functions Along a Continuum

Case management can be best understood as a set of functions that are not static but exist along a continuum ranging from administrative to service functions, as depicted in Figure 9.1. At the administrative end of the continuum, case man-

Review	Gatekeeping	Brokering of Services	Care Coordination	Advocacy	Direct Support	Treatment	Therapist
Performs administrative review of care plans for organizational resource management.	Manages referrals, authorizes payment, performs utilization review.	Establishes helping relationship with family; procures and implements services to meet child and family needs.	Coordinates service to ensure all services are appropriate and addressing the same goals; monitors outcomes.	Serves as an advocate for the family across different child-serving agencies' systems.	Provides a variety of direct supportive services, for example, informal mentoring, transportation.	Provides appropriate assessment and treatment; ensures that interventions meet clinical needs.	Serves as traditional therapist and may assume other helping connections.

ADMINISTRATIVE → **SERVICE**

FIGURE 9.1. Continuum of Case Management Functions.

Source: Adapted from Cole and Poe (1993, p. 65).

agement functions may include utilization management, gatekeeping, and service authorization. Functions in the middle of the continuum include brokering (procuring, implementing) of services, monitoring client outcomes, managing interagency relationships, and advocating for the child and family in different systems. Supportive functions and direct therapeutic services are on the service end of the continuum. In systems of care practice, where the needs of the child and family drive the services, the case manager may perform different functions along this continuum at different times, depending on the changing needs of the child and family and the phase of treatment. For example, direct supportive functions may assume prominence early in the process to facilitate engaging the child and family in treatment, whereas more administrative functions, such as coordination of care and monitoring outcomes, may be more relevant after an individualized service array is put into place. Fluid application of these functions allows for responsiveness to the evolving needs and competencies of the child and family.

Variables Influencing Case Management Functions

Case management approaches differ according to intensity of contact, amount of direct service provided (for example, clinical versus administrative case management), level of intervention (such as client level versus system level), and whose interests shape the intervention (for example, client-centered versus program-driven case management) (Schaedle & Epstein, 2000). Approaches along these dimensions are influenced by a number of variables that have been similarly described in the adult and child case management literature (Evans & Armstrong, 2002; Schaedle & Epstein, 2000; Stroul & Friedman, 1996).

Intensity of case management is influenced by caseload size, frequency of contacts, and direct clinical responsibility. Intensive case management is generally applied to the highest-need clients, who are at risk of needing restrictive and highly expensive services. The more intensive models provide more direct support and clinical roles. For children with serious emotional and behavioral challenges, it has been suggested that optimal caseloads are between five and fifteen (Katz-Leavy, Lourie, Stroul, & Zeigler-Dendy, 1992; Evans & Armstrong 2002). Duration of case management is another variable; it is generally related to the population being served. Children with SED tend to be served for longer periods as compared with those who have more transient problems or fewer multisystem needs (Evans & Armstrong, 2002).

The nature of the organizational context is another important variable. Important aspects of the organizational context as described by Burns, Gwaltney, & Bishop (1995) include team versus individual structure, location, whether the case manager has fiscal and clinical decision-making authority, and auspices (accountability). The case management team tends to be used in more intensive models.Location of case management in an agency providing mental health services as opposed to a managed care organization shifts case management toward client-level rather than system-level functions. Client-centered approaches are enhanced if the case manager has access to flexible funds to provide an individualized service array. Fiscal authority to decide to what extent and for how long those individualized services will be in place may be critical to implementing the service plan. Accountability (that is, to whom the case manager is accountable for process and outcomes) is another critically important and often unrecognized variable. With the advent of public managed mental health care, utilization management models of mental health case management accountable primarily to the mental health organization may be used for cost containment. The most extreme example of the utilization case manager is one who performs reviews over the telephone for gatekeeping purposes. Although in practice, case managers can and do represent multiple interests, the tilt in their role toward representing the interests of the client versus the mental health organization determines whether clinical decision making is driven primarily by the child's and family's unique needs or by resource utilization directives.

ORIGINS OF CASE MANAGEMENT

Case management is not an invention of mental health, but grew out of social service models (Moore, 1990). Its origins can be traced back to the 1960s, when there was rapid growth of human services and programs, with resulting networks of fragmented and uncoordinated services. Case management approaches began to emerge in the 1970s to manage an individual's involvement with the service delivery system and to fill the gaps that had occurred during deinstitutionalization (Intagliata, 1982). At the same time, case management was adopted by the private sector to restrain costs that had been driven up by increased use of mental health services (Sledge et al., 1995). The use of case management as a means of coordinating and increasing access to services spread to other populations, such as the elderly, individuals with traumatic brain injury, and individuals with developmental disabilities. Case management has been used for children with chronic medical illness. The Academy of Pediatrics is now recognizing the need for pediatricians to take on more care coordination functions for their patients who are involved with multiple services (American Academy of Pediatrics Committee on Children with Disabilities, 1999). Child-serving agencies such as child welfare and the educational system employ case management as the locus of accountability and coordination of service delivery. Education legislation such as Public Law 99–142 and the Individuals with Disabilities Education Act provide for case management for children in need of special education services. Public Law 102–321 authorized the Child Mental Health Services Initiative, which is being implemented by Center for Mental Health Services (CMHS). This program identifies case management as an essential function in its system of care grantee sites nationwide.

Use of Case Management with Adult Populations

Until recently, most of the literature on case management focused on adults with SPMI. Case management in adults has been used to address the overuse of inpatient services, poor vocational and social functioning, and quality-of-life issues for adults with SPMI. Assertive community treatment (ACT) is a case management approach based on the Program in Assertive Community Treatment (PACT; Stein & Test, 1980). ACT is a team approach providing case management and comprehensive services to adults with chronic mental illness. In comparative studies, PACT was shown to be associated with decreased hospital days and better functional outcomes, with costs not greater than for traditional services, including broker case management. ACT case managers generally have caseloads of ten to fifteen clients, work in teams, provide most of the direct mental health services, and frequently see their clients outside the office. Case managers who work in the broker model purchase and coordinate services; they generally have caseloads of fifty to one hundred, usually see clients in their office, and have limited hours of availability. A sizable literature comparing these contrasting models has demonstrated the superiority of ACT over broker case management in reducing hospital use and improving housing stability (Bedell, Cohen, & Sullivan, 2000; Holloway & Carson, 2001; Wolff et al., 1997; Ziguras & Stuart, 2000).

The literature demonstrating better outcomes with the ACT model, which includes direct clinical service and use of a team of mental health professionals (including a psychiatrist), suggests that the brokering and linking functions may be less important for adults than the suitability of the treatment provided. The risk of expecting too much from case management and allowing case management to substitute for the services themselves has been pointed out (Sledge et al., 1995). Holloway and Carson (2001) also that note that "case management is not in itself an effective treatment for severe mental illness" (p. 28).

Contrasts Between Children and Adults

Although there are undoubtedly some lessons to be learned from the case management literature in adults, it is not yet clear how these findings apply to children with SED. There are many differences between the two age groups. First, adults with SPMI who are highly symptomatic tend to use psychiatric hospitals, whereas children who are seriously disturbed are served in numerous settings, including residential treatment centers, foster care, intensive alternative educational placements, and juvenile correctional facilities. This difference has both clinical and cost implications. From a clinical perspective, many agencies need to be involved in service planning for seriously disturbed youth, making the care coordination function more critical. From a utilization perspective, reduction of hospital use is not a large cost savings for children and adolescents since they receive restrictive services in multiple systems.

Another difference is that children with SED tend to have diverse internalizing and externalizing clinical problems, necessitating a variety of treatment approaches (Hoagwood, Jensen, Petti, & Burns, 1996; Liao, Manteuffel, Paulic, & Sondheimer, 2001), in contrast to the adult SPMI population, largely made up of individuals with psychotic disorders (Mueser, Bond, Drake, & Resnick, 1998). Thus, interventions need to be more varied. The most significant difference between the two populations, however, is that children exist in the ecological framework of their families and other caregivers (for example, teachers, child care workers, and health care providers). Children's strengths and vulnerabilities develop in the context of their relationships with these caregivers. When parental mental health or addiction problems present barriers to the child's progress, services need to include both child and family. Consequently, children cannot be served without involving the multiple parties who are interested in and responsible for their welfare.

Five agencies are designated by law to serve children: child welfare, mental health, public health, education, and juvenile justice. The educational, child welfare, and juvenile justice systems each plays a significant role in providing services to youth with SED. Moreover, each child-serving agency has its own legal mandates, service protocols, funding priorities, and training and supervisory structures, all of which shape different institutional cultures and practices.

The System of Care Movement

The lack of coordination among these agencies that serve children and adolescents with SED was a significant factor in the genesis of the system of care movement. Several reports on the status of children's mental health services in the 1970s and 1980s documented that children with SED were either not receiving mental health services or were receiving fragmented and uncoordinated services. They were often placed in overly restrictive settings away from their families and communities (Joint Commission on the Mental Health of Children, 1969). The Child and Adolescent Service System Program (CASSP), under the auspices of the National Institute of Mental Health and later CMHS under the Substance Abuse and Mental Health Services Administration, was initiated in 1984 to develop an integrated system of care for youth with SED.

Stroul and Friedman (1986) outlined the system of care concept and articulated core CASSP values and guiding principles that provide a framework for the SOC concept and have guided subsequent system of care reform efforts (see Figure 2.1). The essential elements of this approach are threefold: (1) the types and mix of services are driven by the needs of the child and family from a strengths-based perspective; (2) the locus of services is in the community, derived from multiagency collaboration; and (3) the services offered are responsive to the individual culture and characteristics of the children and families served (Center for Mental Health

Services, 1997). The CMHS Comprehensive Community Mental Health Services for Children and Their Families Program, which has funded over sixty-five system of care demonstration sites across the nation, defines case management as an essential component of systems of care and requires case management for all youngsters offered access to services in grant sites.

The Role of Case Management in Children's Systems of Care

The crucial role of case management in systems of care follows from the CASSP value that services are driven by the unique needs of the child and family. Because of the unavoidable tension between the needs of the individual and the fiscal constraints of the system, true individualization of care may not be accomplished without someone empowered by the system to help accomplish these goals. A system-empowered case manager serves as the locus of accountability to ensure access to needed services, much like Solomon's (1992) characterization of case management as a coordinated strategy on behalf of clients to obtain the services that they need, when they need them, and for as long as they need them.

The following issues that commonly arise in treatment planning for a child with SED highlight the importance of a system-empowered case manager:

- There may be multiple providers who do not communicate with each other, leading to duplication and fragmentation.

- There may be multiple providers who have different conceptualizations of the child's problems, resulting in lack of coherence in the service plan and conflicting treatment approaches.

- The providers may not be targeting the problems that the child or family is most concerned about.

- The child or family may not accept services because their concerns and apprehensions are not being understood or respected. This is especially relevant to minority children and families.

- The child or family may not engage in services because their social or concrete needs (for housing, vocation, or recreation) are not being met.

- Adequate consultation is not available to assist in diagnostic clarification or formulation of the problem, development of an appropriate treatment plan, and problem-solving difficulties in team functioning.

- The services needed (such as specialized services or culturally competent clinicians) may not be available within the service continuum. It has been well documented that minority youth have poorer access than nonminority youth to any mental health services, as well as inadequate access to culturally competent service providers (Pumariega & Cross, 1997; U.S. Department of Health and Human Services, 1999, 2001).

RESEARCH ON CASE MANAGEMENT MODELS IN SYSTEMS OF CARE

Several case management models in children's systems of care have now been described, and there is an emerging evidence base to support case management as a significant intervention in systems of care (Evans & Armstrong, 2002).

The Wraparound Approach

Developed over the past fifteen years, wraparound is an approach to treatment defined as a "planning process involving the child and family that results in a unique set of community services and natural supports individualized for that child and family to achieve a positive set of outcomes" (Burns & Goldman, 1999, p. xiii). Although the wraparound process is not a case management approach per se, it is used in client-centered case management. The wraparound process as described by VanDenBerg and Grealish (1996) includes the following elements:

- Wraparound efforts are based in the community.
- Services and supports are individualized to meet the needs of the children and families rather than being driven by priorities of categorical services.
- Parents are included at every level of the planning process.
- The process is culturally competent and based on unique values, strengths, and social or racial composition of the child and family.
- The process has access to flexible, noncategorical funding.
- The process is implemented on an interagency basis and owned by the larger community.
- The services are unconditional, so that when needs change, the services are modified rather than the child or family being rejected.
- Outcomes are measured so that the process is developed on an empirical scientific basis.

The wraparound model, with its emphasis on individualized, strength-based services, relies on flexible funding to allow for a balance of formal and informal interventions. Wraparound lends itself to nontraditional services, including in-home providers, respite care, and services by paraprofessionals (Burchard, Bruns, & Burchard, 2002). Results of service effectiveness studies suggest that nontraditional services (especially case management, home-based services, and therapeutic foster care) are effective in altering service-level outcomes, such as change in placements and service intensity (Jensen et al., 1999). The role of case manager in service implementation and coordination, monitoring, and advocacy is critical to the wraparound process.

Burns, Goldman et al. (1999) reviewed multiple uncontrolled studies of case management using a wraparound approach. Overall, they concluded, there is emerging evidence for the effectiveness of wraparound, although results often focus on service use rather than clinical status. They noted questions about the integrity of the wraparound interventions, a concern also put forth in Burchard et al.'s recent review of wraparound (2002). They suggested two priority areas for future research on the effectiveness of wraparound: (1) establishing a reliable method to assess fidelity of the intervention and (2) more controlled studies contrasting wraparound with other interventions. The recently developed Wraparound Fidelity Index measuring the presence of wraparound elements appears to have promising psychometric properties (Bruns, Ermold, & Burchard, 2001).

Intensive Case Management Models in New York

The Children and Youth Intensive Case Management model (CYICM) in New York State involved an intensive broker model in which case managers with caseloads of ten were assigned to high-risk youth populations as long as necessary. Case managers' activities, based primarily in the community, included advocacy and direct support, in addition to service coordination. The case managers were available to clients at all times and had access to flexible funds. When compared with a matched comparison group, CYICM led to a decrease in inpatient utilization and decreased high-risk behaviors (Evans, Banks, Huz, & McNulty, 1994).

The family-centered intensive case management (FCICM) model is a team case management approach described by Evans, Armstrong, and Kuppinger (1996) that uses parent advocates and flexible service funds to purchase economic and social supports, along with in-home respite care. The family-centered case manager's aim is to support the skills of family members in functioning as the natural case manager for the child. Evans, Armstrong, Kuppinger, Huz, and Johnson (1998) compared two intensive community-based interventions targeting children who had been approved for out-of-home placement. Children were randomly assigned to two conditions. The first was FCICM, which used a team of case manager and family advocate to provide all care in the home; the second was family-based treatment (FBT), a treatment foster program, which treated the child out of the home. The children in the FCICM were shown to have better clinical and functional outcomes at significantly lower cost than the FBT group. Neither group showed improvement in family functioning at eighteen months (Evans & Armstrong, 2002).

Broker Model: The Oregon Partners Project

The Oregon Partners Project (1990–1995), a Robert Wood Johnson Mental Health Services Program for Youth system of care demonstration program, included a family-centered broker-style case management model with the following elements:

- Access to flexible funding from a pooled fund
- Multiagency service planning teams
- Family participation at all levels
- Caseloads of seventeen
- Case manager fiscal authority to authorize all services except for foster care and school placements
- Close supervision of case managers by child and adolescent psychiatrists

The Oregon Mental Health Division and Portland State University did an evaluation of the Oregon Partners Project (OPP) using a quasi-experimental design comparing case management and flexible funding (OPP) with case managers lacking access to flexible funds or fiscal authority (Gratton, Paulsen, Stuntzner-Gibson, & Summers, 1995). At the twelve-month period, the OPP children were more socially competent; children and caregivers were more satisfied with services and more empowered as families; the service system was more coordinated, comprehensive, and individualized; and less restrictive, community-based alternative services had been developed. The groups did not show differences in clinical outcomes.

EPSDT Early and Periodic Screening, Diagnosis, and Treatment Program versus Home-Based Therapy: Two Wraparound Models

Fallon (2001) compared two wraparound models in Philadelphia. One was a modular model, an early and periodic screening, diagnosis, and treatment (EPSDT) program with a separate evaluator, behavioral specialist, therapeutic support staff, and mobile therapist. The other model, the home-based therapy program (HBT), consisted of a team of two experienced mental health clinicians who did anything and everything needed, including evaluation and therapy. Interestingly, many of the same staff members were involved in both programs, and they shared the same psychiatric consultant. Outcomes at six, twelve, and eighteen months were compared. The two programs had similar overall costs, but youth enrolled in the HBT model showed greater clinical improvement at all measurement points. There was also a significant dropout rate in the EPSDT program. These results suggest that in children with SED, as in adults with SPMI, the clinical case management model may be more effective than the broker model. The less effective

EPSDT model, which delivered more hours of service by more people, recalls Bickman's comment about the Fort Bragg continuum of care project: "More is not always better" (1996, p. 689).

Primary Clinician Case Manager versus Specialist Case Manager

Burns, Farmer, Angold, Costello, and Behar (1996) did a randomized trial of case management in which a dedicated case manager (experimental condition) was compared with case management functions assigned to the primary therapist. They found that designating primary clinicians as case managers did not increase the time they spent doing case management. Youth in the experimental condition reported less alcohol use than in the control condition. In addition, youth in the experimental condition had a richer array of services, used fewer hospital days, remained in treatment longer, and reported greater satisfaction than in the control condition.

THE PRACTICE OF FAMILY-CENTERED CASE MANAGEMENT

Case management guided by the CASSP principles for children's systems of care is child and family centered; we refer to this general approach as family-centered case management.

Philosophy

Family-centered models of case management are particularly compatible with the system of care and wraparound philosophies. These models emphasize the child's and family's strengths as well as needs, and seek to provide the family with the skills and resources needed to care for a child with SED. Family-centered case management uses wraparound principles. It is characterized by fluidity and flexibility, so that the level of services matches the needs of the child and family (whose needs change from day to day). Its aim is to support the family as the natural case manager for the child. Developing and maintaining positive working alliances with parents is the cornerstone of effective case management in work with SED children. The effective case manager also needs to build cohesive service teams that develop a shared understanding of the problems being addressed and agree on appropriate desired outcomes that are meaningful to the child and family.

Ecological Framework

Service planning within systems of care lends itself to using an ecological conceptual framework that maintains a systemic overview. In this framework, the child is understood in the context of the family as well as the school, neighborhood, and larger community environments in which he or she lives (Evans

& Armstrong, 2002). In the child's ecological system, factors such as the parents' untreated medical or addictions problems or changes in their work environment can be understood as significant influences on the child's functioning and therefore appropriate targets for service interventions.

Strength-Based Orientation

In treatment planning, there is a relative weight toward identifying and building on strengths rather than targeting deficits. A strength-based orientation is based on the theory that change proceeds more successfully in a context of competency and as a result of reinforcing successes. A strength-based assessment carefully identifies positive individual traits, abilities, talents, and interests; family values, beliefs, and desires; and the natural supports, friendships, and extended family within the community. Interventions supporting and enlarging on strengths are then designed to meet the unique needs of the child and family.

The Role of Parents and Family Members

Within the past decade, the role of parents, family members, and other caregivers in the care of children with behavioral and emotional disorders has been dramatically reconceptualized. And it could be argued that this will be one of the most abiding contributions of the system of care movement. In a system of care, parents are viewed as experts in the unique characteristics of their children, central to the life and well-being of the child, and the enduring factor in the long term. At the team level, parents act as partners with case managers to drive and manage the service plan. Nationally, families are participating in training and advocacy efforts to bring the family perspective to the program, administrative, policy, and legislative levels. In local systems of care, family-driven outcomes are evident in program evaluation and service delivery products.

Research on the effectiveness of various models must integrate authentic family feedback. When family members were asked by Friesen and Poertner (1995) to identify the aspects of case management most important to them, they reported that parents should have major influence in deciding their own case management role; that a single case manager should have frequent contact with the child, family, and key individuals and be responsible for finding necessary resources; that both parents and the child should be involved in decision making; and that case managers should be committed and accountable to the family and support family functioning.

The Role of the Child and Family Team

The team process itself is at the center of the system of care model. Through the working of the team, family members are empowered to come together as equals with representatives of agencies caring for their children; the team is client centered and works collaboratively through consensus building. Teams include parents, family members, advocates, and others chosen to attend by the family; the clinical case manager; the child and adolescent psychiatrist; and involved providers and child-serving system representatives. Individual roles and responsibilities are articulated, but the overarching role of the team is to work together to document, direct, and revise the individualized service plan comprising the strengths, needs, strategies, and desired outcomes. Such a plan should reduce or eliminate conflicting mandates or approaches. The case manager, modeling active collaboration with parents and family members, provides leadership and direction to the process. Such collaboration creates a plan that is truly dictated by the needs of the family and a process that is supportive and empowering to families.

Use of Nontraditional Interventions

As shown in Figure 9.2, a host of nontraditional interventions can be accessed in an individualized, child- and family-centered service plan. Although these services have sometimes been referred to as wraparound services, that term should be reserved for a comprehensive approach to providing services, including principles and values. These services are typically purchased with flexible funds; however, use of these services may be constrained by state "medical necessity" rules for covered services. In some states, managed Medicaid programs have expanded covered services; however, recent data suggest that these services themselves are still not widely available or may be funded by agencies outside the mental health benefit (Stroul, Pires, & Armstrong, 2001).

Emergency respite services

Crisis workers with twenty-four-hour availability

Culturally specific traditional services

In-home supportive and therapeutic services

Therapeutic foster care

Specialized group homes

Supported independent living

Mental health–supported classrooms

Transportation

Vocational mentoring

Parent training and coaching

Therapeutic mentoring

Flexibly funded incentive plans

Family-selected respite providers

FIGURE 9.2. Examples of Nontraditional Services.

In developing nontraditional interventions, the case manager and family work closely together to identify services that are compatible with the family's attitudes and beliefs, target mutually identified problems and goals, address problems in a strength-enhancing manner, and make use of community supports that have the potential to expand the network of contacts after formal services are completed.

Integration with Other Child-Serving Agencies

This model also takes into account the different service systems that the child and family draw on, including mental health, social services, education, health, substance abuse, vocational services, and recreational services. The coordination function may include sharing of case management tasks across different agencies that are serving a child, or the case manager in a multiagency team may be selected from the agency most involved with the child. Different agency cultures and mandates need to be respected in the interagency team process. For example, child welfare and juvenile justice service planning may be determined by the court system, superseding the team planning process. Workers from other systems may have different treatment philosophies, such as a correctional orientation in juvenile justice, creating disagreements as to what interventions are appropriate. The process of bringing together these differing perspectives to form a functioning team is one of the early tasks of case manager. Successful models of interagency collaboration include service colocation such as school-based mental health programs and sharing of case management functions.

Training and Qualifications of Case Managers

As is the case with mental health counselors, case managers may be educated in the areas of social work, counseling psychology, marriage and family therapy, or other behavioral sciences. Most public agencies receiving Medicaid funding require basic credentialing for mental health professionals, which may vary from a bachelor's degree with relevant experience to the master's degree. However, training in the core functions of case management varies from organization to organization and reflects the model adopted by the specific agency and the local community resources and norms. Competencies in core functions may not be articulated as well as the competencies of the mental health counselor dictated by state licensure boards. A comprehensive, manualized approach is the Child Mental Health Case Management Curriculum (Behar, Zipper, & Weil, 1994).

The Clinical Perspective Informing Case Management

Successful case managers are not merely coordinators and brokers of services, although this function is unquestionably very important for youth involved with multiple agencies. Their work needs to be informed by a clinical understanding and formulation of the child and family's problems, needs, strengths, beliefs, and adaptive capacities. Case managers need to have access to good-quality and appropriately timed psychiatric and psychological diagnostic assessment. Children with SED tend to be diagnostically complex (Liao et al., 2001) with multifactorial disorders that often have biological underpinnings. Even the most comprehensive wraparound approach cannot compensate for a missed or inaccurate diagnosis. Identification of major depression, attention deficit hyperactivity disorder (ADHD), or psychosis, for example, can point to effective pharmacological interventions. If not identified, autism spectrum disorders may result in failure to respond to conventional treatment approaches. Although there are still significant gaps in knowledge about pharmacological agents for children (Jensen et al., 1999), these interventions have shown increasing efficacy for childhood mental health disorders (Pumariega, Del Mundo, & Vance, 2002; U.S. Department of Health and Human Services, 1999). These agents should be made available to the SED population when appropriate. If untreated, those disorders are likely to cause significant symptoms and functional impairment, and these youth may spend more time in restrictive placements. Case managers should have the capacity to triage youngsters with SED for psychiatric assessment and pharmacotherapy. The case manager also needs to facilitate the psychiatrist's integral role in the multidisciplinary team and to advocate for a higher frequency of psychiatric appointments for symptomatic children. In conjunction with the primary therapists and case manager, the psychiatrist can contribute to an accurate clinical formulation from which therapeutic efforts proceed.

The case manager should also have access to second opinions for clarification of difficult diagnostic questions. One such case in our experience involved a severely impaired adolescent with an unusual psychotic disorder refractory to conventional treatment. The case manager was instrumental in acquiring two expert second opinions, which led to a reformulation of the problem, appropriate medication selection and dosage adjustment, and the identification of the optimal treatment milieu, all of which averted further hospitalization.

Similarly, good-quality psychological and neuropsychological evaluations can contribute to the overall understanding of a youth's cognitive, psychological, and adaptive strengths and vulnerabilities. Neurocognitive limitations can lead to lack of progress in both educational settings and mental health interventions. Psychological and psychiatric evaluations yield the most useful results when specific questions are addressed and the process has access to comprehensive information from multiple sources. The case manager, who oversees the overall service plan, can supply comprehensive information and help the family frame the clinical questions for the evaluation.

Activities of a Family-Centered Case Manager

A family-centered case manager begins forming an alliance with the child and family by developing a shared understanding of their problems, assets, and goals for the future. After this understanding is achieved, the child and family and the case manager agree to services and develop a service plan. The case manager then brokers (acquires, develops, and identifies) resources and puts those services into place and ensures that services are delivered in a coordinated manner. Sharing information across settings may be the most crucial aspect of this function. The case manager, in partnership with the family, helps to evaluate the service appropriateness and the child and family's progress. The treatment is supervised and monitored through regular service team meetings. The service plan is modified as needed based on ongoing progress and assessment of changing needs.

The case manager's functions change over time as the child and family's needs change and the service team's functioning matures. For example, whereas initially needs assessment, developing an alliance, and direct support to the family might be the most prominent functions, service development and implementation, along with building a service team, may be most prominent later. As time progresses, facilitating the coordinated operation of a service team, assessing appropriateness of services, and monitoring outcomes may be most prominent. Over time, service utilization considerations need to be incorporated into the decision-making process, because the case manager is also responsible to an organization. In order to avoid case manager conflict of interest, it is helpful to have practice guidelines and supervisory review procedures to ensure cost-efficient utilization of funds.

CLINICAL EXAMPLES OF FAMILY-CENTERED CASE MANAGEMENT

The following case examples adapted from a system of care program illustrate some of the principles of family-centered case management, including individualized services, strength-based treatment planning, service team collaboration, use of nontraditional services, and access to flexible funds. Names and some details were changed to protect confidentiality.

Joseph was a fifteen-year-old Caucasian male when he entered the program. He had been diagnosed with ADHD, oppositional defiant disorder, and posttraumatic stress disorder related to a history of physical abuse and witnessing domestic violence. Although Joseph had been in highly structured alternative schools, they were unable to manage his defiant and aggressive behavior. The family had not used office-based counseling and pharmacotherapy because they were against medication use and had no access to transportation.

After convening the service team to review the family's strengths and needs, the case manager began by engaging a family therapist who met with Joseph and his mother in their home. A youth mentor was then added, initially to provide more positive social experiences for Joseph in his neighborhood. He later took a more therapeutic role, working with Joseph on anger management, especially to decrease physical altercations between Joseph and his mother. Joseph then made the transition to a mentored job experience in a family-owned business. When problems arose in Joseph's attitude toward authority figures, the family's son, who was a professional counselor, was available to help Joseph adopt more constructive behaviors. Joseph's mother developed a trusting relationship with the home-based therapist and allowed a medication evaluation by a physician who came to the home. Joseph had a positive job experience and was able to return to school.

This evolving service plan respected the family's beliefs and addressed real-life needs, eventually resulting in better treatment acceptance. A nontraditional mentored job experience provided a better opportunity than office-based therapy for Joseph to develop needed social skills. Interventions were accessed through the use of flexible funds. Most important, service planning was fluid, changing with Joseph's progress and developmental needs.

Elena, a fourteen-year-old Latina, entered the program after discharge from a psychiatric hospital where she had been hospitalized for a serious suicide attempt complicated by substance abuse. This was her third hospitalization. Elena lived with her Spanish-speaking mother, who had difficulty enforcing any limits or rules for Elena; their relationship was highly conflictual.

The first intervention that the case manager put into place was a Spanish-speaking home-based therapist who helped Elena's mother develop clear expectations and consequences for Elena's behavior. She was also encouraged to seek voluntary involvement by the child welfare agency. The child welfare caseworker was a good match for the family. The service team, facilitated by the case manager, developed a strategy in which the caseworker functioned as the limit setter, enforcing drug and alcohol treatment as a requirement for Elena to stay in the home. Elena was then assigned to a child psychiatrist for both psychotherapy and pharmacotherapy. They developed a stable and grounding therapeutic relationship. Elena returned to school, aided by a flexibly funded incentive plan that allowed her to purchase clothes contingent on regular school attendance.

Important elements of this family-centered plan were the use of culturally competent services, a cohesive and collaborative multiagency team, use of flexible funds to provide incentives for school attendance, and the ability to select a very experienced clinician as primary therapist.

CHALLENGES OF FAMILY-CENTERED CASE MANAGEMENT

The role of a family-centered case manager has challenges as well as opportunities. At the client level, one of the challenges is to meet the child and family's needs without creating dependency, that is, deciding how much service is enough. An alliance must be created between the case manager and family without colluding with less adaptive behaviors, and, similarly, a strength orientation is helpful, but it is also essential not to overlook problems or pathology that needs to be addressed. One should develop a working alliance with the child and family without creating dependency. There may also be a trade-off between allying with and working to preserve a family and protecting a child from maltreatment. It can be challenging to maintain an alliance with a family when the case manager, acting either in a fiscal authority role or as an employee of an organization with fiscal authority, is not able to approve services. However, if the case manager is clear from the start about the need to conserve system resources and the family and team share in this responsibility, the planning process can incorporate the goal of identifying community supports to replace formal treatment gradually.

There are different challenges for the family-centered case manager at the system level. As fiscal considerations in managed care environments become more prominent, keeping families involved in setting system priorities and driving the service plans for their child may be difficult. In addition, in a managed care program responsible for a Medicaid population, guidelines and some degree of uniformity are needed to allocate resources equitably. Nontraditional services, especially if they exceed average costs, may be difficult to get authorized in a managed care environment. In situations where blended funding is not a fiscal reality and some services, especially respite and supportive services, may not be seen as medically necessary, they may be more justifiably seen as responsibilities of the child welfare agency.

The case manager should rely on evidence-based services that are likely to be clinically effective; however, the available evidence base does not cover all possible interventions worthy of consideration. There are increasing numbers of studies of system of care interventions. Burns and Hoagwood (2002) provide a thorough review of community-based interventions used in systems of care. They describe emerging evidence for effectiveness of case management, multisystemic therapy, treatment foster care, school-based prevention programs, and encouraging results for community mentoring. A previous review in the surgeon general's report on mental health (U.S. Department of Health and Human Services, 1999) found evidence for the effectiveness of day treatment but less for hospitalization and residential care, and more data were needed on coaching and skill building. Even armed with information about evidence-based interventions, those interventions may not be available in the case manager's community. Case managers therefore need the skills and organizational support to cultivate new service providers.

THE ROLE OF CASE MANAGEMENT IN MANAGING CARE

During times of rising health and mental health costs, and certainly in times with shrinking tax revenues, cost containment becomes necessary in private and public insurance sectors. There is a need to control the costs of the highest service users, who spend a large percentage of the mental health budget (Ringel & Sturm, 2001). The use of objective guidelines for clinical decision making assumes greater importance to ensure appropriate utilization of resources. The case manager has available new technologies to make level-of-care decisions. Level of care can be conceptualized as a continuum of intensity rather a specific program (Lyons & Abraham, 2001), allowing for a variety of service options. This conceptualization is well suited to the youth in systems of care who need the services of multiple agencies. Lyons and Abraham (2001) describe available decision support and outcome monitoring tools to assist with level-of-care decision making and service planning. Examples are the Severity of Psychiatric Illness (Lyons, 1998) and the Child and Adolescent Level of Care Utilization System (American Academy of Child and Adolescent Psychiatry & American Association of Community Psychiatry, 1999).

Monitoring Outcomes

Case managers, in their role of providing coordination and oversight, are in an ideal position to monitor individual client outcomes. A number of technologies are available to facilitate this process, depending on the specific outcomes targeted in service planning. Clinical and functional outcomes can be measured with instruments such as the Child and Adolescent Functional Assessment Scale (Hodges, 1994), the Child and Adolescent Level of Care Utilization System (American Academy of Child and Adolescent Psychiatry, 2001), or the Children's Global Assessment Scale (Shaffer, Gould, & Brasic, 1983) The Child Behavior Checklist (Achenbach, 1991) continues to be a widely used measure of emotional and behavioral problems. (For a more complete discussion of outcome measures, see Chapter Twenty.)

Methods of tracking client-level outcomes over time have been described in the literature, including the Life Events Timeline and the Monthly Adjustment Summary (Burchard et al., 1995). One method we used is to create a case map to track individual outcomes and expenditures over time (Winters, Maciejewski & Terrell, 1996). Outcomes as measured by quarterly Children's Global Assessment Scale scores assigned by the care coordinator and consulting child psychiatrist were diagrammed against costs and correlated with child, family, and system factors at different time points. The case map in Figure 9.3 illustrates the decreasing costs of services as the twelve-year-old boy improved over time. Client-centered interventions such as home-based family therapy were noted to be associated with improvements.

Tensions Between Managed Care
and Family-Centered Case Management

Many tensions can develop between client-centered approaches and the realities of managed care. Medicaid managed care, especially in early iterations, has tended to adopt private sector managed care methodologies. These include limited

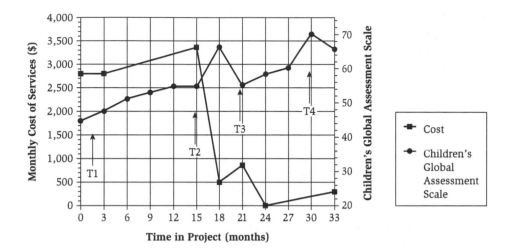

Issues	T1 Enrollment (Age 12)	T2 (15 months)	T3 (18–24 months)	T4 (24–35 months)
Service System	Expelled from school one year prior for legal offense.	Day treatment program adds home-based family therapist.	Return to office-based family therapy after child leaves day treatment program.	Ongoing in-home family intervention through Family Presentation Services arranged.
Child	Diagnosed with SED, enuresis/encopresis. Starts day treatment one month after enrollment.	Symptoms decrease gradually in day treatment.	Returned to mainstream school with 1:1 aide; aide time increased after disruptive behavior worsens.	In self-contained behavior classroom. Starting to be mainstreamed.
Family	Financial, housing stressors; siblings with behavior problems.	Family tentatively engages in family treatment.	Family reluctant to attend sessions.	Father gets job promotion, spends more time at home. Family Preservation Services helps organize home.

FIGURE 9.3. Case Map.

Source: Adapted from Winters, Maciejewski, and Terrell (1996, p. 5).

provider panels and episode-oriented care, all of which are not as applicable to a Medicaid population with high rates of multiple problems and chronic mental health problems. In addition, managed health care is diagnosis driven, an approach that supports pathology-based, in preference to strength-based, approaches. Efforts at cost containment tend to move the system toward uniformity rather than individualization, and potentially toward reduced flexibility or recategorization of services. Administrative overhead costs as well as the need to contain costs may decrease available resources for children and families. Also, decision making in large organizations tends to be centralized, potentially leaving families without a meaningful voice in policymaking. There is also a risk that managed care organizations inappropriately apply adult-oriented strategies to children, leaving out crucial interagency planning structures and family inclusion.

The goal of cost containment in a managed care system has the potential to shift the emphasis from a family-centered case management model to a system-centered utilization management model. The case manager is charged with the responsibility of using system resources equitably across populations, as well as ensuring that individual service plans are cost-efficient. However, it becomes very difficult for the case manager to have accountability to both the managed health organization for service utilization and the client for clinical outcomes. Sledge et al. (1995, p. 1262) note that "utilization review case managers vs. intensive clinical case managers function within a mixed bureaucratic and clinical system of accountability. . . . This can be confusing and the source of considerable strain when the case manager has a mixed clinical and systems-level responsibility and yet is not able to relate directly to the clinical line of authority and accountability."

Case Management in Multnomah County, Oregon

Our experience with a case management program in Oregon illustrates the impact of the transition from a system of care demonstration program to Medicaid managed care. It illustrates the tension between the needs of the client and the system that come into focus in Medicaid managed care. The functions of the case managers gradually shifted from brokering and direct support to increased involvement in documentation and utilization review. The variables of fiscal authority, caseload, and shifts in the organizational environment profoundly reshaped the case manager role.

Robert Wood Johnson Mental Health Services Program for Youth, 1989–1995. Managed care coordinators each served seventeen children with SED and their families. They were master's-level specialist case managers who had fiscal authority, working under a capitation arrangement in which case rates were flexibly distributed across their caseload. They were able to draw from a pool of blended funds, contributed by child welfare, mental health, and education, to fund traditional and nontraditional services. They led consensus-driven, client-centered, multiagency service teams that met quarterly and produced plans of care that described interventions across eight life domains. Each case manager had access to a child psychiatrist for consultation for one hour each week. They partnered closely with parents and provided visits in the home with ongoing coaching and crisis management using the plan of care as an active tool.

Case Management Folded into Fee-for-Service Managed Care, 1995–1996. After the Robert Wood Johnson grant ended, there were fewer case managers (now referred to as intensive case managers), who served the entire Medicaid-eligible child population. The caseloads increased up to fifty, which shifted their functions in a more administrative direction (see Figure 9.1). Service team meetings were held only as needed, and fewer home visits were done. Case managers continued to have fiscal authority and access to flexible funds and nontraditional services. With the advent of Medicaid managed care, the blended fund pool, which previously covered both Medicaid- and non-Medicaid-eligible children in the system of care demonstration project, was now used to cover only non-Medicaid-eligible children. This led to greater emphasis on using Medicaid funds only for services specifically defined as mental health. There were resulting pressures to shift certain costs for services, such as respite care, which had previously been paid out of the blended pool fund, to other service sectors. The amount of child psychiatric consultation per case manager was reduced: service plans were reviewed by the psychiatrist only yearly. Case management shifted to a less family-centered model due to decreased intensity and direct support.

Case Management Under Fully Capitated Managed Care, 1996–2001. Medicaid managed care then moved into a subcapitation arrangement with two provider networks. These networks developed their own specialist case managers, and a majority of the case management was gradually shifted over to the networks. Reimbursement under the capitation rate was not adequate for the high-need population, so the case-managed children were served under fee-for-service. Case managers no longer had fiscal authority. They were required to submit documentation to authorization specialists. Use of nonparticipating (that is, off-panel) providers, who were often providing home-based and culturally competent care, was gradually eliminated to support the fiscal viability of the provider networks. The clinical appropriateness of nontraditional and strength-based services was often questioned, and they were authorized less frequently. High-cost clients were under greater scrutiny, and services were withdrawn in many long-term cases. Plans that had been developed by service teams by consensus were at times modified by authorization specialists according to utilization management criteria, with the result that case managers experienced less effectiveness in implementing family-centered service plans.

FUTURE RESEARCH DIRECTIONS

Given the growth of case management as a primary intervention for children in mental health systems of care, there is a pressing need for more research in this area. Some of the following suggestions for future research directions have been discussed in the children's case management literature (Burns, Gwaltney, & Bishop, 1995; Evans & Armstrong, 2002; Stroul, 1995). The most significant questions relate to which functions of the case manager have the most impact on outcomes. For example, how important is inclusion of direct clinical services as compared with the care coordination function? The adult case management literature suggests that the inclusion of direct clinical services may be an essential element to the efficacy of ACT; however, it is not known whether the same applies to children and their families. A study comparing the broker case management with a clinical case management model for children would be of great interest. A related question of interest is the level of intensity of the service. Caseload, number of contacts, and off-hours crisis availability are variables that could be investigated. Case management models will need to be tested as evidence-based interventions, using manualized approaches applied with adequate fidelity. It has been recognized, however, that case management approaches need to be tailored to their community contexts, and this offers the opportunity to examine different variables and research approaches.

Given the blend of administrative and clinical functions in case management, it is often unclear where case managers best fit. If housed in the managed care organizational structure, they may experience role devaluation, whereas in a provider agency, they may not have the authority to implement an individualized service plan (Burns, Gwaltney, & Bishop, 1995). They need to have influence on the service team to be effective. The accountability of the case manager to the client as opposed to a resource manager acting in the interest of the mental health organization is another variable of interest for research. Given the efficacy of ACT for adults, the case management team should be tested against the individual model of case management. Our experience in Oregon suggests that a team of home-based clinical providers who also do care coordination has been effective for particularly difficult clinical problems that have been refractory to other treatment modalities.

Access to a diverse and culturally competent service array may also have an impact on outcomes, as good case management cannot compensate for lack of access to appropriate services. Qualifications and specialization of case managers are other areas of interest. More research is needed on specialization following the initial findings of Burns et al. (1996) comparing specialist case management with primary therapist case management. Potential advantages of specialization include increased experience, decreased role conflicts, and increased knowledge of community resources; however, an exclusive case management role is a challenging one requiring the ability to tolerate frustration and maintain a clinical perspective without ongoing direct clinical service experience. There is some suggestion of comparable effectiveness of paraprofessional and professional case managers (Ignelzi & Dague, 1995; Simpson, Koroloff, Friesen, & Gac, 1999), but the conditions under which those outcomes are obtained need to be understood better. A final but extremely important variable needing to be examined is duration of case management. The child SED population and their families have chronic, long-term needs that do not occur in episodes and require continuous and long-term care. Given the reality of limited resources, however, open-ended, long-term assignments to intensive treatment conditions are not realistic for large numbers of clients. Thus, it is important to identify how long case management is needed in order to obtain the desired outcomes.

Case management has achieved widespread use in human services, and it is likely to continue to be a highly valued intervention for clinical and fiscal reasons. Case management as a means of bringing order to the treatment process will be needed as long as the principles of human nature and physics apply (that is, chaos rather than order prevails, resulting in uncoordinated treatment efforts). As long as resources are limited and health care costs continue to rise, approaches to managing care will be used. Despite the variety of definitions and models of case management, the functions of a case manager remain fairly consistent across models, although with varying emphases. These functions exist along a continuum of administration to direct service functions. The most flexible and client-centered case management models will allow for fluid movement among those functions. However, variables such as caseload size, team versus individual model, organizational context, and continuity are significant in determining the case management functions.

The utilization model of case management that is accountable to the mental health organization can be at odds with the CASSP principle-guided family-centered case management model. However, there remains a need for both types of case management, and more knowledge is needed about the feasibility of integrating these functions. In the best of worlds, the clinical perspective—what is most likely to result in clinical and functional progress for the child and family—should inform case management activities.

Research is needed in child populations to test whether case management models including direct clinical care (analogous to the adult ACT model) are more successful than broker models, as Fallon's findings (2001) suggest. Expanding methodologies are available to the case manager, allowing for objective assessment of individual and family outcomes, decision making about level of care, as well as manuals for several case management models. As Burchard et al. (2002) noted, case management models will need to be operationalized to allow for comparison of different case management variables.

Finally, although case management is an intervention, it is not itself an adequate treatment for serious emotional, behavioral, and mental disorders (Holloway & Carson, 2001). The reorganization of service delivery and coordination of services will therefore have a limited impact without the use of more empirically tested specific treatments for childhood mental disorders.

References

Achenbach, T. M. (1991). *Integrative guide for the CBCL 4–18, YSR, and TRF profiles.* Burlington: University of Vermont, Department of Psychiatry.

American Academy of Child and Adolescent Psychiatry & American Association of Community Psychiatry. (1999). *Child and Adolescent Level of Care Utilization System, Version 1.1.* Washington, DC: Author.

American Academy of Child and Adolescent Psychiatry Work Group on Systems of Care & American Association of Community Psychiatry. (2001). *Child and adolescent level of care utilization system user's manual.* Washington, DC: Author.

American Academy of Pediatrics Committee on Children with Disabilities. (1999). Care coordination: Integrating health and related systems of care for children with special care needs. *Pediatrics, 104,* 978–981.

Bedell, J. R., Cohen, N. L., & Sullivan, A. (2000). Case management: The current best practices and the next generation of innovation. *Community Mental Health Journal, 36,* 179–194.

Behar, L., Zipper, I. N., & Weil, M. (1994). *Case management for children's mental health: A training curriculum for child-serving agencies.* Raleigh: North Carolina Department of Mental Health, Developmental Disabilities and Substance Abuse.

Bruns, E. J., Ermold, J., & Burchard, J. D. (2001). The wraparound fidelity index: Results from an initial pilot test. In C. C. Newsman, C. J. Liberton, K. Kutash, & R. Friedman (Eds.), *The Thirteenth Annual Research Conference Proceedings: A system of care for children's mental health: Expanding the research base* (pp. 339–342). Tampa: University of South Florida, Louis de la Parte Florida Mental Health Institute, Research and Training Center for Children's Mental Health.

Burchard, J. D., Bruns, E. J., & Burchard, S. N. (2002). The wraparound approach. In B. J. Burns & K. Hoagwood (Eds.), *Community treatment for youth: Evidence-based interventions for severe emotional and behavioral disorders* (pp. 69–90). New York: Oxford University Press.

Burchard, J. D., Hinden, B., Carro, M., Schaefer, M., Bruns, E., & Pandina N. (1995). Using case-level data to monitor a case management system. In B. J. Friesen & J. Poertner (Eds.), *From case management to service coordination for children with emotional, behavioral or mental disorders: Building on family strengths.* Baltimore: Brookes Publishing.

Burns, B. J., Farmer, E.M.Z., Angold, A., Costello E. J., Behar, L. (1996). A randomized trial of case management for youths with serious emotional disturbance. *Journal of Clinical Child Psychology, 25,* 476–486.

Burns, B. J., & Goldman, S. K. (1999). *Promising practices in wraparound for children with serious emotional disturbance and their families.* Washington, DC: Center for Effective Collaboration and Practice, American Institutes for Research.

Burns, B. J., Goldman, S. K., Faw, L., & Burchard, J. (1999). The wraparound evidence base. In B. J. Burns & S. Goldman (Eds.), *Promising practices in wraparound for children with serious emotional disturbance and their families.* Washington, DC: Center for Effective Collaboration and Practice, American Institutes for Research.

Burns, B. J., Gwaltney, E. A., & Bishop, G. K. (1995). Case management research: Issues and directions. In B. J. Friesen & J. Poertner (Eds.), *From case management to service coordination for children with emotional, behavioral, or mental disorders.* Baltimore: Brookes Publishing.

Burns, B. J., & Hoagwood, K. (2002). *Community treatment for youth: Evidence-based interventions for severe emotional and behavioral disorders.* New York: Oxford University Press.

Center for Mental Health Services. (1997). *Evaluation of the Comprehensive Community Mental Health Services for Children and Their Families Program.* Washington, DC: Author.

Cole, R. F., & Poe, S. L. (1993). *Partnerships for care: Systems of care for children with serious emotional disturbances and their families.* Washington, DC: Washington Business Group on Health.

England, M. J., & Cole, R. F., (1992). Building systems of care for youth with serious mental illness. *Hospital and Community Psychiatry, 43,* 630–633.

Evans, M. E., & Armstrong, M. I. (2002). What is case management? In B. J. Burns & K. Hoagwood (Eds.), *Community treatment for youth: Evidence-based interventions for severe emotional and behavioral disorders* (pp. 39–68). New York: Oxford University Press.

Evans, M. E., Armstrong, M. I., & Kuppinger, A. D. (1996). Family-centered intensive case management: A step toward understanding individualized care. *Journal of Child and Family Studies, 5,* 55–65.

Evans, M. E., Armstrong, M. I., Kuppinger, A. D., Huz, S., & Johnson, S. (1998). *A randomized trial of family-centered intensive case management and family based treatment: Final report.* Tampa: University of South Florida.

Evans, M. E., Banks, S. M., Huz, S., & McNulty, T. L. (1994). Initial hospitalization and community tenure outcomes of intensive case management for children and youth with serious emotional and behavioral disabilities. *Journal of Child and Family Studies, 3,* 225–234.

Fallon, T. (2001). *A comparison of two wraparound models.* Paper presented at the American Academy of Child and Adolescent Psychiatry symposium, Houston.

Friesen, B. J., & Poertner, J. (eds.), (1995). *From case management to service coordination for children with emotional, behavioral, or mental disorders.* Baltimore: Brookes Publishing.

Gratton, J., Paulsen, R., Stuntzner-Gibson, D., & Summers, R. (1995). *Oregon Partners Project: Progress and outcomes report.* Paper presented at Building on Family Strengths Conference, Portland, OR.

Hoagwood, K., Jensen, P. S., Petti, T., & Burns, B. J. (1996). Outcomes of mental health care for children and adolescents: I. A comprehensive conceptual model. *Journal of the Academy of Child and Adolescent Psychiatry, 35,* 1055–1063.

Hodges, K. (1994). *Child and Adolescent Functional Assessment Scale.* Ypsilanti: Eastern Michigan University, Department of Psychology.

Holloway, F., & Carson, J., (2001). Case management: An update. *International Journal of Social Psychiatry, 47,* 21–31.

Ignelzi, S., & Dague, B. (1995). Parents as case managers. In B. J. Friesen & J. Poertner (Eds.), *From case management to service coordination for children with emotional, behavioral or mental disorders: Building on family strengths* (pp. 327–336). Baltimore: Brookes Publishing.

Illback, R. J., & Neill, T. K., (1995). Service coordination in mental health systems for children, youth, and families: Progress, problems, prospects. *Journal of Mental Health Administration, 22,* 17–28.

Intagliata, J. (1982). Improving the quality of community care for the chronically mentally disabled: The role of case management. *Schizophrenia Bulletin, 8,* 655–674.

Jensen P. S., Bhatara, V. S., Vitiello, B., Hoagwood, K., Feil, M., & Burke, L. B. (1999). Psychoactive medication prescribing practices for U.S. children: Gaps between research and clinical practice. *Journal of the American Academy of Child and Adolescent Psychiatry, 38,* 557–565.

Joint Commission on the Mental Health of Children. (1969). *Crisis in child mental health.* New York: HarperCollins.

Kanter, J. (1989). Clinical case management: Definition, principles, components. *Hospital and Community Psychiatry, 40,* 361–368.

Katz-Leavy, J., Lourie, L., Stroul, B., & Zeigler-Dendy, C. (1992). *Individualized services in a system of care.* Washington, DC: Georgetown University, Child and Adolescent Service System Program Technical Assistance Center.

Liao, Q., Manteuffel, B., Paulic, C., & Sondheimer, D. (2001). Describing the population of adolescents served in systems of care. *Journal of Emotional and Behavioral Disorders, 9,* 13–29.

Lyons, J. S. (1998). *Severity and acuity of psychiatric illness manual: Child and adolescent version.* San Antonio, TX: Psychological Corporation, Harcourt Brace Jovanovich.

Lyons, J. S., & Abraham, M. E. (2001). Designing level of care criteria. In L. Kiser, P. Lefkovitz, & L. Kennedy (Eds.), *The Integrated Behavioral Health Continuum: Theory and practice.* Washington, DC: American Psychiatric Association Press

Moore, S. (1990). A social work practice model of case management: The case management grid. *Social Work, 35,* 444–448.

Mueser, K. T., Bond, G. R., Drake, R. E., & Resnick, S. G. (1998). Models of community care for severe mental illness: A review of research on case management. *Schizophrenia Bulletin, 24,* 37–74.

Pumariega, A. J., & Cross, T. L. (1997). Cultural competence in child psychiatry. In J. Noshpitz & N. Alessi (Eds.), *Basic handbook of child and adolescent psychiatry* (pp. 473–484). New York: Wiley.

Pumariega, A. J., Del Mundo, A. S., & Vance, B. (2002). Psychopharmacology in the context of systems of care. In B. J. Burns & K. Hoagwood (Eds.), *Community treatment for youth: Evidence-based interventions for severe emotional and behavioral disorders* (pp. 277–300). New York: Oxford University Press.

Ringel, J. S., & Sturm, R. (2001). National estimates of mental health utilization and expenditures for children in 1998. *Journal of Behavioral Health Services Research, 3,* 319–333.

Rosen, A., & Teesson, M. (2001). Does case management work? The evidence and the abuse of evidence-based medicine. *Australian and New Zealand Journal of Psychiatry, 35,* 731–746.

Schaedle, R. W., & Epstein, I. (2000). Specifying intensive case management: A multiple perspectives approach. *Mental Health Services Research, 2,* 95–105.

Shaffer, D., Gould, M. S., & Brasic, J. (1983). A Children's Global Assessment Scale (CGAS). *Archives of General Psychiatry, 40,* 1228–1231.

Simpson, J. S., Koroloff, N., Friesen, B. J., & Gac, J. (1999). *Promising practices in family-provider collaboration.* Washington, DC: Center for Effective Collaboration and Practices, American Institutes of Research.

Sledge, W. H., Astrachan, B., Thompson, K., Rakfeldt, J., & Leaf, P. (1995). Case management in psychiatry: An analysis of tasks. *American Journal of Psychiatry, 152,* 1259–1265.

Solomon, P. (1992). The efficacy of case management services for severely mentally disabled adults. *Community Mental Health Journal, 28,* 163–180.

Stein, L. I., & Test, M. A. (1980). Alternative to mental hospital treatment. I. Conceptual model, treatment program, and clinical evaluation. *Archives of General Psychiatry, 37,* 392–397.

Stroul, B. A. (1995). Case management in a system of care. In B. J. Friesen & J. Poertner (Eds.), *From case management to service coordination for children with emotional, behavioral, or mental disorders.* Baltimore, MD: Brookes Publishing.

Stroul, B. A., & Friedman, R. M. (1986). *A system of care for children and youth with severe emotional disturbance* (rev. ed.). Washington, DC: Georgetown University, Child and Adolescent Service System Program Technical Assistance Center.

Stroul, B. A., & Friedman, R. M. (1996). Service coordination in systems of care. In B. A. Stroul (Ed.), *Children's mental health: Creating systems of care in a changing society* (pp. 3–21). Baltimore: Brookes Publishing.

Stroul, B. A., Pires, S. A., & Armstrong, M. I. (2001). *Health Care Reform Tracking Project: Tracking state health care reforms as they affect children and adolescents with behavioral health disorders and their families—2000 state survey.* Tampa: Research and Training Center for Children's Mental Health, Department of Child and Family Studies, Division of State and Local Support, Louis de la Parte Florida Mental Health Institute, University of South Florida.

U.S. Department of Health and Human Services. (1999). *Mental health: A report of the surgeon general.* Rockville, MD: U.S. Department of Health and Human Services, Substance Abuse and Mental Health Services Administration, Center for Mental Health Services, National Institutes of Health, National Institute of Mental Health.

U.S. Department of Health and Human Services. (2001). *Culture, race, and ethnicity. A supplement to mental health: A report of the surgeon general.* Washington, DC: Substance Abuse and Mental Health Administration, U.S. Department of Health and Human Services.

VanDenBerg, J. E., & Grealish, E. M. (1996). Individualized services and supports through the wrap-around process. *Journal of Child and Family Studies, 5,* 7–21.

Winters, N. C., Maciejewski, G., & Terrell, L. (1996). The case map: A navigational aid for the care manager. *Family Matters,* pp. 2–8.

Wolff, N., Helminiak, T. W., Morse, G. A., Calsyn, R. J., Linkenberg, W. D., & Trusty, M. L. (1997). Cost-effectiveness of three approaches to case management for homeless mentally ill clients. *American Journal of Psychiatry, 154,* 341–348.

Ziguras, S. J., & Stuart, G. W. (2000). A meta-analysis of the effectiveness of mental health case management over twenty years. *Psychiatric Services, 51,* 1410–1421.

PART THREE

WORKING
ACROSS POPULATIONS
AND SETTINGS

CHAPTER TEN

A Conceptual Framework for an Early Childhood System of Care

Robert L. Klaehn
Jan Martner

Two decades ago, Knitzer's groundbreaking *Unclaimed Children* (1982) identified the fragmentation and inadequacy of mental health services for children and adolescents. Friedman and Stroul's *A System of Care for Children with Serious Emotional Disturbances* (1986) was written in response to Knitzer's identification of these service inadequacies. These seminal works led to a series of national initiatives to develop community-based systems of care for children and adolescents, including the federal Child and Adolescent Service System Program and the Robert Wood Johnson Foundation's Mental Health Services Program for Youth. This early work, however, did not address the multiple and frequently changing needs of our youngest children, birth to five years of age.

Similarly, the principles of wraparound have been in use in the United States since the 1970s (VanDenBerg & Grealish, 1996). Strength-based, individualized service planning and other wraparound principles have come into wide use in the community-based, multiagency systems of care that treat children and adolescents with multiple needs. Again, the wraparound process was not initially applied to the care of infants and toddlers and their families.

Knitzer's subsequent work (1996) stimulated national interest in the challenges facing the youngest and most vulnerable children and the importance of

We acknowledge the contributions of Nancy Winters, Andres Pumariega, Mark Chenven, Kieran O'Malley, Al Zachik, and Tom Vaughan, Jr., to an earlier draft of this chapter. We also acknowledge the support of Alexandra Larriva and Gary Delago in the preparation of this chapter.

developing integrated early childhood systems of care. Programs employing system of care principles with very young children are now developing nationwide. Many are also employing the principles of wraparound to meet the needs of infants and toddlers and their families. The resulting body of work will aid in the development of more fully elaborated systems of care for this population.

The biopsychosocial model, familiar to all psychiatrists, is also a comprehensive paradigm that can be adapted to an early childhood system of care. The model integrates state-of-the-art scientific knowledge, current research, and clinical practice to provide a comprehensive approach to evaluation and treatment. The recent book *From Neurons to Neighborhoods: The Science of Early Childhood Development* (National Research Council and Institute of Medicine, 2000) provides in-depth analysis of the science of early childhood development and supports the extended use of the biopsychosocial model to clinical work with infants and toddlers. It also recommends further research and a framework for the application of recent advances in child development to direct service and clinical practice.

One result of the biopsychosocial evaluation is a diagnosis of the child in order to help clinicians and the family communicate effectively about the child's challenges and to guide treatment. Until recently, the *Diagnostic and Statistical Manual of the American Psychiatric Association* (American Psychiatric Association, 1994) was the only diagnostic classification system available. Clinicians found it limited when used with infants and toddlers. The development of the Diagnostic Classification: Zero to Three (DC: 0–3; Zero to Three, 1994) was a significant step forward, providing a functional diagnostic tool for the direction of treatment of very young children. The DC: 0–3 adapted a number of diagnoses such as depression and anxiety to describe these disorders in infants and toddlers better. This advance helps clinicians and families communicate effectively about the child's challenges and treatment.

In addition, the DC: 0–3 introduced the new categories of relationship and regulatory disorders. Coded on Axis II, the relationship disorders categories identify maladaptive interactional patterns between mother and child. The regulatory disorders, according to the *Diagnostic Manual*, "are characterized by the infant or young child's difficulties in regulating behavior and psychological, sensory, attentional and motor or affective processes, and in organizing a calm, alert, or affectively positive state" (Zero to Three, 1994, p. 31).

CORE VALUES FOR AN EARLY CHILDHOOD SYSTEM OF CARE

A truly robust early childhood system of care must be a fusion of the work of Knitzer, Friedman and Stroul, the principles of wraparound, and the application of state-of-the-art scientific and medical knowledge through the biopsychosocial model. This chapter identifies nine core values for an early childhood system of care and examines the challenges of putting these values into practice within the system of care and possible action steps to resolving these challenges (see Figure 10.1).

Support the Optimal Biological, Psychological, and Social Development of Infants and Toddlers and Their Families

The overriding goal of the early childhood system of care is to create an environment in which young children who are at risk and those with established developmental delays or emotional disturbances can achieve optimal biological, psychological, and social development. To use a metaphor from the writings of D. W. Winnicott (1965), the early childhood system of care must support the integrity and continuity of the infant or toddler's "holding environment." Although Winnicott's work talks primarily about the parent-child dyad, a broader application of this concept is useful: include the child and family's community as part of this holding environment. This metaphor is quite compatible with recent writings that support the use of an ecological approach to the design of programs,

---

The early childhood system of care must:

1. Support the optimal biological, psychological, and social development of infants and toddlers and their families.

2. Make families full partners at every level.

3. Provide support for the stability of children's families—biological, adoptive, or foster.

4. Formulate individualized and integrated multiagency service plans with the full participation of the child's family.

5. Value and respect the family's unique social and cultural beliefs and interests in order to provide culturally competent and clinically appropriate services.

6. Intervene without delay to meet the developmental needs of young children.

7. Ensure smooth transitions between service system elements as the child's developmental needs change.

8. Encourage professionals within the system of care to make advocating for the child and family their highest priority.

9. Strive for an ethical balance between protecting the rights of children and supporting the rights of parents.

FIGURE 10.1. Core Values for the Early Childhood System of Care.

Source: Adapted from American Academy of Child and Adolescent Psychiatry's Work Group on Community-Based Systems of Care (American Academy of Child and Adolescent Psychiatry, in press).

interventions, and service plans. An ecological approach requires the consideration of familial, sociological, environmental, economic, educational, and psychological factors in the development of early childhood systems of care and, ultimately, highly individualized child and family service plans (Simpson, Hivanjee, Koroloff, Doerfler, & Garcia, 2001).

Make Families Full Partners at Every Level

True partnership with parents is essential for the coordinated care of infants and toddlers in their natural environment. Since babies cannot speak for themselves, the voices of those who know them best must be central to the treatment planning process. The goal of partnership is supporting and respecting parents as the managers of their infant or toddler's care.

Partnership is the key to true individualization of the infant and family's service plan. It is important to ask the families what they need. For example, the support for grandparents raising small children will be different from the needs of a teenage mother raising an infant on her own. In responding to the family's concerns, the professionals should provide information on existing and potential services and supports that may be available to the family. During service planning for the infant and toddler, special attention should be paid to the inclusion of the needs of parents with developmental disabilities, severe substance abuse, and serious and disabling mental illness. Meeting the developmental needs of the child and protecting his or her attachments must be carefully integrated into the treatment planning of the parents. With regard to another special population, incarcerated parents, the needs of the young child must be carefully balanced with the needs of the parent and the community's need for safety.

Many challenges must be addressed before this value is fully implemented by developing early childhood systems of care. For example, parents must be included in all levels of the system of care. Inclusion is most common, but not universal, at the direct service level; across the country, there are still many places where parents are not included in treatment planning or have to give up custody of their children to obtain needed services. Supporting the participation and voice of teenage parents in the treatment process is an especially difficult task.

Inclusion of parents is even rarer at the administrative levels of systems of care; the input of parents to matters of policy and program design and development is frequently limited or nonexistent. For a true partnership between parents and professionals to exist, parents must participate in numbers large enough to have real influence on the deliberations of the administrative body. They must also be compensated for their time away from work to participate in system of care management.

Another challenge to successful parent-professional partnerships is training for both parents and professionals. Parent advocacy groups must be supported in their efforts to provide access for parents to the information and resources that they require to be a full partner in decision making. Professional training programs must also be supported in efforts to change curriculum or even program philosophy in order to foster a change in attitude toward parent participation in the design of treatment plans and treatment programs.

There are many places to look for potential remedies for this challenge. Though rare in mental health programs, parent participation and partnership is much more frequent in early intervention programs and in Head Start. Model early childhood mental health programs such as the Positive Education Program in Cleveland hire parents whose young children have completed treatment to provide direct service to other parents as part of their early intervention center staff (Simpson et al., 2001). The arbitrary boundary between parent and professional breaks down when parents become members of multidisciplinary treatment teams.

Full integration of the principles of wraparound into a system of care is another potent solution to this challenge (see Figure 10.2). The heart of the wraparound process lies in its child-centered, family-focused orientation toward service delivery. According to Whitbeck, the full participation of children and families in the development of individualized service plans is accomplished through access, voice, and ownership: "Access is defined as the parent and child having valid service options at the inclusion point in the decision making process, Voice is defined as the

---

- Wraparound efforts must be based in the community.
- Services and supports must be individualized to meet the needs of the children and families and not designed to reflect the priorities of the service systems.
- The process must be culturally competent and built on the unique values, strengths, and social and racial makeup of children and families.
- Parents must be included in every level of the development of the process.
- Agencies must have access to flexible, noncategorized funding.
- The process must be implemented on an interagency basis and be owned by the larger community.
- Services must be unconditional. If the needs of the child and family change, the child and the family must not be ejected from services. Instead, the services must be changed.
- An individualized plan of care must be developed and implemented on the basis of an interagency, community-neighborhood collaborative process.
- Outcomes must be determined and measured.

FIGURE 10.2. Elements of the Wraparound Process.

Source: Adapted from VanDenBerg and Grealish (1996), and Kendziora, Burns, Osher, Pacchiano, and Mejia (2001).

parent and child being heard and listened to at all junctures of planning, and Ownership is defined as the parent and child agreeing with and committing to any plan concerning them" (Whitbeck et al., 1993).

True implementation of the wraparound process requires that a new relationship be forged between professionals and parents where the there is mutual respect for each other's strengths and an equal understanding of each other's weaknesses, leading to a fully realized collaboration. Strong parent-professional partnerships are the cornerstone of a strong system of care.

Provide Support for the Stability of Children's Families— Biological, Adoptive, or Foster

The book *From Neurons to Neighborhoods* (National Research Council and Institute of Medicine, 2000) clearly states that current research supports the notion that early environments are an extremely important form of optimal child development and that warm, supportive caregiving is essential. The authors state, "The scientific evidence on the significant developmental impacts of early experiences, caregiving relationships, and environmental threats is incontrovertible. Virtually every aspect of early human development, from the brain's evolving circuitry to the child's capacity for empathy is affected by the environments and experiences that are encountered in a cumulative fashion, beginning early in the prenatal period and extending throughout the early childhood years. The science of early development is also clear about the specific importance of parenting and regular caregiving relationships more generally" (p. 6).

Given the state of current knowledge on the importance of attachments for optimal development, an early childhood system of care must promote the stability of families and community-based caregivers. By emphasizing the importance of stability, the early childhood system of care makes preserving and strengthening the attachment systems of young children its highest priority.

Despite this, infants and toddlers in the child welfare system are at high risk for disruption of their attachments. The numbers of children in out-of-home care through the child welfare system are growing and require attention from the early childhood system of care. According to Goerge and Wulczyn (1998–1999), a child under age five is twice as likely to be in foster care as older children or adolescents. Many of these young children are removed from their mother's care within weeks of birth and are likely to be substance exposed. Once in out-of-home care, it is not unusual for infants and toddlers to have multiple placements prior to their establishment in a permanent placement. Infants are also much more likely to stay longer in out-of-home care than older children do. In addition, infants and toddlers who are removed from the parents' care are less likely to be returned to their parents than older children and more likely to be adopted (Goerge & Wulczyn, 1998–1999).

Another challenge that the early childhood system of care must address is that historically, children in foster care have had significant difficulty accessing mental health services (Knitzer, 1982). This has improved somewhat with welfare reform during the past decade. However, according to Kamerman (1998–1999), four times as much money in 1996 was spent on foster care placements than on family preservation and support services. In order to preserve infant-parent attachments, the early childhood system of care must put a greater emphasis on preventing infants and toddlers from being removed from their home of origin and supporting the maintenance of placements that are made after removal. Every effort must be made to maintain a child in crisis in one foster home rather than allowing multiple placements if the child's behavior becomes problematic. Bringing infants and toddlers in foster care quickly into the wrap-around process may help to avoid these multiple placements.

The work of Charles Zeanah and his colleagues at Tulane University provides another model for mental health intervention with infants and toddlers who are placed in foster care. Zeanah's program in Jefferson Parish, Louisiana, provides comprehensive evaluations of the infants and their biological and foster families. Their recommendations concerning the steps necessary for reunification are provided to the juvenile court, which orders a case plan. Zeanah's team then provides the needed treatment (Larrieu & Zeanah, 1998). When Zeanah and his colleagues compared the recidivism rates for mothers who completed their program with mothers adjudicated for child abuse or neglect in the four years prior to the beginning of the program, they found a marked reduction in the rate of later substantiated abuse allegations on the same child in the intervention group (Zeanah et al., 2001). Such collaborative interventions between mental health providers, the court system, and child welfare are essential for providing the best possible treatment for children in foster care.

Another challenge for the early childhood system of care is providing support for the development and maintenance of the relationship between infants and toddlers and their child care providers. A young child's development may be significantly affected by having a succession of temporary caregivers. Equally troubling is the rising rate of expulsion from multiple day care settings for toddlers with difficult behaviors. Children need dependable relationships that provide a secure base of love, nurturance, and interaction that is responsive. This is difficult to achieve in many community-based child care settings. The centers are challenged by low reimbursement rates, limited availability of trained staff, and very high child-to-staff ratios. Staff have little time for planning or professional development activities. As the child care settings have become overcrowded due to the reforms in welfare statutes, they are less likely to be able to be responsive to a child who presents with behavioral challenges and possibly less willing because they have a waiting list.

The most significant step that can be taken is to recognize the importance of the relationships children develop outside the home and to respect the stability they provide for a child. Some child care centers are beginning to assign children to staff and have the staff stay with the child over time rather than assign the child to rooms by age. Gerber has been an advocate of this type of model for many years. The video *Respectfully Yours: Magda Gerber's Approach to Professional Infant/Toddler Care* provides an excellent description of her beliefs (Far West Laboratory, 1995). For example, she recommends that a child care provider care for a child from infancy to age five rather than assign the child as many as five different providers within one center over the five years. In this model, providers work in teams, with one being primary to each child. Within each team are at least two people who know each child well.

To address staff shortage and turnover concerns due to lack of compensation, many programs have begun to write supplemental funding proposals to raise pay rates and add a benefit package. Health insurance, reduced rates, or scholarships for the staff's children to attend the program or payment for college credit are examples of such added incentives.

Methods to meet the enormous child care staff development and training needs are being developed across the country. California provides an outstanding example of these efforts. The state invested money in the development of a training program and curriculum for infant and toddler caregivers, with the principles of infant mental health at its core (Far West Laboratory, 1995). (Gerber's video is part of this training curriculum.) The state's investment has led to the training of thousands of child care providers in California and other states through a training-of-trainers model. Following the development of this training program, California upgraded its licensing criteria regarding training requirements for child care providers.

Formulate Individualized and Integrated Multiagency Service Plans with the Full Participation of the Child's Family

These individualized service plans must be of appropriate intensity, flexibility, and comprehensiveness to meet the child and family's needs. The family and all providers must agree on a consolidated service plan in order to ensure plans are in place for all identified needs and to avoid fragmentation and duplication of services. An early childhood system of care must arrange services and supports based not on what programs are available but on the family needs. This often requires creative thinking beyond categorical programs and services.

Among the many challenges to this core value, perhaps the biggest challenge to unified service plans for families is the separation between adult (parent) and child mental health programs and systems. Each program and each system develops criteria independent of the others for service plan requirements. Programs typically target adults or children, but not both. This is in part due to funding streams and in part due to the training and expertise of staff who specialize in adult or children's services. It may also be a licensing issue. The delivery of mental health services to children from birth to age five cannot be done out of the context of the adult caregiver. The caregiver is the conduit for the child's therapy. Infant and toddler mental health must consider equally the histories and the capacities of the child and the caregiver. Therefore, the service plan must consider the entire family. This requires that agencies be willing to conduct their work in collaboration rather than in isolation. They must be willing to work together, to blend funding and combine various program requirements into a joint service plan.

In an ideal world of infant and toddler mental health, services would flow from need, not a long list of eligibility criteria. They would be integrated between the adult and children's systems. Billing would not be for either the adult or child client system but the family. The service plan would also reflect this philosophy.

Arizona's 300 Kids Project is one recently established initiative for the development of integrated service planning. The project is an effort to begin implementation of the reforms required by the settlement agreement of the *Jason K. v. Eden* (2001) class action lawsuit. Originally filed in 1991, this lawsuit alleged that Title XIX–eligible children in Arizona were not receiving adequate mental health care. The settlement of this lawsuit is remarkable for the agreement on a set of twelve principles to make publicly funded mental health services more responsive to the needs of children and their families (*Jason K. v. Eden* Settlement Agreement, 2001, pp. 5–7). Two hundred children and their families from Maricopa County (Phoenix) and one hundred children from rural northern Arizona have been selected to participate. These sites have been chosen to test strategies for providing services in accordance with the principles outlined in the settlement agreement, which include collaboration with families, individualized service delivery, improved cultural competency, and use of a best practice approach. Joint treatment planning, increased use of the wraparound process, and streamlined funding mechanisms are expected outcomes of the project. The recent addition of a small number of toddlers and their families to the project will extend these reforms into early childhood services in Arizona.

Another challenge to integrated service planning is that children are often seen in isolation from the family in many mental health settings. With children under age five, it is essential to see the child and family together. Because the work with infants and toddlers is focused on the enhancement of the interaction and the relationship between the infant and toddler and the adult caregivers, they must not be seen in isolation.

One helpful and best practice solution to this challenge is to see families in their home. Home-based service allows the therapist to work with the child and primary caregivers in their natural environment. The Southwest Human Development Good Fit Center in Phoenix, Arizona, provides an excellent model for this type of service delivery. This community-based center serves approximately 270 children from birth to age five and their families, with services funded primarily with Title XIX Medicaid dollars. The center delivers its therapy services in the home unless the family chooses to be served in the center or there are significant safety concerns in the natural environment. The center is actively involved in the 300 Kids Project and is the only agency in that project serving infants and toddlers (www.swhd.org).

Value and Respect the Family's Unique Social and Cultural Beliefs and Interests in Order to Provide Culturally Competent and Clinically Appropriate Services

Culture and ethnicity are fundamental aspects of each individual and shape essentially all aspects of family life. Parenting practices, family structure, and the extent of community participation in the raising of children vary with culture and ethnicity. Cultural values influence beliefs in all aspects of child rearing, including sleeping, eating, toilet training, parental responsiveness, gender and family roles, social development norms, and concepts of independence and autonomy. Standards for discipline and appropriate behavior are also highly culture bound.

Infancy and early childhood are normally times when parents rely on extended family. In some cultures, grandparents may be a coprimary caregiver in caring for an infant. Different cultural groups experience varying stressors in early the child-rearing phase. The families of migrant workers, for example, experience frequent moves and difficulties establishing networks of care and social support. Families experiencing immigration and acculturation may be under additional stress if they lack their usual culturally normative supports for child rearing. Family dynamics also have cultural influences, including variations in gender or generational roles. Service providers must understand and respect these factors in order to be accepted by families and have an opportunity for successful intervention.

Training mental health practitioners on cultural competence does not necessarily result in cultural respect, that is, respect for differing values and cultural responsiveness. It is not enough for funders to require a brief training on cultural competence. The subtleties of cultural disregard are enormous. Program managers and designers must build in practice parameters that address the cultural needs of the program clientele and the program staff. The most successful way to ensure cultural responsiveness in practice is to engage in regular management discussions on this topic and establish culturally related quality indicators and outcome measures. This will facilitate the maintenance of the importance of cultural responsiveness in the forefront of the program's activities.

As the desire to be culturally responsive increases, there is an increasingly large demand for bilingual and minority staff who mirror the clientele to be served. The shortage of qualified bilingual and minority staff is serious, and there is little or no relief in sight. Programs continue to struggle to identify and hire qualified mental health staff. One solution that early childhood programs are employing to deal with this crisis is the utilization of paraprofessionals from the culture of the client family.

The Kmiqhitahasultipon Program, serving the Passamaquoddy tribe of Indian Township, Maine, provides a strong example of culturally responsive early childhood service delivery. The program "offers home-based care consistent with Passamaquoddy approaches to healing and community well-being" (Simpson et al., 2001). Taking its name from the Passamaquoddy words "we remember," the Kmiqhitahasultipon Program primarily uses community providers to deliver individualized services to the infant and family in their home or other local settings. These community providers also assist in linking the family to other services available through the program or from other agencies serving the tribe. The relationships between program staff and the family are often established before the birth of the child in order to address the needs of the child and family from the earliest possible moment (Simpson et al., 2001).

Intervene Without Delay to Meet the Developmental Needs of Young Children

Scientific knowledge indicates that normative early development is the foundation for well-being later in life. Therefore, newborns, infants, and toddlers at risk for developmental delays require expedient intervention to strengthen their development during this highly vulnerable period. Because infant and toddler development is so rapid, any postponement of intervention may result in more serious delays and require more intensive intervention.

Challenges to the implementation of this core value include the lack of linkages between potential points of entry to the rest of the system of care. Especially critical for early childhood are the linkages between pediatricians and family doctors and the system of care: concerns about atypical development and early-onset behavioral problems are likely to come to the attention of a physician before any other community provider. Outreach to primary care physicians is essential to ensure prompt referral of the infant or toddler to the appropriate array of services.

Another barrier to early intervention is the lack of penetration of state-of-the-art knowledge of child development and infant mental health to all levels of the system of care. Dissemination of new learning to direct service providers, program developers, parents, and funders of services will facilitate the design and functioning of the early childhood system of care. For example, research indicates that infants and toddlers with significant behavioral, developmental, or regulatory disturbance will not "just grow out of it," as has been assumed by medical practitioners for many years. In fact, recent research on infants with the DC: 0–3 diagnosis of regulatory disorder finds that symptoms of the disorder persist over time. DeGangi, Porges, Sickel, and Greenspan (1993) found that eight out of nine infants with sleep disturbance, difficulties with self-consoling, mood lability, and distress during transitions and other activities that offer a sensory challenge at age eight to eleven months continued to have developmental or behavioral challenges at four years of age. Incorporating research information such as this into program design might dramatically increase the attention paid to the identification of these conditions in infants and toddlers. Providing this information to parents and parent advocacy groups would potentially increase the number of infants and toddlers who are identified for early intervention.

The Children's Upstream Services Project in Vermont has successfully dealt with this challenge by emphasizing technical assistance as part of its statewide service array. Based in a children's center in Burlington, three early childhood mental health consultants are available to work with child care providers and parents and share their specialized knowledge through workshops and consultation. In addition to their insights into behavioral interventions and child development, they also support the adults involved with their expertise in stress management (Simpson et al., 2001).

Several funding issues also interfere with implementation of this core value. First, preventative care such as early identification and intervention are not funded to the same extent as pathology-driven treatment interventions. Second, third-party payment for mental health services to infants and toddlers is inadequate due to the limited number of reimbursable diagnoses for this age group. Third, traditional reimbursement patterns are not supportive of the community-based interventions that are the mainstay of work with this population.

Technical assistance to program designers, systems administrators, and legislative budget committees showing the effectiveness of early intervention in reducing the frequency of later psychopathology (Olds et al., 1998) may be helping in shifting budgetary priorities in the direction of more preventative care. Obtaining third-party payer reimbursement for DC: 0–3 diagnoses would also support increased therapeutic work with this age group.

Finally, increasing the number of reimbursable community-based therapeutic service codes in state Medicaid plans will also support a broader array of available services. The recent Covered Services Project of the Arizona Division of Behavioral Health Services is one example of this approach to system reform (Arizona Department of Health Services Division of Behavioral Health Services, 2001). The importance of this type of system change should not be underestimated; in the words of John VanDenBerg, one of the pioneers of wraparound, "When the financial incentives line up, systems can change overnight" (personal communication, 1997).

Ensure Smooth Transitions Between Service System Elements as the Child's Developmental Needs Change

The structure of the early childhood system must mirror the developmental needs of the child and family. A child's development is continuous from the moment of conception onward. A responsive early childhood system of care will constantly consider the developmental status of the child and family in order to provide the most appropriate array of services and supports. Providers and agencies must ensure that the needs of the child and family are met as they move through the system of care.

The main challenge to implementation of this core value is that there are often multiple discontinuities between elements of the developing early childhood system of care. Mothers with special needs frequently do not receive intervention and support prior to or after the birth of their child. Children leaving neonatal intensive care units are often lost to follow-up until years later, despite the parents' long-standing concerns about delayed development or behavioral challenges. Infants and toddlers who do receive early intervention services often have disruption of their care when responsibility for continued therapy moves to the school system at age three.

Fragmentation of services frequently occurs due to the different funding streams for early childhood services. For example, a young child receiving services within the mental health system often has difficult accessing speech or occupational therapy, services that are often administered and funded by other child-serving agencies. Different funding and administrative structures also interfere with the coordination of a infant's care with that of the mother or father, who may also be receiving services from providers of adult services.

Once again, these barriers to a seamless service system can be broken down using the principles of wraparound. One of the essential elements of wraparound is that the "services and supports must be individualized to meet the needs of the children and families and not designed to reflect the priorities of the service systems" (VanDenBerg & Grealish, 1996, p. 9). With the focus on providing services to the entire family in a coordinated fashion, barriers between the adult system of care and the early childhood system of care can be broken down. Another essential element of wraparound is that the process have communitywide ownership, that no element of the child-serving system hold itself apart from the full implementation of individualized services for the children and their families. With complete community buy-in, the child and family team, led by the parent or primary caregiver, will be able to break down artificial barriers to needed services.

Care coordination is also essential to navigate the discontinuities between the different programs within the early childhood system of care. There are many models of the delivery of this service. Most often, care coordination is carried out by someone within the mental health system, such as a designated case coordinator or therapist, but it can be carried out by direct service personnel within early intervention, child welfare, or developmental disability programs. In fully mature systems of care, the parent or primary caregiver for the young child may coordinate the care with the assistance and support of the child and family team. Regardless of who provides this service, the person must have cross-agency support to be effective in this task.

Flexible funding and blended funding streams are another tool for making seamless transitions between programs, with the least amount of disruption of service to the infant and family. Access to "flexible, non-categorized funding" is another essential element of wraparound (VanDenBerg & Grealish, 1996, p. 9); without access to flexible funds, child and family teams would have much greater difficulty developing unique ways to support the child and family. Blended funding streams allow cross-categorical services to be delivered. For example, a family preservation program, funded by both child welfare and mental health dollars and staffed with both child protective services workers and mental health providers, is much more likely to be effective in collaboration than two separate agencies with two totally separate funding streams.

A communitywide mechanism for system oversight is also an important tool for breaking down artificial barriers to service delivery. Where systems of care for older children and adolescents have been successful in this regard, there have been interagency protocols that bring together high-level administrators from each child-serving agency in the community. The goals of these collaborative bodies include coordination of care delivery and the removal of barriers that hamper the work of direct service providers. In truly robust systems of care, these coordinating bodies have administered blended funding pools to provide money for wraparound plans or seed money for the development of programs to fill perceived service gaps in the community.

Encourage Professionals Within the System of Care to Make Advocating for the Child and Family Their Highest Priority

Advocacy is an essential component of an early childhood system of care. There must be advocacy for the infant's basic developmental and emotional needs in the face of the legal primacy of parents' rights and the power of organizational and bureaucratic imperatives. There also must be advocacy for the rights and needs of parents with mental illness or an addictive disorder; professionals within the adult mental health system may be inadequately aware of the effects of the adult's treatment on the child and family. Strong advocacy may be necessary to navigate complex systems where interagency linkages are not well established.

Many different individuals and organizations may provide advocacy within an early childhood system of care. Each professional discipline has the responsibility to advocate strongly for its clients. Parent organizations and state interdisciplinary coalitions of concerned professionals also have important roles to play. Within the child welfare system, the guardians ad litem (attorneys appointed by the court to speak for the best interests of the child within the system) have an especially important role in providing advocacy for children in state custody.

One of the primary challenges to full implementation of the core value is adequate training for both professionals and parents. Most professional programs do not graduate system-savvy practitioners who feel comfortable in advocating for services and supports outside their specialty. For example, a mental health therapist may not know how to obtain access to a community food bank for a family or secure flexible funds to help pay for an overdue utility bill. The need for training of guardians ad litem is especially important for children within the child welfare system. They will require specialized training and support from within the early childhood system of care to be truly effective and independent advocates for the developmental needs of the infants and toddlers assigned to them.

Parents can often obtain access to needed information and resources to be effective advocates for their children with the assistance of parent advocacy groups. However, developing systems of care do not always prioritize the funding of these advocacy groups when funding is tight and cut funding to these groups when belt tightening occurs.

Another significant barrier is the lack of understanding that professionals may have of the importance of parent advocacy groups with developing systems of care. Professionals may not be aware of the important role that parents can play in helping other parents and in advocating for system change. *Collaborations: Building Partnerships* (Keys for Networking, 1995), written by a Kansas parents' advocacy group affiliated with the national Federation of Families for Children's Mental Health, describes the role that parent advocacy groups can play within systems of care:

> Self helping parent groups are in a unique position to empathize with the parents who call on them and are accessible in a way that professionals seldom are. . . .These parents almost always become interested in changing the institutions that provide services for their children and reforming the laws that govern these services. An important point is the passion that parents bring to advocacy for large-scale change springs from their own acute, painful experiences. Resourceful parents can make policies, institutions, agencies and governments vibrant with respect for the power of the passion these people have for their children. Professionals must learn that, in partnering with parents, their ability to improve the lives of the children they serve is greatly enhanced.

Clearly, one of the solutions to this challenge is making changes in professional training programs, so that one of their goals becomes producing graduates with the tools to become strong system advocates and partners with parents. Technical assistance to practitioners already in community practice to improve their advocacy skills must also be made a priority. Another solution is for parent advocacy groups and parent providers to become integral parts of the early childhood system of care. Only then will the stage be set for true parent-professional partnerships and the development of true respect by professionals for the contributions that parents can make to the care of children and management of the system.

Strive for an Ethical Balance Between Protecting the Rights of Children and Supporting the Rights of Parents

The ethical issues that may arise within early childhood systems of care are often quite complex. Perhaps the most common ethical dilemma is the decision about the custody of a child who has been removed from the biological parents' home by child welfare authorities. Even more difficult is the decision to terminate parental rights. Making the choice by weighing the legal rights of the biological parents and the developmental and emotional needs of the child is never an easy one, and too often the decision is made without close attention to the ethical issues. The situation has become even more complex with in vitro fertilization, surrogate parenting, and nontraditional families.

Use of medication to treat three- to five-year-old children increased dramatically during the 1990s (Zito et al., 2000). Ethical issues abound in the medication treatment of preschool children for their serious emotional disturbances. For example, does the unknown but potential long-term risk of using powerful medications to help stabilize a young child in the birth, foster, or adoptive home outweigh the known risk to the child's attachments by placement in out-of-home care? Is it ethical to use medication to treat a condition that would respond equally well to more time-intensive and expensive psychotherapeutic interventions?

The challenge for developing early childhood systems of care is to find the time for the discussion of these and other important ethical considerations. Too often, the necessary people, such as the community's religious leaders, do not participate in these difficult decisions. Most medical centers have ethics committees to assist in the deliberation of the complex ethical issues that develop in these settings. For example, these committees often participate in the difficult decision to terminate life support to a significantly premature infant. However, in community settings, there is seldom an ethics committee available to help deal with the difficult decisions that must be made in this environment. The establishment of ethics committees within early childhood systems of care would mark a significant step forward in improving the quality and inclusiveness of decision making with regard to these and other sensitive and difficult issues.

STORY FROM THE COMMUNITY

The following case study illustrates the importance of system of care principles and use of the wraparound process in providing comprehensive care to young children. The child and family team that formed around Chelsea and her family was composed of both professionals and the family's natural circle of support.

Chelsea was first seen at the infant and toddler mental health program at age two years, six months. She was born six weeks prematurely and has had persistent delays

in her speech development. Her parents reported that she has a low tolerance for frustration and severe tantrums that can last for over two hours. She sleeps only four to five hours each night and becomes very upset with any change in routine. When observed in a play group, Chelsea frequently isolates herself, often biting other children who get too close to her. Although the infant and toddler program had provided a family therapist, Chelsea was still on the waiting list for speech and occupational therapy three months after these needs were identified.

The family includes Chelsea, her parents, Ben and Kathy, and her one-year-old brother, Jacob. Ben has been in treatment within the adult mental health system for several years with a severe bipolar affective disorder and has had difficulty finding the right combination of medications to stabilize his condition, leaving him unable to work and help with the children on a consistent basis. Kathy has experience in marketing and advertising, but has had difficulty finding work with the downturn in the economy. Behind on their bills, Ben and Kathy have been forced to move out of their apartment and place their children in an emergency shelter. At the time that a wraparound child and family team was brought together around Chelsea's family, Ben and Kathy had been living out of their car for several weeks.

Ben and Kathy felt that their first priority was finding a new place to live and bringing their family back together. Finding at least part-time employment for Kathy and obtaining support for Ben to assume some child care responsibilities were also important. Chelsea's parents felt that she needed a psychiatric evaluation.

The child and family team consisted of the family's therapist from the infant and toddler program, a representative from the state developmental disabilities program (who controlled access to the needed speech and occupational therapy services), Ben's case manager from the adult mental health program where he had been receiving his services, Ben's elderly parents, the pastor from Ben and Kathy's church, and an experienced family advocate.

Ben and Kathy's pastor reported that their church was willing to support them in finding new housing. A member of their congregation who owned a small apartment complex was willing to donate a two-month stay in a recently vacated apartment while the family was getting back on its feet. Another member of the congregation owned an employment service and was willing to assist Kathy in developing a resumé and help her find work within her field. Yet another member of the church was willing to donate or buy clothing for her job interviews.

The team agreed to support Ben and Kathy's request for a psychiatric evaluation for Chelsea. The developmental disabilities worker and the family advocate agreed to work together to obtain the speech and occupational therapies Chelsea needed. Ben's case manager promised to advocate for Ben with his psychiatrist to change his medications so that Ben would be less drowsy during the day and better able to assist with child care. Ben's elderly parents were willing to come into the home and support their son in caring for his children several days each week. The therapist from the infant and toddler center and the developmental disabilities specialist agreed to work together to increase support into the home. An individualized service plan was written by the child and family team and was used by all agencies within the system of care.

Six months later, Chelsea's family's situation had stabilized significantly. Kathy had been successful in finding a job in her field, and the family's financial situation was improving. Ben's psychiatrist had changed Ben's medication, and Ben was gradually taking a larger role in child care. A psychiatric evaluation for Chelsea had resulted in the prescribing of a medication that improved her sleep and lessened her tantrums to the point where behavioral interventions were more successful. Speech and occupational therapy had been started but were discontinued when Chelsea turned three and aged out of early intervention. The school district told the family that they would not have an opening in their special needs preschool for several months. In the meantime, Chelsea's frustration with being unable to communicate her needs was growing, and her behavior was worsening. Ben's father had recently had a small stroke, and his parents were unable to continue to assist them with child care.

The child and family team reconvened to change the individualized service plan for the family. They agreed to access flexible funding to continue the speech and occupational therapy until Chelsea entered the special needs preschool. The family advocate, working in tandem with Ben and the family's therapist, were successful in moving up Chelsea's entrance evaluation for the preschool by six weeks. Ben's younger brother and his wife agreed to be on call to the family to provide in-home support to Ben and Kathy when needed. Several members of their church agreed to be on call as well.

This story from the community illustrates many of the core values for the early childhood system of care. The central role of the principles of wraparound in accessing needed services and assisting with service transitions is clear. Ben and Kathy are at the center of service planning for Chelsea and the rest of the family. Strong advocacy from the parent advocate, the therapist, and the developmental disabilities specialist was needed to put the plan into action. The early childhood system of care clearly supported the reintegration and stability of this family as its highest priority. Figure 10.3 provides suggestions for professionals who want to deepen their involvement in their local early childhood system of care.

The mission of the early childhood system of care must be to provide early intervention and treatment to infants and toddlers and their families in a coordinated fashion in order to prevent poor attachments, reduce the impact of disorders of development, and decrease the likelihood of psychopathology later in life. The best place to provide this intervention is in the natural environment of the young child and family. The research of Olds et al. (1997, 1998) is strongly supportive of the use of home visitation to reduce the risk of child abuse and neglect and decrease the likelihood of the child's engaging in antisocial behavior later in life. Coordinated service delivery through an early childhood system of care can increase the power of these early interventions.

The early childhood system of care must bring together many disparate voices into one united chorus in support of infants and toddlers. One of the strongest voices in the chorus can be the child psychiatrist, equipped with the tools of expertise in child development, familiarity with the principles of wraparound and systems management, and a willingness to partner with families.

- Identify individuals in your local and state governments with an interest in infant and toddler issues with the goal of influencing public policy and budgetary priorities.
- Participate in wraparound child and family teams.
- Use a strength-based approach to your evaluations of children. Include both strengths and weaknesses of the family in your final report.
- Become more knowledgeable about local family resources, and advocate for more with passion.
- Find creative ways to provide clinical consultation to Medicaid-funded agencies or technical assistance to parent advocacy groups. Consider writing a grant to support your time.
- Reach out to and collaborate with pediatricians and family doctors to bring them into the early childhood system of care.
- Participate in community boards overseeing services for infants and toddlers.
- Support others' grant-writing efforts by becoming a coauthor or by writing a letter of support.
- Partner with parents.

FIGURE 10.3. How Mental Health Professionals Might Participate in Their Early Childhood System of Care.

Perhaps Selma Fraiberg said it best: "We . . . conceive of infant mental health as a province of community mental health which extends beyond the borders of any clinic or social agency" (1980, p. 4). To serve the next generation best, we must serve them early and serve them where they live.

References

American Academy of Child and Adolescent Psychiatry. (in press). *Best practices for early childhood systems of care.* Washington, DC: Author.

American Psychiatric Association. (1994). *Diagnostic and statistical manual of mental disorders* (4th ed.). Washington, DC: Author.

Arizona Department of Health Services Division of Behavioral Health Services. (2001). *Covered services project draft documents.* Phoenix: Arizona Department of Health Services.

DeGangi, G. A., Porges, S. W., Sickel, R. Z., & Greenspan, S. I. (1993). Four-year follow-up of a sample of regulatory disordered infants. *Infant Mental Health Journal, 14,* 330–343.

Far West Laboratory for Educational Research and Development, Center for Child and Family Studies. (1995). *The Program for Infant/Toddler Caregivers' Trainer's Manual, Modules I-IV.* Sacramento: California Department of Education.

Fraiberg, S. (1980). *Clinical studies in infant mental health: The first year of life.* New York: Basic Books.

Friedman, R. M., & Stroul, B. A. (1986). *A system of care for children and youth with severe emotional disturbances* (Rev. ed.). Washington, DC: Child and Adolescent Service System Program Technical Assistance Center, Georgetown University Child Development Center.

Goerge, R. M., & Wulczyn, F. (1998–1999). Placement experiences of the youngest foster care population: Findings from the Multistate Foster Care Data Archive. *Bulletin of Zero to Three: National Center for Infants, Toddlers and Families, 19*(3), 8–13.

Jason K. v. Eden. (2001, Mar. 21). U.S. District Court, District of Arizona, No. CIV 91–261 TUC JMR.

Kamerman, S. B. (1998–1999). Child welfare and the under-threes. *Bulletin of Zero to Three: National Center for Infants, Toddlers and Families, 19*(3), 1, 3–7.

Kendziora, K., Burns, E., Osher, D., Pacchiano, D., & Mejia, B. (2001). *Wraparound: Stories from the field.* Washington, DC: Center for Effective Collaboration and Practice, American Institutes for Research.

Keys for Networking. (1995). *Collaborations: Building partnerships.* Topeka, KS: Author.

Knitzer, J. (1982). *Unclaimed children.* Washington, DC: Children's Defense Fund.

Knitzer, J. (1996). Meeting the mental health needs of young children and their families. In B. A. Stroul (Ed.), *Children's mental health: Creating systems of care in a changing society.* Baltimore: Brookes Publishing.

Larrieu, J. A., & Zeanah, C. H. (1998). Intensive intervention for maltreated infants and toddlers in foster care. *Child and Adolescent Psychiatric Clinics of North America, 7,* 357–371.

National Research Council and Institute of Medicine. (2000). *From neurons to neighborhoods: The science of early childhood development.* Washington, DC: National Academy Press.

Olds, D. L., Eckenrode, J., Henderson, C. R., Kitzman, H., Powers, J., Cole, R., Sidora, K., Morris, P., Pettitt, L. M., & Luckey, D. (1997). Long-term effects of home visitation on maternal life course and child abuse and neglect: Fifteen year follow-up of a randomized trial. *Journal of the American Medical Association, 278,* 637–643.

Olds, D. L., Henderson, C. R., Cole, R., Eckenrode, J., Kitzman, H., Luckey, D., Pettitt, L., Sidora, K., Morris, P., & Powers, J. (1998). Long-term effects of nurse home visitation on children's criminal and antisocial behavior: Fifteen year follow-up of a randomized, controlled trial. *Journal of the American Medical Association, 280,* 1238–1244.

Simpson, J., Hivanjee, P., Koroloff, N., Doerfler, A., & Garcia, M. (2001). *Promising practices in early childhood mental health.* Washington, DC: Center for Effective Collaboration and Practice, American Institutes for Research.

VanDenBerg, J., & Grealish, E. (1996). Individualized services and supports through the wraparound process: Philosophy and procedures. *Journal of Child and Family Studies, 5,* 7–21.

Whitbeck, J., Kimball, G., Olsen, D., Lonner, T., McKenna, M., & Robinson, R. (1993). *An analysis of the interaction among systems, services and individualized and tailored care.* Olympia, WA: Washington Division of Mental Health.

Winnicott, D. W. (1965). *The maturational processes and the facilitating environment: Studies in the theory of emotional development.* New York: International Universities Press.

Zeanah, C. H., Larrieu, J. A., Heller, S. S., Valliere, J., Hinshaw-Fuselier, S., Aoki, Y., & Drilling, M. (2001). Evaluation of a preventative intervention for maltreated infants and toddlers in foster care. *Journal of the American Academy of Child and Adolescent Psychiatry, 40,* 214–221.

Zero to Three. (1994). *Diagnostic classification of mental health and developmental disorders of infancy and early childhood: Zero to three.* Arlington, VA: National Center for Infants Toddlers and Families.

Zito, J. M., Safer, D. J., Dos Reis, S., Gardner, J. F., Boles, M., & Lynch, F. (2000). Trends in the prescribing of psychotropic medications to preschoolers. *Journal of the American Medical Association, 283,* 1025–1030.

CHAPTER ELEVEN

Youth in the Juvenile Justice System

William M. Heffron
Andres J. Pumariega
Theodore Fallon Jr.
Debbie R. Carter

The juvenile justice system in the United States formally began with the Illinois Juvenile Court Act of 1899, which separated children and adolescents from the adults within the penal system. The primary mandate of juvenile court was to act as "kind parents" (in loco parentis), seeking to educate and rehabilitate youth rather than to punish them. In accepting the task of caring for young offenders, the juvenile justice system has been given the most difficult youth to care for, many of whom come from other child-caring systems. (See Schiraldi, 1999, and Center on Juvenile and Criminal Justice, 1999, for further information regarding the history of juvenile justice in the United States.)

The juvenile court remains a civil rather than a criminal system. Juveniles are not charged with crimes and prosecuted; petitions are filed seeking court action. Juveniles are not found guilty; the petition is sustained or dismissed. Juveniles are not sentenced as a punishment; their case disposition reflects the court's view of the best treatment to meet the juvenile's needs.

MENTAL HEALTH AND JUVENILE JUSTICE

Increasing attention has been focused on addressing the mental health needs of youth in the juvenile justice system. Although only a few prevalence studies have been done, some general idea of the scope of the problem does exist (Otto, Greenstein, Johnson, & Friedman, 1992; Edens & Otto, 1997; Faenza & Siegfried,

2001; Atkins et al., 1999). Prevalence rates are reported for a variety of diagnoses and conditions—for example:

- Conduct disorder at over 80 percent
- Substance abuse at up to 70 percent
- Attention deficit hyperactivity disorder at up to 50 percent
- Affective disorders between 2 and 80 percent
- Anxiety disorders up to 41 percent
- Psychotic disorders up to 6 percent
- Personality disorders up to 46 percent
- Mental retardation up to 15 percent
- Learning disabilities and specific developmental disorders up to 53 percent
- Prior mental health treatment: Outpatient treatment up to 66 percent and inpatient treatment up to 26 percent
- Suicidal behavior in up to 26 percent of cases
- Child abuse between 25 percent and 31 percent of cases

Females have different issues that predominate. Delinquent girls show symptoms of anxiety and depression three times more than females in the general population (Kataoka et al., 2001). Depression in adolescent girls has been correlated with crimes against property and other people (Obeidallah & Earls, 1999). Females also have an increased amount of posttraumatic stress disorder. The high prevalence of abuse has been correlated with truancy, violence, risky sexual behavior, prostitution, and running away (Prescott, 1997).

Adolescents from racial minorities are overrepresented in all stages of the juvenile justice system, with increasing representation found as the level of restriction in the system increases (Bilchik, 1999). Data from 1996/1997 illustrate this pattern (information on Hispanics is hard to find because they are frequently listed as white at the time of arrest):

Population: black, 15 percent

Arrests: black, 26 percent

Juvenile court cases: black, 30 percent

Detention: black, 45 percent

Residential placement: black, 40 percent; Hispanic, 18 percent

Waived to adult court: black, 46 percent

The mental health needs of minority youth are often not met or are ignored in the community. They use hospital admissions to a greater degree and outpatient treatment to a lesser degree than white youth do (Isaacs, 1992; Gibbs & Huang, 1998). It falls on the juvenile justice system to address these needs.

Addressing the mental health needs of youth in the juvenile justice system requires an understanding of the aims of both systems. Juvenile justice is primarily interested in reducing recidivism rates, promoting public safety, and providing appropriate services in a cost-effective manner (Greenwood et al., 1994; Andrews et al., 1990). Mental health is primarily focused on the youth and family and aims to manage or cure disorders of thought and affect. In general, the great majority of mental health interventions are seen as voluntary, while those of juvenile justice are not.

The juvenile justice system is complex, and variations exist from state to state. In negotiating the process, a youth can come in contact with the police, prosecutors, defense attorneys, judges, probation officers, detention centers, long-term residential facilities, group homes, foster homes, day treatment programs, and a variety of different agencies, including education, mental health, and social services. A mental health professional working in this area must be aware of the impact of all of these possible interactions.

Detention Services

Juvenile detention can be viewed as a process (Kentucky Department of Juvenile Justice, 2001). Traditionally, the term is used to describe confinement of a youth in a secure facility. The individual is held in temporary and safe custody in order to guarantee his or her appearance in court or in other instances to provide short-term sanctions for illegal behavior. Ideally, detention should offer a variety of helpful services to support a youth's physical, emotional, and social development (Kudart, 2000). The same services can be provided through various detention alternatives. Examples include staff-secure shelters, supervised foster care, community supervision, house arrest with a tracker, and periodic checks with or without electronic monitoring. Most juveniles should be processed in relatively short time, but in reality that does not necessarily occur. Conditions in many centers are overcrowded, resulting in serious safety issues and overuse of restraints (Allen-Hagen, 1993).

Child psychiatrists and other professionals can provide a variety of services to detention. Evaluation and treatment of mental health disorders are clearly necessary. Consultation to juvenile justice staff on how to manage youth with mental health problems is very much needed. Teaching staff about mental health issues and how to deal with them on a very basic level is very much desired. Most juvenile justice workers are eager for the information because their traditional ways of dealing with youth do not work (Boesky, 2001). Assisting in the transition to community-based mental health treatment is also valuable. The previous use of outpatient mental health services by incarcerated youth seems to be less than expected, while their use of out-of-home placements is significantly greater than that of mental health populations (Pumariega et al., 1999).

Because many juvenile justice employees are unfamiliar with psychological and psychiatric terminology, it is essential to use nontechnical language in consultations. The use of examples to explain a point and the willingness to answer questions should be a high priority. It is important to understand how long a youth will remain in the particular detention program so that any recommendations to staff are relevant to the situation.

Residential Services

Long-term residential programs can vary from small facilities of thirty to forty beds to large institutions of over a thousand beds. Ideally, these programs should provide educational and vocational training, individual and group counseling, health care, and mental health care. The quality of services, however, varies from adequate to minimal. Generally, youth stay in the programs for six to twelve months and are then released to less restrictive environments.

Youth in these programs have been adjudicated and are usually considered more serious risks to society. The purposes of these programs are public protection and rehabilitation. The advantage over detention and even short-term hospitalization is in the fact that youth can be served for longer periods of time. The disadvantage is that while many of the adolescents in these programs have mental health issues, they also have serious delinquent behavior. In many facilities, overcrowding has led to increased violence, abuse, suicidal behavior, and use of isolation (Allen-Hagen, 1993).

Mental health professionals can provide significant contributions to these programs, particularly if they have an effective treatment team in place. In residential programs, participating in treatment planning is a good idea. This process gives the clinician a clear idea of the youth's everyday behavior, particularly if direct care workers participate. Evaluation and treatment of youth, consultation, and teaching of staff are again very much in demand. In the treatment planning process, the psychiatrist and mental health professional can be of help in identifying interventions that may be effective with a particular youth. Helping staff determine whether a youth's needs should be met in another setting (say, hospitalization for a suicide attempt or manic symptoms) and recommending treatment interventions after a youth is discharged from the facility are important contributions.

Community-Based Services

The great majority of youth in the juvenile justice system reside in the community, and the most effective interventions to prevent delinquency are community based (Mendel, 2000). Residential programs, even if they manage to change behavior in the institution, have minimal effects on youths' actions once they are discharged. Proven interventions include intensive family-oriented and home-based family counseling services, screening of first-time and second-time offenders with intensive treatment for those deemed at high risk to become chronic delinquents, short-term treatment foster care combined with counseling and parent management training, intensive advocacy services as an alternative to detention, social competence promotion, encouraging community organizations and volunteers to sanction and supervise many delinquent youth, and coordinated care for adolescents with serious emotional disabilities. Working with juvenile justice staff in community settings can be a positive contribution for a clinician Issues of confidentiality need to be addressed since many systems will be involved. Releases of information between agencies have to be signed in order to provide services appropriately.

A good deal of evidence exists on what risk factors predispose youth to violence in adolescence (U.S. Department of Health and Human Services, 2001). For youth ages six to eleven, important factors are committing general offenses, substance use, being male, low family socioeconomic status, antisocial parents, and aggression. For youth ages twelve to fourteen, important factors are weak social ties, antisocial and delinquent peers, gang membership, and committing general offenses. Many effective prevention programs are available (Mendel, 2000; U.S. Department of Education, 2001; U.S. Department of Health and Human Services, 2001). Included are early childhood interventions, school-based prevention programs, therapies with children and families that focus on social competency and parent training, and mentoring.

The surgeon general's report on youth violence recommends a public health approach (U.S. Department of Health and Human Services, 2001). Primary prevention or universal strategies target all youth populations and are aimed at preventing the onset of youth violence and related risk factors. Some effective interventions are skills training and the use of behavioral techniques for classroom management. Secondary intervention or selected strategies target youth populations that have one or more risk factors for violence. Some effective interventions include parent training and home visitation. Tertiary intervention or indicated strategies target youth populations in which violence has already occurred. Some effective interventions include wraparound services and multimodal interventions.

A systems of care approach that involves a wide variety of agencies, families, and neighborhoods in a timely fashion works most effectively. Nontraditional interventions such as multisystemic therapy have been found to be more effective with delinquent populations (Henggeler, Schoenwald, & Pickrel, 1995) because of their use of such contextual systems approaches in combination with cognitive behavioral, supportive, and educational methods.

Delinquents with or without mental health issues usually have their problems after routine office hours, so these community services must be responsive outside usual hours and office settings. Psychiatrists can be involved but must be willing to work with a variety of individuals. All clinicians also need to be willing to inform juvenile probation workers about missed appointments so that interventions can occur quickly.

THE OFFICE OF JUVENILE JUSTICE AND DELINQUENCY PREVENTION COMPREHENSIVE STRATEGY

In 1993, Wilson and the Office of Juvenile Justice and Delinquency Prevention (OJJDP; Wilson, 1994; Wilson & Howell, 1993) outlined a comprehensive, coordinated strategy for addressing juvenile delinquency. In 1995, Howell submitted a 270-page document detailing the elements of this comprehensive strategy. Since 1996, OJJDP has been providing technical assistance for three pilot sites. The Comprehensive Strategy, put forth by OJJDP (Coolbaugh & Hansel, 2000) as the standard of care for juvenile justice, incorporates the philosophy of balanced and restorative justice by employing restitution, community service, and other restorative justice programs when appropriate. This multidisciplinary research-based framework is guided by the following six principles for preventing and reducing high-risk behaviors:

- Strengthening the family in its primary responsibility to instill moral values and provide guidance and support to children
- Supporting core social institutions (schools, churches, youth service organizations, and community organizations) in their roles to develop capable, mature, and responsible youth
- Promoting delinquency prevention as the most cost-effective approach to reducing juvenile delinquency
- Intervening immediately and effectively when delinquent behavior first occurs to prevent delinquent offenders from becoming chronic offenders or from progressively committing more serious and violent crimes
- Establishing a system of graduated sanctions that holds each juvenile offender accountable, protects public safety, and provides programs and services that meet identified treatment needs
- Identifying and controlling the small percentage of serious, violent, and chronic juvenile offenders who commit the majority of juvenile felony level offenses

This type of system of care has a number of goals:

- Mobilize all segments of a community, including its institutions (schools, government, law enforcement, courts and corrections, public and private social service agencies, businesses, civic organizations, and the faith community) and private citizens, to cooperate in a comprehensive approach to reducing juvenile crime.
- Increase coordination and information sharing among all of these agencies.
- Identify and reach populations in need of prevention services.
- Create a continuum of care that allows for graduated sanctions.
- Monitor and evaluate the implementation and impact of these services.

Many of the principles identified fit with a systems of care approach (Stroul & Friedman, 1986):

- An array of services is emphasized.
- Early identification and prevention of delinquent behavior are critical.
- Coordination of care and agency cooperation is desired.
- Use of core social institutions fits with the principle of care in the most normative environment.
- Restrictive interventions are used on only a very small group of individuals.
- Focusing on the family is given first priority.

ROLES FOR MENTAL HEALTH PROFESSIONALS IN JUVENILE JUSTICE

Practicing in a juvenile justice system can offer a variety of experiences ranging from administrative to clinical to teaching and research. A clinician can stay very busy doing evaluations, making treatment recommendations, providing individual and group therapy, prescribing and managing medications, and providing emergency services. We will explore the wide variety of options available to clinicians.

Clinical Practice

A child psychiatrist is usually called on to evaluate a youth for treatment with medications or to look at the effectiveness of medicines currently prescribed. This evaluation can result in much more than a medicine check. The bias of juvenile justice employees tends to be against the use of medications unless they see clear results. Seeing the increasing number of youth who have failed in traditional mental health treatment settings reinforces this bias. As we have seen, many of these adolescents were involved in drug abuse, and they see some of the side effects of psychotropic medicines as a "high." Effects that can be seen as desirable include sedation and perceptual distortions of any kind. If youth have been involved with the mental health system previously, they tend to carry multiple diagnoses and have received many medications. In many instances, it may be prudent to start from the beginning and observe the youth over the longer time available in a residential setting.

Youth workers are eager to have help on how to manage behavior problems. The consultant can use this time productively, talking with staff about interventions to try with any particular youth. Any consultant must spend a considerable amount of time talking with staff in order to confirm what youth say to them. Delinquent youth with mental health issues will still behave in a delinquent manner. Matching what they say with what they really do is an absolute necessity. Issues related to suicidal or self-mutilating behavior are critical. Staff concerns usually relate to whether they are faking symptoms to get out of consequences. Impulsive behavior may be seen as acting oppositional. Assistance in how to deal with these symptoms is usually appreciated (Boesky, 2001). Determining whether the juvenile justice program can handle the situation is a difficult decision. If hospitalization is indicated, the mental health professional usually ends up making the referral. Smoothing the return to juvenile justice is important in preventing a revolving-door effect with the hospital.

Working in the community can be more difficult in some ways because delinquent youth tend to be uncooperative. Coordination between the agencies involved with the adolescents and their families has resulted in lower recidivism rates. A willingness to have a more flexible schedule and to be available to the juvenile justice worker for telephone consultation increases the likelihood of providing effective interventions. Youth in the community are more resistant to taking psychotropic medications because they do not want to be seen as "weak." Having control battles over medication use is not desirable if the goal is to establish a good treatment alliance and adherence by the youth.

Teaching

Mental health professionals working in juvenile justice have a wide area of expertise that they can share with a variety of individuals. Many programs have students rotating through. Other agencies frequently ask for information on treatment or delinquency issues. A critical area is in teaching juvenile justice staff about mental health issues. It is usually better to use case examples and role playing rather than formal lectures. Using medical and psychological terminology usually is not well accepted.

Topics of interest include the following:

- Identification and management of suicidal behavior
- Management of self-mutilating behavior
- Mental health diagnoses
- Medications and their side effects
- Use of isolation and restraint
- When someone should be hospitalized
- How to manage oppositional behavior
- Identification and intervention with malingering

Research

Establishing a sound basis for juvenile justice practice requires that decision making be done on a rational basis. Effective interventions are being identified, but more work needs to be done (Mendel, 2000). Among the areas that need more attention are these:

- Outcomes measurement of various interventions
- Residential versus community treatment
- Effect of intensive after-care
- Effect of in-home services
- Prevention programs
- Empirical identification of those most likely to recidivate
- Studies on sex offenders
- What interventions work
- Prediction of risk to reoffend
- Effectiveness of community versus residential treatment
- Studies on female delinquents
- Prevalence of mental health disorders
- Effects of treatment interventions

Administration

Mental health professionals can be called on to provide expertise in a variety of areas, including policy writing, program quality assurance, personnel issues, committee involvement, treatment protocols, record keeping, dealing with crises, and relationships with other agencies. A number of policy issues are critical—for example:

- Definition of a mental health assessment
- How restraint and isolation should be used
- What comprises a treatment plan
- Identification and management of suicidal behavior
- Roles and duties of mental health professionals
- Treatment techniques
- Use of medications
- Behavior management
- Placement in psychiatric care
- Information sharing

Reviewing the quality of treatment is an ongoing process. Most juvenile justice programs have fairly high staff turnover, and monitoring of treatment helps to maintain quality. The reviewer needs to see that interventions take place and are documented. Treatment planning needs to be documented. Incidents such as suicide attempts, use of restraints and isolation, and injuries to youth or staff need to be reviewed. Often, juvenile justice systems contract or work with other agencies to provide services. The clinician at times will review the quality of those programs also.

Personnel issues sometimes require the advice of the mental health professional. Situations may arise where an employee is unable to function at work, and the supervisor may ask for advice on making a referral for treatment. If an evaluation is done on whether an employee should return to work, the clinician may be asked to translate the report into language that the supervisor can understand.

Mental health professionals are frequently called on to participate in committees on a variety of issues, for example, after-care planning, treatment plan revisions, treatment philosophy of a department, evaluation of outcomes, determination of who is likely to reoffend, treatment protocol revisions, form revisions, and department management meetings.

As new research findings and evidence-based interventions become available, treatment protocols need revision. Clinicians are usually very involved in any changes that are made and can translate the findings to other committee members. Keeping up with changes is an integral part of the job. The professional is also involved in any training of juvenile justice staff concerning any protocol changes.

Mental health professionals generally review quality of record keeping. They also must document their own work. Juvenile justice facilities tend to keep medical records separate from facility records in order to maintain confidentiality.

Mental health in general is considered to be in the medical domain, and any written information is guarded closely. A clinician needs to be able to balance how much should be shared with other staff and how much should remain private. Policies need to be clear on this point.

Unanticipated events occur often with juvenile justice youth, and clinical input on how to manage a situation is often requested. A youth completing suicide is a prime example. It is important to help both the family and the staff involved with the youth deal with the situation. Sometimes complaints are made about the treatment a youth is receiving, and the professional may review the case. At times, when a youth escapes from a facility, the treatment quality is reviewed. Occasionally, a facility may ask a professional not involved in the treatment to review the care of a particularly difficult-to-manage youth and make suggestions. If a youth should die of any cause, a juvenile justice department ought to do a death review and examine the care the youth received. A mental health professional should be involved in the process.

Interacting with other agencies can involve the clinician in a variety of issues. The managing of juvenile sex offenders involves courts, the police, and adult corrections at times. Issues such as Medicaid behavioral health carve-outs can involve mental health, Medicaid, social services, and various consumer groups. If states are involved in interagency collaboration in the treatment of children with serious emotional disturbances (SED), the mental health professional usually represents juvenile justice.

To describe how mental health involvement in juvenile justice has evolved in various states over the past few years, we use examples from Kentucky, South Carolina, and Colorado to highlight the clinical and systems issues involved in mental health services in juvenile justice settings.

THE KENTUCKY STORY

The Kentucky Department of Juvenile Justice (DJJ) was formed in the fall of 1996 as a result of a federal consent decree. Among the provisions of the decree was the institution of adequate mental health treatment. In 1997, a child psychiatrist faculty member at the University of Kentucky Department of Psychiatry was hired to serve as mental health director for the agency, and three doctoral-level psychologists were hired to oversee services in DJJ's three regions. Over the course of a year, psychologists (mostly master's level) were hired to fill treatment director positions at the twelve residential treatment programs across the state. Four of the programs already had facility psychologists. The facilities were scattered around the state and had a capacity of no more that forty youths each. In addition, DJJ contracted with several psychiatrists and the Child Psychiatry Division at the University of Kentucky to provide at least four hours per week of on-site coverage at each of the facilities.

The mental health director is expected to oversee treatment in DJJ, serve as a member of the executive staff, review policies related to treatment and mental health services, assist in hiring personnel, and be available to staff for consultations. Over time, he has also represented DJJ at meetings of the State Interagency Council for Children with SED, Sex Offender Risk Assessment Board, the Mental Health Planning Council of the Kentucky Department of Mental Health, and a series of planning meetings reviewing a possible Medicaid behavioral health carve-out. He has participated in DJJ staff training and training for staff in other departments concerning mental health services at DJJ.

The regional psychologists are expected to clinically supervise the facility psychologists, be available for consultation to staff in their regions, facilitate care of DJJ youth at psychiatric hospitals, teach staff at DJJ and other departments, engage in quality assurance monitoring of treatment at facilities, and serve as members of the regional executive staff. They work together with the mental health director to plan implementation of mental health services at DJJ.

The facility psychologists are expected to work with the superintendents to enhance the treatment programs at the facilities. It has been critical that they develop a good working relationship with the superintendents, and for the most part, this has happened. In the few instances the relationship did not work, the superintendent was replaced by one more supportive of treatment issues. The psychologists assess every youth admitted to their facility, run treatment team meetings, and work with families. In some instances, they supervised youth counselors, but facilities do not require that role now. They also help staff manage youth who might become suicidal, recommend hospitalization if necessary, and facilitate referrals to the facility psychiatrists. They review the use of isolation and restraints on every youth who requires it. The psychologists have been on call for acute clinical incidents occurring on off-hours.

The facility psychiatrists have provided diagnostic assessment and medication management for youth and consultation on difficult cases, and they have been available to staff as requested. They have provided individual and group therapy, participated in treatment team meetings, and in several instances have helped in teaching facility staff about mental health issues.

Once personnel were hired, the majority of new initiatives provided by the mental health staff were directed at attaining compliance with the consent decree. These efforts primarily took place in 1998 and 1999. DJJ used the Massachusetts Youth Screening Instrument (MAYSI I and later the MAYSI II) as initial screening tools for youth in residential facilities. All youth entering were given the screen, which was used primarily to identify areas of concern that could be explored more fully during the actual assessment. The MAYSI was developed in juvenile corrections settings to help identify potential mental health problems (Grisso, Barnum, Fletcher, Cauffman, & Peuschold, 2001).

A great deal of effort was put into revising policies related to treatment issues: the duties of all mental health staff, the screening and assessment process, the process for referrals internally and to outside providers, criteria for the use of restraints and isolation and how these could be extended, and the procedures for dealing with suicide potential. The use of psychotropics on an as-needed basis for behavioral control was forbidden. The forms for treatment planning, documentation of counseling sessions, use of isolation and restraint, suicide watches, and incident reports were made uniform.

By 2000, the last issue related to the consent decree, after-care, took precedence. Most youth in the system live in the community and are maintained there. Youths leaving the residential facility eventually made the transition to the community. Nevertheless, a small number of individuals repeatedly commit crimes and require greater ongoing attention. Developing a program to identify them and provide extra services was critical (Altschuler & Armstrong, 1994; Altschuler, Armstrong, & MacKenzie, 1999). Many mental health professionals were very much involved in the process. Teams of community, residential, and group home staff were created and trained together to provide a seamless transition to each level of care in the system.

In 2001, DJJ examined its system for the treatment of juvenile sex offenders in the community. Several community mental health centers around the state were providing outpatient counseling, but the vast majority refused. Private providers took up the slack but cost much more. Ultimately, DJJ decided to expand mental health services to the community; eighteen positions were created under the regional psychologists. Over time, these clinicians will provide sex offender counseling and consultation to community workers, day treatment programs, and group homes, as well as mental health and substance abuse services.

DJJ is also using some technological innovations to address treatment needs. Since the residential programs are primarily in rural areas, the cost of attending treatment team meetings to DJJ and to families is large. By 2001, all residential facilities, district offices, and regional offices had teleconferencing capabilities. This equipment has allowed community workers and families to attend treatment team meetings at programs that are long distances away. One of the university psychiatrists provides treatment services by teleconferencing to a facility that cannot get a local psychiatrist to come on-site. The use of this system should grow even more as budget constraints limit travel by state employees.

DJJ is also in the process of developing ten state-run regional detention centers to replace all county-run detention centers. These centers will provide services to youth who generally have been warehoused in the locally run facilities. Necessary mental health services are provided by the community mental health centers in the five facilities that are operational now and are expected to do so in the new ones. This process has worked well.

THE SOUTH CAROLINA EXPERIENCE

South Carolina operated a traditional juvenile justice agency for many years. Originally titled the Department of Youth Services, the agency was oriented to limited rehabilitation and community reintegration in its earlier years, including the development of some community-based counseling and diversion services (under its division of community services) and operation of a central institutional facility in the state capital of Columbia (under its division of institutional services). The agency served a population of predominantly poor African American youth who came into early contact with the legal system as a result of their lack of access to mental health and human services; over 75 percent of its detainees and over 50 percent of its parolees were African American.

As state government adopted a more conservative philosophy in the 1980s amid a climate of law and order, the agency's orientation shifted toward a more punitive one, as reflected by its change in title (Department of Juvenile Justice, SCDJJ) and its increasing rates of institutionalization and length of detainments. At its peak, the central detention facility in Columbia served over a thousand youth on a campus built for a capacity of 350 (out of a population of about 12,000 youth served in their communities). The campus itself was composed of cinderblock dorm buildings built for twenty youth but housing up to sixty, surrounded by a state-of-the-art perimeter containment fence that came to be called the "million dollar fence." There were frequent allegations of peer and staff abuse by detainees, as well as the containment of suicidal youth in isolation cells in handcuffs.

Class Action Lawsuit

In 1990, a class action lawsuit (*Alexander S. v. Boyd,* 1997) was brought against the SCDJJ alleging that the conditions of confinement in the detention facility were unconstitutional under the Civil Rights of Institutionalized Persons Act and the Fourteenth Amendment. These included overcrowding, lack of health and mental health services, and lack of educational services. This lawsuit was the catalyst for two major changes in the agency's policy: its reorientation back toward rehabilitation and the community and its development of a close collaborative relationship with the South Carolina Department of Mental Health (SCDMH) in the development of services at both the detention facilities and in the community. The SCDMH had already developed a strong orientation toward interagency and public-academic collaboration that supported these efforts (Bevilacqua, Morris, & Pumariega, 1996).

The consent decree from the U.S. district court outlined a subclass of seriously mentally ill and seriously mentally retarded youth who required specialized mental health services and could not be kept in the detainment facilities and defined the criteria for inclusion using based on the third edition, revised, of the *Diagnostic and Statistical Manual of the American Psychiatric Association* (DSM-III-R; American Psychiatric Assocation, 1987). The criteria included primary disorders defined on Axis I, some personality and learning disorders defined on Axis II, and level of function as defined in Axis V (Global Assessment of Function) of the multi-axial diagnostic manual (see Figure 11.1).

Disorders Included in the Subclass

- Pervasive Developmental Disorder (Autism and others)
- Organic Brain Syndrome (Delirium, Amnestic Disorder, Organic Delusional Disorder, Organic Hallucinosis)
- Schizophrenic Disorders
- Paranoid Disorders (Delusional Disorder, Induced Psychotic Disorder)
- Psychotic Disorder Not Otherwise Specified
- Multiple Personality Disorder
- Major Depression, Recurrent and Single Episode
- Bipolar Disorder (All Subtypes)
- Psychotic Disorders not Elsewhere Classified (Schizophreniform and Schizoaffective Disorder)

Disorders Requiring Low Global Assessment of Function
(score below or equal to 50)

- Eating Disorders
- Attention Deficit Disorder with Hyperactivity
- Other Organic Brain Syndromes (Organic Mood, Anxiety, Personality Disorder and Organic Mental Disorder Not Otherwise Specified)
- Personality Disorders (Borderline, Paranoid, Schizotypal, Schizoid Personality Disorder Not Otherwise Specified)
- Dysthymic Disorder and Cyclothymic Disorder
- Post-Traumatic Stress Disorder

FIGURE 11.1. Subclass Criteria of Youth Who Require Specialized Mental Health Services in South Carolina.

The consent decree also indicated that mental health services needed to be provided for institutionalized youth not meeting the subclass criteria. The early major focus of SCDJJ and SCDMH collaboration became the provision of services for youth in the subclass. The SCDJJ is responsible for identifying the subclass youth, and the SCDMH was deemed responsible for providing clinical services and placement of this population.

Institutional Services Reform

The collaboration on services for subclass youth included the University of South Carolina School of Medicine and the William S. Hall Psychiatric Institute as the major clinical partner. The university and Hall Institute first operated an intensive diagnostic and treatment program in one of the cottages inside the fenced institutional setting, using a blend of clinicians and especially trained juvenile correctional officers. However, it became evident that this capacity was inadequate for the number of youth in the subclass. In addition, it became increasingly difficult to operate a fully staffed program for subclass youth within the fence due to staff shortages among the juvenile correctional staff. This led to the development of a secure intensive residential treatment program on the grounds of the Hall Institute and its eventual replication in two other sites by contract providers. The model that evolved within the secure residential programs was quite successful in reintegrating the youth back into their communities, working closely with their families, community mental health centers, and even the district attorneys who had originally prosecuted the youth.

A special outreach to parents was instituted through a support group sponsored by the South Carolina Alliance for the Mentally Ill, and the South Carolina Mental Health Association provided special advocacy. This effort served to empower families who had been traditionally stereotyped as disinterested in their youth, and they became valuable members of the treatment team as community transition plans were developed. The program also remained available to youth for readmission if they were judged to be at risk for reoffending or relapse in their condition, modeled on the approach used by the Hall Institute forensic program for adults termed not guilty by reason of insanity. The recidivism rates for this program have been extremely low (below 10 percent), which testifies to its success.

In addition to the specialized services for the subclass, SCDJJ greatly enhanced its mental health staffing for its institutions, hiring larger numbers of social workers, psychologists, and psychiatrists (the last also through the university). It also boosted its juvenile correctional officer staffing and its educational and recreational and activity programs, even creating a Reserve Officer Training Corps program within the institutional campus. Eventually, the institutions were regionalized, with smaller campuses opened in the eastern and western parts of the state to decompress the Columbia campus, with a special campus designated for substance abuse treatment.

Community Services Reform

However, the main challenges for SCDJJ remained. Its institutions were highly overcrowded, and its rate of incarceration and incarceration of mentally ill youth remained high, putting much pressure on institutional resources. This was largely due to the deficits of the community programs that served youth prior to incarceration. A study conducted by the university faculty demonstrated high rates of mental illness in a random sample of institutionalized youth, as well as low prior rates of mental health services and high rates of residential services in this population when compared to mental health populations (Atkins et al., 1999; Pumariega et al., 1999). Although the lawsuit exclusively focused on the institutionalized populations of youth, the solution of the crisis in juvenile justice in South Carolina was in the reform of its community programs.

State officials were aware of this and began to lay the groundwork for this reform. Part of it involved curtailing institutionalizing status offenders and parole violators, which involved close collaboration with juvenile and family court judges. A critical component of this reform was the development of community systems of care approaches to addressing the needs of offending youth, again in collaboration with mental health as well as other child serving agencies, and the adoption of community-based interventions to divert youth from institutionalization. For example, SCDJJ and SCDMH were the main sponsors and implementers of the successful work by Henggeler and colleagues in the development of multisystemic therapy, which has demonstrated evidence-based results in diverting youth from institutions (Henggeler, Melton, Smith, Schoenwald, & Hanley, 1993). The state also supported a statewide school-based services initiative through SCDMH to provide early services within schools for youth with challenging behaviors (Motes, Melton, Waithe Simmons, & Pumariega, 1999).

Concurrently, SCDMH engaged in partnerships with SCDJJ and other child-serving agencies in the state to pursue local systems of care as a means of serving youth with serious emotional disturbances more effectively in their own communities and prevent mental health or juvenile justice placements. After examining many areas around the state for potential pilot sites, state officials decided to support the efforts toward a model system of care beginning in the city of Charleston. The Charleston program, eventually called the Village Project, became one of the original Center for Mental Health Services (CMHS) model demonstration sites (funded in 1994), though it has now outlived its original five-year funding cycle. The program is now funded and jointly operated by SCDMH and the Charleston-Dorchester CMHC (CDCMHC), SCDJJ and its Charleston County regional office, and the South Carolina Department of Human Services, with collaboration form the Charleston City Schools and the Medical University of South Carolina. It has become a model for two other CMHS-funded systems of care demonstration projects in South Carolina and many other local children's systems of care initiatives.

The Village Project

The Village Project was developed in the early 1990s in response to the need for interagency collaboration in the delivery of effective child mental health and human services to the population of children and youth in inner-city Charleston. This is a high-risk population of children and their families, many living in poverty and exposed to high levels of drug use and crime. The project was in large part the result of collaboration between the local director of juvenile justice and the director of Children's Mental Health Services. This collaboration, which began at a personal level, extended to the joint development of the project and the eventual inclusion of the other agency collaborators and private clinicians and providers in the area.

The Village Project now operates out of a large storefront shopping area in inner-city Charleston, including colocated offices for each of the collaborating agencies, as well as a large staffing and conference room where interagency and interdisciplinary staffings are held. It provides community-based case management, clinical services, wraparound services, and support services out of this site, as well as school-based programs, after-school programs, community mentoring programs, home-based intervention programs, and even specialty programs for youthful sexual offenders. The project has succeeded not only in obtaining continuing funding for its operation, but in reducing its state hospital use to near-zero levels and cutting its use of inpatient hospitalization and referral to central detention services by over 80 percent (from 15 to 18 percent of all youth served being institutionalized prior to the program to less than 5 percent currently). The program's governance is handled through the Village Coordinating Council, which includes representation of the many collaborating agencies, as well as family advocates, in itself a collaborative venture.

The key elements that appeared to lead to the success of this program were (1) the personal bond developed between the directors of community juvenile justice and children's mental health, (2) the principle of colocation in the community, (3) the involvement of advocates and families as participants and stakeholders in the program, and (4) support with noninterference from state-level administrators. These same elements are also resulting in closer collaboration with Human Services, the schools, and the academic sector.

In addition to the Village Coordinating Council, the following collaborative practices outlined by the program address the interface between juvenile justice and mental health:

• Specialized assessment and treatment services for youth with sexual aggression problems, which include family therapy, group therapy, service coordination, individual therapy, and case management. These are provided as a community-based alternative to institutional care and have succeeded in reducing such care to a minimum. Over three hundred children have been served since 1991, and a study tracking outcomes has found only one youth reoffending so far.

• CDCMHC committed a seasoned clinician-supervisor to serve youth identified as having serious emotional disturbance or serious mental illness under the SCDJJ class action lawsuit to ensure that appropriate services are provided upon community transition.

• Juvenile justice and mental health staff cofacilitate the Village Multicultural Task Force, which has provided cultural competence training and promoted culturally competent practices with staff from all collaborating agencies.

• CDCMHC assigned a staff member to provide services to youth detained at the Charleston County Detention Center.

• CDCMHC located a staff member at the local DJJ offices to provide assessments, service coordination, and therapeutic services to families referred by DJJ.

• Every week at Village Child and Family Consultations, agency staff and family members meet to design care plans and services for youth and families. CDCMHC and DJJ staffs share in the rotation for facilitating these meetings.

• CDCMHC and DJJ are involved in a number of cost-sharing and blended funding arrangements to fund services for youth and families, including residential care and community-based wraparound.

• DJJ, family court, and the state Department of Alcohol and Other Drug Abuse Services operate a youth drug court in Charleston County, using a model of judge as case manager. CDCMHC assigned a master's-level staff member to the program at least two days each week.

• CDCMHC and DJJ developed strong partnerships with families by establishing family support and advocate positions for family members with youth involved in the system of care. A seasoned parent advocate serves as coordinator of these advocacy staff family members for CDCMHC. Most impressive is the role of Sister Miller, a highly charismatic and energetic African American spiritualist who is a parent of youth who have been through juvenile justice. Based on her own experiences with the system, she developed a church-based volunteer network of over sixty family advocates for youth in juvenile justice. She works closely with both agencies and provides support, input, and guidance from the family and community perspectives.

• CDCMHC and DJJ collaborate around youth referred to the many school-based and home-based services operated by the Village Project—school-based counseling, day treatment, after-school vocational services, and in-home counseling and family preservation services—and serve many youth at risk of entering the juvenile justice system. CDCMHC operates services in fifty of seventy-seven schools in Charleston and includes seventeen staff members dedicated to school-based mental health services.

COLORADO DIVISION OF YOUTH CORRECTIONS

A partnership was formed between the Division of Youth Corrections and the University of Colorado Health Sciences Center in 1995 to provide comprehensive mental health services to incarcerated males at Lookout Mountain Youth Services Center (LMYSC), located in Golden, Colorado. The Division of Youth Corrections also had enhanced vendor contracts with several adolescent residential centers and youth mental health and substance abuse treatment programs at the inception of the state-university collaboration project. (These contracts provided specialized secure treatment services for mentally ill offenders at special reimbursement rates.)

In 1994, Division of Youth Corrections (DYC) staff had conducted a campus survey of all youth enrolled at LMYSC, a high-secure correctional facility. The survey, or "one-day snapshot," used the PES 7B, a mental health screening tool used by the state's community mental health systems to determine symptom severity and level-of-care needs. The DYC mental health and security staff used this instrument to capture a profile of the mental health needs of youth present in the population.

Twenty-four males were identified as having a high level of mental health services needs. Staff at LMYSC also determined that many of the twenty-four youth had a history of psychiatric hospitalizations, self-mutilation, and suicide attempts. Although the DYC had contracts with residential programs in a number of local communities, many of the youth at LMYSC could not be placed in the available settings because of the nature of their crime or past failure to progress in less restrictive treatment programs.

In April 1995, the Colorado legislature funded an intensive mental health treatment program at LMYSC at the request of DYS. The existing Closed Adolescent Treatment House was converted in November 1995 to the Cypress Unit. Mental health staff provide crisis intervention coverage twenty-four hours a day, seven days a week.

Program Creation

The program design for the Cypress Unit and campus mental health program incorporated use of outcome principles to design a model of service delivery on the campus. Key components of the design process were early inclusion of stakeholders such as the Colorado Health Care Finance Administration and OJJDP, Department of Adult Corrections, Division of Youth Corrections staff across disciplines, state social service, education and mental health divisions, hospital administrators, youth, families, legislators, and consumer advocacy groups in the design collaboration. In addition, the design team focused on linking treatments, transition into community programs, and fiscal responsibility. For example, due to the high rates of comorbid substance abuse, the Lookout Mountain Campus pursued and obtained certification as a state-licensed drug and alcohol treatment program, which allowed for campuswide incorporation of dual-disordered treatment.

Twenty-four males with co-occurring problems such as major mental illnesses, substance abuse and dependence, and significant antisocial cognitive constructs related to their offenses are referred to the Cypress unit by mental health or security staff from the LMYSC campus. A multidisciplinary team of DYC security staff and master's- and doctoral-level staff provide offense-specific cognitive rehabilitative treatments for property, sex, and violent offenders.

A variety of mental health treatments, including but not limited to pharmacotherapy, crisis intervention, individual, group, and family therapies, are provided. All youth on the campus participate in a cognitive behavioral therapy curriculum and offense-specific and skill-enhancement treatment groups that are co-led by mental health professionals and correctional staff. Individual therapies such as cognitive-behavioral, interpersonal, supportive (psychoeducation), and eye movement desensitization and reprogramming are offered. In addition, the Cypress unit offers three to four individual structural family therapy slots. One of the unique family therapies is a multiple family group therapy program that meets for eight-week semesters. All units also provide this weekly multifamily therapy group. In addition, a weekly family issues group is offered on several units for youth who have no active family contacts or whose families are unable to attend family therapy due to the geographical constraints. All pharmacotherapy services are voluntary; there are no as-needed medications in use. Individual quarterly assessments using informal and formal mental health interviews such as a mental status exam, Diagnostic Interview Schedule for Children (Shaffer et al., 1996), the Symptom Check List-90 (SCL-90; Derogatis, Lipman, & Covi, 1973), and the Colorado Client Assessment Record, a problem checklist and functional measure (Ellis, Wackwitz, & Foster, 1991), are used to track treatment effectiveness.

The on-grounds high school is administered by Metropolitan State College, and college curricula leading to an associate degree, vocational programs with certification requirements, general equivalency diploma, and high school diploma options are available to all youth on campus. All youth are offered intramural activities designed by a recreational therapist and arts and music programs. The high school participates in state-sanctioned sports leagues.

All therapies are employed to maximize each youth's ability to participate in the campus educational programs and social skills–building program, in addition to helping youth gain mastery in managing their mental illness.

The Cypress unit maintains a minimum of five security staff and has two social workers, one psychologist, one psychiatric nurse, and a half-time child psychiatrist who provide mental health and offense-specific services in a multidisciplinary team format. A core treatment team comprises three individuals: a safety and security officer, a Division of Youth Corrections youth service counselor (who has expertise in group therapies and milieu management), and one of the mental health professionals. All units have a medical liaison staff person—either a registered nurse, nurse practitioner, or physician's assistant—who meets with the entire staff and provides medical and behavioral observations to each youth's treatment team.

In 1998, the DYC received additional funding to the Lookout Mountain Project to expand mental health and substance abuse prevention services for an additional thirty-six youth with identified mental illnesses. This additional funding allowed for the creation of additional therapeutic opportunities for the approximately one hundred youth who participate in offense-specific treatment groups co-led by mental health professionals or attended art or music groups. These youth reside in units that have dedicated mental health professional time, seven hours of psychiatric services, twelve hours of psychologist services, and forty hours of social worker services per unit.

Program Evaluation

Several outcomes studies have been done. Recidivism rates for the most severely mentally ill youth are no different from those of the general DYC population. Rehospitalization rates, during time at the Cypress unit and one year after discharge, were lower for the first seventy-five youths completing the program. A 1999–2000 study looked at 111 youths at the Lookout Mountain Campus who received mental health treatment. Global Severity Scale scores on the SCL-90 decreased by ten from entry scores. Initial high scores on the Depression, Anxiety, and Paranoia Scales were reduced to a statistically significant degree. Youth with cognitive disabilities showed similar reductions on these scales. Most of the youth had a significant trauma exposure and reported the issue was addressed in treatment. The mean length of stay was thirteen months.

System Linkages

In order to be able to provide a system of care, both state hospitals provide inpatient support and have dedicated staff liaisons to attend a weekly LMYSC mental health services review meeting. Continuity of care and service provision is ensured by formal memoranda of agreements with the community mental health centers.

Additional funding has been set aside to hire contract mental health specialists at the bachelor's and master's level to provide direct supervision and intensive psychoeducation for youth with significant psychiatric symptoms such as suicidal behaviors or active psychosis. The use of a mental health tracker (who shadows the youth in the community) allows youths to remain in school and continue to work with their treatment team.

Due to the conflicting principles of punishment and health promotion, the campus has embraced an emphasis on using restorative justice principles, peer mentoring, and developing alternatives to seclusion and restraint. The LMYSC campus has a specific protocol to limit seclusion to seven hours a day for youth and follows the state's mental health guidelines for use of seclusion or restraints.

Other DYC Activities

In 1998, the division started an urban and rural detention intervention project to provide services for at-risk youth. Youth receiving the case management, mental health, substance abuse, and tailored school services in this project had minimal recidivism. Several DYC-funded multisystemic therapy programs started throughout the state in 1998 and serve youth in a variety of areas, including diversion, exiting detention, community, residential, and LMYSC. All of the DYC initiatives have broadened the opportunities for mentally ill youth to decrease their morbidity.

A substantial number of youths in the juvenile justice system have mental health needs. Addressing these needs requires the involvement of a variety of disciplines and systems. In the past decade, a body of research has identified interventions that are effective in preventing or mitigating delinquent behavior. Mental health professionals can play an important role in the systems of care that have proven effective. They can also advocate for the use of programs and interventions that work.

References

Alexander S. v. Boyd, No. 96-1950, U.S. Court of Appeals for the Fourth Circuit, Dec. 5, 1996, argued; May 28, 1997, decided.

Allen-Hagen, B. (1993, Apr.). Conditions of confinement in juvenile detention and correctional facilities. *OJJDP Fact Sheet*, 1–3.

Altschuler, D. M., & Armstrong, T. L. (1994). Intensive aftercare for high-risk juveniles: A community care model program summary. *OJJDP Summary*. Washington, DC: U.S. Department of Justice, Office of Juvenile Programs, Office of Juvenile Justice and Delinquency Prevention.

Altschuler, D. M., Armstrong, T. L., & MacKenzie, D. L. (1999). *Reintegration, supervised release, and intensive aftercare*. Washington, DC: U.S. Department of Justice, Office of Juvenile Programs, Office of Juvenile Justice and Delinquency Prevention.

American Psychiatric Association. (1987). *Diagnostic and statistical manual for mental disorders* (3rd ed. rev.). Washington, DC: American Psychiatric Press.

Andrews, D. A., Zinger, I., Hoge, R., Bonta, J., Gendrew, P., & Cullen, F. (1990). Does correctional treatment work? A clinically relevant and psychologically informed meta-analysis. *Criminology, 28,* 369–404.

Atkins, D. L., Pumariega, A. J., Montgomery, L., Rogers, K., Nybro, C., Jeffers, G., & Sease, F. (1999). Mental health and incarcerated youth. I: Prevalence and nature of psychopathology. *Journal of Child and Family Studies, 8,* 193–204.

Bevilacqua, J. J., Morris, J. A., & Pumariega, A. J. (1996). State services research capacity: Building a state infrastructure for mental health services research. *Community Mental Health Journal, 32,* 519–533.

Bilchik, S. (1999). Minorities in the juvenile justice system. In *1999 National Report Series Juvenile Justice Bulletin.* Washington, DC: U.S. Department of Justice, Office of Juvenile Justice and Delinquency Prevention.

Boesky, L. (2001, Mar.–Apr.). Why train juvenile justice staff on mental health issues? *Juvenile Correctional Mental Health Report,* 35–36, 44–45.

Center on Juvenile and Criminal Justice. (1999). 100 years of juvenile justice: Prominent former juvenile offenders salute centennial of children's court. Available on-line at: http://www.cjcj.org/centennial/media.html.

Coolbaugh, K., & Hansel, C. J. (2000, Mar.). The comprehensive strategy: Lessons learned from the pilot sites. *OJJDP Juvenile Justice Bulletin,* 1–11. Available on-line at: http://www.ncjrs.org/pdffiles1/ojjdp/178258.pdf.

Derogatis, L. R., Lipman, R. S., & Covi, L. (1973). The SCL-90: An outpatient psychiatric rating scale. *Psychopharmacology Bulletin, 9,* 13–28.

Edens, J. F., & Otto, R. K. (1997). Prevalence of mental disorders among youth in the juvenile justice system. *Focal Point, 11,* 1, 6, 7.

Ellis, R., Wackwitz, J., & Foster, M. (1991). Use of an empirically derived client typology based on level of functioning: Twelve years of the CCAR. *Journal of Mental Health Administration, 18,* 88–100.

Faenza, M. M., & Siegfried, C. B. (2001). Responding to the mental health treatment needs of juveniles. In G. L. Landsberg & A. Smiley (Eds.), *Forensic mental health: Working with offenders with mental illness* (pp. 47–56). Kingston, NJ: U.S. Civic Research Institute.

Gibbs, J. T., & Huang, L. N. (1998). *Children of color: Psychological interventions with culturally diverse youth.* San Francisco: Jossey-Bass.

Greenwood, P. W., Rydell, C. P., Abrahames, A. F., Caulkins, J. P., Chesia, J., Model, P. E., & Klein, S. D. (1994). *Three strikes and you're out: Estimated benefits and costs of California's new mandatory sentencing law.* Santa Monica, CA: RAND Corporation.

Grisso, T., Barnum, R., Fletcher, K. E., Cauffman, E., & Peuschold, D. (2001). Massachusetts Youth Screening Instrument for Mental Health Needs of Juvenile Justice Youths. *Journal of the American Academy of Child and Adolescent, 40,* 541–548.

Henggeler, S. W., Melton, G., Smith, L., Schoenwald, S., & Hanley, J. (1993). Family preservation using multisystemic therapy: Long term follow-up to a clinical trial with serious juvenile offenders. *Journal of Child and Family Studies, 2,* 283–293.

Henggeler, S. W., Schoenwald, S. K., & Pickrel, S. G. (1995). Multisystemic therapy: Bridging the gap between university- and community-based treatment. *Journal of Counseling and Clinical Psychology, 63,* 709–717.

Howell, J. C. (Ed.). (1995). *Guide for implementing the comprehensive strategy for serious, violent, and chronic juvenile offenders.* Washington, DC: U.S. Department of Justice, Office of Juvenile Justice and Delinquency Prevention. Available on-line at: http://ojjdp.ncjrs.org/pubs/violvict.html#guide.

Isaacs, M. R. (1992). Assessing the mental health needs of children and adolescents of color in the juvenile justice system: Overcoming institutionalized perceptions and barriers. In J. J. Cocozza (Ed.), *Responding to the mental health needs of youth in the juvenile justice system* (pp. 141–163). Seattle, WA: National Coalition for the Mentally Ill in the Criminal Justice System, 1992.

Kataoka, S. H., Zima, B. T., Dupre, D. A., Moreno, K. A., Yang, X., & McCracken, J. T. (2001). Mental health problems and service use among female juvenile offenders: Their relationship to criminal history. *Journal of the American Academy of Child and Adolescent Psychiatry, 40,* 549–555.

Kentucky Department of Juvenile Justice. (2001). *Kentucky juvenile detention system.* Frankfort, KY: Author.

Kudart, K. C. (Ed.). (2000). *National juvenile detention directory, 2000–2002.* White Plains, MD: American Correctional Association.

Mendel, R. A. (2000). *Less hype, more help: Reducing juvenile crime, what works— and what doesn't.* Washington, DC: American Youth Policy Forum.

Motes, P., Melton, G., Waithe Simmons, W., & Pumariega, A. (1999). Ecologically oriented school-based mental health services: Implications for service system reform. *Psychology in the Schools, 36,* 391–401.

Obeidallah, D. A., & Earls, F. J. (1999, July). Adolescent girls: The role of depression in the development of delinquency. *Research preview.*

Otto, R. K., Greenstein, J. J., Johnson, M. K., & Friedman, R. M. (1992). Prevalence of mental disorders among youth in the juvenile justice system. In J. J. Cocozza (Ed.), *Responding to the mental health needs of youth in the juvenile justice system.* Seattle, WA: National Coalition for the Mentally Ill in the Criminal Justice System.

Prescott, L. (1997). *Adolescent girls with co-occurring disorders in the juvenile justice system.* Delmar, NY: National GAINS Center.

Pumariega, A. J., Atkins, D. L., Rogers, K., Montgomery, L., Nybro, C., Caesar, R., & Millus, D. (1999). Mental health and incarcerated youth. II: Service utilization. *Journal of Child and Family Studies, 8,* 205–215.

Schiraldi, V. (1999). The juvenile court centennial: 100 years of giving kids a chance to make a better choice. Available on-line at: http://www.cjcj.org/jpi/csmon080299.html.

Shaffer, D., Fisher, P., Dulcan, M., Davies, M., Piacentini, J., Schwab-Stone, M., Lahey, B., Bourdon, K., Jensen, P., Bird, H., Camro, G., & Regier, D. (1996). The MMH Diagnostic Interview Schedule for Children, Version 2.3 (DISC 2.3): Description, acceptability, prevalence rates, and performance in the MECA study. *Journal of the American Academy of Child and Adolescent Psychiatry, 35,* 865–877.

Stroul, B., & Friedman, R. (1986). *A system of care for severely emotionally disturbed children and youth.* Washington, DC: Child and Adolescent Service System Program Technical Assistance Center, Georgetown University Child Development Center.

U.S. Department of Education. (2001). About Safe and Drug-Free Schools Program. Available on-line at: http://www.ed.gov/offices/OESE/SDFS/aboutsdf.html.

U.S. Department of Health and Human Services. (2001). *Youth violence: A report of the surgeon general.* Rockville, MD: Center for Mental Health Services, Substance Abuse and Mental Health Administration, U.S. Department of Health and Human Services.

Wilson, J. J. (1994). Treatment of juveniles in the criminal justice system. *Juvenile Justice Digest, 22*(15), 1–7.

Wilson, J. J., & Howell, J. C. (1993). *A comprehensive strategy for serious, violent, and chronic juvenile offenders: Program summary.* Washington, DC: U.S. Department of Justice, Office of Juvenile Justice and Delinquency Prevention.

CHAPTER TWELVE

School-Based
Mental Health Services

A Necessity, Not a Luxury

Gayle K. Porter
Glen T. Pearson
Sandra Keenan
Jacquelyn Duval-Harvey

Innovative and nontraditional school-based mental health services are essential to address the emotional, behavioral, and psychiatric issues experienced by millions of children and their families. It is estimated that over 20 percent of all children and adolescents—at least 11 million—have diagnosable developmental, learning, behavioral, and emotional problems, which often have a devastating impact on their interpersonal relationships, academic achievement, and even life span (U.S. Department of Health and Human Services, 1999). And in many poor, urban communities, the estimates are that over 50 percent of the children manifest significant learning, behavioral, and emotional difficulties (Zahner, Pawelkiewicz, De Francesco, & Adnopoz, 1992).

These children are also at increased risk of becoming victims or perpetrators of violence (Lavigne et al., 1998). The victims are vulnerable to depression, suicidal ideation and attempts, anxiety, and posttraumatic stress disorder (PTSD; Bell & Jenkins, 1991; Hill & Madhere, 1996). The aggressors often develop patterns of physical, emotional, or sexual misconduct that range from excessive teasing and bullying to felonious criminal acts (Olweus, 1991).

From one-third to over one-half of all referrals to mental health agencies are for aggressive behaviors or conduct problems, which usually occur in schools (Atkins et al., 1998). In the system of care programs funded through the Comprehensive Community Mental Health Services for Children and Their Families program of the federal Center for Mental Health Services (CMHS), approximately

40 percent of the children have a conduct-related diagnoses-either oppositional defiant or conduct disorders. The stress of living with violence accounts for a significant percentage of these referrals (Bell & Jenkins, 1991). However, less than one-third of those referred receive adequate care, and only 20 to 30 percent of poor and minority children have access to appropriate mental health services (Richardson, Keller, & Shelby-Harrington, 1996). The therapeutic services provided to these children, especially African American children, are often available only after they have entered the juvenile justice system or become eligible for special education (Gibbs & Huang 1998). Minority adolescents are also more likely to use more restrictive and expensive forms of mental health services (partial hospitalization, 34 percent; residential treatment centers, 33 percent) than outpatient treatment (22 percent; Hoberman, 1992).

A variety of barriers make it difficult for children and families to access appropriate mental health care. Inadequate insurance, lack of transportation, misinformation and stigma about mental health services, family management problems, a limited number of outpatient clinics, and long waiting lists are some of the obstacles (Weist, 1997). Thus, for most children, and especially poor and minority youth, schools are the most readily available and easily accessible sites for the provision of a continuum of community-based mental health services (Tuma, 1989; U.S. Department of Health and Human Services, 1999). Schools can foster the development of comprehensive services and integrated care. They also provide a mechanism through which preventive and remedial treatment interventions can be developed and implemented through the collaborative input and effort of multidisciplinary teams, which include parents and children (Atkins et al., 1998).

Although most of the correlates of mental disorders—biological factors, early emotional and behavioral problems, poverty, physical abuse, racism, excessive exposure to media and community violence, poor academic performance, and inadequate or inconsistent parental support and discipline—do not originate in the schools, some of the most effective interventions to reduce or ameliorate their impact have occurred there (U.S. Office of Juvenile Justice and Delinquency Prevention, 1995). The use of evidence-based and best practice clinical interventions, including psychotropic medications and a range of psychosocial treatments, have demonstrated effectiveness in improving treatment outcomes in school-based settings (Elliott, Hamburg, & Williams, 1998; Hoagwood, 2000; Forness & Kavale, 2001). However, all of these preventive, early intervention, and remedial programs required multidisciplinary collaboration.

It is clear that schools are important partners with other agencies and institutions in improving the emotional and behavioral functioning of youth. Many different mental health professionals exist in schools; some are employed by the school system (school counselors, social workers, and school psychologists), and others work on a contract basis in the school but are employed by noneducational vendors (psychiatrists, mental health counselors, clinical psychologists, clinical social workers, art therapists). Contracted services that take place within the school building are referred to as school-based mental health services.

This chapter explores the development, utilization, and effectiveness of school-based mental health services from multiple perspectives and demonstrates how school-employed and -contracted mental health professionals can work collaboratively with others to develop and implement clinical interventions and programs designed to effect positive mental health in youth within grant communities and partnerships.

A HISTORICAL OVERVIEW

Initially, school-based mental health services were designed "to prevent, or at least reduce truancy and delinquency; [and] to rehabilitate poor, disorganized families by providing relief services" (Sedlak, 1997, p. 352) to poor, urban, immigrant, and minority children and families. Over the past century, these services have evolved to interventions that can affect the entire structure and curricula of schools that are racially, financially, and geographically diverse (Sedlak, 1997). What has remained consistent about the provision of these services is that their effectiveness continues to be dependent on the collaboration between traditional school-employed personnel and the agency-employed school-based mental health professionals.

At the beginning of the school-based movement, clinicians were welcomed by school personnel as resources to complement or enhance the services provided by the school social workers (originally called visiting teachers because they went to the families' homes) and school counselors (Reese, 1978). During the 1940s and 1950s, national attention became focused on the emotional problems experienced by children from all socioeconomic levels. Monies from various acts of Congress (Smith-Hughes Act, 1917 and the National Defense Education Act, 1958) reflected the increased involvement of the federal government in shaping and financing school guidance and counseling programs in districts serving families of diverse income levels (Sedlak, 1997).

During the past thirty years, there has been a significant decrease in monies for general support of mental health services (Dryfoos, 1994). Most state and federal funding for supportive services was often mandated to poor, preschool, and special education populations. The administrative responsibility for tracking the paperwork required for government and private funding was increasingly the work of the social workers and school counselors. Caseloads increased dramatically. School social workers and psychologists were often restricted to working with children who were either in or being evaluated for special education. School counselors were often assigned hundreds of children, while paraprofessionals and school-based mental health specialists were allowed to provide on-going clinical services to a manageable caseload (Dryfoos, 1994; Gallagher, 1996; Sedlak 1997).

In addition to changes in the funding priorities, there were increasing social pressures on school social workers and school counselors to take a more passive and egalitarian approach to shaping the values and behaviors of their students (Cusick, 1983; Sedlak, 1997). Many counselors expressed ambivalent feelings about this change in their role. Some were angry over their inability to use their expertise to provide students with accurate and realistic information about college and career choices without being accused of being racist or undermining the students' vocational dreams. Others were jealous of the freedom from administrative responsibilities of outside professionals (Rosenbaum, Miller, & Krei, 1996). An alliance that had expanded the resources available to children families and professionals became seriously damaged.

PROVIDERS OF CONTEMPORARY
MENTAL HEALTH SERVICES IN SCHOOLS

The residual impact of the historical change in the relationship between school-employed and school-based mental health professionals and contemporary demands on all support providers can make communication and collaboration difficult. Most of the providers of school-based services are employed by public or private entities, including school systems, community mental health centers, universities, health organizations, and mental health agencies. All face increasing challenges to their ability to provide appropriate mental health services. The dramatic rise in the number of children who exhibit multiple signs of risk, from academic difficulties to aggressive behaviors, has significantly outpaced the funding required to meet the need (Weist, 1997). The responsibility for meeting this need has often fallen on the already overburdened shoulders of school-employed mental health professionals.

School counselors, especially those in middle and high schools, often are responsible for short-term clinical crisis interventions, as well as vocational and educational planning for hundreds of students. They frequently function as liaisons between administrators, teachers, parents, and the school-based mental health professionals and are perceived to be part of the administrative hierarchy of the school. With their large caseloads and administrative responsibilities, school counselors are often limited to delivering short-term counseling and developmental guidance to the large number of students they serve (Weist, 1997). Their ability to provide ongoing, intensive, clinical interventions to regular education students is very limited. They often refer students who require intensive services to the school-based mental health professionals, who can quickly focus on this smaller subset of students.

Managing the bureaucracy and paper tracking mandated by federal and state rules and regulations for special education is often the responsibility of the school social worker and psychologist (Conoley & Conoley, 1991). They must ensure that children involved in the special education process are appropriately assessed, diagnosed, referred, and treated. Many children who are in special education often need transitional services when they leave their more restrictive setting and return to regular education classes. Those services and longer-term individual, group, or family therapy are often provided by the school-based mental health clinician The use of a single generic billing code for all different types of mental health services delivered by school-based clinical teams proved to be an effective model in the School Based Mental Health Services program of South Carolina. It reduced paperwork and increased integrated service delivery (Motes, Melton, Simmons, & Pumariega, 1999).

Fiscal concerns, especially those related to managed care, often influence the activities of outside providers. Many of the clinical and consulting psychologists, social workers, psychiatric nurses, psychiatrists, and mental health counselors who provide care pay for their services through public (Medicaid) or private insurance. This usually requires that a significant amount of their time be focused on direct or face-to-face interventions with children who have a diagnosed mental health condition. Their time to provide consultations, training, or case management can often be quite limited.

Collaboration between school-employed and school-based mental health providers increases the opportunity to augment and expand the quality and quantity of service that so many students desperately need. The school-employed and school-based professionals are particularly effective when they work as a team to identify the mental health needs of students, provide a continuum of care, integrate services, and create a global school environment conducive to safety.

School-based mental health professionals bridge the discontinuity in mental health services between schools and community agencies. They offer a visible link to the outside world of community resources and serve as a liaison with both the outside agency or hospital that sponsors them and the wider community. These practitioners can provide on-site services to students with mental illnesses or those at risk of developing such illnesses. Their mission is somewhat revolutionary in the sense that they bring to the school mental health services that once appeared inaccessible and unappealing to students. In creating this valuable linkage, they can easily connect students with even more specialized mental health services, which may be offered in the school, community, or student's home, such as psychiatric consultation, family therapy, substance abuse counseling, or case management (Adelman & Taylor, 1993). In addition, some school-based mental health professionals are very proactive in carrying out schoolwide prevention programs around mental health issues and running therapeutic after-school and summer programs for at-risk students.

Despite the many benefits of having a school-based clinician, there are potential problems. The missions of staff and professionals employed by the school and school-based mental health clinicians are usually different. School boards (and their employees) have as their mandate educating youth, while noneducational providers are frequently focused on improving clinical outcomes. Because their employers have different primary goals, it is often more difficult for the school-employed and school-based clinicians to resolve turf issues, differences in clinical approaches, or interpretations of school procedures or regulations. There is also the increased opportunity for students, parents, and even school personnel to engage in what is known as splitting: pitting one professional against the other. However, all of the problems can be avoided or at least minimized by mutual respect, ongoing active collaboration, and a willingness to reassess one's position on any issue routinely.

LEGAL CONTEXT FOR SYSTEM CHANGE

It is helpful to examine the opportunities for system of care collaboration presented with the reauthorization of the Individuals with Disabilities Education Act (IDEA) in 1997 and the existing statutes in Section 504 of the Rehabilitation Act. Some provisions support various aspects of school-based mental health services. Both laws protect students who meet the eligibility requirements. Both require a free appropriate public education, evaluation and assessment, individualized planning, periodic review, parent rights, and due process. Section 504 is civil rights law, which provides protections for equal access to an education that is comparable to that provided to nondisabled students. It requires reasonable accommodations, modifications to the environment, and supports and development activities for the teacher (Miller & Newbill, 1998; Schacht & Hanson, 1999). IDEA requires services and related supports for specially designed instruction.

There are specific requirements under IDEA (U.S. Department of Education, 1999) that are of benefit to both school-based and school-employed mental health providers:

• Section 300.244, Coordinated Services System, allows a school system to use up to 5 percent of its federal dollars to develop and implement a coordinated services system designed to improve results for children and families. This includes developing and implementing interagency agreements for service coordination, case management, linkages to other federal and state programs, such as Medicaid and supplemental security income, and interagency financing strategies for the provision of education, health, mental health, and social services.

• Section 300.235, Permissive Use of Funds, allows nondisabled children to benefit and have access to services or programs that may have been designed for a regular class or education-related setting as long as the child with a disability receives the benefit. Through IDEA, school districts can use special education personnel in classwide or schoolwide behavioral and emotional support programs.

• Section 300.306, Nonacademic Services, requires that school systems take steps to provide nonacademic and extracurricular services such as counseling services, health services, and referrals to agencies.

• Section 300.142, Methods of Ensuring Services, requires each state to establish responsibility for services and other mechanisms for interagency coordination, which helps to define the financial responsibility of each agency for providing services. It clearly states that the financial responsibility of each noneducational public agency, including the state Medicaid agency and other public insurers of children with disabilities, must precede the financial responsibility of the local education agency. This provision has allowed some states to develop a wide array of services that are Medicaid eligible and complement the school-based services.

These provisions facilitate interagency collaboration toward school-based mental health services within the context of community-based systems of care. However, relatively few communities have taken advantage of these statutory and funding opportunities for such collaboration and development of funding. Lack of state funding applied to the development of these services may be a key reason, resulting in unfunded mandates. California and South Carolina (Schacht & Hanson, 1999; Motes et al., 1999) have made some strides toward systemwide collaborations through their approaches to statutory reform and leverage of federal funding through enhanced state funding.

At the individualized student level, Section 300.344, IEP Team, describes the members of an individualized education plan team meeting. There must be an individual who can interpret the instructional implications of evaluation results. School-based and school-employed mental health providers can develop strategies and supports for the child's individualized program. Section 300.24, Related Service, means supportive services that are required to assist a child with a disability to benefit from special education and include psychological services, counseling services, school health services, social work services, and parent counseling and training. These services must be provided by licensed or certified mental health professionals. Through IDEA and Section 504 of the Rehabilitation Act, it is possible for a school district to establish schoolwide or districtwide programs, using interagency agreements, and blended funding to support the development, coordination, and provision of positive behavioral interventions for all students, as well as targeted interventions for the specific needs of a child on an IEP. California (Schacht & Hanson, 1999) has made some modest efforts to promote such co-ordination of behavioral health services through the state statute. These laws are a valuable resource for the creative development of school based mental health services.

SCHOOL-BASED SERVICE DELIVERY MODELS

School mental health clinicians and researchers have developed a wide variety of models for secure delivery. We briefly review these under a series of common headings, in rough order of intensity of services.

Consultation

One of the most widely used school-based interventions is the consultation model. Therapists, usually from outpatient mental health clinics or universities, meet with teachers to discuss children's behavioral and academic performance and plan appropriate interventions. Teachers are often provided didactic information about various learning and emotional disorders (Goldman, Botkin, Tokunaga, & Kylinski, 1997; Atkins et al., 1998).

School-Based Health Clinics

For over twenty-five years, school-based health clinics have provided acute and referral physical health services. Most clinics include some level of mental health services. Their purpose is to provide integrated health care. A multidisciplinary team usually develops treatment plans. The addition of the mental health component has proven very successful. In fact, Dryfoos (1994) noted, "As soon as we open our doors, kids walk past the counselor's office, past the school nurse, past the principal, and come into our clinic to tell us they have been sexually abused or that their parents are drug users" (p. 52).

School-Based Mental Health Centers

In numerous cities, especially in poor and minority communities, specific areas in schools have service centers for programs ranging from violence prevention to bereavement. Many of the directors of these centers believe that collaboration with other school staff is critical in the development of effective, well-coordinated programs (Adelman & Taylor, 1993).

Multiple Systems Model

There is a growing movement to develop comprehensive school-based mental health programs in both rural (Motes et al,, 1999) and urban areas (Flaherty & Weist, 1999; Casat, Sobolewski, Gordon, & Rigsby, 1999). These programs combine coordinated clinical services for children and families in need, consultative services for teachers and school staff, and preventive mental health educational curricula and enrichment programs for the general school population. These have evolved from the collaboration between a school district (or regional or state education department) and a mental health entity, at times in collaboration with other child-serving agencies.

Several other school-based programs have a mental health promotion and prevention orientation and focus. These programs include Slavin's "Success for All," Comer's "Social Development," and Maiger's "Constructive Discipline." Such programs have strong mental health components and often combine clinical services with parent training, tutoring, and day care. These models also emphasize positive opportunities for parents and children to participate in school activities (Atkins et al., 1998).

UTILIZATION AND EFFECTIVENESS OF SCHOOL-BASED MENTAL HEALTH SERVICES

Studies have repeatedly documented the alarming lack of access to or underuse of mental health services by children who have a mental health diagnosis and are seriously emotionally disturbed (Knitzer, 1982; U.S. Health and Human Services, 1999). However, children who do receive mental health services are more likely to use services within the education sector than from their primary care providers or private or clinic-based mental health practitioner. Estimates of service utilization from the school system range from 50 to 80 percent of children who are at risk or who have been diagnosed as having serious emotional disturbances (Bums et al., 1995). Poor families, especially those living in urban areas, had higher rates of attendance and lower rates of premature termination in school-based mental health programs (McKay, 2000; Zahner et al., 1992; Atkins et al., 1998).

Anecdotal reports, studies, and surveys attest to the effectiveness of school-based mental health services in improving clinical outcomes and behavioral functioning. (Hoagwood, 2000; Atkins et al., 1998). Treatment interventions can be effective, whether they are applied to mood disorders or attention deficit and disruptive behavior disorders (Clarke et al., 1995). The use of psychotropic medications or psychosocial interventions, or the combination of both, has proven effective in treating these disorders in school-based settings. Cognitive-behavioral therapy has proven particularly effective in school-based settings with the major clinical disorders, especially depression and oppositional-defiant and conduct disorders (Hoagwood & Erwin, 1997).

TRANSCENDING BARRIERS TO THE DELIVERY OF COLLABORATIVE MENTAL SERVICES

Multidisciplinary, collaborative service delivery can increase resources, decrease fragmentation, and reduce costs, which is particularly important in a managed care environment (Flaherty et al., 1998). Barriers exist that make translating that maxim into a reality very difficult.

Education, training, professional terminology, and mission differences exist among school-employed and school-based providers of service and must be acknowledged, respected, and worked through (Pace, Chaney, Mullins, & Olson, 1995). Feelings of territorial and professional competition can occur in any setting, but school personnel are particularly vulnerable to these feelings because of their high degree of accountability and relatively low level of status and resources (Sedlak, 1997; Flaherty et al., 1998). Conflicting beliefs about issues ranging from confidentiality to the process for reporting abuse can be very divisive, especially when these are compounded by racial and educational differences. Resolving these disputes can be time-consuming and energy draining. The examples of collaboration that follow demonstrate the availability of models and mechanisms to facilitate a more interprofessional collaborative process that can help professionals transcend these barriers.

A PSYCHIATRIST'S PERSPECTIVE

The perspective that follows is based on my (Glen Pearson) personal experience since fall 1993 of providing mental health services to children and families in the public schools, in collaboration with the Dallas Independent School District and with Parkland Health and Hospital Systems.

The original effort began at a single elementary school in the inner city in 1993, when the principal decided she needed mental health services in order to address problems of attendance, discipline, and academic performance. I was at that time program and medical director for child and adolescent services at the public community mental health services agency and volunteered a half-day a week of time at that school.

From that initial exploration evolved a three-way collaboration of the school district, the mental health agency, and the public hospital district to provide health and mental health services throughout the school district. The collaboration began in 1995 and continued until 2000, when the CMHC had to pull out due to constrictions placed on it by the state's experiment in Medicaid managed care. To that point a loyal soldier in the public mental health system, I could no longer countenance continuing in that role and left it for private practice and the opportunity to continue working with the schools.

The Dallas Youth and Family Centers project maintains ten centers, each serving a family of schools, with health, mental health, social services, and youth and family development services. Districtwide, over two hundred campuses and 170,000 students and their families are eligible. Approximately twelve thousand unduplicated families are served in a typical year, about 10 percent of them for mental health services. Independent evaluation of the program by the district's research and evaluation division has shown a significant decrease in attendance problems, a significant increase in academic success, very high levels of student, family, and faculty satisfaction, and a decrease of over 90 percent in disciplinary referrals for students served by the mental health program.

Developmental Issues

In keeping with the principle that the school campus provides an ideal location for community health and human service activities, center services are available to family members of enrolled students (pre-kindergarten through high school graduation) throughout the school life of the child. Developmentally appropriate health, behavioral, and social services are regularly provided to children from about age four to age nineteen (and age twenty-two in cases of developmentally impaired special education students). Providers of professional services at the center must therefore possess a range of knowledge, skills, and techniques appropriate to the gamut of developmental attainment in the service population. A variety of skilled professionals are retained under contract, since very few clinical workers have the inclination, aptitude, and skills required for effective work with children of all ages.

Examples of commonly provided mental health services are family intervention and parent training to families of preschoolers, individual and group social skills training to elementary school-age children, and individual psychotherapy and substance abuse counseling to adolescents. The child and adolescent psychiatrist is the team's leader for all treatments provided and prescribes adjunctive psychotropic pharmacotherapy for some children (the most commonly prescribed agents are stimulants and antidepressants).

Cultural Issues

The ethnic diversity of this inner-city urban school district is reflected in the families served in the centers: Americans all, over half are of Hispanic, about one-third of African, about 8 percent of Anglo-European, and the remainder of Native American, Asian, or Pacific Islander descent. These groups, as well as many subgroups within each, are characterized by widely divergent attitudes toward such crucial variables as family life, health, social services, and spirituality. It behooves a community service program to be competent in the cultures of the populations to which it offers service and the individual providers of service to be competent in the language and culture of each family she or he serves. These are ideals that in practice are extremely difficult to attain (Pumariega & Cross, 1997).

Specific Opportunities

School-based mental health services present a number of important opportunities for the children they serve and for the communities and systems of care they reside in.

Accessibility. Children, family members, and others are all well acquainted with the school campus, and most feel at home there. Stigma is absent, or at least dramatically reduced. When the local community's public mental health center colocated children's services to the public schools, appointment adherence more than doubled (from less than 50 percent to almost 100 percent). Among other benefits, this translates into a significant increase in efficiency and staff productivity.

Earlier Identification and Intervention. These are possible for a range of developmental and behavioral disorders of children when community services are campus based, accessible, and community friendly. From the public health perspective, this represents secondary prevention at its best: mitigating future morbidity through targeted early intervention.

Integration of Service Delivery. From clinic to school to home to community sites, integration of service delivery is uniquely facilitated by the school-based community center. Indigenous neighborhood resources are routinely made a part of treatment plans, and services may be delivered not only in centers but in the classroom, the home, and other community settings that comprise the locus of the family's life.

Broad Participation on Treatment Teams. Broad participation by child, clinician, teacher, counselor, administrator, parents, extended family, and other concerned parties ensures that prescribed interventions are carried out consistently across settings and are continuously, rather than episodically, implemented.

Knowledge of Local School Community. The school-based community service center has an unparalleled opportunity to become a part of the neighborhood and to appreciate, and make good use of, the rich variety of resources there. The center should offer membership on a steering or advisory committee to representatives of parents, community agencies, businesses, service providers, religious faiths, and other community partners.

Measurement of Relevant Outcomes. School districts routinely collect and aggregate data on student attendance, achievement, and disciplinary referrals. Services provided by school-based community centers have been well documented to produce significant improvements in these three areas. Therefore, an existing data system can usually be co-opted to provide relevant outcome data analysis.

Specific Challenges

Of the many problems thought to be inherent in the provision of mental health services in a school-based community site, two, stigma and confidentiality, can be dismissed. Ordinary commonsense attention to patient and family confidentiality is all that is required, bearing in mind that most of the domains in which the child lives are represented on the treatment team. A child's teacher and principal are not authorities from whom confidential information must be withheld; they are treatment team members—people who can help and have a defined responsibility to do so. Should any treatment team member not view all the other members in this same way, there are alliances to build before beginning conversations about planning treatment. Four other areas of concern *do* pose some risk to successful collaboration. Listed in ascending order of increasing threat, they are bureaucracy, controversy, mobility, and funding.

Bureaucracy. The divergent aims, processes, and procedures of the partnering agencies must be negotiated by a core group of representatives of each. These partners must share a realistic respect for the nonnegotiable requirements of their own and the others' agencies, side by side with a healthy skepticism toward the rigidities that are always inherent in large public institutions. Each agency must allow the other partners access to its inner workings in order to discover potential synergetic processes and aims, and avenues toward reducing duplication of efforts. The partner representatives must also share a vision of children's education, families' health, and community mental health as a commitment that is superordinate to mere agency affiliation.

Controversial Health Care Issues. When argued in the public media, controversial health care issues pose a serious risk to the political and financial supports that school-based services require. In Dallas, there have arisen only two such issues: psychopharmacology prescribing practices (which subsided quickly and easily) and reproductive health services for adolescents (which did not, and in its persistence nearly torpedoed the entire coalition).

Population Mobility. Because of Texas's proximity to Mexico and other Central American countries, a majority of public school students are of Hispanic origin. Many (the proportion is unknown) are undocumented, and some travel unpredictably between their Texas homes and their Latino ones, often staying for months—or years—in Mexico, only to reappear in the Dallas schools at a later time. This phenomenon makes continuity of care problematic. A related mobility issue affects indigenous Dallas students among the poorest of the poor: they are often moved from project to project or to homeless shelters. These children may lose access to services, particularly if their families' wanderings cross school district boundaries.

Funding. Always the major nemesis of innovative service delivery, funding lives up to its reputation. The problem was easily solved in the early phases of collaboration between the schools and the other agencies: the mental health and health providers simply relocated already-funded services to the schools. With the advent of Medicaid managed care, the private companies that controlled the funding required encounter and claim documentation from the provider agencies, a data requirement that could not be met by a widely scattered, poorly systematized network of neighborhood service centers without electronic support. In order to survive, the community mental health center was forced to pull out of the collaboration, leaving the school district and the hospital district as the two remaining partners, with the school district having to negotiate the mental health component. Since the district is now spending education dollars on what should be a health care expenditure, it is having to examine the possibility of becoming a network provider for the company that administers the mental health dollars. This is the kind of dilemma that we should expect to continue to confront unless and until the current iteration of health care reimbursement reform has finally failed in the public perception and in the policymaking halls of governments.

Lessons Learned

Each of the opportunities and challenges represents an important lesson learned over several years' experience of providing collaborative services in the schools. In addition to these, mention should be made of the importance of conceptualizing schools as multipurpose community centers in order to take advantage of their strategic location and availability (including after school, weekends, and holidays) and of the necessity of developing an integrated service system for children and families that combines the functions of education, health, child protection, family welfare, mental health, and juvenile justice.

Furthermore (and in consequence of the need for service systems integration), we need to begin to appreciate the irrelevance of the agendas of traditional governmental, professional, and even advocacy organizations. These agencies, well intentioned one and all, are bound by the strictures of traditional thinking and, more important, the bureaucratically created and maintained system of vertically integrated funding: the mind-set is, "This for education, that for health, another for child protection, still another for juvenile justice, and [practically nothing] for mental health." And even those paltry deliberations are framed by the fraudulent assumption that undergirds the current iteration of health care reimbursement policy: that health care is a commodity, like any other, that can be efficiently and profitably traded in the marketplace. These assumptions and practices need to be called into question before a meaningful system of services and supports for American children and families can be built.

THE VIEW OF THE PARENT-EDUCATOR

I (Sandra Keenan) am the parent of a teenager with severe depression and have experienced personally over the past year the need for care coordinated among the school, home, and clinician.

I was also a school-based administrator for over fifteen years and supervised districtwide special education and special services programs. In that role, I had the opportunity to establish working relationships with community-based providers, as the school system was participating in building a community-based system of care. One of the basic principles of a system of care (Stroul & Friedman, 1986) is the provision of services when and where the child and family require. There are many advantages to having mental health services provided in schools or within the local community. Children attend school daily. It makes sense to provide the services where they are. Historically, services have been provided in hospitals, clinics, or private offices of the providers. Appointments were usually scheduled after school or on Saturdays. Many families had scheduling problems due to their own work schedules. By providing the services in the school, the child is already there, and a consistent, predictable schedule for treatment can be established.

Schools can play an important role by providing space, access to a telephone, and a contact person responsible for communicating with the clinician on a regular basis. In addition, once space is established, it can be available for late afternoons or evenings as a meeting place for families and the clinician, if that is more comfortable and convenient for the family. Services delivered in schools also decrease any possible stigma that the child or parent may experience by entering a psychiatrist or clinician's office.

School-Based Teams

It is vital to have someone within the school designated as the contact person for both the family and the therapist. This person provides information on the student's progress and needs on a regular basis to both the clinician and the family. He or she serves as the point person in this triangle of support for the child and family, can request regular updates on the progress of therapy for the child, and makes sure that all written communication and summaries are secured in the student's file.

In addition, the clinician can plan to attend evaluation or review meetings on a routine basis and slowly becomes part of the team. In many situations, the clinician serves as a systems mediator or navigator. He or she assists the child and family in understanding the public school system and what the law requires or provides, and can mediate disagreements between the parties if necessary. The clinician also assists in providing the framework for addressing the mental health needs of the child in a more coordinated manner and can assist in the development of information packets for school personnel and families. These can be made available through parent-teacher organizations, the community public libraries, and churches. The clinician can also assist in developing training curriculum related to children's mental health, both prevention and intervention.

As part of the school-based team, the clinician provides accessibility to an entire network of providers and resources that the school or family may not be accessing. Through the evaluation or assessment process, the clinician can provide the supporting documentation for eligibility for not only school-based services, but services that may be funded through Medicaid or other insurance.

In some cases, the psychiatrist may be linked to a clinic that offers additional services for the family or more intensive services when needed for the child. In 1993, the Westerly Support Services Program established an agreement with Elmcrest Hospital in Portland, Connecticut. It secured the services of a clinical psychologist who worked for a satellite program of the hospital. This psychologist met with high school staff, students, and families as needed and provided options that could be more or less restrictive, depending on what was needed for the child. The day treatment program was one of the options, for full day or partial day, as well as inpatient or outpatient hospital-based services through Elmcrest. The staff at the Westerly program had access to a beeper for the clinician or his staff. Treatment plans were coordinated with all stakeholders, and crisis intervention plans were developed as well. This coordination provided the opportunity for students to experience less restrictive options, because movement to more restrictive locations was already structured as part of their intervention plans. It did not have to be all or nothing in terms of setting.

A different experience in teaming with the child's clinician occurred when the school system set up transition plans for students who were attending another day treatment program and were preparing to return to the public school setting. The child and family had been working with a particular therapist and psychiatrist at the private school. As part of a transition plan, the child and clinician visited the public school setting, attended some meetings with scheduled teachers and other support personnel, and met the clinician who would be providing treatment for the child back in the community. We would help the family find a local provider one to two months prior to discharge. It was important that the student and family feel they had a support base in the local community to assist with any issues that might occur. This also allowed the child's current clinician to cover any concerns regarding this transition with the child. Once the student returned to the public school, he or she continued to see the previous therapist for at least four more sessions to make sure the transition was working. This proved to be very successful, and in several cases, fewer sessions were required.

As a district administrator, I experienced several different ways that medication was prescribed and managed by either the physician or psychiatrist. Usually the child had completed some initial assessment or evaluation, and the physician had made a decision to try a certain medication. The child would have a follow-up appointment usually within six to eight weeks, but sometimes twelve, where the physician would ask the child and family how things were going and if there were any problems taking the medication. There was no connection to the school, what was happening for six hours each day, or if it had any bearing on the child's performance and success in that setting. This type of care and treatment, managed only in the clinic, did not allow for the most comprehensive assessment and measure of the impact of the medication.

The results can be very different within a school district that incorporates protocols for coordinated communication. When we established a school-based support service team, we realized how important medication management was for all children involved in the support program. For most of them, their success in school, at home, and in the community was directly tied to the decrease in symptoms or behaviors that were interfering with school attendance, work completion, and interactions with peers, teachers, and other adults. Therefore, it was imperative that information regarding those three areas was communicated regularly to both the parent and the clinician. This is the best way to make informed decisions about maintaining, altering, or stopping the medication.

Communication Framework and Strategies

I have also experienced the building of a relationship with a therapist as a parent of a teenager with depression and anxiety. As a parent, I want to have a private meeting or session with the psychiatrist to be informed of the evaluation results, suggested interventions and therapy, and the possible use of medication. I want to hear the choices, recommendations, and potential side effects and risks associated with the medication. I want to hear projected goals, approximate timelines, and possible outcomes as a result of therapeutic intervention so we as a family can know what to expect and be prepared. I want to know who to call, when, and what to do if there is an emergency. I want a crisis plan in place. I want to know that someone in the school knows how to interpret the evaluations and assessments and understands the effects of the medication. There needs to be a primary contact person at the school whom I can call when there is a change in my child's status or treatment. I need that person to help advocate on my child's behalf and inform all service providers of the status of treatment and current impact on her program. As a parent, I want the opportunity to provide direct input to the school as well as the psychiatrist, so my child's team has all the information to make better decisions regarding her care.

As a school administrator, we established a set time each week for the clinical psychologist to participate with the school-based team. Any referrals that involved behavioral or emotional concerns were scheduled during that block of time. Any recommendations for evaluations were assigned to the clinician, time permitting. In addition, the clinician scheduled individual and group therapy sessions during their assigned time in the school each week. The clinician maintained monthly clinical summaries outlining impact on outcomes, and copies were made for the file and family.

The primary contact person within the school, usually the school psychologist or school social worker, made sure there was regularly scheduled feedback from teachers and other providers to the clinician. We had negotiated a six-hour block of time each week on a particular day for these services. The clinician was not an employee of the school district. He was paid as a consultant on a monthly basis. This proved to be quite cost-effective. One day a week was the equivalent cost of one clinical evaluation. Many other services occurred during that time, in addition to the completion of evaluations as well.

The school-based support team was able to establish some schoolwide prevention and early intervention programs that provided support not only for the identified children with formal plans, but also served children at risk for developing serious needs. This brought about the creation of planning centers within the school to provide support to children and families. These centers (Woodruff et al., 1998) facilitate the early identification of, and interventions into, problems students are having; staff can then work with students to teach them coping and problem-solving skills to manage their difficulties. These centers also serve to prevent the escalation of inappropriate behaviors by addressing academic, emotional, or behavioral problems before they become crises. The clinician serves an important advisory role in the development of strategies and supports within the center. In addition, he or she assists with referrals for related child or family needs to other providers.

Another component that contributed to effective communication was a quarterly meeting with all program partners to coordinate service delivery. This included school administrators, support personnel, local police, mental health staff, clinician, community-based therapists, juvenile court representatives, and child protective agents. Basically, these meetings served as a quality check to ensure that all agencies were working cooperatively, communicating the appropriate information, and using services for the best results for children and families.

Benefits for Schools, Child, Family, and the Provider

These practices can have positive results for families, the child, and the school. Improved communication and consistent delivery of services provide trust and stability for the child and family. The family and the clinician are partners focusing on the treatment issues and work as a team with the school. The family and school are partners focusing on the child's education and work as a team with the clinician. These partnerships provide coordination of services and an improved level of accountability around service provision.

This coordination benefits the child by providing one system, one network focused on the whole child. The messages and expectations are clear and consistent. It benefits the family by providing a single system to work within. Historically, families had to become case managers for their child and learn all systems. It could become a scheduling and tracking maze.

These practices benefit the school by providing more consistent outcomes for the child and adding to his or her success in the educational program in a more positive way. The school knows the goals and objectives for treatment and understands how it affects daily performance in academics and peer relations.

The clinician receives timely information from a variety of sources and thus has a framework for delivering therapy that can prove to be more consistent. Being part of the school-based team provides a guaranteed consulting slot for a school year and enables the therapist to schedule work in a more predictable manner.

THE SCHOOL-BASED
MENTAL HEALTH ADMINISTRATOR'S VIEW

I (Jacquelyn Duval-Harvey) am the director of the Johns Hopkins school-based program, which is part of the Johns Hopkins Community Psychiatry Department. Prior to my appointment as director, I was a school-based clinician. This program exists as a partnership with other child-serving agencies: the Departments of Social Services, Juvenile Justice, Health, and Police; Families Involved Together (a family advocacy group); and the Baltimore City Public School System. A full array of universal and targeted prevention activities and treatment services is provided on-site. The program has school-based mental health clinicians—professional counselors, psychologists, arts therapists, and social workers—working full time in nineteen schools in East Baltimore. The mental health clinicians provide individual, group, and family counseling and make referrals to other departmental units—in home and outpatient—and other community agencies. Services are provided during the school day, after school, and during the summer. Each school also has a weekly three-hour consultation with a psychiatrist from the Community Psychiatry Department. Psychiatric services (consisting of evaluations, referrals, and medication monitoring) are provided by a psychiatric resident who rotates through the program for one year, beginning in July and ending in June.

As with most other relationships, personal and professional, impressions fostered in the early stages can have a significant impact. As the outsider coming into the school setting and with the knowledge of human behavior that is part of mental health training, the school-based clinician must take responsibility for extending the initial overtures to building the collaborative relationship with school-employed staff. These efforts should be directed at all school employees, not only those involved in the delivery of mental health services.

The activities of the school-based clinician should be focused on demonstrating to school staff that the clinician is committed to becoming a team player and brings expertise that can be beneficial to the education process. New or inexperienced school-based clinicians often miss opportunities to demonstrate commitment to the team membership concept because it typically involves non-job-related activities. For example, the clinician may be asked to monitor a class for a short period. In situations where the service being requested does not have a negative impact on current or future therapeutic relationship with clients, and the clinician has the time or availability to perform the task, it is recommended that he or she do so. Such requests should be viewed as tests of loyalty and trust, which are common for newcomers in schools as well as many other professional settings.

Formal opportunities to demonstrate team membership are also available. In most schools, there is often a group of individuals who come together for the purpose of assisting students who are having difficulty functioning in the classroom. These teams, called student support teams in some areas, usually include a variety of professionals or staff with varied backgrounds. This is the ideal forum for school-based staff to share their clinical expertise as well as receive referrals.

Clinical information and treatment goals must be redefined for relevance in a classroom or school setting. Classroom teachers are more likely to perceive the clinician as supportive and will more willingly contribute to the clinical process if the goals of treatment are clearly articulated using school terminology in addition to or instead of clinical jargon. For example, in communicating with the teacher of a student who is easily frustrated and becomes disruptive, increasing on-task behavior, as opposed to increasing frustration tolerance, should be the stated goal of the interventions.

The clinical outcomes articulated in the mission of the mental health agency that sponsors the school-based clinician can also be revised to reflect those that are more pertinent to academic settings. Increased school attendance leading to improved academic performance and decreased suspensions are outcomes that can be supported by any individual or agency working with school-aged youth.

Another issue that must be addressed administratively by the sponsoring agency prior to involvement in community services is the application of the medical model to the school setting. The school setting provides an ideal opportunity for prevention. However, classification of students into diagnostic categories may seem antithetical to the prevention model. In addition, parents and other family members may be reluctant to respond to the more sensitive questions that are a standard part of a psychiatric evaluation. In the emergency room setting, where there is a crisis or other significant event, the purpose of the evaluation is clear. In other settings, like an outpatient clinic, where the parents or guardians are more likely to have requested assistance, they may also be more willing to provide such information. However, it is less common for questions of such a personal nature, in some cases involving admission of illegal activity (substance use or criminal conduct), to be asked in a school setting. When the evaluation is performed by a psychiatrist or other credentialed mental health professional who is unknown to the family, the accuracy of the information provided is questionable, if the questions are answered at all.

One way to minimize these difficulties is for the permanent school staff to pave the way for the psychiatrist. This can be done by orienting the family to the assessment process and giving them a preview of the questions that will be asked. It is important to inform the parent that there is awareness of the sensitive nature of the questions and to provide an explanation of how the information is used to develop an appropriate treatment plan. It may also be helpful to inform parents that it would be best to inform the evaluator when they prefer not to answer a particular question than to provide inaccurate information since this could result in an ineffective plan.

Providing opportunities for more integration of psychiatry staff into the school setting will also help alleviate this problem. For example, in-service presentations to school staff as well as caregivers on the role of psychiatry in a community setting could allay the misconceptions and the stigma associated with mental illness. Presentations on developmental stages and associated challenges are often well attended while at the same time providing benchmarks for families. Periodic updates on treatment of various disorders using language appropriate to the setting could also contribute to increased understanding. An underlying goal of formal and informal activities should be to indicate that concerns are seen as legitimate and are responded to respectfully. Clinicians who are placed temporarily or for limited periods in schools but whose primary training has occurred in a setting other than a school should value the placement as a site with unique features that will serve to improve their clinical skills. Having the expectation that the school site should fit into previously held beliefs or practice will inhibit learning and can result in less than optimal care of the clients in that setting.

Once the collaborative team approach is in place, the school-based clinician must maintain and enhance this relationship. Timely and appropriate responses to referrals or requests from school staff is an effective strategy. Typically, assistance with crisis intervention is a frequent requirement, particularly when schoolwide behavior management plans are lacking. In these situations, once the crises have been resolved, clinicians can act as consultants to school staff concerning formulation of an effective plan. Staff development to classroom teachers and other school-employed staff is often an additional task for the clinician in the implementation of the behavior management plan.

While there are specific strategies school-based clinicians can employ to collaborate effectively with school staff, there are also pitfalls that can be detrimental to this relationship. Two of the most divisive issues are psychotropic medication and child abuse reporting. The use of medication becomes an even more loaded issue in low-income urban schools located in communities where substance abuse is prevalent. In many cases, the parents or guardians of the students have either firsthand or second-hand knowledge of the negative effects of substance abuse and as a result are often unwilling to consent to the use of psychotropic medication. It is not unusual for school-employed staff to espouse similar viewpoints.

Open discussion about different points of view on this topic is more likely to occur if there is trust and collaboration prior to the surfacing of this issue. It is important for school-based clinicians to provide alternative strategies for symptom management other than medication. Cognitive behavioral approaches that focused on increasing anger management, prosocial skills, and assertiveness were frequently used as alternatives to medication.

The issue of medication will have minimal negative impact on the collaborative relationship if the clinician facilitates clear and frank discussion about the pros and cons of medication and other intervention strategies with an understanding of the family and community's experience in relation to drugs.

The reporting of child abuse is another hurdle that must be managed. Typically, more obvious cases, having to do with trauma or injury to the child, are less problematic. It is more difficult to achieve consensus in cases of neglect, psychological abuse, and corporal punishment. In such cases, the clinician must have a clear understanding of the school system policy concerning these issues. Certain scenarios are common. One situation involves the clinician's being asked to report the abuse, so that the relationship between the school-employed staff and the student's family is not jeopardized. In this case, regardless of the final outcome about who makes the call, the clinician may want to discuss how his or her relationship with families is perceived by school-employed staff. Another scenario involves the clinician's calling in the report without the support of school-employed staff. Regardless of outcome, this situation provides an opportunity to advance the relationship, with the clinician modeling how professionals can disagree on some issues yet continue to work effectively.

It is important to build into the school schedule an opportunity for staff from specialty services, school based and school employed, to reflect on past events and provide and receive feedback with each other and others in the school. A willingness to respect and encourage individuals to function from a strength-based perspective begins with the school-based clinician's maintaining an open mind about personal shortcomings and demonstrating the ability to practice self-improvement.

THE CHALLENGE
OF COLLABORATION

The challenges that families, school personnel, and health professionals face in helping children to develop into caring responsible, competent adults are formidable. Effectively confronting these challenges requires collaboration. Following the strategies described below increases the ability of parents and professionals to use their varied skills and experiences in a complementary, collaborative way to transcend the barriers:

• *Multidisciplinary team meetings.* When possible, the school counselor can take the lead in scheduling meetings on a weekly basis if possible, but certainly at least once a month to triage referrals, decide on prevention and remedial interventions, and develop a process for resolving sticky issues like confidentiality and reporting of abuse (Adelman & Taylor, 1993; Flaherty et al., 1998).

• *Cross-cultural training.* Many school-based programs are in poor, minority, urban areas. The children are often living in single-parent, female-headed households. Recruiting and retaining staff who are from ethnic, minority, groups can be difficult. Thus, many of the mental health staff are like to have a European American background. Training of all mental health staff to be sensitive on matters of race, ethnicity, class, and gender can reduce the level of racial and cultural tension and facilitate open and honest dialogue (Weist, 1997; Pumareiga & Cross, 1997). Because school counselors are more permanent than school-based employees, they can keep track of completed trainings and ensure that new staff are exposed to critical training.

• *Interdisciplinary training and supervision.* Cross-disciplinary training and supervision can facilitate the development of a common language and change the hierarchy that often exists, especially when physicians are part of the team (Flaherty et al., 1998).

• *Open, flexible, attitudes.* The ability to be flexible and respond to situations can be valuable in working with anyone, but especially with people who have a similar goal of helping children but very different methods for achieving that goal.

• *Standardized procedures.* Routine methods for collecting and reviewing information can reduce potential professional and turf conflicts and speed up the process of developing and providing best practice interventions. School counselors, because of their stability and knowledge of school procedures and regulations, are in the best position to ensure that this process is institutionalized.

References

Adelman, H. S., & Taylor, L. (1993). School-based mental health: Toward a comprehensive model. *Journal of Mental Health Administration, 20,* 32–45.

Atkins, M. S., McKay M. M., Arvanitis, P., London, L., Madison, S., Costigan. C., Haney, P., Zevenbergen, A., Hess, L., Bennett. D., & Webster, D. (1998). An ecological model for school-based mental health services for urban low-income aggressive children. *Journal of Behavioral Health Services Research, 5,* 64–75.

Bell, C. C. & Jenkins, E. J. (1991). Traumatic stress and children. *Journal of Health Care for the Poor and Underserved, 2,* 175–185.

Bums, B. J., Costello, E. J., Angold, A., Tweed, D., Stangl, D., Farmer, E.M.Z., & Erkanli, A. (1995). Children's mental health service use across service sectors. *Health Affairs, 14,* 147–159.

Casat, C. D., Sobolewski, J., Gordon, J., & Rigsby, M. B. (1999). School-based mental health services (SBS): A pragmatic view of a program. *Psychology in the Schools, 36,* 403–413.

Clarke, G., Hawkins, W., Murphy, M., Sheeber, L., Lewinsohn, P., & Seeley, J. (1995). Targeted prevention of unipolar depressive disorder in an at-risk sample of high school adolescents: A randomized trial of a group cognitive intervention. *Journal of the American Academy of Child and Adolescent Psychiatry, 34,* 312–321.

Conoley, J. C., & Conoley, C. W. (1991). Collaboration for child adjustment: Issues for school and clinic-based child psychologists. *Journal of Consulting and Clinical Psychology, 59,* 821–829.

Cusick, P. (1983). *The egalitarian ideal and the American high school.* New York: Longman.

Dryfoos, J. G. (1994). *Full service schools.* San Francisco: Jossey-Bass.

Elliott, D. S., Hamburg, B. A., & Williams, K. R. (1998). *Violence in American schools.* Cambridge: Cambridge University Press.

Flaherty, L. T., Garrison, E. G., Waxman, R., Uris, P. F., Keys, S. G., Glass-Siegel M., & Weist, M. D. (1998). Optimizing the roles of school mental health professionals. *Journal of School Health, 68,* 420–424.

Flaherty, L. T., & Weist, M. D. (1999). School-based mental health services: The Baltimore model. *Psychology in the Schools, 36,* 379–389.

Forness, S. R., & Kavale, K. A. (2001, Fall). Are school professionals missing their best chance to help troubled kids? *Report on Emotional and Behavioral Disorders in Youth,* 80–83.

Gallagher, J. J. (1996). Policy development and implementation for children with disabilities. In E. Zigler, S. Kagan, & N. Wall (Eds.), *Children, families, and government: Preparing for the twenty-first century* (pp. 171–187). Cambridge: Cambridge University Press.

Gibbs, J. T., & Huang, L. N.. (1998). *Children of color: Psychological interventions with minority youth.* San Francisco: Jossey-Bass.

Goldman, R. K., Botkin, M. J., Tokunaga, H., & Kylinski, M. (1997). Teacher consultation: Impact on teachers' effectiveness and students' cognitive competence and achievement. *American Journal of Orthopsychiatry, 67*, 374–384.

Hill, H. M., & Madhere, S. A (1996). A multidimensional model or risks and resources. *Journal of Community Psychology, 24*, 26–43.

Hoagwood, K. (2000, Winter). State of the evidence on school-based mental health services—NIMH perspectives. *Report on Emotional and Behavioral Disorders in Youth, 1*3–17.

Hoagwood, K., & Erwin, H. D. (1997). Effectiveness of school-based mental health services for children: A ten year research review. *Journal of Child and Family Studies, 6*, 435–451.

Hoberman, H. M. (1992). Ethnic minority states and adolescent mental health services utilization. *Journal of Mental Health Administration, 19*, 246–267.

Knitzer, J. (1982). *Unclaimed children.* Washington, DC: Children's Defense Fund.

Lavigne, J. V., Arend, I. L., Rosenbaum. D., Binns, H. J., Christoffel, K. K., Bums, A., & Smith, A. (1998). Mental health service use among young children receiving pediatric primary care. *Journal of the American Academy of Child and Adolescent Psychiatry, 37*, 1175–1183.

McKay, M. M. (2000, Winter). What we can do to increase involvement in mental health services and prevention programs. *Report on Emotional and Behavioral Disorders in Youth, 11*–20.

Miller, L., & Newbill, C. (1998). *Section 504 in the classroom.* Austin, TX: Pro-Ed.

Motes P. S., Melton, G., Simmons, W.E.W., & Pumariega, A. (1999). Ecologically oriented school-based mental health services: Implications for service system reform. *Psychology in the Schools, 36*, 391–401.

Olweus, D. (1991). Bully/victim problems among school children: Basic facts and effects of a school-based intervention program. In D. J. Pepler & K. H. Rubin (Eds.), *The development and treatment of childhood aggression* (pp. 411455). Mahwah, NJ: Erlbaum.

Pace, T. M., Chaney, J. M., Mullins, L.L., & Olson, R. A. (1995). Psychological consultation with primary-care physicians: Obstacles and opportunities in the medical setting. *Professional Psychology: Research and Practice, 26*, 123–131.

Pumariega, A. J., & Cross T. L. (1997). Cultural competence in child psychiatry. In J. Noshpitz & N. Alessi (Eds.), *Basic handbook of child and adolescent psychiatry* (Vol. 4, pp. 473–484). New York: Wiley.

Reese, W. J. (1978). Between home and school: Organized parents, clubwomen, and urban education in the progressive era. *School Review, 37*, 3–28.

Richardson, L., Keller, A. M., Shelby-Harrington, M. L., & Parrish, R. (1996). Identification and treatment of children's mental health problems by primary care providers: A critical review of research. *Archives of Psychiatric Nursing, 10*, 293–303.

Rosenbaum J., Miller. S., & Krei, M. S. (1996). Gatekeeping in an era of more open gates: High school counselors' views of their influence on students' college plans. *American Journal of Education, 104,* 257–279.

Schacht, T. E., & Hanson, G. (1999). Evolving legal climate for school mental health services under the Individuals with Disability Education Act. *Psychology in the Schools, 36,* 415–426.

Sedlak, M. W. (1997). The uneasy alliance of mental health services and the schools: An historical perspective. *American Journal of Orthopsychiatry, 67,* 677–682.

Stroul, B., & Friedman, R. (1986). *A system of care for children and youth with severe emotional disturbances.* Washington, DC: Georgetown University Child Development Center, National Technical Assistance Center for Children's Mental Health.

Tuma, J. M. (1989). Mental health services for children: The state of threat. *American Psychologist, 44,* 188–198.

U.S. Department of Education. (1999). *Federal Register Part II, CFR Parts 300 and 303: Assistance to states for the education of children with disabilities and the early intervention program for infants and toddlers with disabilities: Final regulations.* Washington, DC: U.S. Government Printing Office.

U.S. Department of Health and Human Services. (1999). *Mental health: A report of the surgeon general.* Rockville, MD: U.S. Department of Health and Human Services, Substance Abuse and Mental Health Services Administration, Center for Mental Services, National Institutes of Health, National Institutes of Mental Health.

U.S. Office of Juvenile Justice and Delinquency Prevention. (1995). *Guide for implementing the comprehensive strategy for serious violent and chronic juvenile offenders.* Washington, DC: U.S. Government Printing Office.

Weist, M. D. (1997). Expanded school mental health services: A national movement in progress. In T. H. Ollendick & R. J. Prinz (Eds.), *Advances in clinical child psychology* (Vol. 19, pp. 319–352). New York: Plenum.

Woodruff, D. W., Osher, D., Hoffman, C., King, M., Snow, S., & McIntire, J. (1998). The role of education in a system of care: Effectively serving children with emotional or behavioral disorders. In Center for Mental Health Services, *Systems of care: Promising practices in children's mental health* ((Vol. 3). Washington, D.C.: Center for Mental Health Services, Substance Abuse and Mental Health Administration.

Zahner, G.E.P., Pawelkiewicz, W., DeFrancesco, J. J., & Adnopoz, J. (1992). Children's mental health service needs and utilization patterns in an urban community: An epidemiological assessment. *Journal of the American Academy of Child and Adolescent Psychiatry, 31,* 951–960.

CHAPTER THIRTEEN

Youth with
Comorbid Disorders

Kieran D. O'Malley

Comorbid disorders are more likely to prolong the course of mental disorders in youth or necessitate the use of more intensive, restrictive, or additional clinical services than with one disorder alone (U.S. Department of Health and Human Services, 1999; Klaehn, O'Malley, Vaughan, Sowers, & Kroeger, 2002). The complexity of the comorbid disorders often drives and challenges the system of care. The history of wraparound services for severely emotionally disturbed children (SED) acknowledges the need for more comprehensive care to manage the comorbid disorders, which invariably appeared in these children.

GENERAL EPIDEMIOLOGY

Epidemiological studies have shown that young adults in the United States, including those in the mid- to late adolescent period, are twice as likely to suffer a mental disorder as children under twelve years old (Polger & Cabassa, 2001). The current prevalence estimate is that 22 to 23 percent (or 44 million) of the adult population in the United States have diagnosable mental disorders during a given year. This estimate is quoted in the recent surgeon general's report on mental health and comes from two epidemiological surveys: the Epidemiological Catchment Area study of the early 1980s and the National Comorbidity Survey of the early 1990s (Regier, Farmer, et al., 1993; Regier, Narrow, et al., 1993; Kessler et al., 1994; U.S. Department of Health and Human Services, 1999).

The prevalence of mental disorder in children and adolescents is 20 percent (U.S. Department of Health and Human Services, 1999). There is also a subgroup of this population identified with what is called severe emotional disturbances (SED). The United States has 42.6 million uninsured people, and those between eighteen and twenty-five years old are the most mobile and tenuous of groups receiving any health insurance (O'Malley, 2002). Thus, the youth often at the highest risk for mental disorder are at an age when they are most likely to have no medical insurance to enable them to avail of appropriate diagnosis and treatment (Polger & Cabassa, 2001). The compounding complexities of comorbid conditions make the mental disorders in youth particularly challenging to diagnose and treat (Nisbet, 1969).

The comorbidities are divided into four domains: substance use, developmental, medical, and psychiatric.

SUBSTANCE USE DISORDER COMORBIDITY

It has been recognized for a long period that the period of adolescent development is a time when substance use disorders are a pervasive problem. Many studies have demonstrated the negative physical and mental health problems that have arisen as a result of adolescent substance use (Kaminer, 1994; Kaminer & Tarter, 1999). Epidemiological studies have shown a decrease in the age of first diagnosis of substance use disorder, a continued increase in the incidence of substance use among youth, and an increase in the lifetime prevalence of substance abuse and dependence in the general population (Johnson et al., 1999; Lewinsohn, Rohde, & Seeley, 1996). It has been shown that by eighteen years of age, 79.2 percent of youth in the United States have drunk alcohol, and 3.7 percent drink alcohol on a daily basis (Johnson et al., 1999). Furthermore, 44.9 percent of eighteen year olds have used marijuana at least once, with 4.9 percent using the drug daily. The general population prevalence for adults with mental disorder and comorbid substance use disorder is 3 percent in one year, and 6 percent have substance use disorders alone (U.S. Department of Health and Human Services, 1999). However, it has been estimated that the prevalence of psychiatric disorder with comorbid substance use disorder in publicly treated severely mentally disordered populations ranges from 32 percent to 61 percent (Drake & Wallach, 1989; Regier et al., 1990; Breakey, Calabrese, Rosenblatt, & Crum, 1998). Finally, the estimated lifetime exposure rates for inhalants (16.6 percent), stimulants (15.3 percent), hallucinogens (14.0 percent), and cocaine (7.9 percent) illustrate the extent of substance use in youth in the United States (Johnson et al., 1999; Kaminer & Tarter, 1999).

Newer Synthetic Agents

There are several so-called club drugs that merit specific mention: 3, 4 methyl-enedioxymethamphetamine (MDMA, known as Ecstasy), ketamine, and gamma hydroxybutyrate (GHB). These drugs are reputed to have been used by hippies in the 1960s in Ibiza, an island off Spain, and came back into prominence with the 1980s rave and party scene. The use of these club drugs spread to England and entered the American subculture in the late 1980s and early 1990s. Now they are used throughout the world, most commonly in nightclubs and all-night dance parties and at gay circuit parties (McDowell, 1999).

The most pervasive club drug used is Ecstasy, which is ingested orally. Recent estimates of the prevalence of its use in United States vary from 3.1 percent in grade 8, 8.2 percent in grade 12, and 5.5 percent in college (Elliott, 2001). Also, the recent National Household Study of 3.4 million people indicated that 78 percent of the users of Ecstasy reported using other drugs as well.

MDMA damages serotonin (5-HT) neurons in the brains of laboratory animals. It has been shown that the ingestion of MDMA causes a decrease in the serum and spinal fluid levels of 5-HIAAA in a dose-dependent fashion (Shulgin, 1990; McCann & Ricaurte, 1991, 1993). Accumulating scientific evidence is beginning to show that MDMA is neurotoxic to humans (Gold & Miller, 1997; Sprague, Everman, & Nichols, 1998). Studies have demonstrated decreased cerebrospinal fluid 5-HIAA levels and 5-HT2 receptor density (McDowell, 1999). There have also been reports of possible neurocognitive deficits in verbal memory and psychiatric sequelae such as major depression (Creighton, Black, & Hyde, 1991; Elliott, 2001). The drug offers a profound psychological effect that induces an overwhelming feeling of attachment and connection (McDowell, 1999; Elliott, 2001). Practical safety concerns include an awareness that MDMA is contraindicated in anyone taking monoamine oxidase inhibitors (MAOIs) for depression or protease inhibitors for AIDS (Elliott, 2001). The adverse effects of MDMA resemble a combination of the serotonin syndrome and the neuroleptic malignant syndrome with symptoms such as impaired sensorium, hyperthermia, muscle rigidity, and fever.

Ketamine is classified as a dissociative anesthetic. It is still legally manufactured for use by veterinarians and pediatric surgeons as a nonanalgesic anesthetic (McDowell, 1999). It is a close relation to phencyclidine (PCP, or Angel Dust). The recreational use of ketamine began in the 1960s, and its use has steadily continued. Now it is used alone for a paranormal experience or in a social setting such as a rave. It is available as a liquid, converted to powder, and is taken intravenously, intranasally, or orally. Ketamine interferes with the actions of the excitatory amino acid neurotransmitters, especially glutamate and aspartate, which are particularly important in cortical-cortical and cortical-subcortical interactions (McDowell, 1999). It can induce tangential ideas of reference and distort body and space perception. Higher dosages may induce hallucinations or paranoid delusions (Oye, Paulsen, & Maurset, 1992; Garfield, Garfield, & Stone, 1994; Malhotra et al., 1996).

GHB is found naturally in many mammalian cells, and in the brain the highest concentrations are found in the hypothalamus and the basal ganglion (Gallimberti, Spella, Soncini, & Gessa, 2000). It is both a precursor and a metabolite of GABA but does not act directly on the GABA receptor sites (Chin, Kreutzer, & Dyer, 1992). It is ingested orally and causes a pleasant state of relaxation and tranquility, mild euphoria, and loquaciousness (sometimes compared to an alcohol effect). Side effects include drowsiness, dizziness, nausea, and vomiting (McDowell, 1999). As the dose increase, patients may experience loss of bladder control, temporary amnesia, clonus, seizures, and cardiopulmonary depression (Chin et al., 1992; Gallimberti et al., 1989). This drug is commonly used with other substances: alcohol, 77 percent; marijuana, 20 percent; and cocaine, 20 percent.

Prenatal Risk Factors

Youth who have a history of prenatal alcohol exposure may be at biological risk for developing alcohol use disorder because of the alcohol chemical sensitization of the developing brain. Animal studies of prenatal alcohol exposure as early as the mid-1970s had revealed this risk of later alcohol craving (Bond & Di Gusto, 1976; Reyes, Garcia, & Jones, 1985; Dominguez, Chotro, & Molina, 1993). Recent work has commented that the prenatal alcohol exposure is actually a greater risk factor in subsequent adolescent and adult alcohol use disorder than the more conventionally held belief of a family history of alcohol abuse (Baer, Barr, Bookstein, Sampson, & Streissguth, 1998; Kapp & O'Malley, 2001). In a recent study, heavy maternal drinking during pregnancy was found to increase the odds that a twenty-one-year-old offspring will have at least mild alcohol dependence from 5.4 percent to 14.2 percent (Baer, Sampson, Barr, Connor, & Streissguth, in press).

Gender Differences

There may be gender differences in engaging youth with mental disorder and substance use disorder. Although women are more likely than men to seek medical care (Mechanic, 1978), this has apparently not been true for those with comorbid mental disorder and substance use disorder. Gender differences in clinical presentation and treatment access and response have been documented in psychiatric disorders such as schizophrenia (Goldstein & Tsuang, 1990; Franzek & Beckmann, 1992). Also, gender differences have been seen in the clinical presentation and treatment of patients with substance abuse (Weisner & Schmidt, 1992; DeJong, Brink, & Jansen, 1993; Watkins, Shaner, & Sullivan, 1999). Studies have shown that compared to other women and men, young adult women with mental disorder and comorbid substance use disorder are more likely to have been exposed to sexual, physical, or emotional abuse as children (Miller,

Downs, Gondoli, & Keil, 1987; Wallen, 1992; Alexander, 1996; Watkins et al., 1999). This history of childhood abuse and victimization has been seen as negatively affecting the young woman's ability to seek and engage in treatment (Watkins et al., 1999).

Substance Use and Psychiatric Disorders

The link between psychiatric disorders and adolescent substance use can begin in childhood, with conditions such as disruptive behavior disorder conferring an increased risk for later adolescent substance use (Greenbaum, Foster-Johnson, & Petrilia, 1996; Bukstein, Brent, & Kaminer, 1989). The interrelationship between psychiatric disorder and substance use is complicated and not necessarily linear (Weinberg, 1997):

- Psychiatric disorders may precede the substance use disorder in youth.
- The psychiatric disorder may develop as a result of a preexisting substance use disorder.
- The psychiatric disorder may modulate the severity of the substance use disorder (Hill & Muka, 1996; Gomez et al., 2000).
- Both the psychiatric disorder and the substance use disorder may have a common vulnerability or etiology, as is seen in youth with prenatal alcohol exposure or postchildhood sexual or physical abuse (Watkins, Shaner, & Sullivan, 1999; Baer et al., 1998).

The youth or adolescent with a history of childhood sexual abuse may develop severe posttraumatic stress disorder (PTSD), which is coupled with a chronic substance abuse disorder. The substance use seems to have a role in numbing the psychic pain of the early abuse.

Specific psychiatric disorders in youth have been associated with substance use disorder. The most commonly cited disorder is conduct disorder, which usually precedes the substance use disorder. Rates of 50 to 80 percent have been described in youth with substance use disorders (Milin, Halikas, Meller, & Morse, 1991). The association between attention deficit hyperactivity disorder (ADHD) and substance use disorder is probably related to the clinical coupling of the ADHD with conduct disorder (Alterman & Tarter, 1986, although recent studies have suggested that properly treated ADHD decreases the risk of youth substance use disorder (Biederman, Wilens, Mick, & Farone, 1997). Depressive disorders have been shown to have a prevalence of 24 to 50 percent in youth with substance use disorders (Bukstein, Glancy, & Kaminer, 1992; Dreykin, Buka, & Zeena, 1992). Also, anxiety disorders have been demonstrated to have a prevalence varying from 7 percent to more than 40 percent in youth with substance use disorder (Galanter & Kleber, 1999; Kaminer & Tarter, 1999). The relationship between depressive disorder and anxiety disorder and substance abuse is problematic and ever changing. The psychiatric disorders may precede the substance use disorder, or the nature of the acute and chronic intoxication with the substance use may bring on an anxiety disorder or depressive disorder with possible suicidal ideation. Some researchers distinguish between the anxiety disorders and postulate that social phobia brings on the substance use disorder, whereas the substance use disorder can itself bring on panic attacks and generalized anxiety disorder (Health Canada, 2001). A recent Canadian study analyzed the comorbidity of phobic disorders with alcoholism and found that individuals with lifetime alcohol abuse or dependence had two- to threefold increased odds of having a phobic disorder (Sareen, Chartier, Kjewrnisted, & Stein, 2001).

Axis II personality disorders have been studied in youth substance abuse. It appears that there is an association between Cluster B disorders (for example, antisocial, borderline, histrionic, and narcissistic) and substance use disorders. It is often the personality disorders interwoven into the psychiatric and substance use disorders that offer the biggest therapeutic challenge for adolescent psychiatrists. These youth are superficially charming but also manipulative, defiant, and self-defeating. They are forever disappointing, aggravating, and enraging the therapist and can engender many complicated countertransference feelings. They challenge the omnipotence and basic competence of the adolescent psychiatrist or mental health therapist, and it is always important to establish a clinical inventory of the current level of the youth's active substance use addiction, as this generally negates any therapeutic program, not least the compliance with psychotropic medication (Sandler, 1976; Casement, 1980; Kaminer & Tarter, 1999).

The clinical comorbidity between psychiatric disorders and substance use disorders (especially alcohol) has been eloquently described by psychiatrist and psychoanalyst Karl Menninger (1938): "Although there are exceptions, as a general rule the parents of alcoholics . . . are peculiarly unseeing with regard to the sufferings of their children. They think because their child is popular in high school or because he makes a fraternity or an athletic team in college that all is well with him, that peace and contentment fill his heart. Such parents little realize the suffering silently endured (often unconsciously) by well-appearing, well regarded children" (p. 143). Here Menninger captures the often hidden depressive disorder with low self-esteem or the chronic PTSD masked by the chronic alcohol or substance use disorder. The comorbidity of psychiatric disorder and substance use disorder can be subtle in so-called well-functioning youth, but the inevitable legacy of the disorders eventually emerges. Sometimes it is as a suicidal threat or act.

Finally, the general population of mentally disordered patients with substance use disorder has more psychiatric symptoms and distress than the population of mentally disordered without substance use disorder. Also, these patients are hospitalized more frequently, show lower levels of functioning, and are less functionally independent (Brady et al., 1990; Reis, Jaffe, Comtois, & Mitchell, 1999).

This obviously applies to youth as well. The general population of mentally disordered patients with comorbid substance use disorder has demonstrated lower rates of compliance with medication and other treatment recommendations (Brown, Ridgely, Pepper, & Levine, 1989; Lehman, Herron, Schwartz, & Myers, 1993; Kaminer & Tarter, 1999), but this quality is especially an issue in highly mobile and socially fluid youth.

A female teenage patient was seen initially by a psychologist and treated with insight-oriented psychotherapy for chronic depression and feelings of helplessness. Although there was a family loading for affective disorder on both the maternal and paternal sides of the family, the parents were excluded from therapy because of boundary problems. The psychologist suggested that the primary physician prescribe fluoxetine for recurrent mood disorder, and this medication precipitated a manic switch. The patient was then seen by an adolescent psychiatrist and given a presumptive diagnosis of bipolar disorder. The fluoxetine was discontinued, and the teenager was given lithium carbonate. She responded well to this medication. There had been some alcohol and substance use, which served to calm the patient and make her less anxious, but the need for alcohol and substance use decreased as she responded to lithium, and her moods and anxiousness became more controlled. The therapy also included supportive family therapy and parent education sessions, which greatly helped the parents' understanding of bipolar disorder and decreased their anxiety about their daughter's comorbid substance use.

DEVELOPMENTAL COMORBIDITY

Traditionally, developmental disability has been equated with mental retardation, but it is essential to understand that not all developmentally disabled youth are mentally retarded, although all mentally retarded youth are developmentally disabled. It then becomes the functional disability of the youth that is the key to understanding his or her developmental disability (Werner, 1948; Weiss, 1969; Spencer, 1896; Overton, 1984; Cicchetti, 1992). The overall prevalence of mental retardation is 1 percent, although some studies quote a prevalence rate of 3 percent (Munro, 1986; Russell, 1997). This figure does not acknowledge the large populations of developmentally disabled people who have an IQ over 70 (Piaget, 1971).The most striking example are patients with fetal alcohol spectrum disorder (FASD) who have had a recent prevalence estimate of 1 percent (Sampson et al., 1997). The University of Washington Secondary Disabilities Study sample of 415 patients aged six to fifty-one years, with fetal alcohol syndrome (FAS) or fetal alcohol effect (FAE), alcohol related neurodevelopmental disorder (ARND) showed 27 percent of those with FAS had an IQ under 70 and only 9 percent of those with FAE (ARND) had an IQ under 70 (Streissguth, Barr, Cohen, Kogan, & Bookstein, 1996). Recent statistics from Canada enumerated 3.1 million people, or 12.5 percent of the population over twelve years of age, who suffered from a long-term disability or handicap. Similarly, the Canadian National Longitudinal Survey of Children and Youth found that 436,000 youngsters, or 9.3 percent of the general population, were regarded as having special needs, ranging from a learning disability to something as severe and debilitating as a degenerative disease (Health Canada, 1996). Although comparative statistics are not available in the United States, this highlights the problem of attempting to estimate the true population of patients with developmental disability because often the populations of physical and mental disabilities are grouped together (Spemann, 1938; Reese & Overton, 1970).

The impact of a comorbid developmental disability on a youth with psychiatric disorder is also significant. Prevalence rates of psychiatric disorder in populations of patients with developmental disability vary from 40 to 60 percent, except for patients with FASD, who have a prevalence of over 90 percent throughout the life span (Corbett, 1985; Gilberg, Persson, & Grufman, 1986; Reiss, 1990; Einfeld & Tonge, 1996; Russell, 1997; Streissguth et al., 1996; Streissguth & Kanter, 1997; Goldstein et al., 1999; Gilberg & O'Brien, 2000; Streissguth & O'Malley, 2000).

Genetically Inherited Developmental Disorders

The first category of youth and adolescents with developmental comorbidity are those who are born with genetically inherited developmental disorders such as pervasive developmental disorders including autism and Asperger's disorder, Down's syndrome, fragile X syndrome, or velo-cardio-facial syndrome (Waddington, 1957). A brief review of these common disorders shows their distinctive physical features, as well as their unique clinical presentations. Youths with these disorders exist within systems of care, and so some knowledge of their clinical incidence, prevalence, and psychiatric clinical features is warranted if the system of care aspires to incorporate the full range of youth with comorbid disorders (Goldstein & Reynolds, 1999).

Autism. Autism was first described in 1943 by Kanner. It is now generally accepted that autism is a genetic condition rather than a syndrome with diverse organic etiologies (Folstein & Rutter, 1988; Harris, 1995). Current evidence points to the theory that it is not a single gene disorder but a disorder of at least two to ten genes, with a three-gene model being the most likely (Howlin, 2000). The clinical concept of autistic spectrum disorder widens the clinical range and increases the prevalence of the condition to 4 to 5 cases per 10,000. However, the National Autism Society in the United Kingdom suggests a figure of 91 per 10,000 (Howlin, 2000). The rates of the disorder are higher for boys than girls, with ratios of 4 or 5 to 1 (Wing, 1993). The onset is prior to age three years (American Psychiatric Association, 1994).

The physical phenotype of autism is usually normal with no distinguishing pathognomonic signs. The behavioral phenotype and kernel of the disorder is aptly described in the fourth edition of the American Psychiatric Association's *Diagnostic and Statistical Manual of Mental Disorders* (DSM-IV). The condition has three basic areas of disturbance: qualitative impairment in social interaction, qualitative impairment in communication, and restricted repetitive and stereotyped patterns of behavior, interests, and activities.

Although the DSM-IV does not include this condition in the adult section on diagnosis, it is universally recognized that autism continues into adolescent and adult life. Youth present with a range of intellectual functioning, with the modal IQ being in the moderately retarded range and approximately 20 percent having an IQ of 70 or more (Harris, 1995; Howlin, 2000). These youth present a variety of problems in social interaction, with the failure to develop peer relationships causing marked social isolation. The language deficits in social cognition and communication impair the youth's ability to voice distress, and this can lead to severe behavioral outbursts or undiagnosed chronic depression. Adolescence also is a period when medical problems such as seizure disorder may become more frequent (Harris, 1995).

Asperger's Disorder. This was described by Asperger in 1944 and with the development of DSM-IV entered the official psychiatric nomenclature. Asperger felt this disorder to be genetically transmitted, as he noted that the characteristics tended to cluster in families (Harris, 1995; Howlin, 2000). However, no definitive genetic evidence is yet available. The general prevalence is unknown because of the absence of adequate large-scale epidemiological studies. The behavioral phenotype is undistinctive, as with autism. As described in DSM-IV, it includes qualitative impairment in social interactions and restricted, repetitive, and stereotyped patterns of behavior, interests, and activities. The disturbances cause significant impairment in social, occupational, and other important areas of functioning. There is no clinically significant general delay in language or cognitive development.

The absence of language impairment and cognitive impairment is an essential component that separates Asperger's disorder from autism. Nevertheless, a current debate rages over the difference between high-functioning autism and Asperger's disorder, with no definitive clinical, neurochemical, genetic, or structural differences consistently reported. This condition exists through the life span, even though it is included only in the child and adolescent section of the DSM-IV.

Down's Syndrome. J. Langdon Down first described this in 1887. Underlying cytogenetic anomaly (trisomy 21) was identified by J. Lejeune and colleagues in 1958. The incidence is approximately 1 in 600 live births (if no prenatal screening), with 1 in 1,400 at maternal age twenty-five years rising to 1 in 110 at age forty years, and 1 in 30 at age forty-five years. There is also increased incidence if there is a long pregnancy-free interval. It is not listed in DSM-IV.

The physical phenotype of the disorder includes upward- and outward-slanting eyes, epicanthus, a wide nasal bridge, Brushfield spots in the eyes, a large posterior fontanelle, brachycephaly, low nuchal hair, single transverse crease, a large cleft between the first and second toe, and relatively short upper arms. Neonatal hypotonia is usually present, which improves over time. The majority are of short stature. In adolescence, 15 percent are hypothyroid. There is a 1 percent incidence of leukemia. As well, 50 percent have structural heart lesions of varying severity, with 15 percent having full atrioventricular septal defect (AVSD). Seven percent have congenital upper intestinal obstruction of differing degrees. Patients with untreated AVSD can die any time in their late teens or early twenties from respiratory and cardiac failure.

The psychiatric or behavioral phenotype includes cognitive abilities that are variable. About 10 percent are in the low-normal IQ range. Specific speech and language delay is common and is independent of general cognitive ability. Although many children and teenagers do conform to the popular stereotype of being happy, fun loving, and equable, nearly all react adversely to confrontational input, and so-called motivational problems interfere with learning. Approximately 25 percent have features of attention deficit disorder, and autism is another common psychiatric presentation. There is a high incidence of Alzheimer-like dementia with onset around thirty-five years of age (Harris, 1995).

Fragile X Syndrome. Fragile X syndrome (FXS) was first described by Martin and Bell in 1943, who showed a family pedigree with a sex-linked inheritance for learning difficulties and characteristic facial features. About four-fifths of the males with FSX have learning difficulties, and one-fourth of the females are mentally retarded. The FMR-1 gene was identified at the fragile X site (Xq27.3) in 1991. Prevalence estimates range from 0.19 to 0.92 per 1,000. This syndrome is the commonest inherited cause of mental retardation; institutionalized teenagers and young adults may have rates of 2.5 percent to 5.9 percent. FSX is not listed in DSM-IV.

The physical phenotype includes a long face with slightly increased head circumference, a large jaw with large protruding ears, a nasal bridge that is often long and flat with a high-arched palate, and abnormal dermatoglyphics. Microorchidism is present in up to 96 percent of men, which is useful diagnostically after puberty. Hearing and vision problems have been reported. Also, connective tissue dysplasia produces joint laxity, soft velvety skin, and aortic dilation with mitral valve prolapse (Turk, 1992).

The psychiatric or behavioral phenotype includes approximately 30 percent of both males and females with FXS exhibiting significant IQ decline over time. Speech and language development is almost always retarded, with dysfluent conversation, incomplete sentences, echolalia, palilalia, and verbal perservera-tion (Turk, 1992). FXS studies have shown that the onset of puberty is associ-ated with hormonal changes, which can also affect behavior. In adolescence, mood lability and anxiety may become more problematic for both males and females with FXS (Hagerman, 1999). Mood swings, crying spells, and irritabil-ity around the menstrual period can be manifestations of premenstrual syn-drome or late luteal phase dysphoric syndrome, which may be more exaggerated in females with FXS. The anxiety presentations may be quite severe and unre-sponsive to standard psychotropic medications. Finally, aggression is a clinical issue in about 50 percent of the FXS males (Harris, 1995; Hagerman, 1999).

Velo-Cardio-Facial Syndrome. Also called Shprintzen syndrome, this is a dele-tion syndrome. The most commonly deleted region is within the 22q11 and spans about 1.5 million base pairs. The condition is reported to affect between 1 in 3,000 and 1 in 5,000 of the population (Papolos et al., 1996; Murphy & Owens, 1997). It is not listed in the DSM-IV.

The physical phenotype includes hypernasal speech with cleft palate, cardiac anomalies, a characteristic facial appearance with a long face, large nose with large tip and high nasal root, small ears with over-folded helices, and narrow squinting eyes. This syndrome may affect many other tissues and organs, es-pecially those derived from neural crest cells. Other clinical features include transient neonatal hypocalcemia, hypoplasia or aplasia of the adenoids, micro-cephaly, mental retardation, tortuous retinal blood vessels, medial displacement of the internal carotids, Robin sequence, and scoliosis.

The psychiatric or behavioral phenotype includes behavioral excitation, pro-nounced response to threatening stimuli, an enduring fear of situations associ-ated with unpleasant experiences, bland affect, monotonus voice, impaired attention, impairments in social interaction and extremes, and shy or disinhibited behavior. Psychiatric disorders reported in association include psychotic disorders (schizophrenia or schizoaffective disorder) in adolescence (Shprintzen, Goldberg, Golding-Kushner, & Marion, 1992; Pulver et al., 1994). Also seen are ADHD, sepa-ration anxiety disorder, obsessive-compulsive disorder, and cyclothymia. Late-childhood and early-onset bipolar disorder was described by Papolos et al. in 1996. No association has been found between the presence of low-activity cathecol-O-methyltransferase allele and the presence of a psychiatric disorder (Shprintzen et al., 1992; Pulver et al., 1994).

Biological Central Nervous System Insult

This includes adolescents with a history of prenatal, perinatal, and neonatal events constituting a biological insult to the developing central nervous system (CNS). These events either singly or collectively have increased the risk of fu-ture developmental disorder in adolescence and even adulthood (Tjossem, 1976;

Kopp & Krakow, 1983; Rolf et al., 1992; O'Dougherty & Wright, 1992; Streissguth & O'Malley, 2000). This category includes adolescents with a history of prenatal exposure to alcohol, nicotine, or drugs such as cocaine. It also includes adolescents with a history of perinatal hypoxia or fetal distress.

The concept of a "continuum of reproductive wastage" was first coined in 1951 by Lilienfeld and Parkhurst to describe the wide range of lethal (abortion, neonatal death, stillbirth), sublethal (cerebral palsy, epilepsy, hemiplegia), and subtle manifestations of disability (learning disability, hyperactivity, minimal brain dysfunction) that can result from early CNS trauma. After a series of retrospective studies, the term "continuum of reproductive casualty" was employed, which expanded the range of deviant developmental outcomes to incorporate the range of minor motor, perceptual, learning, and behavioral disabilities associated with an early cerebral insult (Pasamanick, Knoblock, and Lilienfeld, 1956; Pasamanick & Knoblock, 1966).

In the Collaborative Perinatal Project of the National Institute of Neurological Diseases and Stroke, 53,000 infants (the products of 56,000 pregnancies) were studied during a six-year period (1959–1965) and received detailed pregnancy, birth, neonatal, four-month, eight-month, early childhood, and elementary school assessments (Broman, Nichols, & Kennedy, 1975). The most consistent predictors of later cognitive competence were maternal education and socioeconomic factors, but documented early brain abnormality, rare neurological conditions, and developmental delay were significant as well. This study highlighted the interaction between the high-risk pregnancies and the poverty and adverse environmental rearing conditions of the infants. It was this critical interaction that increased or decreased the long-term developmental problems of the child extending into adolescence (Niswander & Gordon, 1972; Broman et al., 1975).

Another classical longitudinal study was carried out in Hawaii on the island of Kauai in 1954. In this study, a large multiethnic sample (857 births) was followed from birth through adolescence, with assessments during the mother's pregnancy, at birth, at two years, at ten years, and at eighteen years of age (Werner, Bierman, & French, 1971; Werner & Smith, 1977). The study showed that by eighteen years of age, more than 50 percent of this predominantly lower socioeconomic status sample had learning or emotional problems. Severe perinatal stress was associated with later impairments in cognitive, physical, and emotional functioning, but only when accompanied by adverse environmental stressors. Moderate perinatal stress had a weaker association with later impairments. This study also documented the importance of early child-rearing factors as a crucial variable having an impact on adolescent developmental outcome (Werner & Smith 1977).

The Seattle Longitudinal Prospective Study has carefully documented the developmental outcomes of infants prenatally exposed to alcohol. The study began in 1974 and has followed a cohort from birth to young adulthood with assessments during the mother's pregnancy, neonatal day one and two, and at four, seven, eleven, fourteen, and twenty-one years. It is currently studying the twenty-five-year developmental outcome quantifying the complex psychiatric disorders present. The classic FAS or more recent conceptualization of FASD (Fetal Alcohol Spectrum Disorder) are not in DSM-IV (Streissguth & O'Malley, 2000).

Psychological CNS Insult

This includes adolescents who were exposed to depriving, damaging, or abusive rearing environments. The impact of these environmental factors may be of critical importance in the emotional and physical development of the adolescent (Gottried, 1973; Parmalee, Sigman, Kopp, & Haber, 1975; Werner & Smith, 1977; Sameroff, 1983; O'Dougherty & Wright, 1992). In the early 1960s, many studies tended to show that most children with perinatal hazards developed normally, and the ones who did not develop normally usually came from socially disadvantaged homes (Sameroff & Chandler, 1975). As medical technology progressed, the advent of noninvasive brain imaging techniques began to show that the serious adverse psychiatric and developmental sequelae were evident mainly in the survivors who had experienced periventricular or intraventricular hemorrhage (Stewart, 1983; Rutter & Schopler, 1992). Therefore, the good outcome in the remaining group was mainly a function of their not having experienced perinatal brain damage. The DSM-IV category reactive attachment disorder addresses the social relatedness problems in these children, but does not address the neurodevelopmental implications of the psychological CNS insult in the children or the possible longer-term sequelae for teenagers.

Another major psychosocial adverse event, the early death of a parent, has been linked with subsequent youth and adult depression. Here again, more recent research has revealed that early parental death has a long-term psychiatric vulnerability effect only if it is intertwined with a serious lack of affectionate parental care (Brown, 1988).

A more recent review has surveyed the biological effect of child abuse and neglect on the brain (Glaser, 2000). The process of early brain development is constantly modified by environmental influences. It has been shown by previous animal and human research that there are sensitive periods during early brain development that can negatively or positively affect brain maturation (Glaser, 2000). These sensitive periods can be seen as a small window of vulnerability, need, or opportunity.

Developmental Comorbidity: Too Important to Ignore

Developmental comorbidity in youth is a product of genetic or acquired biological factors, or both. Genetic research is rapidly expanding our knowledge of specific genetic disorders and their neuropsychiatric presentations. Similarly, the public health and psychosocial research is clearly quantifying the long-term neuropsychiatric legacy of prenatal, perinatal, and neonatal insults that have an impact on development. Finally, both genetic and acquired biological factors involved in developmental comorbidity in youth are modulated by the impact of depriving, damaging, or abusive rearing environments. The challenge for mental heath professionals, psychiatrists, educators, social workers, and probation officers in including developmental comorbidity in their system of care program is to find a common language. At the moment, the American Psychiatric Association's standard psychiatric nomenclature DSM-IV all but ignores developmental disability and its psychiatric sequelae from childhood to adulthood. This inhibits adequate cross-discipline descriptions and also is a major barrier to service and research funding for youth with developmental disability.

MEDICAL COMORBIDITY

There are no definitive prevalence figures for general acute and chronic medical illnesses in youth.

Comorbid medical illnesses may present as a psychiatric disorder, increase the morbidity of a preexisting psychiatric disorder, or significantly disrupt the emotional and psychological development of the youth and increase the stress and emotional burden of his or her family.

One of the commonest influences of the chronic medical disorders is one of mimicking or introducing a depressive or even a bipolar disorder. This clinical effect of comorbid medical illnesses on the psychiatric disorder of the youth can be divided into two main components: acute organic reactions and chronic organic reactions.

Acute Organic Reactions

The comorbid medical issues are not just of a chronic nature; many acute medical problems can dramatically change the presentation and response to therapy of a psychiatric disorder (see Figure 13.1). In this medical comorbid condition, the clinical onset is always sudden, although when the condition is minor in degree, it may not reveal itself in an obvious fashion. The majority of acute organic reactions are reversible when the underlying pathology can be remedied. However, some may progress to a chronic organic syndrome, such as when an acute posttraumatic psychotic disorder remediates, only to reveal an underlying enduring amnestic syndrome.

The clinical pictures that result are basically due to the disruption of normal brain function as a result of biochemical, electrical, or mechanical disturbances (Lishman, 1998). The premorbid personality and familial background of the youth will color this clinical picture, especially when the intensity of emotional disturbance or delusional thinking is concerned. This differential aspect of illness behavior is also seen in response to minor infections and affections (Mechanic, 1978).

Neurological Disorders

Huntington's Chorea, complex partial seizure disorder, absence seizure, grand mal seizure, postictal state, Kleine-Levin syndrome

Infectious Diseases

encephalitis, meningitis, HIV infection and AIDS, streptococcal infection, septicemia, pneumonia, influenzas, typhoid, typhus, cerebral malaria, trypanosomiosis, rheumatic chorea, infectious mononucleosis, viral pneumonia, viral or serum hepatitis, subacute meningovascular syphilis

Trauma

acute posttraumatic psychosis

Space-Occupying Lesion

cerebral tumor, subdural hematoma, cerebral abscess

Metabolic Disorders

uremia, liver disorder, electrolyte disturbances, alkalosis, acidosis, hypercapnia, porphyria, remote effects of carcinoma

Endocrine Disorders

hyperthyroid crises, myxedema, Addisonian crises, hypopituitarism, hypo- or hyperparathyroidism, diabetic pre-coma, hypoglycemia

Vascular Disorders

acute cerebral thrombosis or embolism, transient ischemic attack, subarachnoid hemorrhage, hypertensive encephalopathy, systemic lupus erythematosus, iron deficiency anemia, acute intermittent porphyria

Toxic Disorders

alcohol, drugs, benzodiazepines, salicylate intoxication, cannabis, LSD

Vitamin Lack

B12 or folic acid deficiency

FIGURE 13.1. Acute Organic Reactions in Youth.

Sources: Lishman (1998); Papolos and Papolos (1999).

There are six main areas of where an acute medical comorbid condition may affect the clinical presentation of the youth's psychiatric disorder (Lishman, 1998): impairment of consciousness, psychomotor behavior, thinking, memory, perception, and emotion. This involves the presence of a significant medical condition that is poorly controlled or potentially life threatening in the absence of close medical management. This includes uncontrolled diabetes mellitus, debilitating cardiac disease, severe liver disease, severe alcohol withdrawal, or medical complications during pregnancy or the puerperium.

Chronic Organic Reactions

These reactions can be subtle at first, but gradually they begin to have a major psychiatric impact on the person's comorbid psychiatric disorder. They also can lead to a major psychiatric disorder, such as a major depressive disorder or even an eating disorder. Again, it is useful to clinically assess the impact of a chronic organic condition (see Figure 13.2) in the six areas of neuropsychiatric function as suggested by Lishman (1998): impairment of consciousness, psychomotor behavior, thinking, memory, perception, and emotion.

Chronic medical illnesses also have a multilayered impact on the youth and family. These illnesses challenge the autonomy and omnipotence of the youth and can have sustained effects on self-esteem and self-worth. This is a time when identity is being formed, and the youth is planning his or her future. The chronic

---

Neurological Disorders
epileptic dementia

Infectious Disorders
HIV-associated dementia, subacute and chronic encephalitis

Trauma
Posttraumatic dementia

Space-Occupying Lesions
Cerebral tumor, subdural hematoma, central nervous system tumors, lung or brain cancer with metastases

Metabolic Disorders
uremia, liver disease, carcinoma remote effects

Endocrine Disorders
diabetes, hypoglycemia, hyper- or hypothyroidism, Cushing's disease, Addison's disease, myxedema, hypopituitarism, hypo- and hyperparathyroidism, hypoglyemia

Nutrtional Disorders
pernicious anemia, pellagra

Metal Intoxications
manganese, mercury, thallium

Other Diseases
chronic fatigue syndrome, Lyme disease

FIGURE 13.2. Chronic Organic Reactions in Youth.

Sources: Lishman (1998); Papolos and Papolos, 1999).

illness presents a foreshortened future and changes the adolescent's wishes and dreams. Understandably, the youth may become quite severely depressed with feelings of hopelessness and helplessness. The youth has to cope with regular and sometimes invasive medical interventions, such as daily injections of insulin or cytotoxic medications with many unpleasant side effects. Not uncommonly, the youth becomes socially isolated from his or her peer group because of the chronic debilitating effect of the medical illness. He or she has to withdraw from sports or group activities such as band or drama and sometimes enter a life over-powered by a chronic sick role (Mechanic, 1978). The long-term debilitating effects of illnesses such as cystic fibrosis, asthma, or neurological disorders impair the teenager's normal emotional and even physical development (Pearson, Pumariega, & Seilheimer, 1991; Hodapp, 1998). The deviations in physical maturation and growth from the chronic medical disorders can result in major body image problems, especially in teenage girls. Sometimes these body image problems may usher a true psychiatric eating disorder (Pumariega, Pursell, Spock, & Jones, 1986).

The youth's chronic medical disorder also affects the parents, who are often overcome with marked anticipatory grief and unable to come to terms with the anticipated loss of their idealized son or daughter. The family burden or stress of managing the daily routines of medical treatments can take their toll on the most resilient of families. Sometimes daily and weekly schedules of schooling, specialist visits, psychological therapy, occupational therapy, work, or social activities have to become organized around the timing of injections or medications. The logistical problems in organizing these schedules can become almost a full-time job in itself. The compliance or noncompliance of the youth to the prescribed medical treatment can often become a battleground between the parent and the youth. The severe medical incapacity of the youth may force the parent into a reluctant medical caregiver role (Pumariega, Pearson, & Seilheimer, 1993). This family burden may lead to what is called altruistic filicide, where the parent ends the child or teenager's life ostensibly because it is of poor quality. A recent well-publicized case in Canada involved a father who killed his medically and developmentally disabled teenage daughter, Tracy, claiming that the act was because of his compassion and pity for her life (Petersilia, Foote, & Crowell, 2001). The issues of chronic depression or compassion fatigue are very real in parents of youth with chronic medical disorders and become compounded by the presence of other comorbidities (Figley, 1995; O'Malley & Gelo, in press).

PSYCHIATRIC COMORBIDITY

It has been estimated that 20 percent of youth have psychiatric disorders (U.S. Department of Health and Human Services, 1999). The concept of comorbid psychiatric disorders is an appreciation of the clinical observation that a number of psychiatric disorders are frequently linked with one another. It is important to pay attention to these comorbid psychiatric disorders as some of them may appear hidden at first and may be unmasked by treatment—for example, the long-term usage of selective serotonin reuptake inhibitors (SSRIs) in a FASD youth with anxiety disorder unmasking a marked affective instability with a rapid cycling manic depressive quality. Here we look at some of the common psychiatric conditions that have been shown to occur together.

ADHD and Bipolar Disorder

Researchers found that 94 percent of a sample of forty-three children with mania also met the DSM-IIR (American Psychiatric Association, 1986) criteria for ADHD (Biederman, Newcorn, & Sprich, 1991). This becomes especially problematic in adolescents who may exhibit euphoria or excitedness as a result of treatment with psychostimulants for ADHD. It is probably prudent to clarify the family history of the adolescent or youth and see if there is loading for either mood/bipolar disorder or ADHD. Current concepts of early-childhood-onset bipolar disorder are beginning to throw light on the inappropriate response of certain youth to psychostimulants for their supposed ADHD. It is beginning to be shown that the patients showing marked euphoria or excitedness may in fact have a comorbid or even primary bipolar disorder, which necessitates a different psychopharmacological treatment. Some researchers dispute the association between ADHD and bipolar disorder, seeing them as two distinct entities (Kraeplin, 1921; Anthony & Scott, 1960). Other clinicians and researchers feel that the ADHD predates the development of bipolar disorder in some adolescents (Popper, 1996; Geller & Luby, 1997; Carlson, Fennig, & Bromet, 1994; Wozniak & Biederman, 1996).

ADHD with Anxiety Disorder

Many studies have demonstrated the comorbid occurrence of anxiety disorders with ADHD. It is generally accepted that 20 percent of ADHD children and adolescents have differing varieties of anxiety disorder (for example, generalized anxiety disorder, panic attacks, phobic anxiety, or PTSD). The negative response to a pschostimulant may be one of the indicators of a comorbid anxiety disorder, or a difference in test performance and daily school functioning may herald the onset of significant performance anxiety, which inhibits academic function. This performance could have many roots, such as a generalized anxiety or panic attack or even phobic anxiety.

ADHD with Conduct Disorder

Longitudinal studies have shown the presence of conduct disorder with ADHD in adolescents and youth. These youth are more likely to also be involved in substance use, which impairs their function further and leads to possible involvement with the law. The violence and aggression associated with the conduct disorder should not be minimized, as it may involve fire setting, cruelty to animals, or destruction of property. Not uncommonly, the youth with ADHD and conduct disorder has shown oppositional defiant disorder as a child. In these patients, it is imperative to do a full family assessment because the confounding issues of family violence or abuse have a major impact on response to therapy.

Mood Disorder and Anxiety Disorder

Many authors have written about the comorbidity of these two disorders (Maser & Cloninger, 1990; Kendler, 1996). A recent World Health Organization (WHO) collaborative study investigated the form, frequency, course, and outcome of common psychological problems in primary care settings at fifteen international sites. Initially, 25,916 adults who consulted health care services were screened, and then in-depth assessments were done on a sample of 5,438.The diagnostic codes used were from the International Classification of Diseases, Tenth Edition (ICD-10). The prevalence of the mood disorder was 12.5 percent (depression and dysthymia), and anxiety disorder was 7.9 percent for generalized anxiety disorder and 4.1 percent for panic disorder and agoraphobia (Sartorious, Ustun, Lecrubier, & Wittchen, 1996). Nearly half of the patients who had a depressive disorder or an anxiety disorder were not recognized as having either disorder by the primary care physicians who saw them. Also, approximately half of the cases of depression and anxiety appeared in the same patients at the same time (Sartorious et al., 1996).

Mood Disorder and Obsessive Compulsive Disorder

Studies have shown the overlap of these two psychiatric conditions. Sometimes the mood disorder predates the obsessive compulsive disorder (OCD), and at other times, it is the other way round. One major study of 217 children with OCD revealed that 69 percent had mood disorder diagnoses.

Conduct Disorder and Mood Disorder

Studies have indicated the prevalence of the association of conduct disorder and mood disorder. Kutcher, Pareton, and Korenblum (1989) showed the comorbidity of bipolar disorder with conduct disorder in a group of ninety-six adolescent inpatients (Kutcher et al., 1989). This was replicated by Kovacs and Pollack (1995) in their study of twenty-six bipolar youth. The associations of these two disorders have posed some interesting clinical questions. Are conduct disorder symptoms directly associated with bipolar disorder as a co-occurring disorder and therefore implying that they have common genetic origins? Are the conduct disorder symptoms in youth expressed primarily during full episodes of mania or hypomania, implying that these conduct behavior symptoms are motivated and mediated by the mood disorder?

Treatment Implications

The existence of two comorbid psychiatric disorders has many implications for management, not the least being the correct balance of medication. The art and science of this area is to assess carefully for the possibility of two psychiatric disorders. As was shown in the WHO study on depression and anxiety, it was not uncommon to find that the primary physicians did not see the comorbid anxiety with the depression or vice versa (Sartorious et al., 1996). Youth with comorbid psychiatric disorders offer a particular challenge for psychiatrists because these disorders are commonly camouflaged by comorbid substance use.

Long-Term Implications

There may be an association between nonpsychotic psychiatric diagnoses in adolescence and adult-onset schizophrenia. The National Institute of Mental Health (NIMH) Epidemiological Catchment Area Study revealed that adolescents with OCD, social phobia, panic attacks, and schizotypal personality had an increased risk of subsequent schizophrenia. As well as this study, it has been demonstrated that Minnesota Multiphasic Personality Inventory (MMPI) traits of depression, anxiety, internalized anger, social alienation, and withdrawal are associated with increased risk of the future development of schizophrenia. Finally, a prodromal disorder, which includes subnormal IQ, withdrawal, social behavior, conduct and adjustment abnormalities and mild neurological deficits in children and youth has been associated with a higher risk for the onset of schizophrenia (Tien & Eaton, 1992; Steinhausen, Meier, & Angst, 1998; Carter, Parmas, Cannon, Schulsinger, & Mednick, 1999; Johnson et al., 1999; Weiser et al., 2001).

SYSTEM ISSUES IN THE CARE OF YOUTH WITH COMORBID DISORDERS

The history of systems of care may have arisen out of the frequent finding of comorbidity not just in youth, but also adults and children. Psychiatric comorbidity has been consistently implicated in the functional impairment of youth with serious emotional disturbance (Greenbaum et al., 1996; Petrilia, Foster-Johnson, & Greenbaum, 1996). In a recent description of adolescents served in the Center for Mental Health Services system of care programs, for example, significant impairment was found in youth with comorbidity of substance abuse diagnoses and other disorders (Liao, Manteuffel, Paulic, & Sondheimer, 2001). The standardized clinical Level of Care Utilization System (LOCUS) developed by the American Association of Community Psychiatrists came out of a need to address the complex service requirements of adults with mental disorders and comorbid substance use disorders.

A young adult with paranoid schizophrenia is hospitalized in a chronic care institution. He responds well to reality group therapy and standard antipsychotic agents. He is discharged into a halfway house and a few weeks later is found by the police dodging the traffic on a busy freeway. A psychiatric reassessment reveals the deep-rooted comorbid depression with active suicidal ideation and the undiagnosed long-standing alcohol abuse that had masked his depression. The recognition of the comorbid psychiatric disorders with substance abuse precipitated a change in management strategy, with more active involvement of staff trained in addictions.

General Impact on Systems of Care

The existence and complexity of a large clinical population of youth with co-morbid disorders has forced systems of care to collaborate on management. Often this is out of medical or psychiatric necessity because of the acuteness of the clinical problem—for example, a youth with chronic depression and acute symptoms of Ecstasy overdose who passes out in a social service group home facility or an acutely suicidal or aggressive youth with FASD who impulsively tries to hang himself in the locker room while attending a special education class.

An adopted thirteen-year-old Native American teenage girl attending a small town school hits one of her classmates. She explains to the teacher that she "was told to do it." The teenager is suspended from the school pending a psychiatric assessment. The psychiatrist reviews the clinical history, which includes significant exposure to prenatal alcohol with no birth family history of schizophrenia. The patient describes a recurrent male voice that tells her to do things such as hit people and destroy property. She also describes recurrent visual hallucinations of monsters and dark shapes in the room day and night. Sometimes the patient has loss of memory (and possible loss of consciousness) around these events. There has been no history of abuse in the youth. A sleep-deprived electroencephalogram reveals temporal lobe slowing with the possibility of complex partial seizure disorder to be explored. The patient has been previously diagnosed as severe ADHD, but has been unresponsive to standard psychostimulant medication, which appeared to make her worse. The girl is quite emotionally volatile, with her moods changing rapidly on a daily basis. General clinical examination revealed no classic FAS dysmorphology signs but did reveal complex learning and social language deficits consistent with ARND. There was no history of developmental delay in either of her birth parents.

A psychiatric formulation described the teenager as having a psychotic disorder due to general medical condition of prenatal alcohol exposure with clinical evidence of ARND. The differential diagnosis included affective instability due to the general medical condition of prenatal alcohol exposure with clinical evidence of ARND and the possibility of a complex partial seizure disorder, which needs to be out ruled by a pediatric neurologist's assessment. A change of medication to carbamazepine and risperidone has had a sustained positive effect on the teenager, with no further explosive episodes, a decrease in auditory and visual hallucinations, and stability in mood.

The psychiatric consultation enabled the school system, which had expelled her, to be more sensitive to the unseen neuropsychiatric symptoms. School officials are reviewing the previous psychological testing and will be adding neuropsychological testing and age-appropriate testing for psychotic ideation. The consultation also mobilized the local social service system, which has added regular respite care to the multimodal management program of the youth. This acknowledges the complexity of the comorbidity in this youth and the adoptive parents' need for planned relief to avoid compassion fatigue. Ironically, the adoptive father is a senior social service provider and has been aware of his adoptive daughter's complex neuropsychiatric problems for some time. It was the school suspension and subsequent unraveling of the comorbid clinical issues that verified, and validated, the astute father's concerns, as well as mobilizing a multisystem approach to management.

Clinical Impact on Systems of Care

Systems of care services may not have sufficiently trained residential, medical, psychiatric, or psychological personnel who understand the interaction of these different comorbidities; for example the substance abuse staff may have no basic medical knowledge and do not know how to assess hypoglycemia in a youth with a history of drug usage and insulin-dependent diabetes. An adolescent medical hospital outpatient may be unable to follow a complicated medication regime because of unrecognized cognitive problems in memory and computation due to a developmental disability. An adolescent addiction psychiatrist may refuse to assess the addictive risk of a patient with FAS because the patient's problem is organic and not amenable to group therapy. Or a psychologist or social worker who has the responsibility for primary management of a youth with comorbid disorders does not recognize the acute medical risks of certain medications with certain medical or developmental disorders. These would include cardiac problems or seizure problems.

A nineteen-year-old male youth with Asperger's disorder is involved in a supported independent living program in an inner-city community. The program consists of a residential placement in a caregiver home and a daily community program, which consists of volunteer work at a food bank, formal exercise, and social skills group and individual training. He has a history of obsession with fire and matches. The caregiver staff at the home expressed concern to the politic and to the consulting psychiatrist that critical ingredients for making explosives, such as wire, magnesium, and other flammable materials, were missing from a new housing development where the youth had been seen. A community police interviewed the youth and coordinated a search of his bedroom, which turned up only a long cable wire. Further clinical assessment revealed the youth to be acutely depressed because he had been abandoned by his one friend (a youth with similar traits).

The residential placement had broken down largely due to the inexperience of those working in the residential home and their suspicion of the youth. The staff had misunderstood his tendency to hide himself away in his room as a sign that he was guilty of a possible crime, and the youth became irritable and argumentative at the day program and when visiting his parents. It was only when he was clinically assessed by the psychiatrist after a case management meeting that the acute depressive features and acute feelings of low self-esteem and low self-worth were revealed. His friend had abandoned him because he would not cooperate in stealing computer parts to start a small cottage industry in specialized computer parts. His social language deficits (including alexithymia) made it hard for him to express his feelings. After he could be understood and with a small increase in his SSRI, the youth became much more settled.

The community developmental disability staff, community police liaison worker, and the parents were able to see the true depression that the youth had been experiencing, and he was moved to a residential home with more empathetic and better-trained staff. The psychiatric disorder was an important comorbid clinical issue, which had implications across the systems

Youth with comorbid disorders have an ability to shine a bright light on the lack of training and broad clinical competence within agencies. They also challenge the collaboration between medical and nonmedical agencies. Yet their service needs dictate mutual understanding and respect between the agencies. This includes the understanding that no one agency "owns" the youth with comorbid disorder because the very nature of the problems mandates a multisystem approach.

A fifteen-year-old teenage boy with insulin-dependent diabetes and a long history of conduct disorder and depression is living in a social service group home facility. The group home has no nursing, physician, or psychiatrist consultation and relies on a clinical social worker consultant. The staff is constantly bringing the youth to the local hospital emergency department because he passes out regularly in the group home. The youth is not in school because the school is afraid of its liability if he passes out in the school setting and injures himself. Thorough endocrinological and psychiatric assessments are eventually done and reveal that the youth is deliberately injecting himself with higher dosages of insulin as a self-destructive act. The higher insulin causes episodes of severe hypoglycemia, and so the cycle begins. The social service agency had been frozen in a belief that the medical model was not appropriate for this youth and saw the trips to the hospital emergency department as a systemic intervention of aversive therapy that would eventually stop the youth from passing out.

The case was managed when the youth was transferred to a residential facility with nursing staff available to monitor his insulin level daily and with a weekly pediatric and psychiatric consultation available. His depression and acute and chronic suicidal ideation were addressed by more rigorous cognitive behavioral psychotherapy and psychiatric antidepressant therapy. The youth became more settled clinically and returned to school in a regular class.

A collaborative interagency approach is essential when dealing with youth with comorbid disorders. This is really the true essence of management of this patient population. By their very nature, these youth first appear in different agency settings. A youth with developmental disability appears in the school setting. A youth with substance use appears in a drug rehabilitation residential unit.

A youth with a medical disorder appears in a physician's office. And a youth with a psychiatric disorder appears in a psychiatrist's or psychologist's clinic. Only with a clear interagency approach can these youth be properly served.

The impact of comorbid issues ultimately shows in the level of the youth's functional ability. This can be formally assessed using standardized adaptive function instruments such as the Vineland Adaptive Behavioral scales. In the school setting, it will offer a template for the school's individualized education plan (IEP) for the youth. This can often facilitate a shift from a formal academic stream to a more holistic work experience and vocational level. School meetings with the psychiatrist, teacher, parent, and psychologist are a means to fine-tune such an IEP. This model of intradisciplinary case management is also relevant for the youth in juvenile detention or a group home setting. It is imperative to approach the interagency management of the comorbid issues by translating them into the common vernacular of functional ability given all the comorbid constraints.

Here are some examples of system collaboration in youth with comorbid disorders:

Mental health and addictive services: A youth with depression and substance use is managed in a dual diagnosis (psychiatric disorder and addictive disorder) clinic setting.

Mental health and school services: A youth with FAS is placed in a special education class with regular psychiatric consultation.

Mental health and juvenile justice system: A youth with ADHD and conduct disorder is placed on a year's probation for stealing from a department store. He is followed by the probation officer in collaboration with the treating psychiatrist.

Mental health and general medical services: A severely asthmatic youth with chronic depression is followed closely by his pediatrician and psychologist in a consultation liaison clinic. The community psychiatrist is also involved in medication and family therapy management.

Mental health and social services: A youth is removed from his home because of family violence and placed in a group home. He is acutely depressed and abusing alcohol and is managed by collaboration between the social service workers and the community psychiatrist.

The population of youth with comorbid disorders highlights the danger of a single disease specialty model of service. This is a legacy of the traditional medical model, where patients presented with a primary disorder and all their problems were seen as stemming from that one disorder. It is important for psychiatrists and other mental health professionals to embrace the importance of comorbid disorders, which occur across disciplines. An approach seen in some addiction services where youth with neuropsychiatric and neurodevelopmental histories are excluded is a shortsighted assessment. Furthermore, psychiatric disease clinics where everything is attributed to the bipolar disorder or the schizophrenic disorder are out of step with holistic family-centered management. The recognition of the dynamic equilibrium that exists in these youth with comorbid disorders is not only clinically enriching and insightful, but also common sense.

Youth Exhibiting Four Comorbidities

A twenty-three-year-old Native American adult female with alcohol-related neurodevelopmental disorder is diagnosed with a quadruple comorbidity: psychiatric disorder, substance disorder, developmental, and medical.

Psychiatric Disorder

Axis I. Affective instability due to general medical condition of prenatal alcohol exposure with clinical evidence of ARND (DSM-IV)

Differential Diagnosis

- Posttraumatic stress disorder, early onset, and chronic variety with a long history of early physical abuse and physical neglect and the possibility of sexual abuse.
- Substance use disorder. Some evidence of early-onset intermittent alcohol abuse, which may have biological origins in the prenatal alcohol exposure (Baer et al., 1998).
- Somatization disorder (Briquet syndrome). The patient has a history of mild mental retardation and early-onset physical abuse and neglect.

Axis II. Patient has a history of mild mental retardation. Complex Learning disorders with mathematics disorder and disorder of written expression, Evidence of mixed receptive/expressive language disorder. Personality features consistent with borderline personality disorder, which may have a psychological etiology in history of abuse and a biological etiology in history of prenatal alcohol exposure (Seiver & Davis, 1991).

Axis III. History of prenatal alcohol exposure with evidence of ARND. Evidence of alcohol related birth defects (ARBD). Investigation for VSD as an infant. Possible renal disorder, abnormal serum creatinine. Seizure disorder; patient had afebrile seizure at 6 months and 12 months and was treated with phenobarbital for seven years from 1 year to 8 years. Recent grand mal seizure was apparently precipitated by high anxiety (panic attack). Gross and fine motor problems in balance and coordination, suggesting cerebellar dysfunction. Neurocognitive deficits. Patient has problems in visual and auditory memory.

Family and Community Context

Patient is of Haida origin and was adopted into a Caucasian family at 12 years of age. She lives in a small town, and her two adoptive siblings are her actual natural brother and sister. She works occasionally as a caregiver for foster children in the care of her adoptive grandmother, who lives in the same town. The patient has little contact with her birth mother, last one year ago, but very much identifies with Haida customs and traditions. Patient had major problems throughout her school life and was bullied a lot. She failed in many subjects and received a Grade XII Handicapped Certificate.

Medical History

Patient had failure to thrive and evidence of physical and emotional neglect in infancy. There is also a history of recurrent pneumonia and chronic abdominal pain in early childhood. Patient had investigation for possible Ventricular Septal Defect, with a cardiac murmur in infancy.

Psychiatric and Psychological History

At 10 years of age, a child psychiatrist diagnosed the patient with adjustment reaction of childhood and mild mental retardation. Also commented that the cultural factors were an added stressor. No treatment or follow-up.

At 14 years of age, mental health therapist diagnosed posttraumatic stress disorder related to transgenerational alcohol abuse, as well as physical and emotional abuse. Sexual abuse suspected but not disclosed. A psychotherapeutic approach was used to treat the patient's emotional problems and potential for alcohol addiction, as the therapist suspected the patient's sugar craving was related to alcohol addiction.

At 21 years of age, a developmental pediatrician commented on the patient's prenatal alcohol as being contributory to mental handicap. Also commented on the patient's compulsive drinking of water and mouthwash containing alcohol from late childhood. No follow-up.

At 21 years of age, there was a psychiatric hospitalization with a diagnosis of Conversion Disorder. No follow-up.

The patient is currently seeing a counselor in her small town and receiving psychotherapy for posttraumatic stress disorder. There is no previous psychological testing

Current Investigations and Treatment

1. Fasting and 2 hour post-meal blood sugar normal.
2. CBC, thyroid indices, B12, folic acid, liver function test normal
3. Serum creatinine abnormal, low, needs repeat.
4. Urinalysis for routine and microscopic (24 hour urine for creatinine clearance, protein, glucose and calcium may need to be done).
5. Electrocardogram done (normal).
6. Sleep-deprived EEG has been done after recent grand mal seizure, abnormal, but needs repeating after period of anticonvulsant functioning.
7. WAIS Adult IQ test ordered to clarify intellectual verbal and performance achievement. The patient's cognitive functioning has been complicated by the fact that she took phenobarbital for seven years, and this medication is known to have a negative effect on cognitive functioning (Farwell et al., 1990).
8. Vineland Adaptive Behavior Scale to assess functional disability ordered. Functional assessment, best to use Vineland Adaptive Behavior Scales as tested in this patient population. This assesses functional ability in three areas: communication, daily living skills, and socialization.
9. Language assessment, especially of social communication and cognition.
10. Discussion with adoptive mother regarding developmental disability services, including patient's dependency regarding managing her own affairs.

11. Referral to adult neurologist for seizure disorder.
12. MRI of brain to rule out deficits in corpus callosum, cerebellum, and hippocampus.
13. Initial medication: Neurontin 100 mg BID initially for anxiety and seizure control, increased to 300 mg, 100 mg, and 300 mg. Patient took medication for a month and then stopped because her adoptive parents were not supportive of medication.
14. Connect with therapist in town to start dyadic therapy between adoptive mother and patient as they have arguments daily.

Consultations

1. General medical examination by family physician or internist important to rule out any ARBD. Patient is scheduled to have an ultrasound of the kidney to assess for structural abnormalities.
2. Adult neurologist to assess neurological function, because FASD is a chronic neuropsychiatric disorder. Patient has had a grand mal seizure since initial evaluation and has seen an adult neurologist. She is now taking phenytoin.
3. Adult nephrologist will probably need to be consulted to investigate the renal function further and outrule structural problems related to prenatal alcohol exposure.
4. Family therapist to review the family functioning. The patient has been reassessed by a mental health worker who consults to the developmental disability agency, and it has been recommended that she be moved to a supported independent living placement. This will decrease the ongoing defiance to the adoptive mother and acknowledge the young adult's desire for more independence.
5. Vocational rehabilitation agency to arrange residential supported independent living placement and day program to include a job coach. They will also coordinate with the psychiatrist the issues of adult guardianship and trusteeship (for management of mental handicap and developmental disability funding).

This clinical case illustrates a family–centered approach within a multisystem frame (interagency involvement of health care, mental health, social service, vocational rehabilitation, and cultural). It also shows a multimodal treatment model with individual cognitive behavioral therapy, medication therapy, family therapy, and vocational rehabilitation therapy involving a job coach in the future, as well as support for a supported independent living residential placement to help her individuate from her adoptive parents and establish her own competence (O'Malley & Huffine, 2002).

The young woman is still quite emotionally unstable and may need a period of time in hospital for medical and psychiatric stabilization. This may be organized in tandem with the neurologist's follow-up assessment and the nephrologist's assessment.

IMPLICATIONS FOR MANAGEMENT OF
YOUTH IN COMMUNITY SYSTEMS OF CARE

The comorbid clinical issues with youth and the epidemiological evidence showing their 20 percent prevalence of mental disorder should alert psychiatrists and mental health professionals to screen and diagnose this population carefully (Weissman, Sabshin, & Eist, 1999). The clear implications for existing systems of care are that they need to be sensitive to the range and complexity of comorbid disorders in youth. The American Academy of Child and Adolescent Psychiatry (1997) has delineated clear practice parameters for children and adolescents with substance use disorders. The parameters include clear diagnostic assessment, often using different sources, such as school personnel or juvenile justice personnel, and multimodal treatment options such as twelve-step programs, self-help groups (such as Alcoholics Anonymous and Narcotics Anonymous), family therapy, interpersonal or psychodynamic therapy, psychoeducation, cognitive behavior therapy, and medication therapy (including treatment of withdrawal syndrome, antagonist agents, naltrexone and aversion agents, and disulfiram). They address diagnosis and treatment of comorbid psychiatric disorders, but do not substantially address the possible comorbid developmental or medical conditions as they might affect the clinical presentation and treatment of the adolescent or youth with substance use disorder.

It seems that the most problematic and least understood comorbid issues relate to youth presenting with a psychiatric disorder and a developmental disability, especially if the youth is not mentally retarded. This area is complicated by the almost total absence of diagnostic validation in the standard psychiatric nomenclature of the DSM-IV. This absence often invites professionals to minimize the developmental comorbidity or dismiss it completely. Here the patient is often thought to be deliberately defiant or "telling stories." The issue of the youth's functional ability in relation to school, home, or work is an essential part of the assessment of the impact of the developmental disability. Standardized assessment instruments such as the Vineland Adaptive Behavioral scales (VABS) quantify the youth's functioning in areas such as communication, socialization, and daily living skills. Researchers have shown the difference between IQ and functional ability in developmental populations of patients with FAS and FAE (ARND). These patients not uncommonly have an IQ at least 20 points higher than their functional ability as seen on VABS (Streissguth et al., 1996; Kapp & O'Malley, 2001). This is a concept that needs to be incorporated in all systems of care involved with youth who have comorbid developmental disability, as it is often not the IQ or cognitive ability that is the source of the youth's problems but the level of functional ability. This has more subtle societal ramifications in the ability of a youth with a comorbid developmental disability to parent appropriately or the professional help needed to maintain the parenting attachment and involvement. This type of transgenerational issue has been dealt with in a unique parent-child advocate program for substance-abusing and developmentally delayed FASD mothers that started in Seattle and is now replicated in other parts of Washington State as well as Canada (Grant, Ernst, & Streissguth, 1999).

Acute crisis issues such as potential suicide risk are especially complicated and misunderstood in youth with developmental disability (Huggins, Connor, O'Malley, Barr, & Streissguth, 2001; Huggins, O'Malley, Connor, Barr, & Streissguth, 2002). The most common example is a youth with FASD. There are many services for those with a traditional dual diagnosis, such as a psychiatric disorder and a substance abuse disorder, but these services need to incorporate developmentally appropriate assessments and cognitive rehabilitation. Also, the complex acute and chronic medical comorbid conditions are frequently hidden, and it is probably sensible to have a neurodevelopmental dual diagnosis (dealing with developmental disorders and psychiatric disorders) community clinic or hospital unit formally connected with adolescent medical consultation on a regular basis.

The youth with comorbid substance use, developmental, medical, and psychiatric disorders would fit into a holistic neuropsychiatric consultation liaison center of the future. This type of center might be better organized under the umbrella of a neurodevelopmental assessment and treatment facility. Such a center, the Newcomen Centre, existed at Guy's Hospital in London in the late 1970s. The financial and logistical challenges of operating such a multispecialty consultation assessment center are huge, but the potential saving in chronic disability and future expensive medical and psychiatric complications would be a substantial benefit. For the present, it is suggested that there needs to be an involvement of a wider range of physicians, pediatricians, and psychiatrists with varying backgrounds and expertise. Although the systems of care emphasis has its origins in nonmedical management, it is clear that to address youth with comorbid disorders fully, there needs to be a pool of regular collaborative medical and psychiatric consultation. The systems of care movement should not feel threatened by this apparent medicalization because the incorporation of this approach will strengthen their relevance.

The future of neuropsychiatric diagnosis and treatment is already with us. We now have an expanding area of molecular psychiatry. Recent research into comorbid substance use disorder has demonstrated a molecular basis for this disorder. A transcription factor protein found in the nucleus of a neuron in the nucleus accumbens, DELTA Fos B, has been shown to increase sensitivity to cocaine, morphine, and alcohol, as well as to increase the incentive drive for the same substances. This DELTA Fos B protein has been linked to the CdK5 gene (Nestler, 2002). In parallel with this molecular psychiatric research, we are now becoming involved with preimplantation genetic diagnosis (PGD) and subsequent in vitro intervention. A woman with a gene that was all but certain to cause Alzheimer's disease by her forties has just given birth to a baby free of this defect after having her eggs screened and selected in the laboratory (Tanner, 2002). The linking of these later-onset comorbid conditions to molecular and genetic origins will begin to change the role and style of medical and psychiatric intervention. Youth with certain comorbid disorders may become identified at birth or earlier with these techniques, and the ethical decisions about genetic engineering will start to become more complicated and more frequent. These major changes in medical and psychiatric thinking will need to be incorporated in the systems of care.

References

Alexander, M. J. (1996). Women with co-occurring addictive and mental disorders: An emerging profile of vulnerability. *American Journal of Orthopsychiatry, 66,* 61–70.

Alterman, A. I., & Tarter, R. E. (1986). An examination of selected topologies: Hyperactivity, familial, and antisocial alcoholism. *Recent developments in alcoholism.* Vol. 4. New York: Plenum Press.

American Academy of Child and Adolescent Psychiatry. (1997). Practice parameters for the assessment and treatment of children and adolescents with substance use disorders. *Journal of the American Academy of Child and Adolescent Psychiatry, 36* (Suppl.), 140S–156S.

American Psychiatric Association. (1986). *Diagnostic and statistical manual of mental disorders.* (3rd ed., rev.). Washington, DC: Author.

American Psychiatric Association. (1994). *Diagnostic and statistical manual of mental disorders.* (4th ed.). Washington, DC: Author.

Anthony E. J., & Scott, P. (1960). Manic-depressive psychosis in childhood. *Journal of Child Psychology and Psychiatry,* 1(1), 53–72.

Baer J. S., Barr, H. M., Bookstein, F. L., Sampson, P. D., & Streissguth, A. P. (1998). Prenatal alcohol exposure and family history of alcoholism in the etiology of adolescent alcohol problems. *Journal for the Study of Alcohol, 59,* 533–543.

Baer, J. S., Sampson, P. D., Barr, H. M., Connor, P. D., & Streissguth, A. P. (in press). A twenty-one-year longitudinal analysis of the effect of prenatal alcohol exposure on young adult drinking. *Archives on General Psychiatry.*

Beers, M. H., & Berton, R. (Eds.). (1999). *Merck manual.* (2000). 17th ed. Whitehouse Station, NJ: Merck Research Laboratories.

Biederman, J., Newcorn, J., & Sprich, S. (1991). Comorbidity of attention deficit hyperactivity disorder with conduct, depressive and other disorders. *American Journal of Psychiatry, 148,* 564–577.

Biederman J., Wilens, T., Mick, E., & Farone, S. V. (1997). Is ADHD a risk factor for psychoactive substance use disorders? Findings from a four-year prospective follow-up study. *Journal of the American Academy of Child and Adolescent Psychiatry, 36,* 21–29.

Bond, N. W., & Di Gusto, E. L. (1976). Effects of prenatal alcohol consumption on open field behavior and alcohol preference in rats. *Psychopharmacologia, 46,* 164.

Brady, K., Anton, R., Ballenger, J. C., Lydiard, R. B., Adinoff, B., & Selander, J. (1990). Cocaine abuse among schizophrenic patients. *American Journal of Psychiatry, 147,* 1164–1167.

Breakey, W. R., Calabrese, L., Rosenblatt, A., & Crum, R. M. (1998). Detecting alcohol use disorders in the severely mentally ill. *Community Mental Health Journal, 34,* 165–174.

Broman, S. H., Nichols, R. L., & Kennedy, W. A. (1975). *Preschool IQ: Prenatal and early developmental correlates.* Mahwah, NJ: Erlbaum.

Brown, G. W. (1988). Early loss of a parent and depression in adult life. In S. Fisher & J. Reason (Eds.), *Handbook of life stress, cognition, and health* (pp. 441–465). New York: Wiley.

Brown, V. B., Ridgely, M. S., Pepper, B., & Levine, S. (1989). The dual crises: Mental illness and substance abuse: Present and future directions. *American Psychologist, 44,* 565–569.

Bukstein, O. G., Brent, D. A., & Kaminer, Y. (1989). Comorbidity of substance abuse and other psychiatric disorders in adolescents. *American Journal of Psychiatry, 146,* 1131–1141.

Bukstein, O. G., Glancy, I. J., & Kaminer, Y. (1992). Patterns of affective comorbidity in a clinical population of dually diagnosed substance abusers. *Journal of the American Academy of Child and Adolescent Psychiatry, 31,* 1041–1045.

Carlson, G. A., Fennig, S., & Bromet, E. J. (1994). The confusion between bipolar disorder and schizophrenia in youth: Where does it stand in the 1990s? *Journal of the American Academy of Child and Adolescent Psychiatry, 33,* 543–459.

Carter, J. W., Parmas, J., Cannon, T. D., Schulsinger, F., & Mednick, S. A. (1999). MMPI variables predictive of schizophrenia in the Copenhagen High–Risk Project: A 25 year follow-up. *Acta Psychiatrica Scandinavica, 99,* 432–440.

Casement, P. J. (1980). Review of The Therapeutic Environment by R. J. Langs & J. Aronson (1979). *International Review of Psycho-Analysis, 7,* 525–528.

Chin, M. Y., Kreutzer, R. A., & Dyer, J. E. (1992). Acute poisoning from gamma-hyroxybutyrate in California. *Western Journal of Medicine, 1576,* 380–384.

Cicchetti, D. (1992). A historical perspective on the discipline of developmental psychopathology. In J. Rolf, A. S. Masten, D. Cicetti, K. H. Nuechterlein, & S. Weintraub (Eds.), *Risk and protective factors in the development of psychopathology* (pp. 2–28). Cambridge: Cambridge University Press.

Coggins, T. E., Friet, T., & Morgan, T.. (1998). Analysing narrative productions in older school-age children and adolescents with fetal alcohol syndrome: An experimental tool for clinical applications. *Clinical Linguistics and Phonetics, 12,* 221–236.

Corbett, J. A. (1985). Mental retardation: Psychiatric aspects. In M. Rutter & L. Hersov (Eds.), *Child and adolescent psychiatry* (2nd ed., pp. 663–678). Cambridge, MA: Blackwell.

Creighton, F., Black, D., & Hyde, C. (1991). Ecstasy psychosis and flash-backs. *British Journal of Psychiatry, 159,* 713–715.

Davies, K. E. (1989). *The fragile X syndrome.* New York: Oxford University Press.

DeJong, C. A., Brink, W. V., & Jansen, J. A. (1993). Sex role stereotypes and clinical judgement: How therapists view their alcoholic parents. *Journal of Substance Abuse Treatment, 10,* 383–389.

Dominguez, H. D., Chotro, M. G., & Molina, J. C. (1993). Alcohol in amniotic fluid prior to cesarean section delivery: Effects of subsequent exposure to drug's odor upon alcohol responsiveness. *Behavior and Neural Biology, 60,* 129.

Drake, R. E., & Wallach, M. A. (1989). Substance abuse among the chronically mentally ill. *Hospital and Community Psychiatry, 40,* 1041–1046.

Dreykin, E. Y., Buka, S. I., & Zeena, T. H. (1992). Depressive illness among chemically dependent adolescents. *American Journal of Psychiatry, 149,* 1341–1347.

Einfeld, S. L., & Tonge, B. J. (1996). Population prevalence of psychopathology in children and adolescents with intellectual disability. II. Epidemiological findings. *Journal of Intellectual Disability Research, 90,* 99–109.

Elliott, D. (2001). Child psychiatry grand rounds, University of Washington.

Farwell, R. F., Lee, Y. J., Hirtz, D. G., Sulzbacher, S. I., Ellenberg, J. H., & Nelson, J. B. (1990). Phenobarbital for febrile seizures: Effects on intelligence and on seizure recurrence. *New England Journal of Medicine, 322,* 364–369.

Figley, C. R. (1995). *Compassion fatigue: Coping with secondary traumatic stress disorder in those who treat the traumatized.* New York: Brunner/Mazel.

Folstein, S. E., & Rutter, M. (1988). Autism: Familial aggregation and genetic implications. *Journal of Autism and developmental disorders, 18,* 3–30.

Franzek, E., & Beckmann, H. (1992). Sex differences and distinct subgroups in schizophrenia, a study of 54 chronic hospitalized schizophrenics. *Psychopathology, 25,* 90–99.

Galanter, M., & Kleber, H. D. (Eds.). (1999). *Textbook of substance abuse treatment* (2nd ed.). Washington, DC: American Psychiatric Press.

Gallimberti, L., Spella, M. R., Soncini, C. A., & Gessa, G. L. (2000). Gamma-hydroxybutyric acid in the treatment of alcohol and heroin dependence. *Alcohol, 20,* 257–262.

Garfield, J. M., Garfield, F. B., & Stone, J. G. (1994). A comparison of psychological response to ketamine and thiopental-nitrous-oxide-halothane anaesthesia. *Anaesthesiology, 36,* 329–338.

Geller, B., & Luby, J. (1997). Child and adolescent bipolar disorder: A review of the past ten years. *Journal of the American Academy of Child and Adolescent Psychiatry, 36,* 1168–1176.

Gilberg, C., & O'Brien, G. (Eds.). (2000). *Developmental disability and behavior.* Cambridge: Cambridge University Press.

Gilberg, C., Persson, E., & Grufman, M. (1986). Psychiatric disorders in mildly and severely mentally retarded urban children and adolescents: Epidemiological aspects. *British Journal of Psychiatry, 149,* 68–74.

Glaser, D. (2000). Child abuse and neglect and the brain—A review. *Journal of Child Psychology and Psychiatry, 41,* 97–116.

Glashan, T. H. (2001). Co-morbidity of borderline personality disorder with other personality disorders in hospitalized adolescents and adults. *American Journal of Psychiatry, 157,* 2011–2016.

Gold, M., & Miller, N. (1997). Intoxication and withdrawal from marijuana, LSD, and NMDA. In N. Miller, M. Gold, & D. Smith (Eds.), *Manual of therapeutics for addictions.* New York: Wiley.

Goldstein, J. M., & Tsuang, M. T. (1990). Gender and schizophrenia: An introduction and synthesis of findings. *Schizophrenia Bulletin, 16,* 179–183.

Goldstein, S., & Reynolds, C. R. (Eds.). (1999). *Handbook of neurodevelopmental and genetic disorders in children.* New York: Guilford Press.

Gomez, M. B., Primm, A. B., Tzolova-Iontchev, I., Perry, W., Vu, H. T., & Crum, R. M. (2000). A description of precipitants of drug use among dually diagnosed patients with chronic mental illness. *Community Mental Health Journal, 36,* 351–362.

Gottried, A. W. (1973). Intellectual consequences of perinatal anoxia. *Psychological Bulletin, 80,* 231–242.

Grant, T. M., Ernst, C. C., & Streissguth, A. P. (1999). Intervention with high risk alcohol and drug abusing mothers: 1. Administrative strategies of the Seattle model of paraprofessional advocacy. *Journal of Community Psychology, 27,* 1–18.

Greenbaum, P. E., Dedrick, R. F., Friedman, R. M., Kutash, K., Brown, E. C., Lardieri, S. P., & Pugh, A. M. (1996). National Adolescent and Child Treatment Study (NACTS): Outcomes for children with serious emotional disturbance. *Journal of Emotional and Behavioral Disorders, 4,* 130–146.

Greenbaum, P. E., Foster-Johnson, L., & Petrilia, A. (1996). Co-occurring addictive and mental disorders among adolescents: Prevalence research and future directions. *American Journal of Orthopsychiatry, 66,* 52–60.

Hagerman, R. J. (1999). *Neurodevelopmental disorders: Diagnosis and treatment.* New York: Oxford University Press.

Harris, J. C. (1995). *Developmental neuropsychiatry: Assessment, diagnosis and treatment of developmental disorders.* New York: Oxford University Press.

Health Canada. (1996). *National Longitudinal Survey of Children and Youth.* Ottawa, Ontario: Publications Health Canada, Government of Canada.

Health Canada. (2001). *Mental health and substance abuse disorders.* Ottawa, Ontario: Publications Health Canada, Government of Canada.

Hill, S. Y., & Muka, D. (1996). Childhood psychopathology in children from families of alcoholic female probands. *Journal of the American Academy of Child and Adolescent Psychiatry, 35,* 725–733.

Hodapp, R. M. (1998). *Development and disabilities.* Cambridge: Cambridge University Press.

Howlin, P. (2000, Oct.). *Autism and Asperger syndrome.* Paper presented at the Society for the Study of Behavioral Phenotypes, Sixth International Symposium, Venice.

Huggins, J. E., Connor, P. D., O'Malley, K. D., Barr, H. M., & Streissguth, A. P. (2001, June). Suicidal behavior in adults with fetal alcohol spectrum disorders (FASD). In *Proceedings of the Twenty-Fourth Scientific Meeting of the Research Society of Alcohol.* Montreal, Quebec.

Huggins, J. E., O'Malley, K. D., Connor, P. D., Barr, H. M., & Streissguth, A. P. (2002). *Suicidal behavior in fetal alcohol spectrum disorders (FASD): Epidemiologic and clinical issues.* Canada Journal of Psychiatry.

Johnson, J. G., Cohen, P., Skodol, A. E., Oldham, J. M., Kasen, S., & Brook, J. S. (1999). Personality disorders in adolescence and risk of major mental disorders and suicidality in adulthood. *Archives of General Psychiatry, 56,* 805–811.

Kaminer, Y. (1994). *Adolescent substance abuse: A comprehensive guide to theory and practice.* New York: Plenum Press.

Kaminer, Y., & Tarter, R. E. (1999). Adolescent substance abuse. In M. Galanter & H. D. Kleber (Eds.), *Textbook of substance abuse treatment* (2nd ed., pp. 465–474). Washington DC: American Psychiatric Press.

Kapp, F.M.E., & O'Malley, K. D. (2001). *Watch for rainbows: True stories for educators and caregivers of children with fetal alcohol spectrum disorders.* Calgary, Canada: Frances Kapp Education.

Kasen, S., & Brook, J. S. (1999). Personality disorders in adolescence and risk of major mental disorders and suicidality in adulthood. *Archives of General Psychiatry, 56,* 805–811.

Kendler, K. S. (1996). Major depression and generalized anxiety disorder: Same genes, (partly) different environments—revisited. *British Journal of Psychiatry, 168,* (Suppl. 30), 68–75.

Kessler, R. C., McGonagle, K. A., Zhao, S., Nelson, C. B., Hughes, M., Eshleman, S., Wittchen, H. U., & Kendler, K. S. (1994). Lifetime and 12 month prevalence of DSM III-R psychiatric disorders in the United States: Results from the National Comorbidity Survey. *Archives of General Psychiatry, 51,* 8–19.

Klaehn, R., O'Malley, K., Vaughan, T., Sowers, W., & Kroeger, K. (2002). *Child and Adolescent Level of Care Utilization System (CALOCUS) user's manual, Version 1.2.* Washington, DC: American Academy of Child and Adolescent Psychiatry and American Association of Community Psychiatrists.

Kopp, C. B., & Krakow, J. B. (1983). The developmentalist and the study of biological risk: A view of the past with an eye toward the future. *Child Development, 54,* 1086–1108.

Kovacs, M., & Pollack, M. (1995). Bipolar disorder and comorbid conduct disorder in childhood and adolescence. *Journal of the American Academy of Child and Adolescent Psychiatry, 34,* 715–723.

Kraeplin, E. (1921). *Manic–depressive insanity and paranoia.* Edinburgh: E. & S. Livingstone.

Kuo, Z. Y. (1967). *The dynamics of behavior development.* New York: Random House.

Kutchner, S. P., Pareton, P., & Korenblum, M. (1989). Relationship between psychiatric illness and conduct disorder in adolescents. *Canadian Journal of Psychiatry, 34,* 526–529.

Lehman, A. F., Herron, J. D., Schwartz, R. P., & Myers, C. P. (1993). Rehabilitation for adults with severe mental illness and substance abuse disorders. *Journal of Nervous and Mental Disorders, 181,* 86–91.

Lewinsohn, P. M., Rohde, P., & Seeley, J. (1996). Alcohol consumption in high school adolescents: Frequency of use and dimensional structure of associated problems. *Addiction, 91,* 375–390.

Liao, Q., Manteuffel, B., Paulic, C., & Sondheimer, D. (2001). Describing the population of adolescents served in systems of care. *Journal of Emotional and Behavioral Disorders, 9,* 13–19.

Lilienfield, A. M., & Parkhurst, E. (1951). A study of the association of factors of pregnancy and parturition with the development of cerebral palsy. *American Journal of Hygiene, 53,* 262–282.

Lishman, A. W. (1998). *Organic psychiatry: The psychological consequences of cerebral disorder* (3rd ed., pp. 149–155). Cambridge, MA: Blackwell.

Malhotra, A. K., Pinals, D. A., Weingartner, H., Sirocco, K., Missar, C. D., Pickar, D., & Brerer, A. (1996). NMDA receptor function and human cognition: The effects of ketamine in healthy volunteers. *Neuropharmacology, 14,* 301–307.

Maser, J. D., & Cloninger, C. R. (Eds.). (1990). *Comorbidity of mood and anxiety disorders.* Washington, DC: American Psychiatric Press.

McCann, U., & Ricaurte, G. (1991). Lasting neuropsychiatric sequelae of methylenedioxymethamphetamine (ecstasy) in recreational users. *Journal of Clinical Psychopharmacology, 11,* 302–305.

McCann, U., & Ricaurte, G. (1993). Reinforcing subjective effects of 3,4 methylenedioxymethamphetamine (Ecstasy) may be separable from its neurotoxic actions: Clinical evidence. *Journal of Clinical Psychopharmacology, 13,* 214–217.

McDowell, D. (1999). NMDA, ketamine, GHB, and the "club drug" scene. In M. Galanter & H. D. Kleber (Eds.), *Textbook of substance abuse treatment* (2nd ed., pp. 295–305). Washington, DC: American Psychiatric Press.

Mechanic, D. (1978). Sex, illness, illness behavior, and the use of health services. *Social Science and Medicine, 12B,* 207–214.

Menninger, K. (1938). *Man against himself* (p. 143). New York: Harvest Press.

Milin, R., Halikas, J. A., Meller, J. E., & Morse, C. (1991). Psychopathology among substance abusing juvenile offenders. *Journal of the American Academy of Child and Adolescent Psychiatry, 30,* 569–574.

Miller, B. A., Downs, W. R., Gondoli, D. M., & Keil, A. (1987). The role of childhood sexual abuse in the development of alcoholism in women. *Violence and Victims, 2*, 157–172.

Miller, N. S. (1994). *Treating coexisting psychiatric and addictive disorders.* Center City, MN: Hazelden.

Munro, J. D. (1986). Epidemiology and the extent of mental retardation. In C. Staurakaki (Ed.), *Psychiatric perspectives on mental retardation* (pp. 591–624). Philadelphia: Saunders.

Murphy, K., & Owens, M. J. (1997, Nov.). *The behavioral phenotype in velo-cardio-facial syndrome.* Paper presented at the Seventh Annual Scientific Meeting of the Society for the Study of Behavioral Phenotypes, Cambridge, UK.

Nestler, E. R. (2002, Feb. 28). *The molecular basis of addictive states.* Thirteenth Annual Herbert S. Ripley lecture, University of Washington, Seattle.

Nisbet, R. A. (1969). *Social change and history.* New York: Oxford University Press.

Niswander, K. R., & Gordon, M. (1972). *The women and their pregnancies: The collaborative perinatal study of the National Institute of Neurological Diseases and Stroke.* Philadelphia: Saunders.

O'Dougherty, M., & Wright, F. (1992). Children born at medical risk: Factors affecting vulnerability and resilience. In J. Rolf, A. S. Masten, D. Cichetti, K. H. Neuechterlein, & S. Weintraub (Eds.), *Risk and protective factors in the development of psychopathology* (pp. 120–137). Cambridge: Cambridge University Press.

O'Malley, K. D. (2002). *Comparative health care practices: Canada and the U.S.A.: The political and ethical issues in health care delivery.* Manuscript submitted for publication.

O'Malley, K. D., & Gelo, J. (in press). Family stress in parenting a child or adolescent with FASD. *Iceberg: FAS Newsletter.*

O'Malley, K. D., & Huffine, C. (2002). *Family-centred, multi-system and multi-modal management of fetal alcohol spectrum disorders (FASD): Considerations for community psychiatry considerations.* Unpublished manuscript.

O'Malley, K. D., & Nanson, J. (2002). Clinical implications of a link between fetal alcohol spectrum disorder (FASD) and attention deficit hyperactivity disorder (ADHD). *Canadian Journal of Psychiatry, 47*, 349–354.

Overton, W. (1984). World views and their influence on psychological theory and research: Kuhn-Lakatos-Landan. In H. Reese (Ed.), *Advances in child development and behavior* (Vol. 18, pp. 191–226). Orlando, FL: Academic Press.

Oye, N., Paulsen, O., & Maurset, A. (1992). Effects of ketamine on sensory perception: Evidence for a role of N-methyl D-aspartate receptors. *Journal of Pharmacological Experience, 260*, 1209–1213.

Papolos, D. F., Faedda, G. L., Veit, S., Goldberg, R., Morrow, B., Kucherlapati, R., & Shprintzen, R. J. (1996). Bipolar spectrum disorders in patients diagnosed with velo-cardio-facial syndrome: Does a hemizygous deletion of chromosome 22q11 result in bipolar affective disorder? *Genomics, 12*, 1541–1547.

Papolos, D., & Papolos, J. (1999). *The bipolar child: The definitive and reassuring guide to childhood's most misunderstood disorder.* New York: Broadway Books.

Parmalee, A. H., Sigman, M., Kopp, C. B., & Haber, A. (1975). The concept of a cumulative risk score for infants. In N. R. Ellis (Ed.), *Aberrant development in infancy: Human and animal studies* (pp. 113–121). Mahwah, NJ: Erlbaum.

Pasamanick, B., & Knoblock, H. (1966). Retrospective studies on the epidemiology of reproductive causality: Old and new. *Merrill-Palmer Quarterly of Behavior and Development, 12,* 7.

Pasamanick, B., Knoblock, H., & Lilienfield, A. M. (1956). Socioeconomic status and some precursors of neuropsychiatric disorders. *American Journal of Orthopsychiatry, 26,* 594–601.

Pearson, D. A., Pumariega, A. J., & Seilheimer, D. K. (1991). The development of psychiatric symptomatology in patients with cystic fibrosis. *Journal of the American Academy of Child and Adolescent Psychiatry, 30*(2) 290–297.

Petersilia, J., Foote, J., & Crowell, N. A. (Eds.). (2001). *Crime victims with developmental disabilities: Report of the National Research Council, Committee on Law and Justice.* Washington, DC: National Academy Press.

Petrilia, A. T., Foster-Johnson, L., & Greenbaum, P. E. (1996). Serving youth with mental and substance abuse problems. In B. A. Stroul (Ed.), *Children's mental health: Creating systems of care in a changing society* (pp. 493–511). Baltimore: Brookes.

Piaget, J. (1971). *Biology and knowledge.* Chicago: University of Chicago Press.

Polger, M., & Cabassa, L. (2001, Spring). Continuity of mental health care for young adults. *Focal Point,* 11–12.

Popper, C. (1996). Diagnosing bipolar vs. ADHD: A pharmacological point of view. *Link, 13.*

Pulver, A. E., Nestadt, G., Goldberg, R., Shprintzen, R. J., Lamacz, M., Wolyneic, P. S., Morrow, B., Karayiourgou, M., Anatonarkis, S. E., Housman, D., & Kucherlapati, R. (1994). Psychotic illness in patients diagnosed with velo-cardio-facial syndrome and their relatives. *Journal of Nervous and Mental Disease, 182,* 476–478.

Pumariega, A. J., Pearson, D., & Seilheimer, D. (1993). Family and individual adjustment in children with cystic fibrosis. *Journal of Child and Family Studies, 2,* 109–118.

Pumariega, A. J., Pursell, J., Spock, A., & Jones, J. D. (1986). Eating disorders in adolescents with cystic fibrosis. *Journal of the American Academy of Child and Adolescent Psychiatry, 25*(2) 269–275.

Reese, H., & Overton, W. (1970). Models of development and theories of development. In L. R. Goulet & P. Baltes (Eds.), *Life span developmental psychology: research and theory* (pp. 115–145). Orlando, FL: Academic Press.

Regier, D. A., Farmer, M. E., Rae, D. S., Locke, B. Z., Keith, S. J., Judd, L. L., & Godwin, F. K. (1990). Comorbidity of mental disorders with alcohol and other drug abuse. *Journal of the American Medical Association, 265,* 3511–3518.

Regier, D. A., Farmer, M. E., Rae, D. S., Myers, J.,K., Kramer, M., Robins, L. N., George, L. K., Karno, M., & Locke, B. Z. (1993). One month prevalence of mental disorders in the United States and sociodemographic characteristics: The Epidemiologic Catchment Area study. *Acta Psychiatrica Scandinavica, 88,* 35–47.

Regier, D. A., Narrow, W. E., Rae, D. S., Manderscheid, R. W., Locke, B. Z., & Goodwin, F. K. (1993). The de facto US mental and addictive disorders service system. Epidemiologic Catchment Area prospective 1 year prevalence rates of disorders and services. *Archives of General Psychiatry, 50,* 85–94.

Reis, R. K., Jaffe, C., Comtois, K. A., & Mitchell, M. (1999). Treatment satisfaction compared with outcome in severe dual disorders. *Community Mental Health Journal, 35,* 213–221.

Reiss, R. S. (1990). Prevalence of dual diagnosis in community-based day program in the Chicago metropolitan area. *American Journal of Mental Retardation, 94,* 578–585.

Reyes, E., Garcia, K. D., & Jones, B. C. (1985). Effects of maternal consumption of alcohol on alcohol selection in rats. *Alcohol, 2,* 323.

Rolf, J., Masten, A. S., Cichetti, D., Neuechterlein, K. H., & Weintraub, S. (1992). *Risk and protective factors in the development of psychopathology.* Cambridge: Cambridge University Press.

Russell, O. (Ed.). (1997). *Seminars in the psychiatry of learning disabilities.* London: Royal College of Psychiatrists, Gaskell, and Washington, DC: American Psychiatric Press.

Rutter, M., & Schopler, E. (1992). Classification of pervasive developmental disorders: Some aspects and practical considerations. *Journal of Autism and Developmental Disorders, 22,* 459–482.

Sameroff, A. J. (1983). Developmental systems: Contexts and evolution. In P. Muessen (Ed.), *Handbook of child psychology* (Vol. 1, pp. 237–294). New York: Wiley.

Sameroff, A. J., & Chandler, M. J. (1975). Reproductive risk and the continuum of caretaking casualty. In F. D. Horowitz, M. Hetherington, S. Scarr-Salapetek, & G. Siegel (Eds.), *Review of child development research* (Vol. 4, 187–244). Chicago: University of Chicago Press.

Sampson, P. D, Streissguth, A. P., Bookstein, F. L., Little, R. E., Clarren, S. K., & Dehaene, P. (1997). Incidence of fetal alcohol syndrome and the prevalence of alcohol related neurodevelopmental disorder. *Teratology, 56,* 317–326.

Sandler, J. (1976). Countertransference and role-responsiveness. *International Review of Psychological Analysis, 3,* 43–47.

Santostefano, S. (1978). *A bio-developmental approach to clinical child psychology.* New York: Wiley.

Sareen, J., Chartier, M., Kjewrnisted, K. D., & Stein, M. B. (2001). Comorbidity of phobic disorders with alcoholism in a Canadian community sample. *Canadian Journal of Psychiatry, 46,* 733–740.

Sartorious, N., Ustun, T. B., Lecrubier, Y., & Wittchen, H. U. (1996). Depression co-morbid with anxiety: Results from the WHO study on psychological disorders in primary health care. *British Journal of Psychiatry, 168* (Suppl. 30), 38–43.

Seiver, L. J., & Davis, K. L. (1991). A psychobiological perspective on personality disorders. *American Journal of Psychiatry, 148,* 1647-1658.

Shprintzen, R. J., Goldberg, R., Golding-Kushner, K. J., & Marion, R. (1992). Late onset psychosis in velo-cardio-facial syndrome. *American Journal of Medical Genetics, 42,* 141-142.

Shulgin, A. (1990). History of NMDA. In S. Peroutka (Ed.), *Ecstasy: The clinical, pharmacological and neurotoxicological effects of the drug NMDA* (pp. 1–20). Boston: Kluwer.

Spemann, H. (1938). *Embryonic development and induction.* New Haven, CT: Yale University Press.

Spencer, H. (1896). *The principles of biology* (Vol. 2). New York: Appleton. (Original work published in 1862)

Sprague, J. E., Everman, S. L., & Nichols, D. E. (1998). An integrated hypothesis for the serotonergic axonal loss induced by 3,4 methenedioxymethamphetamine. *Neurotoxicology, 19,* 427–441.

Steinhausen, H. C., Meier, M., & Angst, J. (1998). The Zurich long-term outcome of child and adolescent psychiatric disorders in males. *Psychological Medicine, 28,* 375–383.

Stewart, A. (1983). Severe perinatal hazards. In M. Rutter (Ed.), *Developmental neuropsychiatry* (pp. 15–31). New York: Guilford Press.

Streissguth, A. P., Barr, H.M.M., Kogan, J., & Bookstein, F. L. (1996, Aug.). *Understanding the occurrence of secondary disabilities in clients with fetal alcohol syndrome (FAS) and fetal alcohol effects (FAE)* (Tech. Rep. No. 96–0). Seattle: University of Washington, Fetal Alcohol and Drug Unit.

Streissguth, A. P., & Kanter, J. (1997). *The challenge of fetal alcohol syndrome: Overcoming secondary disabilities.* Seattle: University of Washington Press.

Streissguth, A. P., & O'Malley K. D. (2000). Neuropsychiatric implications and long term consequences of fetal alcohol spectrum disorders. *Seminars in Clinical Neuropsychiatry, 5,* 177–190.

Tanner, L. (2002, Feb. 27). Alzheimer's gene screened out in lab: Baby born without it. *Seattle Post-Intelligencer.*

Tien, A. Y., & Eaton, W. W. (1992). Psychopathological precursors and socio-demographic risk factors for the schizophrenia syndrome. *Archives of General Psychiatry, 49,* 37–46.

Tjossem, T. D. (Ed.). (1976). *Intervention strategies for high risk infants and young children.* Baltimore: University Park Press.

Turk, J. (1992). Fragile X syndrome: Recent developments. *Current Opinion in Psychiatry, 5,* 677–682.

U.S. Department of Health and Human Services. (1999). *Mental health: A report of the surgeon general.* Washington, DC: Center for Mental Health Services, Substance Abuse and Mental Health Administration.

Waddington, C. H. (1957). *The strategy of the genes.* London: Allen & Unwin.

Wallen, J. (1992). A comparison of male and female clients in substance abuse treatment. *Journal of Substance Abuse Treatment, 9,* 243–248.

Watkins, K. E., Shaner, A., & Sullivan, G. (1999). Addictions services. The role of gender in engaging the dually diagnosed in treatment. *Community Mental Health Journal, 35,* 115–126.

Weinberg, N. Z. (1997). Cognitive and behavioral deficits associated with parental alcohol use. *Journal of the American Academy of Child and Adolescent Psychiatry, 35,* 1177–1186.

Weiser, M., Reichenberg, A., Rabinowitz, J., Kaplan, Z., Mordehai, M., Bodner, E., Nahon, D., & Davidson, M. (2001). Association between non-psychotic psychiatric diagnoses in adolescent males and subsequent onset of schizophrenia. *Archives of General Psychiatry, 58,* 959–964.

Weiss, P. A. (1969). *Principles of development.* New York: Hafner.

Weissman, S., Sabshin, M., & Eist, H. (Eds.). (1999). *Psychiatry in the new millennium.* Washington, DC: American Psychiatric Press.

Weisner, C., & Schmidt, I. (1992). Genetic disparities in treatment for alcohol problems. *Journal of the American Medical Association, 268,* 1872–1876.

Werner, E. E., Bierman, J. E., & French, F. E. (1971). *The children of Kauai.* Honolulu: University of Hawaii Press.

Werner, E. E., & Smith, R. S. (1977). *Kauai's children come of age.* Honolulu: University of Hawaii Press.

Werner, H. (1948). *Comparative psychology and mental development.* New York: International Universities Press.

Wing, L. (1993). The definition and prevalence of autism: A review. *European Child and Adolescent Psychiatry, 2,* 61–74.

Wozniak, J., & Biederman, J. (1996). A pharmacological approach to the quagmire of comorbidity in juvenile mania. *Journal of the American Academy of Child and Adolescent Psychiatry, 35,* 826–828.

CHAPTER FOURTEEN

Collaboration with Primary Care

Sharing Risks, Goals, and Outcomes in an Integrated System of Care

Katherine E. Grimes

We now have ample evidence of the great need for attention to mental health disorders among the children in the United States, along with the most specific directive in our history from the government to medical leaders to do something about it (Satcher, 2000). It is also clear that the need exceeds the reach of subspecialty providers and that all clinicians who take care of children need to work together for it to be addressed. New uses of federal dollars, such as the expansion of Medicaid via State Children's Health Insurance Program (SCHIP) and early and periodic screening, diagnosis, and treatment program funding of mental health interventions, are being considered to help pay for this care. Coordination of effort and resources is desirable for providers to have the greatest impact. In addition, the idea that physical and mental well-being are linked is supported by both ancient wisdom and the latest biomedical research (Cohen, 2000; Baum & Garofalo, 1999; Carney et al., 2001). Yet we are starting from a distinct disadvantage in this effort due to the lack of established systems to provide integrated care to children and adolescents.

CHALLENGES TO INTEGRATION

Although most clinical services are not intentionally integrated, the effects of pediatric or child psychiatric care are ultimately integrated within the person of the child. Various influences around the child, most importantly the family and secondarily the school, care delivery system, and community cultures, make that integration either easier or more difficult. The predominant health care model now delivers pediatric and child mental health services in settings that are greatly isolated from each other, with a sea of misunderstanding, mistrust, and frustration between them. In order for greater collaboration to occur, we need to understand the reasons for this, which include conflicting traditions, medical expense and managed care, confidentiality, and, most recently, carve-outs.

Conflicting Traditions

Pediatricians and family practitioners are typically trained to expect to interact with the family in an appointment or a crisis and only rarely to see a child alone. Parents are the immediate "customers" of pediatric recommendations, as well as the parties who implement the majority of the interventions (such as clear fluids, wound care, or nebulizer treatments), which mainly take place at home. Pediatricians or family practitioners are the child's first health care provider and are taught that they need to own the case. Consultation is obtained as needed from pediatric subspecialists who perform recognizable and familiar procedures and then report back recommendations to the pediatrician or family practice provider, who conveys them to the family. Finally, communication about the patient among primary care staff or providers is open, expected, and hindered only by time.

Child psychiatrists and mental health clinicians have been trained within a different tradition: they are expected to interact with the individual in an appointment or crisis and rarely meet with the whole family. Parents historically were peripheral to the interventions (such as play therapy, semistructured interviews, and psychotherapy), which mainly occurred in the office. Child psychiatrists traditionally pick up referrals, which they then keep; they rarely see themselves as pediatric subspecialists and do not expect to function under the direction of the primary care provider. The child mental health clinician is unlikely to be in contact with the primary care doctor at the beginning of treatment, psychiatric assessment and treatment processes are often unfamiliar and mysterious to primary care providers, and recommendations at termination are made to the patient and family but rarely passed on to the pediatrician. Communication about the mental health patient between staff members or providers is complicated, hampered by confidentiality issues and hindered by different vocabularies.

Medical Care Expense and Managed Care

Resource and reimbursement patterns shifted in response to the escalating costs of medical care in the 1980s. Private and public purchasers, primarily employer groups but also government programs such as Medicaid and Medicare, rebelled against the unchecked growth of the fee-for-service health care industry with its incentives aligned toward expenditures. In the new climate of health insurance premium reductions and cost control, managed care became a significant force

(Patterson, 1990; Wickizer & Lessler, 1996). The realignment of incentives toward avoiding expenditures altered care patterns almost overnight. Worries about excessively long, even "frivolous" hospitalizations of adolescents swung instead to worries about hospitals shutting down and being able to get children, first, into the hospital and, second, being able to keep them there when they needed care (Sabin & Daniels, 1999; Smoyak, 2000). To some extent, fragmentation of care is unavoidable in most health care delivery models, including traditional fee-for-service, but the onset of managed care and accountability within a financial cap brought new challenges to care coordination. Although some aspects of health maintenance organizations are actually conducive to integrated care, such as a single medical record, colocation of providers, and comprehensive pharmacy data, these benefits were soon eclipsed by the diminished role of local health maintenance organizations (HMOs) and the rise of national managed care companies. The two medical specialties that were historically the lowest paid, pediatricians and child psychiatrists, now had to compete for the same premium dollars within managed care (where adult "employee" and "members" were the major customers and children an afterthought in most service programming).

The squeeze on mental health and primary care providers limited the previous consultation-liaison opportunities, such as team meetings, in both inpatient and outpatient settings. Even time for hallway consults or telephone contacts was slashed as productivity measures, misguidedly focused on face-to-face contact time, were put into place. Providers not only had less time to coordinate with each other; the shift to adult-driven relative value units (RVUs) for reimbursement meant that previous opportunities to participate in more community-based care planning appropriate for children, such as school meetings, became all but nonexistent. Colocation was now less likely; medical records were maintained separately (shared with benefit managers but not colleagues) as providers returned to the private office culture. And although pharmacy benefit data might be joined in one insurance record, individual prescribing clinicians in a network were less able to access the total pharmacy record readily to ensure protection against drug interactions or other risks.

The increased pressure on inpatient settings to limit both admissions and lengths of stay (Fendell, 1994; Lind, Rosenblatt, Attkisson, & Catalano, 1997), coupled with increased pressure on outpatient settings to limit time spent on the telephone or in meetings, resulted in less time for child psychiatrists to review information about a patient before seeing that person, talk with the patient or family when the patient was seen, think about the patient after the appointment, record the encounter, and generate a thoughtful plan.

All of this seriously undermined the intrinsic system capacity to coordinate care for children precisely at a time when external community resources, such as advocacy services developed in the late 1970s and early 1980s, were being phased out or closed due to reduced funding (Duchnowski & Friedman, 1990). Children and families began to feel a stiff breeze blow between the gaps in the service delivery system; and health status reports, such as Kids Count, showed declining scores on protective factors, such as family health insurance coverage (Kids Count, 1999; Massachusetts Institute for Social and Economic Research, 2000).

Confidentiality

The confidentiality of the medical record is another issue that has complicated the delivery of integrated care and led to great controversy between providers and among members of the public. The decade between 1985 and 1995 saw steady advances in the sophistication of computerized medical records. For the first time, doctors working in integrated systems such as HMOs could access unified lab results, prescription records, and consultation notes for their patients regardless of the site where the care was provided. The benefits of such a system seemed obvious: it was much less likely that conflicting medications would be prescribed or that an after-hours provider would be unaware that a patient had recently been seen elsewhere and had an abnormal electrocardiogram. However, paralleling these advances was a deep unease growing among the general public regarding computerized access to personal information and concern about what safeguards were in place to protect privacy (Simmons, 1997).

It is noteworthy that this unease appeared to be primarily driven by adult patient needs and that there are distinct differences between internal medicine and pediatric practices regarding record keeping. Many adults are sensitive about both the possible stigma of mental health treatment itself and the possibility that details from their personal histories might be accessible from the record without their consent. They prefer not to disclose the content of their psychiatric symptomatology to their primary care providers, much less to their allergist or dermatologist, and certainly not at all to their insurer. These consumers pressed for a completely separate mental health record, which would be exempt from most record review and would require a separate release of information signature.

There is no question that the inappropriate intrusion into treatment planning by insurance reviewers and administrators was legitimate fuel for concerns about patient confidentiality. However, pediatricians, often the first to identify mental health conditions in their patients, were frustrated that after requesting a psychiatric consult, they were prevented by the newly modified medical records system from accessing their consultant's report. They were the primary recorders of family system or environmental risk (such as a non-English-speaking parent or problems with parental visitation), and they sought to maintain the traditional comprehensive medical record, warning of fragmented responses to family concerns if health care was not coordinated. Child psychiatrists, meanwhile, were burdened with duplicative and oddly divided record keeping so that medication refills and notes about side effects were no longer likely to be in the same place, making clinical coverage and care decisions both more burdensome and more risky.

Some HMOs, such as Harvard Pilgrim Health Care (HPHC) in Boston, made several sequential modifications in their medical record system within a matter of months in an effort to balance concerns about confidentiality and the need for communication about patient care (Leaning & McDonald, 1997). Each of these changes generated new complaints from dissenting groups that too much or too little information was available. The decision was ultimately made to dismantle the integrated computerized medical record and put notes by mental health staff in separate paper records. This was reassuring to those who felt private information from their therapy sessions was now better protected. However, others feared that unified, comprehensive medical record keeping, one of the elements that support excellence in the delivery of integrated patient care, had been dealt a significant blow. Notes about sexually transmitted diseases or substance abuse could still be included in the medical record if they were made by a primary care clinician. But a child psychiatrist's documentation of symptoms and medication side effects for a patient with attention deficit disorder, for example, could not be read by the child's pediatrician. In the new HPHC system, even mental health providers, working with the same patient but at different sites, were required to use separate, unlinked paper medical record systems.

The optimal way to document and track detailed patient information to support care coordination while protecting privacy remains a challenge. However, the disintegration of the patient record is impractical and undermines one of the great potential clinical quality advantages of an integrated care setting.

Carve-Outs

Notwithstanding all these challenges, the carve-out movement of the mid-1990s offered the most direct assault on the process of delivering high-quality integrated care (Jellinek & Little, 1998; Sharfstein, 2001). The separation of responsibility for mental illness (renamed *behavioral health*) from other forms of illness appeared to promise financial savings for insurers and employers alike. Mental health dollars were theoretically already managed by various means, such as gatekeeping by primary care, limitations on coverage, and newer, and escalating, copays. But managed care companies and physician groups were still struggling to find ways to reduce the cost of mental health service delivery further. They hoped to keep the percentage of the health care dollars spent on mental health to a minimum in order to sustain the overall favorable financial trend of ten years earlier. This was made more difficult in a buyers' market for members. Expensive tests, specialized treatments, and new drugs had been driving costs and expectations up, but employers and other purchasers of care were unwilling to support premium increases. The so-called behavioral health carve-outs, often for-profit companies, promised to manage mental health costs within a separate benefit outside the rest of the patient's care for which the carve-out company would take the financial risk. This was to be accomplished by requiring all authorizations and treatment decisions to be routed through designated behavioral health benefit managers.

The carve-out model quickly became popular with purchasers of health care benefit packages since it appeared to offer a single solution for rising mental health costs, complaints about access to specialists, and the confidentiality problem. As a result of this widespread move to carve-outs, most people now negotiate psychiatric referral and treatment decisions through intermediaries whom they have never met and are unfamiliar with their overall health status.

In addition, the gulf between primary care and child mental health clinicians has only widened as the system offers little or no contact between them. Some child psychiatrists see pediatricians as seeking to compete for their business by prescribing Ritalin and billing for office-based "counseling." Some pediatricians see child psychiatrists as motivated by reimbursement rates alone and unwilling to share responsibility for a child's overall health and well-being. Providers in both groups complain that the other group does not initiate calls regarding care coordination or return them.

Child psychiatrists typically report feeling alienated or cut out of the mainstream health care delivery system, with an associated suggestion of second-class citizenship in the medical world. They resent being pushed into a dangerous, hectic, insurance-driven role of seeing six patients an hour as a "prescriber" rather than that of a highly trained clinician who diagnoses carefully over several hour-long visits and treats using an array of methods, including psychotherapy. They are angered by the added expectation that they work part time in several locations in order to have full-time hours. They are frustrated and distressed at traveling from site to site (unpaid), while maintaining the ethically and clinically required follow-up responsibility and emergency access for each site on their own time, all within the fifteen-minute visit reimbursement rate.

Pediatricians, meanwhile, indicate feeling abandoned and overwhelmed as they are asked to handle children with mental health crises by themselves in the emergency room or board the children on pediatric inpatient units when there is no child psychiatric resource to receive them. They feel pressured to take on the mental health prescription and medication management for these seriously at-risk children, since there is no one else to do it. And they resent the absence of backup from child psychiatrists who have left the larger system to go into cash-only private practices or taken on administrative positions.

Families dealing with carve-outs report confusion and desperation regarding how to get child psychiatric help when they need it. They recognize the difference between getting child mental health advice from a specialist versus from their primary care clinician (Briggs-Gowan, 2000). They have little or no choice regarding mental health providers, due to restricted panels, and the scarcity of doctors or other clinicians who will accept carve-out company reimbursement levels. They note a loss of experience level and expertise in providers who are willing to see their children; training programs have also been hit hard, and intensive clinical supervision is not easily obtained. Many managed care companies have provider lists heavy in adult-trained providers, some willing to see children. Behavioral health utilization managers assign children to be treated by these providers, either when they are unaware of the lack of appropriate training or because they do not have specialty care available in their network. Parents feel solely responsible for any coordination that occurs among providers on behalf of their child, within mental health and across specialties.

NEED FOR INTEGRATION

For patients who themselves have, or whose family members have, adequate physical, emotional and financial resources, these barriers can be overcome or circumvented, although with difficulty. The tenacious, well-connected father will undertake as many telephone calls as necessary to make sure that the specialist his child has been referred to is truly qualified. The wealthy can seek the services they desire directly, without need for authorization. An educated and energetic mother may put in several hours directing the linkage among her daughter's various caregivers and treatments, even double-checking to make sure that her child's medical records were sent and read.

The need for coordination between primary and mental health care is directly proportional to the vulnerability of the patient. That is, the youngest, the oldest, and the sickest patients stand to benefit the most from close communication among the providers of their care. The ensuing risks when this does not happen in such cases are great, not only for the individual patients but for the population in general. These broader population risks can be summarized into three types: health care access, health care disparities, and health care quality, all of which represent reasons for integration of care.

Health Care Access

Among the more recent issues that have contributed to constraints on the delivery of integrated care is appropriate access to mental health and substance abuse providers. Consumer groups and health policy analysts began voicing concerns in the early 1990s about barriers in the path of patients requesting mental health referrals (Fendell, 1994). Many HMOs had attempted to contain mental health costs by requiring referrals from primary care providers (PCPs) or gatekeepers before mental health treatment could be obtained (Costello & Burns, 1988; Grembowski, Novak, & Roussel, 1997). Most children's health problems are self-limited; that is, they resolve with time, regardless of what remedies are undertaken. But problems of a more serious nature or with complications require timely and accurate interventions for optimal results. Access to services is often less dependent on severity of health risk than on social and geographic circumstances. However, even those with comparatively generous health care benefits may suffer with regard to appropriate access to care. All patients and their families in a practice are affected when a small percentage of cases absorb the bulk of their doctor or nurse's time. Sometimes this occurs because these are truly the most severely ill cases. Other times, illnesses have been incorrectly or only partially treated at the outset, and new treatment plans are needed. Sometimes there may have been inadequate levels of patient or family follow-through on the doctor's directions. Regardless of the reason, the rest of the patients have to wait. This engenders a circular problem where some of those people waiting for care experience relapses, deterioration, or prolongation of symptoms that could have been avoided if they had been dealt with more promptly. This is particularly a problem when resources are already very limited, such as is the case nationally and internationally with child psychiatry (American Academy of Child and Adolescent Psychiatry, 1999). In a coherent system of care, where access can be appropriately supported by cross-training of other professionals, and even family members, to recognize clinical symptoms requiring greater expertise, access to subspecialty care is improved. Large medical systems may employ only one pediatric cardiologist, but clinical guidelines, mutual arrangements with other specialties (such as pediatrics or adult cardiology), and informed nursing staff can maintain an appropriate level of responsiveness and access as needed by the population. This is equally possible in child psychiatry, where integration within a larger, competent system would greatly improve appropriate access to care.

Health Care Disparities

In some cases, sufficient educational and financial resources can partially offset the drawbacks of fragmented care, but for others, it is not possible to fill in the gaps personally. Examples of families or children in this group include a young immigrant family struggling to care for a premature infant across a language barrier, a depressed teenage girl who misses appointments set up to improve medication management of her serious asthma, and anyone with complex mental health or medical conditions. Unfortunately, in most modern health care systems, such at-risk populations are the least likely to enjoy integrated delivery of clinical services, thereby perpetuating the disparity in health outcomes for poor children and children of color (Samaan, 2000; Navarro & Shi, 2001; Politzer et al., 2001). The social costs of the increased morbidity within disadvantaged populations readily translate into financial costs for insurers, such as Medicaid and Medicare, and for the taxpayer. Countries and states with significant health care disparities have no winners, only losers (Kennedy, Kawachi, Lochner, Jones, & Prothrow-Stith, 1997).

Health Care Quality

As the U.S. economy has taken a downturn, inpatient and outpatient facilities are closing, and staffing levels are being reduced in settings across the nation. The possibility of addressing availability and quality of appropriate child mental health services issue by increased numbers of specialty clinicians seems unlikely. Continuing with existing approaches appears to lead us into declining quality as resources, human and financial, cannot support those. Instead, we can consider looking at a broader, secondary prevention model, similar to that used in other countries (Belfer & Saraceno, 2002), with a three-pronged approach, which depends heavily on partnership with families. As we increase the population-wide, community-based recognition of child mental health issues, we obtain the opportunity to intervene earlier and manage illness more cost-effectively, with resultant improvement in outcomes for more children and families.

This model for improved child mental health outcomes at the population level depends on three co-occurring processes:

- Patients and families are informed (in their primary language) at all possible venues, such as churches, markets, and public transportation areas, regarding observable health risks and consequent needs in order to sensitize public awareness of child mental health.

- Local screening and early intervention efforts jointly sponsored by primary care and school system teams of nurses, teachers, volunteers, and others can, through their collective availability, shift the cost and morbidity curve to the left so that there are fewer high-end children needing scarce specialty resources.

- Community-based systems of care are created where families, agencies, schools, and informal supports can be linked to child psychiatrists, pediatric neurologists, and others as needed through the use of multidisciplinary protocols and clinical guidelines, along with clearly defined resources, action steps, and care processes for both urgent and routine situations.

In order for such ideal systems to function, there needs to be significant restructuring of roles and reimbursement in the mental health system. A first step in that process is to enhance the relationship between primary care and specialty mental health care for children and adolescents and to identify what supports that relationship requires to function well.

PRINCIPLES AND PRACTICES FOR COLLABORATION

The term *integrated care,* as it is being used here, refers to the delivery of primary and specialty health care, including mental health, within a system that supports a team approach (Call, Wisner, Blum, Kelly, & Nelson, 1997; U.S. Department of Health and Human Services, 2001). There is controversy regarding whether integrated care can best be delivered through outreach specifications placed on primary care (the public health medical home concept) or mental health and substance abuse providers (a variant born from responsibilities assigned to carve-outs when health care was divided into "mental" versus "health"). From either starting point, the underlying premise of an integrated model of care is that clinical interventions, including, but not limited to, medication, have the potential to interact with each other, for both good and for ill. Thus, it behooves the providers of these interventions to understand the implications of such interactions and seek the safest, most efficient combination of treatments for each patient.

Sharing Risks

There have been obvious gains in medical techniques and knowledge in the United States since the era when a community had one doctor providing care house by house, but there have also been losses. One of these is the clear ownership of care. When there is only one provider, things may be overlooked, or there may be too much to do, but there is no "turfing" or turning away from risk or responsibility out of the conviction that it is someone else's job to respond. In most health care settings in the United States today, care delivery is fragmented, and there are no clear owners of outcomes or process. The child mental health specialist does not consider himself or herself responsible for knowing whether a therapy patient gets a hepatitis B shot, and the primary care clinicians do not tend to inquire about suicidal ideation during their review of systems. Examples of successful integration of care, where the risks to the child are regularly shared, include when a pediatrician involves social services due to suspected child abuse or a therapist asks whether the sexually active adolescent patient is using birth control.

However, there is no greater disincentive to such outreach and expanded risk screening than to feel that there is no backup when problems are discovered. Child abuse most often goes unreported when there are underdeveloped response systems. Similarly, a therapist who has no link to medical providers is less equipped to take the next steps to steer her teenage patient toward birth control. It is critical in the encouragement and training of an interdisciplinary team approach to be able to describe clearly what the steps will be when a risk is uncovered and how resources can be accessed. Even the existence of cross-training on a paper protocol can be a resource under these situations, although having a defined person to consult, directly or electronically, is infinitely preferable. Regardless of modality, it is more likely that population and individual health issues will be identified when areas of potential risk are understood by all who encounter the child or adolescent and when there are clear-cut processes for sharing the risk response among providers or a broader team (ideally including family, informal supports, and nonprofessionals).

Additional risk-sharing opportunities occur during the initiation of medications, or regarding the recognition of diagnoses, that span primary and specialty care categories (such as insulin or substance abuse). In these instances, failure to communicate and create shared strategies for patients will waste resources and adversely affect patients, as in the following two case examples:

Unaware of the boy's clinical status, a school social worker recommended anger management classes for a diabetic who was repeatedly hypoglycemic and irritable rather than suggesting his mother talk to the pediatrician about his insulin dose.

Unaware of the teenager's heavy alcohol use, her pediatrician prescribed inappropriate pain medication for her complaints of chronic headache rather than recognize the need for a pain management and addiction treatment approach.

The literal sharing of financial risk can help to underscore the interconnectedness of the care delivery system. Ultimately, all risk sharing works to the benefit of the providers and other members of the caregiving community, as well as to the child or family. The burdens are too large and the need for creativity too great to bear alone. In addition, the involvement of mental health providers has been demonstrated to improve overall health and cost outcomes (referred to as medical cost offset) in several different studies (Shemo, 1985–1986; Thompson & Hylan, 1998). In an ideal collaboration among adults, the child reaps the reward of multiple perspectives; in addition, the joining together to manage the shared risk allows a perfect base on which to build common goals.

Sharing Goals

The most successful method for choosing treatment goals is to ask the family to identify them. We have gone from "doctor knows best," to "remember to talk to the family," to "family-focused" care, which stresses *remember to listen to the family*" (Briggs, 1995; VanDenBerg & Grealish, 1996). Although primary care clinicians are still expected to maintain the protocol for immunizations and choose appropriate antibiotics when needed, other issues in the pediatrician's office are driven by parental concern, such as sleep patterns or school functioning. Eliciting the family's sense of the child, including his strengths and needs, is even more urgent for child mental health and substance abuse clinicians, who do not have the "regular check-up" culture to rely on and must connect with the family quickly or lose a treatment opportunity. Understanding how to hear what the family strengths and needs are is the first step toward choosing treatment goals.

Integrated care takes the list of goals that a family identifies for their child, and that an older child or adolescent identifies for himself or herself, and looks at the distribution of responsibilities for each goal. The family is like the chief executive officer in these settings, with the care community, including the pediatrician or child psychiatrist, as members of the board of directors, working together to implement the family's goals and objectives. In this way, communication among relevant parties is enhanced at the beginning and is not dependent on an emergency. Goals are focused and prioritized with built-in measures for success that allow for correction if they are not being met. Systems partners, such as teachers or social service workers, may be asked to be part of the treatment team; at a minimum, their views need to be understood for the optimal success of the plan.

Unless and until the needs of the members of the care planning team for high school freshman Michael are woven together into a shared mission, the efforts of the players will be at cross purposes with no clear end point or agreed-on measure of success.
The list of these needs might include:

- Michael's wish for his assistant principal to "give him a break."
- His mother's wish to be uninterrupted at work by calls from Michael's school.
- His therapist's concern that Michael may be using both alcohol and marijuana.
- His father's view that alcohol is all right but marijuana is not.
- His pediatrician's discomfort with requests for covert urine screening.

The team mission derived for Michael that all could agree with from such a list might be: "Michael making it safely to tenth grade." Thus, all interventions or modalities (whether therapy or detention) are reviewed in the context of the question, "How does this enhance or decrease the chance that Michael will make it safely to tenth grade?"
Strength-based goals to support this mission could include:

- Recruiting the assistant principal to the team and using his interest to provide information to the family
- Finding a way to involve the family that does not undermine the mother's job security
- Encouraging Michael's (and his team's) increased understanding of the triggers or motivation behind his substance use
- Creating a shared parental assessment of objective risk to Michael if he uses any substances
- Clarifying for other team members the role of the pediatrician (and urine tests)

Interventions tied to these goals might include:

- A school-based liaison to meet regularly with parents (before work) and take over monitoring of student from the assistant principal

- A crisis plan for implementation in school with Michael's father as backup
- An after-school psychoeducational group for Michael on decision making
- A meeting to include the therapist, Michael's parents, and the pediatrician to review actual and relative risks of suspected substances and clarify parental strategy and communication
- Clarification regarding the clinical site policy regarding urine screening and pediatric role in suspected substance abuse

All the while, there would need to be parameters in place, such as summer school if Michael has not mastered certain curriculum items by March, transfer to a more intensive clinical setting for academics if his behavior (including weekend or evening activities which result in emergency room visits) does not improve by January, participation in recreational activities contingent on successful attendance in a twelve-week psychoeducational group for teenagers, and commitment from Michael's family to take part in concurrent family work to pursue his concerns regarding his father's alcohol use and his mother's depression. Michael's pediatrician can justify involvement in these meetings as supporting the goal of the patient's "getting safely to tenth grade," especially because her participation should be outcomes driven. Time spent in meeting every three weeks is less expensive than emergency room visits (under a cap) for inebriation or a residential treatment program for substance abuse.

Sharing Outcomes

No intervention, whether strictly medical or in some other therapeutic realm, should be undertaken without a clear sense of anticipated, or at least hoped-for, specific outcomes. This hardly sounds controversial, but it is actually not typical of child therapies, many of which have been accurately charged by families and primary care providers with being diffuse, nonspecific, and unmeasurable. Linked to the need to tie interventions to goals and monitor outcomes is the need to change interventions based on so-called process measures—indicators along the path of the ultimate outcomes that will address whether the mission was achieved.

In the example, if Michael never attended the after-school group, it would not make sense to leave everything the same and keep noting that he was not attending the group. Either the appropriateness of the intervention would need to be reconsidered, or the rest of the action steps were insufficient to support this intervention's being successful. In other words, something needs to change. This accountability helps support the integrated team's energy and effectiveness rather than having it sink into an atrophied relic of a treatment team that repeats failed strategies.

Child mental health outcomes do not occur in a vacuum but are the reflection of the interplay between risk and opportunity. An integrated clinical approach within an overall community-based system of care allows a wider array of opportunities to modify innate and acquired sources of risk to healthy development for children and adolescents.

To the extent possible, given local variation in health care delivery systems, child mental health and primary care clinicians should seek to build a close collaboration regarding both child population health risks and those of the individual families and children in their care. Integrated clinical care delivery should be a key element for organized systems of care and demanded by family and mental health advocates. There is an increasing body of evidence that strategic, coordinated efforts within a strength-based approach can shift the outcome for otherwise severely at-risk children toward the mean (Duchnowski & Johnson, 1993; Evans, Huz, McNulty, & Banks, 1996; Burns & Farmer, 1996). Not only is this good for the children and families involved, it allows for resources to be reallocated toward earlier recognition and treatment for those who might otherwise not have received care (Cole, 1996). Ultimately, consistent application of this strategy contributes to improvement in the overall health status of the community.

References

American Academy of Child and Adolescent Psychiatry. (1999). *Workforce fact sheet: Critical shortage of child and adolescent psychiatrists.* Available on-line at: http://www.aacap.org/training/workforce/htm.

Baum, A., & Garofalo, J. P. (1999). Socioeconomic status and chronic stress. Does stress account for SES effects on health? *Annals of the New York Academy of Sciences, 896,* 131–144.

Belfer, M., & Saraceno, B. (2002). *Caring for children and adolescents with mental disorders: Setting WHO directions.* Geneva: World Health Organization, Department of Mental Health and Substance Dependence.

Briggs, H. E. (1995). Enhancing family advocacy networks: An analysis of the roles of sponsoring organizations. *Community Mental Health Journal, 31,* 317–333.

Briggs-Gowan, M. J. (2000). Mental health in pediatric settings: Distribution of disorders and factors related to service use. *Journal of the American Academy of Child and Adolescent Psychiatry, 39,* 841–849.

Burns, B. J., & Farmer, E.M.Z. (1996). A randomized trial of case management for youths with serious emotional disturbance. *Journal of Clinical Child Psychology, 25,* 476–486.

Call, K. T., Wisner, C. L., Blum, R. M., Kelly, A., & Nelson, A. (1997). Children with chronic illness and disease in managed care. *Abstract Book, Association for Health Services Research (Washington, DC), 14,* 143–144.

Carney, R. M., Blumenthal, J. A., Stein, P. K., Watkins, L., Catellier, D., Berkman, L. F., Czajkowski, S. M., O'Connor, C., Stone, P. H., & Freedland, K. E. (2001). Depression, heart rate variability, and acute myocardial infarction. *Circulation, 104,* 2024–2028.

Cohen, J. I. (2000). Stress and mental health: A biobehavioral perspective. *Issues in Mental Health Nursing, 21,* 185–202.

Cole, R. (1996). The Robert Wood Johnson Foundation's Mental Health Services Program for Youth. In B. A. Stroul (Ed.), *Children's mental health: Creating systems of care in a changing society* (pp. 235–248). Baltimore, MD: Brookes Publishing.

Costello, E. J., & Burns, B. J. (1988). Service utilization and psychiatric diagnosis in pediatric primary care: The role of the gatekeeper. *Pediatrics, 82,* 432–441.

Duchnowski, A. J., & Friedman, R. M. (1990). Children's mental health: challenges for the nineties. *Journal of Mental Health Administration, 17,* 3–12.

Duchnowski, A. J., & Johnson, M. D. (1993). The alternatives to residential treatment study: Initial findings. *Journal of Emotional and Behavioral Disorders, 1,* 17–26.

Evans, M. E., Huz, S., McNulty, T., & Banks, S. M. (1996). Child, family, and system outcomes of intensive case management in New York State. *Psychiatric Quarterly, 67,* 273–286.

Fendell, S. (1994, Spring). Mental health managed care: MHMA report card mixed: Conflict between profits and consumers. *Massachusetts Mental Health Legal Advisor,* 4–12.

Grembowski, D., Novak, L., & Roussel, A. (1997). Measuring the "managedness" of managed care. *Abstract Book, Association for Health Services Research (Washington, DC), 14,* 126–127.

Jellinek, M., & Little, M. (1998). Supporting child psychiatric services using current managed care approaches: You can't get there from here. *Archives of Pediatric and Adolescent Medicine, 152,* 321–326.

Kennedy, B. P., Kawachi, I., Lochner, K., Jones, C., & Prothrow-Stith, D. (1997). (Dis)respect and black mortality, *Ethnicity and Disease, 7,* 207–214.

Kids Count. (1999). Census data online. www.aefc.org/kidscount.

Leaning, J., & McDonald, K. (1997). Confidentiality guidelines. Internal memorandum to Health Center Division medical staff, Harvard Pilgrim Health Care, Boston.

Lind, S. L., Rosenblatt, A. B., Attkisson, C. C., & Catalano, R. A. (1997). Evaluating the cost-effectiveness for a continuum of mental health care for children. *Abstract Book, Association for Health Services Research (Washington, DC), 14,* 129–130.

Massachusetts Institute for Social and Economic Research. (2000). MISER [database]. Available on-line at: http://www.umass.edu/miser/misover.html.

Navarro, V., & Shi, L. (2001). The political context of social inequalities and health. *Social Science and Medicine, 52,* 481–491.

Patterson, D. Y. (1990). Managed care: An approach to rational psychiatric treatment. *Hospital-Community Psychiatry, 41,* 1092–1095.

Politzer, R. M., Yoon, J., Shi, L., Hughes, R. G., Regan, J., & Gaston, M. H. (2001). Inequality in America: The contribution of health centers in reducing and eliminating disparities in access to care. *Medical Care Research and Review, 58,* 234–248.

Sabin, J. E., & Daniels, N. (1999). Public-sector managed behavioral health care: II. Contracting for Medicaid services—the Massachusetts experience. *Psychiatric Services, 50,* 39–41.

Samaan, R. A. (2000). The influence of race, ethnicity, and poverty on the mental health on children. *Journal of Health Care for the Poor and Underserved, 11,* 100–110.

Satcher, D. S. (2000). Executive summary: A report of the surgeon general on mental health. *Public Health Reports, 115,* 89–101.

Sharfstein, J. M. (2001, Jan. 1–15). Unhealthy partnership. *American Prospect, 12*(1).

Shemo, J. P. (1985–1986). Cost-effectiveness of providing mental health services: The offset effect. *International Journal of Psychiatry in Medicine, 15,* 19–30.

Simmons, J. (1997). Who needs to know? *Healthplan, 38,* 56–60.

Smoyak, S. A. (2000). The history, economics, and financing of mental health care. Part 3: The present. *Journal of Psychosocial Nursing and Mental Health Services, 38,* 32–38.

Thompson, D., & Hylan, T. R. (1998). Predictors of a medical-offset effect among patients receiving antidepressant therapy. *American Journal of Psychiatry, 155,* 824–827.

U.S. Department of Health and Human Services. (2001). *Health Resources and Services Administration Annual Report.* Rockville, MD: U.S. Department of Health and Human Services.

VanDenBerg, J. E., & Grealish, M. E. (1996). Individualized services and supports through the wrap-around process. *Journal of Child and Family Studies, 5,* 7–21.

Wickizer, T. M., & Lessler, D. S. (1996). Containing costs while maintaining quality: An unresolved dilemma for managed care within mental health. *Association for Health Services Research (AHSR) and Foundation for Health Services Research (FHSR) Annual Meeting Abstracts Book, 13,* 61–62.

CHAPTER FIFTEEN

Foster Children in the Child Welfare System

Larry Marx
Marilyn Benoit
Bruce Kamradt

More than 2 million child abuse reports are filed annually on behalf of children in the United States. It is estimated out of those reports that approximately 500,000 to 700,000 children are in foster care each year. Most of these children have been victims of repeated abuse and neglect. Many have not experienced a nurturing, stable environment during their early development. As a result, children and adolescents in foster care have a higher prevalence of physical, developmental, and behavioral health problems than any other group of children. Typically, these health and mental health care problems are unidentified or undertreated. Some of these problems are chronic and will have a continued impact on all aspects of these children's lives even after they exit the child welfare system.

Despite federal, state, and local mandates, child welfare systems in most communities across the United State have difficulty providing the appropriate level of health and mental health services that children and youth in foster care need. In 1997, the Adoption and Safe Families Act (ASFA) set federal standards in multiple domains for this population. One of the key objectives of this legislation was to shorten the timelines for children to receive permanency in placement. Physical and mental health care issues are known to have an impact on the length of time in foster care (Rosenfeld et al., 1997). However, it is challenge for health and mental health professionals to support local child welfare and judiciary systems to meet these federal standards.

Current health care systems are often inadequate to address the complex health care issues of foster children. Financing of these systems has also changed dramatically in recent years, creating different barriers to care. Although federal and state appropriations continue to be major sources of financing for health and human services in the United States, the increasing costs of services for foster care and other publicly funded populations have led many states and local governmental entities to adopt managed care principles. The application of these principles to publicly funded physical and mental health delivery systems for children in foster care has significantly changed their function of providing direct care. Risk sharing and capitation have increasingly transformed these public systems into purchasing and regulatory authorities. Private health and mental health delivery systems are being given greater responsibility for providing direct services to foster children. However, the private sector has historically been designed for children with acute or episodic health and mental health care needs. Thus, the ability of private health systems to provide long-term care for children with multiple needs is limited.

Additional funding for more flexible, specialized services to meet the unique needs of children in foster care is often limited by the categorical requirements that exist within public health, mental health, and child welfare service delivery systems. The inability to pool funding from multiple sources to provide individualized treatment results in the continuation of fragmented, poorly coordinated care. The application of managed care principles to public systems, although holding promise for early identification and prevention of health and mental health issues, has complicated the management of the multiple funding streams that are needed to fund the care plan for each foster child and his or her family.

THE CHILD WELFARE SYSTEM: HISTORY AND CURRENT CHALLENGES

In colonial America, it was not uncommon for abandoned, destitute, and orphaned children to be indentured into nonbiological homes in order to receive training in a trade. By the early 1800s, this practice gave way to the development of huge orphan asylums as a way of caring for these children. Over time, some religious leaders began to denounce large church and state orphanages as warehouses that fostered urban crime. By the 1850s, Charles Loring Brace, a Protestant minister, asserted that placement with families was preferable to the large institutions that were rapidly growing in numbers. Arguing that midwestern farm families were both available and more suitable for these children, he established the "orphan train" movement. In 1893, the Children's Aid Society became the first charitable organization in the United States to support this type of placing-out service for unwanted or abandoned children. From 1854 to 1929, approximately 150,000 children from New York City were relocated to the Midwest, where families short of available labor took them in. It is reported that Brace was confident that relocating to a new home would help these children develop into self-sufficient adults.

This emigration program, which peaked in 1875, became highly criticized and began a steady decline. Compulsory school attendance and the passage of child labor laws during the progressive era are cited as key reasons that this practice ultimately ended in 1930. However, during the orphan train movement, it has been reported that these midwestern families frequently were not screened, many of the families abused these youth by using them as overworked laborers, and the children were separated from their siblings with little or no contact with their biological parents. The Children's Aid Society's agents who made inadequate or infrequent follow-up contacts often ignored these situations. Similar issues remain as areas of concern for children in foster care today.

This movement nevertheless changed the nature of child welfare in the United States. By the early 1900s, huge orphanages closed. In 1909, the first White House conference on caring for dependent children was convened. It is reported that participants argued over whether these children were better off in foster homes near their biological parents or should be sent away from the urban areas in which they resided. They did agree that poverty in itself was not a justification for removal of children from their families.

During this period, many foster care arrangements were made informally between children's biological parents and a relative or friend. Charitable organizations, or the state, located alternative foster parents if needed. Many religious groups felt obligated to form their own agencies whose mission was to find foster families of similar faith to receive these children. The system at that time was voluntary. Parents usually had to seek services on their own, and children were placed back at their biological parents' request once the family's social situation improved.

Not until the 1960s did the expansion of foster care in the United States occur. In 1962, C. Henry Kempe and his associates published an article in the *Journal of the American Medical Association* entitled "The Battered Child Syndrome" and made the point that some children from all socioeconomic backgrounds were being abused or murdered by their biological parents. Although America had traditionally respected family autonomy, the political climate of that decade motivated every state to pass child abuse prevention laws. Abuse and neglect reports, particularly of children in lower-class families, grew dramatically. Unfortunately, state welfare departments had no clear guidelines about how to care for these children. Over many biological parents' objections, these children were placed in foster homes without clear plans to address not only their physical or mental well-being but also under what circumstances these children could return to their biological homes.

By the late 1970s, the number of children being placed in out-of-home care reached an all-time high. Greater recognition of child abuse and neglect by both medical and social service professionals, increased federal funding for health and social welfare services, and broader public awareness of the plight of these children were leading factors for this growth.

In 1980, Congress passed the Adoption Assistance and Child Welfare Act (P.L. 96–272) in response to the increasing numbers of children being placed out of the home and the length of time they remained in foster care without clear permanency plans. The act also highlighted that out-of-home care was being used at a higher rate than were family preservation and support services to the biological families.

The Adoption Assistance and Child Welfare Act mandated child welfare agencies to develop more timely permanency plans, ranging from a variety of options that included returning the child to his or her biological parents, adoption, or long-term foster care and to enforce them within eighteen to twenty-four months of placement. Although federal financial incentives were established for states to change their focus by using greater family preservation and support services to maintain children in their biological homes, most states had significant difficulty meeting these new federal mandates. Most states did not provide additional monies to local communities to expand the models and scope of human services targeted to these multiproblem children and families. There was little recognition on the part of both state and private child welfare agencies that health, mental health, and substance abuse problems directly contributed to the rate of out-of-home care. There was no state acknowledgment that health and mental health services would need to be financed at greater levels to ensure that these children could be maintained safely in their biological homes.

By the 1990s, the national trend of increasing numbers of children entering foster care continued, with an average increased length of time in out-of-home placement. There were high rates of recidivism of children who were returned to their biological parents, only to be placed back by child welfare agencies into the out-of-home care system.

The demographics of children in foster care also changed. There were now larger numbers of infants and preschoolers, an overrepresentation of children of color, children with severe emotional and behavioral problems, and growing numbers of children infected and affected by HIV/AIDS. The families of these children had complex health and mental health issues, particularly substance abuse, that had a bearing on their ability to maintain these children safely in their homes.

In 1993, in response to these trends, Congress created the Family Preservation and Family Support program as part of the Omnibus Budget Reconciliation Act.

The program reiterated the goals of the Adoption Assistance and Child Welfare Act but increased funding for a variety of services, including intensive family intervention that was targeted to family preservation as well as timely reunification of children with their biological families. However, this program had little impact in most states on the number of children entering foster care or a reduction in the length of time they spent in out-of-home care. Large child welfare caseloads, a high turnover of inexperienced or poorly trained social service staff, and a decline in the number of foster families made it difficult to improve services for children and their biological families.

It was not until passage of the ASFA in 1997 that federal legislation clarified and reinforced the wide range of policies and standards that were established after the passage of the Adoption Assistance and Child Welfare Act.

ASFA modified the "reasonable efforts" that states had to make to preserve or reunite families by providing examples of circumstances in which states are not required to keep children with their parents for safety reasons. It established in federal law timelines and conditions for filing petitions for termination of parental rights. States must now file on behalf of any child who has been in out-of-home care for fifteen of the most recent twenty-two months. ASFA set time frames for permanency hearings at twelve months rather than eighteen months with a determination of whether and when a child may return home, placed for adoption, referred for legal guardianship, or another planned permanent living arrangement. It encouraged adoptions by requiring states to document child-specific efforts to place a child for adoption and offering financial incentives to potential parents for adoption of children with special needs in out-of-home care. ASFA expanded the Promoting Safe and Stable Families program by including funding for time-limited reunification and adoption promotion and support services.

The ASFA also allowed states to apply for a Title IV-E waiver, which allows for federal foster care monies that are paid for room and board costs for institutional care to be used flexibly without a foster child having to be placed in such a setting for states to access these funds. This has allowed at least eighteen states to develop innovative programs designed to prevent out-of-home placements, encourage development of community-based services as alternatives to group home and residential treatment, and cofund some of the blended funding community-based mental health programs serving this population

Although the goal of ASFA was to set federal timelines that would both reduce the number of children who entered foster care and the length of time these children spent in out-of-home placement, it has fallen short in addressing the health and mental health issues that affect these outcomes. Without federal and state financial support for health- and mental health–related services, many local child welfare agencies continue to fail in meeting ASFA's requirements.

HEALTH AND MENTAL HEALTH CARE NEEDS
OF CHILDREN IN OUT-OF-HOME CARE

Children in foster care have much higher rates of physical, developmental, and emotional illness when compared to the general pediatric and adolescent population. Halfon, Mendonca, and Berkowitz (1995) found in one study of children with a mean age of three years that over 20 percent had growth abnormalities, 30 percent had neurological abnormalities, and 16 percent had asthma. Fewer than 20 percent of children had no medical problems, and 28.8 percent had three or more conditions. This study also found that over 80 percent of the children had developmental, behavioral, or emotional disorders. Simms (1989) performed multidisciplinary diagnostic evaluations of 113 children from birth through age six. Findings from his sample revealed that 61 percent of the children had developmental delay, 35 percent had chronic medical problems, 14 percent had birth defects, 14 percent demonstrated growth delay, and 40 percent of the children had a behavioral disturbance. Other literature concurs that children in foster care have significant deficits in their health and mental health status (Rosenfeld et al., 1997; Chernoff, Combs-Orme, Risley-Curtiss, & Heisler, 1994; Hochstadt, Jaudes, Zimo, & Schachter, 1987). Foster children can also have an increased frequency of unmet health needs that include inadequate or undocumented immunizations, vision and hearing abnormalities, intellectual or academic problems, and infectious diseases. They can display the full range of psychiatric diagnoses that include posttraumatic stress and other anxiety disorders, disruptive behavioral disorders, attachment disorders, and affective illness.

Most often, foster children come from poor, minority, single-parent families, with members who suffer from high rates of mental illness, substance abuse, homelessness, and chronic physical disability. Many of their biological parents have their own abuse and neglect histories. Their capacity to provide for their children often has been compromised by poor educational opportunities. In addition, these foster children most often come from urban areas with the highest rates of poverty, crime, violence, and drug abuse.

Despite the Child Welfare League of America's *Standards for Health Care Services in Out-of-Home Care* (1988), few child welfare agencies have implemented specific policies or programs to address children's health care needs. With rare exception, child welfare agencies lack specific policies on health care to guide workers. Usually, only the foster children with the most severe and obvious problems receive attention. Foster care agencies have few monitors or the information system infrastructure in place to determine and track whether children and their biological parents are receiving physical and behavioral health care.

Although foster parents can generally meet the basic needs of the children in their care, most are ill prepared to manage the complex health and mental health problems of their children without professional guidance and support. Typically, the children require multiple evaluation and treatment services from a variety of community providers. Given that foster children's medical history may be unknown, it is often difficult or impossible for providers to assemble a complete medical history or record. Biological parents are often either unavailable or cannot provide adequate information about their children. Preexisting health and mental health conditions may not be adequately recognized or treated until the child shows symptoms in placement.

Once a foster child is evaluated, there is often little communication among caregivers about the type and duration of treatment needed for the child's identified problems. This is complicated by the fact that most foster parents are not legally empowered to make major medical or mental health decisions regarding specialized treatment. This authority and responsibility may be unclear depending on the child and biological family's legal status within the local child welfare system. This issue presents a significant barrier to instituting timely interventions.

Current literature suggests that health and mental health services for this population are most effective when there is continuity of care by a primary care provider through the establishment of a medical home (that is, a primary physical health care provider that constitutes comprehensive care). These services should be of high quality, available without obstacles to access, comprehensive and culturally sensitive, and coordinate and integrate different types of services that are developmentally appropriate and individualized for each child. A health care management system should be developed to provide the infrastructure to support this model of service delivery. In addition, an after-care health care plan that addresses continuing health care needs and issues should be developed as the child exits the foster care system (Task Force on Healthcare for Children in Foster Care, 2001). However, the current method of health care financing for these services creates one of the major barriers to the successful implementation of these recommendations.

COORDINATION OF HEALTH AND MENTAL HEALTH CARE FUNDING FOR FOSTER CHILDREN

Children in foster care are higher users of health care services than comparable children, although they may not receive sufficient services and their care is usually more likely to be inadequate, fragmented, and poorly coordinated.

Halfon, Berkowitz, and Klee (1992) examined all California Medicaid claims (Medi-Cal) data for 1988 in children and youth under eighteen years of age to describe the utilization of health services by children in foster care. Although children in foster care represented 4 percent of Medi-Cal children, they accounted for approximately 5 percent of children using Medi-Cal services and 6.7 percent of expenditures. This represented a 23 percent greater utilization rate and 41 percent greater expenditure rate than all children and youth covered by Medi-Cal. Using the entire Medi-Cal population younger than eighteen years of age as a comparison group, children in foster care were higher utilizers of mental health services.

Takayama, Bergman, and Connell (1994) performed an analysis of the 1990 Medicaid program claims data in the state of Washington. A total of 1,631 children in foster care and 5,316 children in the Aid to Families with Dependent Children (AFDC) program from birth through age seven years who were eligible for Medicaid continuously during the study year were examined. The main outcome measures of the analysis were the health care utilization and expenditures classified by types of health service and health care provider and the proportion of children with 1990 expenditures exceeding $10,000 for the year (high-cost children) and most prominent diagnoses associated with their health care utilization. Some results from that study include the following: mean health care expenditures in 1990 were $3,075 for children in foster care compared to $543 for AFDC children; mental health services were used by 25 percent of foster children compared with 3 percent of AFDC children; 8 percent of children in foster care and 0.4 percent of AFDC children were high cost; and among those high-cost children, 59 percent had mental disorders.

Although Medicaid (Title XIX) is the principal funding source for physical and mental services for most children in out-of-home care, other federal financing programs support health and related services to this population. These include Medicaid's early and periodic screening, diagnosis, and treatment (EPSDT), Title V (Maternal and Child Health programs), P.L. 94–142 (Education for the Handicapped Act), P.L. 99–457 (Birth to Three Early Intervention Program), Head Start, Child Nutrition Act, Supplemental Security Income, Katie Beckett (a program that pays for medical services for a disabled child living at home who would be eligible for Medicaid if living in an institution) and Alcohol, Drug Abuse and Mental Health Services Block Grant programs. Given the categorical nature of these and other programs, there is a limited ability for state and local child welfare agencies to coordinate benefits of the Medicaid program with these other funding streams. This inability to pool funding from multiple sources creates a barrier for the state or local child welfare agency to meet the individualized, complex health and mental health needs of each child in out-of-home care.

In addition, Medicaid managed care programs that are operated in many states have placed another layer of complexity on this already fragmented financing strategy. Foster children under the age of nineteen with special needs and funded by other federal qualifying requirements are exempt from compulsory managed Medicaid enrollment. However, any state through a Medicaid 1915(b) waiver may automatically enroll these children into a managed care plan. In addition, under the 1997 Balanced Budget Act (BBA), each state's managed care Medicaid program can employ various service delivery options for

Medicaid-eligible enrollees. Thus, depending on a state's Medicaid plan, the service delivery system that is financed may not adequately address the health and mental health needs of these children.

Although the BBA removed some waiver requirements that states had to fulfill in order to use managed care in Medicaid, it also added numerous protections, including access to emergency services, network adequacy, grievance processes, external quality review, and liability protections for enrollees. Although this has created safeguards for foster children in managed Medicaid plans, it does not ensure that the service network meets the community-based, developmental, or culturally specific requirements of the population.

Most state managed care capitation rates and health care service planning do not always account for the special needs of foster care children. Based on the foster care population's higher utilization of specialty services from multiple child-serving agencies, Medicaid managed care plans may place foster children at considerable risk of receiving fragmented or inadequate care.

In addition, state Medicaid managed care plans that do adequately care for these youth are usually vulnerable to behavioral health care carve-out capitation, which typically does not cover the cost of the intensity or duration of mental health services that are needed. The child welfare systems in many localities offer supportive care to foster children with emotional disturbance through the use of therapeutic foster homes, group homes, or emergency respite for foster parents. However, these supports do not replace the need for traditional mental health services that are limited in most carved-out managed behavioral health care plans. This inability of many child welfare systems to provide or access the appropriate level and intensity of outpatient mental health services based on the child's need has sometimes resulted in foster children's being placed in more restrictive mental health settings, such as residential treatment. Such inappropriate placement has an adverse impact on the length of time that foster children spend in out-of-home care.

MANAGED, INTEGRATED SYSTEM OF CARE MODEL IN THE CHILD WELFARE POPULATION

The development of a fully integrated, managed local system of care model for youth in the child welfare system could address the complex issues facing this population. With the federal mandate to decrease the length of time that children spend in foster care, the complexity and severity of the physical and mental health needs that have a negative impact on permanency planning and the fragmentation in financing, the benefit of an integrated model would be to provide an individualized intervention for each child in care.

Although there are no known national demonstration models of an integrated, managed physical health and mental health within the child welfare system for foster children, the system of care movement for seriously emotionally disturbed children and their families may provide a framework for such a model. Stimulated by the Child and Adolescent Service System Programs (CASSP) of the mid-1980s, the Robert Wood Johnson Foundation and the Center for Mental Health Services of the Substance Abuse Mental Health Services Administration have sponsored the demonstration and replication of system of care models in local communities across the United States. Based on CASSP principles of service delivery and wraparound care philosophy, these local systems of care have demonstrated success in meeting the mental health and human service needs of a multiproblem, multi-need population of seriously emotionally disturbed youth and their families. The framework for these programs can be applied to a managed, integrated model of service delivery that could include physical health care for the foster care population.

Services within this integrated system of care model for foster children must be developmentally appropriate and comprehensive, including flexible and wraparound services to address physical, emotional, social, and educational needs effectively. Service plans would be individually tailored, with unique strengths and needs driving a care plan. The services provided would be in the least restrictive and most normative environment that is clinically appropriate to meet the needs of children or adolescents and their families. Services must be collaborative, coordinated, and integrated among agencies, programs, and service systems responsible for the children in out-of-home care.

Ideally, all the child-serving systems responsible for foster children would fund and actively support collaborative initiatives that would colocate services in child welfare offices, educational settings, and health clinics, as well as focus integration efforts to increase access to and availability of mental health services. These colocation efforts would promote collaborative case management that would increase ease of access to services for foster children and their families that are currently involved with multiple systems.

A proposed policy recommendation is for a single governing authority to be established to oversee an integrated model of service delivery operating within the framework of federal and state statutes for the child welfare population. This would eliminate fragmented policies resulting from multiple governing authorities. Federal, state, and local funding would be consolidated under the control of this local authority, thereby eliminating fragmented funding decisions resulting from multiple funders. Management of the system would be unified and integrated to the maximum extent possible, eliminating duplicative layers of administrative and prescriptive requirements. System management and service providers would be held accountable for ensuring the cost-effectiveness of services in achieving developmentally appropriate outcomes for children and adolescents in foster care.

WRAPAROUND MILWAUKEE: A CASE OF BEST PRACTICES

Wraparound Milwaukee, a coordinated system of community-based care and resources for families of children with complex needs, is operated by the Children and Adolescent Services Branch of the Milwaukee County, Wisconsin's Mental Health Division. The features of this care management model are a provider network that furnishes an array of mental health and child welfare services; an individualized plan of care; a care coordinator management system to ensure that services are coordinated, monitored, and evaluated; a managed care approach including the preauthorization of services and service monitoring; and a reinvestment strategy where dollars saved from acute mental health inpatient or residential care are invested into increased community service capacity.

Since its inception in 1995, Wraparound Milwaukee has blended funding streams and currently operates as a behavioral health care carve-out. It blends funds from a monthly Medicaid capitation, a case rate from county child welfare and juvenile justice funds, a mental health block grant, and reinvestment from Welfare to Work agencies. The capitated rate covers all mental health and substance abuse services, inpatient hospitalization, and residential care. For the child welfare population, foster care, group home, and shelter care costs and nontraditional mental health community services (such as mentors, life skill coaches, and recreational programs) are provided. It does not, however, cover the physical health needs of the population.

Wraparound Milwaukee has been able to demonstrate some remarkable outcomes. Currently serving approximately nine hundred youth per year who have been adjudicated in the child welfare or juvenile justice system, the program has substantially reduced the use of high-end residential and acute psychiatric inpatient services and improved functional and educational outcomes for the population served, while reducing the total cost of service for each youth in care. These savings have been reinvested in community capacity building, which has resulted in an increase in the number of youth served over the life of the program.

The potential benefits of embarking on an integrated physical health and mental health care model similar to Wraparound Milwaukee are numerous. A fully integrated care coordination model would improve the overall health status of foster children by virtue of earlier identification and evaluation of physical and mental health care needs, as well as increased access to appropriate services. This could result in cost containment through better preventative care, reduction in the use of acute care services, improved continuity of care while the child was in foster care, and increased utilization of community-based and natural support systems. Theoretically, the improved health and mental health outcomes from an integrated model would shorten and improve permanency planning for foster children in a local community.

THE ROLE FOR CHILDREN MENTAL HEALTH PROFESSIONALS

A 2002 joint policy statement by the American Academy of Child and Adolescent Psychiatry (AACAP) and the Child Welfare League of America (CWLA) urges that children who are removed from their primary caregivers because of suspected child abuse, neglect, or caregiver impairment receive immediate mental health screening followed by comprehensive psychological or psychiatric evaluation and reassessment given their compelling and urgent mental health needs. This screening and evaluation is to ensure that these children receive prompt and appropriate mental health care. In order to achieve this, the policy statement outlines the following imperatives for mental health screening and evaluation of these children:

- *Screening.* An initial mental health screening should be conducted within twenty-four hours of a child's placement in the care of the child welfare agency. The screening is intended to identify children in urgent need of emergency mental health services, including youth whose behavior may pose a danger to themselves or others. Appropriate training should be provided on the screening protocol, and the individual administering the screening should have on-site or readily accessible mental health supervision. Ideally, the mental health screening will take place as part of a child's health examination on entry into care and be conducted by a health professional with expertise in the developmental and mental health needs of children in foster care. The AACAP/CWLA would encourage states to use Medicaid's EPSDT funding as a vehicle for obtaining health screenings for children entering foster care as developmental and mental health screens are a mandatory component of the EPSDT screening exams.
- *Evaluation.* Children entering foster care and their families should receive a comprehensive psychological or psychiatric evaluation within one month of placement, or sooner, based on the severity of the child's needs as identified in the screening process. Evaluations should be conducted by qualified mental health providers and, where possible, include the active involvement of a psychiatrist trained in child and adolescent psychiatry. The comprehensive evaluation should incorporate the use of developmentally appropriate techniques and tools, be conducted in a comfortable and accessible setting, and address the child's and family's strengths as well as needs. Informed consent should be obtained from the party or parties legally responsible for the child. Where indicated, the child or adolescent ought to be directly involved with procedures such as informed assent and be made a partner to all assessments and treatment.
- *Child focus.* This process should include support for the child that acknowledges and addresses that removal from primary caregivers may constitute a psychological and social crisis for the child and family. The initial screening should seek to understand the child's internal experience of the placement and

the nature of the child's attachments. Placement often suddenly separates a child from everything familiar, including places (home, neighborhood, school) and people (primary caregivers, birth family, other family members, friends). Such sudden and complete loss may result in unrecognized experiences of trauma and bereavement, which can interfere with making new attachments and with the success of the placement. New caregivers may need immediate advice on how to help the child make a positive adjustment. Children may need mental health services to cope with the trauma of placement, even in the absence of symptoms that constitute a psychiatric diagnosis. Children with internalizing problems, such as depression and anxiety, should receive the same consideration for mental health care as those with externalizing problems such as disruptive behavior. A child's wishes about placement and visitation should be ascertained and given as much weight as possible.

Children and adolescents should be evaluated individually, and adequate time and preparation must be devoted to the evaluation so that every child and adolescent has the opportunity to express his or her concerns freely.

• *Family centered.* Approximately 80 percent of children placed outside the home are returned to their family of origin. In order to achieve successful reunification, whenever possible, we must consider the family of origin in assessments and services and supports for children placed in out-of-home care. Assessment and services and supports should be both child focused and family centered. The definition of family includes biological, foster, and adoptive parents, grandparents and their partners, as well as kinship caregivers and others who have primary responsibility for providing love, guidance, food, shelter, clothing, supervision, and protection for children and adolescents (National Peer Technical Assistance Network, 1997). Finally, other persons may be considered members of the family for purposes of assessment and services and supports depending on the family of origin, their culture, ethnicity, and language and the culture of their community.

Professionals are expected to work in partnership with the family for these reasons:

• Assessing the individual strengths and needs of the children

• Assessing the parents' and family's strengths and needs to deal effectively with their children's emotional and mental health needs

• Identifying ways to provide the appropriate mental health services and supports to children and their family effectively and to determine the level of involvement required with the foster family to return the child home

• Determining the level and type of relationship needed between the foster parents and the birth parents to ensure the emotional and mental health needs of the child are met

Some specific decisions need to be made early because they have a strong impact on a child's experience while in foster care:

- If a child and his birth family can be in immediate and continuing contact (face-to-face visitation and telephone) to decrease the trauma of separation
- If the birth parents and foster parents can be expected to communicate with each other to maximize continuity and mutuality in accomplishing therapeutic goals

Initial assessments and follow-up assessments should address these questions as well.

Family members should be considered essential partners for successful treatment unless there is evidence to the contrary. Wherever possible and unless mandated otherwise by the courts, there should always be family involvement in the assessment and reassessment process, the development of the individualized treatment plan, and the treatment and support process. All treatment plans should be individualized for the child and family and include family treatment services and supports as part of the plan unless the courts have restricted access or contact due to safety issues or there is evidence to the contrary. The treatment plan should also be in keeping with the permanency plan for the child, as well as the family service plan. When parents are mandated not to have contact or are not available to have contact with the child, the initial assessment and reassessments must address the impact for the child with recommendations for effective interventions.

Placing a child in out-of-home care automatically expands the definition of their family, at least temporarily, to include the foster parents. This means including the foster parents in the ongoing assessment and treatment and support process. With family-centered practice, when indicated, families are supported and empowered to be an advocate for the needs of their child and for the services that will facilitate the family's being successful in dealing with the emotional and mental health needs of their child. Other key components of family-centered practice include:

- Focusing on the whole family as the unit of attention
- Organizing assistance in accord with the family's strengths while acknowledging but not emphasizing deficits
- Except where a child's safety is at risk, service planning and delivery that takes family priorities into consideration
- Structuring treatment and support service delivery to ensure accessibility, minimal disruption of family integrity, and routine

- Sharing of results of the assessments and reassessments with the birth family when a child is returning home (should this not have been done during out-of-home care) or the adoptive families when a child is being adopted

- *Cultural sensitivity and administration in a culturally competent manner.* The assessment and evaluation of children and their families must take into account the influence of each family's heritage. This includes culture, ethnicity, and religion and consists of race, religion, gender, socioeconomic status, language, sexual orientation, geographical origin and location, and immigration status.

Clinicians and staff who perform assessments should develop specialized knowledge and understanding about the history, tradition, values, family systems, perceptions, communication styles, and artistic expressions of major client groups that they serve (National Association of Social Workers, 2001a). Acquiring this knowledge should be accompanied by a regular assessment of their own personal values, beliefs, and biases in an effort to inform their practice and increase the quality of relationships they have with the children and families they serve (National Association of Social Workers, 2001b).

This cross-cultural knowledge and personal awareness should be considered and applied to all approaches, skills, and techniques when working with children and families (National Association of Social Workers, 2001b). This kind of approach is necessary to understand the stigma and shame that many cultures associate with mental health issues. This insight will help clinicians and staff to better understand the kind of help people seek, the types of coping and communication styles, social supports needed, and the level of resistance to treatment that can be expected from the children and families they serve (U.S. Department of Health and Human Services, 2001).

In all circumstances, special consideration should be given to ensure that there are adequate numbers of clinicians and staff who speak the languages of the client groups served and that procedures are in place for obtaining any needed translation and interpreter services.

In addition, it is necessary to ensure that all screening tools, protocols, instruments, and approaches used in the mental health screening, assessment, evaluation, and treatment process are geared toward the population being served. Given the most recent statistics regarding the racial disparity in individuals obtaining mental health services and those involved with the child welfare system, this commitment to cultural competence is essential to adequately assess and treat the mental health needs of children in the foster care system and their families (U.S. Department of Health and Human Services, 2001).

- *Reevaluations and standardized collection of health information.* All foster children are at serious risk for emotional and psychiatric difficulty and ought to be reevaluated periodically. The appropriate intervals depend on the severity of the child's disturbance and the family's needs and must be determined on a case-by-case basis. Children who are found at initial screening to have emotional or psychiatric difficulties need to be treated and reevaluated at regular intervals. Those in group homes and residential treatment centers usually have been placed in out-of-family foster care because they are already exhibiting more serious behavioral issues and should be receiving intensive interventions. They require closer supervision and more frequent reevaluation.

The timing and frequency of reevaluations need to be consistent with best practices such as AACAP guidelines. Reevaluations should collect standardized information needed to ensure continuity of care.

Children who need psychotropic medications, including psychostimulants, should be reevaluated following the AACAP Policy Statement, "Prescribing Psychoactive Medications for Children and Adolescents," approved on September 20, 2001. During the initial stabilization period, children should be reevaluated frequently and should have immediate access to a psychiatrist if they experience any difficulty adjusting to the medications. Once the child is stabilized on a standard dose of medication, he or she should be reevaluated in a face-to-face interview no less than every three months.

Children and families who are adjusting well to foster care and are in no apparent need of mental health intervention should also be reevaluated in face-to-face interviews at regular intervals—no less than every twelve months or as requested by the child or family. Given the level of vulnerability of children and the potential to be revictimized and traumatized, professionals must evaluate and reevaluate to ensure the ongoing safety and well-being of children in out-of-home care.

Children about to leave the system should be reevaluated. Those who need, or desire, further mental health services should have adequate referral and follow-up plans in place to ensure proper continuity of care. All parties involved in the child's care should be notified of any follow-up appointments. The clinician should follow the standard procedures (locale specific) that are in place to document summary reports and ensure that the child's health data are conveyed to the next provider or caregiver, if this is the case.

These most vulnerable and traumatized of children need and deserve appropriate and effective mental health care. Mental health services ought to be provided by appropriately trained individuals, including the active involvement of a psychiatrist trained in child and adolescent psychiatry. The AACAP/CWLA (2002) urge local, state, and federal authorities to work together with the mental health professions to ensure that these children's mental health needs are met.

CURRENT AND FUTURE DIRECTIONS FOR INTEGRATED MODELS OF CARE

Any model of integrated physical and mental health care for children in the foster care system should incorporate population-based, public health principles that provide for a full, comprehensive array of services while the child is in out-of-home care and after exiting the child welfare system. Although state and local community factors will drive the development of the integration of services, it is imperative that communities begin to understand the complex needs of foster children and their families and begin planning for a service delivery and financing model that will support a seamless system.

There are immediate implementation steps that children service providers and communities can initiate to support the integration of both physical and mental health care into the child welfare system. As stated, immediate screening and provision for preventative interventions for children first entering out-of-home care could decrease the potentially negative impact of immediate removal from their biological families and placement in a new foster care environment. This could increase the stability and quality of the child's relationship with the foster caregiver, reduce the risk of multiple foster home placements, and shorten the time a child spends in the out-of-home care system. Additional benefits of an early screening process include more timely referrals for comprehensive medical, psychiatric, psychological, and educational assessments; early identification and referral of children who require more restrictive levels of mental health care such as inpatient hospitalization; and better support services for foster parents who have difficult-to-manage children.

Given the discontinuity of past medical, mental health, and educational interventions for many children in foster care, it is recommended that both past treatment history (including immunization records) and the results of multi-disciplinary screening and assessment be collated into one comprehensive health "passport" for each child in out-of-home care. This passport can then be used by the multiple provider agencies to direct the type and intensity of services that the child needs for improved functioning and as a continuous medical record to chart the child's progress. Thus, the health passport lays the foundation for a health and mental health care management system, ensuring that all treatment modalities are integrated and monitored.

Treatment interventions must be made available as soon as possible after placement to maximize the foster child's individual physical, emotional, and intellectual development (Schneiderman, Connors, Fribourg, Gries, & Gonzales, 1998). Mental health providers can provide agency-based clinical consultation to assist the child welfare worker in formulating and attaining permanency goals that recognize not only the physical and mental health needs of foster children but that of their biological parents. As needed, the mental health consultant should be available to meet with the foster child, biological and foster parents, and case worker to assist in the ongoing development and monitoring of treatment and service plans that promote the achievement of the permanency plan.

The child mental health clinician can also be incorporated into the child welfare system's home visitation program. The clinician can provide a therapeutic experience for both the foster child and the biological parents while performing an ongoing assessment for the child welfare worker of both the timing and ability of the child to be reunified with the biological parents. The mental health clinician can also assist the biological parents in developing more positive age-appropriate parenting skills while supporting both the child and foster parents in the emotional and behavioral consequences that are precipitated by the visits.

Local child welfare agencies can develop preventive mental health and educational programs in support of the overall care of children in foster care. Preventive programs may help to ameliorate long-term consequences of chronic psychosocial stressors: peer support groups for foster children and their foster parents, increased education about physical and mental health issues for foster families and caseworkers, and the use of foster parent mentors to teach newer foster families more effective strategies of handling problematic behaviors by their foster children. Foster children would benefit from infant and child stimulation programs, reading promotion, and early childhood education. These are in addition to services provided by the child welfare agencies that are directed toward biological families and designed to promote family reunification.

Although most communities nationwide address the needs of children in foster care to various degrees, it is imperative that each community examine the gaps in its own service delivery system. As communities begin to plan for a system of health and mental health services for foster children, financing models can be developed to support the clinical integrity of this continuum of care. It is the integration of all of these factors that in the end should produce what is in the best interests of the child.

References

American Academy of Child and Adolescent Psychiatry and Child Welfare League of America. (2002). *Joint policy statement on mental health screening and evaluation of children in foster care.* Washington, DC: Author.

Chernoff, R., Combs-Orme, T., Risley-Curtiss, C., & Heisler, A. (1994). Assessing the health status of children entering foster care. *Pediatrics, 93,* 541–601.

Child Welfare League of America. (1988). *Standards for health care services for children in foster care.* Washington, DC: Child Welfare League of America.

Halfon, N., Berkowitz, G., & Klee, L. (1992). Children in foster care in California: An examination of Medi-Cal reimbursed health services utilization. *Pediatrics, 89,* 1230–1237.

Halfon, N., Mendonca, A., & Berkowitz, G. (1995). Health status of children in foster care: The experience of the Center for the Vulnerable Child. *Archives of Pediatric Adolescent Medicine, 149,* 386–392.

Hochstadt, N. J., Jaudes, P. K., Zimo, D. A., & Schachter, J. (1987). The medical and psychosocial needs of children entering foster care. *Child Abuse and Neglect, 11,* 53–62.

National Association of Social Workers. (2001a, June). Standards for cultural competence in social work practice. In *Standard 3: Cross-cultural knowledge.* Available on-line at: http://www.naswdc.org/ pubs/standards/ cultural.htm#Standard 2.

National Association of Social Workers. (2001b, June). Standards for cultural competence in social work practice. In *Standard 2: Self awareness.* Available on-line at: http://www.naswdc.org/pubs/standards/cultural.htm#Standard 2.

National Peer Technical Assistance Network. (1997, Nov.). *Family-professional relationships: moving forward together.* Rockville, MD: Office of the Surgeon General, U.S. Public Health Service, U.S. Department of Health and Human Services.

Rosenfeld, A. A., Pilowsky, D. J., Fine, P., Thorpe, M., Fein, E., Simms, M. D., Halfon, N., Irwin, M., Alfaro, J., Saletsky, R., & Nickman, S. (1997). Foster care: An update. *Journal of the American Academy of Child and Adolescent Psychiatry, 36,* 448–457.

Rosenfeld, A., Wasserman, S., & Pilowsky, D. J. (1998). Psychiatry and children in the child welfare system. *Child and Adolescent Psychiatric Clinics of North America, 7,* 515–536.

Schneiderman, M., Connors, M. M., Fribourg, A., Gries, L., & Gonzales, M. (1998). Mental health services for children in out-of-home care. *Child Welfare, 77,* 29–40.

Simms, M. D. (1989). The foster care clinic: A community program to identify treatment needs of children in foster care. *Journal of Developmental and Behavioral Pediatrics, 10*(3), 121–128.

Takayama, J. I., Bergman, A. B., & Connell, F. A. (1994). Children in foster care in the state of Washington: Health care utilization and expenditures. *Journal of the American Medical Association, 271,* 1850–1855.

Task Force on Healthcare for Children in Foster Care. (2001). *Fostering health: Health care for children in foster care.* Lake Success, NY: American Academy of Pediatrics, District II, New York State.

U.S. Department of Health and Human Services. (2001). *Mental health: Culture, race, and ethnicity—a supplement to mental health: A report of the surgeon general.* Rockville, MD: Office of the Surgeon General, U.S. Public Health Service, U.S. Department of Health and Human Services.

PART FOUR

ADMINISTRATION
AND EVALUATION OF
SYSTEMS OF CARE

CHAPTER SIXTEEN

Relationships Between Systems of Care and Federal, State, and Local Governments

Albert A. Zachik
William M. Heffron
Wade Junek
Andres Pumariega
Terry Russell

G overnment can impede or foster the development of systems of care for children and adolescents with mental health needs. Government's policies and the collaboration of its agencies can promote better integrated and more comprehensive services for children. However, if government leaders are not supportive of services based on interagency collaboration, the care of youth can remain disjointed, duplicative, inefficient, and often less effective. This chapter examines the ways in which federal governments and several state and provincial governments in the United States and Canada are promoting the development of systems of care for children and adolescents.

U.S. FEDERAL GOVERNMENT ROLE

The federal government sets broad national public policy for mental health services for children and adolescents. In the United States, policy initiatives can be initiated from the executive branch of government (by the president or one or more of the president's cabinet secretaries) or by a member of the legislative branch in the U.S. Congress (by a member or group of members of Congress).

Federal Government Initiatives: Reports and Documents

The surgeon general, David Satcher, has released several reports that have affected policy and clinical practice in state and local jurisdictions:

- *Mental Health: A Report of the Surgeon General* (U.S. Public Health Service, 1999) resulted from a partnership between the Department of Health and Human Services, Center for Mental Health Services (CMHS), and the National Institute of Mental Health. The report reflected an extensive review of scientific literature on mental health and supported a clear connection between mental and physical health. It emphasized that mental health is an important concern for persons of all ages. It supported several broad courses of action to improve the quality of the nation's mental health, including support for research, work against stigma, ensuring effective service delivery with ease of access, expanding the supply of mental health practitioners, and reducing financial barriers to care.

- *Report of the Surgeon General's Conference on Children's Mental Health: A National Action Agenda* (U.S. Public Health Service, 2000) summarizes the conference held in September 2000. The report spoke of the unmet need for mental health services to children and adolescents and suggested ways to improve care of youth.

- *Youth Violence: A Report of the Surgeon General* (U.S. Department of Health and Human Services, 2001b) examines the risk factors that lead young people to gravitate toward violence, reviews the factors that protect youth from perpetrating violence, and identifies effective research-based preventive strategies and programs.

- *Culture, Race, and Ethnicity: A Supplement to Mental Health: A Report of the Surgeon General* (U.S. Department of Health and Human Services, 2001a) highlights the role that culture and society play in mental health, mental illness, and the types of mental health services people seek. Racial and ethnic minorities are less likely to receive quality care than the general population. The report proposed broad courses of action to remedy the problem.

As with all other surgeon general initiatives, these reports do not prescribe policy directions. However, they highlight the areas of serious need for children and adults with mental illness that future policy should address.

CMHS's Promising Practices monograph series contributes to the national knowledge base by disseminating findings and lessons learned from providing community mental health services to children with serious emotional disturbances and their families. Among the topics covered are family and service provider partnerships in the system of care; new roles for family members; training strategies in systems of care; wraparound approach in systems of care; school involvement in systems of care; and interagency collaboration, governance, accountability, and leadership in systems of care.

CMHS's Child, Adolescent, and Family Branch also provides public information materials through The Caring for Every Child's Mental Health: Communities Together campaign, a national public education and social marketing campaign.

Once federal policy is established, the federal government's grant programs to states and local communities drive and support public policy initiatives in states and local communities that give life to the federal policy.

Federal Government Grant Programs

The CMHS, U.S. Department of Health and Human Services, which is under the Substance Abuse and Mental Health Services Administration's (SAMHSA) in the Department of Health and Human Services, offers several grant opportunities. In the 1980s, the Child and Adolescent Service System Program (CASSP) offered grants to states to hire CASSP directors to foster the development of better services for children with mental health needs. In describing CASSP principles, Stroul and Friedman (1986) note that a system of care should be community based, child centered, family focused, and culturally competent.

Authorized by Congress in 1992, the Comprehensive Community Mental Health Services for Children Program, administered by the Child, Adolescent and Family Branch of CMHS, offers grants to states and local communities to develop systems of care for children and adolescents with mental health needs. These systems of care are required to meet the CASSP principles established by the federal government in 1984. Many service sites throughout the country have been established with funding from this ongoing grant. States and local communities in urban, suburban, and rural areas have used these federal dollars to develop systems of care that meet the CASSP principles. The grants provide money for direct service provision to children and their families or caregivers and administrative costs. Technical assistance from national experts on the development of systems of care is available to service sites at national meetings of all the sites and individually to each site.

A major evaluation component of the programs established at the sites around the country provides useful information on what works for national, state, and local use in policy planning and program development. Service sites are encouraged to share best practices with communities throughout their own state. The federal government requires states to match the federal grant with state dollars in increasing amounts over the five years of the grant. This state funding helps ensure the long-term survival of the model programs after the federal grant ends.

Systems of care are developing and expanding in most states as a result of this national initiative. In the past, mental health providers had hospital and outpatient office-based care to choose from and little in between. As result of these new models of care, children and adolescents and their families now have access to a service system that is better coordinated among state and local agencies, with a fuller array of community services available near a family's home.

The federal government has also pursued smaller grant initiatives in the field of children's mental health. Established in 1981, the CMHS Mental Health Block

Grant program supports comprehensive, community-based systems of care for adults with serious mental illness and children with serious emotional disturbance. These grants are designed to improve access to services for people with serious mental illness, who quickly exhaust available insurance benefits and often turn to their states and the public mental health system for care. With input from state planning councils, states develop annual plans that must include goals, objectives, and performance indicators for improving community-based services. These grants require a percentage to be used for children's services.

In 1991, Healthy Start grants began with demonstration projects to improve infant mortality rates in states by targeting communities where infant mortality is highest. These grants focus on low-income women and their children, putting services where they are easily accessible, tailoring them to the particular community's needs, and integrating them with other services the family may need.

In 1997, Starting Early, Starting Smart grants were developed through the collaboration of SAMHSA, Health Resources and Services Administration, Administration for Children and Families, National Institutes of Health, Department of Education, and Casey Family Programs (a private foundation). These grants support early prevention and intervention programs through a public-private partnership for children from birth to age seven and their families or caregivers. The grants look to develop new knowledge, demonstrate what works, establish community-based partnerships to sustain improved health care and services, and integrate substance abuse and mental health services to improve outcomes for children and their families.

In 1999, the Department of Health and Human Services in collaboration with the Departments of Education and Justice, developed the Safe Schools/Healthy Start grants. School districts get support to help link community-based services and prevention activities into a single comprehensive communitywide approach to school safety.

CMHS's Statewide Family Network Grants Program helps family organizations to develop statewide family networks to support family participation in the mental health planning for their children and strengthen coalitions between parents, policymakers, and service providers.

Federal Services Funding: Medicaid and Its Offspring

Adequate funding remains vital to the growth and sustainability of system of care initiatives. Use of Medicaid funding, with its minimum one-to-one federal dollar match to state dollars, is a key component to sustaining systems of care. The federal government has also supported various Medicaid options and entitlements, which are particularly important for children's mental health funding.

The Early and Periodic Screening, Diagnosis, and Treatment Program (EPSDT) is the child health component of the Medicaid program. Under EPSDT, all eligible children are entitled to periodic screening services, including comprehensive physical examinations and vision, dental, and hearing screens. Mental health screens are also required as part of EPSDT. Mental health screens are supported by statute as well as federal case law from class-action lawsuits over this benefit. All eligible children are entitled to any medically necessary service within the scope of the federal program that is to correct or ameliorate defects, and physical and mental illnesses and conditions, even if the state in which the child resides has not otherwise elected to include that service in its state Medicaid plan. EPSDT gives child and adolescent Medicaid recipients access to many medical and mental health services.

The federal government has supported Medicaid waivers to allow states flexibility in how they provide Medicaid services. A 1115 waiver allows a state to place its Medicaid program under managed care. This has led many states to capitate its Medicaid program to managed care organizations (MCO), paying the MCO a monthly fee to cover all health services for each recipient enrolled in the plan. Many MCOs have subcapitated the mental health services to behavioral managed care organizations (BMCOs). The MCO then pays the BMCO a monthly fee per member to provide mental health service to plan members. There are various ways this waiver option has been used by states, some helpful to the development of systems of care and others not.

A 1915C home and community-based waiver allows the use of Medicaid for community-based care for children and adolescents who are Medicaid eligible based on the child's own income by virtue of long-term placement in psychiatric hospitals. These youth would not normally be eligible for community Medicaid coverage because their family's income level is too high. Under a 1915C waiver, they would be able to use Medicaid for community services if they continue to meet eligibility requirements for institutional level of care but could safely be treated in the community with intense wraparound services.

The Family Opportunity Act has been introduced in Congress to expand Medicaid options for states to cover severely disabled children in middle-income families. Many families whose children have serious mental illness find the costly services vital to the child's health beyond the family's own ability to pay. Many parents have exhausted their resources over years of caring for their child and feel they must give up custody of their child to the child welfare agency to pay for these services. This bill could help prevent the adverse outcome of lack of access to care for seriously ill children and their families.

The federal government also reviews health insurance coverage. Health insurance is available to some families but not to others. The benefit package for mental health services can be rich, more often in public Medicaid programs or barely existent as in some private insurance programs including most federal employee insurance packages.

U.S. STATE GOVERNMENT ROLE

Just as the federal government establishes policy for the nation, state governments establish policy for their particular state. Policy initiatives can begin at various levels of state government. The governor or lieutenant governor can set the tone to develop policy in a given area. The governor can place dollars earmarked for a certain initiative in the budget each fiscal year. A member of a state legislature can propose a bill to establish law related to a policy initiative and, if passed by the legislature, require state government to develop policy under the provisions of the law. Maryland's state legislature passed a law requiring intake officers in the state Department of Juvenile Justice to suggest to families of all youth seen at intake that their child receive a screening for mental health and substance abuse needs. This law helped move the state to improve the mental health and substance abuse services to youth in the juvenile justice system. Often a cabinet secretary or staff from a child-serving department will propose a policy initiative that is carried out throughout the state.

State government also responds to federal government initiatives. States decide to accept or not accept federal grant initiatives. There are good incentives for a state to apply for a federal grant, including flexible funding and technical assistance, but states can choose not to apply if the federal policy is not consistent with the state's current policy direction. However, the incentives offered by the federal government often are strong enough to move a state's policy toward the federal policy approach. Often the state can mold the federal initiative to develop a program more closely matching its individual service philosophy. However, a state's failure to meet a legally established federal entitlement leaves itself open to class action litigation by legal and consumer advocacy groups.

The state government itself offers grant incentives to local jurisdictions to drive and support the state's own public policy initiatives. The state can use its own state dollars or dollars from the state's federal block grant for mental health with federal government approval.

A state can choose to apply to the federal government for a Medicaid waiver. This choice can have a major positive or negative impact on the development of systems of care for children and adolescents with mental health needs and the resultant effect on clinical practice. For example, in a 1115 waiver application, the state chooses how it will provide services to Medicaid recipients and how it will manage Medicaid dollars. Mental health services can be a part of the overall Medicaid plan included with physical health services or carved out separately from physical health services. Mental health services can be provided under a capitated model under the physical health managed care organization or carved out and subcapitated to a separate behavioral health managed care organization. These capitated or subcapitated models can be done with the provider assuming full, partial, or no risk for the cost of care. Another option is to have mental health services carved out but remain a separate fee-for-service system apart from a capitated managed care system, which is the model in Maryland.

Critical to systems of care development in a state is leadership from various important stakeholders. The governor and lieutenant governor, state legislators, child-serving cabinet secretaries and their key staff, mental health commissioners, state child and adolescent mental health directors, consumer and family groups, other advocacy groups, and professional associations are key to the success of policy initiatives. Consumer and family groups like the Federation of Families for Children's Mental Health or local family organizations, the Alliance for the Mentally Ill, and the Mental Health Association are vitally important to the creation and successful passage and implementation of legislation or policy initiatives. Government officials, elected and appointed, all respond to effective advocacy by a state's citizens. Juvenile and family court judges and local community mental health agency directors also play important roles in local and statewide advocacy.

Professional organizations like the local psychiatric society or the local council of the American Academy of Child and Adolescent Psychiatry and other professional groups can advocate similarly and effectively to influence state policy, which in turn affects clinical practice within a state. There have also been numerous advocacy efforts to influence federal and state policies on the development of systems of care for children's mental health by national professional and advocacy organizations. These have included the American Academy of Child and Adolescent Psychiatry's *Guidelines for Children's Managed Mental Health Services* (1996), which many states have used in designing their Medicaid waivers, the National Mental Health Association's report cards of children's managed Medicaid services, and the Annie E. Casey Foundation's 2001 "Kids Count" report of the fifty states' health, mental health, and human services and needs.

Once mental health policy initiatives are developed, it can be critically important to have the policy placed in state law by the state legislature. This provides for more consistent implementation of the policy throughout the state. As state leadership changes with the change of a governor, legislature, cabinet secretaries, or other state officials or staff, statute protects the system of care policies and improvements. It is much harder to change a statute than it is to change a policy.

Continued education of all stakeholders and the general public is important to nurture further growth and refinement of systems of care development throughout the state and its local jurisdictions. Change in any state is slow but steady, and improvement in services to children and adolescents can be attained. Everyone working today in a system of care knows that it takes many years for effective change to occur and be stabilized. This often includes demonstrating both system-level outcomes using data collected by service or funding agencies and client-level outcomes as reflected in the stories of children and families that are shared with influential stakeholders and legislators.

STATE-LEVEL POLICY INITIATIVES

The following examples of policy initiatives in several states and Canada illustrate in practical terms many of the above ideas. These examples also show how government policy affects clinical practice.

Maryland

Maryland adopted the CASSP principles and hired a CASSP coordinator in the 1980s. Several state government leaders, including the governor, key state legislators, and cabinet secretaries, supported a statute creating a subcabinet for Children, Youth and Families. A special secretary works with the secretaries of the other child-serving departments, including the Department of Health and Mental Hygiene (DHMH), Human Resources (social services and child welfare), Juvenile Justice, Education, Housing, and Budget Management. This partnership is mirrored on a local county level and in the City of Baltimore with local management boards (LMB) that have representation from the same public agencies as well as consumers and the private sector. The subcabinet and LMBs on a state and local level foster partnership and collaboration among agencies to develop systems of care for children and adolescents.

In 1998, the Maryland Partnership for Children, Youth and Families was established by executive order of the governor. This group, chaired by the lieutenant governor, is composed of the subcabinet secretaries for children, youth and families, LMB representatives, child advocates, and citizens. The partnership reviews and coordinates policy initiatives for children and adolescents and sets budget priorities for child and adolescent programs. The advocacy of the lieutenant governor and the partnership has been critical to the funding of several new initiatives for children and adolescents in Maryland.

In July 1997, DHMH, under a 1115 Medicaid waiver, brought its Medicaid health services under managed care. Somatic health services and substance abuse services are capitated to several managed care organizations. Mental health services, with the support of the governor, lieutenant governor, key legislators, the secretary of DHMH, and the state's major advocacy groups for mental health and those representing families, were carved out into a fee-for-service system run by the Mental Hygiene Administration (MHA) of DHMH. On July 1, 1997, MHA became responsible for all Medicaid mental health services to all age groups in Maryland. It selected an administration services organization (ASO) in a contractual relationship to pay claims, credential providers, collect data, perform outcome and consumer satisfaction surveys, and perform utilization review. The medical-necessity criteria for services were developed by MHA with key stakeholders. These criteria, as well as the type and rates for specific services offered, are regularly reviewed for refinement based on consumer and provider input.

Any licensed mental health provider is welcome to become a provider in Maryland's public mental health system. The number of providers, including children's providers, increased dramatically in the new public mental health system. Rates for services are comparable to, and often better than, rates in private managed care systems. An increased array of community-based services, including after-school programs, in-home services, school-based mental health services, crisis response systems, mobile treatment teams, off-site clinic services, as well as traditional hospital and residential treatment center services and outpatient therapies, are available in the system. These new community-based services can be integrated with the services provided by other agencies, including schools, juvenile justice, and social services, and integrated into existing early childhood programs to improve wraparound services individualized to a child and family or caregiver's needs. Former state grant dollars are now used to fund public mental health services to uninsured families with a sliding-fee scale. Federal block grants and some state dollars are used to fund services not covered by Medicaid. Consumers, families, and advocacy groups work with MHA to improve the system.

The public mental health system is protected in state statute as a fee-for-service system. Legislative approval would be necessary to capitate the system.

Maryland has taken other initiatives that have supported systems of care and affected clinical practice. Maryland accepted the federal government's Child Health Insurance Program and chose to extend Medicaid services, including public mental health services, to pregnant women and children through age eighteen to 300 percent of the federal poverty level, effectively extending insurance to working poor uninsured families. MHA with Baltimore City and the Johns Hopkins University received one of the first service system grants from the federal government's CMHS. Called the East Baltimore Mental Health Partnership, it provides a model of a system of care approach for children to the state with school-based clinicians in nineteen schools in Baltimore City, service coordination teams for children involved with several agencies, as well as services to Head Start programs and violence prevention initiatives with the city police department.

Maryland has submitted a 1915C Medicaid waiver to the federal government to allow Medicaid coverage to continue for community-based services for children and adolescents in need of residential treatment center (RTC) level of care. The U.S. Congress is currently considering the Family Opportunity Act, which would allow RTCs to be covered under a 1915C waiver, which currently applies only to hospitals and nursing homes. If passed, Maryland's 1915C waiver will make Medicaid public mental health system services available in the community to youth otherwise not covered due to the higher income level of their families.

Maryland continues to look for ways for its public mental health system to be responsive to the needs of its citizens and to integrate with existing programs and services of other child service agencies as well as preschool early childhood services. The flexibility of a fee-for-service model with any willing licensed provider welcome to be a public mental health system provider has caused mental health services to grow in Maryland and had a positive impact.

Kentucky

The Kentucky experience with systems of care began when the Bluegrass area of central Kentucky was included as a site in the original grant from the private Robert Wood Johnson Foundation (RWJ). As part of the process, the state legislature needed to provide matching money and be willing to continue funding a system based on the CASSP principles. In 1992 the legislature created the State Interagency Council (SIAC) for Services to Children with an Emotional Disability, with representatives from the Departments of Families, Mental Health, Social Services, and Education and the Office of the Courts. Comparable regional interagency councils (RIAC) were created. Funding was provided not only for the RWJ grant site but also for statewide implementation of the project, as the grant's effectiveness became apparent. The new approach became known as the Kentucky IMPACT Program.

Kentucky has 120 counties, and having the interagency structure at the state and regional level rather than county level was easier to manage. Over the years, representatives from public health, Medicaid, juvenile justice, and family resource centers have been added. In addition, some local interagency councils (LIAC) were created to address geographical or population needs. The number of children served in the fiscal year ending June 30, 2000, was 5,831 and will remain at that level unless funding increases. The Department of Mental Health estimates that roughly 11 percent of children with complex needs actually receive services.

When the SIAC was first conceived, the functions of mental health, public health, Medicaid, social services, and juvenile justice were all under the same cabinet. In 1996, the cabinet was dismantled and the departments shifted to three cabinets: Health Services, Families and Children, and Justice. The reorganization has caused more service fragmentation and attempts to shift costs to other departments as a negative effect. Nevertheless, juvenile justice has thrived in the new system because it receives more funding and administrative support.

In 1995, to complicate matters further, the state began to toy with a behavioral health carve-out for Medicaid services. In the end, after much expenditure of time and effort, the health services cabinet decided to pass and keep its fee-for-service system for mental health services. Some positive effects of this effort included development of methods to evaluate service effectiveness and a growing recognition that more case management and intermediate-level services were needed in order to reduce the costs of high-end services such as hospitalization and out-of-home residential care.

In 1998, the departments of Mental Health, Community-based Services, and Medicaid Services developed a funding stream, IMPACT PLUS, to develop services to allow children in institutional care to reside in the community. The program grew astronomically and quickly surpassed its budget but did successfully manage to return children to the community. It had been assumed that IMPACT PLUS would be folded into the Medicaid carve-out, but once that effort failed, IMPACT PLUS was eventually managed by the agency that did hospital length-of-stay reviews. IMPACT PLUS seems to serve about half the number of children that IMPACT does and has expanded the continuum of care in the state.

In 1999, building on the structure of the IMPACT Program, the southeastern part of the state received a federal CMHS grant to expand interagency cooperation. The grant is helping to strengthen relationships with schools by providing service teams, including a family liaison in certain selected schools. A heavy emphasis has been placed on cross-training staff from different agencies. A liaison position to the courts and juvenile justice has been created. More crisis stabilization services and therapeutic foster care services to serve children from all agencies have been created.

In the past few years, as new departments have joined the SIAC, more effort has been expended to formalize interagency agreements and try to standardize how referrals to the IMPACT program are made. In the past, these processes seemed more informal. In addition, the SIAC has begun to meet in different locations around the state in order to improve communication between the state and regional representatives. The role of family representatives is being examined so that they can enhance their independence from agencies and express opinions freely.

Tennessee and TennCare

Tennessee had one of the more progressive children's mental health systems in the southern United States. Although the level of funding for children's mental health services in its earlier years was relatively low, Tennessee pioneered some important approaches for later systems development. The Re-Education philosophy of children's mental health services, originated by Hobbs and colleagues (Hobbs & Robinson, 1982) at Peabody College (later of Vanderbilt University) steered the field away from a psychoanalytic approach to the treatment of children and toward a more ecological and behavioral orientation, becoming one of the precursors of the systems of care movement. A signal event in family advocacy took place in Tennessee in the late 1970s when the state cut funding to the first children's psychiatric inpatient unit at Vanderbilt Medical Center. Parents of children served in this program staged an advocacy intervention to keep the program open, including a sit-in and lobbying at the state capitol. This resulted in the provision of Medicaid funding for children's inpatient treatment for the first time in the state, thus saving the program, which continues to exist today.

The 1980s witnessed a rapid expansion of both corporate for-profit health companies based in Nashville (including psychiatric companies) in parallel with the rapid growth of inpatient services for children and adolescents in the state, primarily in the main population centers. Many of these came to benefit from expanded Medicaid funding for mental health services. In the late 1980s, the CASSP initiative in the state contributed to the development of both a Child and Adolescent Office in the state Department of Mental Health and Mental Retardation (now Mental Health and Developmental Disabilities, DMHDD) as well as more advocacy for community-based children's mental health services. These services were developed by the state's community mental health centers that were private, not-for-profit, locally administered entities receiving preferential Medicaid billings and some grants directly from the state, especially for model demonstration programs. These contributed to the development of a broader range of children's services, such as day treatment programs, group homes, in-home services, and even therapeutic nurseries.

The Birth of TennCare. In the early 1990s, Tennessee faced a crisis in health care coverage and funding. The annual cost of Medicaid soared, while its numbers of uninsured individuals grew exponentially, the result of the type of industrialization being pressed by the state, which focused on entry-level jobs without benefits. Many regions in the state, especially rural regions, also lacked adequate primary care medical services. At the same time, the state's considerable health care industry was suffering as a result of the shift toward managed care by private insurers.

State government leaders, led by Governor Ned McWherter, wanted to reform the state's health care system to address its many shortcomings. They watched the health care reform debate within the Clinton administration in 1992–1993 with great interest. Once the reform forces were defeated in Washington, they approached the Clinton administration with an intriguing proposal: to allow Tennessee to become an experiment for health care reform at a state level. Their proposal incorporated many of the Clinton health task force's ideas of fostering managed competition among private health providers, applying managed care technology to control costs and expanding health coverage with the resulting savings. The use of private health entities also benefited Tennessee's hard-pressed health industry. The Clinton administration also saw the opportunity to pursue the reform agenda in an incremental manner and rolled out the 1115 and 1915 Medicaid waiver programs, granting Tennessee the first 1115 waiver for its new TennCare program.

TennCare Structure and Organization. TennCare started as a fully capitated and fully at-risk managed Medicaid program for physical health services, carving out mental heath services initially on a fee-for-services basis. Its plan was eventually to "carve-in" mental health back into the plan, with an overall capitated rate fostering integration of primary care and mental health services. Its benefits paralleled the state employees' health plan, with the state using participation in this plan to leverage provider participation in TennCare.

Initially, multiple MCOs contracted with the TennCare Bureau (the successor of the state Medicaid agency) and had different levels of representation across the state's vast "Grand Divisions" (West, Middle, and East). Problems in implementation in the overall plan, as well as resistance by the powerful community mental health center lobby, led to the revision of the plan to carve in mental health. In July 1996, the state implemented a fully capitated, partial-risk mental health carve-out. This involved two for-profit behavioral health organizations (BHOs) managing the program, community mental health centers as the preferred providers within this program (receiving case rates), and some limited private provider participation (under restrictive credentialing procedures and discounted fee-for-service). The two BHOs eventually merged in 1999. The basic benefit package had limited inpatient and outpatient coverage and a restricted formulary (the latter eventually discarded), while an extended benefits package for people with serious mental illness or emotional disturbances received an extended benefit with limited community-based services.

TennCare's Record. The TennCare program has had significant successes in some areas. It contributed to the expansion of health care coverage to over 600,000 Tennesseans who were previously uninsured, including many children and their families. It provided expanded access to health care, especially primary care services to underserved rural regions (though this has begun to fail due to inadequate reimbursement to primary care physicians). It promoted the expansion of primary care capacity through its innovative use of disproportionate-share Medicaid funding to promote primary care training and services in medical schools and hospitals. It also reduced the rate of increase of the Medicaid budget, saving over $1 billion in state funds and over $2 billion in federal funds over Medicaid during the life of the program. It also provided support for Tennessee's important health care industry.

At the same time, the program has been plagued with many of the shortcomings inherent in fully privatized, first-generation managed Medicaid programs. These have come primarily as a result of its reliance on private for-profit entities for managing care, which used primarily a benefit restriction approach with little support for intensive community interventions, lack of risk adjustment for the multiproblem populations covered under Medicaid, and lack of state oversight over these processes (and resources for such). Chang et al. (1998), in their study of TennCare's performance, found reductions in coverage and services that were especially pronounced for persons with the most severe psychiatric disabilities. They also found considerable shifting of the burden of care to other service sectors, such as criminal justice and human services, as a result of inadequate risk adjustment. Funds previously earmarked for the seriously mentally ill were now spread across the entire covered population. The program has also been plagued with problems with provider credentialing and timely reimbursement, leading to shortages of specialty services in many regions in the state.

Community mental health centers significantly reduced community-based treatment and support services for the most seriously ill individuals and their families. The influence of managed care technologies developed to oversee services delivered to middle-class populations, insufficient funding and lack of standards for intensive community-based services, and emphasis on the basic benefit package for the uninsured over services for traditional Medicaid populations contributed to these changes. The role of the state DMHDD in developing state mental health policy was greatly reduced, while the role of the BHO was greatly expanded.

These factors led to some unintended consequences for children and youth with severe emotional disturbances (SED). The BHO contract was silent on the EPSDT mandate for children under Medicaid, so the state was left without a mechanism for EPSDT implementation. Significant increases in hospitalization (and rehospitalization) and in children entering state custody resulted when families were unable to obtain longer-term intensive treatment services under the basic TennCare mental health benefits. The TennCare reforms left the parallel service system for children in state custody largely intact, even though the child welfare and juvenile justice agencies merged into a combined Department of Children's Services (DCS) in 1997. This parallel system includes large residential, group home, and foster home capacities provided by a system of private providers (and often community mental health centers) under contract to DCS. There have been significant problems in the coordination of care delivered under the basic mental health benefits and services, managed by the BHO and delivered largely by the mental health centers, and the extended services delivered under DCS contract.

Federal class action lawsuits against the state Department of Children's Services (such as the *Brian A.* v. *Sundquist,* 2000, lawsuit over placement turnover and permanency planning) and TennCare (especially the *John B.* v. *Menke,* 1998) lawsuit over the lack of implementation of the EPSDT mandate under TennCare) have been filed and are ongoing (see Chapter Eighteen). These have resulted in retrofits of TennCare that are being implemented. A special carve-out plan, TennCare Select, with a specialized provider network, has been developed for children in state custody or at risk of entering custody. This network also features a series of Centers of Excellence, located at regional academic or specialty medical centers, which provide specialty physical and mental health consultation to primary care providers, Department of Children's Services staff, and community mental health centers. There has been a greater effort to develop targeted case management for children with SED and more intensive community-based services.

In addition to class action litigation, family advocacy is becoming a greater force within the state. Organizations such as Tennessee Voices for Children (founded by Tipper Gore), the Tennessee Mental Health Association, and the Tennessee Alliance for the Mentally Ill have been increasingly vocal over children's mental health needs and pushed to participate in planning meetings between the state, the BHO, and providers. As a result, there have been recent efforts to redevelop interdisciplinary coordination and family advocacy at the community level. At the state level, there has been interagency planning for the development of an interagency system of care for children in state custody involving many stakeholders (including the BHO, MCOs, academic institutions, community mental health centers, and primary care providers) and family advocates. The newly reformed state Department of Mental Health and Developmental Disabilities has worked to reassert its role in policy development and oversight through increased input into the renegotiation of the BHO contract, particularly the implementation of best practice guidelines for adult and child mental health services under the contract.

Future of TennCare. The ultimate irony of TennCare model is that as a result of recent increasing costs of TennCare (and a general shortfall in state revenues), there are now plans to split TennCare into three plans: (1) a plan to cover the traditional Medicaid population (which would be covered as currently), (2) a plan with more limited benefits to cover the uninsurable and uninsured population, and (3) a program to provide vouchers for individuals and families who can buy into their employer health benefits. These changes would reduce overall costs but endanger some of the federal match usually applied to Medicaid-funded health care.

The Tennessee experience serves to highlight the pros and cons of a highly devolved and highly privatized system of care within a politically conservative state. The lessons learned from the TennCare experiment have been valuable for many other states as they followed in their 1115 and 1915 Medicaid waiver programs. Sadly, these lessons have been largely lost for Tennesseans as they look to the future. TennCare appears to be headed into more crisis rather than revision and improvement as a result of state's leaders' reluctance to pursue the tax base for adequate and quality health, mental health, and human services. Current lawsuits, underfunding, and cost-cutting efforts threaten the 1115 waiver itself, and there have been numerous threats by federal judges to return the system to a fee-for-service Medicaid system. Such a default solution would in effect throw out the proverbial baby with the bathwater. Tennessee nevertheless has the fiscal and human resources to reform TennCare to preserve its best aspects while serving the needs of children with SED and their families, as well as other underserved populations. The next few years will be telling in this ongoing saga, with significant implications for American health and human services policy as a whole.

THE CANADIAN EXPERIENCE

The desire to develop a system of care for mental health services for children and youth in Canada is held by provincial and territorial administrators for these services as strongly as state administrators in the United States. Despite some apparent advantages in health care delivery in Canada, achieving this goal is still elusive.

Federal Government Role

The federal government has two main roles in health care in Canada: establishing broad standards of care, usually through agreement with the ten provinces and three territories, and providing a portion of the funding through transfer of funds, usually from the federal income tax systems. The federal Canada Health Act (1988) and its predecessor, the Medicare Act of 1970, require all provinces and territories to provide health care within four fundamental principles: publicly administered, publicly funded, accessible to all, and universal in coverage for hospital and physician services. Other social programs (child welfare and young offender, that is, juvenile justice, services) that serve children and youth were developed in a similar fashion with federal transfer payments and federal/provincial/territorial (F/P/T) agreements that inform the delivery of services.

Historically, the separate F/P/T payments and agreements served both to create and to perpetuate the separate provincial/territorial (P/T) government departments and their subservices that would be brought into a system of care for services for children and youth. The rules and legislation governing the agreements formed one of the major barriers to the creation of a system of care.

Health care services delivery, including mental health services and most social services, are a P/T responsibility. The federal government role is to transfer funds primarily from income tax sources to the P/T governments by agreement and through federal law. Historically, the federal government funded 50 percent of P/T spending on health care and social programs such as child protection services and income assistance for the poor. Hospitals, fee-for-service medical practitioners, and public health were the primary recipients of federal and provincial health care funds through the F/P/T agreements. Thus, hospital-based and private office-based physician services had funding priority.

Traditionally, mental health services were precluded from the health funding formulas, except those provided by private practice physicians or in general hospital psychiatric wards. Consequently, these services have been developed as a matter of funding availability. Historically, outpatient or community mental health services, including those for children and youth, received partial funding through separate federal legislation and a funding agreement focused on the rehabilitation of disabled persons (25 percent of expenditure on a recovery basis from the federal government). More recently, community mental health services have been fully incorporated into total health services delivery and attached to regional service delivery organizations, funded under the 1994 new F/P/T funding formula, the Canada Health and Social Transfer (CHST) fund.

With the CHST, a number of the older F/P/T transfer agreements were amalgamated, and there were fewer strings attached by the federal government to the expenditures. However, the CHST also identified a lesser proportion of health and social expenditures for the P/T governments. In all provinces and territories, the difficulty has been to maintain existing levels of service with fewer and decreasing federal dollars (it was only in 2000 that provinces had a small increase in the CHST). Although there has been an effort to focus funding on effective utilization (only funding services that can be demonstrated to have a positive effect on health), this has not freed up dollars to fund services that were not traditionally a part of the Medicare scheme. Furthermore, although the CHST reduced the significance of one of the major barriers for provinces wishing to create a system of care, the history of separation, provincial legislation, and markedly different departmental culture, models, and administrations were entrenched enough to overcome the potential freedom.

Provincial/Territorial Government Role

In Canada, the provinces and territories are responsible for developing and administering health, education, social, and justice services (although the Criminal Code and Young Offenders Act are federal in scope, administration resides with the P/T governments), including those for children and youth. In most provinces, there are at least three levels of administration (central government, regional management, and local service delivery agencies or organizations) and two models of service delivery (direct public service with accountability to the departmental minister and nongovernment organizations accountable to boards of directors but primarily funded under contract to government departments). Generally there are, within each level, separate organizations for child protection and income assistance, public health, mental health, hospitals, addiction services, jails and community corrections, regional and municipal boards of education, and local schools. This matrix of services—three levels of governance and up to nine types of service organizations—is a major part of the problem when it comes to developing a coherent system of care.

In Canada historically, there have been two forms of mental health services for children and youth. Payments are made to family practice physicians, pediatricians, and psychiatrists on a fee-for-service basis for approved services, usually provided in the doctor's office. As well, larger and regional hospitals have developed pediatric wards and adult psychiatric wards that serve children and youth. In most provinces, there is at least one designated hospital ward usually providing psychiatric services for youth. Many youth are also served in the predominantly adult psychiatric wards of general hospitals. The second set of services developed out of the community mental health programs that were originally established to provide local care for the mentally ill so they did not have to be transferred to provincial mental hospitals or could be discharged from mental hospitals into community care.

Traditionally, physicians have played a greater role in the private office-hospital model than the community mental health model. Steps have been taken to bring these two sets of services together—for example:

- Paying physicians on a daily retainer so that they can participate in case conferences with schools and other service providers, as well as work closely with the community mental health workers.

- Hiring staff in community mental clinics but placing them in the hospital psychiatric ward in order to be responsible for discharge planning and follow-up after discharge.

- Amalgamating the community clinics and hospitals into regional service delivery organizations with a defined geographical mandate.

Child welfare services in Canada developed in the same provincial departments responsible for income assistance for the poor. Since the 1960s, these departments have also been responsible for services for people with mental disabilities, for the development and regulation of day care, and for funding day care on a means-tested basis for people with low incomes. Similar funding arrangements between the F/P/T governments have been in place for each of these program sectors. Significant numbers of the children and youth in child welfare services were discovered to have mental health problems. In order to receive timely services, the child welfare system developed and operated mental health services parallel to those operated by Department of Health–funded organizations and, in some provinces, even exceeding them in size and funding.

Young offender services have developed in Canada as part of the adult corrections services. The federal Young Offenders Act for twelve- to seventeen-year-old youth was passed in 1984, replacing the Juvenile Delinquents Act of 1908. The new act makes room for the judge to order a psychiatric or psychological assessment and for this to be cost-shared with federal funding at the same rate as other justice services. Young offender services may have their own staff of mental health clinicians for their community and detention services.

Education is a P/T responsibility, and there is no federal role in control or funding. P/T governments provide funding and oversee the system of schools that local boards operate. The province of New Brunswick experimented with this model during the 1990s by canceling local boards of education and operating the schools directly as a provincial responsibility. However, in 2000, it reinstituted local boards of education to be responsible to deliver educational services. Many educational services may have a full range of special educational programs that include a full range of mental health clinicians, another parallel mental health service.

In most provinces and territories, the tradition is to have separate government departments or ministries responsible for health (fee-for-service physicians, hospitals, public health, mental health and drug dependency), education (including all forms of special needs), social services (child welfare and income assistance), and justice and corrections. At the regional or community level, there are usually separate offices for each department or ministry and often for each of the subcategories of service. As well, most of the organizations have a mandate for adult as well as child services within their purview. Together, these organizations and agencies provide the services that would be brought together in a system of care in keeping with the use of the term in the U.S. CASSP document, *A System of Care for Severely Emotionally Disturbed Children and Youth* (Stroul & Friedman, 1986). Private for-profit organizations, foundations, and private practice clinicians are not funded by government health care plans (such as social workers and psychologists in private practice) and make a relatively small contribution to overall service delivery.

The Canadian model of service delivery has three main contrasts with the United States:

- Federal and county governments have no direct service delivery role.
- For-profit service delivery organizations and foundations have no significant role except when funded by government under contract.
- The total population is covered by universal health insurance that includes mental health benefits on an equal basis with other components of health.

Although some increased attention has recently been given in Canada to the role of for-profit or private medicine, public support for the fundamental principles remains very high, and any changes are unlikely to affect the services that would constitute the system of care for children and youth.

As evidenced by the national report, *One Million Children* (Commission on Emotional and Learning Disorders in Canada, 1970), and *Admittance Restricted: The Child as Citizen in Canada* (Canadian Council on Children and Youth, 1978), there has been a keen understanding of the need for coordinating services at the policy, planning, and delivery levels. With a universal system administered and funded by one level of government, administrators for child and youth services, including mental health, should in theory find it simpler to create a system of care incorporating the CASSP principles. However, no one approach has had the attention of all. Voluntary mechanisms have been and are still used in many places. Various provinces have developed new approaches to making the system coordinated, coherent, and consumer relevant.

Canadian Provincial Initiatives

Canadian provinces have tried various methods of addressing the problems inherent in the organization of services.

Nova Scotia. Four separate departments control planning and delivery organizations for (1) hospitals, physicians, mental health, public health, and drug dependency; (2) child welfare and income support; (3) juvenile justice and adult corrections; and (4) education and special needs services.

A subdeputy ministerial, nonfunding, provincial policy and coordination committee, the Child and Youth Action Committee (CAYAC), is in place and beginning to function. However, there is an absence of both regional CAYACs with associated mandates, authority, and funding responsibilities to create a system of care. Therefore, service delivery units still remain isolated and dependent on local efforts for coordinating services. The provincial CAYAC is beginning a process of creating a blended mental health service, but in the absence of actually starting it, it is far too early to comment.

Ontario. Ontario has a long history of an integrated ministry at the provincial level for mental health (excluding hospital based mental health units for children and youth), child protection, and young offenders (up to and including age fifteen, leaving sixteen- and seventeen-year-old youth governed by the young offenders legislation but within the adult corrections department). However, there has never been a successful integration of services at the local community level. The Ontario example illustrates that changing central government structure alone is not enough to bring integration to the community level. A number of documents and action plans to bring community integration have floundered at the political level. Community-level services remain as if administered by separate departments of government.

Manitoba. An assistant deputy ministerial interdepartmental Children and Youth Secretariat has full-time staff and some funding for joint administration. As a result, there are a number of specific projects successfully coordinating services.

British Columbia. Since 1997, one government department and thirteen regional operations have been responsible for services for children and youth, including mental health, drug dependency, child welfare, and youth corrections, with one-stop shopping for services and planning at the regional and community levels.

The organization also funds public health offices (80 percent to provide nursing, audiology, speech pathology, and nutrition). A change in government in 2001 resulted in changes to this model, with public health funding and drug dependency programs returned to the minister of health portfolio. Mental health services and juvenile justice services remain under review and may be returned to their original ministries. This recent and major government organizational change is still too new to evaluate its usefulness and effectiveness. However, the British Columbia experience of the past four years serves to remind us that decisions regarding the organization of services for children and youth are primarily political and seldom the result of thoughtful evaluation.

Advocacy Organizations

Government-appointed advocacy organizations such as provincial offices of the ombudsman, children's commissioner, or child and youth advocate have recently become thoughtful watchdogs and strong advocates for change within the overall services that care for children. As yet, they have not had any appreciable effect in helping to create a lasting integrated provincial or territorial system of care–based theory and grounded in evaluation.

National nongovernmental organizations advocating for the needs of all children and youth do not have a long history in Canada. For the most part, the organizations are either professionally based or specific to a disability, dysfunction, type of child, or type of service need. In each case, the concern is more likely to argue for separate or improved services, specific to the identified need or approach.

Barriers to Cooperation

Many factors exist to inhibit the successful incorporation of the CASSP principles and the development of a coherent and coordinated service delivery system for children and youth. The following list is confined to significant barriers within government itself and is meant to serve as illustration of challenges yet to be overcome (these may exist in state jurisdictions as well). It is interesting to note how many of the same factors serve to inhibit government collaboration on children's system of care development in the United States:

- The pre-CHST and longstanding F/P/T transfer agreements acted as incentives to divide child and youth services into groups that maximized financial gain from the federal government. These divisions remain deeply embedded in many provincial governments.
- Government legislation perpetuates the divisions and can inhibit sharing of information, cooperative work, joint services, and competent evaluation.
- Each branch may be divided into regions within a province, but none of the regional branches may have coterminous boundaries. This acts as a tremendous barrier to administrative cooperation.

• Some branches have administrative structures that bring the services in at a deputy ministerial level, and others end several steps further down the hierarchy in another department. Thus, attempts to bring services together for the needs of children may find committee members who have extensive knowledge but no authority meeting with other members who have extensive authority but little knowledge.

• For a variety of historical and ad hoc reasons, resource distribution can distort cooperation. Some service branches may have less than 10 percent of the money of another branch and be unable to bring the resources and support needed to another branch for cooperative efforts. The larger branch may end up funding another parallel service. For example, if children's mental health receives little funding, child welfare, young offender, or special education services may end up running parallel mental health services to meet the needs of their clientele.

• Some governments have no formal child and youth service linkages between the service branches. Cooperative efforts in the regions become very difficult under these circumstances.

• For the most part, desires for cooperation are centered about goals, for example, with service cooperation as the goal. Without goals linked directly to the outcomes for children and youth, the efforts seem more administratively led and philosophical than practical and immediate.

• Governments tend to provide no real rewards for cooperation and have many unplanned disincentives, making the efforts at cooperation too onerous to last.

• A variety of political factors add to the barriers: changes in elected government, leadership changes that are too frequent, a recalcitrant or indifferent leader in one of the branches, lack of public advocacy that reaches the leadership level, lack of knowledge of the issues by those higher in the hierarchy, and even political partisanship.

• A lack of shared vision and indicators of progress on the well-being of children and youth means that the system of care in most jurisdictions has problems both focusing on where it is going and determining whether it is getting there.

The result is that most existing "systems of care" are not true systems but rather collections of services.

FUTURE DIRECTIONS: A SELF-REGULATING SERVICE DELIVERY MODEL FOR CANADA (AND AMERICA?)

What will happen in the future will depend on many unknown factors, but a clear and important factor will be the degree of success of the methodologies set out in this chapter to bring about improved mental health and well-being of the children and youth of a province or territory. Since this outcome is not yet measured routinely, even evaluation of existing methodology is missing its most important indicator.

A self-regulating service delivery system model for child and youth services has been published in "Self-Regulating Service Delivery Systems: A Model for Children and Youth at Risk" (Junek & Thompson, 1999) and by the federal government's Health Canada, *Celebrating Success: A Self-Regulating Service Delivery System for Children and Youth* (2000), by the Federal/Provincial/ Territorial Working Group on the Mental Health and Wellbeing of Children and Youth. The latter publication has recently been distributed by Health Canada to all provinces and territories and is on the Health Canada Web site. This approach is intended to broaden the conceptual models (see Kagan & Neville, 1993, for excellent descriptions of strategies for collective action) available for creating a system of care and is as applicable to Canadian provinces and territories as it is to American states.

The model can be used to understand how services, as existing today, function, but its significance becomes apparent when starting with the model and re-thinking services delivery. The hope is that it will stimulate new thinking and directions for the future.

The essence of this model is that governments start with an outcome-based child and youth-centered vision that all children and youth achieve optimal functioning and well-being as adults. Without a vision, no one knows where they are going.

Four service delivery components then help the governments, service delivery organizations, and the public attain this vision:

• *Outcome measures.* A broad variety of indicators of the health and well-being of children and youth in both the general population and the service user population are collected on a regular basis. Without indicators, it is not possible to know whether services are moving closer to or further away from attaining the vision.

• *Feedback.* The indicators are evaluated, condensed, and published on a regular basis for all in the government, services, and public. This could be in the form of an annual progress report on the well-being of children and youth. It could develop and contain an index of well-being for children and youth to be given the same importance as the gross national product. Without attention to the developmental health of children and youth, the economic wealth of the nation will surely suffer. Without feedback, no one knows what is happening to children and youth or services for them. True accountability is not possible.

• *Incentives and rewards.* Essentially, this is the attribution of value to a product or activity. In this model, the value must be as powerful as profit in a business to drive a better product. The value must be firmly attached to incremental improvements in the health and well-being of children and youth. (Incentives and rewards for improved health and well-being of children should not be confused with the profit an organization makes for a service provided.) Organizations already respond to the many incentives and disincentives of their environment, but the problem, as many have noted, is that they have stronger incentives to focus on other activities, such as making a profit for management, maintaining existence in a time of cutbacks, staying out of trouble with the media, and political pressures from all levels. Furthermore, with the disincentives and barriers in place for cooperative activities, remember the list noted earlier and the fact that outcomes for children and youth are not even measured. It is little wonder that organizational activity is driven by many factors other than the state of children and youth. Without conscious incorporation of positive incentives and rewards, the unconsciously built-in disincentives will continue to rule, and the product of healthier children and youth does not receive motivating value.

• *Executive capacity.* Many models stress the importance of finding a method or bringing those with executive power into a working relationship to improve the cooperative activities and create a system of care. This model is closer to a business model with a product (improving outcomes for children and youth) and a powerful profit (the incentives and rewards). Once the reward is powerful enough and the product clarified, the system will move in that direction, and those who stand to gain the rewards will seek to make the alliances and create the appropriate executive capacity to produce the product. Figure 16.1 illustrates the overall model.

The System in Action

The system is controlled by governments or provincial/state/regional boards and functions, which are under their auspices, in a fairly direct manner. The government/board sets the outcomes (for example, reduced numbers of young offenders or reduced youth drug abuse rates in the community) and the incentives (for example, $1 million or prestigious awards) for jurisdictions or organizations that make the most improvements over baseline values. In practice, governments, service delivery organizations, and the community need to set the outcomes and incentives that are most meaningful to the local conditions.

The model can be developed in a series of steps, with the first step in keeping with most current government demands for accountability. The accountability question, "By what measures of the mental, emotional, or behavioral health and well-being of children and youth would the current government like to be held accountable for the millions or dollars spent in attempts to improve their status?" begins the practice of producing indicators and feedback. Once the practice of indicators and feedback is more common, the next step is to build in the incentives and rewards to accelerate progress for children and youth. (For further details on this model, see Junek & Thompson, 1999.)

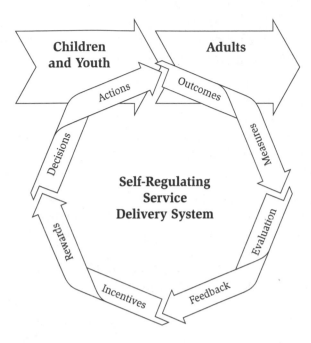

FIGURE 16.1. Self-Regulating Service Delivery System.

Potential Benefits

Once a self-regulating system is in place, there are a number of potential benefits:

- It incorporates the principles of the business model, which have allowed it to be so successful worldwide.

- It addresses and incorporates population health concepts as well as service delivery to individual users.

- It leaves communities and organizations more freedom to develop the structures that best meet their local situation yet stay focused on an overall better outcome for children.

- It accommodates to a wide variety of environmental, social, and economic conditions.

- It is compatible with a wide variety of quality assurance and management tools for organizations.

- The overall government role is simplified to setting the rules, allocating resources equitably, measuring and monitoring indicators, applying and monitoring incentives, and celebrating successes.

- While most service delivery has arisen out of historical precedent and ad hoc solutions, as a model, this system is subject to the testing of hypotheses, including those associated with the potential benefits.

- It is self-regulating and self-perpetuating.

- Above all else, it maintains its focus on direct improvements to the health and well-being of children and youth. This is what is counted, and as always in government, what gets counted is what gets done. It is the potential benefit to children on which this and all models ought to be evaluated.

The future of all countries depends on the developmental health of children. Indeed as Keating and Hertzman (1999), make clear, the nation that does not look after the health and well-being of its children risks reducing the wealth of its citizens.

For those of us who have given many years working and advocating on the behalf of children and who know that the mental health of children ought to be the number one priority of any government services to children and youth, let us hope that we attain enough success that we do not have to pass this struggle down to our own children and grandchildren. Surely it is time for children and youth to have their day in the political sun.

References

American Academy of Child and Adolescent Psychiatry. (1996). *Guidelines for children's managed mental health services.* Washington, DC: Author.

Annie E. Casey Foundation. (2001). *Kids count.* Baltimore: Author.

Brian A. et al. v. Donald Sundquist, Governor of Tennessee, et al. (2000). U.S. District Court for the Middle District of Tennessee at Nashville, Civil Action No. 3-00-0445.

Canadian Council on Children and Youth. (1978). *Admittance restricted: The child as citizen in Canada.* Ottawa: MOM Press.

Chang, C., Kiser, L., Bailey, J., Martins, M., Gibson, W., Schaberg, K., Mirvis, D., & Applegate, W. (1998). Tennessee's failed managed care program for mental health and substance abuse services. *Journal of the American Medical Association, 279,* 864–869.

Commission on Emotional and Learning Disorders in Children in Canada. (1970). *One million children.* Ottawa: Author.

Health Canada. (2000). *Celebrating success: A self-regulating service delivery system for children and youth.* Ottawa: federal/Provincial/Territorial Working Group on the Mental Health and Well-Being of Children and Youth.

Hobbs, N., & Robinson, S. (1982). Adolescent development and public policy. *American Psychologist, 73,* 212–213.

John B. v. Menke. (1998). U.S. District Court for the Middle District of Tennessee at Nashville, Civil Action No. 3-98-0168.

Junek, R. W., & Thompson, A. H. (1999). Self-regulating service delivery systems: A model for children and youth at risk. *Journal of Behavioral Health Services and Research, 26,* 64–79.

Kagan, S. L., & Neville, P. (1993). *Integrating services for children and families— Understanding the past to shape the future.* New Haven, CT: Yale University Press.

Keating, D. P., & Hertzman, C. (1999). *Developmental health and the wealth of nations.* New York: Guilford Press.

Stroul, B. A., & Friedman, R. M. (1986). *A system of care for severely emotionally disturbed children and youth.* Washington, DC: Georgetown University Child Development Center, Child and Adolescent Service System Program Technical Assistance Center.

U.S. Department of Health and Human Services. (2001a). *Culture, race, and ethnicity: A supplement to mental health: A report of the surgeon general.* Washington, DC: Center for Mental Health Services, Substance Abuse and Mental Health Services Administration, Department of Health and Human Services.

U.S. Department of Health and Human Services. (2001b). *Youth violence: A report of the surgeon general.* Washington, DC: Center for Mental Health Services, Substance Abuse and Mental Health Services Administration, Department of Health and Human Services.

U.S. Public Health Service. (1999). *Mental health: A report of the surgeon general.* Washington, DC: Department of Health and Human Services.

U.S. Public Health Service. (2000). *Report of the Surgeon General's Conference on Children's Mental Health: A national action agenda.* Washington, DC: Department of Health and Human Services.

CHAPTER SEVENTEEN

Systems of Care
and Managed Care

Are They Compatible?

Nancy C. Winters
Larry S. Marx
Andres J. Pumariega

The past two decades have seen dramatic changes in the organization and financing of health services, including mental health services. As a result of escalating costs for mental health and substance abuse services, and in part hastened by increased acute inpatient utilization in the 1980s, private and public sectors have adopted managed care as a primary mechanism to contain costs. Managed care can be described as "a technology that can be used to achieve . . . improved efficiency and cost effectiveness" (Stroul & Friedman, 1986, p. 594). It is not a monolithic concept. Managed care describes a variety of approaches to cost containment that include different financing strategies and relationships with providers and state and local governments. Managed behavioral health care exists in different forms and contexts, including both private and public insurance sectors; it can be integrated with physical health (the integrated model) or carved out to a behavioral health managed care organization.

The system of care movement has also evolved and expanded over the past decade, paralleling and more recently intersecting with the development of managed care. Many system of care programs now exist in managed care environments, and others will surely follow suit as they move from grant funding to finding sustainable sources of revenue utilizing existing local and state funding streams. The compatibility of systems of care with managed care is an important area to examine in considering how systems of care might achieve sustainability and broader applicability (Pumariega et al., 1997).

The goals and values driving the development of systems of care and managed care overlap in some areas and diverge significantly in others. The commonalities between the two models have often led to confusion and interchangeable use of the terms. However, the principal aims of the two are different. This chapter elucidates some of the fundamental areas of alignment and possible misalignment of these two methodologies.

The American Academy of Child and Adolescent Psychiatry (AACAP) published one of the first documents (1996) addressing the integration of managed Medicaid with system of care principles and practices (Pumariega et al., 1997). Written as a guide for state purchasers of managed care, it described the governance, benefit design, service features, information management systems, and quality improvement strategies of a Medicaid managed care program that would be consistent with system of care principles. A companion document described strategies for measuring performance and outcomes in managed mental health programs (AACAP, 1998).

Public sector managed care is the focus of this chapter since it has the most applicability to the populations served by systems of care. We also focus on the behavioral health carve-out rather than the integrated model of behavioral health managed care, as the more specialized carve-out model has generally been more supportive of system of care principles and responsive to the needs of more seriously disturbed populations (Stroul, Pires, & Armstrong, 2001).

WHAT IS A SYSTEM OF CARE?

There are different ways of defining *system of care*, and these definitions, when translated to goals and objectives, can result in very different practice models. Is system of care a set of core values and principles, an organizational structure for delivering services, a clinical approach, or a funding mechanism? It can be some or all of these. System of care is, first, a philosophy that is humanitarian in its origins. This philosophy was conceptualized as a response to several well-publicized examinations of the state of children's mental health services in the 1960s and 1970s (Joint Commission on the Mental Health of Children, 1969; Knitzer, 1982), which found that children with serious emotional, mental, and behavioral disorders were often not receiving any services. The services they did receive were fragmented, duplicative, and largely ineffective.

These findings led to establishment of the Child and Adolescent Service System Program (CASSP) in 1984 under the auspices of the National Institute of Mental Health (NIMH) and later the Center for Mental Health Services (CMHS). The philosophy articulated in the CASSP principles (Stroul & Friedman, 1986) was intended to refocus treatment efforts to address the unique needs of children and their families rather than the interests of service agencies, funders, and policy-makers. The CASSP principles assert that services should be child centered and family focused, individualized and flexible, community based, culturally competent, and coordinated and integrated across different agencies. These principles seem to be the right ones for all children and their families in need of mental health services. However, when the system of care philosophy is translated into practice, as it has now been in numerous grant-funded demonstration projects, there has to be a target population identified. Although the humanitarian values of systems of care should apply to the whole population in need of mental health services, the specific methods (here referred to as the system of care model) are best suited to children and youth involved with multiple systems and those who are at risk of out-of-home placement and other restrictive levels of care.

Unfortunately, that clarification does not resolve this conundrum. Although the system of care model was developed for the population of children and adolescents with serious emotional, mental, and behavioral disorders, the additional system of care goal of prevention and early intervention broadens the scope of applicability. Moreover, the system of care goals of parent empowerment, family involvement in treatment planning and system design, and strength-based treatment approaches apply well to all children and families in need of mental health services. And finally, there should be community participation in and ownership of the system regardless of the intensity of need.

WHAT IS MANAGED CARE?

The introduction of health benefits for employees came after the formation of strong labor unions in the 1930s and 1940s, which advocated for improved salary, benefits, and working conditions. From the 1940s through the 1970s, health benefits were seen as a means of attracting qualified workers or as a relatively inexpensive concession to labor, in lieu of wage increases. With the rapid rise in health care expenditures after the 1980s, driven by improved but expensive health care technology and an aging population, employer purchasers looked to prepaid managed health care to control the skyrocketing health care costs of a fee-for-service system.

The early methodology of managed care was to set arbitrary mental health benefit levels, based on large populations of generally healthy adults and children who were infrequent users of mental health services. This methodology was patterned after the success of health maintenance organizations (HMOs), multispecialty groups that mainly provided services to employed middle-class populations. This caught the eye of industry during the mid-1980s, at a time when mental health care costs were rising due to increasing use of psychiatric hospitalization (with the advent of for-profit psychiatric hospitals) and psychotherapy by insured populations.

The success of managed care organizations (MCOs) in controlling general health costs led to the formation of behavioral health organizations (BHOs), which were formed as special entities to handle mental health benefits on a subcontracted or carve-out basis. BHOs rapidly grew during the 1990s and came to manage the mental health benefits of over 100 million "covered lives." They used similar benefit reduction methods (such as reduced reimbursement to providers, preauthorization and concurrent authorization, retrospective denials of necessity, and restricted provider networks) as did the MCOs, sometimes charging MCOs (and employers) a capitated rate. Not surprisingly, some of the same for-profit entities that had operated free-standing psychiatric hospitals rapidly shifted to this more lucrative field.

The costs of mental health services continue to rise, and this is no less true for children. As reported by Ringel and Sturm (2001), the total mental health treatment expenditures for children in 1998 were estimated to be approximately $11.68 billion ($172 per child). This is a threefold increase from the 1986 estimate of $3.5 billion, not accounting for inflation. Medicaid enrollees account for 24 percent ($2.8 billion), children with other public insurance 3 percent ($0.4 billion), and the uninsured for 5 percent ($0.6 billion). Outpatient services account for 57 percent, inpatient services for 33 percent, psychotropic medications for 9 percent, and other services for 1 percent. There has been an increase in the rate of outpatient mental health service use since the 1980s, although only 5 to 7 percent of children receive specialty mental health services, despite estimates that 20 percent of children have a diagnosable mental disorder (U.S. Department of Health and Human Services, 1999). The fact that one-third of the expenditures are used for institutional care (not including residential care) may be related to lack of evidence-based community alternatives (National Advisory Mental Health Council Workgroup on Child and Adolescent Mental Health Intervention Development and Deployment, 2001). Racial disparities in service use persist despite higher rates of need in minority populations. Hispanics are the least likely of all groups to access specialty care (5 percent), even though they and African American children have the highest rates of need (10.5 percent,) according to measures in the National Health Interview Survey (National Center for Health Statistics and Centers for Disease Control and Prevention, 1999).

Fee-for-service (FFS) health care, managed care, and systems of care have contrasting priorities when viewed in terms of access, cost, and quality, often described as the three interrelated apices of a health care triangle. While the first priority of FFS was quality, its costs were high, and access to services was not addressed. Managed care had as its primary emphasis decreasing costs, with an additional goal of increasing access, while quality may have been compromised in the interest of cost efficiencies. Systems of care, which are a component of an overall public health model, emphasize quality first, with titrated access (to identified target populations), and costs dependent on the degree of management. For example, in the Fort Bragg system of care demonstration project (Bickman et al., 1995), costs were high, but utilization was not managed.

Managed Medicaid Mental Health Care

Managed care's impact on community-based systems of care has been felt mostly through its implementation in the Medicaid program. As system of care demonstration projects move into state managed care Medicaid, social and political priorities determine the system; managed cost is the first political priority.

At the same time that American industry struggled with inflation of health care costs, so did the federal government and the states, particularly through the Medicaid and Medicare programs. The budgets for the former program had grown exponentially as a result of similar factors as in private health care, as well as rapidly growing underserved poor and minority populations. In addition to these pressures, there were many political pressures for change in the public funding of health and mental health services. Political forces that emphasized the limitations of centralized government and the benefits of the market economy were gaining greater public acceptance. These trends were expressed in advocacy for privatization of services and shifting of federal responsibility to a more local level, outside government when possible. At the same time, the federal government and the states were under increasing pressure to provide health coverage for increasing numbers of uninsured individuals and families, losing benefits as industry cut back on health care benefits or as they acquired chronic health conditions that placed them in higher-risk (and higher-cost) categories.

The Clinton administration sought to find a solution to the dual problems of health care inflation and rising numbers of uninsured Americans through a comprehensive public-private health care plan. However, the Clinton health plan of 1993 failed to win support in a highly politicized environment. Many state and federal leaders began to consider the idea of pursuing state-level experiments with Medicaid plans, using the evolving managed care industry to help manage public health benefits. This led to expansion of the federal waiver program in the early 1990s, resulting in two basic waivers that states could employ to operate their own Medicaid managed care programs: the 1115 waiver (usually a fully capitated system) and the 1915 waiver (often a partially capitated program keeping specific portions of the health care system on a fee-for-service basis).

Types of Medicaid Managed Care Programs

A wide range of managed Medicaid programs was developed under these waivers. Some states sought to privatize and award their whole Medicaid programs to private managed care companies through management contracts. Many of these even tried to place the managed care companies fully at risk for the financial operation of the program within the capitated rate, while others held them at only partial risk, with clauses for reimbursement of losses. Many managed care companies are now passing the risk for providing care to clinicians through capitation risk-sharing arrangements. Other states used managed care companies only as administrative services organizations, contracting with them for specific services such as claims management, medical necessity determination, utilization review, and provider network development, but under guidelines developed by the state.

A variety of types of managed care entities currently are being used by states to administer their public mental health systems. These include for-profit MCOs, nonprofit MCOs, for-profit MCOs contracting with specialized BHOs (MCO/BHO), nonprofit BHO/MCO, private nonprofit agencies, and government entities. According to the Health Care Reform Tracking Project (Stroul, Pires, & Armstrong, 2001), recent trends include an increase in the number of states using governmental entities as MCOs, a trend toward the use of specialized BHOs, and continued high use of for-profit entities, which are being used in 70 percent of states (Stroul et al., 2001).

HOW DO THE GOALS OF SYSTEMS OF CARE AND MANAGED CARE COMPARE?

As shown in Table 17.1, systems of care and managed care share some common goals and objectives, although they may be conceptualized differently.

Identification of Target Populations

Each system has brought clearer definition to the term *target population* through identifying the clients for whom they are accountable. Systems of care were developed for the population of children and adolescents with serious (or severe) emotional disturbance (SED), generally defined as a mental, emotional, or behavioral disorder causing significant impairment in the important areas of the child or youth's functioning. Specific systems of care have targeted subgroups of these youngsters, for example, youth involved with the child welfare or juvenile justice systems and especially youth at risk of out-of-home placement. The system of care model, emphasizing interagency coordination and case management, is particularly relevant to this high-need population. Managed care Medicaid is responsible for the entire eligible population and other groups assigned to the MCO by the state mental health agency. Tension may result from efforts to balance the needs of a smaller high-risk population with the needs of the larger population.

Table 17.1. Goals of Systems of Care and Managed Care

System of Care Goals	Managed Care Goals
Serve children and adolescents with serious emotional and behavioral disorders	Serve entire eligible population
	Cost containment
Broad array of community-based services	Reduce use of costly services
Family involvement at multiple levels	Increase access
Individualized, flexible care	Expand service array
Interagency treatment and service planning	Improve quality
Service coordination	Improve accountability
Cultural competence	Increase access to preventive services
Accountability for outcomes	
Prevention and early identification	

Comprehensive Array of Services

Both systems of care and managed care emphasize access to a comprehensive array of services. However, in systems of care, the service array is individualized and uses a variety of traditional and nontraditional services, including home-based and culturally diverse interventions. Traditionally, medical insurance has funded well-established categorical services in hospital or office settings. Most managed care plans include established, categorically defined mental health services in their continuum of services. They tend to limit their providers to those within a network panel. In the interest of cost containment, managed care uses standardized utilization protocols that may further reduce opportunities for development of individualized services.

Utilization of Community-Based, Least Restrictive Services

Managed care and systems of care are both interested in using less restrictive mental health interventions, but for different reasons: in systems of care, the aims are humanitarian, whereas in managed care, the primary motivation is cost containment. The system of care value of providing care in the most normative setting is based on the belief that children's physical, psychological, and social development is best supported in the family environment. Here, the relevance of earlier versus more mature managed care strategies is in evidence. Earlier models and some that continue in the private sector mostly focused on cost savings, whereas more mature managed care approaches emphasized cost-effectiveness or value, often defined as quality over cost. Both are committed to taking finite resources and using those to maximize capacity, but they diverge in the values underlying how those resources are applied, that is, what is weighted in outcomes.

Increasing Access

Both systems have the goal of increasing access to care. However, as in other objectives, systems of care are oriented to the individual or the specific target group, whereas managed care is population based. Systems of care focus on particular high-need and underserved groups; managed care defines access through population-based service utilization data, or penetrance. Both require a single point of access to services: through a care coordination model in systems of care and a gatekeeper model in managed care.

Service Flexibility

Service flexibility is a key element for systems of care, as embodied by the wrap-around planning approach (VanDenBerg & Grealish, 1996). Wraparound is an approach to service planning rather than a set of services and emphasizes individualized and strength-based approaches, family empowerment, unconditional care, achievement of outcomes, cultural competence, and community-based services. The wraparound approach is committed to doing whatever it takes, regardless of cost, to improve the lives of the children with SED and their families. Interventions are often defined less by psychopathology than by psychosocial needs.

These strength-based approaches do not fit easily into the medical necessity criteria employed in managed care as stipulated by federal Medicaid regulations. The medical model continues to operate in many managed care systems, limiting more family-centered or ecological approaches (Woolston, Berkowitz, Schaefer, & Adnopoz, 1998; Friesen & Koroloff, 1990). More mature public managed care has been able to find ways to cover flexible services, but the availability of these services has not been fully achieved (Stroul et al., 2001).

Family and Consumer Involvement

Partnership with families is one of the core values in systems of care. Services are family centered, and families are active participants as stakeholders in every level of the system. As Friesen and Stephens (1998) noted, families are involved not only as recipients of services, but as partners in service planning, system design and implementation, quality improvement, program evaluation, and service providers.

In standards set for managed care by the National Committee for Quality Assurance (NCQA), the roles of consumers are outlined in the domains of consumer rights, satisfaction, and empowerment through involvement in program design and quality improvement (*Standards and Surveyor Guidelines for the Accreditation of MBHOs*, 2000). This vision has not yet been actualized; as noted by Sabin, O'Brien, and Daniels (2001), "The consumer's voice is still little heard and rarely effective in current managed behavioral health practice" (p. 1303).

Coordination of Care

Both systems of care and managed care use care coordination and intensive case management, but for different reasons. In systems of care, care coordination is used to (1) identify and implement appropriate services, (2) ensure that all services address the same goals, (3) integrate multiprovider and multiagency interventions, (4) monitor effectiveness of services, and (5) modify plans when they are not working. In managed care, the goal is to reduce overutilization of expensive services and provide cost-efficient services to high-need populations. This often results in case management at a distance, based on arbitrary utilization protocols. The model in systems of care is client centered, whereas the managed care model is system driven. This presents challenges when the case manager tries to represent both interests (also see Chapter Nine).

Cultural Competence

Community-based systems of care began as a way of addressing mental health disparities as well as enfranchising underserved ethnic minority groups (a significant segment of the population) within systems of care. These cultural competence needs were defined by Cross, Bazron, Dennis, and Isaacs (1989).

More recently, culturally competent care has been advocated by many as a manner of increasing care efficiency and accountability, that is, to improve access and acceptability of services and prevent adverse or disparate outcomes for ethnic and racial minorities (such as suicide, homicide, institutionalization, school dropout, or teen pregnancy), which lead to increased health and psychosocial costs.

Unfortunately, private managed care has been significantly behind in recognizing the value of culturally competent approaches. Some companies have tried to address this somewhat superficially by increasing covered lives or attempting to improve relations with minority communities. A few have gone as far as paying for traditional healing services, but as inexpensive alternatives to more costly comprehensive services rather than integrated into such care. In some cases, BHOs have disproportionately excluded minority providers and community-based organizations serving ethnic minority populations from provider panels, reducing access to culturally competent services (Center for Mental Health Services, 2001). The HHS health disparities initiative and the surgeon general's supplement on mental health, race, ethnicity, and culture have progressively uncovered disparities in health and mental health among ethnic minority populations. Minority populations have significantly less access to any mental health services and certainly to culturally competent services (Pumariega, Glover, Holzer, & Nguyen, 1998; U.S. Department of Health and Human Services, 2000).

There is still much work to be done in the development of culturally competent services within managed care and systems of care contexts. Culturally competent practices need to be integrated at all levels of a managed system of care, particularly within its care management processes. Provider panels need to be open and to include culturally diverse providers. Development of a culturally diverse provider community should be an area of performance accountability for the managed care organizations (American Academy of Child and Adolescent Psychiatry, 1998). Culturally competent practices need to be addressed at all levels of clinical and support services (such as triage procedures, diagnostic assessment, care planning, case management, treatment implementation, and linguistic support and translation services) and system processes (such as governance, quality improvement, management information systems, and staff training and development).

Consumers will need to hold managed care systems accountable for meeting these cultural competency standards. Consumers and families will also have to advocate for the MCO to be held accountable for outcomes that are meaningful to them, not only to funders, policymakers, and stockholders in the case of for-profit MCOs. The Center for Mental Health Services' cultural competence standards for managed care provide useful operationally defined standards to guide managed care organizations in their implementation of culturally competent practices (Center for Mental Health Services, 2001; also see Chapter Five).

Accountability for Quality and Outcomes

Quality of care is a primary goal for both systems of care and managed health care; however, given the complexities of different constituencies' interests, it can be difficult to sort out what defines quality. The attributes of quality are defined as structure, process, and outcomes. National standard-setting agencies like the NCQA focus on only a few mental health quality indicators in their "report card" measures (England & Cole, 1998). Early quality monitoring in managed care focused on structure and process indicators, such as the time to access crisis services. More recently, managed care has been moving toward outcome accountability.

Although both systems of care and managed care endorse outcome measurement, the system of care philosophy is directed toward individualized, clinical goal achievement that promotes normal development, while most managed care programs focus on population-based outcomes and cost containment or efficiencies.

Successful systems of care programs address community-relevant outcomes that include both client-level and system-level outcomes (also see Chapter Twenty). Jacobsen and Cervine (2001) describe a decade of systems of care development in Santa Cruz County, California. By identifying specific clinical, fiscal, and system outcomes at each stage of system development, they were able to decrease hospital use and decrease residential, foster care, and juvenile justice placements. The authors compare systems of care development to tending a garden: one needs to continually adjust system goals and expectations to social and political influences (weather) and community demographics (soil). Program accountability is achieved through systematic quality monitoring and program evaluation.

Early Identification and Prevention

Both systems of care and managed care place value on preventive and early identification measures, although this goal is slow to be realized in both. The majority of systems of care programs have not included children under age six, although it is increasingly acknowledged that this young and vulnerable population would benefit significantly from the system of care approach (Knitzer, 1998). Some managed care characteristics may result in limitations of services to this early childhood age group. These include arbitrary benefit limits; medical necessity criteria that do not cover diagnoses appropriate to infants (such as the Diagnostic Classification of Mental Health and Developmental Disorders of Infancy and Early Childhood: 0–3; Zero to Three, 1994); lack of integration of mental health services with primary care and early education; and failure to address parental social and mental health needs.

The goals of prevention and early identification include potential cost offsets derived from decreased general medical services, less need for crisis-based intensive services, as well as lower costs in the educational, child welfare, and criminal justice systems. However, these outcomes require a long time frame, which may not be consistent with managed care's generally short-term orientation, geared to corporate benefit managers looking for short-term cost reduction (Jellinek & Little, 1998) and short contract periods (Heflinger & Northrup, 2000).

HOW DO THE METHODOLOGIES OF SYSTEMS OF CARE AND MANAGED CARE COMPARE?

As with goals and objectives, there are also commonalities and differences in methodologies of systems of care and managed care, as indicated in Table 17.2.

Financing Mechanisms

As mental health care systems have matured, both systems of care and managed mental health care emphasize capitation and case rate models as financing strategies and thus incentives to providers to use more flexible services. However, many public and private managed mental health programs are still designed to provide episodic mental health services rather than the continuous care needed for more chronic mental health conditions. They each develop their own benefit structures that are usually based on actuarial studies of historical utilization patterns of their respective populations. Unfortunately, many public

Table 17.2. Strategies in Systems of Care and Managed Care

	Systems of Care Strategies	Managed Care Strategies
Source of funds	Multiple: Medicaid, state and local general funds, contributions by other child-serving systems	Medicaid and mental health agency funds; other system contributions to a small extent
Financing	Case rate Case rate plus fee for service Blended funding	Non-risk-based (fee for services) Risk based: capitation, case rates, risk sharing Enhanced benefit package
Service strategies for high-risk populations	Intensive case management Community-based wraparound services Psychosocial necessity criteria for services; strength-based approaches	Intensive case management Community-based wraparound services outside managed care Medical necessity criteria
Interagency relationships	Interagency governance and policy setting Blended funding	Interagency coordination protocols
Providers	Culturally diverse Family members and paraprofessionals	May be limited to providers in provider network Variable degrees of diversity
Stakeholder involvement	Families represented at all levels of system (for example, service planning, system design, performance monitoring)	Use of family advocates, family involvement in advisory groups, requirements for family involvement in service planning
Accountability	Individual child and family outcomes Specified program outcomes (for example, reducing out-of-home placements)	Total population expenditures Access to services Patterns of service utilization
Data	Cost, including cross-agency expenditures, outcomes	Total cost of services tracked but other encounter data inadequate; few data on cost shifting

mental health systems have experienced multiple challenges in attempting to capture the true costs of providing services for their population. These barriers have included inadequate information systems within the mental health agency, pent-up demand for mental health services because of lack of access to care, and an inability to track mental health utilization in other service settings (such as primary care and schools). Politics, state mental health appropriations, and federal Medicaid policies are also significant determinants of funding levels. At times, this has resulted in public managed behavioral health care plans setting benefit limits that are not adequate to meet the mental health and substance abuse needs of more chronically mentally ill individuals. This has been true for children and youth with serious emotional disturbance.

Although Medicaid is the principal source of funding for public mental health services, children and youth enrolled in systems of care are usually eligible to receive funding for related services from other sources. Many of these sources are tied to other child-serving state or county agencies that operate under separate mandates with different eligibility requirements and performance expectations. In order to create a more substantial benefit design, these funds should ideally be blended with Medicaid funds; however, this is not easily achievable since in many communities, Medicaid recipients' benefits may be administered by different entities. For example, in California, each county can choose to administer the Medicaid benefit for its publicly insured population itself or to contract it out to a different fiscal agent. In Wisconsin, most county-managed Medicaid recipients are enrolled in prepaid health plans that either administer the mental health benefit or carve out the benefit to a managed care system. This additional level of complexity continues to perpetuate the fragmentation of services that is frequently experienced by these more severely ill populations.

Interagency Relationships

In systems of care, one of the child-serving agencies usually takes the lead in managing all of the blended funds available to serve the population. If the lead agency does not have the authority to oversee each child's Medicaid benefit as part of this pooled funding, this agency may not be capable of ensuring that the child and family's service needs are well coordinated. In order to provide coordinated care, it is important that each system of care establish a governance structure that fosters a single purchasing and regulatory authority that can oversee the provision of care. This administrative service organization must have a formal relationship with the state Medicaid agency as well, to ensure that the Medicaid benefit, if not part of the funding mechanism, is well coordinated. This authority can also oversee that the interagency agreements within this governance structure are contractually well defined, the services provided by each agency are consistent with system of care philosophy, and there is a formal continuous quality management program that monitors system performance.

Given states' and local governments' efforts to contain costs for this population, a shared governance model could ideally reduce administrative duplication with a potential reinvestment of savings into building greater community mental health capacity. For counties that can elect to manage their Medicaid mental health benefit themselves or contract it to an outside managed care entity, this may provide additional incentive to assume leadership with the other child-serving agencies in forming a shared governance model.

Strategies at the Service Level

Strength- and community-based services emphasized in systems of care rely on natural supports, as well as the use of culturally diverse, family, and paraprofessional providers. These providers may not be included on managed care network panels and may also have difficulties with credentialing requirements. MCOs often assign clients to specific provider networks or agencies, limiting consumer choice. The assignment of clients to specific agencies can limit opportunities for selection of culturally appropriate services. More mature managed care looks at flexible services and is able to expand service categories through capitation waivers. Capitation rates and risk-sharing arrangements may be adverse for community agencies, which require some capital investment to develop the diversity of community-based services needed for the broad psychosocial needs of the more seriously ill population.

Stakeholder Involvement

In grant-funded systems of care programs, there have been clear contractual requirements for family and consumer involvement at service planning and system levels. Families have taken leadership roles with systems of care in system design, program evaluation, and training (Osher, van Kammen, & Zaro, 2001). This level of involvement is more difficult to duplicate in larger managed care systems, which are more financially driven and bureaucratic. Consumer groups and advocacy organizations have included the requirement that consumers assume an integral role in the governance and oversight functions of managed care organizations (Sabin, 2000).

Inclusion of other child-serving agency stakeholders in the planning and governance of a managed mental health system is hampered by limited availability of interagency financing mechanisms and the financial incentives to shift costs to other sectors (Heflinger & Northrup, 2000).

Accountability Approaches

To meet the goals of different constituencies of the system of care, the managed behavioral health care organization must be accountable for achieving desired outcomes. The following section discusses various strategies for incorporating accountability in system design.

Goals of Different Constituencies. In the system of care model, the goals of different constituencies (or system stakeholders) are represented in every phase of system development. Ideally, system design starts with negotiation around desired outcomes of different constituencies. This minimizes the risk of lack of support of a crucial stakeholder further along in the process. Stakeholders in the system include the children and families who are consumers of services, mental health and substance abuse service providers, other child-serving systems (such as child welfare, juvenile justice, education, and health), community members, taxpayers, legislators, and other policymakers. The goals of children and family members usually relate to improved clinical and functional outcomes and decreased family burden; legislators and other policymakers usually emphasize cost and service utilization outcomes (also see Chapter Twenty). Other child-serving systems generally share the goals of cost containment and decreased utilization of restrictive services in their own systems. However, they are also accountable for outcomes as determined by their own legal and agency mandates, for example, permanency planning requirements for young children in the child welfare system and public safety for the juvenile justice system.

Performance-Based Contracting. With the application of managed care principles to Medicaid populations, purchasing authorities have instituted different methods of contracting with providers to achieve their financial outcomes. Different types of performance-based contracting have been implemented as incentives to providers to provide less costly interventions as opposed to relying on more restrictive levels of mental health treatment such as inpatient hospitalization and residential treatment. A variety of risk-sharing arrangements have been implemented as utilization management techniques. These have included full-risk capitated contracts to MCOs or integrated service delivery networks, establishment of risk corridors between the mental health Medicaid agency and MCOs or providers, and performance-based holdback clauses in provider contracts if specified outcomes are not achieved by the end of the contract period.

In full-risk capitation contracts, the purchasing authority sets a per member per month behavioral health payment rate for each Medicaid enrollee in its population. A total monthly amount for the entire enrolled population is passed to the managed care organization or integrated service delivery network. These organizations are then held completely financially accountable to manage and provide the range of covered mental health and substance abuse services under that Medicaid plan. At the end of the contract period, the managed care entity can retain any cost savings as a result of its financial and clinical management or is held financially liable for all costs for the population that exceeded the mental health capitation payment.

In shared-risk corridor arrangements, the purchasing authority establishes with the managed care entity or provider a percentage of payment share risk.

Together, both the purchasing authority and the managed care entity manage the total allotted Medicaid benefit for the covered population. If there are cost savings, each partner is entitled to its predetermined percentage to invest as each sees fit. If there are expenditures over the available revenue, each partner is financially accountable for its percentage share of the shortfall.

In holdback contracting arrangements, the purchasing authority delineates outcome indicators and thresholds it expects subcontractors to meet by the end of the contracting period. Typically, the purchasing authority specifies in the contract the percentage that will be withheld from the total amount of the contract (usually 5 percent) until the end of the contract period. If the subcontractor is able to meet the thresholds for these indicators, it receives the holdback at the end of the contract period. Obviously, an unsuccessful subcontractor does not receive the additional monies.

Although there can be multiple variations to these financing mechanisms, including a fee-for-service-component, the main thrust of changing the historical contracting relationship between the Medicaid agency and its subcontractors is to make entities other than the Medicaid authority accountable for achieving cost efficiencies while maintaining the quality of care for its population. Although these financial arrangements may encourage more innovative, flexible service intervention strategies, they also influence which services are offered to the Medicaid population based on the financial relationship between the Medicaid agency and its subcontractors.

Purchasing Specific Outcomes. States may purchase specific targeted outcomes to achieve important social and financial goals such as cost containment and reduction of restrictive service utilization. Programs able to demonstrate savings through the use of community-based intensive outpatient (and less expensive) alternatives to higher-cost residential or inpatient services have the greatest chance of sustained funding and public support. One example was in the California AB377 Evaluation Project, which was one of the first systems of care evaluations to demonstrate reduction of residential group home placements through interagency partnerships and community-based services (Rosenblatt, Attkisson, & Fernandez, 1992; also see Chapter Twenty).

Use of Information Systems. In order to demonstrate these cost and service utilization outcomes, programs must have the data systems necessary to calculate expenditures and cost savings across all mental health service components and also across other child-serving systems. Jacobsen and Cervine (2001) note that one of the biggest challenges in tracking pertinent information across systems is "breaking the mold of each bureaucracy managing its own information in disparate computer systems" (p. 130). They describe the development of a cross-system database that tracked all pertinent information about children in residential or foster placements, including type and location of placement, cost, and length of stay.

Another challenge facing public mental health systems is development of sophisticated information systems allowing for accurate actuarial data to aid in the more realistic setting of case and capitation rates for the high-need population. Some private sector MCOs have developed excellent systems to document clinical and financial results (Ogles, Trout, Gillespie, & Penkert, 1998); however, the data collected, especially reflecting service utilization, must be an accurate reflection of utilization for the population. For example, in the Fort Bragg transition to managed care, for example (described below), the managed care contractor measured new admissions to any level of care rather than the number of children served in a year, artificially inflating data on access, one of the contracted performance measures (Heflinger & Northrup, 2000).

IMPACT OF MANAGED MEDICAID ON CHILDREN'S MENTAL HEALTH SERVICES

By the late 1980s and early 1990s, as states and other governmental entities sought to control the increasing costs of Medicaid programs, many moved toward implementing managed care principles. Managed care approaches were relatively new in mental health at that time, and those that existed had been developed with adult and private sector populations in mind. Strategies for care and cost management were developed with middle-class populations of children and families in mind, who have personal and financial resources to compensate for restrictions to care access and utilization. Traditional managed mental health programs were not designed to cover the lives of children with limited family resources, histories of multiple inpatient hospitalization for mental health problems, and frequent utilization of other high-cost services such as residential treatment.

In some instances, when this methodology was applied in the "first generation" of managed Medicaid mental health, adults with severe mental illness and children with serious emotional disturbance exhausted their managed Medicaid mental health benefits and were moved out of the Medicaid-funded mental health system into public sector agencies such as child welfare and the correctional system (Heflinger & Northrup, 2000; Chang et al., 1998). This reinforced the historically fragmented and poorly coordinated care for children with serious emotional disorders. There was little incentive to provide integrative, multimodal interventions in the least restrictive mental health treatment environment. Intensive community-based services (such as day treatment programs, school-based programs, crisis intervention, and home-based intervention) were not covered under the mental health benefit and rapidly dwindled (Heflinger & Northrup, 2000).

The case management services provided by these managed care contractors was telephonic case management "at a distance" by workers who had little understanding of community resources and the clinical and support needs of these children (Jellinek & Little, 1998). There was also an adverse impact at the practitioner level. Not only was reimbursement for services reduced for populations that were already challenging to serve, but there were significant increases in bureaucratic procedures that increased practitioner administrative burden (Chang et al., 1998).

As a result of these negative impacts, many states have had to face litigation over the impact of their managed Medicaid programs on children, for violating the early periodic screening, detection, and treatment (EPSDT) Medicaid mandate designed to address the multiple needs of children enrolled in this program and contributing to significant increases in their state custody populations (see Chapter Eighteen). Many states using managed care companies as contractors reduced their involvement in administration, oversight, and policymaking around public mental health services, thus reducing consumer and provider input into system design and operation.

There have also been some benefits from the implementation of managed Medicaid programs in states, especially second- and third-generation programs, which used more community-friendly approaches. For example, some Medicaid mental health programs have incorporated increased key stakeholder involvement in managed care planning, special provisions for children with serious behavioral needs (such as intensive case management and enhanced benefit packages), and an expanded array of home- and community-based services (Stroul, Pires, & Armstrong, 2001).

The current shortfalls in state budgets pose a significant threat to managed Medicaid mental health programs. Proposed cuts to Medicaid benefits packages and Medicaid-funded community mental health programs are likely to affect the poorest of the mentally ill population, which is predicted to result in more individuals moving into the correctional system (Goldman, 2002).

INTEGRATION OF SYSTEMS OF CARE AND MANAGED CARE: ALIGNMENT AND MISALIGNMENT

The Health Care Reform Tracking project was initiated in 1995 to examine the impact of public sector managed care on children and adolescents with behavioral health disorders and their families (Stroul et al., 2001). This project, now in its fifth year, surveyed state Medicaid agencies about their managed care reforms. The findings are instructive, although with the caveat that they rely on self-report questionnaires completed by representatives of the system being surveyed, that is, representatives of state Medicaid offices. In the most recent report, Stroul et al. (2001), set out the following findings:

- Families and key stakeholders had significant involvement in fewer than half the reforms.

- More populations needing extensive services are being covered.

- More states include special provisions for children with serious mental health needs, such as intensive case management, an enhanced benefit package, or interagency coordination protocols; however, only 20 percent of states incorporate risk-adjusted rates for this population.

- There has been an increase in the use of for-profit MCOs, particularly in integrated designs; the increase in governmental entities as MCOs has been mostly in carve-outs.

- Although a broader array of services is being covered, many services applicable to higher-need populations are not covered within the managed care system—for example, wraparound services, respite, therapeutic foster and group care, residential treatment, school-based mental health services, transportation, family support, and other home-based services.

- Although over half of managed care reforms have reported expanded home- and community-based service coverage, there has reportedly been no expansion in service availability, apparently related to lack of service capacity.

- Carve-outs are significantly more supportive of systems of care than integrated reforms, incorporating a broad array of services, family involvement, and interagency service coordination strategies.

- Financial participation of other agencies is low. For example, the child welfare system contributes resources in only 21 percent of reforms; other systems contribute in fewer than 10 percent of reforms.

- Cost shifting is found in two-thirds of reforms, with carve-outs most likely to experience cost shifting from other child-serving systems to the managed care systems; however, only 16 percent of reforms are tracking and monitoring cost shifting.

- Level-of-care criteria have not been used to achieve consistency in decision making.

- Medical necessity criteria that allow for consideration of psychosocial and environmental factors at the state level are more narrowly applied at the MCO level.

- In most states, managed care has not expanded the availability of culturally diverse providers.

Stroul and her colleagues concluded that publicly financed managed care is a developmental process that presents both opportunities and challenges for children's behavioral health care. The assumption that managed care would save money has not been borne out, because original estimates were based on an underserved population (and did not taken into account costs of increasing access), costs have shifted from hospital to residential treatment, initial funding levels were too low, and financial risk assumed by MCOs was too high. Also, there have been few modifications in financing to protect the highest-need populations from receiving too little care. The authors also note that states need to become better purchasers through including performance expectations as contractual provisions.

Some of the problems in alignment result because MCOs have not had access to adequate information systems to define what the true needs of the population are and what the true costs are likely to be. Difficulties in separating child data from adult data add to the complexity, as well as incorporating the costs of services from different agencies. The financial incentives involved are also problematic. Market forces rather than professional principles have driven the bidding for managed care contracts, with the lowest bidder for monthly per member costs often being awarded the contract, resulting in no choice other than to restrict services (Jellinek & Little, 1998).

Other problems in alignment between systems of care and managed care result from the differences between goals of different constituencies. For example, the primary goal of family members, particularly those involved with SED children, is to improve the child's functioning and decrease family strain and burden, whereas the tax-paying public (and, by extension, legislators), as well as the state contracting agency, may be most concerned with cost and service utilization. Often the goals and the different constituencies are at odds. It has been recommended that states and counties negotiate with providers regarding what services and outcomes they are going to purchase and that these become specific contractual performance indicators.

HOW SYSTEMS OF CARE FARE UNDER MANAGED CARE: CASE EXAMPLES

The state examples that follow illustrate issues of integration between managed care and system of care, including sustainability of system of care programs when integrated into managed care, and managed care's ability to support system of care principles and approaches.

Wraparound Milwaukee

In existence since 1995, Wraparound Milwaukee was created from a six-year, $15 million Center for Mental Health Services grant to the Children and Adolescent Services Branch of the Milwaukee County, Wisconsin's Mental Health Division. Wraparound Milwaukee defines itself as a publicly operated care management organization (CMO) that focuses only on providing a range of mental health, substance abuse, social, and other supportive services to children and adolescents up to age eighteen who are identified by child welfare or juvenile justice as being at immediate risk of placement in a residential treatment center or psychiatric hospital based on serious emotional, behavioral, or mental health needs.

Wraparound Milwaukee shares many characteristics of other MCOs that are a type of managed care entity. These include the use of a sophisticated management information system to oversee the delivery of care; enrolling a well-defined population of high service utilizers; operating with pooled funding from multiple child-serving agencies, insurance providers, and other sources; overseeing an extensive provider network to deliver services; providing case management based on wraparound care philosophy; utilizing continuous quality improvement practices and measurable outcomes to monitor program effectiveness; and having available a well-organized family advocacy component.

Wraparound Milwaukee's governance is under the auspices of the Milwaukee County Health and Human Services Department, with the Milwaukee County Mental Health Division within that department designated as the administrative entity. Key child-serving agencies contracting with Wraparound Milwaukee for this population include the Bureau of Milwaukee Child Welfare (a state-administered, privately operated child protection service system), Milwaukee County Delinquency and Court Services (a county-operated probation services for delinquent youth), Division of Health Care Financing (a state agency administering all Medicaid services, including all special managed care programs), and Milwaukee County Mental Health Division-Children's Branch (which is responsible for overseeing public mental health services for children and youth in Milwaukee County). Other key local and state cooperating agencies that do not provide direct funding to Wraparound Milwaukee but provide services through existing programming include the local school districts within the county; Milwaukee County Adult Mental Health Division, which provides some alcohol and other substance abuse services as well as transition services for young adults; and the State Bureau of Mental Health, which provides technical assistance and other services.

Although Wraparound Milwaukee serves approximately six hundred youth at any point during a fiscal year, these youth represent the subgroup of both the child welfare and juvenile justice populations with the highest service needs and costs. By 1997, all youth in this group who historically had been adjudicated into residential treatment were now placed in Wraparound Milwaukee, which then determined their placement and service needs. When Wraparound Milwaukee assumed responsibility for the residential treatment population of youth, a unique funding arrangement was developed to meet the high level of service need. Funds were pooled by Wraparound Milwaukee from these contracting entities through the use of case rates and capitation formulas to create maximum flexibility and meet the overall costs of these youth. Wraparound Milwaukee also bills Medicaid directly for crisis services. Other funds are available through a mental health block grant, supplemental security income, private insurance companies, and reinvestment from welfare-to-work agencies.

All funds are managed by Wraparound Milwaukee as the CMO and are available to the youths and their families through the child and family team process. This process is overseen by a care coordinator who, in partnership with the family, develops a plan of care and chooses from an extensive fee-for-service community-based provider network a full array of services that meets the youth's and family's individualized goals. In addition to care coordination and the child and family team process, Wraparound Milwaukee relies on its mobile urgent treatment team (MUTT) to intervene during a family crisis situation that might result in a child's being removed from his or her home, school, or the community. Each child enrolled in Wraparound Milwaukee has a safety plan that is developed by the family with the care coordinator to guide MUTT providers in the event of a crisis. MUTT also reviews requests for all inpatient psychiatric hospital admissions and operates an eight-bed group home and several foster homes capable of providing short-term crisis stabilization (of up to fourteen days) while MUTT and the care coordinator work with the family for the return of the child. MUTT's availability has allowed Wraparound Milwaukee to nearly eliminate the use of inpatient psychiatric care for most of the children enrolled in the program. Other key components to Wraparound Milwaukee's success have been the effective use of family advocacy, informal services and natural supports, and wraparound resource teams that provide specialized consultation services for youth with clinically complex and challenging needs (for example, firesetters and juvenile sex offenders).

Wraparound Milwaukee's fiscal office uses various managed care strategies and techniques with a sophisticated Internet-based management information system with modules for enrollment, service authorization, claims adjudication and processing, automated plans of care, on-line invoicing, general ledger, utilization review, and report writing.

Oregon and the Oregon Health Plan

Under the leadership of Governor John Kitzhaber and with active participation by Oregon physicians (including psychiatrists), Oregon developed and implemented the Oregon Health Plan (OHP) for its Medicaid population. The impetus for development of the plan occurred in 1987 when a special request was made to fund a bone marrow transplant for a Medicaid-eligible child with leukemia. It was determined by the legislature, when Governor Kitzhaber was then the president of the state senate, that the $100,000 cost for this procedure would be better spent on prenatal care (McFarland, George, Pollack, & Angell, 1993). This decision led to a public process that determined the basic health care benefits that would be made available to all Medicaid-eligible citizens.

Like other states, Oregon was faced with the problem of a large uninsured population. As a response, the primary objective of the OHP was to expand Medicaid eligibility and access to health care services to a wider population. This was accomplished by defined limits on the Medicaid benefit package through a priority ranking of medical diagnoses. In this participatory process, the most treatable psychiatric disorders, ranked along with physical health conditions, fell within the covered diagnoses (Sabin, 2000). In 1993, Oregon was granted a 1115 Medicaid waiver, allowing the OHP to be implemented in 1994 as a fully capitated health care program. The behavioral health benefit of the OHP was phased in over the next three years. The state, as the purchasing authority, contracted with different MCO structures in each Oregon county to administer the mental health benefit for their population.

In Multnomah County, the largest urban center in the state, the contractual relationship between the state and county MCOs had a significant impact on the system of care operating at that time. In 1990, prior to the implementation of the OHP, Oregon and Multnomah County were awarded one of eight demonstration grants from the Robert Wood Johnson Foundation's Mental Health Services Program for Youth (Oregon Partners Project) to develop a community-based system of care for SED children and their families. During the implementation of that grant, each county managed care coordinator served approximately seventeen SED children and their families. These coordinators were master's-level, specialist case managers who had fiscal authority to draw from a pool of blended funds contributed by child welfare, mental health, and education to fund traditional mental health and wraparound services. Pooled funds were made available under a state-run capitation arrangement.

In the initial stage of the OHP phase-in, the state decided to award contracts to three different MCOs in Multnomah County to administer the children's mental health outpatient carve-out benefits. Importantly, children's residential services were excluded from managed care. One contract was awarded to the county government and the other two to private organizations. This strategy set up a competition that was ultimately not productive for the MCOs and created a confusing system for consumers, who were assigned to mental health plans based on their primary health care assignment. This adversely affected the community-based system of care. Although the intensive case managers (as they were now called) continued to have fiscal authority, the blended funding pool no longer covered Medicaid children. Medicaid-eligible children's mental health costs were differentiated from non–mental health needs, with pressure to shift these costs to other service sectors. By 1996, both of the private MCOs terminated their contracts with the state due to adverse financial risk, leaving the county as the sole MCO.

The county's MCO developed a subcapitation arrangement with two provider networks, but the capitation rate proved to be insufficient to cover the seriously ill population, especially children with SED. A fee-for-service structure that was tightly managed by utilization-style case managers was adopted for this subpopulation. The two provider networks developed their own specialist case managers, and a majority of the case management for SED children and their families was shifted to the two networks from the county. This further fragmented the service delivery system for this population since the private networks had limited access to flexible funds to provide for the level of intensity of services that these children and families required. The subcapitation arrangement between the county and the two provider networks ultimately failed. The county MCO had a large and costly administrative structure that duplicated the administrative structure of the provider networks. The provider networks also felt that their capitation rates were inadequate to support a risk-bearing arrangement.

In 2001, with successful advocacy and new county leadership, the three largest community mental health providers (primarily of adult services) merged and formed a new, larger nonprofit integrated service delivery network that has become the primary BHO for the county. The county reduced its administrative structure in order to free up more funds for the BHO. The county is financially accountable for psychiatric inpatient utilization. In order to control costs, it has instituted aggressive disposition planning with the inpatient programs and intensive case management for patients who have been discharged. The provider BHO has as a contracted task in the first year of this contract to provide enhanced outpatient services as a way to start reducing high adult inpatient utilization. Although the county and the BHO will develop a shared-risk model in the second year of the contract period, the primary performance measure for this new business model will be decreasing adult inpatient costs. In its efforts to contain costs by reducing administrative overhead, the county has had difficulty separating its role as the mental health authority (safety net and quality assurance functions) from its managed care functions. The two components currently are under single leadership, making it difficult to address areas of potential conflict between these two functions.

In the process of evolving to the single MCO–single BHO scenario (as a way to contain costs in adult inpatient services), the interests of children have taken a back seat. This is evidenced by the fact that the large, recently formed BHO does not include several of the established child mental health provider agencies or culturally specific mental health agencies that provide services to minority children and their families. It is not yet clear how these agencies and those that provide alcohol and drug treatment services will relate fiscally to either the primary BHO or the county MCO.

One of the casualties in this evolution of the public mental health system to managed Medicaid was the Oregon Partners Project. Although some elements of the program were maintained (also see Chapter Nine), including flexible funding, case management, and blended funds for some uninsured children, the following changes in the SOC model occurred:

- Loss of blended funding for Medicaid-eligible children
- A shift to a utilization management style of case management
- Decreased family involvement at the case planning and policy level
- Abandonment of the protocol for quarterly interagency service team meetings
- Restriction to a limited network provider panel
- Restriction to specific types and quantities of wraparound services
- Increased use of residential treatment as compared with the original project, which strongly emphasized community-based services

The Partners Project was considered innovative at the time, especially for its financing strategies. Managed care coordinators' roles integrated clinical and financial accountability (England & Cole, 1998). It still stands as a potential model for integrating a system of care as a component in a larger managed care system. Its lack of sustainability may have been related to its integration (at the end of the grant period) back into a premanaged care system that was in transition. During the initial phase-in of managed Medicaid, the county and provider community were struggling to develop new technologies to help them manage care for the entire eligible population. Seen as an overly generous program that targeted a limited number of children, there was little support for sustaining the model. An additional disincentive for sustainability was that the managed care system did not include residential services. Therefore, there was no financial incentive to divert children from residential treatment or other out-of-home placements.

Another factor interfering with sustainability was that community mental health providers had not been brought in fully as stakeholders of the system of care. There was little community education about the system of care model and the CASSP principles, and the project used many out-of-network providers (because they were more available for home-based services), which led to concern that funds were being drained from the network agencies. The challenges of sustaining systems of care during transitions to managed care point to the importance of involving all stakeholders in each stage of system of care development and to address directly the tensions between goals of different constituencies.

Transition from the Fort Bragg Demonstration to Managed Care in North Carolina

The Department of Defense's Fort Bragg Child and Adolescent Mental Health Demonstration in North Carolina (1990–1995) was one of the early systems of care projects. Serving children and adolescents eligible for the Civilian and Medical Program for the Uniformed Services (CHAMPUS), the service delivery structure incorporated a continuum of individualized mental health services, centralized intake, ongoing case management for children involved in intensive services, and high-quality comprehensive assessment and treatment (Heflinger & Northrup, 2000). The program resulted in a number of positive findings, including increased access, more responsive services, higher satisfaction, and fewer disruptions in service (Duchnowski, Kutash, & Friedman, 2002). However, there were no differences in clinical outcomes and the costs were greater compared with the comparison sites (Bickman et al., 1995, 2000). The latter has been attributed to the lack of fiscal incentives for controlling cost (Foster, Kelsch, Kamradt, Sosna, & Yang, 2001; see also Chapter Twenty).

After the demonstration ended, there was interest in curtailing costs while preserving the quality of services in the system of care. Heflinger and Northrup (2000) describe results of a study examining the impact on the system of care after a capitated managed behavioral health contract was awarded to a for-profit managed care company to serve the CHAMPUS-eligible population. The contract stipulated a benefit package encompassing comprehensive services, including outpatient, hospital, residential, partial hospital, and intermediate services, such as day treatment, therapeutic group homes, crisis group homes, and in-home services.

Heflinger and Northrup described a variety of impacts of this transition from a system of care to managed care. First, overall service utilization fell significantly, from 7 to 4 percent of eligibles. Interviews with families indicated that they experienced barriers to accessing services, primarily related to a new required copayment. Intermediate service use went down, and it became clear that difficult-to-treat children were being shifted to the public sector. Community capacity to maintain intermediate services fell as utilization of those services was curtailed. Barriers to outpatient services were created by preauthorization requirements and disruption of continuity of services.

Stakeholders expressed concern that the contractor's philosophy was based on a medical model as opposed to a rehabilitative model that would promote children's well-being in multiple settings. Coordination of services with agencies representing these settings, such as schools, was discouraged by lack of payment and discontinuation of comprehensive treatment teams. A frequently mentioned concern was the lack of access to psychiatrists and a long waiting time between referral and appointment. Since the contractor was not contractually responsible for clinical outcomes, stakeholders felt that the system represented managed costs, not managed care. Ratings on service system goals were similar to or worse than they had been with the traditional fee-for-service program that predated the Fort Bragg system of care demonstration. A wide group of community providers rated service coordination more negatively after the managed care contract. The Department of Social Services reported less support for children in foster care placements with wraparound service needs, especially the seriously disturbed adolescent population.

In their conclusions, Heflinger and Northrup (2000) caution that clinical needs should not be overshadowed by cost containment in managed care systems. They also highlight the risk of excluding beneficiaries with chronic behavioral health needs. They emphasized the role of contract development and monitoring, recommending the use of an accountability-focused contract with comprehensive performance measures. The purchaser must have the resources and data systems needed to monitor quality of care and beneficiary outcomes. They also note that specific contract requirements are needed for promotion of prevention and early intervention activities, the benefits of which require a longer time frame to realize. Especially important is inclusion of clinical appropriateness and quality-of-care expectations, for without these quality-of-care performance requirements, the shifting of risk to the contractor can provide a financial incentive to offer as few services as possible.

The central question of this chapter is whether systems of care and managed care are compatible. The answer is that they are theoretically compatible, but true integration of the two has yet to be realized in most mental health systems. Systems of care and the more recent evolution of public managed care have significant commonalities of philosophy and aims (Scholle & Kelleher, 1998). Both were a response to a fragmented service delivery system, both support community-based rather than restrictive placements, and both advocate the use of information management systems to enhance coordination of care. When successfully integrated, as in the Wraparound Milwaukee Care Management Organization, systems of care and managed care represent strategies for increasing comprehensiveness of services, improving quality of care, expanding services to populations in need, and offering cost-effective services capable of achieving outcomes for which they are accountable.

The aims of more evolved managed care approaches, however, have yet to be realized in the majority of states. Managed care has not yet moved beyond managed costs to address quality-of-care issues. Increased accountability for outcomes will be necessary to move these systems into managed quality (Jellinek & Little, 1998). There are inherent differences in aims and objectives that create tensions between managed care and systems of care. The most significant are the financial incentives for managed care to control costs by restricting service utilization.

Purchasers will need to develop the resources and sophistication to implement contracts that monitor quality of care and outcomes along with cost.

Another difference arises from target populations. Systems of care focus on comprehensively meeting the needs of individuals within a high-risk population, whereas managed care must allocate resources efficiently to the entire eligible population. There are usually not enough resources to provide the best outcome for each individual. Therefore, decisions must be made that are, in effect, rationing and will be experienced by some as withholding of care. It is essential to have a careful and inclusive process to decide under what circumstances and for which populations service restrictions are acceptable. Restricting the care offered to seriously impaired child or adult populations, for which current capitated contracts may offer incentives, is not an acceptable strategy for cost control, as it has been shown to result in higher rates of incarceration and use of other service systems (Chang et al., 1998; Heflinger & Northrup, 2000). Fragmentation is another problem that emerges when only one funding stream is being managed in managed mental health systems (Hoge, Jacobs, Thakur, & Griffith, 1999).

Given the fundamental differences between systems of care and managed care, the most relevant question is how to achieve the best possible degree of integration and compatibility between the two. Figure 17.1 suggests some infrastructure and practices needed to support system of care goals under managed care. Although behavioral health carve-outs are described as generally more responsive to mental health needs, the managed care program that replaced the Fort Bragg system of care (Heflinger & Northrup, 2000) suggests that behavioral carve-outs are not in themselves successful solutions without adequate accountability. Other problems that have been described in managed care reforms such as TennCare in Tennessee (Chang et al., 1998), include excessive bureaucracy and administrative cost burden, inadequate risk adjustment for the seriously mentally ill population, and siphoning payments for profits, all of which are not compatible with preserving resources to serve the highest need population.

While the available evidence suggests that governmental entities such as MCOs may be perceived by stakeholders as more responsive to seriously disturbed populations than commercial MCOs (Stroul et al., 2001), all managed care entities would benefit from more training related to the needs of seriously disturbed children, especially those involved with juvenile justice and child welfare. The inclusion of families as full partners in managed care design, implementation, and monitoring is another system of care emphasis yet to be realized in managed care. Inherently financially driven, managed care organizations are likely to include families as full partners at the policymaking level as meaningful partners only with aggressive advocacy by family and consumer groups.

Another area limiting system of care integration with managed care is the narrow application of medical necessity criteria, which fails to support strength-based treatment models and limits the ability to address psychosocial issues.

- Adequate accountability of the MCO for client-relevant outcomes
- Financing arrangements that allow for risk-adjusted rates for the SED population
- Meaningful family and consumer involvement at every level of the system
- Well-trained, culturally competent, and diverse, credentialed providers and culturally competent processes
- Skilled case managers and care coordinators who are versed in family-centered and strength-based approaches; familiar with community resources; able to lead an inter-agency child-family team; able to develop and be guided by a clinical formulation of the problems; able to identify and procure appropriate services; able to continuously monitor appropriateness of services; and able to access expert consultation
- Use of objective measures to guide clinical decision making, particularly level-of-care decisions, such as the Child and Adolescent Level of Care Utilization System (American Academy of Child and Adolescent Psychiatry and American Association of Community Psychiatry, 1999; Klaehn, O'Malley, Vaughan, & Kroeger, 1999)
- Bring utilization management strategies down from the population level to center on clinical planning for the child and family
- Less narrowly applied definitions of medical necessity
- Reduction of administrative and bureaucratic MCO and BHO costs
- Effective interagency planning processes and financing mechanisms, including blended funding
- Specific contracted expectations for quality of care, services to high-need populations, consumer involvement, and prevention and early intervention activities

FIGURE 17.1. Infrastructure and Practices Needed to Support System of Care Goals Under Managed Care

Federal challenges around the use of Medicaid funds for services not classified as meeting medical necessity criteria could lead to regression in the development of flexible service designs (K. McGinty, personal communication, 2002). The interface with other child-serving systems will have to be addressed, as the evidence suggests that there is significant cost shifting occurring in both directions, and financial contributions by other agencies is decreasing (Stroul et al., 2001). This can lead only to continued fragmentation and duplication of efforts, the very conditions leading to systems of care reform.

Development of sophisticated information systems allowing for accurate actuarial data would facilitate more realistic setting of case and capitation rates for the seriously impaired child population. Longitudinal data allowing for analysis of cost savings through prevention and early intervention efforts will be needed to support these initiatives. There also needs to be recognition of the economic and humanitarian benefits of supporting the families of seriously disturbed children in their efforts to balance work and parenting roles (Friesen, 2000; Rosenzweig, Brennan, & Ogilvie, 2002).

Another area needing investigation is how the fiscal and clinical priorities for children's mental health fare in larger adult-oriented managed care systems. Children, especially younger children, are a vulnerable population and are at risk of being underserved. Funds for children's mental health services are at risk of being raided to fund overspending on adult services. How services are administered and organized for children within larger systems should be examined specifically.

The evidence base concerning integration of managed care with systems of care is limited. Much of the available information is based on self-report methodology. Although these methods have their place, they need to be supplemented with more objective, less biased measurement approaches, as well as systematic inclusion of perspectives of other system stakeholders, as occurred in the study of Fort Bragg's transition to managed care (Heflinger & Northrup, 2000). Especially important to capture are data on expenditures in other systems.

More systematic research needs to be done regarding what specific managed care methodologies, including different financing and risk-sharing approaches, are best suited to serve the high-need child population targeted by systems of care. Contracts will need to incorporate expectations that managed care systems provide high-quality care and use the expanding array of evidence-based interventions (Burns & Hoagwood, 2002; Osher, Koyanagi, Pires, McCarthy, & Webman, 1997). Finally, it is imperative that federal funding of systematic evaluations of systems of care continues at an adequate level, so that the evidence base concerning stakeholder-determined outcomes and financial viability of system of care models in managed care environments can be expanded.

References

American Academy of Child and Adolescent Psychiatry Work Group on Community-Based Systems of Care. (1996). *Best principles for managed Medicaid RFPs.* Washington, DC: American Academy of Child and Adolescent Psychiatry.

American Academy of Child and Adolescent Psychiatry Work Group on Community-Based Systems of Care. (1998). *Best principles for measuring outcomes in managed Medicaid mental health programs.* Washington, DC: American Academy of Child and Adolescent Psychiatry.

American Academy of Child and Adolescent Psychiatry Work Group on Community-Based Systems of Care and American Association of Community Psychiatry. (1999). *Child and adolescent level of care utilization system, version 1.1.* Washington, DC: Author.

Bickman, L., Guthrie, P., Foster, E. M., Lambert, E. W., Summerfelt, W. T., Breda, C., & Heflinger, C. A. (1995). *Managed care in mental health: The Fort Bragg experiment.* New York: Plenum.

Bickman, L., Lambert, E. W., Andrade, A. R., & Penaloza, R. V. (2000). The Fort Bragg continuum of care for children and adolescents: Mental health outcomes over five years. *Journal of Consulting and Clinical Psychology, 68,* 710–716.

Burns, B. J., & Hoagwood, K. (2002). *Community treatment for youth: Evidence-based interventions for severe emotional and behavioral disorders.* New York: Oxford University Press.

Center for Mental Health Services. (2001). *Cultural competence standards in managed care mental health services. Four underserved/underrepresented racial/ethnic groups.* Washington, DC: Center for Mental Health Services, Substance Abuse and Mental Health Administration, U.S. Department of Health and Human Services.

Chang, C. F., Kiser, L. J., Bailey, J. E., Martins, M., Gibson, W. C., Schaberg, K. A., Mirvis, D. M., & Applegate, W. B. (1998). Tennessee's failed managed care program for mental health and substance abuse services. *Journal of the American Medical Association, 279,* 864–869.

Child Council Workgroup on Intervention Development and Deployment. (2001). *Blueprint for change: Research on child and adolescent mental health.* Bethesda, MD: National Advisory Mental Health Council, National Institute of Mental Health. Available on-line at: http://www.nimh.gov/child/blueprin.pdf.

Cross, T., Bazron, B., Dennis, K., & Isaacs, M. (1989). *Towards a culturally competent system of care: A monograph on effective services for minority children who are severely emotionally disturbed.* Washington DC: Georgetown University Child Development Center, National Technical Assistance Center for Children's Mental Health.

Duchnowski, A. J., Kutash, K., & Friedman, R. M. (2002). Community-based interventions in a system of care and outcomes framework. In B. J. Burns & K. Hoagwood (Eds.), *Community treatment for youth: Evidence-based interventions for severe emotional and behavioral disorders* (pp. 16–37). New York: Oxford University Press.

England, M. J., & Cole, R. F. (1998). Preparing for communities of care for child and family mental health for the twenty-first century. *Child and Adolescent Psychiatric Clinics of North America, 7,* 469–481.

Foster, E. M., Kelsch, C. C., Kamradt, B., Sosna, T., & Yang, Z. (2001). Expenditures and sustainability in systems of care. *Journal of Emotional and Behavioral Disorders, 9,* 53–62.

Friesen, B. J. (2000). Points of tension: Mental health administration in a managed care environment. In R. J. Patti (Ed.), *The handbook of social welfare management* (pp. 461–480). Thousand Oaks, CA: Sage.

Friesen, B., & Koroloff, N. M. (1990). Family-centered services: Implications for mental health administration and research. *Journal of Mental Health Administration, 17,* 13–25.

Friesen, B. J., & Stephens, B. (1998). Expanding family roles in the system of care: Research and practice. In M. H. Epstein, K. Kutash, & A. Duchnowski (Eds.), *Outcomes for children and youth with behavioral and emotional disorders and their families: Program and evaluation best practices* (pp. 231–259). Austin, TX: Pro-Ed.

Goldman, E. M. (2002). State budgets slash public mental health net. *Clinical Psychiatry News, 30,* 8–9.

Heflinger, C. A., & Northrup, D. A. (2000). What happens when capitated behavioral health comes to town? The transition from the Fort Bragg demonstration to a capitated managed behavioral health contract. *Journal of Behavioral Health Services and Research, 27,* 390–405.

Hoge, M. A., Jacobs, S., Thakur, N. M., & Griffith, E.E.H. (1999). Ten dimensions of public-sector managed care. *Psychiatric Services, 50,* 51–55.

Jacobsen, D., & Cervine, D. (2001). A magic growth formula for mental health services in Santa Cruz County. In M. Hernandez & S. Hodges (Eds.), *Developing outcome strategies in children's mental health* (pp. 115–136). Baltimore, MD: Brookes Publishing.

Jellinek, M., & Little, M. (1998). Supporting child psychiatric services using current managed care approaches: You can't get there from here. *Archives of Pediatrics and Adolescent Medicine, 152,* 321–326.

Joint Commission on the Mental Health of Children. (1969). *Crisis in child mental health.* New York: HarperCollins.

Klaehn, R., O'Malley, K., Vaughan, T., & Kroeger, K. (1999). *Child and Adolescent Level of Care Utilization System (CALOCUS): User's manual (Ver. 1.1).* Washington, DC: American Academy of Child and Adolescent Psychiatry.

Knitzer, J. (1982). *Unclaimed children: The failure of public responsibility to children and adolescents in need of mental health services.* Washington, DC: Children's Defense Fund.

Knitzer, J. (1998). Early childhood mental health services: A policy and systems development perspective. National Center for Children in Poverty, Columbia School of Public Health.

McFarland, B. H., George, R. A., Pollack, D. A., & Angell, R. H. (1993). Managed mental health in the Oregon Health Plan. *New Directions for Mental Health Services, 59,* 41–54.

National Center for Health Statistics and Centers for Disease Control and Prevention. (1999). *National Health Interview Survey.* Available on-line: http://www.cdc.gov/nchs/htm.

Ogles, B. M., Trout, S. C., Gillespie, D. K., & Penkert, K. S. (1998). Managed care as a platform for cross-system integration. *Journal of Behavioral Health Sciences and Research, 25,* 252–268.

Osher, T. W., Koyanagi, C., Pires, S., McCarthy, J., & Webman, D. (1997, Oct.). Child and family focus: Working together to develop integrated systems of care. *Behavioral Healthcare Tomorrow, 6,* 1–8.

Osher, T. W., van Kammen, W., & Zaro, S .M. (2001). Family participation in evaluating systems of care. *Journal of Emotional and Behavioral Disorders, 9*, 63–70.

Pumariega, A. J., Glover, S., Holzer, C. E., & Nguyen, N. (1998). Utilization of mental health services in a tri-ethnic sample of adolescents. *Community Mental Health Journal, 34*, 145–156.

Pumariega, A. J., Nace, D., England, M. J., Diamond, J., Mattson, A., Fallon, T., Hanson, G., Lourie, I., Marx, L., Thurber, D., Winters, N., Graham, M., & Wiegand, D. (1997). Community-based systems approach to children's managed mental health services. *Journal of Child and Family Studies, 6*, 149–164.

Ringel, J. S., & Sturm, R. (2001). National estimates of mental health utilization and expenditures for children in 1998. *Journal of Behavioral Health Services Research, 3*, 319–333.

Rosenblatt, A., Attkisson, C. C., & Fernandez, A. J. (1992). Integrating systems of care in California for youth with severe emotional disturbance: II. Initial group home expenditure and utilization findings from the California AB377 Evaluation Project. *Journal of Child and Family Studies, 1*, 263–286.

Rosenzweig, J. M., Brennan, E. M., & Ogilvie, A. M. (2002). Work/family fit: Voices of parents of children with emotional and behavioral disorders. *Social Work, 47*, 415–424.

Sabin, J. E. (2000). Managed care and health care reform: Comedy, tragedy, and lessons. *Psychiatric Services, 51*, 1392–1396.

Sabin, J .E., O'Brien, M. F., & Daniels, N. (2001). Strengthening the consumer voice in managed care: II. Moving NCQA standards from rights to empowerment. *Psychiatric Services, 52*, 1303–1305.

Scholle, S. H., & Kelleher, K. J. (1998). Managed care: Opportunities and threats for children with serious emotional disturbance and their families. In M. H. Epstein, K. Kutash, & A. J. Duchnowski (Eds.), *Outcomes for children and youth with behavioral and emotional disorders and their families: Programs and evaluation best practices* (pp. 659–684). Austin, TX: Pro-Ed.

Standards and Surveyor Guidelines for the Accreditation of MBHOs. (2000). Washington, DC: National Committee for Quality Assurance.

Stroul, B. A., & Friedman, R. M. (1986). *A system of care for children and youth with severe emotional disturbance* (rev. ed.). Washington, DC: Georgetown University Child Development Center, National Technical Assistance Center for Children's Mental Health.

Stroul, B. A., Pires, S. A., & Armstrong, M. I. (2001). *Health care reform tracking project: Tracking state health care reforms as they affect children and adolescents with behavioral health disorders and their families—2000 State Survey.* Tampa, FL: Research and Training Center for Children's Mental Health, Department of Child and Family Studies, Division of State and Local Support, Louis de la Parte Florida Mental Health Institute, University of South Florida.

U.S. Department of Health and Human Services. (1999). *Mental health: A report of the surgeon general.* Rockville, MD: U.S. Department of Health and Human Services, Substance Abuse and Mental Health Services Administration, Center for Mental Health Services, National Institutes of Health, National Institute of Mental Health.

U.S. Department of Health and Human Services. (2000). *Culture, race, and ethnicity: A supplement to mental health: A report of the surgeon general.* Washington, DC: U.S. Department of Health and Human Services, Office of the Surgeon General, Substance Abuse and Mental Health Administration.

VanDenBerg, J. E., & Grealish, M. E. (1996). Individualized services and supports through the wrap-around process. *Journal of Child and Family Studies, 5,* 7–21.

Woolston, J. L., Berkowitz, S. J., Schaefer, M. C., & Adnopoz, J. A. (1998). Intensive, integrated, in-home, psychiatric services: The catalyst to enhancing outpatient intervention. *Child and Adolescent Psychiatric Clinics of North America, 7,* 615–633.

Zero to Three. (1994). *Diagnostic classification of mental health and developmental disorders of infancy and early childhood: Zero to three.* Arlington, VA: National Center for Infants, Toddlers and Families.

CHAPTER EIGHTEEN

Systems of Care Under Legal Mandates

Thomas Vaughan
Andres J. Pumariega
Robert Klaehn

Consent decrees are agreements entered into by an entity and a group of plaintiffs to address a grievance addressed by the plaintiffs in a lawsuit against the entity. The consent decree specifies the conditions under which the entity is to address those grievances to prevent the suit from proceeding to court. In the case of mental health services for children, these consent decrees can be entered into by various state agencies, such as departments of human resources, juvenile justice entities, state Medicaid agencies, departments of education, and other entities charged with the welfare of children. This chapter explores class action lawsuits and resulting consent decrees and their impact on systems of care for children's mental health.

AREAS OF CLASS ACTION LITIGATION AND SYSTEMS OF CARE

Class action litigation that affects children's systems of care usually stems from the lack of responsiveness by state or local government to children's health and human service needs. Federal legislation (often based on constitutional principles) often sets out mandated services that states must meet to address these needs. These mandates often accompany federal funding to states for the provision of these services. These funds frequently require matching state funding that competes with other state priorities. The usual pathway for class action litigation involves the identification of patterns of violation of the federal law through service deficits, with advocacy attorneys indemnifying representatives of the affected class. A number of approaches are usually attempted before proceeding to the filing of a lawsuit in federal court. Court-brokered settlement is the most frequent outcome, with court-appointed mediators or masters to broker and monitor the implementation of the settlement of the consent decree. If mediation fails and the court rules against the state, a court-ordered plan is set forth with a court-appointed master to administer implementation. These lawsuits can be appealed to the U.S. Supreme Court, though in practice relatively few are.

The benefits of class action litigation around children's systems of care are multiple. They often overcome bureaucratic inertia in implementing mandated and necessary services and the lack of political will to make the necessary resources available. They also help to set verifiable minimum standards for mandated services, as well as a participatory structure and process for program implementation.

There are risks and limitations inherent in class action litigation around children's systems of care. The greatest risk is a possible negative court decision, setting back advocacy efforts. Alienation of state officials (executive and legislative) from advocates and professionals is also a potential outcome, with resultant lack of buying of reforms by state government. The nature of monitoring and supervision of consent decrees is time limited, though many class action cases have been continued for many years, even decades. There is also a limit to the scope and precedent of rulings within the federal district that a court covers, unless it is appealed to a higher level, with the ultimate impact determined by the U.S. Supreme Court.

We will review the different forms of class action litigation with an impact on children's systems of care and their current status (Bazelon Center for Mental Health, 1998, 1999, 2001a).

Individuals with Disabilities Education Act and Section 504

The Individuals with Disabilities Education Act (IDEA), previously Public Law 94–142, provided the rights for children and youth with disabilities that interfere with learning to receive special educational services. This has perhaps been the main area of litigation in the area of children's health and human services. A number of class actions resulting from IDEA have direct implications for mental health services within school settings.

Some of these lawsuits provided for states to offer an array of mental health services for children with serious emotional disturbances. *Cordero by Bates* v. *Pennsylvania Department of Education* addressed a school district's failure to provide appropriate educational placement, including mental health services, leading to deterioration and loss of custody. *Felix* v. *Waihee* (Hawaii Departments of Education and Health) addressed systems inadequacies for children with serious behavioral health needs. One of the most famous class action lawsuits dealing with children's systems of care, *Willie M* v. *Hunt* (North Carolina government) dealt with the lack of services for violent and assaultive youth with serious emotional disturbances and led to the mandated implementation of a system of care for children within this subclass.

A series of class action lawsuits under IDEA deal with the provision of specified services to children with serious disturbances for addressing educational needs. These included suits that mandated parental and family therapy outside the school setting (San Lorenzo Unified School District and Belcherton Public Schools), in-home services and behavior management (*Krinchinsky* v. *Knox County Schools, Taunton Public Schools, Burke County Board of Education* v. *Denton, Hunger* v. *Leininger,* and *Seattle School District*), and recreational activities outside school (*San Lorenzo Unified School District* and *East Windsor Board of Education,* though they were denied).

Some lawsuits even mandated residential services coverage under IDEA. In *Burlington* v. *Department of Education,* the federal district court set two standards for receiving residential services under IDEA. First, the individualized education plan (IEP) does not meet the Rowley standard ("reasonably calculated to enable the child to receive educational benefits"; *Board of Education* v. *Rowley*), and second, the plaintiff must demonstrate that the proposed placement is appropriate. Another lawsuit, *Hall* v. *Shawnee Mission School District,* failed when the Rowley standard was easily met. The *County of San Diego* v. *California Special Education Hearing Office* lawsuit set three tests for placement appropriateness for a child within school: (1) the placement is supportive of the child's education; (2) the child has medical, social, or emotional problems; and (3) the placement is primarily to aid the student to benefit from special education.

IDEA lawsuits are important tools for securing school-based mental health services such as attendant care, counseling, and other supports. The services that are mandated are limited to those providing some educational benefit (services before and after school are often rejected). Residential services are often available only after surmounting legal hurdles and in the face of obvious neglect by schools. In pursuing these lawsuits, parents often deal with significant stigma from the courts and its officers, as witnessed in the tone of court transcripts.

Medicaid Litigation

The main issues involved in Medicaid litigation are federal regulations on medical services for the needy, particularly the early periodic screening, detection, and treatment (EPSDT) entitlement for children eligible for Medicaid. This entitlement requires states to provide "necessary health care, diagnostic services, treatment, and other measures . . . to correct and ameliorate defects and physical and mental illnesses and conditions" (42 U.S.C. Sec. 1396(r)(5)). There have been no published decisions on access to mental health services because most cases have been settled or are in litigation.

Larry K. v. *Snider* (Pennsylvania) was the first case on a state's failure to comply with EPSDT. The parents sued rather than give up custody of their child due to lack of adequate mental health services. Pennsylvania did not include many needed services in its Medicaid fee schedule. The state settled by paying for medically necessary residential and wraparound services. In *Emily Q.* v. *Belshe* (California), which is ongoing, a similar case was presented around provision of home- and community-based services. The plaintiff's complaint details the concept of wraparound services as services deemed necessary. In a preliminary injunction, the defendants were required to provide "preventive and rehabilitative services" to children under age twenty-one, which included therapeutic mental health services. This case has educated states and local officials on the scope of mental health services required under EPSDT.

French v. *Concannon* (Maine) set important precedents around medically necessary services under Medicaid and EPSDT for children and youth. It primarily dealt with the issue of access to home-based mental health services. The court dismissed the lawsuit but retained jurisdiction to ensure that defendants complied with the terms of a letter spelling out necessary changes. It also ruled that children with mental health and mental retardation needs will receive the following under Medicaid and EPSDT: timely case management, presumption of medical necessity for services in the treatment plan, prompt services (within six months), services not denied or delayed by lack of matching or seed money, a resource directory and best efforts to develop resources, and the removal on annual caps on habilitation services.

There have been other significant rulings in Medicaid and EPSDT cases in various lawsuits. *D.R.* v. *Concannon* (Maine) required that the state promptly provide medically necessary mental health services for children previously screened. In *Scott* v. *Snider,* that court ruled that EPSDT should cover all conditions and services and requires outreach, complete screening, and expanded services. In *Bond* v. *Stanton,* the court ruled that the state of Indiana did not sufficiently define the screening package to ensure needy children got screenings intended by Congress. In *Tallahassee Memorial Regional Medical Center* v. *Cook,* the court ruled that the state must pay for psychiatric inpatient care for adolescents when it failed to provide less restrictive placement due to funding or bureaucratic hurdles. The court in *Salazar* v. *District of Columbia* ruled that the District's EPSDT program failed the requirements for informing, screening, follow-up treatment, scheduling, transportation assistance, and due process for covered children and youth.

Given current proposals in Congress and the federal government to loosen state requirements under Medicaid to ease regulatory and entitlement burdens on states, this is an area of litigation that will need to be closely watched.

Medicaid Managed Care

The main issue addressed in these lawsuits is the requirement for states to meet Medicaid and EPSDT entitlements under managed care waivers (1115 and 1915). *Jason K.* v. *Griffith* (Arizona) was the first to examine a state's implementation of EPSDT under a Medicaid mental health managed care system. It involves over twenty thousand Medicaid-eligible children identified as needing mental health services but not receiving them as required by EPSDT.

Two other similar lawsuits involving managed Medicaid and EPSDT have involved the TennCare program in Tennessee. In *John B.* v. *Menke,* which is ongoing, there is a consent decree against the state for failing to provide outreach, screening, and treatment for physical and mental conditions under EPSDT. Two independent studies were required on whether children in state custody were receiving proper EPSDT services and whether children received appropriate mental health services before entering state custody. Both studies were negative against the state, one citing that 6 percent of children came into state custody because of a need for mental health services. The state first tried to remedy the situation by levying a small fine on the contract managed care (MCO) and behavioral health care (BHO) organizations for failure to provide services, but this solution was not accepted. A more comprehensive plan is being developed with the appointment of a court master, which involves a new carve-out plan for children in state custody or at risk of entering state custody, as well as regional academic centers providing consultation, and involved a direct suit against the BHO for failure to provide adequate residential treatment, with a youth being traumatized by his mother's refusal to pick him up from inpatient care. The BHO was sued for contract and tort, Consumer Protection Act violations, due process, and Medicaid EPSDT violations. The BHO has agreed to pay for the educational portion of care.

Metts v. *Houston* deals with due process rights and medial-necessity definitions. The settlement has useful guidelines on monitoring a managed care system. The plaintiff's attorney is to review all notices of denials, reductions, and terminations of services. The state must conduct a random review of these notices every three months; it must also conduct random telephone surveys on whether HMOs are denying claims verbally and not in writing. The individual's case manager cannot be the same one who also reviews requests for outpatient services.

Americans with Disabilities Act Lawsuits

The main issues in contention in these lawsuits are the requirements under the Americans with Disabilities Act (ADA), particularly Section 504. This law prohibits discrimination based on disabilities in areas of employment, public services, education, public accommodations, and telecommunications. Title II of the ADA applies to all public entities, with no individuals with a disability being excluded from participation in any services of such entities. It also has an integration mandate, under which services must be administered in the most integrated manner and setting. The law challenges unnecessary institutionalization.

One of the main areas of focus under ADA litigation is the unnecessary relinquishment of custody by parents in order to obtain necessary services for their children as well as unnecessary institutionalization. *Key* v. *State of Washington Department of Social and Health Services* directly addresses custody relinquishment under ADA. It found in favor of the state in ruling that children are not deemed excluded from a benefit due to a disability as a result of a finding of dependency to obtain residential services. However, it did find that the state's system offended family values, since it encourages parents to go on public assistance to get help for their child. In *Elizabeth* v. *Texas Department of Protective and Regulatory Services,* the court rejected a similar claim that involved children with severe developmental disorders being placed in long-term residential services instead of family settings.

However, the recent U.S. Supreme Court ruling on *Olmstead* v. *L.C.* (Georgia) set an important precedent for the requirement for community-based services to prevent unnecessary institutionalization. This case was brought by two women with mental illnesses and mental retardation confined in Georgia psychiatric hospitals long after professionals determined they were ready for discharge due to lack of community settings. The Supreme Court found that unnecessary institutionalization violated the integration mandate of ADA. The Court also found that the state may rely on the assessments of its own professionals whether an individual can be served in the community. The state may not impose community services on individuals who do not want them. However, the state is not required to transfer an institutionalized person to the community if doing so fundamentally alters the state's program. There is clear application from this law to the development of systems of care, and advocacy groups such as the Bazelon Center (2001a) are currently working to advance the implications of *Olmstead.*

Child Welfare Litigation

Litigation involving child welfare systems involves a variety of issues. Earlier lawsuits focused on the high frequency of children being given up for state custody as a result of inadequate health and mental health services, defined under ADA, Medicaid, and EPSDT Federal legal mandates.

More recently, there has been an increasing focus on issues of lack of stability and consistency of placements for children in state custody. *R. C.* v. *Hornsby* (1991) became the landmark lawsuit in the area, addressing the civil rights of a child placed in foster care after his parents' divorce and his unfortunate ordeal in extended state custody. R. C. was placed in multiple and inappropriate placements, many of them mental health residential placements. The Adoption and Safe Families Act Child, passed by Congress in 1997, codified many of the lessons from the R. C. lawsuit. It specifically addresses the responsibility of states to provide both stability in placements and timely permanency planning for children in foster care.

A more recent class action lawsuit in Tennessee, *Brian A.* v. *Tennessee Department of Children's Services,* focused on these very mandates of the federal law. The settlement of this lawsuit has involved a commitment by the Tennessee Department of Children's Services to a benchmark of no more than two placements of any child within a year and for completion of either family reunification to termination of parental rights within a two-year period of custody.

As the population of children in child welfare custody grows and their special needs are increasingly recognized, this promises to be a growing and important area of class action litigation (also see Chapter Fifteen).

Civil Rights of Institutionalized Persons Act Lawsuits

Civil Rights of Institutionalized Persons Act (CRIPA) lawsuits stem from federal legislation based on the Fourteenth Amendment to the U.S. Constitution, which asserts that people who are institutionalized have due process rights regardless of the reason for their internment. States are responsible for health and mental health services, physical conditions, and even education for individuals institutionalized against their will. Such individuals are not eligible for federal funding that covers these services for noncommitted individuals, such as Medicaid, Medicare, education funding, and housing assistance. In previous years, these lawsuits involved the conditions within long-term inpatient state psychiatric settings, though this has been a lesser focus since deinstitutionalization. More recently, the focus has been on adults and youth in detention and incarceration facilities, with the main child and adolescent focus being on the juvenile justice system.

CRIPA lawsuits have cited states for inadequate health and mental health services, overcrowding, inadequate educational services, and even inadequate nutrition in institutional facilities. Multiple other federal mandates are also at issue within CRIPA lawsuits, including IDEA, the ADA, and Section 504. There have been over fifty CRIPA lawsuits so far involving state juvenile justice systems in federal court. Most recently, lawsuits in Louisiana and Georgia have attracted national attention to the plight of detained juveniles, including increasing awareness of the high prevalence of mental health needs of youth in this population (Atkins et al., 1999; Pumariega et al., 1999). In Chapter Eleven on collaboration with juvenile justice, the authors discuss experiences with the impact of two significant CRIPA lawsuits: *Alexander S.* v. *South Carolina Department of Juvenile Justice* (1996) and *United States* v. *Kentucky* (1995) on mental health systems.

CONSENT DECREES AND THEIR EFFECTS ON CHILD PSYCHIATRIC PRACTICE

The two examples of federal class action lawsuits we examine here had a significant impact on their respective systems of care.

R. C. v. *Hornsby*: The Alabama Experience

The first statewide reform of a child welfare system in the United States was accomplished by a consent decree in response to a suit filed by the Bazelon Center for Mental Health and the Law, the American Civil Liberties Union of Alabama, and the Southern Poverty Law Center. The class action lawsuit *R. C.* v. *Hornsby* was filed in 1988 against the Department of Human Resources of Alabama (DHR) and its commissioner, Andy Hornsby, on behalf of an eight-year-old boy, R. C. The case never went to trial. However, in a consent decree of 1991, the plaintiff's lawyers and the state agreed to a set of values and principles for total reform of Alabama's child welfare system.

R. C. was taken into the state's custody after his parents divorced. He was sent to a series of psychiatric institutions, even though he was not diagnosed with any serious emotional disorder. He spent much of his time in locked isolation rooms, heavily drugged. R. C.'s father protested this treatment and was promptly barred from visiting his son. A year and a half later, after a lawsuit was filed on R. C.'s behalf, the state's welfare agency returned R. C. to his father, offering no assistance to either the boy or his father.

Those values and principles agreed to by the state of Alabama and its Department of Human Resources were those espoused in the Child and Adolescent Service System Program (CASSP) principles and recently reiterated in the settlement of the *Jason K.* suit in Arizona. They are based on preserving family integrity, bringing all necessary services, including mental health services, to the child and his family in their home or the least restrictive setting possible, and developing an individual service plan (ISP) with the input and direction of the child and family.

This system reform was to be based on bottom-up change that required that the structure of the system and the way it responds are not defined at bureaucratic conference tables in the state offices in Montgomery, the capital of Alabama, but at the point of service to the consumer—in the homes of the children and their families and in the local offices of the county DHR. Partnerships among DHR workers, families, foster parents, communities, and the providers of all the services, including mental health services, that a child and family need are required in order to be compliant with the consent decree, which is continually monitored by court-approved personnel.

The results of the county-by-county bottom-up system reform are impressive. From 1991 to 1995, when the number of children in foster care nationally rose by 12 percent, Alabama's foster care census fell by 22 percent. Children's stay in out-of-home placement dropped from an average of 438 days to fewer than 100. Seven years after the R. C. settlement, the new system of care is in full operation in two-thirds of the state's population. Findings from the monitors of compliance to the decree confirm that child welfare workers and their supervisors take pride in engaging families and building on their strengths to meet children's needs effectively. Families report satisfaction about the quality of services and their relationships with caseworkers. Foster families and providers of services, including mental health services, view themselves as part of a team working together to support families and children.

The R. C. reform is not without problems, particularly in some of Alabama's largest population areas. In these urban areas, there is a disproportionately high rate of truancy and teenage pregnancy relative to children who are not in foster care. The DHR offices in these counties have had to cope with a mix of poverty, substance abuse, and emotional disturbance in both parents and children. Communities and families there were less involved than in other counties, and caseworkers were overwhelmed. However, with intensive advocacy by the plaintiff's attorneys and the flexibility fostered by the R. C. decree, innovative approaches have started to show success in these counties. Recently, the largest county in Alabama, Jefferson County, received a system of care grant from the Center for Mental Health Services of the Substance Abuse and Mental Health Services Administration, and the rate of system reform there has greatly accelerated since the principles of systems of care complement those stipulated in the R. C. consent decree synergistically.

Jason K. v. *Griffith*: The Arizona Experience

In 1991, *Jason K.* v. *Griffith* was filed in federal court, alleging that the children and adolescents in Maricopa County (Phoenix) who qualified for service under Title XIX of the federal Medicaid statute were not receiving adequate mental health care. Six years later, the defendants and the plaintiffs, represented by the Arizona Center for Disability Law and the Bazelon Center for Mental Health Law, agreed to the appointment of an independent review panel to study the children's mental health care system and determine the adequacy of the available services. These services came under the administration of the state in 1997, after the bankruptcy of ComCare, the locally based managed care entity. In 1998, this panel, led by Ivor Groves, published its report, which indicated that in many respects, the services available were not meeting the community's needs. The review panel found that the initial evaluation completed on children and adolescents entering the system was "not sufficiently sensitive to appropriately and consistently triage all children into appropriate care that provides the right services with appropriate intensity and continuity to achieve results" (Independent Review Panel, 1998, p. ii). The lack of adequate services was especially acute for children with the most serious emotional disturbances. The Independent Review Panel found that "the system does not have the capacity to consistently and effectively address the special need/multiagency children (child welfare, developmentally disabled, juvenile justice, and seriously impaired families) that make up 30–40% of the membership and require coordinated and well-planned evaluation and interventions" (Independent Review Panel, 1998, p. ii).

Following the release of the Independent Review Panel's report and a court-ordered stay of the litigation, the Arizona Division of Behavioral Health convened a multidisciplinary work group to revise standards for the initial assessment and evaluation of children and adolescents entering publicly funded mental health services. Three child psychiatrists volunteered their time to participate in the drafting of the work group's final report. Released in June 1999, the report used the American Academy of Child and Adolescent Psychiatry's Practice Parameters for the Psychiatric Assessment of Children and Adolescents (1995) and for the Psychiatric Assessment of Infants and Toddlers (1997) as the backbone of the revised standards for assessment. Language supportive of the use of strength-based assessments was also included in the final draft of the document. The work group also strongly recommended increased support for family participation in the treatment planning process, that wraparound services be used to avoid multiple placements, and that collaborative special teams be formed around children with multiple needs involved in multiple systems. With the stay still in place, three implementation work groups (on assessment, family issues and collaborative special teams) were established in fall 1999 to carry the reforms forward.

January 2000 proved to be a critical juncture for the reform efforts. Only days into the new year, the state terminated Groves's contract two months before he was scheduled to reevaluate the child mental health system in Maricopa County, now administered by ValueOptions, an out-of-state, for-profit managed care company. Following this decision, plaintiffs and defendants began preparing for trial. It was into this heated environment that the American Academy of Child and Adolescent Psychiatry's Work Group on Community-Based Systems of Care came into Phoenix late in the month to present a conference, "Children's Mental Health—A System of Care Approach." This conference, presented by child psychiatrists involved in systems reform nationwide along with local discussants, provided a much-needed forum for dialogue.

In February 2000, reform efforts resumed as the presiding judge on the case ordered that Groves's contract be restored and that both sides resume their work on negotiating a settlement. The Independent Review Panel began its reassessment of children's mental health services in Maricopa County the following month, conducting in-depth reviews of the treatment of forty-one children within the system. Among the tools used for this assessment were two products of the

American Academy of Child and Adolescent Psychiatry: the Child and Adolescent Level of Care Utilization System (CALOCUS), developed in cooperation with the American Association of Community Psychiatrists (AACAP and AACP, 1999), and the Best Principles for Managed Care Medicaid RFP's (AACAP, 1996). When the Independent Review Panel's follow-up review was released in June 2000, it found that 40 to 65 percent of the children receiving treatment continued to be served inadequately. It was the panel's strong sense that "major new strategies will be required for improving daily practice of behavioral health services to achieve an acceptable level of consistent performance within a reasonable time period" (Independent Review Panel, 2000, p. 80).

Following the release of Groves's second review, the work of the Collaborative Special Teams Work Group took on added importance. Composed of child mental health providers from multiple disciplines, administrators from state agencies, and parents, the work group met regularly through the winter and spring of 2000 to draft an Arizona-grown strategy for meeting the needs of children with serious emotional disturbances and their families. Modeled on child and family teams from the wraparound model, the collaborative special teams model sought to provide individualized services to those children most in need. The work group, chaired by a child psychiatrist, stressed the need to identify children at risk for losing their current placement and moving to a higher level of care to be the focus for these teams. Special emphasis was placed on the need for stable placement for children under the age of five and on assisting older adolescents as they move into the adult mental health system. The work group's final report, submitted to the Children's Inter-Governmental Agreement Executive Committee (Children's IGA) in June 2000, made a number of recommendations for continued system reform: that a recognized expert on the wraparound model be retained to provide training to practitioners in the field and that the curricula of the training programs for child-serving professionals be changed so that "graduates understand and operationalize the principles of collaboration, family-centered assessment and Wraparound" (Arizona Division of Behavioral Health Services, 2000, p. 7). The Children's IGA, now charged by the governor with the implementation of reforms, accepted the work group's report without revisions in September 2000 and invited the child psychiatrist and a parent from the work group to join them in these efforts.

Momentum for reform continued to build in the fall of 2000 as a new head of the state Division of Behavioral Health Services was appointed and the 300 Kids Project was started. This project, with one hundred children from rural northern Arizona and two hundred children from suburban Phoenix, was designed to provide the sites where these new collaborative strategies for individualization of care were to be developed. A training Request for Proposal for the 300 Kids Project was awarded to Vroon VanDenBerg to provide wraparound training statewide in January 2001.

The Academy of Child and Adolescent Psychiatry continued its interest and involvement in these reforms, when the plaintiffs and an Arizona member of the academy requested that it file an amicus brief in support of the reform efforts. Although the amicus brief was never needed in court, the willingness of the academy to become involved in this way added to the momentum for settlement.

The *Jason K.* lawsuit was settled out of court in March 2001. The settlement agreement is precedent setting because it is the first to require the reform of a state children's mental health system operated under the principles of managed care. According to a press release from the Bazelon Center for Mental Health Law (2001b), the settlement is also unique in its approach by "spelling out in a legal document a vision defining the purpose of behavioral health services and a set of . . . principles for improving the quality of these services" (p. 1):

1. Collaboration with the child and family: Respect for and active collaboration with the child and parents is the cornerstone to achieving positive behavioral health outcomes.

2. Functional outcomes: Behavioral health services are designed and implemented to aid children to achieve success in school, live with their families, avoid delinquency, and become stable and productive adults.

3. Collaboration with others: When children have multi-agency, multi-system involvement, a joint assessment is developed and a jointly established behavioral health services plan is collaboratively implemented.

4. Accessible services: Children have access to a comprehensive array of behavioral health services, sufficient to assure that they receive the treatment they need.

5. Best practices: Behavioral health services are provided by competent individuals who are adequately trained and supervised. Behavioral health services are delivered in accordance with Guidelines adopted by the Arizona Division of Behavioral Health that incorporate evidence-based "best practices."

6. Most appropriate setting: Children are provided behavioral health services in their home and community to the extent possible.

7. Timeliness: Children identified as needing behavioral health services are assessed and served promptly.

8. Services tailored to the child and family: The unique strengths and needs of children and their families dictate the type, mix, and intensity of behavioral health services provided.

9. Stability: Behavioral health service plans strive to minimize multiple placements.

10. Respect for the child and family's unique cultural heritage: Behavioral health services are provided in a manner that respects the children and

parents' cultural traditions and heritage. Services are provided in Spanish to children and parents whose primary language is Spanish.

11. Independence: Behavioral health services include support and training for parents in meeting their child's behavioral health needs, and support and training for children in self-management.

12. Connection to natural supports: The behavioral health system identifies and appropriately utilizes natural supports available from the child and parents' own network of associates, including friends, and neighbors, and from community organizations, including service and religious organizations [*Jason K.* v. *Eden* settlement agreement, 2001, pp. 5–7].

These principles have provided the basis for ongoing system reform in Arizona. Efforts to implement the principles of wraparound and interagency collaboration continue to change mental health treatment practices across the state slowly. A recent expansion of community-based services covered under the state Medicaid plan will strongly support these efforts.

There are many lessons to be learned from the Arizona experience. An important one is that volunteer work groups with diverse memberships, including parents, state administrators, and mental health professionals from many disciplines, can contribute meaningfully to system reform when they are given a clear mandate and support. Perhaps the most important lesson is that the threat of a consent decree may be as effective in promoting system reform as the actual decree itself. When all parties to the dispute accept the need for change and reform efforts gain momentum, the legal process has served its purpose without ever having gone to trial.

GUIDELINES FOR PRACTICING IN SYSTEMS OF CARE UNDER CONSENT DECREES

Following are recommendations stemming from our collective experiences in practicing in systems of care undergoing class action litigation or under consent decrees.

Know the Details of the Agreement

While most consent decrees have in common some aspects that are similar and that generally follow those principles that are outlined in the CASSP principles (Stroul & Friedman, 1986), each state, each agency, and each consent decree have elements that are unique. In order to practice comfortably within these consent decrees, the specific features of each document must be known. Obtaining a copy of the consent decree will be most helpful in determining what role can be most comfortable for a child psychiatrist.

Child psychiatrists are more frequently being asked to participate in the stake-holder groups that determine the conditions of the settlement agreements. Thus, those aspects of care unique to child psychiatrists are being included in these decrees. They include the necessity for a comprehensive biopsychosocial assessment and treatment plan and specific attention to medically oriented interventions, such as the appropriate use of psychotropic medications for the plaintiff population.

Being aware of what specific services are provided as a result of these consent decrees and what providers are credentialed to provide these services can make child psychiatrists and other mental health professionals more specific in recommendations for evaluation and treatment, whether as an individual provider or a consultant to other providers. The array of services and the variety of providers vary from state to state and from consent decree to consent decree.

The nature of the monitoring process should be kept in mind when practicing within the consent decree. The specific outcome measures used to track compliance with the consent decree may be well intentioned but occasionally misinformed. If, for example, one of the outcome measures is to strive for a reduction in use of psychotropic medications within a plaintiff population without taking into account specific diagnoses that are responsive to those medications, individual clients may be deprived of appropriate therapies. However, the focus of attention on the avoidance of inappropriate medication of clients, to be monitored by the agent of the settlement agreement, can provide the child psychiatrist with additional leverage to use in demanding judicious use of medications. They can also call for the use of medications only within the context of a comprehensive treatment plan designed by the interdisciplinary team working with the plaintiff population.

Know the Stakeholders to the Agreement and Their Political Agendas

Identify the plaintiff group, and establish an effective relationship with families with whom you will be working under the consent decree. It is not unusual that these are consumers, clients, and patients who have felt neglected, ignored, and even abused by the caring system involved in the consent decree. Were that not true, the lawsuit and the consequent consent decree would have been unnecessary. Thus, professional humility is indicated when approaching these children and their families. An open, honest, and nondefensive attitude can allow the child mental health professional to establish a trusting relationship with these consumer groups. Much mutual learning can occur by adapting an attitude of empathy for clients who have found it necessary to seek legal redress for their children's mental health needs.

Familiarity with the stakeholders within the state government or within the other agencies involved in the consent decree is important. To avoid an adversarial relationship and foster one of cooperation calls for some appreciation of the agencies' culture and how that culture can change as a result of political change, change of agency head, or an election result. One of the reasons that the R.C. reform effort succeeded in Alabama was that DHR's leadership was strongly committed to the guiding principles laid out in the consent decree. In fact, the director of Alabama's child welfare system received a national award from his peers for his stewardship of the reform effort. When a later director appointed by a new administration began to dismantle much of the infrastructure that supported the reform effort, the plaintiffs prevailed in maintaining the reform effort only through a return to court. The staunch support of the county DHR directors resulted in a unanimous vote of no confidence in the new state DHR director's leadership and management. A court order continuing the reform effort labeled the effort by the new political administration to dismiss the consent decree as only a shift in political winds. The judge's opinion to continue the consent decree was upheld on appeal.

Know the Specific Provisions of the Agreement That Influence Clinical Practice

Once a suit has been filed, the provisions of the consent decree can be greatly influenced by enlightened and well-informed child psychiatrists. Aspects of the decree addressing assessment and treatment can be modeled after the practice parameters from the Academy of Child and Adolescent Psychiatry (1995, 1997). The structure of services within a managed care framework can be modeled after guidelines provided within publications addressing Medicaid managed care from the Academy of Child and Adolescent Psychiatry, such as *The Best Principles for Managed Medicaid Care RFPs* (1996). Such input from child psychiatry prior to the implementation of a consent decree can ensure that comprehensive services can be based on best practices within the field and can avoid the implementation of narrow or inappropriate guidelines. Child psychiatrists practicing in Arizona and from the AACAP were useful in shaping the consent decree in that state.

Once a consent decree has been implemented and a child psychiatrist is participating in the system of care as a provider or consultant, then such materials as the CALOCUS training manual (Klaehn, O'Malley, Vaughan, & Kroeger, 1999) and the practice parameters from the AACAP (1995, 1997) can be of great assistance to child psychiatrists and other clinicians. They provide support for adhering to those principles in that decree that require the least restrictive treatment for setting and for appropriate clinical services for a given client-patient or the whole lawsuit class of consumers. The CALOCUS instrument can be particularly effective in assisting with placement and level-of-care decisions often cited in consent decrees. For example, the consent decree for *Felix* v. *Waihee* in Hawaii explicitly recommends the use of CALOCUS in the design and operation of mandated services under the consent decree. Using this variety of instruments and documents, a child psychiatrist or other mental health professional who chooses to function in a service delivery system that is driven by the implementation of a consent decree can do so comfortably and know that professional standards are fully supportive of his or her efforts.

Be Mindful of Professionalism and Ethics Under a Consent Decree

In spite of everyone's best efforts, the original intent of the consent decree can be subverted. Sometimes in response to media pressure, political pressure or whim, economic downturn, budgetary constraints, or a variety of other influences, the original intent of a consent decree can be lost, and professionals, including child psychiatrists and families, are asked to function in an untenable fashion. Under such pressure, the participants in a system may be asked to perform outside their professional integrity and professional ethics. When such circumstances occur, as they did six years into the R. C. decree in Alabama, the only reasonable recourse is to resort to whatever remedy is available: appeal to the monitor or master who oversees the compliance with the consent decree, consult with the plaintiff attorneys in concert with the original members of the class action suit, and reactivate the suit for noncompliance on the part of the agency if there is no acceptable ethical resolution. Although the intent of child psychiatric and mental health endeavors within such systems is to avoid adversarial positions whenever possible, it is not always possible, and one must be willing to take on an advocacy position when necessary.

References

Alexander S. v. Boyd. (1996). U.S. Court of Appeals for the Fourth Circuit, No. 96-1950, No. 96-2509, Argued Dec. 5, 1996, Decided May 28. 1997.

American Academy of Child and Adolescent Psychiatry. (1995). Practice parameters for the psychiatric assessment of children and adolescents. *Journal of the American Academy of Child and Adolescent Psychiatry, 34,* 1386–1402.

American Academy of Child and Adolescent Psychiatry. (1996). *Best principles for managed Medicaid RFPs: How decision-makers can select and monitor high quality programs.* Washington, DC: Author.

American Academy of Child and Adolescent Psychiatry. (1997). Practice parameters for the psychiatric evaluation of infants and toddlers (0–36 months). *Journal of the American Academy of Child and Adolescent Psychiatry, 36*(Suppl.), 21S–36S.

American Academy of Child and Adolescent Psychiatry and the American Association of Community Psychiatrists. (1999). *Child and adolescent level of care utilization system, version 1.1.* Washington, DC: Authors.

Arizona Division of Behavioral Health Services. (2000, June 14). *Final report of the Collaborative Special Teams Work Group.* Phoenix: Arizona Department of Health Services, Division of Behavioral Health Services.

Atkins, D. L., Pumariega, A. J., Montgomery, L., Rogers, K., Nybro, C., Jeffers, G., Sease, F. (1999). Mental health and incarcerated youth. I: Prevalence and nature of psychopathology. *Journal of Child and Family Studies, 8,* 193–204.

Bazelon Center for Mental Health and the Law. (1998). *Making child welfare work: Forgoing new partnerships to protect children and sustain families.* Washington, DC: Author.

Bazelon Center for Mental Health and the Law. (1999). *Relinquishing custody: The tragic failure to meet children's mental health needs: Litigation strategies.* Washington, DC: Author.

Bazelon Center for Mental Health and the Law. (2001a). *Merging systems of care principles with civil rights law: Olmstead planning for children with serious emotional disturbance.* Washington, DC: Author.

Bazelon Center for Mental Health and the Law. (2001b). *Groundbreaking settlement reforming managed mental health care for Arizona children ends federal lawsuit.* [press release].

Independent Review Panel. (1998). *Report on the independent study of behavioral health services for Title XIX eligible children in Maricopa County, Arizona.* Tallahassee, FL: Human Systems and Outcomes.

Independent Review Panel. (2000). *Follow-up review of behavioral health services for Title XIX eligible children in Maricopa County, Arizona.* Tallahassee, FL: Human Systems and Outcomes.

Jason K. v. Eden Settlement Agreement. (2001, Mar. 20, 2001). No. CIV 91–261 TUC JMR. United States District Court, District of Arizona.

Klaehn, R., O'Malley, K., Vaughan, T., & Kroeger, K. (1999). *CALOCUS user's manual: Child and adolescent level of care utilization system.* Washington, DC: American Academy of Child and Adolescent Psychiatry and American Association of Community Psychiatrists.

Pumariega, A. J., Atkins, D. L., Rogers, K., Montgomery, L., Nybro, C., Caesar, R., & Millus, D. (1999). Mental health and incarcerated youth. II: Service utilization in incarcerated youth. *Journal of Child and Family Studies, 8,* 205–215.

Stroul, B. A., & Friedman, R. M. (1986). *A system of care for children and youth with severe emotional disturbance* (rev. ed.). Washington, DC: Georgetown University Child Development Center, National Technical Assistance Center for Children's Mental Health.

United States v. Kentucky. (1995). Civil action No. 3 (95 CV 7575).

Cases Cited

Belcherton Public Schools. (1997). 26 IDELR 961 (S.E.A. Mass.).

Board of Education v. Rowley. (1982). 458 U.S. 176, 206–207.

Bond v. Stanton. (1981). 655 F.2d 766 (7th Cir.).

Brian A. et al. v. Donald Sundquist, Governor of Tennessee, et al. (2000). No. 3-00-0445 (M.D. Tenn.).

Burke County Board of Education v. Denton. (1990). 895 F.2d 973 (4th Cir.).

Burlington v. Board of Education. (1985). 471 U.S. 359.

Cordero by Bates v. Pennsylvania Department of Education. (1992). 795 F. Supp. 1352.

County of San Diego v. California Special Education Hearing Office. (1996). 93 F.3d 1458 (9th Cir.).

D. R. v. Concannon (1991). No. 90-483 DA (D. Ore).

East Windsor Board of Education. (1994). 20 IDELR 1478 (S.E.A. Conn.).

Elizabeth B. v. Texas Department of Protective and Regulatory Services et al. (1995). No. SA-94-CA-0050 (W.D. Tex.).

Emily Q. v. Belshe. (1998). No. 98-4181 WDK (AIJX) (C. D. Calif.).

Felix v. Waihee (Hawaii Departments of Education and Health). (1993). No. 93-00367DAE.

French v. Concannon. (1998). No. 97-CV-24-B-C (D. Me.).

Hall v. Shawnee Mission School District. (1994). 856 F. Supp. 1521, 1530 (D. Kansas).

Hunger v. Leininger. (1994). 15 F.3rd 664 (7th Cir.).

Jason K. v. Griffith (1991). 836 F. Supp. 694, 699 (D. Ariz.).

John B. v. Menke. (1998). No. 3-98 0168 (M.D. Tenn.).

Key v. State of Washington Department of Social and Health Services. (1994). No. CS-93-0131-FVS (E.D. Wash.).

Krinchinsky v. Knox County Schools. (1992). 963 F.2d 847 (4th Cir.).

Larry v. Snider. (1993). No. 91-680 (E.D. Pa).

Metts v. Houston. (1998). No. 97-CV-4123 (E.D. Penn).

Olmstead v. L. C. (1999). 119 S. Ct. 2176.

R. C. v. Hornsby. (1991). No. 88-11-11TON (M.D. Ala.).

Salazar v. District of Columbia. (1996). 938 F. Supp. 926 (D. Ariz).

San Lorenzo Unified School District. (1997). 26 IDELR 331 (S.E.A. Calif.).

Scott v. Snider. (1992). No. 91-CV-7080 (E.D. Pa.).

Seattle School District. (1990). 16 EHLR 1478 (S.E.A. Mass.).

Tallahassee Memorial Regional Medical Center v. Cook. (1997). 109 F.3d 693 (11th Cir.).

Taunton Public Schools. (1997). 27 IDELR 108 (S.E.A. Mass.).

Willie M. v. Hunt (North Carolina Government). (1980). No. CC-79-294 (W.D.N.C. 1980) (consent decree; see also Willie M. v. Hunt, 657 F.2d 55 (4th Cir. 1981).

CHAPTER NINETEEN

Systems of Care
Demonstration Projects

Innovation, Evaluation,
and Sustainability

E. Wayne Holden, Rolando L. Santiago
Brigitte A. Manteuffel, Robert L. Stephens
Ana Maria Brannan, Robin Soler
Qinghong Liao, Freda Brashears
Susan Zaro

The Comprehensive Community Mental Health Services Program for Children and Their Families is the federal government's principal response to the service needs of the estimated 4.5 to 6.3 million children in the United States who have a serious emotional disturbance (Friedman, Katz-Leavy, Manderscheid, & Sondheimer, 1999). The program provides grants to states, communities, territories, and Native American tribes to improve and expand their systems of care to meet the needs of children and adolescents with serious emotional disturbances and their families. These include children and youth with a serious emotional disturbance from birth to age twenty-one who currently have, or at any time during the past year had, a mental, behavioral, or emotional disorder of sufficient duration to meet diagnostic criteria specified in the *Diagnostic and Statistical Manual of Mental Disorders* (DSM–IV; American Psychiatric Association, 1994). In addition, this diagnosis must have resulted in functional impairment that substantially interferes with or limits one or more major life activities. The program is administered by the Child, Adolescent, and Family Branch within the Substance Abuse and Mental Health Services Administration's Center for Mental Health Services.

The first four grant communities were funded by this demonstration program in 1993. By 2001, the initial annual investment of $5 million had grown almost tenfold to a cumulative $464 million, the largest federal investment ever in community-based mental health services for children and their families. To date, sixty-seven grants have been awarded, each for a period of five to six years (see

Figure 19.1). As of September 2002, 53,289 children and their families had been served in these federal demonstration sites.

This program is the translation of the system of care approach first articulated by Stroul and Friedman in 1986 and now a major organizing force shaping the development of community-based children's mental health services in the United States. At its inception, this approach signified a new model of working with children and families. The model included a comprehensive spectrum of mental health and other necessary services and supports guided by a set of principles. Although the actual components and organizational configurations of the system of care may differ from community to community, the model calls for individualized, family focused, and culturally competent services and supports. These should be community based and accessible and provided in the least restrictive environment possible through a collaborative, coordinated interagency network.

To explain how systems of care are intended to work, a theory-based logic model was developed with input from program stakeholders across the country (Hernandez & Hodges, 2000). The logic model articulates the underlying assumptions that guide service delivery strategies and are believed to be critical to producing change and improvement in children and families. It has three core elements—population, strategies, and outcome—as well as a mission statement, guiding principles, and an evaluation and feedback cycle (see Figure 19.2). The mission statement addresses the need for intensive community-based services for children with serious emotional disturbances and their families. The guiding principles provide a foundation on which system of care strategies are built. These strategies are grounded in a community ownership and planning process that engages multiple partners. As depicted in the far right of the framework, outcomes are organized into practice, child and family, and system outcomes. The model is not static or linear; it includes an evaluation and feedback cycle, making use of the best and most current research, and incorporates concepts of internal evaluation, quality improvement, adaptation, and accountability.

This federal demonstration program has resulted in widespread implementation of the system of care approach and principles. Since its inception, the potential for children and their families to receive mental health services and supports in their own communities has grown, as have the number of providers and stakeholders knowledgeable about and committed to delivering services using a system of care approach. Grant-funded communities have expanded their service arrays, adding new services such as mentoring, respite, and family support, and tailoring others to meet the specific needs of their communities (Vinson, Brannan, Baughman, Wilce, & Gawron, 2001). Breaking with the past, the norm in the grant communities is for families to be partners in service planning and provision and, in many grant communities, in evaluating services

(text continued on page 438)

Grantee Sites of the Comprehensive Community Mental Health Services Program for Children and Their Families

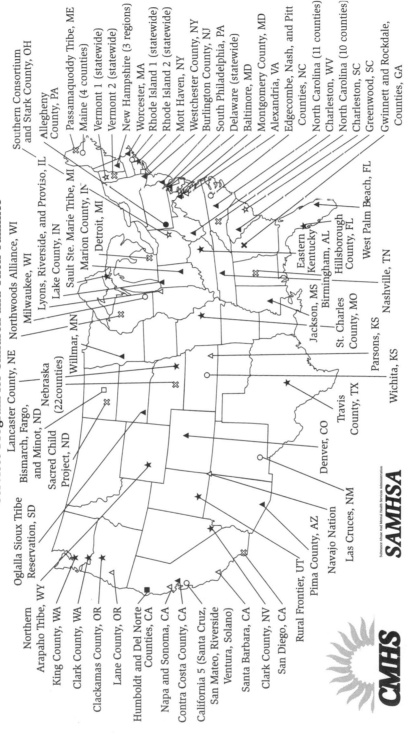

Oglalla Sioux Tribe Reservation, SD
Lancaster County, NE
Northwoods Alliance, WI
Milwaukee, WI
Lyons, Riverside, and Proviso, IL
Lake County, IN
Marion County, IN
Detroit, MI
Sault Ste. Marie Tribe, MI
Southern Consortium and Stark County, OH
Allegheny County, PA
Passamaquoddy Tribe, ME
Maine (4 counties)
Vermont 1 (statewide)
Vermont 2 (statewide)
New Hampshire (3 regions)
Worcester, MA
Rhode Island 1 (statewide)
Rhode Island 2 (statewide)
Mott Haven, NY
Westchester County, NY
Burlington County, NJ
South Philadelphia, PA
Delaware (statewide)
Baltimore, MD
Montgomery County, MD
Alexandria, VA
Edgecombe, Nash, and Pitt Counties, NC
North Carolina (11 counties)
Charleston, WV
North Carolina (10 counties)
Charleston, SC
Greenwood, SC
Gwinnett and Rockdale, Counties, GA

Bismarck, Fargo, and Minot, ND
Nebraska (22counties)
Sacred Child Project, ND
Willmar, MN
Eastern Kentucky
Birmingham, AL
Hillsborough County, FL
West Palm Beach, FL
Jackson, MS
St. Charles County, MO
Nashville, TN
Parsons, KS
Wichita, KS
Travis County, TX
Denver, CO
Las Cruces, NM
Navajo Nation
Pima County, AZ
Rural Frontier, UT

Northern Arapaho Tribe, WY
King County, WA
Clark County, WA
Clackamas County, OR
Lane County, OR
Humboldt and Del Norte Counties, CA
Napa and Sonoma, CA
Contra Costa County, CA
California 5 (Santa Cruz, San Mateo, Riverside Ventura, Solano)
Santa Barbara, CA
Clark County, NV
San Diego, CA

SAMHSA
Substance Abuse and Mental Health Services Administration

CMHS

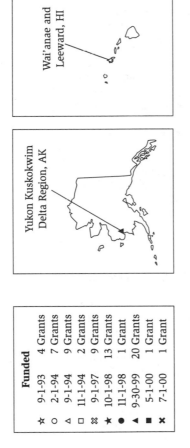

FIGURE 19.1. The Grant Communities Funded by the Comprehensive Community Mental Health Services for Children and Their Families Program.

Comprehensive Community Mental Health Services
Program for Children and Their Families:

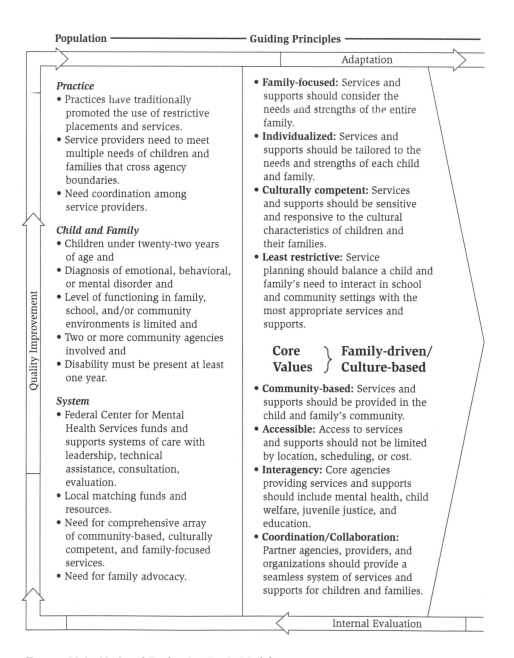

FIGURE 19.2. National Evaluation Logic Model.

The Mission The Comprehensive Community Mental Health Services Program for Children and Their Families encourages the development of intensive community-based services for children with serious emotional disturbance and their families based on a multi-agency, multidisciplinary approach involving both the public and private sectors.

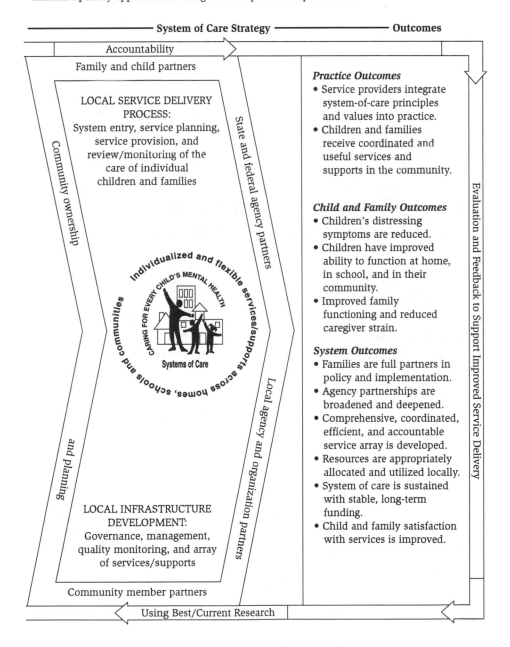

FIGURE 19.2. National Evaluation Logic Model. *(continued)*

(Osher, van Kammen, & Zaro, 2001). There is a growing recognition of the importance of natural support systems within culturally diverse communities and the advantage of adapting services to be congruent with them (Cross, Earle, Echo-Hawk Solie, & Manness, 2000). More is known about how to embed new interventions in service organizations (Burns, 2002), and many child-serving agencies across the country have become committed to providing services in a new way that involves interagency collaboration and leads to more individualized and less restrictive services. In some cases, changes in policies at the state and federal levels have led to legislation that supports system change, both within and beyond the grant communities (Holden, De Carolis, & Huff, 2002). Finally, system of care proponents have been able in some instances to harness managed care technologies to further system of care goals (Stroul, Pires, Armstrong, & Zaro, 2002).

The National Evaluation of the Comprehensive Community Mental Health Services Program for Children and Their Families

The Center for Mental Health Services within the Substance Abuse and Mental Health Services Administration has a strong commitment to promoting knowledge development and application. Reflecting this commitment, a national cross-site evaluation of the Comprehensive Community Mental Health Services Program for Children and Their Families began in 1994. The evaluation responds to the legislation authorizing the program. It calls for an annual evaluation to describe the children and families served by the system of care initiative; assess how systems of care develop and what factors impede or enhance their development, measure whether children served through the program experience improvement in clinical and functional outcomes and whether those improvements endure over time and why, determine whether the consumers are satisfied with the services they receive, and measure the costs associated with the implementation of a system of care and determine its cost-effectiveness. Besides responding to the legislation, the evaluation serves as a laboratory for addressing many of the questions described above. Findings from the evaluation also can provide information on which to base future treatment, programmatic, funding, and policy decisions (Holden et al., 2002).

Any mental health services evaluation must be undertaken with the recognition that a complex set of factors determines the outcomes for a particular child and family. Key questions often posited in mental health services and research are: What works, for whom, and under what conditions? These questions are not easy or straightforward to answer. The service system is one critical factor, but others, such as child and family characteristics and the quality of treatment, must be taken into consideration as well (Burns, 2001, 2002). The national evaluation is designed to address many complex and related dimensions of effectiveness. It is longitudinal in nature; children and families are followed over time so that changes in outcomes can be understood from a developmental point of view. It includes a comprehensive assessment of outcomes across several domains. The service delivery systems are also assessed over time, so that their developmental trajectories can be better understood. This includes identifying the ingredients necessary to sustaining systems of care, whether system-level changes result in concomitant practice-level changes, and how families engage in systems of care. Other critical questions addressed by the evaluation include whether systems of care are more effective than traditional service systems in improving outcomes for children with serious emotional disturbances and whether providing community-based mental health services and supports to this population is cost-effective. This level of complexity is necessary to understand the relationships between system, practice, and individual outcomes, recognizing that changes at different levels can occur simultaneously. The evaluation is comprehensive and includes the sixty-seven grantees, the children and families served by the programs, service providers, and partner agencies (Holden, Friedman, & Santiago, 2001b). It also includes information from nonfunded comparison communities. The number of grantees and participants and number of components and variety of methodologies incorporated into the evaluation is extensive.

In addition to the core components of the study, other special studies have been added to the evaluation as additional questions about effectiveness have emerged over time. The Federation of Families for Children's Mental Health has collaborated with the national evaluation team at ORC Macro to conduct a study on family involvement in evaluation (Osher, van Kammen, & Zaro, 2001) and a family-driven research study that examines how youth and family engagement in a system of care affect child and family outcomes. A special study on the effects of managed care on the demonstration projects (Stroul et al., 2002) was also conducted. A sustainability study is underway to assess the potential of funded grant communities to sustain their systems of care beyond their federal grant period and provide information that will be useful to federal and state policymakers as well as local systems of care to enhance sustainability. In the future, a study will assess the effectiveness of an evidence-based treatment within a system of care. This will allow for the determination of the additive contributions of a focused, evidenced-based treatment to the effectiveness of the entire system of care.

SUMMARY OF RESULTS OF THE NATIONAL EVALUATION

The results of the national evaluation have been reported in annual reports to Congress on the program (Center for Mental Health Services, 1997, 1998, 1999, 2000, 2001), special issues of journals (Holden & Brannan, 2002; Holden, Friedman &

Santiago, 2001a), and individual journal articles (Hodges, Doucette-Gates, & Kim, 2000; Hodges & Kim, 2000; Hodges, Doucette-Gates, & Liao, 1999; Walrath, dosReis, et al., 2001; Walrath, Mandell, et al., 2001). In several instances, grantees have used national evaluation data to address questions of local significance, and reports of these analyses have been published (Catalano, Lind, Rosenblatt, & Attkisson, 1999; Robertson et al., 1998; Rosenblatt & Rosenblatt, 1999; Rosenblatt & Furlong, 1998; Rosenblatt et al., 1998; Walrath, Mandell, & Leaf, 2001; Walrath, Nickerson, Crowel, & Leaf, 1998; Walrath, Sharp, Zuber, & Leaf, 2001; Wood, Chung, et al., 1998; Wood, Furlong, Casas, & Sosna, 1998). This section summarizes some of the most recent analyses conducted that address specific components of the national evaluation.

Development of Systems of Care

The national evaluation has placed a strong emphasis on evaluating the implementation of each demonstration program. This has been accomplished through the development of an innovative system of care assessment protocol designed to (1) describe approaches used by grant communities to implement system of care principles, (2) document the extent to which system of care principles are achieved within each grant community and across grant communities, and (3) track system development over time. This type of assessment is particularly challenging because the system of care approach and philosophy can be operationalized differently, depending on the prior experience, makeup, and needs of individual grant communities.

The initial protocol for the system of care assessment was developed for and implemented within the twenty-two demonstration grant communities that were awarded their funding in 1993–1994 (Vinson et al., 2001). Based on an overriding conceptual framework that included infrastructure and service delivery domains, sixteen separate system of care attributes were evaluated. To collect information on each attribute, a variety of data collection strategies were used, including semistructured interviews, protocols for recording observations and abstracting data from case records, and a review of selected site documents. For each site, data were collected by two trained site visitors during a three- to four-day site visit. During the site visit, interviews were conducted with a wide variety of stakeholders in the system of care. Each respondent was asked his or her perspective on system functioning and operations in relation to the attributes. For example, interview guides for case managers, agency administrators, families, site directors, and other respondents all contained questions about family involvement in the system of care to assess the degree to which the system of care embodied the family focus attribute. Both qualitative and quantitative data were collected on each attribute. Each grant community was visited annually for four years.

Results from the initial twenty-two grantees provided support for the implementation of system of care principles within the demonstration sites (Center for Mental Health Services, 1997, 1998, 1999; Vinson et al., 2001). On an aggregate level, system improvement was generally displayed across the five years of federal funding on each of the sixteen attributes. A wide range of governance bodies and interagency structures was used to support the development of policies and initiatives such as colocation of services, use of individualized service plans, strategies to promote cultural competence, and dedicated case management to promote coordination of more traditional mental health and innovative services. A number of challenges were also detected for the initial twenty-two grantees. Some grant communities had difficulty developing a full continuum of care due to local funding constraints. Family involvement worked well in service delivery but was an ongoing challenge to maintain in the governance and infrastructure of these programs. Specific and systematic strategies for the assessment and integration of strengths into service delivery were also a continuing challenge.

The system of care assessment protocol underwent significant revision based on a newly devised conceptual framework in 1999 (Holden, Brannan, Brashears, Gilford, & Connor, 2001) and is being used to evaluate the forty-five currently funded communities. The new protocol uses a similar site visit approach, but attempts to evaluate the eight key system of care characteristics (see Figures 19.3 and 19.4) across both the infrastructure and service delivery domains.

Assessment of grant communities with the revised protocol has also yielded important findings regarding system of care development. The revised assessment protocol was used to assess three comparison study pairs, which includes federally funded systems of care matched with comparison communities that have not received federal funding to build a system of care (Brannan, Baughman, Reed, & Katz-Leavy, 2002). As expected, comparisons of system scores across paired sites suggested that the federally funded sites came closer than the comparison sites to the ideals articulated in the principles. Seventy-five percent of the quantitative scores for the federally funded systems of care were at or above the adequate level for system of care principles; only 23 percent of the scores for the comparison communities were at or above a similar level. In addition, for 90 percent of the scores, federally funded communities scored higher than the comparison communities. There was less variability in scores across the funded systems of care and greater variability across the comparison sites' scores. Some movement toward the system of care approach was demonstrated in the comparison sites, however, despite their lack of funding. The systems of care performed especially well on the principles of interagency involvement and community-based service delivery. Although they generally performed better than the comparison sites, the systems of care continued to struggle in their system-level quality improvement efforts and in culturally competent service delivery. A more detailed discussion of the differences between these pairs of grantee communities on the system of care assessment can be found in Brannan et al. (2002).

Family-focused—The recognition that: (1) the ecological context of the family is central to the care of all children; (2) families are important contributors to, and equal partners in, any effort to serve children; and (3) all system and service processes should be planned to maximize family involvement.

Culturally competent—Sensitivity and responsiveness to, and acknowledgment of, the inherent value of differences related to race, religion, language, national origin, gender, socio-economic background, and community-specific characteristics.

Interagency—The involvement and partnership of core agencies in multiple child-serving sectors including child welfare, health, juvenile justice, education, and mental health.

Community-based—The provision of services within close geographical proximity to the targeted community.

Accessible—The minimizing of barriers to services in terms of physical location, convenience of scheduling, and financial constraints.

Coordination/collaboration—Professionals working together in a complementary manner to avoid duplication of services, eliminate gaps in care, and facilitate the child's and family's movement through the service system.

Individualized—The provision of care that is expressly child centered, that addresses the child's specific needs, and that recognizes and incorporates the child's strengths.

Least restrictive—The priority that services should be delivered in settings that maximize freedom of choice and movement, and that present opportunities to interact in normative environments (e.g., school and family).

FIGURE 19.3. Definition of System of Care Principles.

The revised protocol is being used to assess system of care development for the forty-five currently funded grantee communities. Each community is being assessed three times across its five-year funding cycle to evaluate the development of service systems across time. As of August 2001, thirty-six of the forty-five communities had participated in their initial assessment, twenty-three communities had participated in two assessments, and nine communities had participated in three assessments. The most recent assessments indicate that system of care principles are being operationalized consistently within these communities (Center for Mental Health Services, 2001). The majority of grant communities consistently scored above the midpoint range across all eight system of care principles in both the infrastructure and service delivery domains. Grant communities consistently scored highest on the principles of family focused, accessible, and individualized

Framework for Assessing Infrastructure Domain

	Governance	Management and Operations	Service Array	Quality Monitoring
Family Focused				
Culturally Competent				
Interagency				
Community Based				
Accessible				
Collaborative/Coordinated				
Individualized				
Least Restrictive				

Framework for Assessing Service Delivery Domain

	Entry into Services	Service Planning	Service Provision	Care Monitoring
Family Focused				
Culturally Competent				
Interagency				
Community Based				
Accessible				
Collaborative/Coordinated				
Individualized				
Least Restrictive				

FIGURE 19.4. Framework for Revised System of Care Assessment.

care and consistently scored lowest on the principles of cultural competence and interagency collaboration. Grant communities with multiple assessment visits have displayed stability across system of care principles and growth in several areas over time.

Children and Adolescents Participating in the Program

Since the beginning of the national evaluation, data have been obtained on demographic and clinical characteristics of children and families as they enter services in the system of care programs. Demographic characteristics for 4,039 children entering services for the twenty-three sites funded initially in 1997 and 1998 were reported in the 2001 annual report to Congress (Center for Mental Health Services, 2001). Children entering services came from a broad racial and ethnic distribution with high rates of single-parent and impoverished families. These children and families were experiencing multiple problems at services entry and as an aggregate had histories of high risk and family challenge.

Sixty percent of the children were white, 23 percent were African American, 12 percent were American Indian, 10 percent were Hispanic, 1.1 percent were Asian American or Pacific Islander, and 6 percent were of other racial and ethnic background. Forty-five percent of the children were in the custody of their mother only, and 25 percent were in the custody of both parents or one biological parent and one step-parent. The average number of children living in one household was three. The average age of caregivers was approximately forty, and the educational level of caregivers was low. Although 37 percent of caregivers earned a high school diploma or equivalency, 26 percent failed to complete high school. Poverty is a salient issue for families involved in systems of care. Forty-nine percent of the children lived in households with an annual income of less than $15,000.

Information on referral sources indicated that 29 percent of the children were referred by mental health agencies, 19 percent were referred by juvenile justice agencies, 18 percent by schools, 13 percent by child welfare or child protective services, 11 percent by caregivers or youth themselves, and 11 percent by others, such as family friends, physical health clinics, and substance abuse clinics.

Children had differing needs and challenges when they entered system of care programs. The most frequently reported problems were noncompliance (40 percent) and physical aggression (39 percent), followed by academic problems (28 percent), hyperactive-impulsive behaviors (25 percent), and attentional difficulties (23 percent). Other frequently reported problems included poor peer interaction (20 percent), sadness (19 percent), anxiety, property damage, extreme verbal abuse, police contacts, and poor self-esteem (16 percent for each of the last five problems). In addition, 80 percent reported two or more presenting problems. The average number of presenting problems reported was four.

A major criterion for entry into system of care services is the presence of a diagnosis. Diagnostic information was collected at a child's entry into the system of care based on criteria from the DSM–IV (American Psychiatric Association, 1994). Thirty-four percent with valid diagnostic information were reported to have ADHD, followed by oppositional defiant disorders (27 percent), mood disorders (including depression, 25 percent), adjustment disorder (17 percent), and conduct disorders (11 percent). Overall, 44 percent of the children had two or more diagnoses. Seventy percent of the children were reported to have at least one child risk factor at entry into system of care programs. The most frequently reported child risk factor was having run away from home (35 percent), followed by having been physically abused (29 percent), having had a previous psychiatric hospitalization (28 percent), having used substances (24 percent), and having been sexually abused (21 percent). Fourteen percent of caregivers reported that their child had made a suicide attempt, and 8 percent of caregivers reported that their child had been sexually abusive to others. In addition to child risk factors, caregivers reported family risk factors experienced by members of the children's biological families. Almost all children (94 percent) were exposed to at least one family risk factor, significantly higher than those with at least one child risk factor (70 percent). Fifty-five percent of the caregivers reported three or more family risk factors experienced by children's biological families. Of all family risk factors, history of substance use was the most frequently cited risk factor (66 percent), followed by mental illness (51 percent), domestic violence or spousal abuse (49 percent), felony conviction (47 percent), and previous psychiatric hospitalization (30 percent). Forty-six percent of children had biological parents who had received treatment for substance abuse.

Benefits of the Program for Children and Their Families

Across all grant communities, children with serious emotional disturbances between the ages of five and seventeen and a half years, who did not have a sibling in the study and had a caregiver willing to consent to the participation of their child (if age eleven or older) and their own participation, were eligible to participate in the longitudinal outcome study. Caregivers (persons with primary caretaking responsibility during the assessment period) and children were enrolled in the study across the second, third, and fourth grant years and could not be followed beyond the end of the funding period. Data were collected primarily by direct interview with caregivers and youth eleven years and older, although some data were also collected from records or from clinicians. These data included demographics, the child's clinical characteristics, living situation, educational indicators, juvenile justice indicators, behavior (Child Behavior Checklist, CBCL; Achenbach, 1991a; Youth Self-Report, YSR; Achenbach, 1991b) and functioning (Child and Adolescent Functional Assessment Scale, CAFAS; Hodges, 1990), and caregiver and youth satisfaction with services. In each grant community, the number of children enrolled in services, and consequently in the evaluation, varied and was affected by the size of the funded community and the nature of the program implemented. In addition, communities employed implementation strategies that addressed local differences in levels of service system characteristics, informed-consent requirements, population needs, interest in additional measures, available resources, and other local characteristics.

Among twenty-one of the twenty-two communities receiving five-year program grants in 1993 and 1994, the outcome study was implemented using a simple pretest-posttest replacement design. (One community did not participate due to limited local staff to conduct the evaluation over a large, rural geographical area.) Interviews were conducted at baseline, six months, one year, and annually for up to thirty-six months as long as the child remained in system of care services. A service exit interview was also conducted. Data were obtained from school systems, juvenile justice records, or service providers. In addition to the measures cited above, the Family Empowerment Scale (FES; Koren, DeChillo, & Friesen, 1992) was administered initially but was later dropped. Children who exited services or were lost to follow-up were replaced by new children entering services. In total, 18,884 children and their caregivers were enrolled in the outcome study. Follow-up data were collected on 8,065 children at six months, 5,995 children at twelve months, 2,580 children at twenty-four months, and 644 children at thirty-six months. Due to the limited number of children evaluated at thirty-six months, longitudinal analyses were limed to outcomes at twenty-four months.

Children who stayed in services in the communities funded in 1993 and 1994 showed considerable improvements in their assessed behavior and functioning. Their internalizing, externalizing, and total problem scores decreased significantly from intake to 2 years (*internalizing problems*: $F(3, 2,379) = 70.29, p < .001$, *externalizing problems*: $F(3, 2,376) = 73.73, p < .001$, and *total problems*: $F(3, 2,379) = 99.79, p < .001$). Change over time in individual behavioral and emotional problems was also examined using the Reliable Change Index (RCI) (Jacobson & Truax, 1991; Speer & Greenbaum, 1995; Jacobson, Roberts, Berns, & McGlinchey, 1999), a statistic that compares a child's scores at two different points in time and indicates whether a change in scores shows clinically significant improvement, stability, or deterioration. From intake to two years, 44.8 percent of children exhibited clinically significant improvement using the CBCL. Of those, 56.7 percent fell below the clinical cutoff for CBCL total problems T-scores at two years compared to 6.7 percent at intake. Children's total CAFAS scores, providing a measure of overall functioning, also declined substantially from intake to two years ($F(3, 3,324) = 58.99, p < .001$), with the greatest improvement in functioning occurring in the first six months in services.

Improvements to two years for children remaining in services were also found on specific functional measures. Children's living situations increased in stability, with the percentage of children living in one living situation increasing from 57.5 percent at intake (n = 10,082) to 72.9 percent at one year (n = 4,019) and 73.6 percent at two years (n = 1,816). School attendance improved ($F(3, 2,961)$ = 3.82, $p < .01$), as did school performance ($F(3, 1,968)$ = 8.72, $p < .001$). These improvements were continuous to one year; however, there was less improvement in school performance and a decline in attendance from one year to two years. Contacts with law enforcement fell among these children, with reported contacts with law enforcement as a result of one or more violations of the law falling from 29.5 percent during the year prior to intake (n = 7,724) to 20.7 percent during the year prior to their two-year assessment (n = 1,417).

Among the twenty-three grant communities funded in 1997 and 1998, the evaluation design was modified so that children could be followed both while they remained in services and after they exited services, and children were not replaced if they were lost to follow-up. Assessment periods were changed to reflect consistent six-month intervals, so that caregivers and youth age eleven and older were assessed at intake and every six months thereafter for up to thirty-six months in and out of services. Slight changes were made in the measures administered. A strength-based assessment of children's behavior, the Behavioral and Emotional Rating Scale (BERS; Epstein & Sharma, 1998), was added, as were three family measures (Family Assessment Device, FAD; Epstein, Baldwin, & Bishop, 1983; Family Resource Scale, FRS; Dunst & Leet, 1987; Caregiver Strain Questionnaire, CGSQ; Brannan, Heflinger, & Bickman, 1998) and a caregiver report of services received during each six-month period. Changes in data collection also included updating the satisfaction measure, obtaining educational information from caregivers rather than school records, and obtaining information about youth juvenile justice contacts, delinquent behavior, and substance use directly from youth age eleven years and older. As of April 2001, 2,388 children had been enrolled in the outcome study, and follow-up data had been collected on 943 children at six months, 484 at twelve months, and 180 at eighteen months.

New measures added to the evaluation of communities funded in 1997 and 1998 have contributed additional information about service experiences, children's strengths, children's substance use, and family characteristics. The BERS provided new information about children's strengths and indicated improvement in strengths at six months (85.5 at intake versus 90.23 at six months, t = –9.36, df = 725, $p < .001$). Clinically significant improvement in strengths was found among 49 percent of children, with 63 percent of children who improved having average or above-average strengths at six months. Caregivers reported a range of service experiences, with most children having received individual therapy (78.5 percent), case management (68.6 percent), assessment (64.0 percent), and medication treatment and monitoring (60.7 percent) in the first six months. Caregivers also reported increased family resources, decreased strain associated with caring for children with serious emotional disturbances, and improvements in family functioning, although youth did not agree with caregivers on all improved areas of family functioning.

Decreases in CBCL and CAFAS scores were again observed among children enrolled in services in communities funded in 1997 and 1998, as were improvements in residential stability, school performance and attendance, and involvement with the juvenile justice system. Average total CBCL scores fell from 69.6 at intake to 65.4 at six months ($t = 11.61$, $df = 628$, p < .001), with 36 percent of children showing clinically significant improvement. Average total CAFAS scores fell from 103.3 at intake to 84.8 at six months ($t = 10.52$, $df = 961$, $p < .001$). Regular school attendance increased from 67.9 percent at intake to 72.3 percent at six months, and passing grades (C or better) increased as well. Children whose school attendance had declined at six months were more likely than those whose attendance improved to be failing all or about half of their classes ($x^2 = 54.22$, $df = 9$, $p < .001$). Fewer youth were accused by the police of breaking the law, arrested, convicted of crimes, or sent to a detention center or jail at six months, and fewer children reported using cigarettes, alcohol, or marijuana. Among children who had lived in restrictive settings at intake, 21 percent lived in two-parent households, 23 percent lived in mother-maintained households, and another 9 percent lived in the homes of relatives or friends at six months.

Longitudinal Comparison Study

The longitudinal comparison study of the national evaluation was first implemented in 1997. Three funded communities were selected for participation from the group of twenty-two that were initially funded in 1993–1994 and were systematically matched with three comparison communities that had not received federal funding to build a system of care. Children and families entering services in each community were enrolled in a comprehensive study that evaluated system of care development, services experiences, outcomes across a number of dimensions, and services received, as well as costs associated with those services. The study contributes to nearly a decade of research designed to determine the efficacy of systems of care for improving child and family outcomes. While the evaluation and research literature has consistently demonstrated the positive effects of system reform, it is less clear whether these system-level changes translate into greater symptom improvement for children served in systems of care than for those served in more traditional service delivery systems (U.S. Department of Health and Human Services, 1999; Farmer, 2000).

One limitation of previous work has been the narrow focus on clinical outcomes as the relevant measure of a system of care's effectiveness. Even more important for assessing effectiveness are improvements in indicators of functioning in school and in the community. Obviously, a need exists to develop evidence of the mechanisms through which system changes affect changes in outcomes for individual children and families. Farmer (2000) observed that there has been a shift in focus as system-building initiatives have grown from their historical roots. While the initial principles of a system of care (Stroul & Friedman, 1986) have continued to drive these initiatives, an emphasis on individual-level outcomes as measures of effectiveness has replaced the initial focus on macrolevel changes and system performance. However, the complexity of the interventions that are implemented, the lack of clarity in defining how effectiveness should be determined, and the lack of well-defined theories of change as the basis for intervention development have all contributed to the difficulty of evaluating the effectiveness of a system of care at the individual level (Friedman & Hernandez, 2002).

The primary research question addressed by the longitudinal comparison study is:

- To what extent can observed changes in child and family outcomes be attributed to differences in service delivery approaches?

Secondary research questions follow from this:

- Do outcomes change over time?
- If outcomes do change over time, is there a differential rate or magnitude of change as a function of treatment delivery approach?
- Are there subgroups of children and families for whom a system of care is more effective?

As noted previously, analyses of system of care assessment data from these studies indicate that system of care principles are being more fully operationalized in funded communities compared to comparison communities (Brannan et al., 2002). In addition, specific services experiences at the level of children and families are more consistent with major system of care principles for children and families receiving services within the funded versus control communities (Center for Mental Health Services, 2000; Hernandez, Gomez, Lipien, Greenbaum, Armstrong, & Gonzales, 2001). Services experiences that were more consistent with major system of care principles were also significantly related to greater emotional and behavioral symptom reduction at twelve months postservice entry (Stephens, Holden, & Hernandez, in press). Children in systems of care experienced high levels of system of care principles in their services, and their symptom severity did not vary as a function of their experiences. Yet children in matched comparison communities had more variable experiences of system of care principles in their services, and their symptom severity decreased as their experiences of the principles increased.

Data collection in the Phase I comparison study ended in the fall of 2001. The overall retention rate of 84 percent for participants across the three pairs of communities was strong compared to other similar longitudinal studies (Angold, Costello, Burns, Erkanli, & Farmer, 2000; Bickman, Summerfelt, & Noser, 1997;

Hamner, Lambert, & Bickman, 1997). Results of clinical measures at intake showed that the typical child in the study had serious behavioral and emotional problems (Center for Mental Health Services, 2001). Preliminary outcome analyses to date have focused on the Stark County—Mahoning County, Ohio, comparison pair. The Stark County system of care was most effective for children with serious emotional disturbances who have the most severe delinquency symptoms at intake—those children who are a primary focus for the system of care approach. Supporting this finding, children with multiple juvenile justice charges before study entry in the Mahoning County matched comparison community were significantly more likely to have multiple charges after entering services than their counterparts in the Stark County system of care community. Children in the Stark County system of care also showed greater improvements in school-related variables, such as need for special education services and numbers of suspensions. They reported higher levels of affiliation with prosocial peers across the twenty-four months of the study than children in the Mahoning County site.

Children and families served at the Stark County children's mental health center received more than twice as many services in the first eighteen months after study entry as children and families served at the more traditional Mahoning County children's mental health center. More intensive case management was apparent in Stark County and reflected how the children's mental health center within the system of care collaborates with other providers in coordinating services, providing a continuous service experience with minimal gaps. While the Stark County children's mental health center within the system of care spent more to deliver mental health services to children in the study, less was spent in Stark County by other child-serving providers for children in the comparison study, with the largest difference coming in juvenile justice placements. Cost offsets are being explored in further comprehensive analyses.

USES OF NATIONAL EVALUATION DATA

The National Evaluation of the Comprehensive Community Mental Health Services Program for Children and Their Families has been designed to provide information for broad audiences at multiple levels to improve the development of systems of care and mental health service delivery for children and their families. Within the funded programs, the data have been used to track the evolving parameters of the populations entering services, evaluate the effectiveness of individualized service plans, assess the effectiveness of specific services that are delivered, and generally evaluate program development as it pertains to the operationalization of system of care principles. Local-level uses of data are designed to improve effectiveness through an outcomes accountability feedback loop (Hernandez, Hodges, & Cascardi, 1998; Woodbridge & Huang, 2000) and provide local-level information for leveraging resources that are essential to sustaining programs once federal funding dissipates. A similar feedback loop exists at the federal level, where evaluation data are used, in part, to shape the provision of technical assistance and other supports necessary for facilitating program development and to sustain federal funding. Sustainability at both the local and national levels requires providing information to a broad range of audiences who influence the public policy process.

The funded programs in the initial phase of this initiative used a wide range of strategies to achieve fiscal sustainability. These included redirecting existing resources, pooling funds across child-serving agencies, reinvesting saved resources, and leveraging managed care (Foster, Kelsch, Kamradt, Sosna, & Yang, 2001; Koyanagi & Feres-Merchant, 2000; Stroul et al., 2002). Several of these programs were able to influence state policy regarding children's mental health services so that continued funding would be available to support the growth and further development of system of care initiatives for children and their families. Fiscal sustainability, however, represents only one portion of the lasting impact of system of care demonstration programs. Philosophical and procedural sustainability are concepts that are much harder to assess yet may have at least as much impact as fiscal resources on the further evolution and change of system of care concepts at the community level. Training professionals across agencies who are involved in direct service provision in system of care procedures and concepts and educating key community members such as agency administrators and legislators of the value and effectiveness of community-based services for children with serious emotional disturbance are critical to achieving philosophical and procedural sustainability. Having an impact on training programs in education, mental health, child welfare, and juvenile justice (Meyers, Kaufman, & Goldman, 1999) is also important for developing a greater appreciation for systems of care principles and procedural skill sets at the more formative stages of professional development. The public-academic liaison approach developed by the PEN-PAL program (McCammon, Spencer, & Friesen, 2001), one of the initial twenty-two grantees, is an excellent example of a collaborative partnership between community-based services and academic training programs that has had mutual benefit for university-based training, community-level practitioners, and family members.

Evaluation data provide the information necessary for identifying effective innovations within the system of care umbrella and disseminating these innovations across communities. The system of care model provides the flexibility that is necessary so that community-level characteristics can shape the development of individual systems, and creativity and innovation can be important drivers of the process of developing effective individualized, community-based, and culturally competent services. Almost continual innovation and creativity, however, can present significant risks to the system of care approach in an era where evidence-based approaches to children's mental health care are being emphasized with increasing frequency (U.S. Department of Health and Human Services, 1999; Burns, Hoagwood, & Mrazek, 1999; Hoagwood, Burns, Kiser, Ringeisen, & Schoenwald, 2001; Schoenwald & Hoagwood, 2001). Expanding the evidence base for systems of care requires a greater focus on systematizing and replicating key system of care procedures, as well as integrating constructs from evidence-based practice into the system of care model. Sustainability of the infrastructure and service array in the future is dependent on the success that occurs with this integration and the ability of research and evaluation protocols to clearly identify and replicate the key elements that are critical to sustaining effective community based practice.

National evaluations of large federal demonstration programs are time-consuming and costly endeavors that require substantial coordination between federal offices that manage these programs, evaluation teams at the local and national levels, and grant communities. Many procedural details need to be put into place and maintained for these evaluations to have the optimal chances for success. Without comprehensive evaluation information, however, the level of implementation of programs cannot be monitored effectively, and the aggregate outcomes expected from these programs may be impossible to detect. Evaluation data provide the information necessary for shaping and influencing program and policy development with consistency of information across demonstration grant communities, contributing to an overall understanding of program effectiveness. There are many challenges associated with conducting a national evaluation of an initiative of the size and scope of the Comprehensive Community Mental Health Services Program for Children and Their Families. These ongoing challenges evolve across time as overall program implementation follows its own evolutionary course in the rapidly changing world of community-based mental health services for children and their families. Many of these challenges are similar to those encountered in other attempts to evaluate the effects of socially complex services in community settings (Wolff, 2000), including the numerous difficulties encountered in measuring complex and innovative approaches that are being implemented in community-based service delivery settings with less than clear boundaries and shifting organizational parameters.

The 1999 surgeon general's report on mental health (U.S. Department of Health and Human Services, 1999) documents the progress that has been made and the resources devoted to transforming the nature of service delivery for children with serious emotional disturbances and their families. The report calls for a refocusing of research from system-level changes and performance to an examination of the effects of system change on individual outcomes. It questions the degree to which changes at the system level have affected clinical outcomes and provides a context for the further refinement and evaluation of systems of care. Having a better understanding of this question of effectiveness is especially important in an era of managed care, accountability, and constrained federal and state spending on mental health services.

In shifting the focus from system-level change to individual-level change, however, it is important to keep in mind the historical context for the system of care approach. Initial system-building efforts were focused on the philosophy, organization, and processes of delivering services. These efforts have been very effective: the goals have been taken seriously; political support, legislation, and resources have been forthcoming; and the service delivery system for children with serious emotional disturbances has greatly improved over two decades (Friedman, 2001). This shift in focus from system change to individual-level change requires clarification about what is meant by outcome and effectiveness. Recently, Farmer (2000) detailed some areas in which answers to current questions would be of benefit in highlighting the effectiveness of these programs. For example, what interventions are most likely to be effective for which outcomes? Is improved consumer satisfaction an indication of effectiveness? Are short-term or long-term changes in individual child and family functioning required for a system or service to be effective? How are outcome domains linked together, and are some more important than others? She points out the need to develop a realistic consensus about appropriate outcomes for this seriously impaired population and realistic time frames for achieving these outcomes. These and other questions will be important targets to address as research and evaluation methodologies are crafted for future work that addresses the effectiveness of the system of care approach.

References

Achenbach, T. M. (1991a). *Manual for the Child Behavior Checklist and 1991 profile.* Burlington, VT: University of Vermont Department of Psychiatry.

Achenbach, T. M. (1991b). *Manual for the Youth Self-Report 11–18 and 1991 Profile.* Burlington, VT: University Associates in Psychiatry.

American Psychiatric Association. (1994). *Diagnostic and statistical manual of mental disorders* (4th ed.). Washington, DC: Author.

Angold, A., Costello, E. J., Burns, B. J., Erkanli, A., & Farmer, E.M.Z. (2000). Effectiveness of nonresidential specialty mental health services for children and adolescents in the "real world." *Journal of the American Academy of Child and Adolescent Psychiatry, 39,* 154–160.

Bickman, L., Summerfelt, W., & Noser, K. (1997). Comparative outcomes of emotionally disturbed children and adolescents in a system of services and usual care. *Psychiatric Services, 48,* 1543–1548.

Brannan, A. M., Baughman, L. N., Reed, E. R., & Katz-Leavy, J. (2002). System-of-care assessment: Cross-site comparison of findings. *Children's Services: Social Policy, Research, and Practice, 5,* 37–56.

Brannan, A. M., Heflinger, C. A., & Bickman, L. (1998). The Caregiver Strain Questionnaire: Measuring the impact on the family of living with a child with serious emotional disturbance. *Journal of Emotional and Behavioral Disorders, 5,* 212–222.

Burns, B. J. (2001). Commentary on the special issue on the national evaluation of the Comprehensive Community Mental Health Services for Children and Their Families Program. *Journal of Emotional and Behavioral Disorders, 9,* 71–76.

Burns, B. J. (in press). Reasons for hope for children and families: A perspective and overview. In B. Burns & K. Hoagwood (Eds.), *Community treatment for youth: Evidence-based interventions for serious emotional and behavioral disorders.* (pp. 1–16). New York: Oxford University Press.

Burns, B. J., Hoagwood, K., & Mrazek, P. J. (1999). Effective treatment for mental disorders in children and adolescents. *Clinical Child and Family Psychology Review, 2,* 199–254.

Catalano, R. A., Lind, S. L., Rosenblatt, A., & Attkisson, C. C. (1999). Unemployment and foster home placements: Estimating the net effect of provocation and inhibition. *American Journal of Public Health, 89,* 851–855.

Center for Mental Health Services. (1997). *Annual report to Congress on the evaluation of the Comprehensive Community Mental Health Services for Children and Their Families Program, 1997.* Atlanta, GA: Macro International.

Center for Mental Health Services. (1998). *Annual report to Congress on the evaluation of the Comprehensive Community Mental Health Services for Children and Their Families Program, 1998.* Atlanta, GA: Macro International.

Center for Mental Health Services. (1999). *Annual report to Congress on the evaluation of the Comprehensive Community Mental Health Services for Children and Their Families Program, 1999.* Atlanta, GA: ORC Macro.

Center for Mental Health Services. (2000). *Annual report to Congress on the evaluation of the Comprehensive Community Mental Health Services for Children and Their Families Program, 2000.* Manuscript under review, U.S. Department of Health and Human Services.

Center for Mental Health Services. (2001). *Annual report to Congress on the evaluation of the Comprehensive Community Mental Health Services for Children and Their Families Program, 2001.* Manuscript under review, U.S. Department of Health and Human Services.

Cross, T., Earle, K., Echo-Hawk Solie, H., & Manness, K. (2000). *Cultural strengths and challenges in implementing a system of care model in American Indian communities.* Washington, DC: Center for Effective Collaboration and Practice, American Institutes for Research.

Dunst, C. J., & Leet, H. E. (1987). Measuring the adequacy of resources in households with young children. *Child: Care, Health and Development, 13,* 111–125.

Epstein, M. H., & Sharma, J. (1998). *Behavioral and Emotional Rating Scale: A strength-based approach to assessment.* Austin, TX: PRO-ED.

Epstein, N. B., Baldwin, L. M., & Bishop, D. S. (1983). The McMaster Family Assessment Device. *Journal of Marital and Family Therapy, 9*(2), 171–180.

Farmer, E.M.Z. (2000). Issues confronting effective services in systems of care. *Children and Youth Services Review, 22,* 627–650.

Foster, E. M., Kelsch, C. C., Kamradt, B., Sosna, T., & Yang, Z. (2001). Expenditures and sustainability in systems of care. *Journal of Emotional and Behavioral Disorders, 9,* 53–62.

Friedman, R. M. (2001). The practice of psychology with children, adolescents, and their families. In J. N. Hughes, A. M. La Greca, & J. C. Conoley (Eds.), *Handbook of psychological services for children and adolescents* (pp. 3–23). New York: Oxford University Press.

Friedman, R. M., & Hernandez, M. (2002). The national evaluation of the comprehensive community mental health services for children and their families program: A commentary. *Children's Services: Social Policy, Research, and Practice, 5,* 67–74.

Friedman, R. M., Katz-Leavy, J. W., Manderscheid, R. W., & Sondheimer, D. L. (1999). Prevalence of serious emotional disturbance: An update. In R. W. Manderscheid & M. J. Henderson (Eds.), *Mental health, United States, 1998* (pp. 110–112). Rockville, MD: U.S. Department of Health and Human Services.

Hamner, K. M., Lambert, E. W., & Bickman, L. (1997). Children's mental health in a continuum of care: Clinical outcomes at 18 months for the Fort Bragg Demonstration. *Journal of Mental Health Administration, 24,* 465–471.

Hernandez, M., Gomez, A., Lipien, L., Greenbaum, P. E., Armstrong, K., & Gonzalez, P. (2001). Use of the system-of-care practice review in the national evaluation: Evaluating the fidelity of practice to system-of-care principles. *Journal of Emotional and Behavioral Disorders, 9,* 43–52.

Hernandez, M., & Hodges, S. (2000). *Turning ideas into action using theory based frameworks.* Tampa, FL: Department of Child and Family Studies, Louis de la Parte Florida Mental Health Institute, University of South Florida.

Hernandez, M., Hodges, S., & Cascardi, M. (1998). The ecology of outcomes: System accountability in children's mental health. *Journal of Behavioral Health Services and Research, 25,* 136–150.

Hoagwood, K., Burns, B. J., Kiser, L., Ringeisen, H., & Schoenwald, S. K. (2001). Evidence-based practice in child and adolescent mental health services. *Psychiatric Services, 52,* 1179–1189.

Hodges, K. (1990). *Child and Adolescent Functional Assessment Scale (CAFAS).* Ypsilanti: Eastern Michigan University, Department of Psychology.

Hodges, K., Doucette-Gates, A., & Kim, C. (2000). Predicting service utilization with the Child and Adolescent Functional Assessment Scale in a sample of youths with serious emotional disturbance served by Center for Mental Health Services-funded demonstrations. *Journal of Behavioral Health Services and Research, 27,* 47–59.

Hodges, K., Doucette-Gates, A., & Liao, Q. (1999). The relationship between the Child and Adolescent Functional Assessment Scale (CAFAS) and indicators of functioning *Journal of Child and Family Studies, 8,* 109–122.

Hodges, K., & Kim, C. (2000). Psychometric study of the Child and Adolescent Functional Assessment Scale: Prediction of contact with the law and poor school attendance. *Journal of Abnormal Child Psychology, 28,* 287–297.

Holden, E. W., & Brannan, A. M. (Eds.). (2002). Special Issue: Evaluating systems of care: The Comprehensive Community Mental Health Services for Children and Their Families Program. *Children's Services: Social Policy, Research, and Practice, 5,* 1–74.

Holden, E. W., Brannan, A. M., Brashears, F., Gilford, J., & Connor, T. (2001, Aug.). *System-of-care assessment: A comprehensive measure to evaluate community based service systems.* Paper presented at the 109th annual meeting of the American Psychological Association, San Francisco.

Holden, E. W., De Carolis, G., & Huff, B. (2002). Policy implications of the national evaluation of the Comprehensive Community Mental Health Services for Children and Their Families Program. *Children's Services: Social Policy, Research, and Practice, 5,* 57–65.

Holden, E. W., Friedman, R. M., & Santiago, R. L. (Eds.). (2001a). Special issue: The national evaluation of the Comprehensive Community Mental Health Services for Children and Their Families Program. *Journal of Emotional and Behavioral Disorders, 9,* 1–80.

Holden, E. W., Friedman, R. M., & Santiago, R. L. (2001b). Overview of the national evaluation of the Comprehensive Community Mental Health Services for Children and Their Families Program. *Journal of Emotional and Behavioral Disorders, 9,* 4–12.

Jacobson, N. S., Roberts, L. J., Berns, S. B., & McGlinchey, J. B. (1999). Methods for defining and determining the clinical significance of treatment effects: Description, application and alternatives. *Journal of Consulting and Clinical Psychology, 67,* 300–307.

Jacobson, N. S., & Truax, P. (1991). Clinical significance: A statistical approach to defining meaningful change in psychotherapy research. *Journal of Consulting and Clinical Psychology, 59,* 12–19.

Koren, P. E., DeChillo, N., & Friesen, B. J. (1992). Measuring empowerment in families whose children have emotional disabilities: A brief questionnaire. *Rehabilitation Psychology, 37,* 305–321.

Koyanagi, C., & Feres-Merchant, D. (2000). *For the long haul: Maintaining systems of care beyond the federal investment.* Washington, DC: Center for Effective Collaboration and Practice, American Institutes for Research.

McCammon, S. L., Spencer, S., & Friesen, B. (2001). Promoting family empowerment through multiple roles. *Journal of Family Social Work, 5,* 1–24.

Meyers, J., Kaufman, M., & Goldman, S. (1999). *Promising practices: Training strategies for serving children with serious emotional disturbance and their families in a system of care.* Washington, DC: Center for Effective Collaboration and Practice, American Institutes for Research.

Osher, T. W., van Kammen, W., & Zaro, S. M. (2001). Family participation in evaluating systems of care: Family, research, and service system perspectives. *Journal of Emotional and Behavioral Disorders, 9,* 63–70.

Robertson, L. M., Bates, M. P., Wood, M., Rosenblatt, J. A., Furlong, M. J., Casas, J. M., & Schwier, P. (1998). The educational placements of students with emotional and behavioral disorders served by probation, mental health, public health, and social services. *Psychology in the Schools, 35,* 333–346.

Rosenblatt, J. A., & Furlong, M. J. (1998). Outcomes in a system of care for youths with emotional and behavioral disorders: An examination of differential change across clinical profiles. *Journal of Child and Family Studies, 7,* 217–232.

Rosenblatt, J. A., Robertson, L. M., Bates, M. P., Wood, M., Furlong, M. J., & Sosna, T. (1998). Troubled or troubling? Characteristics of youth referred to a system of care without system-level referral constraints. *Journal of Emotional and Behavioral Disorders, 6,* 42–54.

Rosenblatt, J. A., & Rosenblatt, A. (1999). Youth functional status and academic achievement in collaborative mental health and education programs: Two California care systems. *Journal of Emotional and Behavioral Disorders, 7,* 21–30.

Schoenwald, S. K., & Hoagwood, K. (2001). Effectiveness, transportability, and dissemination of interventions: What matters when. *Psychiatric Services, 52,* 1190–1197.

Speer, D. C., & Greenbaum, P. E. (1995). Five methods for computing significant individual client change and improvement rates: Support for an individual growth curve approach. *Journal of Consulting and Clinical Psychology, 63,* 1044–1048.

Stephens, R. L., Holden, E. W., & Hernandez, M. (in press). System-of-care practice review scores as predictors of behavioral symptomology and functional impairment. *Journal of Child and Family Studies.*

Stroul, B. A., & Friedman, R. M. (1986). *A system of care for children and youth with severe emotional disturbances* (Rev. ed.). Washington, DC: Georgetown University Child Development Center, Child and Adolescent Service System Program Technical Assistance Center.

Stroul, B. A., Pires, S. A., Armstrong, M. I., & Zaro, S. (2002). The impact of managed care on systems of care that serve children with serious emotional disturbances and their families. *Children's Services: Social Policy, Research, and Practice, 5,* 21–36.

U.S. Department of Health and Human Services. (1999). *Mental health: A report of the surgeon general.* Washington, DC: U.S. Government Printing Office.

Vinson, N., Brannan, A. M., Baughman, L., Wilce, M., & Gawron, T. (2001). The system of care model: Implementation in twenty-seven communities. *Journal of Emotional and Behavioral Disorders, 9,* 30–42.

Walrath, C., dosReis, S., Miech, R., Liao, Q., Holden, E. W., De Carolis, G., Santiago, R., & Leaf, P. (2001). Referral source differences in functional impairment levels for children served in the Comprehensive Community Mental Health Services for Children and Their Families Program. *Journal of Child and Family Studies, 10,* 385–397.

Walrath, C. M., Mandell, D. S., & Leaf, P. J. (2001). Do children with different referral sources, diagnoses and demographic profiles respond differently to mental health treatment? *Psychiatric Services, 52,* 196–201.

Walrath, C. M., Mandell, D. S., Liao, Q., Holden, E. W., De Carolis, G., Santiago, R. L., & Leaf, P. J. (2001). Suicide attempts in the Comprehensive Community Mental Health Services for Children and Their Families Program. *Journal of the American Academy of Child and Adolescent Psychiatry, 40,* 1197–1205.

Walrath, C. M., Nickerson, K. J., Crowel, R. L., & Leaf, P. J. (1998). Serving children with serious emotional disturbance in a system of care: Do mental health and non mental health agency referrals look the same? *Journal of Emotional and Behavioral Disorders, 6,* 205–213.

Walrath, C. M., Sharp, M. J., Zuber, M., & Leaf, P. J. (2001). Serving children with serious emotional disturbance in urban systems of care: Referral agency differences in child characteristics in Baltimore and the Bronx. *Journal of Emotional and Behavioral Disorders, 9,* 94–105.

Wolff, N. (2000). Using randomized trials to evaluate socially complex services: Problems, challenges and recommendations. *Journal of Mental Health Policy and Economics, 3,* 97–109.

Wood, M., Chung, A., Furlong, M. J., Casas, J. M., Holbrook, L., & Richey, R. (1998). What works in a system of care? Services and outcomes associated with a juvenile probation population. *Journal of Juvenile Law and Policy, 2,* 63–71.

Wood, M., Furlong, M. J., Casas, J. M., & Sosna, T. (1998). A system of care for juvenile probationers. *Journal of Juvenile Law and Policy, 2,* 5–9.

Woodbridge, M., & Huang, L. (2000). *Using evaluation data to manage, improve, market, and sustain children's services.* Washington, DC: Center for Effective Collaboration and Practice, American Institutes for Research.

CHAPTER TWENTY

The Role of Outcomes in Systems of Care

Quality Improvement and Program Evaluation

Barbara J. Friesen
Nancy C. Winters

Accountability for outcomes—holding service providers and systems responsible for the results of the resources they expend to provide services to children with emotional, behavioral, and mental disorders—is an essential requirement for systems of care. Without the ability to demonstrate effectiveness and contain costs, no system improvement efforts will be sustained in today's political and economic climate. In addition, the life course of children with emotional and behavioral disorders, especially those whose problems are severe and persistent, can take a sharp turn for the better, or involve continuing dysfunction and distress, depending on the quality and effectiveness of the services and supports provided to them. The outcomes for these children will also have important social and economic implications for the communities in which they live.

Despite the urgency of demonstrating good stewardship of public funds, identifying, measuring, and achieving outcomes in a system of care is a daunting assignment. For the most direct encounter, that of one service provider and a child, establishing a plausible causal relationship between the actions of the provider and changes in the child's symptoms, behavior, or other outcomes requires accounting for the many other forces in the child's life that may influence the child's behavior, such as family or classroom expectations and support, peer relationships, or substance abuse. The difficulties of defining and tracking outcomes are greatly multiplied in a complex community-based system of care.

This chapter reviews major issues related to outcomes in community-based systems of care for children with emotional, behavioral, or mental disorders.

The discussion of outcomes in systems of care can be framed in relation to the following questions: "What are we trying to achieve?" (what are the important outcomes?), "Who says so?" (who gets to define success?), and "How are we doing?" (what do we know about efforts to formulate, measure, and achieve outcomes in systems of care to date?).

EVALUATION CHALLENGES IN SYSTEMS OF CARE

Establishing, evaluating, and using outcomes in systems of care are complicated by four important circumstances:

- The research traditions in children's mental health
- The need to understand systems of care as complex, multilevel, dynamic phenomena
- Real differences in values and beliefs on the part of various constituencies about the proper goals and outcomes of systems of care
- A large gap between the current knowledge base about service effectiveness and practice in most communities

Mental Health Research Traditions

Until recently, research in children's mental health focused primarily on basic research or on the symptoms, diagnoses, and functioning of children with mental disorders, often to the exclusion of other systems, such as the family, schools, or neighborhoods. When the primary system of the family was included in conceptualizations and research, it was often considered as either a context to understand the child's disorder or a target for change (Friesen & Stephens, 1998). The result of this focus is that most of the measure development in children's mental health was focused on clinical phenomena affecting individual children. In addition, measures of clinical phenomena have historically emphasized symptoms and neglected the realm of adaptive functioning, the importance of which has been increasingly recognized, as evidenced by the addition of functional impairment criteria for diagnosis in the most recent edition of the *Diagnostic and Statistical Manual of Mental Disorders* (DSM-IV; American Psychiatric Association, 1994).

Multilevel Dynamic Systems

With the advent of federal support for the concept of system change on behalf of children with serious emotional, behavioral, or mental disorders (Lourie, Katz-Leavy, DeCarolis, & Quinlan, 1996; Stroul & Friedman, 1996), change efforts expanded to include multiple levels of attention and intervention, such as child and family, organizational and interorganizational, and the entire system of care. These multilevel, dynamic phenomena outstripped research models, measures, and methods. Increasingly, concepts were identified as important in systems of care (for example, family participation and empowerment, wraparound services, interagency coordination, strengths-based assessment, and cultural competence) for which there were no corresponding measures.

Multiple Constituencies

The importance of taking the perspectives of stakeholders both inside the system of care (families, youth, clinicians, administrators) and those not directly involved (funders, policymakers, the public at large) is a well-established principle of social planning and evaluation, emphasized by many experts in the published literature on systems of care (Duchnowski, Kutash, & Friedman, 2002; English, 2002). In fact, Hernandez and Hodges (2001b) state that a major influence on service delivery strategies in systems of care is the increasing emphasis placed on the integration of multiple perspectives. The reasons for including multiple stakeholders range from values (such as parents' rights to be involved in decisions about their children) to practical and political concerns about what will happen if relevant stakeholders are not included. At a general level, it is relatively easy to agree that a variety of constituencies should be included in establishing the goals and outcomes of community change efforts. In truth, however, inclusion of a full range of stakeholders is not an established practice in many communities working to establish a system of care (Simpson, Koroloff, Friesen, & Gac, 1999).

This lack of inclusion is related to both a low level of explicit planning with regard to the goals and outcomes of services and to the difficulties (political and practical) of eliciting, managing, and synthesizing feedback from constituencies that may have unrelated, or even conflicting, ideas about appropriate outcomes in the system of care. In fact, different child-serving agencies involved in systems of care (for example, child welfare and juvenile justice) may have legal mandates that prevent them from having the same objectives. Burns, Hoagwood, and Maultsby (1998) acknowledge the potential conflict that may exist across constituencies with regard to outcomes, but note that without such inclusion, there may be low compliance (presumably on the part of youth, families, and clinicians) or, if funders and policymakers do not agree with the outcomes selected and measured in the system of care, service providers may not get paid. Cost and utilization of services as system performance indicators have assumed a central role in decision making about the awarding of managed care contracts and whether to continue funding demonstration systems of care. Programs that are able to demonstrate costs savings through use of alternatives to higher-cost residential or inpatient services are more likely to receive continued funding.

Knowledge-Practice Gap

A discrepancy between what is known about service effectiveness and the mental health and social service practice in many communities is the fourth circumstance that complicates the ability to establish and achieve desired outcomes. Hoagwood, Burns, and Weisz (2002) propose steps to increase the use of evidence-based practice in community settings. They note that some organizations, such as the American Academy of Child and Adolescent Psychiatry and the American Academy of Pediatrics, have adopted practice standards but still face challenges in getting them adopted into everyday practice. A system development process that involves choosing new interventions to be implemented or existing interventions to be expanded is a superb opportunity to incorporate the best information available about what works (Kutash & Rivera, 1996). This should increase the likelihood of congruence between desired and actual results. Several recent publications provide summaries of current knowledge that system of care planners can use (Burns & Hoagwood, 2002; Epstein, Kutash, & Duchnowski, 1998; Hoagwood, Burns, Kiser, Ringeisen, & Schoenwald, 2001; Jensen, Hoagwood, & Petti, 1996; Kutash & Rivera, 1996).

DEFINING OUTCOMES

Of the many possible outcomes that can be identified in community-based systems of care, those that constitute the foundation for all system-building efforts are concerned with the lives of children and their families. The following two case examples, set thirty years apart, give us a glimpse into the experiences of children and families with receiving mental health services.

Billy entered a day treatment program in 1970 at age four when his working parents sought help from their pediatrician when they could not find day care for him because he was not toilet trained. His language development was delayed by two years, and he was distractible, had frequent temper tantrums, and was difficult to comfort. Billy's parents, who had immigrated from an Eastern European country ten years previously, were very upset about the problems of their only child and often in conflict about how to raise him.

Billy entered a day treatment program, which also provided couples therapy for his distressed parents. After four years' treatment at approximately $85,000 per year, he had made some gains in language and social skills but was still not fully toilet trained. At the age of eight, he entered a special education program for children with developmental disabilities, and he remained in segregated special education classrooms until he was nineteen years old.

Now, thirty years later, Billy lives with his parents, for whom he is still a puzzle and disappointment. He has no friends and spends his days wandering the neighborhood looking for opportunities to play with younger children, with whom he has more in common than his chronological peers. The family is quite isolated at least in part because Billy's parents feel deep shame about his condition and are reluctant to appear in public with him.

Hugh, fifteen years old in the year 2000, had a number of problems that caused great disruption in his family's life and caused him great unhappiness. Hugh has a primary learning disability and other developmental problems of unknown origin, episodes of rage with occasional violence, and difficulty sleeping, and he was refusing to attend school when his parents approached the mental health system asking for residential treatment. The county in which he lived had instituted team planning, an intensive wraparound approach, which was offered to Hugh's family as an alternative to out-of-home placement. Hugh's parents were reluctant to try team planning, which they perceived as just another roadblock to getting the care that Hugh needed. However, they agreed to try the new approach for two months.

The planning team, which included Hugh and his parents, identified and implemented the following steps: Hugh received review and adjustment to his medications and an after-school companion so that he could participate in intramural sports. In addition, the team approached Hugh's school to work out a modified attendance plan, since most of Hugh's behavioral outbursts occurred at the end of the school day. Respite services were provided to Hugh's parents.

Within a month, Hugh was going to school regularly, was able to be involved in the sports that were so important to him, his sleep patterns were more regular, and he was having many fewer outbursts at school and at home. Hugh's parents felt supported by the team and the services that they received, and they no longer thought that residential care was necessary. Hugh's mother explained, "He still has the same problems, but he's going to school and sleeping through the night, and we're able to have a reasonable family life again. We're very happy with the services that we received."

These two vignettes raise a number of questions, including, "What are the outcomes important to children and families receiving services?" and "What accounts for the different outcomes in these two cases?" In both cases, the children's behavioral problems presented significant challenges to their families. Each had underlying developmental deficits requiring modifications in their environments; each would benefit from a treatment orientation individually tailored to his needs. In the first case, a costly long-term intervention was used that was not ultimately successful in helping the child achieve age-appropriate adaptive functioning. This may have been related to the lack of fit of the treatment orientation. In the second case, a wraparound approach was used that identified the youth's problems with school attendance and sleep as specific target areas for intervention. Improving those areas of his functioning was helpful in reducing the burden and sense of isolation experienced by his parents.

When outcomes are developed in the context of community values, with broad-based community participation, there will be variation across communities in the outcomes they choose to emphasize and the strategies they evolve to work toward their goals. Despite this expected variation, however, it is instructive to review some existing outcome frameworks that researchers and policy analysts have suggested.

At one level, defining what we want to accomplish may seem relatively simple. For example, Rosenblatt's suggestion (1993) that the outcome of services should be that children are "at home, in school, and out of trouble" is sensible, pragmatic, and likely to have broad appeal. These first-level functional indicators fail to capture the full array of desired outcomes.

Hoagwood, Jensen, Petti, and Burns (1996) propose that children should be as free of psychopathology as possible; function well at home, in school, and in the community; experience a positive quality of life; benefit from a supportive environment; and experience as little of restrictive and coercive living situations as possible. They propose a conceptual model for children's mental health outcomes, arguing that it is difficult and awkward to fit thinking about children's mental health into outcome models developed for adults. They emphasize the developmental needs and processes of children in a conceptual framework with five domains:

- Symptoms and diagnoses (for example, depression, anxiety, distractibility)
- Functioning (ability to adapt to the demands of home, school, and community environments)
- Consumer perspectives (for example, quality of life, satisfaction, family strain)
- Environments (for example, stability of home, school, or neighborhood, social support)
- Systems (characteristics of services, organizational relationships, costs)

They suggest a focus on the environment in which children grow and develop as context for understanding the child's symptoms and functioning, as containing forces that may interact with or be affected by child's symptoms and functioning, and as malleable systems that may be altered to support or directly affect children. They also present consumer perspectives as a discrete domain as a way of emphasizing the importance of the perspectives of children, youth, and families. The systems domain of the framework encompasses both service-related and organizational- and cost-related variables.

Our discussion of outcomes is framed within the four domains proposed by Hargreaves and Shumway (1989) as adapted by the National Institute of Mental Health (NIH Guide, 1994): (1) clinical, (2) rehabilitative, (3) humanitarian, and (4) public welfare. This framework has been adapted to children's mental health by Rosenblatt (1998), who uses the outcome domains of clinical status, functional status, life satisfaction and fulfillment, and safety and welfare. Rosenblatt's domains all pertain directly to child and family outcomes, while this framework

(NIH Guide, 1994) includes outcomes in the category of public welfare that address issues of public concern such as cost and public safety. This framework does not preclude a dynamic view of child mental health outcomes.

Clinical outcomes as a domain are parallel to Rosenblatt's (1998) category of clinical status, which includes both physical and mental health, and the domain symptoms and diagnoses proposed by Hoagwood et al. (1996), which include distractibility, impulsivity, depression, and anxiety as examples.

Rehabilitative outcomes encompass the concept of functional status (Rosenblatt, 1998) and functional outcomes (Hoagwood et al., 1996), which relate to the ability to assume a variety of roles across multiple settings. Adaptive functioning and social competence are related concepts. For children and youth, primary settings are home, school, peer group, and neighborhood. Indicators related to a child's functioning include the extent to which a child can be a contributing member of a family, learn in school, and have positive social relationships with adults and peers. Critical to this domain are the important environmental characteristics that can support a child's functioning (Hoagwood et al., 1996), such as stability at home and in school, absence of violence, and the availability of social supports. The concept of adaptive functioning implies a relationship between the child's vulnerabilities and the demands and resources in the child's environment. This broadens the locus of concern beyond the child and family and introduces the importance of identifying modifications in the family, school, and peer environments that will address the child's needs. For example, the impact of a child's disability may be significantly lessened by a simple restructuring of a classroom.

Humanitarian outcomes include parent and youth satisfaction, quality of life, and family issues such as the impact that the child's needs and behaviors may have on the family system (for example, family roles and caregiver strain, the ability of parents to be employed).

Public welfare outcomes include system results such as the cost of services, number of days that children are in the community versus restrictive settings (that is, service utilization), and changes in interorganizational relationships. Outcomes of broader public concern may include cost-effectiveness, school attendance, recidivism, and the ability of youth and other family members to be productively employed (and tax paying).

STAKEHOLDERS' PERSPECTIVES ON OUTCOME DOMAINS

Table 20.1 displays the four outcome domains as viewed by five important stakeholder groups, along with our estimates of the degree of investment each group might have in each domain. This representation generalizes about each stakeholder group and so does not capture the variation that undoubtedly exists within groups.

Table 20.1. Orientation of Stakeholders to Mental Health Outcome Domains

	Clinical (Symptoms and Diagnosis)	Rehabilitative (Adaptive Functioning, Social Competence)	Humanitarian (Satisfaction, Quality of Life, Caregiver Strain)	Public Welfare (Cost, Service Utilization, School Attendance, Employment, Productivity)
Child or youth	High	Medium to high	High	Low
Family	High	High	High	Medium
Service system, providers	High	High	Medium to high	High
Funders, policymakers	Low	High	Low	High
Society at large	Low	High	Low	High

Source: Adapted from Friesen (2000).

As reflected in Table 20.1, youth, families, and service providers share similar values about what the outcomes of mental health services should be. They are all likely to be invested in relief from clinical symptoms, although possibly for different reasons. Young people want freedom from discomfort and from interference with relationships, especially with peers. Parents and other family members often hope that their son or daughter will find relief from distressing internal states, as well as from behaviors that are dangerous or upsetting to themselves and others. Clinicians are also oriented toward symptom relief as a major goal of their work. Funders, policymakers, and society at large may not be particularly invested in symptom relief (unless the symptoms are accompanied by bothersome or dangerous behavior), perhaps because they do not have intimate experience with the distress associated with emotional disorders and mental illness.

All stakeholder groups are likely to value adaptive functioning and social competence, reflected in the rehabilitative domain. Outcomes such as the ability of children to live at home with their families, attend school, and function competently in social situations are likely to be seen as benefiting children and families, as well as contributing to the public good. The importance of addressing adaptive functioning, in addition to symptom relief, is highlighted by evidence that improved psychosocial functioning does not necessarily correlate with symptom resolution in some disorders (American Academy of Child and Adolescent Psychiatry, 1998; Geller, Zimmerman, Williams, Bolhofner, & Craney, 2001; Weiss & Hechtman, 1993).

Humanitarian outcomes, such as quality of life for children and families, youth and caregivers' satisfaction with services, and the impact on families of living with and struggling to find appropriate services for their children are likely to be valued most by those who are directly affected by them, by clinicians, and, increasingly, by the entire system of care, especially when satisfaction measures are required as a part of quality assurance processes. Unless they are linked to other outcomes of interest, especially those with financial implications (such as the ability of parents to be fully employed), funders, policymakers, and society at large are likely to have relatively low interest in outcomes in this domain.

Family members are concerned with the cost of services as they pertain to their own situations; many families are bankrupted by the high cost of services, especially hospitalization and other out-of-home treatment. Individual families may be less concerned with system-level indicators such as the cost per child or school attendance rates. However, as representatives of family organizations take their place on policy councils and other decision-making bodies in systems of care, they are increasingly developing a systemwide perspective (Osher, deFur, Nava, Spencer, & Toth-Dennis, 1998). Table 20.2 applies the outcome domains framework to the cases of Billy P. and Hugh T.

Representatives of the service system, especially administrators and community partners, along with funders, policymakers, and the general public, will have high interest in the public welfare domain, especially in demonstrations of cost reductions and cost-effectiveness. The growing application of managed care methodologies to public mental health has placed additional emphasis on cost and service utilization outcomes. In the current era of decreasing public revenues, programs unable to demonstrate cost-effectiveness are likely to be short-lived. Sustainability of systems of care programs depends on their acceptance of accountability for outcomes, setting of clear and measurable goals, and investment of stakeholders in program evaluation (Overstreet, Casel, Saunders, & Armstrong, 2001).

Programs must also have the data systems necessary to calculate expenditures and cost savings, including the cost impact across other child-serving systems. Cross-system cost analysis is necessary to identify potential cost shifting to other service sectors and to increase the motivation of agencies to participate in blended funding (Hodges et al., 2001). Long-term tracking of pre- and postprogram data may also be necessary to capture cost trends accurately.

In addition, financial incentives must be aligned appropriately with the goals of the service system in order to achieve desired outcomes. One example is the reduced use of costly out-of-home placements (for example, residential, hospital,

Table 20.2. Mental Health Outcome Domains for Case Examples

	Clinical	*Rehabilitative*	*Humanitarian*	*Public Welfare*
Billy P.	Slow developmental progress; appropriateness of traditional treatment model unclear	At age thirty-four, Billy has no friends, no organized social or recreational activity, no job	Mother works less than full time to accommodate Billy's need for supervision; family isolated; parents' satisfaction with mental health services low	Costly day treatment program did not produce desired outcomes; mother's underemployment reflected in community economic issues; living at home, not in institutional care
Hugh T.	No change in underlying developmental disorder; aggression, sleep patterns improved with targeted interventions (medication adjustments, change in school environment)	Social and academic functioning improved; Hugh returned to school, participates in intramural sports	Team planning approach improved quality of life for entire family; high family satisfaction with services	Living at home, not in institutional care; cost of team planning intervention less than residential treatment

and foster care) achieved by many systems of care projects (Hodges, Woodbridge, & Huang, 2001; Overstreet et al., 2001; Rosenblatt, 1998). Savings from the reduced use of these services, available to invest in community-based services, provide an incentive for further reductions. An example of misalignment is in Oregon, where day and residential programs have historically been funded separately from the rest of children's mental health services. Although there is a small-scale pilot project to explore alternate funding pathways, the managed care Medicaid program has little financial incentive to decrease the use of residential treatment and may even have an incentive to shift higher-cost clients to residential care. Although no one would endorse this as a desirable outcome, the financial misalignment tilts the system in that direction.

There are a great many potential outcomes within these four domains, and it is feasible to focus on and measure adequately only a few of them. As system planners prepare to engage in a planning process in which a variety of stakeholder groups will be involved, it is important to remember that the definition of success in mental health is both value laden and highly political (Friesen, 2000). Major stakeholders in the system of care (children and youth, families, service system representatives including service providers, funders, policymakers, and society at large) may have different ideas about what services should be delivered and different expectations about the results of the services. The outcome domains themselves may be at odds, as well as different constituencies being at odds about which should be the primary system objectives.

English (2002) emphasizes the importance of all concerned with improving services, including policymakers, to be clear about what they expect from services provided. Specifically, he suggests that each constituency clarify what is expected from which component of service—for example, "Clinical outcomes such as remission of symptoms . . . should be expected of clinical interventions. Improved living conditions . . . should be expected of support services such as housing, day care, transportation, and income support" (p. 307). He suggests that conflicting expectations need to be eliminated through public dialogue.

WHAT DO WE KNOW ABOUT SERVICE AND SYSTEM EFFECTIVENESS?

Although much is still unknown about either the efficacy or the effectiveness of many interventions, both traditional and newly developed, system of care planners now have available several summaries of outcomes that will make it easier to make informed choices. These summaries include evidence about both individual treatment approaches designed to affect clinical and functional outcomes and the results of efforts to evaluate selected aspects or entire systems of care.

Services

Authors in a recent publication by Burns and Hoagwood (2002) were invited to address what is known about six comprehensive interventions: case management (Evans & Armstrong, 2002), the wraparound approach (Burchard, Bruns, & Burchard, 2002), multisystemic therapy (Schoenwald & Rowland, 2002), treatment foster care (Chamberlain, 2002), mentoring (Vance, 2002), and family support and education (Ireys, Devet, & Sakwa, 2002). Information is also provided about two targeted interventions: best practices in special education (Epstein & Walker, 2002) and a cognitive-behavioral approach to address traumatic stress and substance abuse (Fairbank, Booth, & Curry, 2002). Pumariega, Del Mundo, and Vance (2002) address psychopharmacology in the context of systems of care, and Burns, Compton, Egger, Farmer, and Robertson (2002) provide a comprehensive annotated bibliography addressing the evidence for diagnostic-specific psychosocial and psychopharmacological interventions.

Summarizing the evidence base for the interventions reviewed in Burns and Hoagwood (2002), Hoagwood et al. (2002) conclude that the evidence base is stronger for multisystemic therapy, treatment foster care, and some forms of intensive case management when these interventions are faithfully implemented. Lack of fidelity in implementation has been shown to compromise effectiveness (Henggeler, Pickrel, & Brondino, 2000). Other services, including wraparound, some special education services, and mentoring, show promise of positive results but require more research.

In addition to knowing about positive evidence-based interventions, it is also important to note that studies of traditional outpatient therapy (Jensen et al., 1996) and out-of-home treatments such as hospitals, residential treatment centers, and group homes, do not support their long-term effectiveness; some interventions may even produce undesirable results (Hoagwood et al., 2001).

One significant challenge in the application of evidence-based interventions to community settings, described by Hoagwood et al. (2002) as the "research to practice problem" (p. 332), is that efficacy studies performed in university settings do not mesh well with the realities of clinic or community-based care. They propose the Clinic/Community Intervention Development Model (CID) to accelerate the pace at which interventions can be developed, adapted, and tested in a variety of practice settings.

Systems

Rosenblatt (1998) summarizes the results of efforts to evaluate entire systems of care. He presents the results of system of care evaluations in twenty communities in relation to five outcome categories: clinical, functional, life satisfaction, safety and welfare, and cost/utilization. Improvement in clinical status was found in all of the nine evaluations that measured these outcomes. Functional status improved in the eleven communities that included measures of this outcome. Satisfaction (usually satisfaction with services) was apparent in all of the six evaluations that measured it. Five system of care evaluations had improved results in the Rosenblatt's safety/welfare domain, most often as represented by reduced arrests. Seventeen system of care evaluations reported cost/utilization data; all but one of these reflected reduced costs of care.

The exception to positive findings in the areas of clinical and functional outcomes and cost occurred in the study of the continuum of care established by the Department of Defense Civilian Health and Medical Program for the Uniformed Services (CHAMPUS) program at Fort Bragg, North Carolina (Bickman et al., 1995), which used a quasi-experimental design that included two comparison sites at other army bases. Although children in the intervention site showed improvement on clinical and functional measures, their progress was not significantly different from children receiving services in a traditional mental health system. In addition, the cost of care was higher in the demonstration site. The results of this study, which is the most comprehensive effort to assess the outcomes of a system of care to date, have generated considerable controversy. A number of alternative explanations have addressed the results that Bickman and colleagues (1995) reported about the lack of difference between the demonstration and comparison sites on clinical and functional outcomes. Hoagwood (1997) commented on the comparability of the intervention sites, noting that the two conditions were not appreciably different in adequacy and coordination of services offered. Friedman and Burns (1996) pointed out that the results for youth with the most severe disorders were more positive, although that assertion was disputed by Bickman and his colleagues in a later analysis (Hamner, Lambert, & Bickman, 1997). Weisz, Han, and Valeri (1997) raised the possibility that the interventions themselves may not have been effective. Foster, Kelsch, Kamradt, Sosna, & Yang (2001) pointed out that the Fort Bragg project was not an adequate test of the system of care model in that it lacked key elements, including multisector coordination of services and management of costs and service utilization. Duchnowski et al. (2002) note a number of positive findings for the demonstration program at Fort Bragg, including increased access, more responsive services, higher satisfaction, and fewer disruptions in service. They conclude that the Fort Bragg evaluation has served to underline the importance of program theory and has stimulated a much-needed focus on practice-level issues.

The importance of a theory-of-change framework for system of care evaluations has become apparent as both conceptual frameworks and evaluation designs have become more thoughtful and sophisticated. Although it seems logical that system designers and evaluators would have explicit expectations about the results expected from specific services or clusters of services, much of the evaluation of community mental health services and systems of care has been conducted without such specification until recently, although logic modeling and theory-based evaluation have been recommended for over thirty years (Rogers, Petrosino, Huebner, & Hacsi, 2000). Fortunately, great progress in both concepts and methods of developing theory-based accountability (Hernandez & Hodges, 2001b) have been made and are available in the literature (Hernandez, 2000; Hernandez & Hodges, 2001b; Rogers et al., 2000; Weiss, 1995). Theory-of-change analysis should include working premises, interventions, expected changes, and both short- and long-term outcomes. These approaches can function at multiple levels, including that of the individual practitioner.

Once desired outcomes have been identified, system planners and evaluators are faced with the task of identifying appropriate measures of the variables and constructs they have selected. The scope of this chapter does not permit a complete review of available measures; the reader is referred to recent publications that discuss some commonly used measures for outcome domains (Burns & Hoagwood, 2002; Hernandez & Hodges, 2001a; Rosenblatt, 1998). For the clinical domain, a number of system of care evaluations have used versions of the Child Behavior Checklist (Achenbach, 1991) and the Moods and Emotions Scale of the Child and Adolescent Functional Assessment Scale (CAFAS; (Hodges, 1994), the Diagnostic Interview Schedule for Children (DISC; Shaffer, Fisher, Piacentini, Schwab-Stone, & Wicks, 1989), the Children's Global Assessment Scale (Shaffer, Gould, & Brasic, 1983), and Conner's Parents and Teacher Rating Scales (Conners, 1973). In the rehabilitative domain, child functioning is often assessed using the Roles Performance Scales of the CAFAS (Hodges, 1994). Instruments available to assess strengths include the Behavioral and Emotional Rating Scale (Epstein & Sharma, 1998) and the Child and Adolescent Strengths Assessment (Lyons, Kisiel, & West, 1997). A useful tool to assess level of service in relation to the child and family needs is the Child and Adolescent Level of Care Utilization System (CALOCUS; Klaehn, O'Malley, Vaughn, & Kroeger, 1999). Other indicators available at the community level may include school attendance and dropout rates, juvenile arrest and diversion rates, teen pregnancy rates, and other health indicators. Measures for variables in the domain of humanitarian outcomes include a number of tools assessing youth and family satisfaction (Anderson, Rivera, & Kutash, 1998), family empowerment (Koren, DeChillo, & Friesen, 1992) and family quality of life (Crowley & Kazdin, 1998). System of care planners and evaluators may also choose to measure the degree to which parents' ability to be employed is affected by their situation or other concepts considered important by various stakeholders.

These measures are useful at the practice level to improve quality of services. In addition, rating scales assessing clinical symptoms can be used to monitor individual response to treatment. Some commonly used measures include the Children's Depression Inventory (Kovacs & Beck, 1977), the Children's Yale-Brown Obsessive-Compulsive Scale (Scahill et al., 1997), and the Revised Children's Manifest Anxiety Scale (Reynolds & Richmond, 1978). Use of rating scales may enhance treatment effectiveness, as illustrated by the NIMH Collaborative Multisite Multimodal Treatment Study of Children with attention deficit hyperactivity disorder (MTA Cooperative Group, 1999), which demonstrated that use of rating scales and dose adjustment protocols yielded better outcomes than community psychopharmacological treatment.

THE ROLE OF FAMILY PARTICIPATION IN OUTCOMES

It follows naturally from the core system of care value of family centeredness that families should play an integral role in outcome evaluation. Friesen and Stephens (1998) provide a framework for the multiple roles for families in systems of care that can also be useful in thinking about family participation in outcomes:

- Context
- Targets for change and recipients of service
- Partners in the treatment process
- Service providers
- Educators and trainers of professionals, students, and other family members
- Advocates and policymakers
- Evaluators and researchers

In the role of providing the primary environmental context for children, families of children with emotional or behavioral disorders experience a great deal of strain in all aspects of their lives, especially in the fit between work and family. Rosenzweig, Brennan, and Ogilvie (2002) describe the significant difficulties that these parents experience in attempting to fulfill their daily work and family responsibilities, resulting from inadequate access to needed child care, after-school care, respite, and other community-based services. Providing needed respite and child care services to reduce tensions between work and family obligations is likely to result in better outcomes and may lessen the utilization of residential and hospital resources (Brannan, Heflinger, & Bickman, 1997).

The role of partner in the treatment process entails parents' and other caregivers' being actively involved in planning, implementing, and evaluating services for their child. The degree of active participation by families in service planning is believed to influence outcomes positively, through identification of appropriate goals, achievement of better service fit, and increased treatment acceptance (McCammon, Spencer, & Friesen, 2001; Pullman, 2002).

Increasingly, families are also assuming roles as evaluators in systems of care. In a recent study of family participation in the CMHS projects, Osher, van Kammen, and Zaro (2001) found that family members were taking an active role in multiple aspects of program evaluation, including modification of questionnaires, data collection and analysis, sharing data with families, and, to a somewhat lesser extent, review and utilization of data. It was perceived that family participation, especially by serving as culturally competent interviewers, improved the quality of data collected and ultimately would improve the services provided. Vander Stoep, Green, Jones, and Huffine (2001) describe a parent-driven evaluation model in the King County Blended Funding Project in which parents were involved as full research partners. Families on the evaluation team helped to develop instruments consisting of visual depictions that were perceived as more accurate reflections of how well children's needs across life domains were being met.

Finally, as English (2002) suggests, families can critically influence policy-making in their advocacy role because "their vested interest in treatment outcomes encourages both persistence and the desire to learn about state-of-the-art services" (p. 314).

THE SYSTEM OF CARE PLANNING PROCESS

Armed with an understanding of the values of various stakeholders and with knowledge about effective interventions and tools to measure desired outcomes, system planners will be ready to embark on a process for setting goals and identifying outcomes for the system of care. Steps or stages in this planning process are as follows:

1. Identify relevant constituencies and form a work group (Hernandez & Hodges, 2001b). We recommend including system evaluators from the inception of the planning process so that the ability to monitor the intended systems changes and outcomes can be built into system design efforts and information systems.

2. Gather information and feedback about the system (both system strengths and service gaps). Information can be in many forms: existing reports or need assessments, extrapolations from national studies to community circumstances, indicators such as dropout rates, school achievement, juvenile crime, preschoolers' readiness to learn, and cost information from existing information systems. The choice of information will, of course, be related to the overall goals and circumstances of the planning process. Caution should be exercised with need assessments that begin with a particular intervention or program and then solicit information from community members about whether they need such a service. The first problem with this approach is that it is an example of goal displacement, with a focus on particular interventions that are popular, or seen as desirable for some reason rather than beginning with demonstrated need, and then fitting services to needs.

3. Plan and implement a process to identify a mission, and establish goals and outcomes. This step requires a process that allows for receiving and synthesizing input from many groups and individuals. It may require considerable negotiation and will involve much hard work. Some communities may wish to locate an outside facilitator who is familiar with children's mental health and community planning processes.

4. Develop a working diagram of a theory of change for the community systems. This includes a brief statement of the mission, target population, working premises, interventions, expected change, and short- and long-term outcomes.

5. Identify the necessary resources to support system change and expansion.

6. Craft and formalize the interagency agreements necessary to create and sustain a comprehensive system of care.

7. Build necessary organizational infrastructure, and train administrators and staff in new interventions and ways of working that reflect the system of care mission.

8. Create a working model of system flow, paying attention to access, intake, triage, and ways to connect children and families with services and resources. This step also requires attention to issues of utilization review and quality assurance.

9. Begin implementation. Carefully monitor the fidelity of interventions to be sure that they are being implemented as intended.

10. Use evaluation tools to monitor progress and provide feedback, so that interventions stay on track and problems are identified early.

11. Assess the degree to which intended outcomes are being achieved. Publicize results often and widely, using them strategically to attract resources for system sustainability and expansion.

Table 20.3 shows how two communities might identify their mission, population, interventions, expected change, and outcomes. To simplify this illustration we have chosen to use more specific rather than more global examples. Therefore, the examples are not inclusive of all children in a community; the system that is developed for serving each identified population will be part of the larger system of care planning, and one planning process might result in several diagrams focused on particular populations.

As illustrated in Table 20.3, the community A work group identified a mission that reflects Rosenblatt's summary of desired outcomes (1993): "Children should be at home, in school, and out of trouble." For this theory of change diagram, the major focus is on just two of these: children at home and in school. Concern about an increasing number of children being referred for out-of-home treatment and escalating costs for hospital, residential care, and group home placements led to this choice. Although the focus is on keeping children at home and in school, the support and intervention they receive could potentially affect other areas as well(for example, juvenile justice involvement).

Community A work group members made two assumptions. The first was that increased availability of intensive, community-based services and supports would help children manage their behavior, increase the ability of school personnel and families to intervene effectively, and provide necessary support for children and families, thus reducing the need for out-of-home placement. The second assumption was that if families were centrally involved in planning services, for their own children and at the system level, services would be more relevant and appropriate; they would achieve a better fit between needs and services.

Members of community A decided to introduce two multifaceted interventions that were not available, a wraparound approach based on work by VanDenBerg and others (Burchard, Burchard, Sewell, & VanDenBerg, 1993; VanDenBerg & Grealish, 1996) and multisystemic therapy (Henggeler et al., 2000). Both interventions

Table 20.3. Program Theory Models for Two Communities

	Population	Working Premises	Interventions	Expected Change	Short-Term Outcomes	Long-Term Outcomes
Community A mission: Children at home, in school, out of trouble	Children at risk of out-of-home placement because of behavior, family stress, inability to obtain appropriate community services for child	Increased availability of intensive, individualized community-based interventions will reduce need for out-of-home placement Full family participation in planning will improve fit between needs and services	Wraparound services to provide needed structure, supervision, support for children and families Multisystemic therapy for those with highest need Respite services	Families and schools better able to support child More at-risk children live at home and in their communities Children better able to manage their emotions and behavior; experience success in school, at home	Decreased out-of-home placement costs Measurable improvements in child functioning (for example, school grades, attendance, family and peer relationships) Reduced family stress, normalization of lives for entire family.	Child able to move successfully to higher education, work, assume range of adult roles Parents remain fully employed, balance work with family life

Community B mission: All young children enter kindergarten ready to learn					
All preschool children and their families in the community	Availability of developmental screening services will lead to healthier development, better school readiness	Universal screening for four and five year olds	Parents and teachers gain knowledge and skills to support, intervene with young children; children gain in social, cognitive, behavioral domains	Higher proportion of children entering kindergarten able to succeed	School-age children experience school success; learn academic and life skills
Children who have or are at risk for emotional, behavioral, or mental disorders	Early childhood mental health services are best provided in natural settings (for example, home, day care, preschool)	Basic training and consultation for parents, child care providers, preschools		Children with mental health needs and their families have service plans, intervention, and support to promote success	Schools have higher graduation rates, lower need for intensive special programs
		Direct mental health services at home; educational settings for highest need			

employ an individualized approach to planning and delivering services for children and their families and can potentially address a broad range of children's needs. Although both approaches require an investment in training and supervision, it was decided to reserve multisystemic therapy (which requires a high degree of supervision and monitoring) for children and families with the highest need. In addition, as work group members listened to families describe their experiences, an apparent link emerged between stress related to children's extremely disruptive and sometimes violent behavior and families' requests for residential treatment. In response to this information, the work group added respite services to the core program.

The changes expected as a result of the interventions were reduction in clinical symptoms, better child functioning and increased school success, and reduced caregiver stress. The work group, which included the evaluator, reviewed a number of measures to select the outcomes they wanted to assess, and agreed to use both the Behavioral and Emotional Rating Scale (Epstein & Sharma, 1998) and the Child and Adolescent Strengths Assessment Scale (Lyons et al., 1997) to inform a strengths-based assessment. The Child and Adolescent Functional Assessment Scale (Hodges, 1994) was chosen to measure both changes in clinical status (Moods and Emotions Scale) and functioning (Role Performance Scale). In addition, the work group examined several instruments that might be used to measure impact on the family (Brannan et al., 1997; Messer, Angold, Costello, & Burns, 1996; Sheras & Abidin, 2002; Yatchmenoff, Koren, Friesen, Gordon, & Kinney, 1998).

Community B used a similar planning approach but chose to focus on young children in their first explicit system of care development process. There was considerable conflict among work group members about the proposal to focus on young children—in particular, to focus on all children in the community—not just those at risk of or those showing early signs of emotional or mental disorder. Proponents of focusing more clearly on children with obvious mental health needs argued that children with diagnosed mental disorders are underserved and should be given a priority for system of care development and expansion of services. Those who favored the focus on young children and their families saw political and practical advantages to beginning with young children. They pointed out that considerable interagency planning and cooperative services for early childhood already existed and that there was a strong base of collaboration on which to build. They also argued that it is very difficult to interest legislators in deep-end services and that a focus on young children and promotion of school readiness would be easier to sell to the public as a whole. In addition, work group members were able to identify several possible outside funding sources that were interested in health promotion and school readiness.

A major fear of family members and providers concerned about children with existing mental health problems was that funds and other resources would be taken from current services and reassigned to early intervention. A compromise was finally struck. With help from an expert facilitator and with the direct involvement of administrators responsible for such program decisions, the group crafted an agreement that nearly all agreed to support. The agreement included the intention to support the healthy development of all children from birth to age nineteen, and to provide comprehensive, coordinated, community-based services to children and youth who have emotional, behavioral, or mental disorders and their families. It was also agreed that system of care development would use existing resources, and funds would not be reassigned from other programs to enhance early childhood intervention.

In the current political and fiscal climate, systems of care are increasingly being held accountable for demonstrating outcomes that meet expectations of various stakeholders of the system, especially those responsible for making policy and funding decisions. It is crucial in the planning process to involve multiple stakeholders in setting the goals and objectives of the service system. The process of negotiating outcomes with funders, stakeholders, and other policymakers to resolve competing interests and objectives, although cumbersome, is essential. If some stakeholders expect a goal to be accomplished that is not possible, there will be later problems, including failure to obtain continued funding or loss of support of constituents critical to the system of care.

In system planning, it is important to be clear about the expected outcomes at the client (child and family) and system level and to develop a theory-based expectation of change as a result of system interventions. In order to develop system objectives representing the interests of the multiple relevant stakeholders, we recommend use of a framework that includes the domains of clinical, rehabilitative, humanitarian, and public welfare outcomes.

Although much of the research on systems of care has focused on the level of service delivery and organization, it is also clear that achieving desired outcomes cannot take place if interventions at the practice level are not effective. The growing literature on evidence-based interventions is useful in community settings, along with methodologies for applying and testing them in those settings. These approaches will need to be systematically and thoughtfully incorporated into community-based service systems.

With regard to program evaluation, we offer the following guidelines:

- Involve the evaluator from the beginning of the planning process. At this early stage, the evaluator can help with development of a theory of change and suggest useful tools for program monitoring and evaluation.

- Choose an evaluator who understands system of care concepts, or the resulting system may not be what the constituents wanted.

- To increase relevance and applicability of the goals and methods of the evaluation, be sure the evaluation is part of the system rather than contracted out to an outside evaluator. To facilitate this internal process, there needs to be an ongoing evaluation work group. Evaluation results should also be available to clinicians for quality improvement.

- Families have important roles to play in program evaluation and quality improvement efforts: defining outcomes, helping to select family-relevant assessment tools, collecting and analyzing data, and using and interpreting evaluation results.

The process of measurement may be overwhelming to the system. It is important to focus on those few things one can measure adequately rather than doing special studies that are not feasible. Finally, one need not feel alone in the process of evaluating systems of care program effectiveness. There are many places in the country doing program evaluation of systems of care, and there is an increasing amount of support available. Helpful resources include Hernandez and Hodges (2001a) on outcome strategies and the National Technical Assistance Center of the Georgetown University Child Development Center. In addition, there are two publications providing a review of measures for evaluating outcomes in systems of care that were available at the time of publication (Cross, Urato, Lyons, & Cavanaugh, 1996; Cross, McDonald, & Lyons, 1997).

References

Achenbach, T. M. (1991). *Integrative guide for the CBCL 4–18, YSR, and TRF profiles.* Burlington: University of Vermont, Department of Psychiatry.

American Academy of Child and Adolescent Psychiatry. (1998). Practice parameters for the assessment and treatment of children and adolescents with depressive disorders. *Journal of the American Academy of Child and Adolescent Psychiatry,* 37 (Suppl.), 63S-83S.

American Academy of Child and Adolescent Psychiatry Work Group on Community-Based Systems of Care. (1998). *Best principles for measuring outcomes in managed Medicaid mental health programs.* Washington, DC: American Academy of Child and Adolescent Psychiatry.

American Psychiatric Association. (1994). *Diagnostic and statistical manual of mental disorders* (4th ed.). Washington, DC: Author.

Anderson, J. A., Rivera, V. R., & Kutash, K. (1998). Measuring consumer satisfaction with children's mental health services. In M. H. Epstein, K. Kutash, & A. Duchnowski (Eds.), *Outcomes for children and youth with behavioral and emotional disorders and their families: Program and evaluation best practices* (pp. 455–481). Austin, TX: Pro-Ed.

Bickman, L., Guthrie, P., Foster, E. M., Lambert, E. W., Summerfelt, W. T., Breda, C., & Heflinger, C. A. (1995). *Managed care in mental health: The Fort Bragg experiment.* New York: Plenum.

Brannan, A. M., Heflinger, C. A., & Bickman, L. (1997). The Caregiver Strain Questionnaire: Measuring the impact on the family of living with a child with serious emotional disturbance. *Journal of Emotional and Behavioral Disorders, 5,* 212–222.

Burchard, J. D., Bruns, E. J., & Burchard, S. N. (2002). The wraparound approach. In B. J. Burns & K. Hoagwood (Eds.), *Community treatment for youth: Evidence-based interventions for severe emotional and behavioral disorders* (pp. 69–90). New York: Oxford University Press.

Burchard, J. D., Burchard, S. N., Sewell, R., & VanDenBerg, J. (1993). *One kid at a time: Evaluative case studies and description of the Alaska Youth Initiative Demonstration Project.* Juneau: State of Alaska, Division of Mental Health and Mental Retardation.

Burns, B. J., Compton, S. N., Egger, H. L., Farmer, E.M.Z., & Robertson, E. B. (2002). An annotated bibliography of evidence for diagnostic-specific psychosocial and psychopharmacological interventions. In B. J. Burns & K. Hoagwood (Eds.), *Community treatment for youth: Evidence-based interventions for severe emotional and behavioral disorders* (pp. 212–276). New York: Oxford University Press.

Burns, B. J., & Hoagwood, K. (Eds.). (2002). *Community treatment for youth: Evidence-based interventions for severe emotional and behavioral disorders.* New York: Oxford University Press.

Burns, B. J., Hoagwood, K., & Maultsby, L. T. (1998). Improving outcomes for children and adolescents with serious emotional and behavioral disorders: Current and future directions. In M. H. Epstein, K. Kutash, & A. Duchnowski (Eds.), *Outcomes for children and youth with emotional and behavioral disorders and their families* (pp. 685–707). Austin, TX: Pro-Ed.

Chamberlain, P. (2002). Treatment foster care. In B. J. Burns & K. Hoagwood (Eds.), *Community treatment for youth: Evidence-based interventions for severe emotional and behavioral disorders* (pp. 117–138). New York: Oxford University Press.

Conners, C. K. (1973). Rating scales for use in drug studies with children. *Psychopharmacology Bulletin, 23,* 24–84.

Cross, T. P., McDonald, E., & Lyons H. (1997). *Evaluating the outcome of children's mental health services: A guide for the use of available child and family outcome measures* (2nd ed.). Boston: Judge Baker Children's Center.

Cross, T. P., Urato, M., Lyons, H. W., & Cavanaugh, D. (1996). *Measuring how we care: Tools for assessing children's mental health services, programs and systems.* Boston: Judge Baker Children's Center.

Crowley, M. J., & Kazdin, A. E. (1998). Child psychosocial functioning and parent quality of life among clinically referred children. *Journal of Child and Family Studies, 7,* 233–251.

Duchnowski, A. J., Kutash, K., & Friedman, R. M. (2002). Community-based interventions in a system of care and outcomes framework. In B. J. Burns & K. Hoagwood (Eds.), *Community treatment for youth: Evidence-based interventions for severe emotional and behavioral disorders* (pp. 16–37). New York: Oxford University Press.

English, M. J. (2002). Policy implications relevant to implementing evidence-based treatment. In B. J. Burns & K. Hoagwood (Eds.), *Community treatment for youth: Evidence-based interventions for severe emotional and behavioral disorders* (pp. 303–326). New York: Oxford University Press.

Epstein, M. H., Kutash, K., & Duchnowski, A. (Eds.). (1998). *Outcomes for children and youth with emotional and behavioral disorders and their families: Programs and evaluation best practices.* Austin, TX: Pro-Ed.

Epstein, M. H., & Sharma, J. M. (1998). *Behavioral and Emotional Rating Scale (BERS).* Austin, TX: Pro-Ed.

Epstein, M. H., & Walker, H. M. (2002). Special education: Best practices and First Step to Success. In B. J. Burns & K. Hoagwood (Eds.), *Community treatment for youth: Evidence-based interventions for severe emotional and behavioral disorders* (pp. 177–197). New York: Oxford University Press.

Evans, M. E., & Armstrong, M. I. (2002). What is case management? In B. J. Burns & K. Hoagwood (Eds.), *Community treatment for youth: Evidence-based interventions for severe emotional and behavioral disorders* (pp. 39–68). New York: Oxford University Press.

Fairbank, J. A., Booth, S. R., & Curry, J. F. (2002). Integrated cognitive-behavior therapy for traumatic stress symptoms and substance abuse. In B. J. Burns & K. Hoagwood (Eds.), *Community treatment for youth: Evidence-based interventions for severe emotional and behavioral disorders* (pp. 198–211). New York: Oxford University Press.

Foster, E. M., Kelsch, C. C., Kamradt, B., Sosna, T., & Yang, Z. (2001). Expenditures and sustainability in systems of care. *Journal of Emotional and Behavioral Disorders, 9,* 53–62.

Friedman, R. M., & Burns, B. J. (1996). The evaluation of the Fort Bragg demonstration project: An alternative interpretation of the findings. *Journal of Mental Health Administration, 23,* 128–136.

Friesen, B. J. (2000). Points of tension: Mental health administration in a managed care environment. In R. J. Patti (Ed.), *The handbook of social welfare management* (pp. 461–480). Thousand Oaks, CA: Sage.

Friesen, B. J. & Stephens, B. (1998). Expanding family roles in the system of care: Research and practice. In M. H. Epstein, K. Kutash, & A. Duchnowski (Eds.), *Outcomes for children and youth with behavioral and emotional disorders and their families: Program and evaluation best practices* (pp. 231–259). Austin, TX: Pro-Ed.

Geller, B., Zimmerman, B., Williams, M., Bolhofner, K., & Craney, J. L. (2001). Adult psychosocial outcome of prepubertal major depressive disorder. *Journal of the American Academy of Child and Adolescent Psychiatry, 40,* 673–684.

Hamner, K. M., Lambert, E. W., & Bickman, L. (1997). Children's mental health continuum of care: Clinical outcomes at 18 months for the Fort Bragg demonstration. *Children's Mental Health, 24,* 464–471.

Hargreaves, W. A., & Shumway, M. (1989). Effectiveness of mental health services for the severely mentally ill. In C. A. Taube, D. Mechanic, & A. Hohmann (Eds.), *The future of mental health services research.* Washington, DC: U.S. Government Printing Office.

Henggeler, S. W., Pickrel, D. G., & Brondino, M. J. (2000). Multisystemic treatment of substance-abusing and dependent delinquents: Outcomes, treatment fidelity, and transportability. *Mental Health Services Research, 1,* 171–184.

Hernandez, M. (2000). Using logic models and program theory to build outcome accountability. *Education and Treatment of Children, 23,* 24–40.

Hernandez, M., & Hodges, S. (Eds.). (2001a). *Developing outcome strategies in children's mental health.* Baltimore: Brookes Publishing.

Hernandez, M., & Hodges, S. (2001b). Theory-based accountability. In M. Hernandez & S. Hodges (Eds.), *Developing outcome strategies in children's mental health* (pp. 21–40). Baltimore: Brookes Publishing.

Hoagwood, K. (1997). Interpreting nullity: The Fort Bragg experiment—A comparative success or failure? *American Psychologist, 52,* 546–550.

Hoagwood, K., Burns, B. J., Kiser, L., Ringeisen, H., & Schoenwald, S. K. (2001). Evidence-based practice in child and adolescent mental health services. *Psychiatric Services, 52,* 1179–1189.

Hoagwood, K., Burns, B. J., & Weisz, J. R. (2002). A profitable conjunction: From science to service in children's mental health. In B. J. Burns & K. Hoagwood (Eds.), *Community treatment for youth: Evidence-based intervention for severe emotional and behavioral disorders.* New York: Oxford University Press.

Hoagwood, K., Jensen, P. S., Petti, T., & Burns, B. J. (1996). Outcomes of mental health care for children and adolescents: I. A comprehensive conceptual model. *Journal of the Academy of Child and Adolescent Psychiatry, 35,* 1055–1063.

Hodges, K. (1994). *Child and Adolescent Functional Assessment Scale.* Ypsilanti: Eastern Michigan University, Department of Psychology.

Hodges, S., Woodbridge, M., & Huang L. N. (2001). Creating useful information in data-rich environments. In M. Hernandez & S. Hodges (Eds.), *Developing outcome strategies in children's mental health,* (pp. 239–255). Baltimore: Brookes Publishing.

Ireys, H. T., Devet, K. A., & Sakwa, D. (2002). Family support and education. In B. J. Burns & K. Hoagwood (Eds.), *Community treatment for youth: Evidence-based interventions for severe emotional and behavioral disorders* (pp. 154–175). New York: Oxford University Press.

Jacobsen, D., & Cervine, D. (2001). A magic growth formula for mental health services in Santa Cruz County. In M. Hernandez & S. Hodges (Eds.), *Developing Outcome strategies in children's mental health.* Baltimore: Brookes Publishing.

Jensen, P. S., Hoagwood, K., & Petti, T. (1996). Outcomes of mental health care for children and adolescents: II. Literature review and application of a comprehensive model. *Journal of the Academy of Child and Adolescent Psychiatry, 35,* 1064–1077.

Klaehn, R., O'Malley, K., Vaughn, T., & Kroeger, K. (1999). *Child and Adolescent Level of Care Utilization System (CALOCUS): User's manual (Ver. 1.1).* Washington, DC: American Academy of Child and Adolescent Psychiatry.

Koren, P. E., DeChillo, N., & Friesen, B. J. (1992). Measuring empowerment in families whose children have emotional disabilities: A brief questionnaire. *Rehabilitation Psychology, 37,* 305–321.

Kovacs, M., & Beck, A. T. (1977). An empirical-clinical approach towards a definition of childhood depression. In I. G. Schulterbrandt & A. Raskin (Eds.), *Depression in children: Diagnosis, treatment and conceptual models.* New York: Raven Press.

Kutash, K., & Rivera, V. R. (Eds.). (1996). *What works in children's mental health services? Uncovering answers to critical questions.* Baltimore: Brookes Publishing.

Lourie, I. S., Katz-Leavy, J., DeCarolis, G., & Quinlan, W. A. (1996). The role of the federal government. In B. A. Stroul (Ed.), *Children's mental health: Creating systems of care in a changing society* (pp. 99–114). Baltimore: Brookes Publishing.

Lyons, J. S., Kisiel, C. L., & West, C. (1997). Child and Adolescent Strengths Assessment (CASA): A pilot study. *Family Matters, 3,* 30–33.

McCammon, S. L., Spencer, S. A., & Friesen, B. J. (2001). Promoting family empowerment through multiple roles. *Journal of Family Social Work, 5,* 1–24.

Messer, S. C., Angold, A., Costello, E. J., & Burns, B. J. (1996). The Child and Adolescent Burden Assessment (CABA): Measuring the family impact of emotional and behavioral problems. *International Journal of Methods in Psychiatric Research, 6,* 261–284.

MTA Cooperative Group. (1999). Fourteen-month randomized clinical trial of treatment strategies for attention-deficit hyperactivity disorder. *Archives of General Psychiatry, 56,* 1073–1086

NIH Guide. (1994, Feb. 11). Research transition grant program in mental health services. *NIH Guide, 23.* Available on-line at: http://grants1.nih.gov/grants/guide/rfa-files/RFA-MH-94-007.html.

Osher, T. W., deFur, E., Nava, C., Spencer, S., & Toth-Dennis, D. (1998). *New roles for families in systems of care. Systems of care: Promising practices in children's mental health,* 1998 Series, Volume I. Washington, DC: Center for Effective Collaboration and Practice, American Institutes for Research.

Osher, T. W., van Kammen, W., & Zaro, S. M. (2001). Family participation in evaluating systems of care: Family, research, and service system perspectives. *Journal of Emotional and Behavioral Disorders, 9,* 63–70.

Overstreet, D. W., Casel, G., Saunders, T., & Armstrong, M. I. (2001). Florida's use of accountable innovation. In M. Hernandez & S. Hodges (Eds.), *Developing outcome strategies in children's mental health* (pp. 97–114). Baltimore: Brookes Publishing.

Pullman, M. (2002). *Family participation in educational and service planning: Brief measures.* Regional Research Institute for Human Services, Portland State University, Portland, OR.

Pumariega, A. J., Del Mundo, A. S., & Vance, B. (2002). Psychopharmacology in the context of systems of care. In B. J. Burns & K. Hoagwood (Eds.), *Community treatment for youth: Evidence-based interventions for severe emotional and behavioral disorders* (pp. 277–300). New York: Oxford University Press.

Reynolds, C. R., & Richmond, B. O. (1978). What I think and feel: A revised measure of children's manifest anxiety. *Journal of Abnormal Child Psychology, 6,* 271–280.

Rogers, P. J., Petrosino, A., Huebner, T. A., & Hacsi, T. A. (Eds.). (2000). *Program theory in evaluation: Challenges and opportunities.* San Francisco: Jossey-Bass.

Rosenblatt, A. (1993). In home, in school, and out of trouble. *Journal of Child and Family Studies, 2,* 275–282.

Rosenblatt, A. (1998). Assessing the child and family outcomes of systems of care for youth with serious emotional disturbance. In M. H. Epstein, K. Kutash, & A. Duchnowski (Eds.), *Outcomes for children and youth with emotional and behavioral disorders and their families* (pp. 333–362). Austin, TX: Pro-Ed.

Rosenzweig, J. M., Brennan, E. M., & Ogilvie, A. M. (2002). Work/family fit: Voices of parents of children with emotional and behavioral disorders. *Social Work, 47*(4), 415–424.

Scahill, L., Riddle, M. A., McSwiggin-Hardin, M., Ort, S. I., King, R. A., Goodman, W. K., Cicchetti, D., & Leckman, J. F. (1997). Children's Yale-Brown Obsessive Compulsive Scale: Reliability and validity. *Journal of the American Academy of Child and Adolescent Psychiatry, 36,* 844–852.

Schoenwald, S. K., & Rowland, M. D. (2002). Multisystemic therapy. In B. J. Burns & K. Hoagwood (Eds.), *Community treatment for youth: Evidence-based interventions for severe emotional and behavioral disorders* (pp. 91–116). New York: Oxford University Press.

Shaffer, D., Fisher, P., Piacentini, J., Schwab-Stone, M., & Wicks, J. (1989). *Diagnostic Interview Schedule for Children (DISC-2.1).* New York: New York State Psychiatric Institute.

Shaffer, D., Gould, M. S., & Brasic, J. (1983). A children's global assessment scale (CGAS). *Archives of General Psychiatry, 40,* 1228–1231.

Sheras, P. L., & Abidin, R. R. (2002). *Stress Index for Parents of Adolescents (SIPA).* Lutz, FL: Psychological Assessment Resources.

Simpson, J. S., Koroloff, N., Friesen, B. J., & Gac, J. (1999). *Promising practices in family-provider collaboration. Systems of care: Promising practices in children's mental health,* 1999 Series, Volume II. Washington, DC: Center for Effective Collaboration and Practices, American Institutes of Research.

Stroul, B. A., & Friedman, R. M. (1996). The system of care concept and philosophy. In B. A. Stroul (Ed.), *Children's mental health: Creating systems of care in a changing society* (pp. 3–21). Baltimore: Brookes Publishing.

Vance, J. E. (2002). Mentoring to facilitate resiliency in high-risk youth. In B. J. Burns & K. Hoagwood (Eds.), *Community treatment for youth: Evidence-based interventions for severe emotional and behavioral disorders* (pp. 139–153). New York: Oxford University Press.

VanDenBerg, J. E., & Grealish, M. E. (1996). Individualized services and supports through the wrap-around process. *Journal of Child and Family Studies, 5,* 7–21.

Vander Stoep, A., Green, L., Jones, R. A., & Huffine, C. (2001). A family empowerment model of change. In M. Hernandez & S. Hodges (Eds.), *Developing outcomes strategies in children's mental health.* Baltimore: Brookes Publishing.

Weiss, C. H. (1995). Nothing as practical as good theory: Exploring theory-based evaluation for comprehensive community initiatives. In J. Connell, A. Kubisch, L. Schorr, & C. Weiss (Eds.), *New approaches to evaluating community initiatives* (pp. 65–92). Washington, DC: Aspen Institute.

Weiss, G., & Hechtman, L. T. (1993). *Hyperactive children grown up* (2nd ed.). New York: Guilford Press.

Weisz, J. R., Han, S. S., & Valeri, S. M. (1997). More of what? Issues raised by the Fort Bragg study. *American Psychologist, 52,* 541–545.

Yatchmenoff, D. K., Koren, P. E., Friesen, B. J., Gordon, L. J., & Kinney, R. F. (1998). Enrichment and stress in families caring for a child with a serious emotional disorder. *Journal of Child and Family Studies, 7,* 129–145.

CHAPTER TWENTY-ONE

Training Child and Adolescent Psychiatrists and Child Mental Health Professionals for Systems of Care

Kaye L. McGinty
John M. Diamond
Michael B. Brown
Susan L. McCammon

The lack of sufficient trained staff to implement community-based services for children is one of the problems facing communities wishing to implement an integrated system of care (Pires, 1996). Mental health professionals working with children and families in the community mental health system represent a number of disciplines, including psychiatry, psychology, counseling, nursing, social work, and marriage and family therapy. Changing perspectives on the importance of mental health services in schools (Adelman & Taylor, 1998) underscore the importance of including school mental health professionals (school counselors, school psychologists, school social workers, and special education teachers) to the list of professionals who will benefit from knowledge of system of care principles.

Criticism of traditional practices does not imply these services were provided by incompetent or uncaring clinicians (Sheridan & Gutkin, 2000). The criticism, rather, is aimed at how problems are conceptualized and the structures and processes employed in service delivery. Implementing system of care principles involves a change in how services are delivered. One way to promote changes in professional practice is to focus on training (Rosenfield, 2000). Therefore, altering the curriculum and field practice in training programs is a necessary step in changing practice.

SYSTEM OF CARE TRAINING OBJECTIVES

Stroul and Friedman (1986) provided the conceptual framework on which system of care principles are based. The Child and Adolescent Services System Program (CASSP) principles are largely philosophical in nature and involve key aspects of the system of care and how intervention is conceptualized. The task that followed was to develop specific competencies that enable mental health professionals to implement the system of care principles in service delivery.

One of the most clearly articulated sets of guidelines was developed through the Pennsylvania CASSP Training and Technical Assistance Institute (Hansen et al., 1999). The child, family, and community core competencies involve developing basic knowledge in each of the areas, along with the skills of implementing this knowledge into practice. In addition to these core competencies, mental health professionals need to know about the strategies that families find most helpful in providing successful interventions (Worthington, Hernandez, Friedman, & Uzzell, 2001). Finally, mental health professionals in training need to be able to understand and use a variety of evaluation strategies to evaluate interventions with individual families and the effectiveness of programs (McCammon, Cook, & Kilmer, in press; Nastasi, 2000). This knowledge and skill base will serve mental health professionals in providing care to children with serious mental health problems and their families.

Core Child, Family, and Community Competencies

The guidelines developed by Hansen et al. (1999) cover key competencies necessary to function in a system of care for children and families. They involve knowledge of normal developmental expectations, psychiatric diagnostic criteria, and effective interventions (including crisis intervention strategies). Professionals need to learn how to gather information through formal as well as informal assessments in order to address behavior concerns. Training programs must help trainees learn about and be sensitive to cultural differences, and use cultural strengths in developing effective interventions. Training programs should provide opportunities for trainees to use this information to develop individualized services that are culturally sensitive and employ the least restrictive service options for interventions.

Families are usually the primary support for children with serious emotional disorders. The core family competencies are the knowledge and skills that enable the professional to work effectively with families. Training programs should ensure that trainees learn about the structure, development, and dynamics of families and how children's emotional disorders affect family functioning. Professionals in training should know the risk factors for families, understand how to help reduce the probability of crises, and intervene when crisis occurs. Family assessment, basic family intervention skills, and working with couples are important skills to be covered in training programs. Trainees must be able to provide referrals where necessary and work collaboratively with other providers to serve families.

The core community competencies represent the knowledge and skills that are necessary for the practitioner to use formal and informal community resources, while working collaboratively with others in the community, as a team with the child and family. Trainees should learn to identify the child's and family's perspective of the community and assist the family in becoming effective advocates in the community. Developing skills to assess the community's family serving systems and helping families access the least restrictive services and supports are important skills to be taught by training programs. Professionals in training should learn how to engage and maintain collaboration with community resources in a culturally sensitive fashion.

Families' Perspectives on Service Provision

A strong alliance between families and service providers is essential for effective services. Worthington et al. (2001) describe practices in community-based services that families and providers found were associated with successful outcomes for families. While families and providers identified specific services as effective, the manner in which services were delivered was equally important. Service providers in training need to be familiar with the processes of engaging with families, the service elements that promote success, and how the values of the system of care can be demonstrated through service delivery.

Engagement is the process by which families and providers develop and maintain a connection, while simultaneously demonstrating and communicating information, needs, attitudes, and values. Engagement is fostered by starting where families are now and addressing the basic needs of the family. Understanding the importance of identifying the families' stated needs and taking prompt action to meet them is a critical learning step for providers in training. Often the basic needs are not behavioral in nature, but can include such things as transportation or medical care. Trainees must learn how to establish a partnership between providers and families that provides support yet empowers families to solve their own difficulties, leading to increased commitment to treatment and greater skill development. Providers need to learn how to involve families in the design and implementation of the treatment process in a fashion that is different than most providers learn in a traditional training program.

Traditional clinical services (medical and mental health treatment) are an important component of care for families with children with serious mental health problems. Mental health professionals typically learn these traditional clinical services in their training programs. Providers in training need to understand the role of traditional clinical services as well as collateral clinical services. These include a variety of treatment modalities and settings, such as drug and alcohol rehabilitation, residential services, and crisis intervention. In addition to these clinical services, providers must become familiar with the importance and utilization of nonclinical services (such as transportation or job coaching) that are important to the quality of life of the child and family and enhance the success of intervention. Learning how to individualize the clinical and nonclinical services for each child and family is important. The ability to provide these services in a positive, collaborative fashion that builds on family strengths is an important skill to promote.

Finally, training programs need to teach the organizational and operational structures and values that guide effective service provision. Effective services include flexible funding systems, community-based services, and continuity of care. Trainees must learn how to advocate effectively for families with other organizations in the community. In order to advocate effectively, the trainee needs a working knowledge of the cultures of the various child service agencies: legal mandates, organizational structure, funding, and staffing and practice models. Then the coordination of care, which is an especially important aspect of system of care approaches, can be ensured. To ensure that appropriate care is provided, families must have consistent access to services and integration of nonclinical and clinical services. Finally, mental health providers must hone skills in developing natural and community supports that extend opportunities for intervention while involving the family more deeply in the community.

Research, Reflection, and Program Evaluation

Mental health providers need to understand how to develop research programs that provide new knowledge for practitioners and academicians. Training programs should provide exposure to a variety of research methodologies necessary for understanding the efficacy of interventions (see Kratochwill & Stoiber, 2000, for a progressive model of intervention research). Applied research also provides an excellent venue for modeling the cross-discipline collaboration necessary to permit further understanding of and cooperation among the varied disciplines of mental health providers.

In addition to training in intervention research, training programs must provide professionals in training with exposure to strategies to evaluate practice. Program evaluation helps determine the level of acceptability to participants, the degree to which the program was implemented as designed, and the effectiveness of the program (Nastasi, 1998). This information is critical to ensure that programs are successful in reaching their goal of assisting families and children. Integrating empirical models into the evaluation of practice may also enhance the decision-making capacity of practitioners and sustain their commitment to effective practices (Kratochwill & Stoiber, 2000).

In order to train a new workforce that will be able to incorporate these system of care training objectives into their practice in a competent and collaborative way with other professionals and parents, it is crucial to find ways to integrate the objectives and practices into the ongoing training of different disciplines.

TRAINING COMPONENT INITIATIVES FOR MENTAL HEALTH WORKFORCE PREPARATION

Efforts to strengthen the preparation of psychiatry residents to function more effectively in systems of care have been developing on a parallel track with other mental health disciplines. Although university training programs have been criticized for their failure to update training to meet current service delivery demands (Meyers, Kaufman, & Goldman, 1999), there have been initiatives to adjust training models such as the programs participating in the North Carolina Public-Academic Liaison (NC PAL; Shelton & Baumhover, 2002). In a number of universities in the University of North Carolina system, participants from the disciplines of marriage and family therapy, nursing, psychiatry, psychology, recreation therapy, and social work have been working to integrate system of care values into their training programs for mental health professionals. Initiatives have included integration of system of care concepts into existing course work, seminars, and grand rounds; the development of new courses; and the development of interdisciplinary field and practicum settings (McCammon, Cook, & Kilmer, in press).

Integration of System of Care Concepts into Existing Curricula

In 1996, the American Academy of Child and Adolescent Psychiatry (AACAP) Task Force on Community-Based Systems of Care for Seriously Emotionally Disturbed Children developed guidelines for residency programs to implement educational experiences and to promote competencies needed to function in these new systems (AACAP, 1996). The CASSP principles were identified as the basic principles underlying the development and function of the system of care. In order to promote these training guidelines, the task force recommended that traditional curricula be supplemented or enriched to provide relevant experiences. Special didactic curriculum components were suggested, including emphasizing systems theory, social factors, cultural competence training, epidemiology, system of care conceptual literature, core spiritual concepts, concepts of quality assurance and total quality management, use of management information systems, health care financing and administration, and leadership principles.

This call for development of state-of-the-art curricula to meet contemporary human service needs has been sounded by other professional groups as well. Zlotnik (1998a) noted the activity of social work education programs to prepare social workers and other human service professionals for new paradigms of service delivery. Methods of curriculum update and revision include adding course objectives regarding system of care principles and practices to core professional training courses; adding such materials to didactic presentations, course texts, and readings; and using innovative teaching methods. Two innovative teaching methods that have been used are interdisciplinary faculty collaboration and the participation of parents of children with serious emotional problems.

Development of New Courses

In addition to the curriculum infusion of existing courses approach, several of the NC PAL universities have developed a new course on interdisciplinary collaboration in serving children with serious emotional problems and their families. This course is taught by faculty from marriage and family therapy, nursing, psychology, and social work and includes students from those disciplines. A description of the development of the course at East Carolina University, including issues implementing and sustaining the course, is offered elsewhere (Dosser, Handron, McCammon, Powell, & Spencer, 2001). Although students and faculty from a number of disciplines have participated, only one child and adolescent psychiatry resident has been able to participate due to scheduling constraints (Handron, Diamond & Zlotnik, 2001). Interdisciplinary training has been emphasized as an important but difficult undertaking in health care (Bellack & O'Neil, 2000). In child and adolescent psychiatry residency programs, this is primarily accomplished during case conferences or seminars where various child mental health professionals and trainees participate in a specific activity.

An equally important teaching innovation has been the involvement of parents in curriculum development and teaching. A combined child and adolescent psychiatrist–family advocate training experience has been developed for child and adolescent psychiatry residents of the University of Pennsylvania. A parent representative of a family advocacy group (Parents Involved Network of Pennsylvania) and the state child and adolescent psychiatric consultant (Office of Mental Health and Substance Abuse Services) develop and present a system of care curriculum to the residents. Their main goal is to provide didactic system of care training jointly with a parent and psychiatrist actively modeling the Pennsylvania CASSP principles and system of care values (G. R. Hodas, personal communication, Jan. 12, 2002).

In the NC PAL initiatives, the group has developed various versions of the parents in residence (PIR) concept, in which university faculty partner with parents of youth with mental health concerns to revise and update university curricula and coteach classes. (The initial development of the PIR at East Carolina University is described by Osher, deFur, Nava, Spencer, and Toth-Dennis, 1999.) Students have been very enthusiastic in their ratings of the parent involvement in the classes, and the courses have been enriched by the parents' contributions. Coteaching has been one way to model partnership with parents and has proved to be helpful in faculty development as well.

Coteaching with parents in university courses provides an opportunity for students to understand the parent's experience while witnessing parent-professional collaboration. In a graduate psychology course, Psychotherapeutic Interventions with Children and Families, parents of youth with severe emotional disturbances (SED) served as guest faculty. At the end of the course, one student commented, "I always viewed parents who were 'un-invested' in their children's lives as uncaring. However, after viewing and experiencing the frustration that Lucy [a parent] felt and seeing how she gave up at times, I realized that the 'experts' may be the cause of the appearance of a parent not caring."

Practica, Field Experience, and Clinical Rotations

One of the most powerful training components has been the attention to integrating system of care experience into field-based training experiences. This has often involved using existing practica, internships, and clinical rotations, but new field experiences have been created too (McCammon et al., in press). All system of care training experiences must be careful to address the practice differences inherent in using this new philosophy. In order to accomplish this task, six areas should be emphasized: partnering with families, attending to caregiver stress, service planning, interdisciplinary collaboration, outcomes and accountability, and supervision.

Partnering with Families. In traditional practice, theoretical dogma often led to professionals bickering and families feeling uncomfortable. But if families are truly partners, they will participate in the treatment process. Treatment options are presented, and family values become an integral part in the medical decision making process. Evidence-based practices are discussed, with families choosing interventions based on outcomes that have the most meaning to them.

Perhaps the paramount skill in this new paradigm is partnering with families. This can be done only if certain building blocks for family participation are available in the system. Indeed, the families must participate in all parts of the system of care (Bronheim, Keefe, & Morgan, 1998). To become an effective partner, all trainees must become comfortable with the presence of parents and family members in all aspects of clinical operations. They may find family advocates accompanying families to appointments, and they may discover that unique family values are coloring the choice and interest of treatments. This concept of family participation in all aspects of administration and treatment is not something residents are exposed to often in medical schools. Developing an acceptance of this paradigm is likely to require exposure in clinical rotations and through modeling whereby residents can observe their mentors and colleagues engaging in these new partnerships. In the clinical setting, residents need to learn how to listen to families and engage them in a decision-making method that takes into consideration both evidence-based best practices in the field and the values of the family.

In the following example, Joe, a six-year-old boy, comes to the clinic with a problem that has been poorly responsive in the past to traditional interventions. The family requests interventions that are not mainstream, and the resident works with the family to achieve their goals. This ability to partner with families is critical in maintaining a positive relationship with the family.

Joe is severely autistic. The school is complaining of his high activity level, and the child has had previous adverse reactions to methylphenidate. The family has read on the Web, and heard from other families, that high doses of B vitamins may be both safe and effective in reducing the disruptive symptoms. They want to try this remedy.

After an evaluation, the resident presents information on what is likely to be most effective and explains the lack of controlled studies on vitamins for this problem. However, the family insists they want to try an alternative treatment. The resident, who has listened to the family and has adopted a partnering attitude, is able to explain the possible risks of high-dose vitamins, but also can counsel the family on how to conduct a vitamin trial safely so that they can evaluate together how effective it has been.

Attending to Caregiver Stress. A number of studies have documented the life disruptions and demands faced by parents rearing children with serious emotional and behavioral problems. Trainees should be exposed to the growing body of literature on family burden (Reisser & Schorske, 1994), parental burden (Angold et al., 1998), caregiver strain (Brannan, Heflinger, & Bickman, 1997), caregiver stress (McDonald, Poertner, & Pierpont, 1999), and family impact (Farmer, Burns, Angold, & Costello, 1997). These areas acknowledge the impact of the acute and long-term demands of caring for the identified child in the context of all the responsibilities a parent may carry. Brannan, Heflinger, and Bickman (1997) observed that elevated caregiver strain was associated with use of inpatient hospitalization and extended use of intermediate services. They noted that clinical outcomes for youth are likely to be affected by caregiver strain as it challenges caregivers' ability to bring children to treatment, make and implement service plans, and maintain gains in the natural environment.

Instruction is needed that cues trainees to look for mechanisms and supports to help parents continue caring for their children and protect the health and well-being of the parents and siblings. Sometimes trying to identify burden amelioration or parent support services helps to identify gaps in the community care system.

Staff of a five-day-per-week residential treatment program reported to a mother on her child's stormy week when she came to pick him up for the weekend. "At times, it took three staff to restrain him when he was out of control. Good luck this weekend!" they said. The crisis plan simply stated that if the boy could not be contained over the weekend, the mother should take him to the emergency department. The mother was perplexed. "I am a single mom, with two other children. If he is out of control, how do I get him into the car and drive to the hospital, with two other children in tow?" A resident understood the dilemma and called through the group home staff roster to identify staff who could be on call. All of the staff were either ill or planning to be out of town. A gap in the care system was identified, and the resident gained a deeper understanding of the challenges this single mother faced.

Service Planning. Functional assessment skills are vital to working with children and families. It is not sufficient to make clinical diagnoses focusing on pathology and weaknesses. Child and adolescent psychiatrists need to sharpen their ability to work with the team in order to help identify the strengths and weaknesses of the child and family. This will further the understanding of the problem and how it affects the functioning of the individual child and family. The child's functional level can then be codified by the DSM-IV global assessment of functioning scale of the *Diagnostic and Statistical Manual of Mental Disorders* (American Psychiatric Association 2000) and other standardized methods (Hodges, 1990). Then the current level of care can be determined based on the child's functioning, using an instrument such as the Child and Adolescent Level of Care Utilization System (Klaehn, O'Malley, Vaughn, & Kroeger, 1999). It is important for the resident to understand that movement within a system of care is dependent on changes in the level of functioning, as well as diagnostic symptomatology. Once the resident appreciates functional assessment, he or she can proceed to the next step of treatment planning. This system of care orientation emphasizes the attention to the partnership with the child and family, while focusing on the improvement in the child's functioning.

Dr. Read, a first-year child and adolescent psychiatry resident, evaluates an eleven-year-old boy with aggressive behavior at school. He makes the diagnosis of attention-deficit/hyperactivity disorder (ADHD), combined type, and recommends treatment with stimulant medications. Although he has obtained information of severe problems at home and in the neighborhood, he does not consider the child's functional assessment to determine the current level of care. Since the child has been diagnosed only with ADHD, Dr. Read assumes the child should be assigned to a lower level of care.

Three weeks later, the child comes to the emergency clinic after carrying a gun to school. The social worker and parent are upset that their concerns were not heard and ask for a new doctor. Dr. Read could attempt to continue treating the child by first admitting his mistake and then establishing a better rapport with the family. This illustrates the value of paying close attention to the level of functioning and eliciting feedback from the parent and social worker about treatment recommendations.

Treatment planning requires an understanding of different treatment modalities and community resources. In addition, the importance of the psychiatrist's knowledge of the individual family's culture, values, and beliefs is vital in approaching this process with the family. In a system of care, treatment planning takes place in a team with the family, traditional service providers, and nontraditional community members (VanDenBerg & Grealish, 1996). Each member of the team contributes to the process by sharing his or her own unique perspective of the child and family. In this way, strengths-based treatment planning is promoted in the system of care. By participating in these teams, residents can appreciate the benefits and challenges of this process (McGinty, McCammon, & Koeppen, 2001). Furthermore, the resident has the luxury of having supervisors and mentors for guidance throughout this process. Supervisors need to remember that the strengths-based approach to patient care is a major paradigm shift for most residents. Therefore, trainees need additional guidance to integrate their previous training in adult psychiatry (with its emphasis on acute care, severe psychopathology, and biological treatments), their current training in development and child and adolescent psychiatry practice, and their individual practice styles in order to function optimally in a system of care.

Strengths can be a challenge to identify, especially for youth who have begun to see themselves as losers. The team approach to strengths-based treatment planning is a valuable tool for educating residents.

The team met about the fourteen-year-old girl who was having more problems in school. Although her obsessive symptoms were decreasing, she was still very self-conscious and had difficulty with her peers. Few personal strengths had been identified. An astute resident looking for her strengths noticed her drawing skills during a medication evaluation session and later asked the child and other team members about this skill. A lively discussion followed, and the girl expressed a desire to pursue art further. A community mentor, a local art professor, was recruited, and within a year, the girl was exhibiting her artwork at the local art museum and her school. She had made a few friends through this activity and was functioning better in school. The resident noted later in supervision that this team experience taught her the value of using the system of care principles.

Interdisciplinary Collaboration. Interdisciplinary collaboration is crucial to the functioning of a system of care. Collaboration is a complicated process, and there are multiple skills for residents to learn to achieve competence in this area, including basic consultation, interpersonal dynamics, and systems theory. Furthermore, professional development issues naturally arise during this type of interaction. Residents typically have various personal reactions to this level of interdisciplinary collaboration. Indeed, some of their reactions may obstruct the process of collaboration. This may be viewed as resistance, ignorance, or lack of professional development. These potentially obstructive reactions may be based on the resident's prior experiences with physicians as the clinical leader, the emphasis on psychopharmacology and neurobiology, the circumscribed prescriber role for psychiatrists, and the lack of support for nondirect service roles.

Supervisors can use the system of care model itself to work with trainees on their collaboration skills. This involves creating a safe environment for discussion, helping residents identify their strengths and weaknesses, and being available for supervision that is provided in a respectful and timely manner.

Trainees require exposure to collaboration, as well as modeling, to learn how to work with a team as an effective team member. This may be an intimidating process for residents who are in a learner role. The supervisor will need to help the residents assess their reactions to team interactions and recognize personal versus professional issues. Processing their failures and successes with team communication should be encouraged with residents so that they can become more effective participants and, hence, better clinicians. Perhaps one of the hardest lessons to learn in the teamwork for residents is to provide input and assistance without giving a solution. Ultimately, all participants of the team hope that the child and family will become more successful and be able to function with less help from the team. Residents can benefit from watching a family move through this process gradually. Excellence in collaborative skills also requires the skill to work with multiple agencies, which at the minimum requires an understanding of the role for each agency.

Interdisciplinary collaboration is one of the most difficult skills for residents to master, and they will need help from their supervisors in dealing with the personal and professional issues that arise during their mastery of this skill.

Dr. Jones had just started a new rotation at a residential treatment center where all treatment decisions were made with the team model. The resident sighed, knowing that this rotation would test her patience. The next day, she had to attend a two-hour team meeting about the problems in a child's home. The resident did not think she needed to be involved in a meeting with social services when she was not the person who could solve the dilemma. Up to this point, her training experience had involved traditional office-based evaluations and treatment.

Her supervisor used this experience to explore her response and challenge some of her assumptions. The supervisor decided to spend more time with the resident to address these issues during this rotation. Afterward, the supervisor called the residency director to emphasize the importance of training toward system of care principles in all resident experiences.

Outcomes and Accountability. A neglected aspect of training is related to outcomes and accountability. Unfortunately, for-profit managed care has led to pervasive beliefs that accountability is simply a way to limit services or avoid payment for services. However, none of the work done in a system of care will be fruitful if effectiveness is not measured. Trainees must understand that outcome evaluations are an integral part of practice. Residents need to become familiar with designs of outcome evaluations, data collection, and quality improvement concepts.

A basic tenet of project evaluation is that outcomes should be relevant and accessible to significant stakeholders in the system of care and that outcome information should be used to improve service planning and delivery (Diamond, McGinty & Mattsson, 1998). For example, in a CASSP demonstration project, data analysis was conducted explicitly for the purpose of quality improvement. The targeted population was at high risk for removal from the home, yet clinicians did not rate the behaviors as severely impairing. Twenty-one percent of the sample did not have a Total Problem Score on the Child Behavior Checklist (Achenbach, 1991a, 1991b) within the clinical range. Nonetheless, half of the "nonclinical range" subjects were receiving special education services, suggesting significant difficulty in school. These data were presented to the project management committee for a reexamination of entry criteria. The intent was to determine whether some children were overidentified for inclusion in the project, or whether some children have psychopathology recognized more by the school than the parent or clinician (Diamond et al., 1998).

Residents need to be involved in these evaluation processes. It could take the form of an ongoing project during training for a grand rounds presentation, or they could participate in clinic administrative meetings to plan these data collection endeavors.

At the University of North Carolina, Greensboro, participants have linked a local service system Quality Improvement (QI) Study with the university's human service training efforts (MacKinnon-Lewis, Arbuckle, Claes, & Shelton, 2001). The QI study, which supplemented data gathered in a federally funded system of care enhancement initiative, addressed two questions: it examined the development of the system of care for serving children and families and assessed whether services were delivered in accordance with CASSP Principles. With this evaluation feedback, the faculty of the Social Work Department were able to modify the social work methods course work. Their curricular modifications included additional didactic material and practice rehearsal to facilitate three processes: the child buy-in to the service plan, incorporation of identified strengths and informal supports into intervention strategies, and developing crisis plans.

Another realm for participation in outcome evaluations is through service testing, a spot-checking procedure for probing front-line practice by investigating the status of a sample of families in a geographical area. Although not true quantitative research, it is a mechanism to understand baseline status and the impact of a program (Groves & Foster, 1995). A resident who participates in this kind of evaluation would learn about the components of a system of care in detail as it operates, or does not, in a particular community. The protocol involves randomly selecting a child and then finding out how the child's and family's needs have been addressed in the community. The child would be one for whom multiagency involvement was required.

Supervision. A critical component to the education of trainees in this new philosophy is supervision by practitioners who have the experience and desire to use the philosophy. Supervision with a systems orientation is reportedly essential to develop not only clinical skills, but also systems evaluation, consultation, and intervention skills. Modeling, supervision, and mentorship may be more easily provided by child and adolescent psychiatrists with significant roles in system of care. The ideal training setting for the resident may be one in which the system of care is an entrenched part of the local mental health program. However, most likely, the system of care is incomplete or perhaps even non-existent for resident training. This does not mean residents will not be able to learn these concepts. All clinical settings provide the opportunity to examine where CASSP principles may have been incorporated. Furthermore, they allow for a critical examination of how CASSP principles could be applied, how the setting may meet the needs of children and families if they were applied, and what barriers exist to the implementation of system of care principles. Even without a structured system of care, the use of interdisciplinary supervision would better facilitate the appreciation of strengths and expertise of different mental health and child service professionals, as well as help to expand the exposure to different theoretical viewpoints. Residents and other trainees would then leave that program with an understanding of how a system of care should function and could become advocates for the development of system of care wherever they may choose to practice.

Clinical Rotations. The AACAP task force guidelines (1996) recommended supplementing or enriching clinical curricula to provide system of care training experiences.

Rotations allowing longitudinal experiences with youth who are chronically mentally ill or emotionally disturbed with multiple agency involvement and multiple developmental needs are especially valuable. Dartmouth Medical School has a program for child and adolescent psychiatry residents to follow patients throughout the child services community in different settings and levels of care. The Dartmouth residents are part of a crisis intervention and brief therapy team that is responsible for seeing all children under eighteen years of age needing acute psychiatric care in Burlington, Vermont, and surroundings. The resident might see a child at a school, a hospital emergency room, or an outpatient office. The resident works with the child and family using a variety of modalities as part of a treatment team until the child is stabilized and has a community-based treatment plan in place. This provides the resident with the opportunity to work with the same child and family over time as the child moves through different levels of care and is involved with many different agencies (R. J. Racusin, personal communication, Dec. 17, 2001).

Many programs have attempted to provide community-based intensive services rotations. At East Carolina University, residents work in a combination day treatment–residential treatment facility for five- to twelve-year-old children with daily school system contact and frequent contact with social services. The resident participates in many experiences at this site, including psychiatric consultation, school consultation, family therapy, individual therapy, group therapy, and team meetings. This coordinated treatment experience helps the resident appreciate the multiple treatment needs of seriously emotionally disturbed children and how the coordination of the services and providers can function best to help the child and family. These are also sites that are more likely to model the partnership with the family and other agencies.

Residents can also benefit from independent system of care rotations. During these rotations, the resident works directly with the child service providers in their respective agency and learns about the agency mission, function, roles, procedures, programs, and working experiences. This experience has been valuable for residents in furthering their understanding of specific agency missions and roles, the broader system issues, and learning how to work among them. Furthermore, they have been able to provide consultee-oriented consultation to help agency personnel navigate system issues and learn how to access mental health treatment. Experiences collaborating with advocacy groups have also been suggested. Most trainees want experiences that can be meaningful, and this frequently means direct contact with a child and family. At East Carolina University, residents visit with a local nonprofit agency that matches parents of developmentally disabled children with support parents. The residents work with parent advocates but do not have direct contact with the child or family. The residents have reported positive experiences with the parent advocates, but without the family contact, it seems too abstract for the residents. It may be more effective if the parent advocates were actively involved with a family currently in treatment with the resident.

EVALUATION METHODS FOR
SYSTEM OF CARE TRAINING AND CURRICULUM

The areas covered in a standard evaluation of trainees and curricula are specific knowledge, general knowledge, thinking skills, attitudes, and values. The knowledge and skills assessment for system of care training should be included in the general assessment of knowledge for all child mental health professional trainees.

Knowledge and skill development alone is not sufficient for child mental health professionals to practice within system of care. The AACAP Task Force identified ten attitudes that child and adolescent psychiatrists need for community-based systems practice. Many of these attitudes are embraced by most trainees, including a well-grounded identity as a child and adolescent psychiatrist, flexibility and resourcefulness, consistency and tenacity, acceptance and openness to diversity, and awareness of personal strengths and limitations. Residents and faculty have been more challenged by attitudes such as welcoming of family members as resources and partners; recognizing the value of consumer input into programs and policies; willingness to adapt interventions to the unique needs and circumstances of the child and family; awareness of and respect for the knowledge, expertise, and perspectives of other mental health and child services professionals; and willingness to tolerate disagreement from families and allied health professionals. These attitudes can be difficult to modify and shape, but are dealt with by faculty modeling, as well as participating in clinical experiences with patients, their families, and teams. Residents may be confused by the modeling or team interaction they observe, but it leads to fruitful supervisory sessions. Furthermore, the combination of didactic instruction and clinical exposure may be helpful in changing attitudes.

In an attempt to teach medical students about system of care principles, a pre-posttest was designed to evaluate the effectiveness of didactic sessions and clinical exposure. The implication from this process was that the combination of didactic sessions and clinical exposure was more effective than didactic sessions alone in changing attitudes toward families and the physician partnership with families (McGinty & Diamond, 2000).

Another set of studies focusing on attitudinal changes in trainees has addressed the attitudes of professionals-in-training on parents. McCammon, Johnson, Groff, Spencer, and Osher (2000) reported positive attitudinal changes in master's-level social work students following class sessions taught by parents of children with emotional and behavioral disabilities. Following those sessions, the students were less likely to agree with parent-blaming statements and more likely to endorse the value of psychotropic medication for children and adolescents and open sharing of information with parents.

As a means of measuring how well students master these objectives, many professional associations are encouraging training programs to establish learning outcomes for their students. For example, the National Association of School Psychologists (2000) has established domains of training and practice that involve both knowledge and skills. Rather than focusing only on course grades or credits earned, training programs must ensure that their graduates are able to demonstrate the mastery of program learning goals. A variety of methods of learning outcomes are suggested, including supervisor ratings, portfolios of work products, case studies, and standard examinations (Waldron, Prus, & Curtis, 2001). As training programs include more system of care principles in the curriculum, it is important to develop explicit student learning outcomes along with methods to measure these outcomes. In addition to providing assurance that the program's graduates can perform the activities for which they are being trained, this information can be used by the program as it considers changes in curriculum or practical experiences.

Various medical education organizations have also begun to encourage the establishment of learning outcomes as a response to concerns that young physicians are less equipped than they need to be to meet the perceived societal health care needs (Medical School Objectives Writing Group, 1999). In an effort to address the preparedness of residents, the Accreditation Council for Graduate Medical Education (2000) mandated that all residency review committees incorporate six general competencies into their requirements: patient care, medical knowledge, practice-based learning and improvement, interpersonal and communication skills, professionalism, and systems-based practice. As of January 1, 2001, all child and adolescent psychiatry residency programs have been required to develop at least one written core competency in each of the six areas and begin documenting the demonstration of this competence for each resident by graduation using various evaluation techniques. Although competency evaluation at graduation is important, the skills in working in a system of care need to be evaluated throughout the training years. It should not be expected that they will be learned in a specific rotation; rather, they should be cultured throughout the training experience.

One competency, systems-based practice, is specifically related to system of care practice. An example of the main learning outcome for systems-based practice developed by the AACAP Work Group on Training and Education is:

> At regular intervals, the child and adolescent psychiatry resident should demonstrate progressive attainment of systems-based care competencies such as working in a mutually respectful manner, displaying knowledge of the diverse systems involved in the treatment of children and adolescents, integrating multiple systems of care in treatment planning and collaborating in a shared treatment plan, and advocating for children and adolescents in various systems of care. The resident should demonstrate competence in child psychiatric treatment and consultation across multiple systems and agencies upon graduation [Sexson et al., 2001].

The work group also suggested specific knowledge, skill, and attitude objectives, along with possible evaluation methods. The evaluation methods suggested include supervisory reports, chart reviews, training portfolio, observation of resident performance, performance on exams and presentations, and satisfactory evaluations from collaborating professionals. This move toward the demonstration of competency focuses attention on developing practical evaluation methodology.

FUNDING OF SYSTEM OF CARE TRAINING

Adequate funding for training is necessary to sustain these efforts to educate child mental health professionals in the system of care philosophy.

Most residency program directors have embraced the task of training residents in the system of care model. However, many have found difficulties in funding trainee time to participate in these types of activities. This follows a trend of mental health providers being perceived primarily as direct service providers, with fewer opportunities to be compensated for the time involved in collaboration with other professionals, or collaboration with multiple agencies. The AACAP task force guidelines (1996) suggested that system of care training be provided by supplementing traditional curricula. Indeed, some programs have provided the training experiences with funding that is already available. For instance, rotations at existing sites (residential treatment centers, day treatment sites, intensive outpatient rotations, school based mental health clinics) have been used to include the objectives and training components described previously. Other programs have had the benefit of adequate state or medical school funding to provide a combination of existing rotations and additional, independent system of care rotations. Yet another mechanism is to have specific rotation sites designed to serve a specific section of the system of care (for example, juvenile justice sites, school-based mental health sites, or social services sites). These agencies then reimburse the academic department for the clinical care provided during the rotation.

Innovative ways of funding system of care teaching are needed in university settings. The NC PAL initiative has been fortunate in the past several years to receive support through contracts with the Child and Family Services Section of the North Carolina Division of Mental Health, Developmental Disabilities and Substance Abuse Services. Although this state financial support is not currently available, there is a strong precedent for university-state partnerships to support training, which we hope will be resumed in the future (see McCammon et al., in press, for a discussion of state-university linkages). Another way to support system of care teaching is to recruit faculty for joint positions with community agencies and individual universities, thereby developing system of care faculty positions within academic departments (this has occurred at the University of Kentucky). Once interested faculty are in place, they need to pursue additional funding to continue to support the system of care training efforts. Currently, the NC PAL participants are seeking federal and foundation grant funding to sustain the PAL initiative. In the meantime, the training initiatives at East Carolina University continue through university support of faculty effort and with the help of a psychology department alumnus whose donation is being used to provide stipends for parents who coteach and serve as guest faculty for classes.

The future of system of care implementation efforts depends on continued innovation and creative approaches to support these training efforts and sustain faculty participation. Incorporating system of care principles into mental health training efforts is consistent with other current initiatives to enhance training. For example, the focus on family-centered care in training physicians and other health professionals is compatible with system of care philosophy and practices (*Advances in Family-Centered Care*, 1999). The emphasis on interprofessional training in health care and the service-learning model are also movements within higher education that are compatible with updating mental health professional training (McCammon et al., in press). Piggybacking system of care training with these initiatives may provide support for curriculum enrichment, as well as opportunities for additional interdisciplinary collaborations to teach more students about this philosophy.

Zlotnik (1998b) offers recommendations for future actions that should occur in the university, in the community, and with university-community partnerships to enhance preparation of professionals. They emphasize that professional education and continuing education are tools that are critical in maintaining a well-prepared workforce, "because learning is a continuous process and the world we live in is always changing" (p. 139).

References

Accreditation Council for Graduate Medical Education Outcome Project. (2000). *ACGME General Competencies Version 1.3(9.28.99).* Chicago: Author.

Achenbach, T. M. (1991a). *Manual for the Child Behavior Checklist/4–18 and 1991 profile.* Burlington: Department of Psychiatry, University of Vermont.

Achenbach, T. M. (1991b). *Manual for the Teacher's Report Form and 1991 profile.* Burlington: Department of Psychiatry, University of Vermont.

Adelman, H. S., & Taylor, L. (1998). Mental health in schools: Moving forward. *School Psychology Review, 27,* 175–190.

Advances in Family-Centered Care. (1999). *5*(1).

American Academy of Child and Adolescent Psychiatry. (1996). *Guidelines for training towards community-based systems of care for children with serious emotional disturbances.* Washington, DC: Author.

American Psychiatric Association. (2000). *Diagnostic and statistical manual of mental disorders* (4th ed. rev.). Washington, DC: Author.

Angold, A., Messer, S. C., Stangl, D., Farmer, E.M.Z., Costello, E. J., & Burns, B. J. (1998). Perceived parental burden and service use for child and adolescent psychiatric disorders. *American Journal of Public Health, 88,* 75–80.

Bellack, J. P., & O'Neil, E. H. (2000). Recreating nursing practice for a new century. *Nursing and Health Care Perspectives, 21,* 14–21.

Brannan, A. M., Heflinger, C. A., & Bickman, L. (1997). The Caregiver Strain Questionnaire: Measuring the impact on the family of living with a child with serious emotional disturbance. *Journal of Emotional and Behavioral Disorders, 5,* 212–222.

Bronheim, S. M., Keefe, J. L., & Morgan, C. C. (1998). *Building blocks of a community-based system of care: The communities CAN experience* (2nd ed.). Washington, DC: Georgetown University Child Development Center, Center for Child Health and Mental Health Policy.

Diamond, J. M., McGinty, K. L., & Mattsson A. (1998). A system of care: Data analysis and quality improvement implications. In C. J. Liberton, K. Kutash, & R. M. Friedman (Eds.), *Tenth Annual Research Conference Proceedings: A System of Care for Children's Mental Health: Expanding the Research Base* (pp. 415–418). Tampa: Florida Mental Health Institute.

Dosser, D. A., Jr., Handron, D. S., McCammon, S. L., Powell, J. Y., & Spencer, S. S. (2001). Challenges and strategies for teaching collaborative interdisciplinary practice in children's mental health care. *Families, Systems and Health, 19,* 65–82.

Farmer, E.M.Z., Burns, B. J., Angold, A., & Costello, E. (1997). Impact of children's mental health problems on families: Relationships with service use. *Journal of Emotional and Behavioral Disorders, 5,* 230–238.

Groves, I., & Foster, R. (1995). *Service testing: Assessing the quality and outcomes of systems of care performance through interaction with individual children served.* Paper presented at the Annual Research Conference, Louis de la Parte Florida Mental Health Institute, Research and Training Center for Children's Mental Health, Tampa, FL.

Handron, D., Diamond, J., & Zlotnik, J. L. (2001). Challenges of providing interdisciplinary mental health education. *Journal of Family Social Work, 5,* 49–62.

Hansen, M., Anderson, C., Gray, C., Harbaugh, S., Lindblad-Goldberg, M., & Marsh, D. T. (1999). *Child, family, and community core competencies.* Harrisburg, PA: PA Child and Adolescent Service System Program Training and Technical Assistance Institute.

Hodges, K. (1990). *The Child and Adolescent Functional Assessment Scale* (rev.). Ypsilanti: Eastern Michigan University, Department of Psychology.

Klaehn, R., O'Malley, K., Vaughn, T., & Kroeger, K. (1999). *CALOCUS user's manual: Child and adolescent level of care utilization system.* Washington, DC: American Academy of Child and Adolescent Psychiatry and American Association of Community Psychiatrists.

Kratochwill, T. R., & Stoiber, K. C. (2000). Uncovering critical research agendas for school psychology: Conceptual dimensions and future directions. *School Psychology Review, 29,* 591–603.

MacKinnon-Lewis, C., Arbuckle, M. B., Claes, J., & Shelton, T. (2001). Connecting training and service through quality improvement. In C. Newman, C. Liberton, K. Kutash, & R. M. Friedman (Eds.), *The Thirteenth Annual Research Conference Proceedings: A System of Care for Children's Mental Health: Expanding the Research*

Base (pp. 287–289). Tampa: University of South Florida, Louis de la Parte Florida Mental Health Institute, Research and Training Center for Children's Mental Health.

McCammon, S. L., Cook, J. R., & Kilmer, R. P. (in press). Integrating systems-of-care values into university-based training. In D. T. Marsh & M. A. Fristad (Eds.), *Handbook of serious emotional disturbance in children and adolescents.* New York: Wiley.

McCammon, S., Johnson, H. C., Groff, D., Spencer, S., & Osher, T. W. (2000). The power of parent-professor partnerships. In C. Newman, C. Liberton, K. Kutash, & R. M. Friedman (Eds.), *The Thirteenth Annual Research Conference Proceedings, A System of Care for Children's Mental Health: Expanding the Research Base* (pp. 287–289). Tampa: University of South Florida, Louis de la Parte Florida Mental Health Institute, Research and Training Center for Children's Mental Health.

McDonald, T. P., Poertner, J., & Pierpont, J. (1999). Predicting caregiver stress: An ecological perspective. *American Journal of Orthopsychiatry, 69,* 100–109.

McGinty, K. L., & Diamond, J. M. (2000). Teaching system of care principles in child and adolescent psychiatry clerkships. *Academic Psychiatry, 24,* 93–98.

McGinty, K., McCammon, S. L., & Koeppen, V. P. (2001). The complexities of implementing a wraparound approach to service provision: A view from the field. *Journal of Family Social Work, 5,* 95–110.

Medical School Objectives Writing Group. (1999). Learning objectives for medical student education-guidelines for medical schools: Report I of the Medical School Objectives Project. *Academic Medicine, 74,* 3–18.

Meyers, J., Kaufman, M., & Goldman, S. (1999). *Promising practices: Training strategies for serving children with serious emotional disturbance and their families in a system of care.* Washington, DC: Center for Effective Collaboration and Practice, American Institutes for Research.

Nastasi, B. K. (1998). A model for mental health programming in schools and communities: An introduction to the mini-series. *School Psychology Review, 27,* 165–174.

Nastasi, B. K. (2000). School psychologists as health care providers in the 21st century: Conceptual framework, professional identity, and professional practice. *School Psychology Review, 29,* 540–554.

National Association of School Psychologists. (2000). *Standards for training and field placement programs in school psychology.* Washington, DC: Author.

Osher, T., deFur, E., Nava, C., Spencer, S., & Toth-Dennis, D. (1999). *New roles for families in systems of care.* Washington, DC: Center for Effective Collaboration and Practice, American Institutes for Research.

Pires, S. (1996). Human resource development. In B. Stroul (Ed.), *Children's mental health: Creating systems of care in a changing society.* Baltimore: Brookes Publishing.

Reisser, G. G., & Schorske, B. J. (1994). Relationships between family caregivers and mental health professionals: The American experience (pp. 3–26). In H. P. Lefley & M. Wasow (Eds.), *Helping families cope with mental illness.* New York: Harwood.

Rosenfield, S. (2000). Commentary on Sheridan and Gutkin: Unfinished business. *School Psychology Review, 29,* 503–504.

Sexson, S., Sargent, J., Zima, B., Berensin, E., Cuffe, S., Drell, M., Dugan, T., Fox, G., Kim, W. J., Matthews, K., Sylvester, C., & Pope, K. (2001). Sample core competencies in child and adolescent psychiatry training: A starting point. *Academic Psychiatry, 25,* 201–213.

Shelton, T., & Baumhover, L. (2002). North Carolina public-academic liaisons: Facilitating collaboration between university and community. In C. Newman, C. Liberton, K. Kutash, & R. M. Friedman (Eds.), *The Fourteenth Annual Research Conference Proceedings, A System of Care for Children's Mental Health: Expanding the Research Base* (pp. 421–427). Tampa: University of South Florida, Louis de la Parte Florida Mental Health Institute, Research and Training Center for Children's Mental Health.

Sheridan, S. M., & Gutkin, T. B. (2000). The ecology of school psychology: Examining and changing our paradigm for the 21st century. *School Psychology Review, 29,* 485–502.

Stroul, B. A., & Friedman, R. M. (1996). The system of care concept and philosophy. In B. A. Stroul (Ed.), *Children's mental health: Creating System of Care in a changing society* (pp. 265–280). Baltimore, MD: Brookes Publishing.

VanDenBerg, J. E., & Grealish, E. M. (1996). Individualized services and supports through the wraparound process: Philosophy and procedures. *Journal of Child and Family Studies, 5,* 7–21.

Waldron, N., Prus, J., & Curtis, M. (2001). *A guide for performance-based assessment, accountability, and program development in school psychology training programs.* Washington, DC: National Association of School Psychologists.

Worthington, J., Hernandez, M., Friedman, B., & Uzzell, D. (2001). *Systems of care: Promising practices in children's mental health* (Vol. 2). Washington, DC: Center for Effective Collaboration and Practice, American Institutes for Research.

Zlotnik, J. L. (1998a). Preparing human service workers for the 21st century: A challenge to professional education. In S. J. Jones & J. L. Zlotnik (Eds.), *Preparing helping professionals to meet community needs.* Alexandria, VA: Council on Social Work Education.

Zlotnik, J. L. (1998b). A look toward the future: Lessons learned. In S. J. Jones & J. L. Zlotnik (Eds.), *Preparing helping professionals to meet community needs.* Alexandria, VA: Council on Social Work Education.

THE EDITORS

Andres J. Pumariega, M.D., is professor and director of child and adolescent psychiatry at the James H. Quillen College of Medicine, East Tennessee State University. He was the founding chair of the Work Group on Systems of Care of the American Academy of Child and Adolescent Psychiatry (AACAP) from 1994 and co-chair from 1999 through 2001. He currently chairs the Community Psychiatry Committee of the AACAP. He has published broadly in the areas of systems of care and cross-cultural child psychiatry, and has been granted numerous awards for his work.

Nancy C. Winters, M.D., is assistant professor of child and adolescent psychiatry and pediatrics and director of the Child and Adolescent Psychiatry Residency Program at the Oregon Health and Science University. She is one of the founding members of the American Academy of Child and Adolescent Psychiatry Work Group on Community-Based Systems of Care and has served as co-chair since 1999. Her publications and research interests span a broad range of topics, including systems of care.

THE CONTRIBUTORS

Deborah Anderson is the program administrator for Opportunities for Family Leadership in Frankfort, Kentucky, and serves as the staff adviser on family leadership to the commissioner of Kentucky's Department for Mental Health and Mental Retardation Services. She has been active in helping to create a network of parents of children with severe emotional disabilities throughout Kentucky.

Marilyn Benoit, M.D., is president of the American Academy of Child and Adolescent Psychiatry. She is a clinical associate professor of psychiatry at Georgetown University Medical Center and at Howard University Hospital, where she is the program director of children's psychiatric services. She is a national advocate for children, testifying before congressional committees on a range of issues pertaining to the welfare of children.

Barbara Brady, L.C.S.W., is the administrator of early childhood and child abuse mental health programs in the Behavioral Health Division of the Department of Community and Family Services, Multnomah County, Oregon. She has been active in system of care policy and practice development activities with a special focus on early childhood and child abuse. Her Early Childhood Mental Health Program received the American Psychiatric Association's 2001 Silver Certification of Significant Achievement Award.

Ana Maria Brannan, Ph.D., is a senior research associate at the Center for Mental Health Policy at Vanderbilt University. She was previously a senior scientist at ORC Macro and is currently a consultant to the National Evaluation of the Comprehensive Community Mental Health Services for Children and Their Families funded by the Substance Abuse and Mental Health Services Administration.

Freda Brashears, M.S.W., a senior scientist at ORC Macro, manages the systems-level assessment team for the National Evaluation of the Comprehensive Community Mental Health Services for Children and Their Families funded by the Substance Abuse and Mental Health Services Administration.

Michael B. Brown, Ph.D., is associate professor of psychology and director of graduate studies in the School of Psychology at East Carolina University. His teaching and research interests include consultation and collaboration, professional issues for school psychologists, and children with learning, behavior, and health problems.

Debbie R. Carter, M.D., is assistant professor of psychiatry at the University of Colorado Health Sciences Center, associate residency training director in the Division of Child Psychiatry, and director of the Forensic Adolescent Consultation and Treatment Services in Programs for Public Psychiatry. She is a member of the Work Group on Systems of Care of the American Academy of Child and Adolescent Psychiatry and the board of directors of the American Association of Community Psychiatrists.

Mark Chenven, M.D., is a board-certified child and adolescent psychiatrist and a cochair of the American Academy of Child and Adolescent Psychiatry's Work Group on Systems of Care for Seriously Emotionally Disturbed Children and Their Families. He is vice president for clinical operations at Vista Hill, a nonprofit human services provider organization with a focus on prevention and early intervention programming.

John M. Diamond, M.D., is associate professor of psychiatry and director of the Division of Child and Adolescent Psychiatry at the Brody School of Medicine at East Carolina University. He works in multidisciplinary programs focusing on high-risk youth and substance-abusing adolescents. His research interests include quality improvement and service delivery and systems of care. He was one of the original members of the Work Group on Community-Based Systems of Care of the American Academy of Child and Adolescent Psychiatry.

Jacquelyn Duval–Harvey, Ph.D., is the director of the School Based Program of the East Baltimore Mental Health Partnership at Johns Hopkins Hospital/University, which provides therapeutic services to inner-city schools in Baltimore. She is also an adjunct professor at George Mason University faculty and serves on a variety of boards and committees that support the health and well-being of children and adolescents.

Theodore Fallon, Jr., M.D., M.P.H., is in private practice in Pennsylvania. He has done research in epidemiology and health services research and is principal investigator for two federally funded national studies: one examining the best practices of juvenile justice and mental health collaboration and the other field-testing the Child and Adolescent Level of Care Utilization Scale.

Barbara Friesen, Ph.D., is professor in the Graduate School of Social Work and director of the Research and Training Center on Family Support and Children's Mental Health at Portland State University in Oregon. Since the beginning of the Child and Adolescent Service System Program in 1984, she has worked to gather and disseminate information about the perspectives of family caregivers and youth about their experiences of seeking and receiving mental health and other services.

Katherine E. Grimes, M.D., M.P.H., is a health policy researcher, clinical program director, and member of the faculty in the Cambridge Health Alliance Department of Psychiatry, an affiliate of Harvard Medical School. She is a child and adolescent psychiatrist with additional training in pediatrics. She has been involved at the national level for many years in the American Academy of Child and Adolescent Psychiatry, including membership in the Work Group on Systems of Care and the Work Group on Health Care Finance and Reform.

William M. Heffron, M.D., is director of mental health services for the Kentucky Department of Juvenile Justice and an associate professor of psychiatry in the Child Psychiatry Division at the University of Kentucky College of Medicine. He represents juvenile justice on the State Interagency Council for Services to Children with an Emotional Disability and on the Mental Health Services Planning Council and is a member of the Work Group on Systems of Care of the American Academy of Child and Adolescent Psychiatry.

E. Wayne Holden, Ph.D., is a vice president at ORC Macro, where he oversees the children's mental health and health communication practice areas. He is officer in charge of the National Evaluation of the Comprehensive Community Mental Health Services for Children and Their Families funded by the Substance Abuse and Mental Health Services Administration. He is also a clinical associate professor in the Department of Psychiatry and Behavioral Sciences at the Emory University School of Medicine.

Charles Huffine, M.D., is assistant medical director of child and adolescent programs at the King County Mental Health, Chemical Abuse and Dependency Division; medical director for King County's SAMHSA Children's Mental Health Initiative grant activities, including a blended funding program; and coordinator of Health 'N' Action, a King County initiative giving voice to youth in the system of care.

Wade Junek, M.D., is a child and adolescent psychiatrist in Halifax, Nova Scotia, where he is on staff at the IWK Health Centre and Dalhousie University. He is a member and secretary-treasurer of the Canadian Academy of Child Psychiatry and of its Advocacy Committee and served on the Federal/Provincial/Territorial Working Group on the Mental Health and Well-Being of Children and Youth.

Bruce Kamradt, M.S.W., has been the director of Children's Mental Health Services for Milwaukee County for the past twelve years. He also serves as the director of Wraparound Milwaukee, a public managed care system serving nearly six hundred children with severe emotional problems and their families that is a national model for systems of care design.

Sandra Keenan, M.Ed., is the senior education adviser to the Technical Assistance Partnership for Child and Family Mental Health, which supports federal grant–funded community-based system change for children with emotional and behavioral disorders and their families. She has been nationally recognized for the development of districtwide behavioral support programs that benefit all children and has published widely on school-based support programs for children with emotional and behavioral needs.

Robert L. Klaehn, M.D., is the medical director for the Division of Developmental Disabilities, Arizona Department of Economic Security. He has been a member of the American Academy of Child and Adolescent Psychiatry's Work Group on Systems of Care since 1995. He was the principal psychiatric consultant for the Stark County Center for Mental Health Services systems of care demonstration site in rural Ohio at its inception.

Qinhong Liao, M.Ed., a senior scientist at ORC Macro, manages the data management team for the National Evaluation of the Comprehensive Community Mental Health Services for Children and Their Families funded by the Substance Abuse and Mental Health Services Administration.

Ira S. Lourie, M.D., a child and adolescent psychiatrist, is a partner in the Human Service Collaborative, an organization that provides consultation, technical assistance, and training in areas of human service policy and service system development. He is also medical director of AWARE of Anaconda, Montana, an agency for troubled children; psychiatric consultant for two other agencies that provide community-based and wraparound services; and assistant clinical professor of child psychiatry at the Georgetown University School of Medicine.

Brigitte A. Manteuffel, Ph.D., is the principal investigator at ORC Macro for the National Evaluation of the Comprehensive Community Mental Health Services for Children and Their Families funded by the Substance Abuse and Mental Health Services Administration.

Jan Martner, M.S.W., is director of the Family Health and Wellness Department of Southwest Human Development, Phoenix, Arizona. She has over twenty years of experience working with infants, toddlers, and their families in a wide variety of settings, including programs for children with special needs, Head Start, research and demonstration projects, and private practice.

Larry Marx, M.D., is the medical director for the Department of County Human Services, Multnomah County, Oregon. He is an active partner in Wraparound Milwaukee, one of the Center for Mental Health Services model demonstration sites, as medical director of Aurora Behavioral Health. He is one of the founding members of the Work Group on Community-Based Systems of Care of the American Academy of Child and Adolescent Psychiatry.

Susan L. McCammon, Ph.D., is professor of psychology and director of the East Carolina University Social Sciences Training Consortium, which promotes curriculum development and training for improving the system of care for children with serious emotional problems and their families. She is a consultant to child and family services in the local community mental health center and a member of the local child and family community collaborative.

Kaye L. McGinty, M.D., is associate professor of psychiatry and director of child and adolescent psychiatry residency training at the Brody School of Medicine at East Carolina University. Her research interests include systems of care and quality improvement in child mental health systems.

Kieran D. O'Malley, M.D., is a child and adolescent psychiatrist specializing in community-based approaches with people with developmental disorders. He is acting assistant professor and adjunct faculty in the Department of Psychiatry and Behavioral Sciences, Fetal Alcohol and Drug Unit, Henry M. Jackson School of International Studies, Canadian Studies Centre, University of Washington, Seattle. He is a member of the Work Group on Community-Based Systems of Care of the American Academy of Child and Adolescent Psychiatry.

Glen T. Pearson, M.D., is medical director for the Dallas Public Schools Youth and Family Centers and chief psychiatrist for the Dallas County Juvenile Probation Department. He is past president of the American Society of Adolescent Psychiatry and is the author or coauthor of a number of publications on diagnosis and treatment of child and adolescent mental and emotional disorders.

Gayle Porter, Ph.D., is a principal research assistant and a senior mental health adviser for the Technical Assistance Partnership (TAP) of the American Institutes for Research, which provides technical assistance to the over forty-five sites of the Comprehensive Community Mental Health Services for Children and Their Families program. She has given numerous presentations on topics related to children's mental health, especially poor and minority children.

Kenneth M. Rogers, M.D., M.S.H.S., is an assistant professor of psychiatry at the University of South Carolina School of Medicine. His research and clinical work has been on the development and evaluation of mental health services for youth in the juvenile justice system.

Terry Russell, Ph.D., is a consultant in the development of health and social programs for children and youth. In British Columbia, he developed the provincial child and youth mental health program and was responsible for planning and funding community health services for children and youth.

Rolando L. Santiago, Ph.D., is the acting deputy branch chief and director of program evaluation at the Child, Adolescent, and Family Branch within the Federal Center for Mental Health Services at the Substance Abuse and Mental Health Services Administration and principal project officer for the Comprehensive Community Mental Health Services for Children and Their Families program.

Robin Soler, Ph.D., a senior scientist at ORC Macro, manages the site liaison team for the National Evaluation of the Comprehensive Community Mental Health Services for Children and Their Families funded by the Substance Abuse and Mental Health Services Administration.

Robert L. Stephens, Ph.D., a senior scientist at ORC Macro, manages the Longitudinal Comparison Study of the National Evaluation of the Comprehensive Community Mental Health Services for Children and Their Families funded by the Substance Abuse and Mental Health Services Administration.

Beth A. Stroul, M.Ed., is vice president and cofounder of Management and Training Innovations, a consulting firm located in McLean, Virginia, and serves as a consultant in the area of mental health policy. She has completed numerous research, evaluation, policy analysis, and technical assistance projects related to service systems for children and adolescents with emotional disorders and their families and published extensively in the field of children's mental health.

Elizabeth Terrell, L.P.C., is the assistant program director of the Larimer Center for Mental Health Child and Family Program in Fort Collins, Colorado. In 1990, she became the original care coordinator for the Partners Project, a Robert Wood Johnson system of care demonstration project located in Multnomah County, Portland, Oregon. She has presented nationally on family involvement as a potent lever of change in systems of care.

Thomas Vaughan, M.D., is vice president for mental health for the Children's Health System of Alabama in Birmingham and senior child psychiatrist for the Birmingham site of the Comprehensive Community Mental Health Services for Children and Their Families program. He provides consultation to community schools, juvenile courts, and community-based mental health agencies, as well as treatment for children, adolescents, and their families. He is also a member of the American Academy of Child and Adolescent Psychiatry Work Group on Community-Based Systems of Care.

Albert A. Zachik, M.D., is a practicing child and adolescent psychiatrist in Bethesda, Maryland. He is a member of the American Academy of Child and Adolescent Psychiatry's Work Group on Community-Based Systems of Care. He is director of the Office of Child and Adolescent Services, State of Maryland, Department of Health and Mental Hygiene, Mental Hygiene Administration, and on the clinical faculty at Georgetown University School of Medicine and the Johns Hopkins University School of Medicine.

Susan Zaro, M.P.H., a vice president at ORC Macro, manages special studies and projects for the National Evaluation of the Comprehensive Community Mental Health Services for Children and Their Families funded by the Substance Abuse and Mental Health Services Administration.

NAME INDEX

A

Abidin, R. R., 478
Abikoff, H., 125
Abrahames, A. F., 226
Abraham, M. E., xviii, 190
Abreu, J., 90
Achenbach, T., 130, 134, 190, 445, 472
Adelman, H. S., 254, 257, 272, 487
Adinoff, B., 281
Adnopoz, J., 108, 117, 250, 258, 387
Aichhorn, A., 118
Alexander, M. J., 279
Alfaro, J., 332, 337
Allen-Hagen, B., 226, 227
Altarriba, J., 92
Alterman, A. I., 280
Aluwahlia, S., 135
Aman, M., 137, 138
Ambrosini, P., 132, 135
Anderson, C., 488
Anderson, D., 35
Anderson, J. A., 472
Andrade, A. R., 404
Andrews, D. A., 226
Angell, R. H., 402
Angelo, A., 154, 258
Angold, A., 182, 195, 449, 478, 494
Angst, J., 295

Annon, K., 94
Anthony, E. J., 293
Anton, R., 281
Aoki, Y., 165, 209
Applegate, W., 365
Arbuckle, M B., 498
Arend, I. L., 250
Armenteros, J., 127
Armstrong, K., 449
Armstrong, M. I., 174, 180, 183, 184, 194,
    381, 385, 387, 397, 407, 438, 439, 451, 467,
    468, 469
Arroyo, W., 87
Aslami, B., 94
Astrachan, B., 175, 176, 192
Atkins, D. L., 132, 225, 227, 420
Atkins, M. S., 36, 250, 251, 257, 258
Attkisson, C. C., 22, 318, 395, 440
Azar, V., 95

B

Baer, J. S., 279, 280
Bailey, J., 365
Baker, A., 94
Balderrama, H., 96
Baldwin, L. M., 447
Ballenger, J. C., 281
Banks, S. M., 154, 155, 180

SUBJECT INDEX